C++ Programming Today

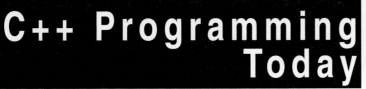

Barbara Johnston

Albuquerque Technical Vocational Institute

Prentice Hall

W9-CGK-956

Upper Saddle River, New Jersey
Columbus, Ohio

Library of Congress Cataloging in Publication Data
Johnston, Barbara
    C++ programming today / Barbara Johnston.
        p. cm.
    Includes bibliographical references and index.
    ISBN 0–13–085375–5
    1. C++ (Computer program language)   I. Title.

  QA76.73.C153 J644 2002
  005.13′3—dc21   2001021354

Vice President and Editor in Chief: Stephen Helba
Assistant Vice President and Publisher: Charles E. Stewart, Jr.
Assistant Editor: Delia K. Uherec
Production Editor: Alexandrina Benedicto Wolf
Design Coordinator: Karrie Converse-Jones
Cover Designer: Frank Gonzales
Production Manager: Matthew Ottenweller

This book was set in Times and Helvetica by York Graphic Services, Inc. It was printed and bound by Von Hoffmann Press, Inc. The cover was printed by Phoenix Color Corp.

Prentice-Hall International (UK) Limited, *London*
Prentice-Hall of Australia Pty. Limited, *Sydney*
Prentice-Hall Canada, Inc., *Toronto*
Prentice-Hall Hispanoamericana, S.A., *Mexico*
Prentice-Hall of India Private Limited, *New Delhi*
Prentice-Hall of Japan, Inc., *Tokyo*
Prentice-Hall Singapore Pte. Ltd.
Editora Prentice-Hall do Brasil, Ltda., *Rio de Janeiro*

Microsoft Visual C++® is a registered trademark of Microsoft Corporation.

10 9 8 7 6 5 4 3 2
ISBN: 0–13–085375–5

In memory of

My mother, Elizabeth H. Johnston
My pal Carol's mother, Anne H. McCreary
My canine co-author, Noel Maxam White-Johnston

I miss you every day.

Foreword

Software can be found in almost all aspects of our lives. Systems such as banking, medicine, payroll, airline reservations, billing, utilities, traffic control, elevators, and school records all depend on their software working reliably and accurately. Our military also depends on software. Military systems include stealth technology, night vision, Ground Positioning Systems (GPS), phased array radar, adaptive optics, and laser systems, to name a few. How's the weather? The weather tracking and forecast methods depend on computer networks around the world. Do you want to fly to Phoenix? You can't without the aircraft's fly-by-wire working correctly and the Federal Aviation Administration (FAA) air traffic control systems in place. Your cell phone, programmable microwave oven, and electronic ignition system in your car are all controlled by software.

The software development process is very important. To produce reliable software, within budget and according to specification, a disciplined approach must be used. The basic step-by-step approach presented in *C++ Programming Today* is at the root of all software development processes. This approach includes stating the problem clearly, determining the input and output information, working the problem by hand, developing an algorithm that reaches the solution, and finally testing the system with a variety of data. This text's software engineering concepts and "rules of thumb" (understand the problem, understand the language, work when you're rested, don't get mad, etc.) are necessary starting points for learning to program in any language.

It is possible for students who become software programmers and engineers to join development teams or support many system users. Communication with fellow team members and customers is an important part of a programmer's life. Aside from writing error-free code, programmers must follow directions, procedures, and specifications.

The C++ programmer never stops learning. *C++ Programming Today* is an excellent starting point for the future programmer. My former student, Barbara Johnston, has written an easy-to-read, technical text with style and a dash of humor. The object-oriented examples are helpful and the complex topics are clear. I know readers of this text will learn the C++ language and will acquire practical information needed in today's programming environments.

Dr. Delores M. Etter
Deputy Under Secretary of Defense, Science and Technology
Office of the Director, Defense Research and Engineering

Preface

C++ Programming Today was written for the individual who is interested in learning to program in C++. You may be

- A college student studying for an associate's, a bachelor's, or master's degree.
- A community college student working toward an associate's degree.
- An employee interested in becoming a programmer at your company.
- A retired individual interested in learning to write programs for fun.

Whatever your situation, if you are ready to learn computer programming, *C++ Programming Today* is for you.

C++ Programming Today Is Easy to Read

This text was classroom tested for more than a year at the Albuquerque Technical Vocational Institute, the largest community college in the state of New Mexico. The students were quite helpful in pointing out the difficult portions and they suggested better ways to explain certain topics. Their input ensured that the technical jargon of the book was written in plain English. What does that mean? A principal goal was to write a C++ programming text that would be easy to read and to understand. When a topic is hard or confusing, the readers are warned.

    The students and reviewers alike agree that the readable style of *C++ Programming Today* is top quality!

How Much Math Do You Need?

I do not assume that you have had any recent math courses or that you remember much of the mathematics you knew at one time. It is true that many programming applications require rigorous mathematics, but you will not need that here—just multiplication, division, addition, and subtraction. You won't find a summation using Greek letters in this book!

Examples Are Easy to Understand

Some of the C++ topics can be difficult to grasp, but the examples presented here have been designed for easy understanding. We Keep It Simple, Sweetie (KISS) so that you can concentrate on the details of the C++ language. Most of us learn new skills in the same way: with examples and practice. Our KISS programs include writing messages to the screen, adding monthly telephone bills, and modeling shopping activities, parking meters, vending machines, and silly dice games. These examples help demonstrate how C++ with object programming is performed.

Light on the Math, Heavy on the C++ Concepts

We need just a simple review of mathematics, but this does not mean that we will tread lightly on the C++ language. This book tackles some complicated programming topics; virtual functions and inheritance aren't for babies. Pointers (a powerful programming tool) are used whenever possible. Class relationships—a topic barely touched on in other texts—is given its own chapter with numerous examples. This text covers not only classes and objects but also shows how to create arrays of objects and pass these arrays to functions. You will learn how to pass the addresses of objects to functions and access members through pointers.

Great Features in *C++ Programming Today*

I give practical, commonsense programming tips. Some are listed here:

- The programmer's do's and don'ts: guidelines illustrate what to do and not to do in your programming endeavors.
- Troubleshooting sections provide insight into common mistakes and pitfalls.
- Writing code the right way is important, but sometimes seeing code written incorrectly can be informative, too. Right and wrong, good and bad examples are here in *C++ Programming Today*.
- Four icons are used throughout the text to highlight good and bad program examples and caution and troubleshooting tips.

Good Programming Practice!   Stop! Do Not Do This!

Be Cautious!   Troubleshooting Tip

- Building programs in a step-by-step manner is described.
- Tips for working with data arrays are provided.
- Compiler errors and warnings are shown in both Microsoft Visual C++ Version 6.0 and the GNU C++ Compiler.
- Helpful ideas concerning the type of programming error and resulting compiler warnings/errors or program behavior are given.
- A wide variety of program examples, ranging from short one-liners to multi-file, multi-object, medium size programs, are included.
- Complete programs, such as accessing the computer system time as a seed for the random number generator or shuffling and dealing playing cards, are provided. The reader is welcome to use any of these as a starting point for further expansion.

C++ Programming Today Has Information Not Found in Other Texts

Many of the *C++ Programming Today* appendixes contain information and demonstration programs for the day-to-day programmer. Summary tables for function use are found throughout the text. There are several unique appendixes, including:

- Getting Started with Visual C++ and the Visual C++ Help.
- File Input/Output, showing sample programs for working with text and binary files.
- How to use the Microsoft Visual C++ Debugger.
- Building multifile programs.
- C++ Keyword Dictionary, containing the sixty-three C++ keywords, with a description and example of how each keyword is used.

Two CD-ROMs Accompany *C++ Programming Today*

Two compact disks are included with this book. One CD is a copy of the Microsoft Visual C++ Version 6.0, Introduction Edition, which may be installed on a personal computer and used to build and run C++ programs. This software includes the Visual C++ development tools as well as an excellent C++ language reference.

The second CD contains the source code for all the program examples in this text. These examples are organized into Microsoft Visual C++ project folders, and each project is located in its respective chapter folder. These source code folders should be copied onto your hard disk and accessed through Visual C++. The source code files (including *.cpp and *.h files) are text-based and ready to be copied to other C++ development environments.

Ancillary Package

- *Laboratory Manual for C++ Programming Today* (ISBN 0-13-093660-X) provides a large variety of complete programming problems for students. It contains assignments beginning with Chapter 2, Getting Started, through Chapter 11, Inheritance and Virtual Functions. As with any programming language, it is necessary for students to be given problems where they can build codes "from the ground up." The programming tasks in this lab manual present easily understood problems that challenge the new programmer to explore and use the language features.

- *Instructor's Manual to accompany C++ Programming Today* (ISBN 0-13-092392-3) provides the solutions to the Review Questions and Problems found at the end of each chapter. The manual, which is available free of charge to instructors using the text for a course, provides discussion and insight into topics that beginning C++ students may find difficult or confusing. Complete program source codes for all programming problems in the text are provided on an accompanying CD-ROM.

- Companion Website, www.prenhall.com/johnston

- Prentice Hall Test Manager (ISBN 0-13-093669-3)

ISO C++, Not Visual C++

The programs included in this text are written according to the International Standards Organization C++ standards. You may run (or modify and run) these programs on any computer system that has ISO standard C++ software. The Microsoft Visual C++ software is included so that you may load it on your personal computer at home and practice writing C++ programs. The appendixes cover how to build and debug a program in Visual C++. You can create and run these programs using the Microsoft Visual C++ Console Application.

The Visual C++ environment also provides the programmer with the necessary tools for writing Microsoft Windows applications. The Windows application programs typically have a graphical user interface, driven by selecting menu items or by clicking the mouse. Visual C++ has an entire object-oriented framework, known as the Microsoft Foundation Class (MFC), for writing these applications. This text does not present in-depth material on MFC or Windows application programming. A brief overview of MFC may be found in Chapter 12, Advanced Topics in C++.

Life After *C++ Programming Today*

Master the concepts in *C++ Programming Today*. With them you will find yourself well prepared to tackle Windows programming using Microsoft Foundation Class Library, start learning Java™, or simply continue working on more C++ problems.

Bon Voyage!

Barbara Johnston

Acknowledgments

"Would you consider writing a textbook?" This suggestion came from my Prentice Hall book rep, Celeste Nossiter. She and I had exhausted our search for an appropriate text for the C and C++ students at Albuquerque Technical Vocational Institute (TVI). After I stopped laughing and realized she was serious, I did eventually submit a textbook proposal to her. Before long, Charles Stewart, my Prentice Hall Publisher, was on my home-phone speed dial.

So many people to thank. First and foremost, my family—Janis, Maddie, and Hannah Banana, who were never jealous of the large time requirement, and who endured Crabzilla as she worked on this book. I appreciate the ongoing interest and support of my dad, John Johnston; my sister Lucy (and husband John) Snell; and my little brother Bob (and wife Janet) Johnston. Very special thanks go to my good friends and fellow OptiCAD Corporation engineers: Mike Abernathy, Ed Sklar, and Carolyn Galceran, who supported their team member in this writing effort. The project never would have been attempted without the support of Mike and Ed. My close friends Susan Furney and Melissa Williams provided encouragement and the use of their computer for testing purposes. I give special thanks to Dr. Janis White, my housemate, for her helpful advice, technical direction throughout this entire project, and her excellent spaghetti dinners!

Two special people are my gold-star support team—Aunt Mary and Claire. My aunt, Mary J. Culbertson, supplied her impeccable proofreading, editing, and grammatical skills. Aunt Mary read every single chapter and appendix many, many times. She smoothed out the rough sentences, rearranged sections to improve the flow, and made sure my style was consistent. She worried over the placement of commas so that I could worry about content. She made sure that my quotations and punctuation were accurate and that I didn't dangle my participles or split my infinitives. Although she claims not to be technical, she made several insightful suggestions to improve my presentation of the C++ language. She is a very important behind-the-scenes person and here is a *big* thank you, Aunt Mary!

Claire C. Jaramillo was my student when I began this project and she has since completed her associate degree in programming. She now works as a programmer in TVI's Computer Information Technology Department. Claire offered to read through the chapters before the classroom students received them. Her continued guidance and insight into what works and what doesn't—from the *student's* perspective—are widely incorporated into this text. Claire took the time to help and I thank her for that.

This text would not be possible without the help of my students at Albuquerque Technical Vocational Institute, New Mexico's largest community college. These students range from programming students, CAD designers and animators, to engineers and software developers from industry. For several semesters these students "test-drove" the chapters and program problems. My students were open and honest, careful with their remarks, and free with their criticisms. Because of their comments and advice, chapters were rewritten, reorganized, renamed, and reworked. To avoid the risk of excluding someone, I wish simply to thank all of my students.

I want to give special thanks to Christine Burns and Derek Fontes for their hard work during the eleventh hour in getting the program source files built into Microsoft Visual C++ projects. They did a great job in organizing the software and the program index. Also, Christine ran all the broken programs through the GNU C++ Compiler. I want to thank and acknowledge Frank Gonzales, musician, graphic artist, and C++ programming student, for his creation of the cover artwork and signal-light icons used in the text. Thanks to Wayne Bennett for helping us select the color palette for the text. A very special thank you to Nancy Koschmann Seemann, my long-time friend and fellow programming instructor, for sharing her excellent proofreading skills and insight.

The TVI Technologies Department deserves recognition for its continued support and interest. Dr. Richard Birkey, Dean, has been most enthusiastic about this project from the beginning. Paul Quan, Director of Computer Technologies, managed to rework my schedule to ensure that I was teaching the appropriate courses that supported this book. Steve Benavidez, Associate Dean, was and still is quick with a smile and an encouraging word. The Lab techs in the E100 lab, including Todd Edgel, Cheryl Brinkley, and Gary Johnson, were most helpful. I feel very fortunate to work with this group of individuals.

I would like to thank the following reviewers for their positive feedback and valuable suggestions: Larry Bernstein, Stevens Institute of Technology, NJ; Susan Garrod, Purdue University, IN; Hayward H. Franklin and G. Harrison Hilt, Albuquerque Technical Vocational Institute, NM; Cynthia Herrera, Advanced Technical Alliances, NM; George Peters, St. Clair College of Applied Art and Technology, Canada; Steven Smith, El Paso Community College, TX; and Asad Yousuf, Savannah State University, GA.

I am grateful to my editorial team at Prentice Hall. Charles Stewart found the time to return my phone calls and to keep my spirits up. Delia K. Uherec, my Prentice Hall Assistant Editor, has been enthusiastic and helpful. I admire her "can-do" attitude. Alex Wolf, Production Editor, and the Prentice Hall production team deserve special thanks for their help and patience.

Barbara Johnston

Contents

1

C++ Overview and Software Development 2

Key Terms and Concepts 2

Chapter Objectives 2

Welcome! 3

1.1 What Is C and What Is C++? 6
A Brief Overview and History of C and C++ 7
C/C++ Is a Compiled Language 8
Why Do Programmers Love C++? 8

1.2 What Do You Mean by *Object-Oriented*? 10
A C++ Program Is Not Automatically Object-Oriented 10
An Easy Example of an Object-Oriented Program 11
Object-Oriented Software Is Better 11

1.3 Structured Design Versus Object-Oriented Design 12
ATM—Structured Approach 12
ATM Object-Oriented Approach 13

1.4 Software Construction Techniques: An Overview 16
How Not to Program 16

1.5 Troubleshooting 17
What Is Wrong with My Program? 18

Review Questions and Problems 18

2

Getting Started: Data Types, Variables, Operators, Arithmetic, and Simple I/O   20

Key Terms and Concepts   20

Keywords and Operators   20

Chapter Objectives   20

The Big Picture   21

2.1   Programming Fundamentals   21
      Algorithm Design   22
      Steps to Programming Success   24
      Practice: How to Give a Cat a Bath   25
      Rule of Thirds   25
      How to Program   27

2.2   Terminology and Project Construction   28
      Construction Steps   28

2.3   General Format of a C++ Program   29
      Hello World! Program   29
      Comments   30
      Preprocessor Directives   30
      The main Function   31
      Function Header Line   31
      C++ Statements   31
      How's the Weather?   32
      Whitespace Characters and Flexible Style in C++   32
      Language Syntax and Compiler Errors   34
      C++ Keywords   36
      Upper- and Lowercase Sensitive   37
      Good Style   37
      Love My Style   37
      One Last Comment on Comments   38

2.4   Programs and Data: Balls and Sticks   38

2.5   Data Types in C++   39
      Shelves = Memory, Containers = Data Types, Labels = Variable
        Names   40
      Data Type Modifiers   42
      Troubleshooting: How Big Is the Integer?   42

2.6   Variable Declaration in C++   43
      Naming Rules in C++   44
      Where Can You Declare Variables?   44

2.7   Operators in C++   45
      Precedence of Operations   45

Assignment Operator   46
Arithmetic Operators   48
Increment and Decrement Operators   53
Accumulation Operators   56
Other Operators in C++   57

2.8   Miscellaneous Topics: #define, const, and casting   57
#define   57
The const Modifier   59
Are consts Better Than #define?   60
Data Casts   61

2.9   Keyboard Input and Screen Output   64

2.10   Practice   64
Troubleshooting: Equation Placement   64
Calculate the Volume of a Cylinder   65
Modulus and Feet and Inches   66
Character Data As Decimal, Hex, and Octal and ios Formatting   67

Review Questions and Problems   68

3

Control Statements and Loops   72

Key Terms and Concepts   72

Keywords and Operators   72

Chapter Objectives   72

Decisions, Decisions!   73

3.1   Relational and Logical Operators   74
Evaluating Expressions and Precedence of Operators   75

3.2   if Statements   77
if else Statements   79
Troubleshooting: Use Braces with if Statements   80
if—else if—else Statements   81
Inefficient Programming Techniques   83
if else: This Old Man Program Example   84
Nested if else Statements   86
The ? Operator   87

3.3   switch Statement   88
Troubleshooting: Don't Forget to Break Your Switch   88

3.4   Loops in General   90
To Brace or Not to Brace?   91
You Can't Get Out of an Infinite Loop   91

3.5 for Loop 91
Do Not Alter the Loop Index 93
for Loop Examples 94

3.6 while Loop 95
while Loop Examples 96

3.7 do while Loop 97
do while Examples 98

3.8 Troubleshooting 100
Four Common Mistakes 100
Troubleshooting: My Loop Won't Stop 103
Troubleshooting: Semicolons and Braces 104
Troubleshooting: Misplaced else, Illegal else, Unexpected End of File 106
Debugging Your Program 108

3.9 Summary 108
The Indenting Convention 108

3.10 Practice 108
Time Conversion 110
Numbers 111
Output Patterns 113

Review Questions and Problems 116

4

Pointers, Addresses, and the Indirection Operator   122

Key Terms and Concepts 122

Keywords and Operators 122

Chapter Objectives 122

Parking and Pointers 123

4.1 Importance of Pointers 123

4.2 Data Variables and Memory 124
sizeof Operator 124
Reserving Memory 126
Computer Memory and Hex 126

4.3 Address Operator: & 127

4.4 Pointers 129
Pointers and the Address Operator 130
Little Red Riding Hood and the White House 132
Pointers and the Indirection Operator 132
Mixed Up Pointers 135

4.5 Where Are We Going with Pointers? 137
Functions in C++ Return One Piece of Data 138
Efficient Handling of Large Data Structures, Arrays, and Classes 138

4.6 Summary 139
Do Pointers Early and Often 140

4.7 Practice 141
WriteHello and Pointers 141
Knick-Knacking and Pointers 141
How Big Is Your Pyramid and Pointers 142

Review Questions and Problems 143

5

Functions   Part I: The Basics   148

Key Terms and Concepts 148

Keywords and Operators 148

Chapter Objectives 148

Building Houses, Building Software 149

5.1 Functions in C++ 149
Life Before Functions 149
Life with Functions 150
Functions Are Good 152

5.2 Functions: Basic Format 152
Four Simple Functions 152
Calling and Called Functions 154

5.3 Requirements for Writing Functions 154
How Old Are You? 155
Function Prototype 156
Function Calls 157
Function Header Lines and Function Bodies 158
Call by Value 160
Another Program Example 160
Review General Format of Functions 162
Troubleshooting: Type Mismatch 164
Troubleshooting: Data Type in Call Statement 167
Function Requirements and C++ Libraries 168

5.4 Local, Static, and Global Variables 168
Local Variables 168
Troubleshooting: Forgetting to Declare Variables 169
Static Variables 170
Global Variables 171

Global Variables Are Dangerous   172
Troubleshooting: Global Variable y1 and math.h   173

5.5   Pointers and Functions   174
Review Call by Value   174
Two Values from a Function?   174
Brief Review of Pointers   175
Call by Reference: Variable's Address to a Function   176

5.6   Summary   180

5.7   Practice   180
IsItPrime   180
Random Numbers   185
Time Conversion   185
Cats and Dogs   188

Review Questions and Problems   191

6

Arrays   196

Key Terms and Concepts   196

Keywords and Operators   196

Chapter Objectives   196

Run Faster! Jump Higher!   197

6.1   Using Single Data Variables   197

6.2   Array Fundamentals   197
Arrays in C++ Are Zero Indexed   200
Arrays Are Not Automatically Initialized   200
One-Dimensional Array Initialization   200
for Loops and Arrays   201

6.3   A Free Pointer with Every Array   202
Array Pointers   204

6.4   One-Dimensional Arrays and Functions   206
Arrays and Their Pointers   206
Passing One-Dimensional Arrays to Functions   206
Array Averaging Program   207
Troubleshooting: You Can't "return" an Array from a Function   209

6.5   Character Strings   213
Character String Initialization   213
The Null Character   214
Character String Input   217
Reading Both Numeric and Character Data   224
Character String Functions Provided in C++   225

6.6 Multidimensional Arrays 226
Two-Dimensional Array Initialization 228
Nested for Loops and Two-Dimensional Arrays 230
Utility Costs Program with Two-Dimensional Array 230

6.7 Multidimensional Arrays and Functions 233
Revisit Utility Costs Program 233
Snow White: Two-Dimensional Array of Names Program 234

6.8 Array Out of Bounds 235
Array Out of Bounds == Big Trouble 237

6.9 Filling Arrays from Data Files 237

6.10 Summary 238

6.11 Practice 238
Favorite Word 238
How's the Weather? 241

Review Questions and Problems 245

7

User-Defined Data Types, struct, and enum   250

Key Terms and Concepts 250

Keywords and Operators 250

Chapter Objectives 250

Building a Fort 251

7.1 Customized Data Types 251
Grouping Data Together 251
structs and enums 252

7.2 Data Structures 253
Review the Concept of a Data Type 253
Creating and Declaring Structures 254
Structure Tags 255
Data Structures Without Tags 256

7.3 Accessing Structure Elements 257
Boxes 257
Accessing Structure Elements 257

7.4 Structure Arrays 261
Structure Array Examples 261

7.5 Structures Within Structures 264
Race Program with a Time Structure 264
A Structure with Two Structures 266

7.6   Copying Structures   269

7.7   Structures and Functions   270
Starting Time Program   270
Averaging Two Points Program   272

7.8   Call by Reference: Structure Address to a Function   274
Pointers and Functions: Quick Review   274
Filling and Returning Student Data Structure   275
Right-Arrow Operator Versus Dot Operator   276
Programmer's Shortcut   278
Bird-Watching Program   280

7.9   Structure Arrays and Functions   281
The Bottom Line   281
Array of Student structs Program   282

7.10   Enumerated Data Types   283
enums Create Numbered Lists   286
enums: Assign and Compare   288
Troubleshooting enums: Choose enum Values Carefully   293
Money Makes the World Go 'Round   293
Input and Output for enum Data   295

7.11   Enumerated Data Types and Functions   297
Optics Part Example and Error Code   297

7.12   Multifile Programs   301

7.13   Practice   301
What Time Is It?   301
Show Me the Cards   303
Fun Dog Shows   305

Review Questions and Problems   307

8

Functions   Part II: C++ Function Enhancements   314

Key Terms and Concepts   314

Keyword   314

Chapter Objectives   314

Leaving the Structured World Behind   315

8.1   Function Review   316
Basic Requirements   316
Call by Value   316
Calling and Called Functions   316
Call by Reference: Variable Address to a Function   317

Global Variables and Functions   319
Four Methods for Getting Data to and from Functions   319

8.2   Call by Reference Using Reference Parameters   320
Call by Reference with Reference Parameters   321
Reference Variable Arrays   329

8.3   Overloaded Functions   330
In the Old C Days   330
Overloaded Functions   332

8.4   Variable-Length Parameter List Functions   333
DrawLines Program   335
Parameter Order   335
Troubleshooting: Overloaded Functions   338
Can You Mix and Match Overloaded Functions?   341

8.5   Inline Functions   343

8.6   Summary   344

Review Questions and Problems   345

9

Classes and Objects   354

Key Terms and Concepts   354

Keywords and Operators   354

Chapter Objectives   354

Wax On, Wax Off   355

9.1   Object-Oriented Principles and Definitions   355
A Brief Introduction   355
Principles of an Object-Oriented Language   358
Objects Are Real-World Things   359
Object Definition   360

9.2   Classes and Objects   361
Object-Oriented Analysis: Characteristics, Behaviors, and Functions   361
Object-Oriented Design   363
Structured TennisBall   365
Class Declaration   366
TennisBall Class   367
How to Get Values into the Data Members   370

9.3   Writing Member Functions   375
Two Different Formats/Locations   373
Class Sphere Example   375

9.4   Class Constructors   377
How to Initialize Class Data Members   377

Class Constructor Functions   378
Constructors and the Seven-Day/Twenty-Four-Hour Clock   379
Constructor Notes   381
Two Dates Program   382

9.5   Class Destructors   385

9.6   A Simple Example   387
Common Stumbling Blocks   387
The Gadgets Program   388
Troubleshooting: Common Errors with Classes   391

9.7   Array of Objects   397
Array of PhoneList Objects   397
Array of Objects and Show Me the Cards   400

9.8   Overloaded Operators and Objects   403
Unary Overloaded Operators   404
Prefix Versus Postfix with Increment/Decrement Operators   405
Binary Overloaded Operators   406

9.9   Pointers and Classes   413
Program Examples   414

9.10   Summary   421
Comparing Structures and Classes   421

9.11   Practice   423
Big, Bigger, Biggest Football Players   423

Review Questions and Problems   428

10

Class Relationships   436

Key Terms and Concepts   436

Chapter Objectives   436

It's Time to Have Fun!   437

10.1   Object Model and Class Relationships   437

10.2   *Using* C++ Language Classes   438
iostream   439
C++ String Class   439
C++ Numeric Classes   439
using namespace std   440
Simple namespace Example   440

10.3   *Having* and *Using* User-Defined Classes   442
Example 1   443
Example 2: DicePlayer Has Dice   451

Example 3: A Track_Coach Has a StopWatch; the StopWatch Uses a
   MasterClock   455
Example 4: Cola Vending Machine   459

10.4   Summary   469

Problems   470

11

Inheritance and Virtual Functions   474

Key Terms and Concepts   474

Chapter Objectives   474

Parents and Children   475

11.1   Why Is Inheritance So Important?   475
   Counter Class Example   475
   Inheritance Is the Answer   477

11.2   Inheritance Basics   478
   Counter and NewCounter Example   478
   Protected Members   482
   Employees, Bosses, and CEOs   484

11.3   Access Specifier Specifics   495

11.4   Multiple Inheritance   496

11.5   Inheritance, Constructors, and Destructors   497
   Review of Constructors and Destructors   497
   Base and Derived Classes and Constructor Functions   497
   Base and Derived Classes and Destructor Functions   498
   Parameter Passing and Base and Derived Constructor Functions   499
   Troubleshooting: Inheritance   507

11.6   Inheritance Program Examples   509
   The Animals Program   510
   Shuffle and Deal the Cards   513
   Object-Oriented Program Design   514
   Class Declarations   518

11.7   Polymorphism and Virtual Functions   526
   Polymorphism—One Interface, Many Forms   526
   What Is a Virtual Function?   528
   Purely Virtual Functions   531
   How Are Virtual Functions Useful?   531

11.8   Summary   536

Review Questions and Problems   537

12

Advanced Topics in C++   542

Key Terms and Concepts   542

Keywords and Operators   542

Chapter Objectives   542

The Tip of the Iceberg!   543

12.1   Dynamic Memory Allocation   544
     Overview   544
     New and Delete Operators   545
     What if New Fails?   548

12.2   Star Wars   550
     Allocating Memory for a Two- or Three-Dimensional Array   550
     Passing an Address to a Function and Beyond   556

12.3   Exception Handling   557
     KISS Examples   558
     Exception Handling with New Operator   560

12.4   Microsoft Foundation Class Library (MFC)   562
     Brief Overview   562
     Build a Beeping Windows Program in a Few Mouse Clicks   563

12.5   The Java™ Programming Language   565
     Java™ Is C++ Without Pointers   566
     Hello World in Java™   566

12.6   Summary: Templates, Standard Template Library, and Friends   567

Appendices

A   Getting Started with Visual C++   569

B   C++ Keyword Dictionary   585

C   Operators in C++   601

D   ASCII Character Codes   602

E   Bits, Bytes, Memory, and Hexadecimal Notation   607

F   File Input/Output   614

G   C++ String Class   628

H   Multifile Programs   639

I   Keyboard Input, Screen Output   649

J   Microsoft Visual C++ Debugger   663

K   Program Index   673

Bibliography   686

Glossary   687

Index   699

C++ Programming Today

1

C++ Overview and Software Development

KEY TERMS AND CONCEPTS

ANSI/ISO standard
C++ class
compiler
functions
GCC GNU C Compiler
linker
object
object-oriented program
operators
pointers
portable language
software development steps
software development skill set
source code
standardized libraries
structured programming
top-down
Visual C++

CHAPTER OBJECTIVES

Introduce this text to the reader.

Present the history and an overview of the C and C++ languages.

Illustrate the concept of object-oriented programming.

Compare structured program design and object-oriented program design.

Help the programmer begin thinking about all aspects of building software.

Welcome!

You are about to embark on a wonderful journey. Learning to write computer programs with the C++ programming language will bring you a wonderful sense of accomplishment. When you become an efficient C++ developer, technical career doors will open for you and many programming paths will become available. C++ is a cornerstone in today's programming environment. Whether you are writing controllers for robots, implementing elegant user interfaces, building high-speed graphics for games, interfacing into databases, or learning the Java programming language for Internet and Web application, C++ is where it all starts.

But beware! Programming—in any language—is not for everyone. Ahead in the journey are speed bumps, potholes, clear-air turbulence, and fog. A successful programmer uses many skills, including logical thinking and troubleshooting. At times, success seems to depend on just plain luck. If you are already familiar with another programming language and are now learning C++, you are aware of all these factors. If C++ is your first programming language, you will find these pearls of wisdom to be true soon enough.

Software Developer Skill Set

Aside from learning C++, there are several other skills a student must learn to be a successful software developer and to contribute fully to a development or maintenance job. A few of these skills are listed in Table 1-1.

A software developer must also be a student of other fields. For any software job, the developer needs to become knowledgeable regarding the activities concerning the software while working closely with non-software experts on a project. For example, to write an inventory control and tracking system for an international company, the software team must have a good idea of all aspects of the business. Software developers are not expected to be experts in everything, but they should expect to keep learning new things long after school is out.

software development skill set
the necessary skills a person should possess to become a successful programmer

3

Skill	Where It Is Used
Documentation	All software needs to be documented well and be easy to read. Documentation describes what the program is doing, the logic that is used, how the user interacts with the program, and any special methods used to solve the problems. You should write your software assuming it will be used for years to come. Can someone read your software and know what you were doing?
Communication	Software developers must be able to communicate with team members, customers, and end users. Software projects often go through several design stages. Formal design and requirements documents are written before any code is built.
Quick learners	Software developers often work with experts in other fields who need to have software written. The software developer must gain some level of understanding of the new concepts before he or she is able to build the software. Often programming requires the use of mathematics, and the programmer should be familiar with mathematical concepts.
Debugging	It is vitally important to learn debugging skills when developing software. Debuggers aid in finding problems in software.
Troubleshooting	Debugging "broken" code is common. Good analysis/troubleshooting skills are invaluable.
Testing	Always think about how to test your software. Are you covering all the cases? Testing is one of the most important aspects of software development, but it is the most often neglected.

A Few Details Concerning This Text

Concepts, Order of Presentation   Chapters 2 through 7 present the nuts and bolts of the C/C++ language without any object-oriented discussions. It is important to learn about different types of data, how to code mathematics, and how to get data in and out of a program (Chapter 2). We need to be able to have our code perform branching statements and loops (Chapter 3). Chapter 4 presents an introduction to pointers—handy little devices found everywhere in C and C++ code. Chapter 5 teaches us how to separate our code into individual modules known as functions. Chapter 6 introduces the concept of an array—a list or grouping of data variables and, finally, Chapter 7 slides us into working with data structures.

The mechanics of writing object-oriented software are based on these concepts. One must be comfortable working with functions and structures before venturing into classes and objects. Program design using objects is difficult enough without struggling with the fundamentals of calling a function. Therefore, we will be working through the topics in a somewhat structured manner.

Visual C++

Microsoft's C++ development environment

Accompanying CDs with This Book   Two compact disks are included with this book. One CD is a copy of the ***Microsoft Visual C++*** Version 6.0, Introduction

Edition, which may be installed on a personal computer and used to build and run C++ programs. This software includes the Visual C++ development tools as well as an excellent C++ Language Reference. Appendix A, "Getting Started with Visual C++", covers the Visual C++ system requirements, software installation, all of the necessary steps to creating and running a simple project, and how to access the help feature. (The debugger tool is described in Appendix J.)

The second CD contains the source code for all the program examples in this text. These examples are organized into Visual C++ project folders, and each is located in its respective chapter folder. The reader should copy the project folders onto her or his hard drive. The projects may be opened using Visual C++, or the source files can be copied and compiled in other C++ environments.

ISO C++, Not Visual C++   The programs included in this text are written according to the International Standards Organization C++ standards. You may run (or modify and run) these programs on any computer system that has ISO standard C++ software. The Microsoft Visual C++ software is included so that you may load it on your personal computer at home and practice writing C++ programs. The appendixes cover how to build and debug a program in Visual C++. We will be creating and running our programs by using the Microsoft Visual C++ Console Application.

The Visual C++ environment also provides the programmer with the necessary tools for writing Microsoft Windows applications. The Windows application programs typically have a graphical user interface, driven by selecting menu items or by clicking the mouse. Visual C++ has an entire object-oriented framework, known as the Microsoft Foundation Class (MFC), for writing these applications. This text does not present in-depth material on MFC or Windows application programming. A brief overview of MFC may be found in Chapter 12, Advanced Topics in C++.

Program Examples, Output, Errors, and Warnings   This book also includes a wide variety of program examples—short one-liners to multifile, multiobject, medium-size programs. Some are complete programs, and the reader is welcome to use them as starting points for further expansion, such as accessing the computer system time as a seed for the random number generator or shuffling and dealing playing cards. You will find many examples of code that are written incorrectly and hence do not build and execute. (Sometimes seeing the wrong way is more informative than seeing the right way.) We illustrate the wrong code and then the software error and/or warning messages.

For each program example where an error or a warning occurs, there are two examples of C++ messages. Each "broken" program has been run through the Microsoft Visual C++ Version 6.0 as well as through GCC, the *GNU C Compiler* that compiles C++ files with a cc extension. The GCC used for this text was version 2.91.66 running under a Redhat Linux, Release 6.1 operating system. We used the default compiler settings. The Web site for this free software is www.gnu.org.

GCC GNU C Compiler
C++ development environment produced by the GNU project

Johnston's Rules for Programmers

As a team member of a commercial firm engaged in building and developing software, I am acquainted with technology skills needed in the marketplace. And as a member of the faculty of a technical and vocational community college, I have learned ways to help students master these skills. Teaching beginning C and C++ students for many years has brought an understanding of the trials and tribulations that the new C++ student encounters.

Drafts of this text were used for four semesters by beginning (Chapters 1–6) and advanced (Chapters 7–11) programming students. These students were quite open about what they needed in the text to aid them in learning to program in C++, what they liked and did not like, and what was helpful and what was confusing. Past students who are now working as C/C++ programmers or are continuing their education have provided even more suggestions and advice.

A common theme for all these students is their belief in a set of rules we develop at the beginning of each programming course. We refer to them as either the "Nine Commandments for Programmers" or the "Johnston Rules for Programmers." They are:

> Keep your cool (don't get mad).
>
> Work when you are rested (don't program when you are tired).
>
> KISS your software (keep it simple, sweetie).
>
> Give help/get help.
>
> Study and know the rules for the language (syntax).
>
> Learn the development environment and tools (we'll concentrate on Visual C++).
>
> Understand the problem you are trying to solve.
>
> Build and test your software in steps.
>
> Save early/save often (back up your computer programming files often).

A tenth rule might emphasize, "Patience, patience." You can apply this maxim immediately, for several topics need to be covered before we reach the core of the C++ language. Read on, and principles which now seem disjointed will come together shortly.

1.1
What Is C and What Is C++?

Often there is a misconception concerning the C and C++ languages. Students wishing to learn the C++ language do not sign up for a C course. Students who need to learn the C language do not enroll for a C++ course. Colleges offering a series of C++ courses inevitably have students asking for a C course. What to do?

The C language was developed originally by Bell Laboratories and standard-ized by the ***American National Standards Institute (ANSI)*** in 1989. In 1990 the ***International Standards Organization (ISO)*** adopted the ANSI standard. You can think of the ISO standard as the governing laws for C++. Just as it is illegal to drive your car through a red light, it is "illegal" to "return" an array from a function.

The language has been expanded to include the ability to build object-oriented software. When a student learns the C++ language, he or she is learning C, too. The entire C language is wrapped up in C++. The "if" statement and "for" loop are essentially identical in C and C++. C has structures; C++ has structures and classes (which are necessary for objects). C++ has overloaded functions and opera-tors, whereas C does not. Structures? Functions? Operators? At this stage it is not necessary for you to know what these things are; however, it *is* important to realize that C++ contains all of the C language features and more!

ANSI/ISO
American National Standards Institute/International Standards Organization

A Brief Overview and History of C and C++

In the early 1970s at the Bell Laboratories, C was used originally as a programming language for operating systems, including Bell Labs' UNIX. However, C quickly became a popular, general-purpose programming language because it offered pro-grammers the basic tools for writing many types of programs.

How C Was Named   Everyone wants to know how the C language acquired its name. To appreciate how C was named, one needs to examine the historical aspects of the language. C is the result of a development process that began in the early 1960s with ALGOL 60, then Cambridge's CPL in 1963, Martin Richard's BCPL in 1967, and Ken Thompson's B language in 1970 at Bell Labs. Many of C's principal concepts are based in BCPL, and these concepts influenced the B and C languages.

The Evolution of C and C++   For many years the C software supplied with the UNIX operating system was the standard C software. Brian W. Kernighan and Den-nis M. Ritchie (C's original designers) published the book, *The C Programming Language* (Prentice Hall, 1978), which describes this version of C. In 1978, aside from the UNIX versions of C, Honeywell, IBM, and Interdata also offered applica-tion production software for the C language.

As C grew in popularity and computer hardware became more affordable, many versions of the C language were created. (Rumor has it that at one time there were twenty-four different versions of C!) Hardware vendors offered their own ver-sions of C, but there was no standard for the language. In 1982 an American National Standards Institute committee was formed to create the ANSI standard for the C language. This standard was adopted in 1989 and ensured that developers of C software used the same rules and procedures.

In 1994 extensions and corrections to the ISO C standard were adopted. The new features in the C language standard included additional library support for for-eign character sets, multibyte characters and wide characters. Extensions to the C language, providing an improved version of C as well as supporting object-oriented programming methodologies, were designed originally by Bjarne Stroustrup of AT&T Bell Labs. These extensions to the C language became known as the C++ language. A working draft of the ISO C++ standard was created in 1994 and adopted in November 1997.

C/C++ Is a Compiled Language

To build a program in C or C++, a programmer must go through many steps. Aside from defining the problem requirements and designing and entering the code on the computer, the programmer must have the computer build an executable file. We will cover all these various steps in detail later. For now, it helps to understand that when you type your program into the computer, you are entering *source code.* Source code contains the actual lines of C or C++ statements that give the program direction. A *compiler* is a computer program that reads the source code, and if the code is "grammatically correct," the compiler produces machine code.

C++ provides libraries that contain functions a programmer can use in his or her programs. For example, an input and output library provides tools for writing messages to the screen and receiving values that are entered from the keyboard. The next build step uses a *linker,* which literally links or hooks the machine code and library code together and binds it into an executable file—one that "runs" the program. Figure 1-1 illustrates these steps.

If you write a program for a personal computer, it must be compiled and linked on a PC. If the program is to run on a UNIX box, it must also be compiled and linked on that machine. This action of requiring only ISO C++ source code to be compiled and linked on various types of computers is known as code portability. A standardized language is a *portable language,* meaning that the source does not need to be changed when moved from one type of machine to another.

Two additional points must be noted. First, if a programmer uses (in his or her code) custom libraries that are specific to a certain operating system or machine, this code will not be portable across machines. For example, Visual C++ provides customized libraries for working with Windows. If the program source code uses these custom-Windows functions, the code will not be portable to a UNIX machine. Second, we should make a distinction between C++ and Java. C++ is portable across machines, but the code must be compiled and linked for each machine—without requiring changes to the source code. This is different from the way Java works. Java's code requires you to write it and build it once; then this built-version of Java will run anywhere.

Why Do Programmers Love C++?

The C++ language provides a wide variety of useful and powerful tools. These tools include data variables for handling numeric (both whole numbers and numbers with decimal precision) and character (text) data, as well as *pointers*—which are variables that "point" to other variables. There are a large number of *operators*

---

source code

file(s) that contain the C/C++ statements that provide program instructions

compiler

a software program that reads source code and produces object or machine code

linker

software program linking machine code and library code to form an executable file

portable language

language in which the source code need not be changed when moved from one type of computer to another

pointers

variables that "point" to other variables

operators

symbols that direct certain operations to be performed, such as + for addition, = for assignment

Source code file: AddTwoNums.cpp

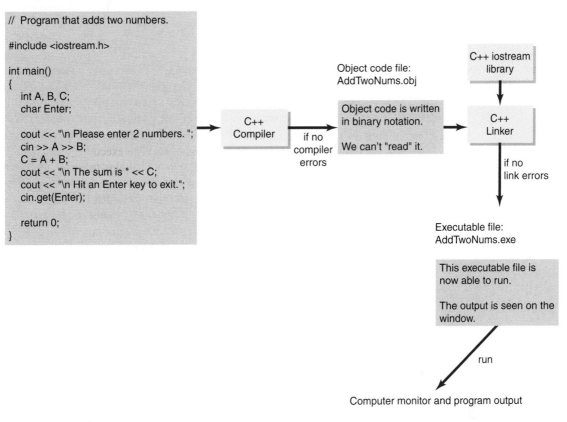

```
// Program that adds two numbers.

#include <iostream.h>

int main()
{
    int A, B, C;
    char Enter;

    cout << "\n Please enter 2 numbers. ";
    cin >> A >> B;
    C = A + B;
    cout << "\n The sum is " << C;
    cout << "\n Hit an Enter key to exit.";
    cin.get(Enter);

    return 0;
}
```

C++
Compiler

if no
compiler
errors

Object code file:
AddTwoNums.obj

Object code is written
in binary notation.

We can't "read" it.

C++ iostream
library

C++
Linker

if no
link errors

Executable file:
AddTwoNums.exe

This executable file is
now able to run.

The output is seen on the
window.

run

Computer monitor and program output

Please enter 2 numbers 5 6
The sum is 11

Hit an Enter to exit.

Figure 1-1
Program Build Steps, Compile, Link, and Run

(symbols that perform certain actions) in C++. For example, the + symbol adds numbers, the * multiplies numbers, etc. Basic decision and control structures enable a program to branch to different code statements or loop over statements.

In addition, C++ allows programmers to write their code in discrete modules, known as *functions.* These functions enable a programmer to organize his or her code and separate tasks logically. An entire group of functions can be grouped into separate files or even built into libraries, enabling procedures to be organized logically. For example, if your program contains many mathematical calculations, it is possible to separate each calculation in its own function and place all the functions in a separate "Calc" library. This action helps to keep your program size from becoming too large and unwieldy.

C++ also provides the programmer with the ability to customize his or her own data variables so that the program data can be organized and grouped as a single unit. We can't forget that there are many *standardized libraries* that provide useful functions for mathematics, file input/output, text operations, and other tools.

But the best part of the C++ language is the fact that we can write programs that use classes and objects. Once you get the "hang" of object-oriented programs, you will never want to use any other technique. What's more, our classes can have babies. Yes, it is possible to use a class as a "parent" or base class and create a "child" or derived class. The technical term for this is inheritance.

functions

discrete modules or units of code that perform specific tasks

standardized libraries

libraries included as part of the C++ language

1.2
What Do You Mean by *Object-Oriented*?

Simply put, *object-oriented programming* means that the program is based on real-world things (objects)—designed and built to model how these things interact instead of how the data flows through a program. If you are an experienced structured programmer, you may find this object business a new and very different way of thinking about program design. If you are new to the field of computer programming, you may find thinking in terms of objects a natural way to lay out program components.

object-oriented programming

program design based on the use of real-world items (objects) and the manner in which these objects interact

A C++ Program Is Not Automatically Object-Oriented

If you write a program in the C++ language, it may or may not be an object-oriented program. *For a program to be object-oriented, it must contain objects.* In the old days (before object-oriented software was available), C programs were designed according to data flow and what had to happen to the data. A common design scenario is this: start the program, find and open the data file, read in the data from the file, make use of the data, calculate the necessary output, write a report, close the data files. This type of program design is known as *top-down* or

structured or top-down programming

program design based on the flow of the data through the program *structured.* Of course, it is possible to write a structured program in C++, but it is not object-oriented.

An Easy Example of an Object-Oriented Program

An object-oriented program design takes a whole different approach. Instead of the step-by-step data flow through the program, an object-oriented design requires that the programmer identify the items (often real-world things) that are needed to perform certain tasks in the program. These items (objects) perform the various tasks for the program. It may be helpful to visualize different people as objects that perform different jobs. Each person (object) has a certain job description plus the necessary tools to perform his or her tasks. This job description is contained in what is known as a *C++ class.* An instance of a class is an *object.*

For example, a program scenario can be built with two objects. First, we create the "job descriptions" for our objects. This task is accomplished by using class descriptions. (Chapter 9 is where we learn all of the class details.) Our Reader_Writer class has the information, tools, and know-how for opening, reading from, writing to, and closing data files. Our second "worker" is a Calculator. The tasks of a Calculator class are to perform whatever mathematics is needed on the data and produces "answers." Let's have a Reader_Writer object named Martha, and a Calculator object named Don.

As our program runs, Martha opens and reads data from the files. She passes the data to Don. Martha doesn't care about anything else in the program. Files are her whole life. Don, on the other hand, doesn't care about files; he simply waits for the data to be passed to him and he performs the math and determines the "answers." Once the answers are passed back to Martha, she writes the answers into a file and closes it. Martha worries about file input and output; Don worries about calculations.

C++ class
fundamental unit in object-oriented programming that contains the "job description" for a program object

object
single instance of a class

Object-Oriented Software Is Better

The C++ language is the C language with the additional necessary features and extensions so that the programmer can build object-oriented software. Object-oriented design and implementation is a more natural way to think about problem solving. Using objects, a team of programmers can identify and assign program tasks to different classes. The program then creates the required number of objects. Each object has its job description contained in a class definition. It is relatively easy to modify the class and thus correct or change an object's task. Object-oriented software techniques have grown in popularity because this process revolves around a well-defined approach and lends itself to producing maintainable, reliable, and reusable software.

Commercial software vendors have a wealth of software tools that C++ software developers can purchase and incorporate into their own projects. Graphics packages, file translators, and complicated computer-aided design tools are just a few. What is so wonderful is that these commercial software products are all object-oriented based. If you need a fancy translator, you simply include a translator object in your code (we can call it Bud), and Bud brings with him all the translator tools we need. We simply ask Bud to perform certain translation tasks. We do not need to modify our existing code except to ask Bud to do things for us. Isn't that great!?

Software development projects have a notorious history of being delivered late, exceeding the budget, and not meeting the desired specifications. Then, once the software is in place, if the people who wrote it are not available to maintain and modify it, it is nearly impossible to correct errors or to add new features. Correctly designed and implemented object-oriented code makes software easier to maintain, modify, and expand.

Programmers need to understand that just using the C++ language does not ensure perfect code. It is easy to write "spaghetti code" in C++. (*Spaghetti code* is a term used by programmers for code that is impossible to follow and understand—like trying to unravel a single strand from a plate of spaghetti.) For the programmers to learn how to write object-oriented software correctly, the software must be carefully designed and use the many object-oriented principles. Later chapters in this text will discuss more detail about designing object-oriented programs.

1.3
Structured Design Versus Object-Oriented Design

Let's do an example in both a structured format and an objects format. This example does not contain C++ code but just lays out the design and flow of the program. Need cash? Where is the nearest automatic teller machine (ATM)? Here we model a few of the ATM tasks.

ATM—Structured Approach

To design an ATM program in a structured approach, we need to list the steps a customer takes to use the ATM. Once the steps are identified, we determine what routines are needed. This is shown in Table 1-2.

In this structured ATM, we can have a main loop that starts when the card is inserted. Once the card is validated, this loop basically asks the user to choose a transaction, calls the appropriate transaction function, and asks the user if he or she would like another transaction. This process seems straightforward and uncomplicated. But what if you need to hook in camera controls? What if a new printer is installed? What if a new type of transaction is added? The guts of the main loop will require rewriting and complete testing.

User Action	Required Routine	Additional Supporting Routines
Insert card into slot	Card Reader to obtain information off the magnetic strip.	Check for errors if card is inserted into slot incorrectly. Validate the ATM card.
Enter PIN	Read PIN and validate bank customer.	Contact ATM network and send/receive data.
Choose transaction	Present transaction options and process transactions.	Contact ATM network, verify transaction, and obtain customer account balances.
Get money	Dispense money to customer.	Before dispensing, check that ATM has enough money to dispense.
Make deposit	Unlock deposit slot and receive envelope.	Check that envelope has been inserted into slot.
Obtain receipt	Print receipt and form-feed to customer.	Return card to user. Turn on beeping sound so customer will not forget the card.

ATM Object-Oriented Approach

An object is a real-world item that has certain characteristics and behaviors. Instead of separating the ATM program into routines such as ReadTheCard, Validate TheUser, ListTransactionOptions, DispenseMoney, and PrintReceipt, our ATM program can be divided into separate objects. (Do not think about the program flow now.) Several obvious parts are associated with an ATM—a card reader object, a printer object, a camera object, a keypad object. For the ATM program, other not-so-obvious objects include a customer object, an ATM controller object, a network object, and others. The ATM objects are illustrated in Figure 1-2, and Table 1-3 lists the characteristics and behaviors of these objects.

In an object-oriented design the various program objects are identified. For each object, the type of data required and functions for that data are identified. Certain objects may contain other objects or merely use their services. Another point is that the objects tell each other what to do or pass information between them.

To withdraw money from our object-oriented ATM, the different objects perform their tasks. (*Note:* This ATM example is strictly fictional. No real ATM code or design has been used. Any semblance of reality is strictly coincidental.) In object-oriented programming, the key is identifying the objects and designing the program with the object in mind instead of using the traditional top-down approach. See Table 1-4.

Figure 1-2
ATM Objects

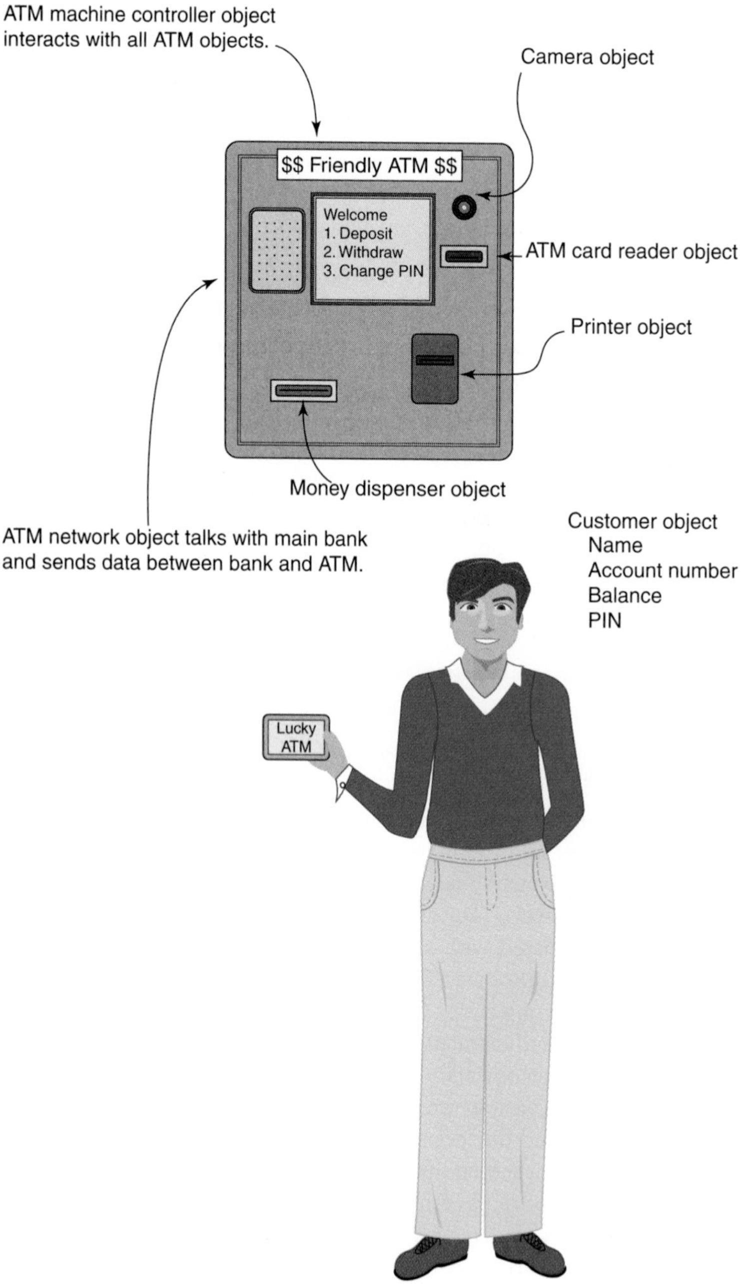

ATM machine controller object interacts with all ATM objects.

Camera object

$$ Friendly ATM $$

Welcome
1. Deposit
2. Withdraw
3. Change PIN

ATM card reader object

Printer object

Money dispenser object

ATM network object talks with main bank and sends data between bank and ATM.

Customer object
    Name
    Account number
    Balance
    PIN

Lucky
ATM

TABLE 1-3
Objects for Object-Oriented ATM Program

Object	Characteristics and Behaviors
Customer	Person who has a name, address, phone, social security number, bank, account number, PIN, and account balances and selects desired transaction.
ATM card reader	Accepts a card and reads data from the ATM card. Can eject card as well.
ATM controller	Interacts with all ATM objects. Queries customers, receives data from the card reader, contacts the ATM network, issues requests to the money dispenser and printer.
ATM network	Contacts network, uses network communication protocol, passes data from the controller to and from the mother bank.
Money dispenser	Gadget stuffed with $20 bills that dispenses exact amount of money.
Printer	Prints receipts, formats all output.
ATM camera	Video camera captures images of customer and can timestamp videotape.

TABLE 1-4
Object-Oriented ATM Program Flow for Withdrawing Money

Object	Task
Customer	Inserts ATM card into card reader.
Card reader	Reads the data off of the magnetic strip on the card. Tells the ATM controller that there is a customer. Passes the data to ATM controller.
ATM controller	ATM controller asks ATM camera to timestamp video. Asks the customer to enter his or her PIN. Accepts the PIN; asks the ATM network object to contact the mother bank and passes customer data to the ATM network object.
ATM network	Contacts the mother bank, passes data to the bank, and awaits reply. Network accepts the reply from the bank. Passes the reply to the ATM controller.
ATM controller	If customer is a valid bank customer, presents list of transaction options. If customer is not a valid bank customer, controller prints message to the screen. Asks the card reader to return the card.
Customer	Now selects withdraw money option.
ATM controller	Asks the money dispenser object to dispense requested money. Writes account information into ATM log.
Money dispenser	Passes requested money to customer.
ATM controller	Asks printer object to print receipt. Asks card reader to return card to the customer.

1.4
Software Construction Techniques: An Overview

Imagine that you are having your dream house built, and you have hired a contractor. The first day on the job the contractor shows up at your vacant lot and drops off piles of lumber, bags of cement, and rolls of wires. He leans the roll of your new living room carpeting against a tree. He stacks the windows on top of each other in the back, has the sheet-rock, electrical fixtures, plumbing items, and doorknobs lying on the dirt. Then he asks you where you want the kitchen. Moreover, he brings his crew to the site of the new house, and they are asking each other how to use the tools, reading how-to books, and looking at the wires and electrical outlets, wondering how they hook together.

Sounds silly? This scenario should never happen! The contractor has a blueprint of your house, and he knows what you want. He knows how much lumber and cement and wire to have on hand and doesn't have items delivered until it is the right time to use or install them. His builders know how to use equipment properly and understand construction techniques. The contractor knows there is a certain order in which things must happen. He makes sure the cement is dry before putting up the frame!

Building software and building houses take similar approaches. Before you start hammering two-by-fours together on your house frame, or writing your functions, you must know what you want to build. What are the requirements and what is the program supposed to do? Just as the contractor builds your house in logical steps, software must be built in logical steps, too.

As students first start learning to program, they often make common mistakes with disastrous results. A student who would never build a house without a blueprint may sit down at the computer and start building software without a plan. Just as a contractor never will put on the roof until he is sure the walls are strong enough to hold it, students never should hook together complicated software modules without testing each piece.

How Not to Program

It is important to learn how to crawl before walking, and to walk before running, and much of this text covers the C++ fundamentals of crawling and walking. In watching babies learn to crawl, walk, and run, adults sometimes have to let them fall a few times. There are all sorts of lessons awaiting beginning C++ programmers. However, just as a responsible parent will keep a watchful eye on the toddler, it is only right to provide beginning C++ programmers with a few pointers.

The following chapters of this book provide troubleshooting information concerning the language. Table 1-5 describes many steps to avoid while programming. I have compiled this table after watching many, many beginning C++ programmers tackle programming assignments in the wrong way.

1.5
Troubleshooting

If your car does not start, what do you do? You follow a logical set of steps to determine the problem. Is your battery dead? Do you have enough fuel? Is there a loose wire? Tracking down a software problem also involves asking simple questions and examining the program to find the error.

What Is Wrong with My Program?

This common phrase is heard in computer labs everywhere. The computer is unforgiving at times and does exactly what you tell it. Many mistakes can be avoided if a student will learn and follow the "nine commandments of programming" and try not to fall into the habit of doing the "don'ts" listed in Table 1-5.

▌ **TABLE 1-5**
Don'ts and Do's for Programmers

Don't	Do
Don't go directly to the computer, start typing in code, and assume you will be able to figure out the program as you go along.	DO: Write down on paper what you need to do.
Don't avoid testing the easy stuff.	DO: Simple functions may seem obviously correct. Spending five minutes checking a two-line function may save you hours of work later.
Don't depend on the compiler to ensure that your code is written correctly. The compiler will allow code to compile but will result in run-time errors.	DO: Understand every single line of code you enter into your program.
Don't avoid comments in your code. You will be amazed how something that seems so clear is not clear a few days later.	DO: Write simple, clear comments explaining your program logic.
Don't type in your entire program before compiling. Often one or two errors will result in many compiler errors.	DO: Build your program in steps, stopping and testing each step as you go.
Don't type in random braces if your program won't compile.	DO: Indent your code and line up your braces.
Don't get mad! When you find yourself getting frustrated with the program, it's time to leave it alone for a while. Go get a soft drink or coffee, take a walk, do the dishes.	DO: Work on your program when you are rested and it is quiet. Programming requires concentration, and interruptions often cause you to lose your train of thought.
Don't wait to start your program until the last moment, even if you do work well under pressure.	DO: Plan to work on your program over the course of several days. This strategy will give you time to rethink problems and refine the work as needed.

And so the journey begins. Again, look out for the hazards ahead because one must be wary and cautious when programming.

▌ REVIEW QUESTIONS AND PROBLEMS

Short Answer

1. When and where was the C language invented?

2. Why was it important for the ANSI committee to standardize the C language?

3. What type of programming techniques does C++ provide that the C language does not?

4. For what purpose was the C language originally designed?

5. What is meant by building and testing software in steps?

6. If a feature is found in the C language, is that feature in C++? Is the reverse true?

7. Describe the basic steps in designing and building software.

8. Why is it often heard that the UNIX operating system looks a lot like C?

9. Why is it important to learn all the tools in your development environment?

10. Name three skills programmers must have besides the ability to write software.

Problems

For questions 11–14, describe an object-oriented model for each item. Identify characteristics and behaviors of each item in terms of computer software; that is, assume you will be writing object-oriented software controls for each of these items.

11. Toaster with light-to-dark control.

12. Digital clock with alarm.

13. Baseball pitching machine. Assume the machine can be set to throw a curve ball, sinker, or slider.

14. Lawn sprinkler. Assume that the sprinkler system contains a single circuit of sprinklers with a simple timer control.

2

Getting Started: Data Types, Variables, Operators, Arithmetic, and Simple I/O

KEY TERMS AND CONCEPTS

algorithm
associativity
bit and byte
case sensitive
casting
comment
data type
#define
function header line
identifiers and naming rules
#include
keywords
lvalue and rvalue
operators
precedence of operations
preprocessor directive
rule of thirds
syntax
value
variables and declaration
whitespace

KEYWORDS AND OPERATORS

char, const, double, float
int, long, short, unsigned
* / % + - =
+= -= *= /= ++

CHAPTER OBJECTIVES

Indicate how to begin designing software by developing a step-by-step approach (algorithm) to a solution.

Introduce new terminology and software construction fundamentals.

Present a general format for a C++ program.

Understand the concept of a data type in the C++ language.

Demonstrate how to declare and to use a variable in a C++ program.

Explore the various C++ operators and how these operators are used in a program.

Illustrate the correct and incorrect methods of coding arithmetic in C++.

Notice how a C++ program writes data to the screen and receives data from the keyboard.

Describe compiler errors and warning messages.

Introduce the four icons to the reader:

 Good Programming Practice!

 Be Cautious!

 Stop! Do Not Do This!

 Troubleshooting Tip

The Big Picture

Programs and programming languages take many forms. There are programs that operate on mainframe computers maintaining airline reservations for hundreds of flights and thousands of travelers. Banking, insurance, and tax records can be found on mainframes. Programs run on personal computers that provide people with application tools for bookkeeping, mathematical calculations, computer design packages, and image processing. Now you can access the Internet, perform professional word processing, or make your own greeting cards—thanks to powerful and easy to use programs. Microsoft Visual C++ is a program, too! Some programs run on customized microprocessors. These programs often control hardware such as robots, assembly line components, and motor controls for various tasks. The software developers (programmers) who write these programs, for the most part, take the same production steps.

Such procedures involve taking an idea, determining all the necessary behaviors and actions, writing the software instructions, building the program according to the structure required by the language, and testing it to ensure the end results are what were originally desired. The majority of this text involves learning how to write the C++ language software instructions—but it is important to keep the big picture in mind.

2.1
Programming Fundamentals

The first order of business for a programmer-wannabe is to understand that programming requires problem-solving skills. If you enjoy getting into the details of how to make something work, you have chosen the right career. Programmers are often presented with a problem or some sort of desired end result. ("Could you just make the computer do this?") The programmer must understand the problem or the goal and then come up with a plan of how to achieve it. Recognize that this plan will not be problem-free.

Algorithm Design

Building and testing your software in steps is an essential habit for a software developer. Something else must be mentioned while we're on the topic of software construction, and that is algorithm development. An ***algorithm*** is a process or a set of rules or steps to follow for solving a problem. It is important that you create a set of steps that solves the problem before you sit down and start entering source code.

algorithm
process or set of rules
followed to solve a
problem

Let's look at a few examples. Suppose you had to write a program that reads lines of text from a data file. Your program should count the number of times the word *sheep* is found. How will you solve this problem? There are several approaches you can take. Figure 2-1 illustrates one. You can read each line of text into your program and then search the line letter by letter for the letter "s." If you find an "s," check the next letter to see if it is an "h." If that letter is an "h," check

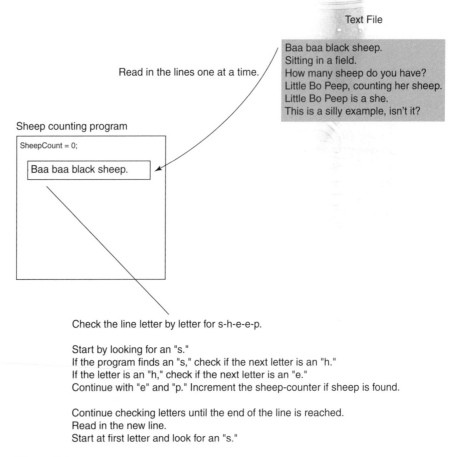

Text File

Baa baa black sheep.
Sitting in a field.
How many sheep do you have?
Little Bo Peep, counting her sheep.
Little Bo Peep is a she.
This is a silly example, isn't it?

Read in the lines one at a time.

Sheep counting program

SheepCount = 0;

Baa baa black sheep.

Check the line letter by letter for s-h-e-e-p.

Start by looking for an "s."
If the program finds an "s," check if the next letter is an "h."
If the letter is an "h," check if the next letter is an "e."
Continue with "e" and "p." Increment the sheep-counter if sheep is found.

Continue checking letters until the end of the line is reached.
Read in the new line.
Start at first letter and look for an "s."

Figure 2-1
Algorithm for Counting the Word *sheep* in Lines of Text

the next for "e," and so on. If you find the five letters you need, increment a sheep-counter. This scheme of checking the letters is an algorithm. (There are, of course, other algorithms for counting sheep.)

What steps are needed for determining the total surface area of a cylinder? (Yes, math problems are everywhere in programming.) Pop the top of your favorite tasty beverage and refresh yourself as we examine how to determine how much wrapping paper it would take to cover the beverage can. Look at Figure 2-2. We need to know two pieces of information: the cylinder's radius and height. We break

We need to know the radius of the cylinder.

We need to know the height.

If we examine the can as three parts, we can find the total area.

Total surface area of our "tasty beverage" cylinder =

area of top
PI * R * R

area of bottom
PI * R * R

Rectangular area of the center part of the cylinder =
top circumference * height =
PI * diameter * height =
PI * 2 * R * height

Figure 2-2
Algorithm for Determining the Surface Area of a Cylinder

the cylinder into three separate pieces: the top, side, and bottom portions. Using the radius and height, we can calculate the total surface area.

Steps to Programming Success

How do you become a good problem solver? Problem solving requires one to be methodical and careful. Let's create our own problem-solving algorithm with basic steps to aid us in understanding the problem and reaching a solution. In general, these steps are as follows.

Step 1. Read the problem statement. Make sure you understand everything about the problem and what it is that you are being asked to do. Do not worry about *how* you are going to solve the problem; just understand *what* is the problem and the desired results.

Step 2. Plan your solution. What are the main components of your problem? List them. What are the steps that you must take to reach your programming goal? Think through each of the steps and develop a plan for each one. It is not necessary to lay out every detail at this stage, but major aspects must be considered. You can write out a plan in a diagram (called a flow diagram) or describe your plan in short phrases (known as pseudocode).

Step 3. Test. As you work toward your solution, identify items that can be individually tested and develop a plan to test the entire program. How will you know that your program is working correctly? Just because you are getting answers from the software doesn't mean that your answers are correct! Always think about testing your software while you are designing and building it.

Step 4. Implement the planned solution. Now's the time to start typing. Once you have clearly defined steps in mind, and on paper, too, it is time to begin writing the program components. Test your software whenever possible. Expect to encounter programmatic details you hadn't thought of. Minor changes may be written as you go. You may need to revisit step 3 and develop more of the solution away from the computer. (*Note:* To enter the program and run it requires that you be familiar with the C++ language and development environment.)

Step 5. Got bugs? Most of us usually have bugs in our new software. The important thing is that you know that your program is not working correctly. If you know you have a problem, you are halfway to the correct solution. (Spend time learning the debugging tools for your development environment. It is time well spent!) The best way to stomp on a software bug is to start at a point where you see the bug and work backward. Run the debugger and watch what the code is doing. After all, you know what the code *should* be doing.

Step 6. Document what you have written. Documentation involves writing comments in your source code that explain what you did.

Practice: How to Give a Cat a Bath

A practical example is useful in learning a new concept. Our practical example is to problem solve and determine how to give a cat a bath. Your cat needs a good shampoo and rinse because he's been hanging out under the car. He sleeps on your pillow—your sheets are filthy.

1. Read the problem statement many times. The cat needs to be bathed. The cat is dirty and shampoo must be used to remove the grease.

2. Plan your solution. The main components are the cat, the sink, water, and shampoo. Fill the sink with warm water and place the cat into the sink. Shampoo must be rubbed into the cat's fur and the cat must be scrubbed until clean. Then rinse all the shampoo off the cat. The cat is then towel-dried. Drain the sink and clean the area. Bandages may be needed afterward. It is safe to expect that the ten-pound cat will have the strength of a 150-pound man and possess eighteen sharp claws. Figure 2-3 illustrates this solution in both pseudocode and flow diagram.

3. Test. How will we know our cat-bathing program is working? Our program will be a success if (a) the cat becomes clean and is not injured in the process, (b) the kitchen is intact when we are finished, and (c) we are not visiting the emergency room afterward.

4. and 5. Implement the planned solution and correct bugs. (a) Prepare the sink area by clearing it of all items that may be knocked into the sink. (b) Obtain shampoo, towels, thick leather gloves, and a strong, able-bodied assistant. (c) Run warm water into the sink in preparation for inserting the cat. (d) Coax the cat from under the car. (*Note:* Fetching the cat from under the car is a different problem and is not addressed here.) (e) Put the cat into the sink. (f) Obtain the wet cat from under the couch. (g) Holding the cat firmly, place the cat into the sink again. (h) Gently pour water over the cat and rub in the shampoo. (i) Rinse. (j) Stand back and on the count of three, you and the able-bodied assistant let go of the wet cat and quickly step away from the sink. (k) Apply bandages to able-bodied assistant and yourself, if necessary.

6. Document. Write the list of steps for bathing the cat and add any bits of information that the next cat-bather will find useful.

Rule of Thirds

Many professional software developers profess that a programming project timeline should be divided into three parts. The ***rule of thirds*** states that the first third of the project time should be spent on program specifications and requirements, planning the user interface, and creating the necessary algorithms and test plans. The middle block of time is spent actually entering the program into the computer and testing

rule of thirds
theory stating that software project time should be divided into three parts: designing, writing, and implementing/testing

Flow Diagram

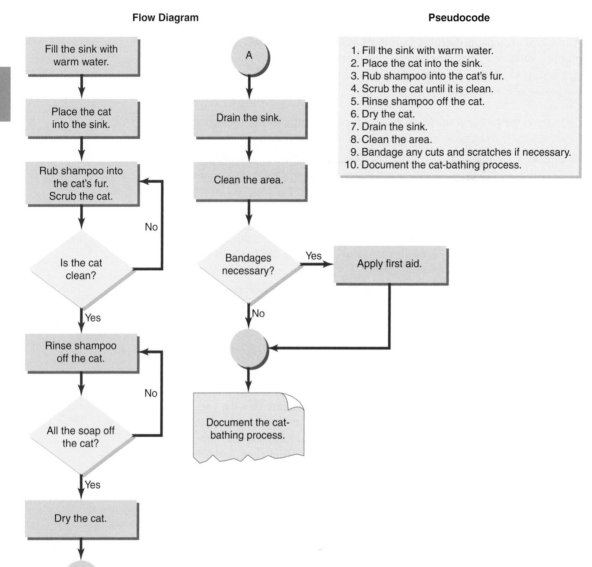

Pseudocode

1. Fill the sink with warm water.
2. Place the cat into the sink.
3. Rub shampoo into the cat's fur.
4. Scrub the cat until it is clean.
5. Rinse shampoo off the cat.
6. Dry the cat.
7. Drain the sink.
8. Clean the area.
9. Bandage any cuts and scratches if necessary.
10. Document the cat-bathing process.

Figure 2-3
Pseudocode and Flow Diagram for Bathing a Cat

each piece. The last block of time is reserved for system integration and testing. This period is used for testing the overall system and ensuring that the software performs as required.

 It is especially important for beginning programming students to recognize the rule of thirds and to spend time studying the language and the programming problem. At this stage of your programming career, entering the C++ statements and getting the program to run is the challenge, since you are new to the language. A misplaced semicolon can cost a new programmer hours (or days).

Try to avoid the temptation of doing all your thinking about your program at the keyboard. Get away from the computer, go to your favorite hangout, and put your thoughts on paper as you treat yourself to a snack.

How to Program

Table 2-1 provides a formal summary of the steps required for designing, building, testing, and integrating a software project. These steps are applicable for beginning C++ programming assignments as well as large, multi-team programming efforts.

TABLE 2-1
Summary of Software Development Steps

Development Concept	Task at Hand	Do
Concept validation	Getting started	Understand program's job and all requirements. Make a list!
Preliminary design	Blueprint	Identify logical steps for building the program. Identify objects and how objects will relate to each other. Find good stopping points. Decide how you will test each step.
Secondary design	Refine the blueprint	Write out the program framework. Write the complicated individual modules on paper first. Do this away from the computer!
Interface requirements	Fitting the parts together	If you are working on a team or on a large program, decide how all the parts will fit together and interact. Write down the interfaces so there is no confusion.
Prototype	Start construction	Build your program in steps. Set up a framework and test to make sure that it works. Don't continue until it all works correctly.
Functional testing	Test as you go	You may build test routines for sections of your code. You can control input/output and ensure that routines work properly.
Module integration	Integrate in steps	Integrate working sections in pieces. If sections have been tested individually, this task should be straightforward.
System integration and testing	Run the program from beginning to end	Once it is integrated, run the program through all the various cases.

Let's keep the big picture in mind here—it is necessary to make the program work, make it work correctly, and then make it work better.

Terminology and Project Construction

Part of learning any new skill involves learning new terminology. Computer programmers seem to have developed their own language. (RAM is not a male sheep, a bug is not an insect, surfing is not performed on the ocean, and a mouse is not a little mammal.) Table 2-2 presents several programming terms and phrases and their meaning.

Construction Steps

Computer systems that provide for C++ program construction may have different approaches for organizing and maintaining the programs physically. Some systems, such as UNIX-based workstations or older versions of personal computer–based

TABLE 2-2
Common Programming Terms and Phrases

Term	Meaning
bug	General catchall word meaning the program is not running correctly.
code	This term can refer to the textual-based phrases written in C++ that represent a program (or portion of a program). Code can refer to a single line, such as "a line of code" or the entire program. Also, it can refer to program file contents such as "machine code" or "executable code."
compiler	Actual software (such as Microsoft Visual C++) that reads C++ statements. It checks that the statements are written with the correct syntax. The compiler produces object or machine code.
debugger	A tool in the software development package (such as Microsoft Visual C++) that allows the programmer to run the program one step at a time and to examine program portions. A debugger is used to track down bugs.
executable	The machine language file that the operating system reads. The operating system performs instructions based on the commands in this file. The executable file constitutes the program.
linker	Software that combines all the required files together and builds an executable file.
object code	File produced by a compiler. The source code file is translated into machine language.
source code	The text-based file containing C++ statements. The source code is read by the compiler.
syntax	The correct way in which the language's words and symbols are put together so that they have meaning to the C++ language. It may be thought of as the "grammar" and "punctuation" rules for the language.

compilers, allow a one-file program to be compiled, linked, and run. Most programs actually have the code separated into many files. For these programs, C++ and the computer systems require more information concerning the program and files. In the personal computer environment, Microsoft Visual C++ requires that the program be contained in a ***project***. The project keeps track of all the files that are required for the program. In the UNIX world, a ***make file*** is a convenient way to tell the compiler what files and libraries are needed.

> **project**
> the Visual C++ component that keeps track of all files needed for a program

It is time to study Appendix A, "Getting Started with Visual C++." This appendix covers installing the Visual C++ software. Once the software is installed, we go through creating a project; writing a short program; and compiling, linking, and running it. How to access the Visual C++ Help is also presented.

> **make file**
> specifies the files and libraries for a program in the UNIX environment

2.3
General Format of a C++ Program

A C++ program consists of several basic components, whether the program consists of a few lines or is large and complicated. Later we will build large programs using several source files, but to get us started, let's do Hello World.[1]

Hello World! Program

In our first program, we write **hello world!** on the screen. This program consists of one function (modular block of code) named main, and other lines of code are necessary, too. This program is also presented in Appendix A, "Getting Started with Visual C++." The source code for our Hello World! program is shown in Program 2-1.

```
//Program 2-1   Getting Started with hello world!
//This is our first program.

#include <iostream.h>
int main()
{
        cout << "hello world! \n";
        return 0;
}
```

---

[1]Hello World! is the first program in Kernighan and Ritchie's *The C Programming Language*. In their honor, it will be our first program as well.

Comments

The first two lines in the example are comment lines.

```
//Program 2-1   Getting started with Hello World!
//This is our first program.
```

comment

lines in source code, ignored by the compiler, in which programmers may write information concerning the file or program

Comment lines are written into the source file by the programmer to relay information concerning the code—information such as titles, file data, or explanations about what the software is doing. The compiler ignores all comment lines in a program. There are two ways to write comments in C++.

```
//This is one way to write a comment.
//The compiler ignores everything from
//to the end of the line.
```

These // comments are especially convenient for one-line comments. A second way to write a comment is:

```
/* Here is another way to write a comment.
The compiler ignores everything between the
beginning slash-star and the ending star-slash.   */
```

This comment style is convenient for writing multiple-line comments because it needs only the /* at the start and */ at the end of the comment lines.

Preprocessor Directives

The next line:

```
#include <iostream.h>
```

preprocessor directive

lines, such as #include or #define lines, in the source code that give the compiler instructions

#include

preprocessor directive telling the compiler to read the given file

is known as a *preprocessor directive*. The directives give the compiler instructions. The most common type of directive includes additional statements in the program. The preprocessor directive statements usually are at the top of the file. In Hello World! we need to include the iostream library because it contains the necessary functions to write text to the screen. The iostream function information is in a file named *iostream.h*. The *#include* statement tells the compiler that this short program uses one or more of the iostream functions. (All of the C++ preprocessor directive statements are shown in Appendix H, "Multifile Programs.")

The ISO Standard C++ language provides many libraries with all types of functions for programmers to use. If your program needs to find a square root, the sqrt() function is in the math library. The program needs to include the *math.h* file at the top of the source file, like this:

```
#include <math.h>         //used for sqrt function
```

The main Function

The line

```
int main()
{
```

is the starting point for a C++ program. When the program begins to run, the operating system (which runs the program) starts performing the actions directed by the C++ statements. Our C++ programs will contain a main function, and the operating system knows to look for it. Think of the main function as the "program director" giving orders to other program components via calls to functions (or through the use of objects). The lion's share of the program activities is not performed in the main function.

Function Header Line

It is never too early to begin learning function details, so let's spend a bit more time examining the following line:

```
int main()
```

This line also is known as a ***function header line***. The first line of any function is a function header line specifying the function name and input and output information. The general format for a function header line is:

function header line
the first line of any
function in C/C++

```
return_type  function_name (input parameter list)
```

where return_type (int in Hello World!) is the type of data that the function passes to whomever calls it. The input parameter list is the list of data that is passed into the function. In C++ the main function returns an integer value to the calling process (the operating system). We use this standard function header line for our programs. (Chapter 5 contains more details on function header lines.)

All C++ functions have an opening brace { after the function header line; at the end of the function is a closing brace }. These braces enclose the statements of the function. Braces are used extensively in C++.

C++ Statements

A C++ statement is part of the program that is issuing a command to be executed. It specifies an action that must occur. Our Hello World! program has two C++ statements.

```
cout << "hello world!";
return 0;
```

This cout statement is written according to the C++ language rules and ends with a semicolon; many, but not all, statements in C++ end in a semicolon. The return 0; statement is located at the end of the main function. The return type for the main function is an int (integer). The main function uses this return statement to pass a zero to the operating system at the conclusion of the program.

How's the Weather?

Our second sample program (Program 2-2) contains several cout statements and both types of comment styles. The program writes three statements to the screen. The \n is an escape sequence, which causes the output to be printed to the next line on the screen. (Appendix I, "Keyboard Input, Screen Output," covers escape sequences in detail, along with other program input/output material.) The program output is:

It is cloudy today.
Maybe it will rain.
I like sunny, warm weather!

Figure 2-4 illustrates the source code and the screen output. Note that the comments are seen only in the source code, and the text information in the cout statements is seen in the program output.

Whitespace Characters and Flexible Style in C++

whitespace

spaces (blanks), tabs, line feeds, enter key, control characters, vertical tabs, and form feed characters

Whitespace characters are defined to be spaces, carriage returns, line feeds (the Enter key), tabs, vertical tabs, and form feeds. For the most part, the C++ compiler ignores whitespace characters. Why is this important to the C++ programmer? It means that the compiler allows the programmer to write his or her code with the

```
/* Program 2-2   How's the weather? Our second program.
   This program will write a few weather-related statements to the screen.      */

#include <iostream.h>
int main()
{
     // Weather information
     cout << "\n It is cloudy today.";
     cout << "\n Maybe it will rain.";
     cout << "\n I like sunny, warm weather!  \n";
     return 0;
}
```

//Source code: weather.cpp

```
/* Program 2-2   How's the weather? Our second program.
   This program will write a few weather-related statements to the screen.    */

#include <iostream.h>

int main()
{
   // Weather information

   cout < < "\n It is cloudy today.";
   cout < < "\n Maybe it will rain.";
   cout < < "\n I like sunny, warm weather!";
   return 0;
}
```

◄·················· Comment lines

◄·················· Preprocessor directive

◄·················· Function header line

◄·················· Single line comment

◄·················· C++ statements

Program output (seen on the computer screen in a window)

```
It is cloudy today.
Maybe it will rain.
I like sunny, warm weather!
```

Computer monitor

Figure 2-4
How's the Weather? Source Code and Program (Screen) Output

use of a wide variety of styles and formats. (The compiler is very particular about the syntax, of course, but style is up to the programmer.) Are you stylish?

Unlike the COBOL or FORTRAN languages, which have restrictions about what data must be in which column and restrictions for the length of lines, C++ statements can be written in virtually any format. For example, our Hello World! program could be written on one line, as shown in Program 2-3. The How's the Weather? program could be entered in the file like Program 2-4.

```
//Program 2-3    Our hello world! program written in one line.
//This is our first program.
#include <iostream.h>
int main(){ cout << "hello world!    \n"; return 0;}
```

```
/* Program 2-4    This is a second way to write the Weather program.
In this program  we'll write a few weather statements to the screen.*/
#include <iostream.h>
int main() { // Weather information
cout <<   " \n It is cloudy today. ";cout << "\n Maybe it will rain.";cout <<
"\n I like sunny, warm weather!  \n";return 0;}
```

The second versions of the Hello World! and How's the Weather? programs compile without error because the C++ compiler does not require the programmer to start each statement on a new line. Both programs produce the same output as their initial versions. However, it is obvious that the source code for both is difficult to read.

Well-written comments are quite significant! Comments make the source code easier to read, and they document what the code is doing. Without comments, the programmer has difficulty remembering what he or she was doing, and it is almost impossible for a new person to read and understand the code at a later date. Too many comments, however, can obscure the code.

syntax
grammatical rules required by the language

Language Syntax and Compiler Errors

The flexibility feature for your C++ style does not mean that you may write C++ statements in just any old way. C++ must be written with correct *syntax*, but the spacing does not matter. What do we mean by a syntax rule? A syntax rule is a rule for writing the language. If C++ requires the word #include to be in lowercase letters, then a syntax error is found if you used all caps (#INCLUDE). For example, this source code contains several syntax errors and does not compile:

```
//Program 2-3x  Our hello world! program with INCORRECT SYNTAX will
not compile.

#INCLUDE<iostream.h>       //#include cannot be all capital letters
int Main ()                // main must be all lowercase
{
   COUT << "hello world!";               //cout must be lowercase
   return 0                              //missing ;
}
```

The Microsoft Visual C++ and GCC compilers do not understand the incorrectly written #include statement. Visual C++ reports this error:

```
Compiling...
Ch2HelloError.cpp
c:\cbook\testcases\ch2helloerror.cpp(3) : fatal error C1021: invalid preprocessor command 'INCLUDE'
Error executing cl.exe.
Ch2HelloError.obj - 1 error(s), 0 warning(s)
```

The GCC reports:

```
login1:johnston:~/gnu:$ g++ G++_Ch2_helloerror.cc
G++_Ch2_helloerror.cc:10: syntax error before '.'
G++_Ch2_helloerror.cc:12: undefined or invalid # directive
```

When the #include statement is corrected, we see the following:

```
//Program 2-3x  Our hello world! program with INCORRECT SYNTAX will not compile.

#include <iostream.h>                //#include is now correct
int Main ()                          // main must be all lowercase
{
   COUT << "hello world!";        //cout must be lowercase
   return 0                        // missing ;
}
```

The Microsoft Visual C++ now reports these three errors:

```
Compiling...
Ch2HelloError.cpp
c:\cbook\testcases\ch2helloerror.cpp(6) : error C2065: 'COUT' : undeclared identifier
c:\cbook\testcases\ch2helloerror.cpp(6) : error C2297: '<<' : illegal, right operand has type char [13]
c:\cbook\testcases\ch2helloerror.cpp(8) : error C2143: syntax error : missing ';' before '}'
Error executing cl.exe.

Ch2HelloError.obj -  3 error(s), 0 warning(s)
```

GCC reports:

```
login1:johnston:~/gnu:$ g++ G++_Ch2_helloerror.cc
G++_Ch2_helloerror.cc: In function 'int Main()':
G++_Ch2_helloerror.cc:15:  'COUT' undeclared (first use this function)
G++_Ch2_helloerror.cc:15: (Each undeclared identifier is reported only once
G++_Ch2_helloerror.cc:15: for each function it appears in.)
G++_Ch2_helloerror.cc:17: parse error before '}'
```

Compilers do the best they can in determining syntax errors. As you will soon learn, however, the compilers cannot read your mind. *The programmer must take the time to learn the correct syntax for C++ and thus be able to spot the compiler errors quickly.*

2

Two Helpful Hints: The Microsoft Visual C++ compiler always shows comments in green, words that are reserved by the language in blue, and statements in black. If you are entering a reserved word (keyword or pre-processor directive), such as #include, it should be in blue. If the word is not in blue, double-check the way you have entered it. Second, the error is often located on the line above the referenced line. If you get a compiler error and the referenced line appears to be correct, look above that line for the error.

C++ Keywords

keywords

reserved words in the language that have specific syntax and actions

The C++ language has many reserved words known as ***keywords***. These keywords have specific meaning for the language and may not be used by the programmer as names for variables or functions. Each keyword has specific syntax and actions associated with it. For example, the two keywords *switch* and *case* might be popular variable names in electronics or inventory programs. However, C++ reserves these two words for its own use (*switch* is a conditional statement and *case* is a label). The C language contained thirty-one keywords. The C++ language expanded that list to sixty-three. Appendix B, "C++ Keyword Dictionary," shows all of the C++ keywords as well as short usage examples and a text reference. Table 2-3 shows the sixty-three keywords in C++.

▌ TABLE 2-3
C++ Keywords

asm	auto	bool	break	case	catch
char	class	const	const_cast	continue	default
delete	do	double	dynamic_cast	else	enum
explicit	export	extern	false	float	for
friend	goto	if	inline	int	long
mutable	namespace	new	operator	private	protected
public	register	return	reinterpret_cast	short	signed
sizeof	static	static_cast	struct	switch	template
this	throw	true	try	typedef	typeid
typename	union	unsigned	using	virtual	void
volatile	while	wchar_t			

Upper- and Lowercase Sensitive

Another feature of C++ is that it is *case sensitive*. C++ recognizes the difference between uppercase and lowercase letters. The operating system knows to look for the main function, and the C++ compiler automatically recognizes a function named main. However, the compiler does not know what a Main or MAIN function is (unless the programmer creates user-defined functions). The same holds true for naming variables or functions in C++. (We cover naming rules later in the chapter.) Remember that the C++ compiler sees the variables total, Total, and TOTAL as three separate variables.

case sensitive
C++ recognizes upper- and lowercase letters are different

Good Style

As mentioned before, it is indeed necessary for the programming student to develop a readable style when writing source code. This legible style includes writing descriptive comments, choosing appropriate variable names, and indenting the source code from the start of a programming project. Always assume that someone else needs to read your code and figure out what you are doing. Students often write their code and "make it pretty" later. Time spent making it pretty initially is time saved when trying to debug compiler errors.

Love My Style

Programs 2-5 and 2-6 illustrate how important good style can be when trying to read source code. Both of these programs compile with no error and write the same output to the screen. Which program would you rather read?

In the first Love My Style program (Program 2-5), the comments are jammed against the C++ statements, making both the statement and comment hard to see. Also, the comments do not tell the reader anything helpful about the program. In the second program, the comments contain more information about the program and obvious or redundant comments are omitted. Throughout this text, we will work on code and commenting style techniques.

```
//Program 2-5 Coding style you love to hate./*This program will write
stuff to the screen.*/

#include <iostream.h>//iostream library
int main(){/* cout output statements*/
cout<<"\nI am a programmer.";//write out I am a programmer
cout<<"\nThis is great code.";
cout<<"\nDo you like my style?  I am all done now. \n"; return 0;//end of program }
```

```
/* Program 2-6 Coding style you love to love.
   This program will write programming comments to the screen.   */

#include <iostream.h>                  //needed for cout statement
int main()
{
    cout<<"\nI am a programmer.";      //write style comments to screen
    cout<<"\nThis is great code.";
    cout<<"\nDo you like my style?  I am all done now.  \n";
    return 0;
}
```

One Last Comment on Comments

Your comments should explain your thought process and logic. The following comment:

```
#include <iostream.h>     //include the iostream library
```

does not tell the reader why the library is included, and it is too close to the end of the #include statement. In the line below, the comment is offset from the source line and explains why this library is needed in the program:

```
#include <iostream.h>           //needed for cout statement
```

Try to ensure that your comments help the reader understand what you are writing instead of wasting space and effort explaining the obvious.

2.4
Programs and Data: Balls and Sticks

Imagine that you get a job at a gymnasium and are in charge of the equipment room. This gym supports many different sporting activities including golf, tennis, racquetball and squash, baseball, softball, basketball, and medicine ball. Medicine balls are big leather balls weighing anywhere between two and sixty pounds. One game of medicine ball involves two people tossing the ball back and forth.

Gym members come to your equipment room to check out whatever type of equipment is required for their sport. This room is a busy place, and when you see the equipment room, you find 200 loose balls rolling around on the floor. Bats, golf clubs, and racquets are piled in a corner. How do you find one golf ball in all that clutter?

Let's assume that your storage room is large enough so that you can build shelves along the walls. You need to have each piece of equipment contained in its own slot on a shelf. (If the bats, clubs, and racquets stick out a bit, that's okay.) Let's also assume that there is a variety of shelf containers and slot fixtures that easily attach on the shelf. These shelf containers come in various sizes, from golf-ball small to medicine-ball large. You order the shelving material and container fixtures. The next day (of course, you ordered on-line and paid the next-day shipping fee), you set up your shelves. Then you adjust your shelf containers and slot fixtures so that each ball and each stick fits nicely in its own slot. You must keep track of all your bats, balls, clubs, and racquets; you name each slot and container with a unique name, and you know the address (location) of each.

Now, think of each ball and stick as a single piece of program data. Data come in different sizes and types. Programs need "containers" to store all the program data. You, as the programmer, need to determine how many "containers" are required, select the appropriate types of containers, and give each container a name. The details of where the containers are located are handled by the operating system—you do not have to worry about that.

As you are designing your program and thinking through the logical steps, you must also ask yourself what types of data the program will handle. Will the program need "containers" for numeric data or textual data? How many different containers are required in the program? What level of accuracy (number of decimal places) is required? A bookkeeping program needs only two or three decimal places; on the other hand, an airborne radar system requires twenty decimal places.

2.5
Data Types in C++

If you are writing a banking program, it probably has a variety of data including name and address information; balance, deposit, and withdraw amounts; account numbers; personal identification numbers; and transaction counters. The money data need to be numeric—the name and address information must be textual (or character) data. It is important to have decimal-place accuracy for the money (to keep track of pennies), but our transaction counter can be a whole number.

The C++ language provides a variety of data types for the programmer. A *data type* is a type of "container" that can hold a specific kind of program data. For each piece of data in your program, you must specify the appropriate type of container that must be used—depending on the type of data. For example, a customer's name needs to be stored in characters (*char*), money information must be stored in either a *float* or a *double* (to maintain the decimal portion), and transaction numbers can be stored as *integers*. Table 2-4 lists the basic data types provided by C++.

data type
type of "container" that holds program data, including int, float, double, char, and bool

char
data type for variables that contain a single character

float
data type for variables containing up to five digits of decimal precision

double
data type for variables containing up to ten digits of decimal precision

int
data type for variables containing whole numbers

Basic Data Types in C++

Data Type	Name	The Data It Contains	Example
char	char or character	A single character	a
int	integer	A whole number (no decimal point)	43
float	float or floating point	A number with six to seven digits of precision	14.937453
double	double	A number with thirteen to fourteen digits of precision	3.14159265294753
void	void	Empty or nothing Specifies function as returning no values	is presented later
bool[a]	boolean	Stores values of true or false	true
wchar_t[a]	wide character	Holds wide characters (16 bits)	Japanese character

[a]*Note:* Not defined in the C language.

Shelves = Memory, Containers = Data Types, Labels = Variable Names

A programmer must designate the type of data container (data type) and name (variable) for each piece of data in the program. When the program executes, physical memory in the computer system is set aside for each piece of data. You may think of the storage shelves as the memory in your computer. Selecting the appropriate type of container to place on the shelf is analogous to specifying a data type in your program. (Remember that containers hold different things.) Placing the label on the container and giving the variable a name serve a similar purpose because you know the name of the container/variable.

To understand the different data types and the range of values they may hold, we need to introduce the concept of a *byte*. The byte is the basic unit of computer memory. The byte consists of eight *bits*. A bit is a unit of data that exists in one of two states. We often refer to a bit as being either a 1 or a 0. Check Appendix E, "Bits, Bytes, Memory, and Hexadecimal Notation," for further discussion.

The ISO Standard C++ language specifies the minimum number of bytes of storage that each data type must reserve and use for storing values. These reserved bytes dictate how big a value may be stored. (Back to the equipment room analogy: if your shelf container is only four inches wide, you can't fit the medicine ball in that slot.)

Figure 2-5 illustrates how the number of bits dictates the number of unique bit-combinations. For a value to be stored, it must be represented by a unique bit pattern. A 1-byte storage container can have only 2^8, or 256, unique bit combinations. Figure 2-6 takes this concept a bit further. If a data type reserves 2 bytes, then there

byte

the basic unit of computer memory consisting of eight bits

bit

a unit of data that exists in one of two states, such as 1 or 0, on or off

Bits	Possible Bit Combinations	Unique Values	
1	0	0	The number of unique values can be calculated by 2^n, where n = number of bits.
	1	1	$2^1 = 2$ combinations
2	00	0	
	01	1	$2^2 = 4$ combinations
	10	2	
	11	3	
3	000	0	
	001	1	
	010	2	$2^3 = 8$ combinations
	011	3	
	100	4	
	101	5	
	110	6	
	111	7	
8	00000000	0	
	00000001	1	$2^8 = 256$ combinations
	⋮	⋮	
	11111111	255	

Figure 2-5
Number of Bits Dictate Number of Unique Combinations

Bytes	Bits	Possible Combinations	Signed Range	Unsigned Range
1	8	256	−128 to 127	0 to 255
2	16	65,536	−32,768 to 32,767	0 to 65,535
4	32	4,294,967,296	−2,147,483,648 to 2,147,483,647	0 to 4,294,967,295

$2^8 = 256$ combinations
$2^{16} = 65,536$ combinations
$2^{32} = 4,294,967,296$ combinations

Figure 2-6
More Bytes Equals a Larger Range of Values

TABLE 2-5
Data Types Defined by the ANSI/ISO C Standard

Keyword	Minimum Bytes of Memory	Minimal Precision (Range in Visual C++)
char	1	−128 to 127
unsigned char	1	0 to 255
signed char	1	−128 to 127
int	2 or 4[a]	−32,768 to 32,767 −2,147,483,648 to 2,147,483,647
short int	2	−32,768 to 32,767
unsigned short int	2	0 to 65,535
unsigned int	2 or 4[a]	0 to 65,535 0 to 4,294,967,295
long int	4	−2,147,483,648 to 2,147,483,647
unsigned long int	4	0 to 4,294,967,295
float	4	6 digits, i.e., 0.xxxxxx $3.4 \text{ E} \pm 38$ (7 digits in Visual C++)
double	8	10 digits, i.e., 0.xxxxxxxxxx $1.7 \text{ E} \pm 308$ (15 digits in Visual C++)
long double	10	10 digits, i.e., 0.xxxxxxxxxx $1.2 \text{ E} \pm 4932$ (19 digits in Visual C++)

[a]Represented in Microsoft Visual C++.

are 16 bits for storage. Four bytes result in 32 bits of storage space. Examining the possible combinations shows how reserving more bytes results in a larger number of combinations, and hence larger values (a wider range of values) may be stored.

Data Type Modifiers

C++ allows the use of modifiers to create many more data types (or specialized containers). The modifiers include the terms (keywords in C++) *short*, *long*, and *unsigned*. The complete list of the data types is shown in Table 2-5. The ISO C++ standard does not specify the exact amount of storage that the C++ program must use for the various data types, but it does specify the minimum. The programmer must be aware that sizes and ranges may vary.

Troubleshooting: How Big Is the Integer?

The ANSI/ISO standard specifies that data types must meet certain requirements but does not specify exact ranges. One data type that can vary between systems is the integer. On systems with 16-bit architecture (such as older personal computers),

On June 4, 1996, an unmanned Ariane 5 rocket launched by the European Space Agency exploded just forty seconds after liftoff. The rocket was on its first voyage, after a decade of development costing $7 billion. The destroyed rocket and its cargo were valued at $500 million. A board of inquiry investigated the causes of the explosion and in two weeks issued a report. The cause of the failure was a software error in the inertial reference system. Specifically, a 64-bit floating point number (i.e., a double) relating to the horizontal velocity of the rocket with respect to the platform was converted to a 16-bit signed integer. The number was larger than 32,768, the largest integer that can be stored in a 16-bit signed integer, and thus the conversion failed.

*This Ariane 5 launch is a classic study of a system failure due to software. The excerpt is adapted from the Computer Arithmetic Tragedies page of the Penn State University Web site (http://www.math.psu.edu/dna/455.f96/disasters.html). The full failure report, *The ARIANE 5 Flight 501 Failure Report* by the inquiry board can be seen at http://java.sun.com/people/jag/Ariane5.html. A search on the Internet for "Ariane 5 Failure" will result in many references.

integers typically had a 16-bit (2-byte) integer. On the newer personal computers, with 32-bit architecture, the integer is 4 bytes. Visual C++ has 4-byte integers. The bottom line? If your system is using a 2-byte int, the maximum value it can represent is 32,767. If your program needs to count the attendance at a National Football League game, the program needs to be using a 4-byte integer (long int on older systems). Always be aware of the size and value range of your system's integer.

2.6
Variable Declaration in C++

A *variable* is an actual location in memory that has been set aside for use by the program and it is referenced by a specific name. Variables contain *values* that may be modified by the program. The program must *declare* a variable by stating the type of data it is to contain (int, float, double, etc.) and give the variable a name. This declaration is performed only once in a function, and then the variable is ready to be used as often as needed. (*Note:* Variable scope is discussed in Chapter 5, which covers global, local, and static variable properties.)

A *variable declaration* statement must have a data type and a variable name. The basic format is:

```
data_type variable_name;
```

For example, in our banking program the money, count, and check number variables could be declared as follows:

variables
memory locations reserved by the program for storing program data

value
actual data stored in the variable

variable declaration
C++ program statement dictating the type and name for a variable

```
//Declaration of variables for banking program
float balance;
float deposit;
float withdraw;
int transaction_count;
int check_number;
```

In these statements we are setting up three floating point variables—balance, deposit, and withdraw—and two integer variables—transaction_count and check_number. When you run this program, five separate memory locations are reserved, one location for each variable. It is valid to have several variables and one data type on one line, such as:

```
//Declaration of variables for banking program
float balance, deposit, withdraw;
int transaction_count, check_number;
```

Naming Rules in C++

In C++, an *identifier* is the name of a user-defined object, a variable, a function or a label. *Identifier naming rules* are listed below. It is always a great idea to use descriptive names for your program items.

- Names may contain letters (A to Z, a to z), numbers (0 to 9), or underscores (_).
- The first character must be a letter or an underscore. Convert_to_dollars or HEADER_H are valid names.
- Names cannot contain any symbols, such as ~!@#$%^&*()-+=\|'", nor can they have any spaces.
- Keywords cannot be used as variable names.
- Identifiers may be any length, but only 1,024 characters are significant.

Table 2-6 shows examples of valid and invalid variable names.

Where Can You Declare Variables?

Variables in C and C++ can be declared in three places in a program: inside a function, outside a function, and in a function header line. Where the declaration occurs dictates what parts of the program can see and have access to the variable values. This access is known as the scope of a variable and is discussed fully in Chapter 5.

C++ requires that a variable be declared before it is used, which makes sense because you need to have a storage container set up before you can store a value. Also, C++ allows variable declaration within conditional statements—but these variables are visible only to the code within the block of statements. These C++ rules for

TABLE 2-6
Valid and Invalid Variable Names

Variable Name	Valid or Invalid	If Invalid, Why?
`balance`	Valid	[Not applicable]
`transaction amount`	Invalid	Contains a space
`convert_2_$`	Invalid	No symbols like $
`_My_Money`	Valid	[Not applicable]
`4_temperature`	Invalid	Cannot start with number
`auto`	Invalid	Cannot be a keyword
`My_auto`	Valid	[Not applicable]

the location of variable declarations differ from the C program rules. In a C program, variable declarations inside a function must be made before other C statements.

2.7
Operators in C++

The C++ language has many operators, which provides wonderful flexibility for the programmer. (A complete table of C++ operators appears in Appendix C.) *Operators* are symbols that represent certain instructions or commands. A simple addition example shows the arithmetic operator + and the assignment operator =.

operators
symbols that represent certain instructions or commands in C++

```
//Operator Example Addition
sum = x + y;
```

A second example shows temperature conversion using operators:

```
//Operator Example Temp Conversion
F_temp = 9.0/5.0 * C_temp + 32.0;
```

This statement is interpreted as "first divide 9 by 5, then multiply by C_temp and add 32, and then assign the result into F_temp."

Precedence of Operations

Precedence of operations (or order of operators) in C++ means simply which operation is performed first, which is performed second, and so on, in a program statement. A program statement may contain multiplication, addition, parentheses, division, and subtraction. There must be a convention for the C++ compiler to follow

precedence of operations
set of rules that dictates the order in which operations are performed

TABLE 2-7

Arithmetic and Assignment Precedence of Operations

Priority	Operator Type	Operator	Associativity
Highest	Primary	() [] . →	Left to right
	Arithmetic	* / %	Left to right
	Arithmetic	+ -	Left to right
Lowest	Assignment	=	Right to left

for obtaining a consistent result. Table 2-7 is an abbreviated version of Appendix C and illustrates the precedence for arithmetic and assignment operators.

Let's look at the temperature conversion example again.

```
F_temp = 9.0/5.0 * C_temp + 32.0;    //Operator Example Temp Conversion
```

In this expression, there are four operators: =, /, *, and +. The multiplication (*) and division (/) operators have the highest priority (there are no primary operators in this expression). When this program is executed, these two operations are performed before the others. But which one gets carried out first? *Associativity* tells us. For the arithmetic operators, the associativity is "left to right," meaning that the operator *on the left in the expression* is performed first. So the computer will divide 9.0 by 5.0 and then multiply by the value in the C_temp variable. The addition is done next. The assignment operator finishes by placing the result from the calculations into F_temp.

associativity

specifies the order of operations if operators have the same priority

The use of a set of parentheses, which are primary operators, changes the order of operations.

```
F_temp = 9.0/5.0 *(C_temp + 32.0);    //Temp Conversion with ()'s
```

The operations inside the parentheses are executed first, following the precedence of operations. In this statement, the addition is performed first. Next, the division occurs, followed by the multiplication and assignment.

Figure 2-7 illustrates several equations written in C++. Based on the precedence and associativity of the operators, arrows indicate the order in which each calculation is performed.

Assignment Operator

In C++ the assignment operator (=) takes the value on the right side of the equals sign and places it in the variable on the left side. The following code shows two assignment statements; the numeric value 1534.34 is placed in balance and the value of y is placed into x.

```
balance = 1534.34;
x = y;
```

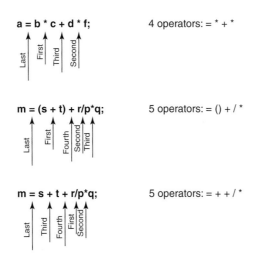

a = b * c + d * f;   4 operators: = * + *

m = (s + t) + r/p*q;   5 operators: = () + / *

m = s + t + r/p*q;   5 operators: = + + / *

Figure 2-7
Precedence and Associativity of Operators

It is possible to have many assignment operators in one expression. Remember, the associativity for the assigment operator is right to left. In this example, we are placing 0 into c, then the value of c into b, and then b into a.

```
a = b = c = 0;        //valid assignment setting a, b, c to 0
```

Assignments in Declarations   It is valid to assign values to variables in the declaration statements. These statements are all acceptable for programmers to use.

```
float x, y;        // declare variables
x = 3.4;           // now assign in separate statements
y = 73.8234;
```

These statements may be combined into one statement:

```
float x = 3.4, y = 73.8234;    // declare and assign
```

Data Types and Stored Values   When values are assigned into C++ variables, the type of variable dictates what is actually stored in memory. The compiler does not give warnings when the value that is stored into a variable is not what is entered in the assignment statement.

```
double x = 15;                 // x will actually be stored as 15.0000000000000
float pi = 3.141592653589793;  // pi will be stored as 3.141593
int money = 435.83;            // integer money will have 435 stored
```

The integer data type contains only whole numbers. The decimal portion is truncated (*not* rounded). Neither the decimal nor the digits to the right of it are stored.

lvalue and rvalue   Often programmers see messages concerning lvalue and rvalue. An *lvalue* is an object that can be on the left side of the assignment operator. An *rvalue* can be on the right side of the assignment operator. C++ expects certain items to be on the left and right sides of the assignment operator. Invalid lvalue error messages are given for these expressions in this short program.

lvalue
an entity that may be found on the left side of an assignment operator

rvalue
an entity that may be found on the right side of an assignment operator

```
//Program 2-x    COMPILE ERRORS    lvalue errors
#include <iostream.h>
#include <math.h>
int main()
{
        double x = 25.0, y;
        double a = 5.0, b = 6.0, c;

        5.2 = x;      // can't assign from right to left
        a + b = c;    // can't have addition on left of = sign
        sqrt(x) = y;  // can't call sqrt on left of = sign
        return 0;
}
```

The Microsoft Visual C++ compiler reports these errors:

```
Compiling...
Ch2LValueErrors.cpp
C:\CBook\TestCases\Ch2LValueErrors.cpp(8) : error C2106: '=' : left operand must be l-value
C:\CBook\TestCases\Ch2LValueErrors.cpp(9) : error C2106: '=' : left operand must be l-value
C:\CBook\TestCases\Ch2LValueErrors.cpp(10) : error C2106: '=' : left operand must be l-value
Error executing cl.exe.

Ch2LValueErrors.obj - 3 error(s), 0 warning(s)
```

GCC errors:

```
login1:johnston:~/gnu:$ g++ G++_lvalueerrors.cc
G++_lvalueerrors.cc:In function 'int main()':
G++_lvalueerrors.cc:14: non-lvalue in assignment
G++_lvalueerrors.cc:15: non-lvalue in assignment
G++_lvalueerrors.cc:16: non-lvalue in assignment
```

Arithmetic Operators

C++ provides five arithmetic operators: multiplication (*), division (/), addition (+), subtraction (−), and modulus (%). The first four operators are self-explanatory, but the modulus operator is new to many C++ programmers. The modulus operator must have integer operands, and it returns the whole number remainder in a division. Figure 2-8 illustrates how both the modulus and division operators work.

Beginning programmers frequently see no use for the modulus operator; however, it is a very convenient operator. For example, if you need to know if an integer is odd or even, the number could be mod'ed with 2 and the result checked for 0 (the number is even) or 1 (the number is odd). This scheme is used to determine if a number is evenly divisible by 10 (or any integer). An integer mod'ed with 10 returns 0 if the number is evenly divisible by 10.

Intermediate Results with Arithmetic Operators   C++ has a simple rule for a programmer who is working with the four arithmetic operators. If the two values on which the operator is working (known as operands) are integers, the result is an integer. If the operands are floats or doubles, the result is a double. If there is one integer and one double or one integer and one float, the result is a double. (Modulus operator works on and returns only integers.) Table 2-8 summarizes this rule.

A problem occurs when two integers are divided and an integer result is generated. The result from the division is an integer. It does not matter to what type of variable the division is being assigned. Figure 2-9 illustrates this C++ feature.

Troubleshooting Using Fractions (Temp and Volume)   The intermediate results rule can cause programmers an incredible amount of grief when working with fractional calculations. If a number in an expression is entered without a deci-

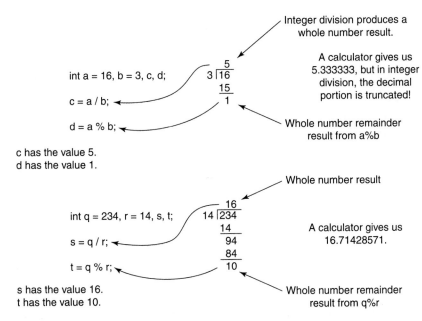

Figure 2-8
Modulus and Division Operators

TABLE 2-8

Intermediate Results with Arithmetic Operators

Operand Data Types	Result Data Type	Example	Result
Both integer	int	5 * 4	20
		16/3	5
		7 + 8	15
		8 − 2	6
		17 % 5	2
int float int double	double	5 * 4.0	20.0000000000000
Both float/double	double	5.0 * 4.0	20.0000000000000

An integer divided by an integer produces an integer result.

```
int a = 16, b = 3, c;
float x;

c = a/b;   // c has the value 5
x = a/b;   // x has the value 5.000000

int q = 234, r = 14, s;
float y;
s = q/r; //s has the value 16
y = q/r;
// y has the value 16, no rounding is performed
```

$$\begin{array}{r} 5.\overline{3333333} \\ 3\overline{)16} \end{array}$$

A calculator gives us 5.333333. But in integer division, the decimal portion is truncated!

$$\begin{array}{r} 16.\overline{71428571} \\ 14\overline{)234} \end{array}$$

Figure 2-9

Intermediate Results from Integer Division

mal point, it is treated as an integer. Programmers forget this fact and write code using algebraic-type expressions.

Suppose we need to code the Celsius to Fahrenheit conversion equation. This conversion is

$$Fahrenheit = \frac{9}{5}Celsius + 32$$

The correct way to write this in C++ is:

```
F_temp = 9.0/5.0 * C_temp + 32.0;       //be sure 9.0/5.0 have decimal values!!!
```

If the fractional portion of this expression is incorrectly written as "9/5" the integer division results in 1, *not* 1.8, as our calculator gives us. This value, 1, is then multiplied by C_temp, and 32 is added to it. The result in F_temp is 132.0, *not* 212.0. Program 2-7 demonstrates the problem. The output is shown on page 51.

```
//Program 2-7   Two Ways to Calculate Temperature
#include <iostream.h>
int main ()
{
        double celsius = 100.0;
        double farenOK, farenNOTOK;
        cout << "\n Two Temperature Conversions  100 C to 212F";
        cout << "\n 100 Degrees Celsius is 212 Degrees Fahrenheit\n";

        farenOK = 9.0/5.0*celsius + 32.0;
        cout << "\n Using correctly coded  9.0/5.0 ==> F = " << farenOK;

        farenNOTOK = 9/5*celsius + 32.0;
        cout << "\n\n Using incorrectly coded 9/5 ==> F = " << farenNOTOK;

        cout << "\n\n Boy what a subtle thing! \n\n";

        return 0;
}
```

Two Temperature Conversions 100 C to 212F
100 Degrees Celsius is 212 Degrees Fahrenheit

Using correctly coded 9.0/5.0 ==> F = 212

Using incorrectly coded 9/5 ==> F = 132

Boy what a subtle thing!

Consider another example where integer division can yield an incorrect numeric result. The volume of a sphere is:

$$V = \frac{4}{3}\text{pi}*r^3$$

The fraction 4/3 must be coded as 4.0/3.0 (or 4./3.) to ensure correct results. Program 2-8 shows the difference that can be found between a right and wrong calculation. The output is:

Two Sphere Volume Calculations
The volume of a sphere of radius = 1 is 4.1888

Using correctly coded 4.0/3.0 ==> vol = 4.18879
Using incorrectly coded 4/3 ==> vol = 3.14159

WOW, another subtle error!

```
//Program 2-8  Two Ways to Calculate Sphere Volume
#include <iostream.h>
#include <math.h>                      //needed for power function
int main ()
{
        double radius = 1.0;
        double volumeOK, volumeNOTOK;
        double pi = 3.14159265;

        cout << "\n Two Sphere Volume Calculations"
                "\n The volume of a sphere of radius = 1 is 4.1888";

        volumeOK = 4.0/3.0 * pi * pow(radius,3);           // 4.0/3.0 OK!
        volumeNOTOK = 4/3 * pi * pow(radius,3);            // 4/3 is wrong!

        cout << "\n\n Using correctly coded 4.0/3.0 ==> vol = " << volumeOK;
        cout << "\n Using incorrectly coded 4/3 ==> vol = " << volumeNOTOK;

        cout << "\n\n WOW, another subtle error! \n\n";
        return 0;
}
```

When to Use math.h   The many mathematical functions of C++ include a
square root, raising a number to a power, trigonometric functions, and others. Often
beginning programmers believe the math library must be included if any math is to
be performed in a program. Remember, there are five arithmetic operators that are
part of the C++ language—multiply, divide, add, subtract, and modulus. The math
library is not needed to perform any of these five operations. If the programmer
needs a square root or tangent function for his or her program, the math library
must be included in the source code, along with the other preprocessor commands,
as shown here.

```
#include <math.h>
```

Arithmetic in C++ and Algebra   Frequently, algebraic expressions need to be
written in C++ code. C++ code looks similar to algebra. C++ has parentheses ( )
and dot operators, but they have different meanings in C++ than in algebra. Table
2-9 illustrates common mistakes made when writing algebraic expressions in C++.

Operator Precedence and Math Expressions   Keep the operator precedence in mind when you code equations. You can leave out a necessary set of
parentheses and obtain an error, or clutter your coding with far too many sets of
parentheses. Break up complicated equations into two or three steps because it is

TABLE 2-9

Algebraic Equations and C++ Expressions

Algebra	C++: The Right Way	C++: The Wrong Way
$v = (a + b)(c - d)$	`double v,a,b,c,d;` `v = (a + b) * (c - d);`	`double v,a,b,c,d;` `v = (a + b)(c - d); //Note 1`

$SA = \text{pi} \cdot \text{radius}^2$	`double SA, pi, rad;`
	`SA = pi * rad * rad;`
	`//OR  See Note 2.`
	`SA = pi * pow(rad,2);`
		`double SA, pi, rad;`
		`SA = (pi)(rad)(rad);//Note 1`
		`//OR`
		`SA = pi * rad **2;// Note 3`
		`SA = pi * rad ^2;// See Note 3`

$a = \dfrac{c + b}{x - y}$	`double a, b, c, x, y;` `a = (c+b)/(x-y);`	`double a, b, c, x, y;` `a = c + b/x - y;    //Note 4`
$m = \dfrac{\sqrt{x \cdot y}}{w}$	`m = sqrt(x * y)/w;  //Note 2`	`m = sqrt(x.y)/w;    //Note 5`

Note 1: To perform multiplication, the * operator must be used. The ()() does not mean multiplication in C++.

Note 2: The math.h library needs to be included to use the square root and power functions.

Note 3: The rad**2 or rad ^2 are not valid ways to do exponentiation in C/C++.

Note 4: Division has higher priority; b/x would be done first.

Note 5: The dot operator (.) is not multiplication in C++.

easier to debug discrete steps rather than a massive equation. Tables 2-10 and 2-11 illustrate several equations and two methods of writing them in C++.

Troubleshooting Fractional Calculations Figure 2-10 shows four different fractional calculations illustrating integer division and how values are stored in variables. It is easy to read a series of fractions in an equation and assume that the computer will calculate the final answer in the same manner that we do on a calculator. The order of precedence dictates that parentheses expressions are performed first. When the developer is using multiplication and division, the order of operations is from left to right. Learn the precedence of operations and associativity!

Increment and Decrement Operators

The increment $(++)$ and decrement $(--)$ operators are useful because they provide a quick way to add or subtract one (1) from a variable. Table 2-12 illustrates how these operators are used.

Beginning C++ programmers often ask about the placement of the operator and if there is a difference between the following two statements:

```
++i;
i++;
```

▌ **TABLE 2-10**
Poor and Error-Prone Techniques of Writing Equations in C++

Algebra	Poor and Error Prone

$V = \dfrac{4}{3}\text{pi} \cdot r^3 + \text{pi} \cdot r^2 h$	`//include math library for sin and sqrt`
	`double vol, r, h, pi = 3.14159265;`
	`vol = ((4/3)*pi*pow(r,3))+(pi*(r*r)*h);`
	`//See Note 1.`

$f(x) = \sin(x - 0.3) + \sqrt{x - y}$	`//include math library for sin and sqrt`
	`double f, x, y;`
	`f(x) = (sin(x - 0.3)) + (sqrt(x-y));`
	`// See Note 2.`

Note 1: We will get integer truncation with 4/3; extra () not needed.
Note 2: We cannot name variables f(x), and extra () not needed.

▌ **TABLE 2-11**
Better Techniques for Writing Equations in C++

Algebra	Better; No Errors

$V = \dfrac{4}{3}\text{pi} \cdot r^3 + \text{pi} \cdot r^2 h$	`//include math library for sin and sqrt`
	`double vol, r, h, pi = 3.14159265;`
	`double temp1, temp2;    //temporary vars`
	`temp1 = 4.0/3.0*pi*pow(r,3);`
	`temp2 = pi*pow(r,2)*h;`
	`vol=temp1 + temp2;`
	`// See Note 1.`

$f(x) = \sin(x - 0.3) + \sqrt{x - y}$	`//include math library for sin and sqrt`
	`double f_of_x, x, y;`
	`f_of_x = sin(x - 0.3) + sqrt(x-y);`
	`// See Note 2.`

Note 1: There are separate addition terms and shorter equations.
Note 2: Valid variable names are used and extra () are removed.

The order of operations and integer division can bring unexpected results.

float X;	int W;	float Z;	int Y;
X = 28/5 * (10/3) * (1/2); 3 0 5 * 3 * 0 15 * 0 0	W = 28/5 * 10/3 * 1/2; 5 * 10/3 * 1/2 50/3 * 1/2 16 * 1/2 16/2 8	Z = 36.0/5.0 + 13/3 + 3/5; 7.2 + 4 + 0 11.2	Y = 36.0/5.0 + 13/3 * 3/5; 7.2 + 4 * 3/5 7.2 + 12/5 7.2 + 2 9.2
Value of X: 0.00000	Value of W: 8	Value of Z: 11.200000	Value of Y: 9

Remember: The variable type on the left side of the equals sign does not alter how the calculations are performed on the right side. The calculations are performed step by step in the order of operator precedence.

Figure 2-10
More Fractional Calculations

TABLE 2-12
Increment and Decrement Operators

Operator	Job	Format	Equivalent To
Increment ++	Add 1 to operand	++i; i++;	i = i + 1;
Decrement −−	Subtract 1 from operand	−−i; i−−;	i = i - 1;

TABLE 2-13
Pre-Fix and Post-Fix Increment and Decrement Operators

Operator	Job	Format	Equivalent To
Prefix increment	Add 1 to i and then assign i into m.	m = ++i;	i = i + 1; m = i;
Postfix increment	Assign i into m and then add 1 to i.	m = i++;	m = i; i = i + 1;
Prefix decrement	Subtract 1 from i and then assign i into m.	m = --i;	i = i - 1; m = i;
Postfix decrement	Assign i into m and then subtract 1 from i.	m = i--;	m = i; i = i - 1;

The answer is, there is no difference. When the increment or decrement operator is used with a variable, as shown in Table 2-12, there is no difference; however, there is a difference when the operators are used in an assignment statement. The prefix operator will increment and/or decrement and then assign; whereas the postfix operator will assign and then increment and/or decrement. See Table 2-13.

Prefix and postfix operators should be used with fear and trepidation! Very nasty bugs (bugs that are hard to find) can result if the operators are used incorrectly.

Accumulation Operators

The accumulation operators (+=, −=, *=, and /=) provide quick ways to write assignment expressions when it is necessary to accumulate values. For example, there are two ways to add a value to a sum variable:

```
sum = sum + x;          //one way to write
sum += x;               // using the += accumulation operator
```

Table 2-14 summarizes these operators.

▌TABLE 2-14
Accumulation Operators

Operator	Use Format	Equivalent To
+=	sum += x;	sum = sum + x;
-=	bal -= withd;	bal = bal - withd;
*=	q *= r;	q = q * r;
/=	m /= n;	m = m / n;

▌TABLE 2-15
Additional Operators in C++

Operator	Operator Type	Refer To
& | ^ - >> <<	Bitwise operators	A complete C++ reference
& *	Address and indirection operator	Chapter 4
<= < >= > == !=	Relational operators	Chapter 3
&& || !	Logical	Chapter 3
? :	Conditional operator	Chapter 3
[]	Array operator	Chapter 6
. →	Dot and right arrow operator	Chapter 7
:: :	Scope operators	Chapters 9 and 11

Other Operators in C++

Several operators in C++ are not covered in this chapter but are discussed in other sections of this book. Operators and corresponding text sections are listed in Table 2-15.

2.8
Miscellaneous Topics: #define, const, and casting

#define

The #define is a preprocessor directive (as is #include) that gives the compiler instructions. Usually the statements are located at the top of the file. The *#define* statement is a symbolic constant and allows the compiler to perform a straight substitution in the code when it is compiled. The form of the #define statement is:

#define
preprocessor directive, compiler symbolic substitution

```
#define  symbolic_name character_sequence
```

Note that there is no semicolon at the end of the statement. An example of a #define is:

```
#define  PI  3.14159265
```

The #define statements are not actual C++ statements that perform an instruction but are compiler substitutions and are performed when the code is compiled. The #define is convenient for coding numeric constants.

If the programmer needs to have numeric constants, the software is written with #define statements as shown in Program 2-9. When the compiler reads and builds the object code for this program, it substitutes the character sequence from the #define statement directly into the code where the symbolic_name appears. For example, whenever the compiler sees the symbolic name PI in the source code, it simply substitutes 3.14159265.

```
//Program 2-9 Using #defines
#include <iostream.h>
#define PI 3.14159265
#define  MyPay  25.00
int main()
{
        float area_circle, r = 10.0, TotalPay;
        area_circle = PI * r * r;
        TotalPay = MyPay * 40.0;
        cout << "\n The value for pi is " << PI;
        cout << "\n The value for MyPay is " << MyPay << endl;
        return 0;
}
```

PI and MyPay are not data variables! They are simply symbolic constants. If we could read the machine code, the main function would look like this:

```
int main()
{
        float area_circle, r = 10.0, TotalPay;
        area_circle = 3.14159265 * r * r;
        TotalPay = 25.00 * 40.0;
        cout << "\n The value for pi is " << 3.14159265;
        cout << "\n The value for MyPay is " << 25.00 << endl;
}
```

Common C++ conventions are to use capital letters for #define constants and to place them at the top of the file so they are easy to locate. These #define statements are used for defining important numbers or identifying data files in a program, such as:

```
#define MAX 100
#define FILE_IN    "A:\data\input.dat"
#define HOURLY_RATE 8.50
```

The const Modifier

C++ has an access modifier, *const*, that is used in variable declaration statements. When used in a declaration statement, the constant's variable initial value remains the same throughout the program. Generally, no C++ assignment statement may modify the value. The form is:

const
modifier specifying that the variable is to remain a constant value

```
const data_type variable_name = initial_value;
```

An example is:

```
const double x = 7.1111;
```

The value in the const variable must be assigned when declared and the program then is not allowed to change this value. The following short program illustrates how different compilers implement this rule.

```
//Program 2-x Changing a const variable  COMPILE ERROR
#include <iostream.h>
int main ()
{
       const double x = 7.1111;   //declare x to be a constant value

       x = 6.2;      //now try to change it

       cout << "\n X = " << x;

       return 0;
}
```

Visual C++ reports that the left-hand value is a const object (and hence not change-able by the program):

Compiling...
Ch2ConstVar.cpp
C:\CBook\TestCases\Ch2ConstVar.cpp(7) : error C2166: l-value specifies const object
Error executing cl.exe.

Ch2ConstVar.obj - 1 error(s), 0 warning(s)

GCC reports this:

```
login1:johnston:~/gnu:$ g++ G++_Ch2constvar.cc
G++_Ch2constvar.cc: In function 'int main()':
G++_Ch2constvar.cc:14: assignment of read-only variable 'x'
```

Are consts Better Than #define?

The const modifier and #define statement both provide the programmer a method
for fixing a value and using it throughout the entire program. But there is one fundamental difference! The const modifier specifies that a variable's value may not be
changed. The #define statement is merely a symbolic substitution that the compiler
performs behind the scenes. The short program in Program 2-10 points out the difference in implementation. Both the APPLE and banana values remain constant
throughout the program:

APPLE = 12
banana = 8

The banana variable is treated like any other variable in C++ (except the value cannot be changed). The variable may be seen in the debugger and may be passed
between functions. APPLE is not a variable at all; it is just a set of characters.
Whenever the compiler sees APPLE, it replaces it with 12.

Great discussions can ensue around the question of whether or not the use of
#define is good style. Because const variables can be seen in the debugger, their
values are not a mystery. On the other hand, #defines are easy ways to set values in
one location, and they do not need to be passed between functions. What you do is
up to you.

```
//Program 2-10 const versus #define
#include <iostream.h>

#define APPLE   12
int main()
{
        const int banana = 8;

        cout << "\n  APPLE = " << APPLE;

        cout << "\n banana = " << banana << endl;

        return 0;
}
```

Data Casts

Variable Assignment Problems   C++ assignment operators are happy to copy the value of one variable into another as long as the two variable data types are the same. In this expression:

```
variable1 = variable2;
```

the value in variable2 is copied into variable1 if these two variables are the same type—such as integers, floats, doubles, structures, or classes (but not arrays). If the two data types are not the same, the compiler will either present a warning (allowing the conversion) or will give an error.

The Visual C++ compiler will give warnings if numeric data types are not the same, but it is possible that the data from one variable can be assigned into another variable. Assigning a double into an integer causes a warning and the decimal precision is lost.

```cpp
//Program 2-x Data conversion warnings
#include <iostream.h>

int main()
{
        double x = 3.5;
        int y;
        y = x;    //3 is placed into y

        cout << "\n The value in X is " << x << " and Y is " << y;

        return 0;
}
```

Visual C++ issues this warning:

Compiling...
Ch2ConversionsWarns.cpp
C:\CBook\TestCases\Ch2ConversionsWarns.cpp(8) : warning C4244: '=' : conversion from 'double' to 'int', possible loss of data

Ch2ConversionsWarns.obj - 0 error(s), 1 warning(s)

GCC reports a similar warning:

login1:johnston:~/gnu:$ g++ G++_Ch2_conversionswarns.cc
G++_Ch2_conversionswarns.cc: In function 'int main()':
G++_Ch2_conversionswarns.cc:14: warning: assignment to 'int' from 'double'

The output shows the truncation effects:

The value in X is 3.5 and Y is 3

It is possible for the programmer to tell the program to convert one data type into another. This conversion is known as a data cast.

casting

an operation in which the value of one type of data is transformed into another type of data

Data Casting   The concept of ***casting*** a variable (or *data cast*) is an operation in which the value of one type of data is transformed into another type of data. The general form of a cast is:

```
(data_type) expression
```

where data_type is the new type of data for that expression, such as:

```
(int) x
```

Applying the cast from double to an integer in the data conversion warnings program eliminates the truncation warning. The cast is written as shown in Program 2-11.

```
//Program 2-11 Data Casting Stomps Conversion Warnings
#include <iostream.h>

int main()
{
        double x = 3.5;
        int y;

        y = (int)x;   //cast x into an int
        cout << "\n The value in x is " << x << " and Y is " << y << endl;

        return 0;
}
```

The program output is:

The value in x is 3.5 and y is 3

The decimal portion of the double value is lost, and the integer value in Y is 3. Casting does not change the fact that the mechanics of placing a double value into an integer still deletes the decimal portion; however, we see no compiler warnings in Visual C++:

An example using the integer division problem illustrates when a cast is help-ful. In the code below is an integer variable whole_number that (for some reason) we need to divide by two so that the result is a double. For the division to issue cor-rect results, we need to cast the integer values into doubles. Let's first examine the program result when a cast *isn't* performed:

```cpp
//Program 2-x              Data Casting
#include <iostream.h>              // casting not performed-> give the wrong answer
int main()
{
        double result;
        int whole_number = 7;
        result = whole_number/2;

        cout << "\n The result of this division is " << result;
        return 0;
}
```

The output shows that integer division occurred and the result contains the value 3:

The result of this division is 3

Now we cast the whole_number into a double, and we see the correct results:

```cpp
result = (double)whole_number/2;    //Here is the cast
```

The output is:

The result of this division is 3.5

Another example of a cast is shown in the code below, where a character variable's value is cast into an integer (refer to Appendix D, "ASCII Character Codes," and the practice section of this chapter):

```cpp
char letter;
int number;
letter = 'A';          //The ASCII code represents A as 65.
number = (int)letter;  // The value in letter is cast into an int--number now has 65.
```

2.9
Keyboard Input and Screen Output

To begin writing programs, we need to learn how to enter data from the keyboard and to write output to the screen. The C++ iostream library makes this task easy. Already we have written **hello world!** using the cout function. In real-world situations, this type of screen output/keyboard input is impractical. User interfaces to programs are typically Windows-based and mouse-driven, or data is read from a file or database. *But* these same concepts for reading data from a keyboard are exactly the same concepts for reading text data from a data file. (Appendix F presents the text-based file input and output information, along with binary file information. We'll reference Appendix F when we learn about arrays in Chapter 6.)

Appendix I presents many short program examples for writing output to the screen and reading data from the keyboard. These concepts revolve around the idea of a data stream, which can be thought of as a stream of characters going from the program to the screen, or as a stream of characters coming in from the keyboard. The only real catch is how the C++ language handles the Enter key (newline) from the keyboard (or the end-of-line marker in a data file). Remember that some input functions (cin and get) leave the Enter key in the stream and others remove it (getline). This material is presented in Appendix I so it will be easy to locate. Spend a few minutes reading this appendix. For beginning writers of C++ programs, this keyboard input and screen output is just what is needed!

2.10
Practice

Troubleshooting: Equation Placement

A common mistake made by beginning programmers is placing equation statements in the upper part of the program and then assuming that the program knows how to use the equations when needed. This practice is not correct! The equations must be placed in the code where they are to be executed once all the variables are known.

In Program 2-12, the equations for the diameter and area of a circle are placed where the variables are declared. This code compiles without error, but when the program is executed, the equations are performed before the radius value is entered. Since the radius value has not been set, you can expect incorrect results for the area and diameter values.

```
//Program 2-x Incorrect Equation Statement Placement
#include <iostream.h>
#define PI 3.14159265

int main()
{
```

```
        float area_circle, diameter,radius;
        area_circle = PI * radius * radius;      //Misplaced Equation Statements :-(
        diameter = 2.0 * radius;


        cout << "\n Enter the radius value for the circle. ";
        cin >> radius;
        cout << "\n The diameter of the circle is " << diameter;
        cout << "\n The area of the circle is " << area_circle << endl;
        return 0;
}
```

The correct placement for the equation statements is illustrated in Program 2-12.

Calculate the Volume of a Cylinder

The short program in Program 2-13 asks the user to input the height and radius of a
cylinder. It calculates the volume of the cylinder and prints the output in tabular
form. If the user entered 15 for the height and 12 for the radius, he or she would see
the following output:

Cylinder Volume Results

Radius	Height	Volume
12.0000	15.0000	6785.8403

```
//Program 2-12  Correct Equation Statement Placement
#include <iostream.h>
#define PI 3.14159265

int main()
{
        float area_circle, diameter,radius;

        cout << "\n Enter the radius value for the circle. ";
        cin >> radius;

        area_circle = PI * radius * radius;   //Equations Statements :-)
        diameter = 2.0 * radius;
        cout << "\n The diameter of the circle is " << diameter;
        cout << "\n The area of the circle is " << area_circle << endl;
        return 0;
}
```

```
//Program 2-13 Practice with Input/Output to calc volume of a cylinder.
#include <iostream.h>                      // needed for cout and cin
#include <iomanip.h>                        //needed for setw()

int main()
{
      float pi = 3.14159265, radius, height, volume;

      cout << "\nPlease enter the height and radius of a cylinder: ";
      cin >> height >> radius;

      volume = pi * radius *radius *height;       //calculate volume
      cout.setf(ios::fixed | iso::showpoint);     //write w/ 4 digits of prec
      cout.precision(4);
      cout << "\n\n Cylinder Volume Results" << endl << setw(12)<<
      "Radius" << setw(12) << "Height" << setw(12) << "Volume" << endl << setw(12) <<
      radius<<setw(12) << height << setw(12) << volume << endl;
      return 0;
}
```

Modulus and Feet and Inches

The usefulness of integer division and the modulus operator is demonstrated in the short program of Program 2-14. We ask the user to enter a whole number of inches (such as 80), and the program converts this distance into feet and inches (6 feet, 8 inches). By dividing 80 by 12, we determine the whole number of feet (6) and the modulus operator 80%12 gives us the inches, which is the whole number remainder, 8.

```
//Program 2-14  Convert Total Inches to Feet & Inches.
#include <iostream.h>
int main()
{
      int user_inches,in, ft;
      cout << "\n Enter Inches (whole number) ==>";
      cin >> user_inches;

      ft = user_inches/12;         //integer division gives us feet
      in = user_inches%12;         //modulus gives us inches

      cout << "\n  Result  "<<ft<<" ft and " << in << " inches." << endl;

      return 0;
}
```

Character Data As Decimal, Hex, and Octal and ios Formatting

The casting operation is the key to being able to write character data as decimal, octal, and hex. In Program 2-15, we ask the user to enter a character and then cast it into an integer. Using the ios formatting flag to format the data, we can then see the user's character represented in the three various formats. (Refer to Appendix D, "ASCII Character Codes.")

```
//Program 2-15  Casting Chars into Ints, Octals, and Hex
#include <iostream.h>

int main ()
{
        char character;
        int int_char;

        cout << "\n Enter the character to be converted ==> ";
        cin >> character;

        cout << "\n\n Your Character  " << character << " is  " ;
        int_char =(int) character;    //cast into an integer
        cout << int_char << " (in decimal)  ";
        cout.setf(ios::oct);
        cout << int_char << " (in octal)  ";
        cout.unsetf(ios::oct);
        cout.setf(ios::hex);
        cout << int_char << " (in hex)  " << endl;
        cout.unsetf(ios::hex);

    return 0;
}
```

The program converts the letter A to the following values:

Enter the character to be converted ==> A
Your Character A is 65 (in decimal) 101 (in octal) 41 (in hex)

REVIEW QUESTIONS AND PROBLEMS

Short Answer

1. Describe the differences between a compiler error and a link error.

2. Name five keywords in C++.

3. What is the difference between a data type and a variable?

4. What is meant by precedence of operations?

5. What is the purpose of an #include statement?

6. Where is an escape sequence used?

7. What library contains the setw() manipulator?

8. What is the purpose of a project in a C++ development environment?

9. What are the two types of comment styles in C++?

10. What is the range of values for a 4-byte integer?

11. Identify valid variable names for the following, and state why the invalid names are not allowed.

x	X	convert-2-pds	_header_h	9_lives
bird brain	$_for_nothing	1_4_U	U_4_1	SleepingDogs

Debugging Problems

For the source code examples in Problems 12 to 14, identify the compiler errors, and state what is needed to eliminate the error(s).

12.
```
#Include <iostrem.h>
int main
{
        float x;
        y = +8.0;
}
```

13.
```
#include<iostream.h>
int main()
{
        int a,4_for_Fun;
        cout << Enter a;
        cin >> a;
```

```
            4_for_Fun = a;
            return 0;
}
```

14.
```
// This is a little program
that calculates a modulus answer.
int main()
{
        float x,y,answer;
        answer = x%y;
        cout << "\n\n answer = << answer;
        return 0;
}
```

Reading the Code

What values will be in the boxes (these represent the computer's memory) once the lines of code in Problems 15 to 17 have been performed? (Be sure to show decimal points and full precision if the variable type is capable of holding that data!)

15.
```
int main()
{
        float x = 4.12345678901230, z = 2;
        int a = 6, b = 6.882;
        double r = 3.12345678901234567;
```

x	z	a	b	r

16.
```
int main()
{
        float x = 234.12345678901230, z = 22.8;
        int a = 44417, b = -0.333 , c = -5;
        double r = 3.12345678901234567;
        long e = 99999;
        char f = '+';
```

x	z	a	b
c	r	e	f

17.

```
int main()
{
        float a = 4.0, b = 8.0, c = 1.5;
        int x = 5, y = 7.5, z = 19.0;
        float  q, r;
        int s, t;

        s = x + z/y*c;
        t = b/a * b*x + c;
        q = y * a+a * c;
        r = z % x+b/a;
```

a	b	c	x	y
z	q	r	s	t

For Problems 18 to 21, write an algorithm to determine the final solution. Your algorithm should be listed in a step-by-step manner.

18. Determine the number of cans of paint needed to paint three rooms of a house (walls and ceiling). Each room is 12 feet × 10 feet with 8-foot ceilings. Each room contains a 4-foot × 5-foot window and a 3-foot × 7-foot door. A can of paint is 1 gallon and covers 250 square feet.

19. Calculate the number of gallons of water in a circular pond. The pond is 20 feet across (diameter) and 3 feet deep. A cubic foot of water contains approximately 7.5 gallons of water.

20. Explain how you would write a program that reads in a line of text and writes it out so the letters are in reverse order. For example, if the line is, "I love C++!", "!++C evol I" is the new way it is written.

21. Given a whole number, explain how you would determine if it is either odd or even.

Programming Problems

22. Write a complete C++ program that demonstrates integer division and the modulus operator. Write a program objective to the screen and then ask the user to enter two integer values. Perform the division and modulus operations on these two numbers and assign the results into integers. Then repeat the operations and assign the results into float variables. Write the two values and four operation results to the screen. Use four decimal places of precision for the floating point values. Include descriptive comments.

23. The area of a regular octagon is

$$Area\_Octagon = 4.828a^2$$

where a is the length of one side. Write a complete C++ program that asks the user to enter the size of the octagon (side), and calculate and print the area to three decimal places of accuracy. Use a #define statement for the multiplicative constant (4.828) and the pow (see math.h library) function to find the side-squared value.

24. The volume of a pyramid is:

$$Vol\_Pyramid = \frac{A*h}{3}$$

where A is the area of the base and h is the height. Write a complete C++ program that asks the user to enter the necessary information about the pyramid, calculate the volume, and print the results (to two decimal places) as well as all dimensional information.

3

Control Statements and Loops

KEY TERMS AND CONCEPTS

binary operator
branch
conditional statement
evaluate a condition
logical operator
loop
loop altering statement
loop index
nested statements
operand
relational operator
same as operator
ternary operator
unary operator

KEYWORDS AND OPERATORS

break
case
default
do
else
for
if
switch
while
logical operators (&& || !)
relational operators (>= > <= <)
relational operators (== !=)
conditional operator (? :)

CHAPTER OBJECTIVES

Present the concept of program control and logic statements.

Illustrate relational and logical operators in C++.

Demonstrate conditional branching statements using if and switch statements.

Compare the similarities between if and switch statements.

Describe the three methods of loop controllers: the for, while, and do while statements.

Show examples of good coding style.

Demonstrate how the proper use of code indention makes the code easy to read and to debug.

Present the common compiler errors made because of missing braces.

Decisions, Decisions!

Any computer programming language must provide methods for checking conditions and making decisions in the program. We need the tools to know if A is greater than B, N is the same as P, Q is equal to R, or S is equal to T. We need the ability to perform statements if certain conditions are met. For example, if the program asks the user to select a menu item, one through five, we need to be able to determine which item was selected and to perform the correct statements. We also need our program to rerun portions of the program. Rerunning portions of a program requires the code to loop back to a statement and repeat certain lines of code. The C++ language provides efficient tools for performing these tasks. A summary of C++ evaluation and loop tools is shown in Table 3-1.

TABLE 3-1
Summary of C++ Evaluation and Loop Tools

Task	Example	Tool
Evaluating a condition	Is A less than B? Is N greater than O and Q the same as P?	relational and logical operators
Branch to correct statements	Pick a menu item and execute the correct statements associated with that menu option.	if statements switch statements
Repeat or loop	Write out "hello world" ten times.	while loop for loop do while loop

3.1
Relational and Logical Operators

relational operator
an operator that evaluates >, >=, <, <=, ==, and != conditions

logical operator
an operator that evaluates AND, OR, or NOT conditions

In C++ *relational* and *logical operators* are used to evaluate conditional statements. A *conditional statement* is used to determine the state (or states) of a variable (or variables). The result of the evaluation is a 1 (true) or a 0 (false). Relational operators are shown in Table 3-2; logical operators are shown in Table 3-3. Relational and two logical operators (AND, &&, and OR, ||) are binary; a *binary operator* expects two values or *operands*. The NOT operator (!) is a unary operator; a *unary operator* requires only a single operand. See Figure 3-1.

TABLE 3-2
Relational Operators in C++

Relational Operator	Tests For	Example
>	greater than	A > B Is A greater than B?
>=	greater than or equal to	A >= B Is A greater than or equal to B?
<	less than	A < B Is A less than B?
<=	less than or equal to	A <= B Is A less than or equal to B?
==	same as	A == B Is A the same as B?
!=	not the same as	A != B Is A not the same as B?

TABLE 3-3
Logical Operators in C++

Logical Operators	Tests For	Example
&&	AND	A && B Return 1 if both A and B are 1; otherwise return 0.
||	OR	A || B Return 1 if either A or B is 1.
!	NOT	!A If A is 1, it is changed to 0. If A is 0, it is changed to 1.

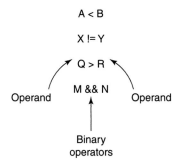

A < B

X != Y

Q > R

Operand   M && N   Operand

Binary
operators

The NOT operator is unary and requires one operand.

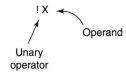

! X

Operand

Unary
operator

Figure 3-1
Binary and Unary Operator Examples in C++

conditional statement

statement in which a
condition is evaluated
and the result
determines which path
the program control
takes

binary operator

operator that requires
two operands

3

operand

C++ operators work on
operands—in the
expression a + b, a and
b are operands and +
is the operator.

unary operator

an operator requiring
only one operand, such
as an increment
operator, ++ or --

Evaluating Expressions and Precedence of Operators

It is possible to write conditional statements using both relational and logical operators. Table 3-4 illustrates several combinations of these types of statements. When a
programmer writes relational and logical statements in C++ (as in arithmetic operations), the precedence and associativity of operators dictate the order of the operations. Table 3-5 presents the precedence and associativity for several operators. (See
also Appendix C, "Operators in C++.") The math operator precedence is higher
than that for relational operators, and the relational operator precedence is higher
than that for logical operators. These facts are important when writing conditional
statements.

▌ TABLE 3-4
Examples of Relational and Logical Statements

Testing For	Example
Is A greater than B and C greater than D?	(A > B && C > D)
Is E greater than H or E greater than D?	(E > H || E > D)
Is A the same as M or the same as Q?	(A == M || A == Q)
Is B greater than C and C less than E?	(B > C && C < E)

TABLE 3-5
Arithmetic, Relational, and Logical Precedence of Operations

Priority	Operator Type	Operator(s)	Associativity
Highest	Primary	( ) [ ] . →	Left to right
	Unary	++ -- & * !	Right to left
	Arithmetic	* / %	Left to right
	Arithmetic	+ -	Left to right
	Relational	< <= > >=	Left to right
	Relational	== !=	Left to right
	Logical	&&	Left to right
	Logical	||	Left to right
Lowest	Assignment	=	Right to left

Example 1

5 + 8 < 14 − 2 || 6 > 3

The + and − have highest precedence.
The + goes first (it's on the left).

13 < 14 − 2 || 6 > 3

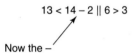

Now the −

13 < 12 || 6 > 3

Next the <

0 || 6 > 3

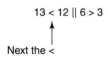

Now the >

0 || 1

Last, the OR operator

1

Example 2

6 + 7 >= 12 && (3+4) > 2 * 4

The ( ) is primary and will be performed first. 3 and 4 are added.

6 + 7 >= 12 && 7 > 2 * 4

Multiplication now has the highest precedence.

6 + 7 >= 12 && 7 > 8

The addition is performed next.

13 >= 12 && 7 > 8

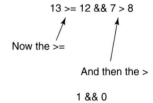

Now the >=

And then the >

1 && 0

Last, but not least, the AND

0

Figure 3-2
Relational and Logical Operators: Simple Examples

When relational and logical operators are used in an expression, the end result is either a 1 (true) or a 0 (false). Figure 3-2 presents two examples using both relational and logical operators. It shows the manner in which C++ comes to a resultant value. Remember that C++ evaluates only one operator at a time.

3.2
if Statements

C++ provides a flexible if statement structure, which allows the programmer to build almost any series of conditional statements. The if statement is based typically on a relational and/or logical expression, which evaluates to a 1 or a 0. The general form of the if statement is shown below:

```
if(Condition)
{
    //These statements are executed if Condition is true or
    //skipped if Condition is false.
}
```

If the condition is true, the statements within the braces are executed. If the condition is false, the statements are skipped. For example, in the code below, "a" is greater than "b" and the condition is true, so the phrase "hello world" is written to the screen. See Figure 3-3 for an illustration.

```
int a = 7, b = 4;
if(a > b)
{
    cout << "\n hello world";
}
```

The braces do not have to be on new lines. The following format is also correct.

```
if(Condition){
    //statements are executed if Condition is true
}
```

If there is only one statement to be executed, the braces are not required. The previous sample of code can be written like this:

```
int a = 7, b = 4;
if(a > b)cout << "\n hello world";
```

The condition is evaluated and if it is true, the statements are executed.
If it is false, the statements are skipped.

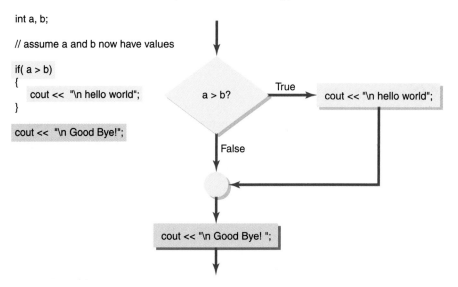

```
int a, b;

// assume a and b now have values

if( a > b)
{
    cout << "\n hello world";
}

cout << "\n Good Bye!";
```

Figure 3-3
if Statement

or like this:

```
int a = 7, b = 4;
if(a > b)
        cout << "\n hello world";
```

The braces are needed if more than one statement is to be executed, such as:

```
int a = 7, b = 4;
if(a > b)
{
        cout << "\n hello world";
        cout << "\n I love C++ programming!";
}
```

This code shows an if statement where the angle is checked to see if it is between 0 and 90 degrees. If the angle is within this range, we convert the angle to radians. If the angle is outside this range, the equation is skipped.

```
if(angle >= 0.0 && angle <= 90.0)
{
        radians = angle * 3.14159265/180.0;
}
```

if else Statements

For situations where something must be done if the condition is true and something else if the condition is false, C++ provides if else statements. Here is the general format:

```
if(Condition)
{
        //these statements done if Condition is true
}
else
{
        //these statements done if Condition is false
}
```

Once again, the braces are needed if more than one statement is executed. If only one statement is executed, the braces are not needed, as shown here:

```
if(Condition)    This statement is performed if the Condition is true.;
else    This statement is performed if the Condition is false.;
```

or

```
if(Condition)
        This statement is performed if the Condition is true.;
else
        This statement is performed if the Condition is false.;
```

In this next example we are checking whether a number is positive or not positive (zero or negative). We need to check only if the number is positive because any values that are zero or negative will fall in the else statement. Figure 3-4 shows the flow of the program statements.

```
if(number > 0)
{
        cout << "\n The number is positive!";
}
else
{
        cout << "\n The number is zero or negative!";
}
```

Since we are executing only one statement for each condition, this code can also be written as:

The condition is evaluated and if it is true, the first statements are executed.
If it is false, the second statements are executed.

```
int number;

// assume number now has a value

if( number > 0)
{
    // first set
    cout <<  "\n The number is positive!";
}
else
{
    // second set
    cout << "\n The number is zero or negative.";
}

cout <<  "\n Good Bye!";
```

number > 0 ?

True

cout << "\n The number is positive! ";

False

cout << "\n The number is zero or negative. ";

cout << "\n Good Bye! ";

Figure 3-4
if-else Statement

```
if(number > 0)
        cout << "\n The number is positive!";
else
        cout << "\n The number is zero or negative!";
```

It is strongly recommended that C++ programmers always use braces to enclose statements in their if else statements. It is permissible not to use the braces when an if statement has a single statement. For any compound if else or if else if format, always use the braces!

Troubleshooting: Use Braces with if Statements

A veteran C++ programmer tells the story of spending more than a day trying to find a bug in his optics design code. The error was due to the fact that he did not have braces in an if else statement, which had multiple lines in the else portion. The code in his program had been written like this:

```
//Actual manner in which the code was written.
if(optics_condition)
        some_optics_statement;            //Line 1
else
        a_different_optics_statement;     //Line 2
        a_third_optics_statement;         //Line 3
```

In this code, if the optics_condition is true, he wants Line 1 to be performed. If the condition is false, he wants to skip Line 1 and execute Lines 2 and 3. In fact, the following statements show how C++ interprets the code:

```
// How it is run in C++
if(optics_condition)
        some_optics_statement;            //Line 1
else
        a_different_optics_statement;  //Line 2


a_third_optics_statement;       //Line 3
```

This code worked well when the optics_condition was false, because Line 1 was skipped and Lines 2 and 3 were executed as planned. The problem occurred when the condition was true. Here Line 1 was executed, then the else and Line 2 were skipped, but Line 3 was executed. (Remember, when no braces are used, C++ is built to assume that just the single statement is associated with the if else statements.) By executing Line 3 accidentally when the condition was true, his program was fouled up. He had unhappy users, and it cost him a day to track down the bug! The code should have been written like this:

```
if(optics_condition)
{
        some_optics_statement;   //Line 1
}
else
{
        a_different_optics_statement;   //Line 2
        a_second_optics_statement;      //Line 3
}
```

if—else if—else Statements

The C++ programmer can cascade a series of condition-checking if statements by incorporating the else if structure. The basic format of the if—else if statement is:

```
if(Condition1)
{
        //Condition 1 statements
}
else if(Condition2)
{
        //Condition 2 statements
}
else
{
        // else statements
}
// Rest of Program statements
```

When executed, the program checks the first condition and, if it is true, executes the Condition1 statements that follow the if statement. Once these statements are completed, program control jumps to the Rest of Program statements. If Condition1 is false, then Condition2 is checked. If Condition2 is true, the Condition2 statements are performed and then the control jumps to the Rest of Program statements. Once the program has found one true condition and executes the statements for that condition, program control jumps to the statement at the end of the if block. If none of the conditions are true, the statements in the else are performed. The programmer may cascade many if else series of checks, as shown in Figure 3-5.

Note the following about the else statement: (1) It is not necessary to have an else block; you may have an if statement, an if—else if statement block, or series of if—else if—else if statements. (2) You may have only one else statement in an if block.

In the following sample code, we check to see if a number is positive, zero, or negative. If the number is not positive and it is not zero, it has to be negative.

```
//Example check to see if a number is positive, zero, or negative.
//Efficient use of if else if statements
if(number > 0)
{
        cout << "\n It is positive!";
}
else if(number == 0)
{
        cout << "\n It is zero!";
}
else
{
        cout << "\n It is negative!";
}
```

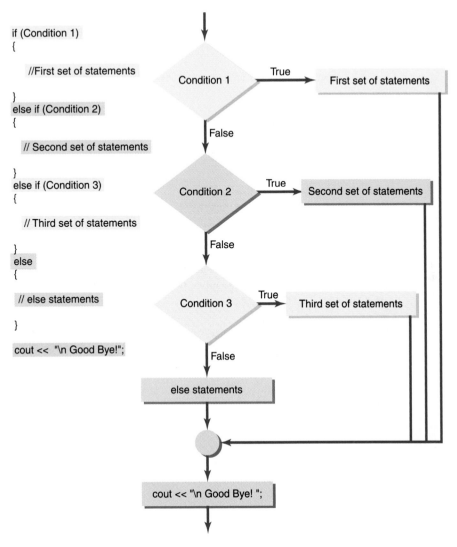

```
if (Condition 1)
{
    //First set of statements

}
else if (Condition 2)
{
    // Second set of statements

}
else if (Condition 3)
{
    // Third set of statements

}
else
{
    // else statements

}
cout <<  "\n Good Bye!";
```

Figure 3-5
Cascading if—else if Statements

Inefficient Programming Techniques

Beginning programmers sometimes forget that program control falls into the else statements if none of the conditions are true. They make extra work by either checking all the possible cases or checking each case individually. The following two examples have the same programmatic results but incorporate unnecessary checking.

```
//Example: check if a number is positive, zero, or negative.
//This uses an extra (unnecessary) else if statement.
if(number > 0)
{
        cout << "\n It is positive!";
}
else if(number == 0)
{
        cout << "\n It is zero!";
}
else if (number < 0)                    // this check is not necessary
{
        cout << "\n It is negative!";
}
```

The second example uses three independent if statements. It is the most inefficient way to write software because it guarantees that the program executes all three if statements. If the number is positive, there is no need to perform the zero or negative checks!

```
//Example:  check if a number is positive, zero, or negative.
//Uses three separate if's when a set of if-else's will do the trick!
if(number > 0)
{
        cout << "\n It is positive!";
}
if(number == 0)
{
        cout << "\n It is zero!";
}
if (number < 0)
{
        cout << "\n It is negative!";
}
```

if else: This Old Man Program Example

We can use a popular children's rhyme and C++ together to illustrate how a program can use a set of if else statements efficiently and perform error checking as well. We see the first four lines of the famous "This Old Man" nursery rhyme. In case you have forgotten it, here it is again:

This old man, he played one, he played knick-knack with his thumb. *
This old man, he played two, he played knick-knack with my shoe. *
This old man, he played three, he played knick-knack on my knee. *

This old man, he played four, he played knick-knack at my door.*
*Chorus: With a knick-knack, paddy whack, give the dog a bone, this old man
came rolling home.

Program 3-1 asks the user to enter an integer. If it is between one and four, we write out the appropriate knick-knack information. If the user enters any other number, we write an error message. Using an if—else if—else block of statements allows invalid entries to be trapped in the else condition. If we code this with a series of individual if statements, we need to do separate checking for any values less than one and greater than four. By using the if—else if—else format, error trapping is easy.

```cpp
//Program 3-1 Knick-Knack Example program with if else
#include <iostream.h>
int main()
{
        int number;
        cout << "\n Please enter an integer for knick-knacking.   ";
        cin >> number;
        cout << "\n He played knick-knack";
        if(number == 1)  //write out knick-knack information
        {
                cout << "with his thumb.  \n";
        }
        else if(number == 2)
        {
                cout << "with my shoe.  \n";
        }
        else if(number == 3)
        {
                cout << "on my knee.  \n";
        }
        else if(number == 4)
        {
                cout << "at my door.  \n";
        }
        else                    // error check, any other number is not valid
        {
                cout << "\n Whoa! He doesn't play knick-knack there!  \n\n";
        }
        return 0;
}
```

Nested if else Statements

nested statements
one set of statements
located inside another
set of statements

It is possible to *nest* if statements within if statements. A nested if statement is simply an if statement as part of the code inside portions of another if statement, like this:

```
if(Condition)  //    first condition
{
    if( Another Condition )     //this is the nested if statement
    {
        //  statements
    }
    // more statements
}
```

In C++, it is possible to nest most types of statements.

In Program 3-2, the user is asked to enter a number. If the number is zero or negative, we just report that. If it is positive, we report only if the number is between 1 and 10.

```
//Program 3-2  Nested if statements sample program
#include <iostream.h>
int main()
{
    int number;
    cout << "\n Please enter an integer   ";
    cin >> number;
    if(number > 0)  //positive number
    {
        cout << "\n The number is positive" << endl;

        if(number >= 1 && number <= 10)
        {
            cout << "and it is between 1 and 10" << endl;
        }

    }
    else
    {
        cout << "\n The number is zero or negative" << endl;
    }
    return 0;
}
```

The ? operator

The C++ language has a ? operator called a ternary operator. A ***ternary operator*** requires three operands. This ? operator functions like the if else statement, with some restrictions. Let's review an if else example:

ternary operator

an operator that requires three operands

```
int moon, star;
star = 50;
if(star > 100)
       moon = 200;    //if star is greater than 100, moon is 200, else moon is zero
else
       moon = 0;
```

In this example, star is not greater than 100; so the else statement is performed and moon is assigned the value of zero.

The format of the ? operator is shown below:

```
Expression1 ? Expression2 : Expression3;
```

The Expression1 is evaluated and if it is true, Expression2 is assigned in Expression1. If Expression1 is false, Expression3 is assigned. The following statements are equivalent to the if else statements above.

```
int moon, stars;
stars = 50;
moon = stars > 100 ? 200 : 0;
```

A second example with the ? operator illustrates a quick way to set a value to either true or false. First, let's show the code in an if else format. We set the value LightsOn to true if the value for Lfound is true.

```
int LightsOn, Lfound;
// code sets the Lfound value
if(Lfound == 1)
       LightsOn = 1;
else
       LightsOn = 0;
```

The ternary operator provides a way to perform this check and assignment in one line.

```
int LightsOn, Lfound;
// code sets the Lfound value
LightsOn = (Lfound) ? 1 : 0;
```

The ? operator does not produce easy-to-read code. It is presented here for completeness, but it is not a format that we encourage beginning C++ programmers to use.

3.3
switch Statement

The switch statement provides an alternate method for doing a series of condition checks and statement executions. It is ideally suited for checking conditions where the value of an integer or character dictates which statements are to be performed. The basic form of the switch is shown below:

```
switch(variable)
{
      case value1:
            //statements 1
            break;
      case value2:
            //statements 2
            break;
      //have all case statements before default
      default:
            //statement n
} //close brace
```

In a switch statement, the value of the variable is examined (an expression may be used and evaluated too). If the value is one of the values in the case statements, the associated statements are performed. The break; statement causes the program to jump to the closing brace. If none of the case values are found, the statements in the default statement are performed. The Knick-Knack program can be written by using a switch statement instead of the if statements. See Program 3-3.

Program 3-4 asks the user to enter a year, and the FamousYears program will check to see if any famous event occurred in that year and writes that information to the screen.

Troubleshooting: Don't Forget to Break Your Switch

Forgetting to include the break statement is a common mistake! If the programmer forgets the break statement, the program continues executing the case statements without breaking out of the switch. For example, if you coded the switch, as shown in red on the next page, and the user entered a 2, the following would be the output:

He played knick-knack with my shoe. on my knee. at the door.
Whoa! He doesn't play knick-knack there!

```
//Program 3-3   Knick-Knack Example program with switch
#include <iostream.h>
int main()
{
     int number;
     cout << "\n Please enter an integer for knick-knacking";
     cin >> number;

     cout << "\n He played knick-knack ";
     switch(number)  //write out area that will be knick-knacked.
     {
          case 1:
               cout << "with his thumb.  \n";
               break;
          case 2:
               cout << "with my shoe.  \n";
               break;
          case 3:
               cout << "on my knee.  \n";
               break;
          case 4:
               cout << "at my door.  \n";
               break;
          default:
               cout << "\n Whoa! He doesn't play knick-knack there!   \n";
     }
     return 0;
}
```

```
cout << "\n He played knick-knack on ";
switch(number)  //Incorrectly coded switch, no break statements!
{
     case 1:
          cout << "with his thumb";
     case 2:
          cout << "with my shoe";
     case 3:
          cout << "on my knee";
     case 4:
          cout << "at the door";
     default:
          cout << "\nWhoa! He doesn't play knick-knack there!";
}
```

```
//Program 3-4  Famous Year Program with switch
#include <iostream.h>
int main()
{
     int year;
     cout << "\n Please enter your favorite year    ";
     cin >> year;

     cout << "\n Your year: " << year << " is famous for  ";
     switch(year)  //check for a famous year
     {

         case 1492:
             cout << " Columbus and his boat ride! \n ";
             break;
         case 1776:
             cout << " a convention in Philadelphia! \n";
             break;
         case 1969:
             cout << " a guy taking a walk on the moon! \n";
             break;
         default:
             cout << "\n ...too bad. Nothing famous happened in that year.\n" ;
     }
     return 0;
}
```

3.4
Loops in General

loop

series of C++
statements that enable
the program to repeat
line(s) of code until a
certain condition is met

A *loop* is a fundamental tool for all programming languages. It involves the ability to have the program loop over or repeat statements. This iterative process may be set up so that the loop is executed a predetermined number of times or until a certain condition is met. For example, a program that calculates yearly totals for utility use performs calculations for the twelve months of the year, whereas a program that sets a thermostat needs to continue checking the temperature until a certain temperature is met and the system is then turned on or off.

The C++ language provides three methods for performing loops: the for loop, the while loop, and the do while loop. All loops in C++ have either a *loop index*, counter variable, or stopping variable, and the following steps must be taken:

loop index
variable used as a counter in a loop

1. An initial assignment for the loop counter or stopping variable.
2. A condition such that, when it is true, it will cause the loop to be executed, and when it is false, it will cause the program to quit performing the loop.
3. *Loop altering statement* that will adjust the counter or stopping variable.

loop altering statement
line of C++ code that changes the value of a variable used in the condition-checking decision for a loop

3

To Brace or Not to Brace?

All three loop formats in C++ require opening and closing braces if the loop is to execute more than one statement. No braces are required if the for and while loops execute only one statement. (The brace requirement is exactly the same as that for the if statements.) In this text, we use braces for our loops and encourage readers to do the same. Using braces with loops and ifs, and indenting code within the braces, makes the code easier to read and aids the programmer in debugging problems.

You Can't Get Out of an Infinite Loop

An infinite loop occurs when a loop starts but the counter limit or stopping condition is never met and the loop never stops executing. (You get checked in but you can't check out of an infinite loop!) A program starts running and then seems to hang or pause forever, when actually the loop is executing. This situation often requires the programmer to use the Control-Alt-Delete sequence to stop the program execution.

Recommendations! Always be sure the loop conditions are reasonable and that, once the loop starts, it will be able to stop. Also, save your program before you run it. If you have an infinite loop and you must kill the program, your recent additions to the file may not be saved automatically. (The Microsoft Visual C++ compiler defaults to saving files before running them.)

3.5
for Loop

The for loop is a convenient C++ statement for use when the programmer knows exactly how many times the statements must be repeated. This loop structure has the following format:

```
for(initial condition; condition; increment)
{
    //statements are executed if condition is true
}
```

Here is an example of writing *hello world* to the screen fifty times:

```
//write hello world 50 times
int i;
for(i = 0; i < 50; ++i)
{
    cout << "\n hello world";
}
```

The for loop, illustrated in Figure 3-6, first executes the initial condition, which is usually an assignment statement. Here the integer "i," acting as the loop counter or loop index, is assigned a value of zero. The condition is then checked: Is i less than 50? Yes, so the statement(s) within the braces are performed. At the end of the statements, the program performs the increment (it adds 1 to i) and checks the condition again. If the condition is true, the statements within the braces are

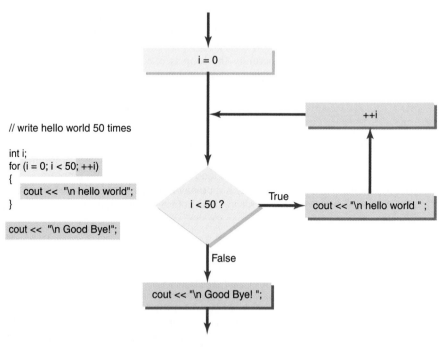

Figure 3-6
for Loop

executed again. If the condition is false, program control then goes to the statement after the closing brace.

It is possible to use the decrement operator instead of the increment operator to vary the loop variable. This loop writes the numbers 100 to 1 to the screen.

```
//write numbers 100 to 1
int ctr;
for(ctr = 100; ctr > 0; --ctr)
{
    cout << "\n The counter =" << ctr;
}
```

In for loops, the assignment statement is performed and the condition is checked. If the condition is false, the loop does not execute, as seen here:

```
int t;
for(t = 0; t < 0; ++t)    //this loop will not execute
{
      //loop statements
}
```

The above examples are by far the most commonly used forms of the for loop, but the programmer can use various forms and more complicated logic. The control for the for loop can be based on the value of two or more variables. The example below illustrates this situation:

```
int x,y;
for(x = 0, y = 100; x != 50 && y > 30; ++x, --y)
{

    //statements are executed if condition is true
}
```

The comma can be used to string together the initialization and increment/ decrement statements. The condition may use logical operators for complicated conditional checks, but beginning programmers should avoid using this type of program code.

Do Not Alter the Loop Index

Programmers should not tinker with the loop counter inside the for loop. This loop structure is built to initialize and to check the condition and increment if the loop statements have been performed. It is poor practice to use creative logic in a for loop. In the example below, the index "k" is altered inside the loop. This alteration results in an infinite loop because "k" never reaches the value of 10.

```
int k;
for(k = 1; k < 10; ++k)          //an infinite loop  BAD EXAMPLE!!!! DO NOT DO THIS!!
{
        //loop statements
        k--;
}
```

for Loop Examples

HowManyHellos   The HowManyHellos program in Program 3-5 asks the user to enter the number of "hellos" he or she wishes to see. The program has a variable for the user's value as well as a counter for the for loop that keeps track of the times the loop has executed.

Writing the Alphabet   We need to write the letters of the alphabet (in capital letters). We wish to write the letters in four rows so that the output looks as shown here:

A	B	C	D	E	F	G
H	I	J	K	L	M	N
O	P	Q	R	S	T	U
V	W	X	Y	Z		

We can use a for loop and the ASCII character codes to access the letters directly. For example, the letter "A" is stored as a 65. To write an "A," we cast a 65 into a character in the cout statement. (Consult Appendix D, "ASCII Character Codes," to see the full range of codes.) To write the alphabet on four lines, we use a counter to

```
//Program 3-5  HowManyHellos and for loop
#include <iostream.h>

int main()
{
        int counter, howmany;
        cout << "\n How many hellos would you like to see?    ";
        cin >> howmany;
        for(counter = 0; counter < howmany; ++counter)  //loop executes howmany times
        {
                cout << "\n Hello!";
        }
        cout << "\n That's a lot of hellos!  \n";
        return 0;
}
```

```
//Program 3-6 Writing the ABC's
#include <iostream.h>
#include <iomanip.h>                      //for setw()
int main()
{
     int letter_ctr, i;
     cout << "\n We're going to write our ABC's  ";

     letter_ctr = 0;
     for(i = 65; i < 91; ++i)             //A = 65, Z = 90
     {
          cout << setw(6) << (char)i;         // write a letter
          letter_ctr++;                       // incr letter counter
          if(letter_ctr == 7)                 // newline if we've written 7
          {
               cout << endl;
               letter_ctr = 0;
          }
     }
     cout << "\n Now I've said my ABC's. Won't you sing along with me? \n\n";
     return 0;
}
```

keep track of how many letters we have written to the screen. Seven letters are written on three lines, with the remaining five characters on the last line. Once we have written seven letters, we write a newline character and reset the counter. See Program 3-6.

3.6
while Loop

The while loop is needed when the programmer does not know how many times a loop is to be executed. The while loop can also be used to perform a loop an exact number of times. The format of the while loop is shown below and is illustrated in Figure 3-7.

```
while(condition)
{
     //these statements done if condition is true
}
```

```
// write hello world 50 times

count = 0;          // initialize count to zero

while (count < 50 )
{
    cout <<  "\n hello world";
    ++ count;       // loop altering statement
}

    cout <<  "\n Good Bye! ";
```

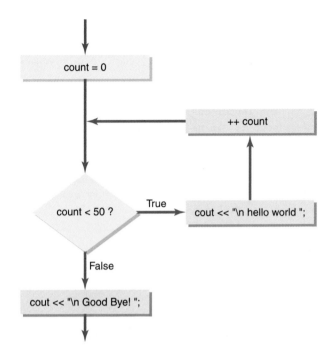

Figure 3-7
while Loop

The while loop checks the condition and if it is true, the loop statements are performed. If the condition is false, the statements are skipped.

To avoid becoming stuck in an infinite loop, a more complete form for this loop includes an initialization statement and a loop altering statement, as shown here when we write *hello world* to the screen fifty times.

```
int count = 0;                  //important to set up initial condition
while(count < 50)               //condition check
{
        cout << "\n hello world";
        count++;                        //alter the loop counter
}
```

while Loop Examples

In the following examples, we must remember to set up an initial condition for the loop counter. If we forget to assign the initial condition, there is no telling what might be in the memory allocated for count. Also note that there must be a loop altering statement inside the while loop or we find our program stuck in an infinite loop.

A Lovely Poem Consider a program that illustrates how the while loop runs until the correct stopping condition is found. Remember, as long as the condition is true, the loop executes. In Program 3-7, we write out a poem and ask the user if he or she would like to see it again. As long as the user wants to see it, we keep writing it.

Note that we initialize the answer to "y" so that the loop runs the first time. After we write out our lovely poem, we ask the user if he or she would like to see it again. Once the user has entered his or her answer, the program then checks the condition in the while statement. As long as the condition is true, the loop executes.

```
//Program 3-7   while loop and Poetry program
#include <iostream.h>

int main()
{
        char answer = 'y';   //initialize answer to y(yes)
        while(answer == 'y' || answer == 'Y')   //keep going until not yes
        {
                cout << "\n Roses are red \n Violets are blue" <<
                "\n I Love C++ \n How about you?";

                cout << "\n\nWant to see my poem again? y=yes, n=no   ";
                cin >> answer;
        }
        cout << "\n OK, all done. Goodbye.";
        return 0;
}
```

HowManyHellos Program 3-8 illustrates how an expression with variables can be used in the conditional portion of a while loop. The HowManyHellos program is rewritten by means of a while loop. Take a moment to review the for loop version of this program. Note that the counter must be initialized and incremented in separate lines of code—as opposed to the for loop, where these statements are all performed on one line.

3.7
do while Loop

The third type of loop structure in C++ is the do while loop. It is very similar to the while loop except that the condition check is performed at the end of the loop. The loop statements are always performed at least once—unlike the for and while loops, where the condition must be true before the loop is executed. Refer to Figure 3-8.

```
//Program 3-8  HowManyHellos and while loop
#include <iostream.h>

int main()
{
        int counter, howmany;
        cout << "\n How many hellos would you like to see?    ";
        cin >> howmany;

        counter = 0;
        while(counter < howmany)    //loop executes howmany times
        {
                cout << "\n Hello!";
                ++counter;
        }
        cout << "\n That's a lot of hellos!    \n";
        return 0;
}
```

```
do
{
        //loop statements
} while(condition);
```

The program executes the loop statements and then checks the condition. If
the condition is true, the program control returns to the do statement and executes
the loop statements again. As in the while and for loops, you must initialize your
counter or stopping condition and have loop altering statements. We can write *hello
world* fifty times using a do while loop.

```
int count = 0;
do
{
        cout << "\n hello world";
        count++;
} while(count < 50);
```

do while Examples

A Lovely Poem   Throughout this book, the problem descriptions usually request
that the user be allowed to loop back to the beginning of the program if he or she
wishes. This request allows the user to continue to loop through the main portion of

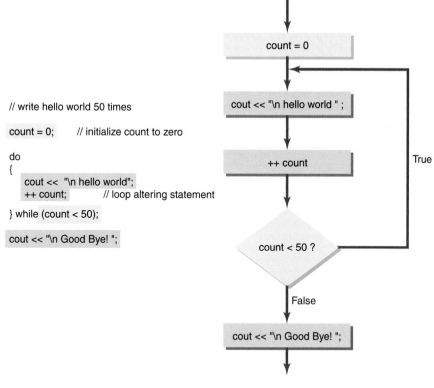

```
// write hello world 50 times

count = 0;        // initialize count to zero

do
{
    cout <<  "\n hello world";
    ++ count;            // loop altering statement
} while (count < 50);

cout << "\n Good Bye! ";
```

Figure 3-8
do while Loop

the program as many times as desired. The do while loop is perfect for this type of application.

Our poetry program appears again in Program 3-9. This time the program makes use of the do while loop format. The statements within the loop are executed once and then the conditional statement is evaluated.

Writing the Alphabet   In this example, we write the lowercase letters of the alphabet to the screen. We use a do while loop and write the letters in five rows so that the output looks as shown here:

a	b	c	d	e	f
g	h	i	j	k	l
m	n	o	p	q	r
s	t	u	v	w	x
y	z				

```
//Program 3-9  do while loop and Poetry
#include <iostream.h>


int main()
{
        char answer; /*no need to initialize since we'll ask the user
                         before we check the condition */
        do
        {
                cout << "\n Roses are red \n Violets are blue" <<
                "\n I Love C++ \n How about you?";

                cout << "\n\nWant to see my poem again?  y=yes, n=no  ";
                cin >> answer;
        } while(answer == 'y' || answer == 'Y');    //keep going until not yes

        cout << "\n OK, all done. Goodbye.";
        return 0;

}
```

We use the same scheme as the for loop version of this program. The lower-case letters are found in ASCII codes 97 (a) to 122 (z). To write the alphabet in five lines, we use a counter to keep track of how many letters we write to the screen (six letters on four lines, with the last two on the fifth line). See Program 3-10.

3.8
Troubleshooting

Four Common Mistakes

Programmers often write complicated conditional statements. Relational and logical operators can be tricky! C++ has strict syntactical rules for writing these statements. Beginning programmers tend to make four mistakes discussed in the following sections.

First Mistake: X > Y && Z   Suppose a programmer needs to check if X is greater than both Y and Z. Each phrase of a conditional statement must be written completely. Remember, relational operators have a higher precedence than logical operators—extra parenthesis are not required. The correct way to write this statement is:

if(X > Y && X > Z) //correct way to write this condition statement

```
//Program 3-10 Writing the abc's with a do while loop
#include <iostream.h>
#include <iomanip.h>                        //for setw()
int main()
{
     int letter_ctr, int_to_ascii;
     cout << "\n We're going to write our abc's   \n";
     letter_ctr = 0;
     int_to_ascii = 97;
     do
     {
          cout << setw(6) << (char)int_to_ascii; // write a letter
          int_to_asci++;                            // incr integer to ASCII number
          letter_ctr++;                          // incr letter counter
          if(letter_ctr == 6)                 // newline if we've written 7
          {
               cout << endl;
               letter_ctr = 0;
          }
     }
     while(int_to_ascii < 123);          //keep looping until we reach one past z

     cout << "\n\n Now I've said my abc's. Won't you sing along with me? \n\n";
     return 0;

}
```

The following statement shows a common mistake when writing complicated statements:

```
if(X > Y && Z)       //incorrect way!!
```

The compiler does not give an error on this statement. When the code is executed, the right side of the AND operator will always be true as long as Z is not zero.

A programming student was attempting to check the condition of a variable to see if it was either 0 or 1. He wrote his statement as follows:

```
if(x == 0 || 1)             // incorrectly written
```

When he ran his program, the statement was never found to be false. Why? The OR requires either the left side or the right side to be 1 (true) to return true. Since the right side of the OR operator was a 1, the statement was always evaluated to be true. The correct way to write this statement is:

```
if(x == 0 || x == 1)                //correct
```

Second Mistake: A = B Is Not A == B   The relational operator, ==, evaluates the two operands to see if they have the same value. The assignment operator, =, assigns the value on the right to the variable on the left. Programmers either forget this or mistype the statement. For example:

```
while(a = b)        // assign b into a
while(a == b)       // checking to see if a and b have same value
```

This simple error can cause a huge amount of programming grief!

---

same as operator ==
an operator that compares the two operands to determine if they are the same

assign operator =
an operator that copies the value of the right operand into the left operand

Recommendation!   Programmers should get in the habit of calling the == operator the *same as operator* and the = operator the *assign operator.* Too often students use the word *equals* for both concepts and inadvertently use the = operator when they mean the == operator.

Third Mistake: A || B && C || D Is Really A || (B && C) || D   The AND (&&) operator has a higher precedence than the OR (||) operator. If a conditional statement uses both && and ||, it is necessary to use a set of parentheses to ensure that the conditions are evaluated in the correct order. For example, if the programmer needs to check if A or B is true and if C or D is true, then the correct way to write the statement is as follows:

```
if( (A || B) &&  (C || D))  //written correctly.
```

In the above statement, the items inside the parentheses will be evaluated first, and results for the A, B and C, D conditions will be rendered. Then the AND condition will be evaluated. Below is a common mistake:

```
if( A || B && C || D)  //incorrectly written
```

A more complex example using the relational operators is shown in Figure 3-9. Notice that without the parentheses, the evaluation steps occur in the wrong sequence and the results are different.

Fourth Mistake: floats Are Not the Same As ints   When you are evaluating floating point or double variables to determine if the values are the same, using the same as operator does not guarantee accurate results. Integer values are stored precisely in memory and will evaluate correctly when using the == operator, but floating point and double variables will have a small inaccuracy due to the manner in which decimal precision values are stored. The code below illustrates this problem, using an if statement:

102   Chapter 3 ▌ Control Statements and Loops

Parentheses must be used to ensure correct evaluation. Three examples follow.

Figure 3-9
AND and OR Logical Operators Have Different Precedence of Operation.

```
float x = 10, y = 10, z;   // x and y may be stored in memory as 10.000001
z = x + y;                 // z is actually 20.000002
if ( z == 20)              // z is not the same as 20, this condition is false.
```

To evaluate two floating point or double values for sameness, the programmer should check for a small difference. In the following sample, we use the fabs function, which is the absolute value function (returns a positive value), for floating point and double values to obtain the positive value of the difference.

```
float x = 10, y = 10, z;
z = x + y
if ( fabs(z - 20) < 0.000001 )   // use the fabs for absolute value
                                 //if small difference, assume z is 20
```

Troubleshooting: My Loop Won't Stop

Two beginning programmers were attempting to have their programs continue to ask the user for input until the user wanted to stop. Sounds simple, doesn't it? Although their techniques, illustrated below, are different, both had the same error. Can you find it?

```
// Scott's Loop that wouldn't stop.   :-(
#include <iostream.h>
int main()
{

     int go = 1;
     while(go = 1)
     {
          // Programming details have been left out.
```

```
                cout << "\n Would you like to go again?  1 = yes, 0 = no";
                cin >> go;
        }
        cout << "\n\n See you Homie";
        return 0;
}


// Sarah's Loop that wouldn't stop.    :-(
#include <iostream.h>
int main()
{

        char answer;
        do {
                // Programming details have been left out.

                cout << "\n Would you like to go again? y = yes, n = no";
                cin >> answer;
        }while(answer = 'y');
        cout << "\n\n Good bye.";
        return 0;

}
```

Microsoft Visual C++ issues a warning if it encounters an assignment statement when it is expecting a conditional expression. In both Scott's and Sarah's programs, the compiler issued a warning on the first build:

```
Compiling...
Ch3Scott.cpp
c:\ch3scott.cpp(6) : warning C4706: assignment within conditional expression
Linking...

TestCases.exe - 0 error(s), 1 warning(s)
```

The GCC compiler did not warn us, and the loop subsequently repeated itself. If the programmer does not pay attention to the compiler warning(s), he or she may miss the message. It is worthwhile to do a Rebuild All in Visual C++ every so often and check every warning that is issued.

Troubleshooting: Semicolons and Braces

One of the nastiest little bugs that strikes a program is caused by the programmer accidentally placing a semicolon after the parentheses, like the examples shown in red on the next page. In both cases, the compiler believes there is only one statement to be executed and ignores the braces.

```
//Program 3-11 Semicolons and Warnings!!!!   DOES NOT RUN CORRECTLY
#include <iostream.h>
int main()
{
        char answer;
        int count = 0;
        if(count == 50);            //<===YIKES!   ();
        {
                cout << "\n Count is too big" <<
                            "\n You won't get a hello from me.";
        }
        cout << "\n Did you like them apples?  y or n  ";
        cin >> answer;
        cout << "\n Now you get 10 hellos.\n";

        while(count < 10);                        //infinite loop here!
        {
                cout << "\n hello world ";
        }
        return 0;
}
```

```
if(x > 5) ;
{
        //if statements
}
```

or

```
while(count < 6 );
{
        //while statements
}
```

When this situation occurs, the statements within the if statement braces are executed because the "empty" statement is executed only if the condition is true. In the case of the while loop, the program gets stuck in an infinite loop because the empty statement is executed until the condition is false—which never happens. In the case of the if statement, the Microsoft Visual C++ compiler warns the programmer that an empty statement has been found. An example appears in Program 3-11.

When this code is compiled, Visual C++ issues the following warning concerning the if count statement:

Compiling...
Ch3SemiColon_Warnings.cpp
C:\CBook\TestCases\Ch3SemiColon_Warnings.cpp(8) : warning C4390: ';' : empty controlled statement found; is this the intent?
Linking...

TestCases.exe - 0 error(s), 1 warning(s)

No errors or warnings are issued by GCC. Visual C++ is warning the programmer about the if statement, but it does not warn about the while statement. When this program runs, the programmer sees the following output:

Count is too big
You won't get a hello from me.
Did you like them apples? y or n

The "Count is too big" statements are executed because the semicolon at the end of the if statement is the empty statement. As far as the program is concerned, the statements after that semicolon should be executed—no matter what the results of the if condition. Once the user types in an apple response, the program then hangs in an infinite loop.

Remember that it is legal in C++ to have a single statement executed after a conditional expression. Always take a few minutes to read each warning, and always look at your condition statements to be sure the loop or if statement is in the desired format.

Troubleshooting: Misplaced else, Illegal else, Unexpected End of File

Style is important when programming if statements, switch statements, and loops! Beginning programmers often view the requirement of aligning the opening and closing braces and indenting code as an after-the-fact task. If the program has complicated logic, however, there will be many pairs of braces in the source code. You will not be able to see all the braces on the screen while editing. It is good practice to develop the habit of aligning the braces and indenting the code within the braces as you enter your C++ statements.

The most common mistake programmers make is not having complete sets of braces when using the if else, switch, and loop statements. The compiler does its best to match up the opening and closing braces, and it will attempt to report the location where it suspects the missing brace should be placed. But compilers are not perfect!

To gain a feel for debugging code with poor style, here is a shortened version of the Knick-Knack program. This code will generate the two compiler errors shown below it. Can you spot the problem?

```
//Program 3-x  Short Knick-Knack Program with compiler error
#include <iostream.h>
int main()
{
int number;
cout << "\n Please enter an integer for knick-knacking";
cin >> number;
cout << "\n He played knick-knack on ";
if(number == 1)  //Write out knick-knack information.
{
cout << "his thumb";
}
else if(number == 2)
{
cout << "my shoe";
else
{
cout << "\n whoa! He doesn't play knick-knack there!";
}
return 0;
}
```

The Visual C++ compiler displays the following messages:

Compiling...
ch3cerror.cpp
C:\ch3cerror.cpp(17) : error C2181: illegal else without matching if
C:\ch3cerror.cpp(23) : fatal error C1004: unexpected end of file found
Error executing cl.exe.

TestCases.exe - 2 error(s), 0 warning(s)

GCC reports this error:

login1:johnston:~/gnu:$ g++ G++_Ch3_2.cc
G++_ ch3cerror.cc: In function 'int main()':
G++_ ch3cerror.cc:26: parse error before 'else'

Always indent the code statements within each set of braces. Also, be sure that the opening brace is in the same column as the closing brace. There are several compiler errors that relate to either missing or extra braces. These errors are illegal else, misplaced else, missing brace, compound statement missing }, or unexpected end of file. If your code will not compile due to one or more of these errors, chances are excellent that you have either too few or too many braces.

> **Microsoft Visual C++ Tip!** To determine the partner of an opening or closing brace, place the cursor on a brace and holding down the control (ctrl) key, press the brace key. The editor will then show which it believes is the partner brace.

Debugging Your Program

If you haven't already, now is the perfect time to learn the debugging tools that accompany your development environment. Refer to Appendix J, "Microsoft Visual C++ Debugger."

3.9
Summary

Tables 3-6 and 3-7 summarize the if else and switch statements as well as the types of loops available in C++. These tables can be used as guides for selecting the most appropriate statements for a given task.

The Indenting Convention

> *Three, six, nine,*
> *the goose drank wine,*
> *the monkey chewed tobacco on the streetcar line.*[1]

This popular rhyme has helped at least one programmer with her programming. She used the values 3, 6, 9, 12, 15, etc., as the indention values—tab stops—when aligning statements within a function; that is, the first brace set was in column 1 and all code was indented to column 3. When the next opening brace was entered, the code following that brace was indented to column 6. Having some form of indention style and using it consistently makes the code much easier to follow and debug.

3.10
Practice!

In the first examples presented in this section, we build the program in two steps to illustrate how programs should be built in stages. (In reality, your programs should be built in many stages.) Write a small portion of the code and run it to ensure that it behaves correctly before continuing to write the program. Beginning students often try to enter the entire program in one step and then are faced with a multitude of errors.

---

[1]This children's rhyme continues with "the line broke, monkey got choked, and they all went to heaven in a little row boat."

TABLE 3-6

if, if else, if else—if else, switch Summary

Decision Type	When to Use	Basic Format
if	If a condition is true, perform statements; if the condition is false, skip statements.	```if(condition)\n{\n //statement\n}```
if else	If a condition is true, perform certain statements; if the condition is false, perform different statements.	```if(condition)\n{\n // true condition statements\n}\nelse\n{\n // false condition statements\n}```
if else—if else	If the first condition is true, perform statements and jump to end. If the first condition is false, check the next condition. If it is true, perform statements and jump to end. Continue to check until a condition is true. If no condition is true, perform else statements. Can use complicated logic. *Note:* else is not required.	```if(condition1)\n{\n // true condition1 statements\n}\nelse if(condition2)\n{\n // true condition2 statements\n}\nelse\n{\n // neither condition is true\n}```
switch	The switch may be used if the value for which you are checking is simple numeric (i.e., 1, 2, 3, etc.) or character (i.e., a, b, c, etc.). Switch will evaluate the expression for a value and performs the case that matches the value. Default statements correspond to else statement in if else structure. *Note:* Default is not required.	```switch (expression)\n{\n case value1:\n //statements for value 1\n break;\n case value2:\n // statements for value 2\n break;\n default:\n // no case matches\n}```

3

TABLE 3-7
for, while, and do while Loop Summary

Loop Type	When to Use	Basic Format for Writing 1 to 10
for	Use the for loop if you know exactly how many times the loop should execute. The condition must be true for it to run.	```int i;\nfor(i = 1; i <= 10; ++i)\n{\n cout << "\n i =" << i;\n}```
while	Use the while loop when a loop must continue to run until a condition has been met. The condition must be true for it to run.	```int i = 1;\nwhile(i <= 10)\n{\n cout << "\n i =" << i;\n ++i;\n}```
do while	Use the do while loop when the loop statements must run at least once. The condition will be checked after the first pass, and the loop will continue as long as the condition is true.	```int i = 1;\ndo\n{\n cout << "\n i =" << i;\n ++i;\n} while(i <= 10);```

Time Conversion

This first sample practice program is a time-conversion program that presents the user with three choices:

1. Convert time (in hours, minutes, and seconds format) to total seconds.
2. Convert total seconds to hours, minutes, and seconds.
3. Exit the program.

error trap

programmer's term that means to have the program be on the lookout for invalid or incorrect situations

The program will **error trap** (alert the user) if there is an incorrect input value and loop until the user is finished.

Phase 1: Program Flow   In this first phase, we will ask the user for his or her choice and get the loop portion executing before adding any of the time conversion statements. Notice in Program 3-12 that the opening and closing braces are in the same column and that the code is indented consistently. It is easy to see that all the braces have a partner.

Phase 2: Add the Complicated Components   Now that the loop is working, add the time-conversion statements. The complete program is seen in Program 3-12, Phase 2.

```
//Program 3-12 Practice! Time Conversion
//Phase 1 -- Program Flow Only

#include <iostream.h>
int main()
{
    int choice;

    do{
        cout << "\nPlease pick your choice:  \n1= Convert H:M:S to second" <<
        "\n2= Convert second to H:M:S  \n3 = Exit\n\n";
        cin >>choice;
        switch(choice)
        {
            case 1:
                cout << "\n You entered a 1 ";
                break;
            case 2:
                cout << "\n You entered a 2  ";
                break;
            case 3:
                cout << "\n You entered a 3  (and will exit)   \n";
                break;
            default:
                cout << "\n Oh I don't do that choice! Try again! ";
        }
    }while(choice != 3);
    cout << "\n Bye Bye!";
    return 0;
}
```

Numbers

In this second practice program, we ask the user to enter a number from 1 to 1,000. We will use a while loop and set the initial value of the answer to yes to get the loop started. Inside the loop, we will check first to see if the user's value is within the specified range. The else portion of this if statement will write the out-of-range message. If the user number is within the specified range, the modulus operator will be used to determine if the number is divisible by 2 or 3.

Phase 1: Program Flow   We will write just the loop and in-range number-checking statements.

Phase 2: Additional Features   Once the Phase 1 portion is working, we will add the additional variables and nested if statement.

```cpp
//Program 3-12 Practice! Time Conversion  Phase 2, complete program
#include <iostream.h>
int main()
{
    int choice,hr, min, sec, totalsec;
    char colon;
      do{
            cout << "\nPlease pick your choice:  \n1= Convert H:M:S to second" <<
            "\n2= Convert second to H:M:S  \n3 = Exit\n\n";
            cin >>choice;

            switch(choice)
            {
                case 1:
                    cout << "\n Enter time in H:M:S format, such as 3:26:33 ";
                    cin >> hr >> colon >> min >> colon >> sec;
                    totalsec = hr*3600 + min*60 + sec;
                    cout << "\n Your time in seconds is " << total
                    sec;break;
                case 2:
                    cout << "\n Enter total seconds, such as 3440 ";
                    cin >> totalsec;
                    hr = totalsec/3600;
                    totalsec = totalsec - hr*3600;
                    min = totalsec/60;
                    totalsec = totalsec - min*60;
                    sec = totalsec;
                    cout << "\n Your time is " << hr << ":" << min << ":" <<
                    sec;
                    break;
                case 3:
                    cout << "\n You have chosen to exit.  \n";
                    break;
                default:
                    cout << "\n Oh I don't do that choice! Try again! ";
            }
    }while(choice != 3);
    cout << "\n Bye Bye!   \n";
    return 0;
}
```

```
//Program 3-13 Numbers and More Practice!
// Phase 1  Program Flow only
#include <iostream.h>
int main()
{
       int number;
       char answer = 'y';

       while(answer == 'y')
       {
               cout << "\nPlease enter a number from 1 to 1000  ==> ";
               cin >> number;
               if(number > 0 && number < 1001)          //number is within range
               {
                       cout << "\n IN RANGE---Your number  is " << number ;
               }
               else
               {
                       cout << "\n Your number is out of range!!   ";
               }
               cout << "\n Want to go again?  y = yes, n = no  ";
               cin >> answer;
       }
       cout << "\n Bye Bye!";
       return 0;
}
```

Output Patterns

No C++ textbook is complete without at least one pattern output problem. We start
with an easy pattern and then list a few hints to help with the not-so-easy patterns in
the exercises.

Write a program that prints the pattern shown below to the screen. Your program should ask the user to enter the character he or she wishes to use in the pattern
and the number of lines. (Limit the number of lines to twenty.) Here is a sample
output using the + character and six lines:

```
+
++
+++
++++
+++++
++++++
```

```
//Program 3-13 Numbers and More Practice!
#include <iostream.h>
int main()
{
        int number, mod2,mod3;
        char answer = 'y';
        while(answer == 'y')
        {
                cout << "\nPlease enter a number from 1 to 1000  ==> ";
                cin >> number;
                if(number > 0 && number < 1001)          //number is within range
                {
                        mod2 = number%2;                    // is it divisible by 2 or 3?
                        mod3 = number%3;
                        if(mod2 == 0 || mod3 == 0)
                        {
                                cout << "\n Your number " << number << " is divisible by ";
                                if(mod2 == 0) cout << "2 !";
                                if(mod3 == 0) cout << "3 !";
                        }
                }
                else
                {
                        cout << "\n Your number is out of range!!  ";
                }
                cout << "\n Want to go again?  y = yes, n = no  ";
                cin >> answer;
        }
        cout << "\n Bye Bye!";
        return 0;
}
```

The trick with any of these pattern problems is to write the pattern on a piece of paper and note the process. The number of rows will be controlled by one for loop, and the number of characters on each line will be controlled by either a for or a while loop. (More complicated patterns may take two or more inner loops to write the pattern lines.)

In Program 3-14, the row number represents the number of characters on that line—that is, row one has one character, row two has two characters, and so on. The inner loop limit is the outer loop's counter value.

```
//Program 3-14 Writing a Simple Pattern
#include <iostream.h>
#include <iomanip.h>                      //for setw()
int main()
{
      int NumRows, i, j;
      char MyChar;

      cout << "\n Write a simple pattern.   ";
      cout << "\n Enter the character for your pattern     ";
      cin >> MyChar;
      cout << "\n How many rows?  1 - 20     ";
      cin >> NumRows;

      for(i = 1; i <= NumRows; ++i)
      {
          cout << endl;       //start on a new line

          for(j = 0; j < i; ++j)
          {
              cout << MyChar;             // write the char
          }
      }
      cout << "\n\n Oh, what a pretty pattern!          \n\n";
      return 0;
}
```

The output shows $ in 9 rows:

Write a simple pattern.
Enter the character for your pattern $

How many rows?   1 - 20   9

$
$$
$$$
$$$$
$$$$$
$$$$$$
$$$$$$$
$$$$$$$$
$$$$$$$$$

Oh, what a pretty pattern!

To reverse the pattern, you need to write leading blanks on each row. In a five-row pattern, the first row contains four blanks and one character, the second row contains three blanks and two characters, the third row contains two blanks and three characters, etc. Here is the reversed pattern:

```
    +
   ++
  +++
 ++++
+++++
```

There is a new inner for loop that writes out the leading blanks for each row. Since the outer loop index (i) is the number of characters and NumRows is the total characters on a line, NumRows minus i is the number of blanks required for each line.

```cpp
for(i = 1; i <= NumRows; ++i)
{
      cout << endl;         //start on a new line

      for(j = 0; j < NumRows - i; ++ j)              //write blanks
      {
            cout << " ";
      }

      for(j = 0; j < i; ++j)
      {
            cout << MyChar;               // write the char
      }
}
```

▌ REVIEW QUESTIONS AND PROBLEMS

Short Answer

1. Describe the precedence of operations for the relational and logical operators.

2. What is the difference between a unary and a binary operator?

3. What is the best technique for checking whether a floating point value is the same as zero?

4. When are braces required in an if statement?

5. Is it possible to nest a switch statement inside an if statement?

6. What are the three different methods for performing a loop in C++?

7. Why is a loop altering statement necessary in a while loop?

8. What type of loop always performs the loop statements at least once?

9. What is (are) the consequence(s) if you forget to break your switch?

10. Name the four keywords associated with a switch statement.

Debugging Problems: Compiler Errors

Identify the compiler errors in Problems 11 to 14 and state what is wrong with the code.

11.
```
int a = 7, b = 9, c = 2;
If(a << b)
{
     c == b;
}
```

12.
```
int 3_for_me = 3, quick_4
switch(3_for_me)
{
     Case 7: cout << "hello"; break;
     case 8: cout << "goodbye"; break;
}
```

13.
```
float inventory, case;
inventory = 8;
if(inventory = 3)
{
    case = inventory;
    inventory = 0;
}
```

14.
```
int Hurry = 17, m, n, o;
if(m < n)
     o = Hurry;
     n = o;
else
     m = Hurry;
```

Debugging Problems: Run-Time Errors

Each of the programs in Problems 15 to 17 compiles but does not do what the specification states. What is the incorrect action and why does it occur?

15. Specification: Write out Hello World twenty-five times. Each hello begins a new line.

```
#include <iostream.h>
int main()
{
        int i = 1;
        while(i < 25)
                cout << "\nHello World";
                ++i;
        return 0;
}
```

16. Specification: Check to see if the user's input is a 0 or a 1. If it is a 0 or a 1, write out Hello World.

```
#include <iostream.h>
int main()
{
        int user_input;
        cout << "\nEnter an integer.";
        cin >> user_input;
        if(user_input == 0 || 1)cout << "\nHello World";
        return 0;
}
```

17. Specification: Check to see if the user's input is 1, 2, or 3. Write out the numeric word (such as ONE) if it is within range; otherwise, write OUT OF RANGE.

```
#include <iostream.h>
int main()
{
        int user_input;
        cout << "\nEnter an integer.";
        cin >> user_input;
        switch(user_input)
        {
                case 1:
                cout << "\nONE";
                case 2:
                cout << "\nTWO";
                case 3:
                cout << "\nTHREE";
                default: cout << "OUT OF RANGE";
        }
        return 0;
}
```

Reading the Code

In Problems 18 and 19, what will be the output from the source code?

18.

C++ Code	Output

<pre>int x = 10, y = 6, ctr = 0;
 	
cout << "Hi There!" << endl << endl;
while(ctr < 3)
{
   cout << x << y;
   ++ctr;
   y--;
}
do {
      cout << "\nI Love C++!";
}while(ctr < 3);</pre>	

19.

C++ Code	Output

<pre>int a = 5, b = 8;
while(a < b)
{
   cout << "\n Red";
   ++a;
}
do
{
   cout << "\n Blue";
   ++a;
}while(a < 6);
cout << "\n END!";</pre>	

Programming Problems

For Problems 20 to 24, incorporate a loop so that the user can continue inputting values until he or she is finished. Then have the program write out a good-bye message so the user can exit the program.

20. Write a complete C++ program that asks the user for a number between 0 and 100 (0 and 100 are out of range.) If the number is between 1 and 9, write out the words ONE DIGIT BIG! If it is between 10 and 99, write out the words TWO DIGITS BIG! Your program should state if the user's number is outside the requested range. If it is, write out the phrase OUT OF RANGE.

21. Write a complete C++ program that asks the user to enter a date in the month/day/year format, such as 4/25/2001. Check to ensure that the date is valid. (You may use another rhyme for assistance in this task: thirty days hath September, April, June, and November. All the rest have thirty-one, excepting February alone, and that has twenty-eight days clear, and twenty-nine in each leap year.)[2] If the date is valid, convert it to the day number in the year. For example, January 31 is the thirty-first day of the year, and February 1 is the thirty-second day of the year. Recall that a year is a leap year if it is evenly divisible by 4—except in century years, which are leap years only if they are divisible by 400.

22. Write a complete C++ program that asks the user to input a character. Using the ASCII character set as a guide, state whether the user's character is a digit (0 to 9), a letter (a to z or A to Z), or a symbol.

23. Write a complete C++ program that converts distance values. The program should give the user three options: convert a whole number of inches to feet and inches, convert feet and inches to decimal feet, or exit. For example, 80 inches is 6 feet, 8 inches; and 5 feet, 6 inches is 5.5 feet. Write the decimal feet to three decimal places.

24. Write a complete C++ program that prints out one of the output patterns shown below.

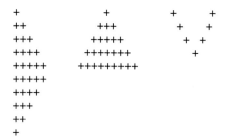

Ask the user for a symbol and the number of lines (limit 1 to 20). If the user enters an invalid number of lines, issue a message and ask the user if he or she would like to see another pattern. If the answer is yes, have the program loop back to the point in the code where it asks for the lines and the symbol.

---

[2] A common saying dating back perhaps to *Holinshed's Chronicle of England*. There have been many modifications since 1577.

4

Pointers, Addresses, and the Indirection Operator

KEY TERMS AND CONCEPTS

assigning address into a pointer
hex address
hexadecimal notation
memory
memory efficient programming
pointer
pointer declaration
stack

KEYWORDS AND OPERATORS

address operator, &
indirection operator, *
sizeof

CHAPTER OBJECTIVES

Illustrate the concept of a pointer, which is a variable that holds another variable's address.

Demonstrate how data variables and computer memory are related.

Introduce the address operator, which returns a variable's hex address.

Show how the pointer can be used to access another variable's contents with the indirection operator.

Present an overview of how pointers are used in C++ programs and why pointers are so important.

Parking and Pointers

Remember when you were learning to drive a car? You went to a parking lot with an experienced driver and practiced driving. You went forward and turned corners and stopped. You may never have driven the car in reverse the first time out. After a few lessons you started backing out of the driveway or a parking space.

Learning to work with pointers in C++ is like learning to drive a car in reverse. Just as backing a car is an inevitable part of driving, pointers are an inevitable part of C++. In certain programming situations, a pointer (or two) is the only tool available to solve the problem. Pointers may seem difficult at first, but once you become familiar with them and do some simple exercises, you will see how they work and you will learn how to use them.

The work we do with pointers in this chapter is just like the parking lot phase of learning how to drive a car in reverse. We will write one-function programs that show how pointers work. The real usefulness of pointers will be evident once we start working with functions.

4.1
Importance of Pointers

To become fluent in the C++ language, a programmer must speak "pointers" as naturally as he or she speaks his or her native language. A **pointer** is a variable that holds a memory address. Pointers are everywhere in C++ code! Pointers are the most efficient method to use when working with large data structures or classes. Arrays are inherently passed to functions through the use of a pointer. Pointers make it possible to avoid duplicating large data items within a program. Also, many key concepts for developing Windows application programs are based on pointers.

pointer
variable that holds the hex address of another variable

There is a high probability that you, as a C++ programmer, will be working with pointers in all of your code. Unfortunately, pointers have a reputation with beginning C++ programmers as being a difficult topic to grasp. Initially, pointers seem to be more trouble than they are worth. However, past students subsequently claim that you can't have too much practice with pointers.

Before we introduce pointers, we also need to discuss data variables, memory, and addresses.

4.2
Data Variables and Memory

When data variables are declared in a program (such as int x;), physical memory in the random access memory (RAM) is reserved for the variable. The number of memory bytes that are actually used depends on the data type of the variable. Table 4-1 (a duplication of Table 2-5 in Chapter 2) lists all the data types and the bytes reserved, as dictated by the ISO C++ standard.

sizeof

an operator that returns the number of bytes reserved for the variable or for data type

sizeof Operator

C++ provides the *sizeof* operator, which returns the number of bytes reserved for either a data type or a variable. The form for the sizeof operator is:

▌ TABLE 4-1
Data Types Defined by the ANSI/ISO C Standard

Keyword	Range	Digits of Precision	Bytes of Memory
char	−128 to 127	[Not applicable]	1
unsigned char	0 to 255	[Not applicable]	1
signed char	−128 to 127	[Not applicable]	1
int	−32,768 to 32,768 −2,147,483,648 to 2,147,483,647	[Not applicable]	2 or 4[a]
short int	−32,768 to 32,767	[Not applicable]	2
unsigned short int	0 to 65,535	[Not applicable]	2
unsigned int	0 to 65,535 0 to 4,294,967,295	[Not applicable]	2 or 4[a]
long int	−2,147,483,648 to 2,147,483,647	[Not applicable]	4
unsigned long int	0 to 4,294,967,295	[Not applicable]	4
float	3.4 E ± 38	6	4
double	1.7 E ± 308	10	8
long double	1.2 E ± 4,932	10	10

[a]Represented in Microsoft Visual C++.

```
sizeof variable_name;          //for a variable value () optional, but convenient
sizeof (data_type);            //for a data type (must be in parentheses)
```

In the short program of Program 4-1, we use the sizeof operator to determine the bytes of memory reserved for five popular data types.

```
//Program 4-1   sizeof
#include <iostream.h>
int main()
{
    char c;
    double d;
    float f;
    int i;
    long l;

    //Use sizeof with data types
    cout << "Number of bytes for these data types in Visual C++."
            << "\n Using sizeof with data types:"
            << "\n    char " << sizeof(char)
            << "\n  double " << sizeof(double)
            << "\n   float " << sizeof(float)
            << "\n     int " << sizeof(int)
            << "\n    long " << sizeof(long) << endl;

    //Use sizeof with variables
    cout << "\n\n Now use sizeof with data variables:"
            << "\n    char " << sizeof c
            << "\n  double " << sizeof d
            << "\n   float " << sizeof f
            << "\n     int " << sizeof i
            << "\n    long " << sizeof l << endl;
}
```

The output is shown below:

Number of bytes for these data types in Visual C++.
 Using sizeof with data types:
   char 1
 double 8
   float 4
    int 4
   long 4

Now use sizeof with data variables:
    char 1
    double 8
    float 4
    int 4
    long 4

Reserving Memory

In the following three declaration statements, memory space is reserved for these six variables—4 bytes of memory for each float and int, and 8 bytes for each double in Visual C++.

```
float x,y;          //4 bytes reserved for each float and int
int i,j;
double q,r;         //8 bytes reserved for each double
```

memory

physical location in the computer that provides storage space for program data

stack

the portion of the computer memory where local program variables are stored

hexadecimal notation

the notation for showing how computer memory is referenced

hex address

the address of a memory location of a variable

The computer actually reserves **memory** for the variables on the memory **stack**, and the first variable that is declared is placed at the far end of the stack. The stack is a region of memory reserved for program variables. Data variables are stacked into memory, and the first variable—because it is located at the end of the stack—has the highest address. We will not worry about the stack, but when the memory locations are examined, we see that the last declared variable (in this case "r") has the lowest memory address. Figure 4-1 illustrates how the six variables in the declaration statements above are reserved in memory. The boxes in Figure 4-1 represent the memory for each variable.

Computer Memory and Hex

Computer memory is addressed by using **hexadecimal notation**. (For a discussion of hexadecimal notation, see Appendix E, "Bits, Bytes, Memory, and Hexadecimal Notation.") In a 32-bit environment (such as Microsoft Visual C++), the addresses are 4 bytes long. A memory location might have the **hex address** of 0x0066FDF0.

In Figure 4-2, the six variables in the declaration statements above are shown with memory addresses. This diagram assumes that the memory address for the first byte of variable "r" is located at 0x0066FDD8. Each of the six variable addresses is shown.

If we assign values to the six variables, as shown in the code below, each value is stored in memory. In Figure 4-3 the variable values are written in the boxes. Floating point variables have six digits of precision, doubles have at least ten, and integers are whole numbers.

```
//assign values into the variables
x = 1;
y = 2;
i = 3;
j = 4;
q = 5;
r = 6;
```

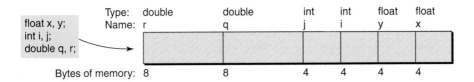

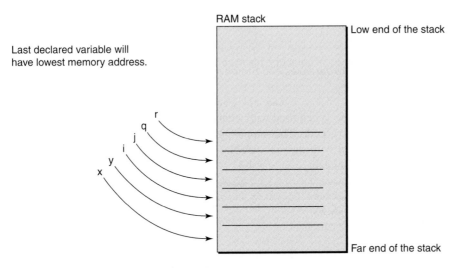

Figure 4-1
Memory Reserved for Data Variables on the Stack

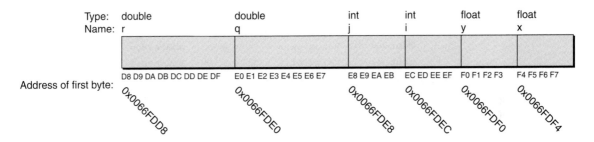

Figure 4-2
Data Variables and Hexadecimal Addresses

4.3
Address Operator: &

Data types, such as floating point, integers, and char, each hold (or contain) a type of data such as numeric or character. Each variable declared in C++ has a data type, name, value, and address. To access the address, C++ provides the

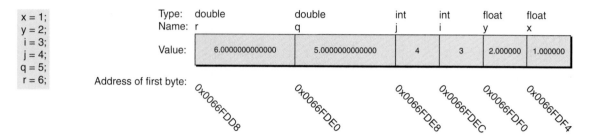

```
x = 1;
y = 2;
i = 3;
j = 4;
q = 5;
r = 6;
```

Figure 4-3
Values Assigned into Variables and Stored in Memory

4

address operator, &
returns the hex address
of the memory location
for a variable

address operator, &. When used with a data variable, the address operator gives the address of the data variable. The sample program in Program 4-2 shows the address operator being used with the six variables to write out the memory addresses for each variable. Refer again to Figure 4-3.

```
//Program 4-2  Address Operator Program and Output
#include <iostream.h>
int main()
{

        float x = 1, y = 2;        //declare and assign values
        int i = 3, j = 4;
        double q = 5, r = 6;
        cout.setf (ios::fixed);
        cout.precision(7);
        cout << "\n Value of x = " << x << " Address = " << &x;
        cout << "\n Value of y = " << y << " Address = " << &y;
        cout << "\n Value of i = " << i << " Address = " << &i;
        cout << "\n Value of j = " << j << " Address = " << &j;
        cout.precision(14);
        cout << "\n Value of q = " << q << " Address = " << &q;
        cout << "\n Value of r = " << r << " Address = " << &r <<endl;
}
```

Here is the output from this program:

Value of x = 1.000000 Address = 0x0066FDF4
Value of y = 2.000000 Address = 0x0066FDF0
Value of i = 3 Address = 0x0066FDEC
Value of j = 4 Address = 0x0066FDE8
Value of q = 5.0000000000000 Address = 0x0066FDE0
Value of r = 6.0000000000000 Address = 0x0066FDD8

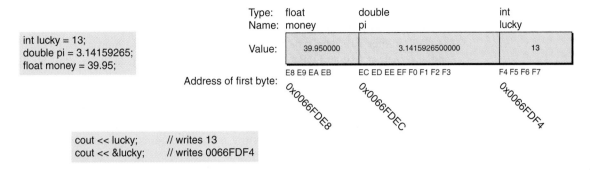

```
int lucky = 13;
double pi = 3.14159265;
float money = 39.95;
```

Type:	float	double	int
Name:	money	pi	lucky
Value:	39.950000	3.1415926500000	13
	E8 E9 EA EB	EC ED EE EF F0 F1 F2 F3	F4 F5 F6 F7

Address of first byte: 0x0066FDE8   0x0066FDEC   0x0066FDF4

```
cout << lucky;      // writes 13
cout << &lucky;     // writes 0066FDF4
```

Figure 4-4
The Address Operator Returns the Hex Memory Address of the Data Variable

4

Another short program (shown in Program 4-3) illustrates the use of the address operator. The output, which appears below, shows the associated memory and is diagrammed in Figure 4-4.

Here are just the addresses!
&lucky = 0x0066FDF4
&pi = 0x0066FDEC
&money = 0x0066FDE8

```
//Program 4-3  Address Operators with lucky, pi, and money variables
#include <iostream.h>
int main()
{
    int lucky = 13;
    double pi = 3.14159265;
    float money = 39.95;
    cout << "\n Here are just the addresses!";
    cout << "\n &lucky = " << &lucky <<
            "\n    &pi = " << &pi <<
            "\n &money = " << &money << endl;
}
```

4.4
Pointers

All data types in C++ are designed to hold certain kinds of data, and specific operations are allowed if they are relevant to the data types. For example, an integer variable may contain a whole number. The arithmetic and modulus operations are allowed for integer variables. The computer reserves 4 bytes of memory for storing the value for each integer.

A pointer is a data type in C++, and it is designed to hold a hexadecimal address, such as 0x0066FDF4. A pointer in a C++ program is assigned the address of a specific variable. When the pointer variable contains another variable's address, it is said that the pointer "points to" that variable.

Pointers do not have their own keyword, such as int, float, or double, but pointers have specific declaration statements. The program and the pointer need to know what type of variable-address the pointer contains. A pointer variable is declared by specifying the data type to which it will be pointing. The asterisk operator (*) is used in the declaration. Here is the format:

```
data_type *variable_name;
```

An example of a pointer declaration is:

```
float *x_ptr;
```

Many naming conventions are used with pointer variables to help the programmer remember which variables are pointers. A naming convention is a general agreement or customary practice used for naming variables, but it is not a rule in C++. Three conventions are listed below:

```
float *x_ptr;     // use the extension _ptr
float *pX;        // use lowercase p with capital letter
float *p_x;       // use prefix p_
```

Here we declare two integer variables and two pointers:

```
int count, temp;
int *count_ptr, *temp_ptr;
```

We have named our pointers count_ptr and temp_ptr so that we can keep track of which pointer variable belongs with which integer. C++ does not automatically assign the correct address into the correct pointer. The address assignment is the job of the programmer, and the programmer's tool is the address operator: &.

Pointers and the Address Operator

The address operator (&), when used with a variable name, returns the address of the variable. Using the address operator is one way to assign addresses into pointer variables. For example, the following code shows how we assign the addresses into the pointers for count and temp.

```
int count, temp;
int *count_ptr, *temp_ptr;
count_ptr = &count;
temp_ptr = &temp;
```

After this code is executed, the count and temp have not been assigned any values; whereas, the pointer variables count_ptr and temp_ptr now contain the addresses of the count and temp variables. The data values in the pointer variables are the addresses of the integers.

Program 4-4 illustrates the declaration of variables, including pointers, assigning addresses, and then printing the value and addresses of the variables. Figure 4-5 illustrates this concept as well. All pointer variables in a 32-bit environment are 4 bytes in size, no matter what type of variable they are pointing to, because all addresses are 4 bytes. In this example, the a_ptr and b_ptr are both 4 bytes in size, even though the b_ptr will be pointing to an 8-byte variable. The output is shown below:

VARIABLE	VALUES	ADDRESSES
a	75	0x0066FDF4
b	82	0x0066FDEC
a_ptr	0x0066FDF4	0x0066FDE8
b_ptr	0x0066FDEC	0x0066FDE4

In Figure 4-5 the pointer variables have been assigned the addresses of the variables. These hexadecimal addresses are shown in the boxes of the pointer vari-

```
//Program 4-4   Variables, Addresses, and Pointers
#include <iostream.h>
#include <iomanip.h>
int main()
{

        int a = 75;
        double b = 82;
        int *a_ptr;
        double *b_ptr;
        a_ptr = &a;             //assign addresses of variables into pointers
        b_ptr = &b;
        cout << "\nVARIABLE          VALUES          ADDRESSES\n" <<
                "\n a      " << setw(12) << a << setw(12) << &a <<
                "\n b      " << setw(12) << b << setw(12) << &b <<
                "\n a_ptr " << setw(12) << a_ptr << setw(12) << &a_ptr <<
                "\n b_ptr " << setw(12) << b_ptr << setw(12) << &b_ptr << endl;

}
```

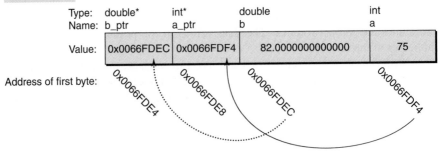

```
int a = 75;
double b = 82;
int *a_ptr;
double *b_ptr;
a_ptr = &a;
b_ptr = &b;
```

Figure 4-5
Pointers Are Assigned the Variable Addresses

ables. Notice that the address of "a" is the value of the a_ptr, and the address of "b" is the value of b_ptr.

Little Red Riding Hood and the White House

Little Red Riding Hood had to travel through the woods to reach her destination: her grandmother's house. Now we can assume she knew how to get to her grandmother's house. In fact, she probably always referred to this location in the woods as "grandmother's house" and, as far as Little Red Riding Hood was concerned, the address (if any) didn't matter.

We can take the opposite approach when traveling to a location. Instead of traveling to a place such as grandmother's house, if we know the address we can just navigate our way to that location. For example, you can go to 1600 Pennsylvania Avenue, Washington, D.C., knock on the door and see what's for dinner.

In C++ programming, we access a memory location by using the name of the variable—much like Little Red Riding Hood does by going to her grandmother's house. This method is how all of our programs have accessed data so far. It is possible (and necessary) to access variables in memory just by using the address of the variable. In fact, at times we do not even know the name of the variable we are accessing; all we know is its address.

indirection operator,*

an operator, when used with a pointer, directs the program to the address held in the pointer variable

Pointers and the Indirection Operator

Now it is time to introduce the ***indirection operator***, the asterisk (*), which is a pointer's best friend. The indirection operator, when used with a pointer variable that contains an address, is telling the program, "Go to the address that I am holding." It can be used either to assign a value where the pointer is pointing or to get a value where the pointer is pointing. It can look like the following:

```
*x_ptr = 3;    //assign value 3 into the variable where x_ptr is pointing

m = *y_ptr;    /*get the value in the variable to which y_ptr is pointing and
                 assign it into m */
```

The pointer with an indirection operator can either put or get values in or out of the variable to which the pointer is pointing. This pairing of the pointer variable and indirection operator gives us a way to access directly variables that would otherwise be off limits to us. (This part is important!)

Program 4-5 places values into two variables by using pointers and the indirection operator. We then print some results. Figure 4-6 illustrates the process.

```
//Program 4-5  Addition, Pointers, and Indirection Operator
#include <iostream.h>
int main()
{
        int a, b, c;
        int *a_ptr = &a, *b_ptr = &b, *c_ptr = &c;   //declare and assign addresses

        *a_ptr = 5;    //assign values where pointers are pointing
        *b_ptr = 7;
        *c_ptr = *a_ptr + *b_ptr;   /* using pointers to access the values in a and b
        add them and place answer into c, using *c_ptr */

        //write out values using
        cout << "\nAddition using pointers to access variables. \n" <<
               *a_ptr << " + " << *b_ptr << " = " << *c_ptr;
}
```

The output is shown below:

```
Addition using pointers to access variables.
5 + 7 = 12
```

Remember, a data variable has a value and an address. A value is what the variable holds. The address is the memory location of that variable and is always referred to in hex notation. A pointer is a data variable that holds the address of another variable. (The pointer variable has an address, too.)

Step 1: 5 and 7 are placed in the location to which the pointers are pointing.

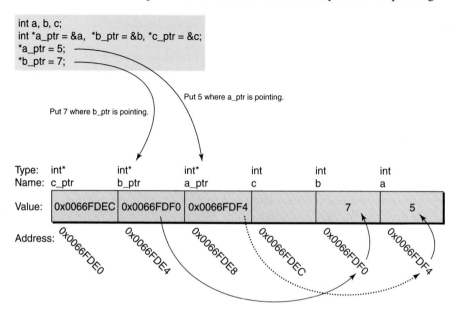

Step 2: Values pointed to by a_ptr and b_ptr are retrieved and added together.

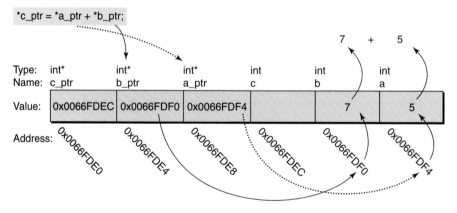

Figure 4-6
Accessing Data Values Using Pointers and the Indirection Operator

Step 3: Sum is placed in the location to which c_ptr is pointing.

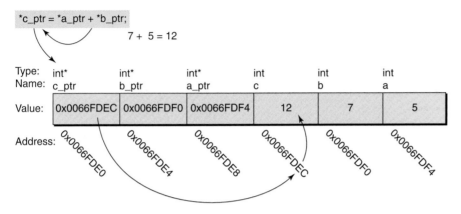

Figure 4-6 (continued)

In Program 4-6, we declare four variables, assign values using the pointers, and write out all the pointer information. Refer to Figure 4-7 for illustration. The output is shown below:

Ptr Name	Value	Address	Pointing to
m_ptr	0x0066FDF4	0x0066FDF0	4
p_ptr	0x0066FDEC	0x0066FDE8	3.14159

Mixed Up Pointers

You may ask the question, "What if I accidentally assign an integer address into a double pointer?" As it turns out, most compilers will stop you from doing this illegal operation. Look at the following sample program, where we attempt to assign an integer variable's address into a double pointer and a double variable's address into an integer pointer.

```
//File:   Ch4MixedUpPtr.cpp
//Program 4-x   Assign the wrong address into a pointer

#include <iostream.h>

int main()
{
```

```
//Program 4-6   What are pointers pointing to?
#include <iostream.h>
#include <iomanip.h>

int main()
{
//set up variables and assign addresses into pointers
      int m , *m_ptr = &m;
      float p, *p_ptr = &p;

//assign values where the pointers are pointing
      *m_ptr = 4;
      *p_ptr = (float)3.14159;

//write each pointer's value, address and what the pointer is pointing to

      cout << "\nPtr Name    Value    Address    Pointing to  \n" <<
          "\n m_ptr    " << m_ptr << setw(12) << &m_ptr
              << setw(10) << *m_ptr <<
            "\n p_ptr    " << p_ptr << setw(12) << &p_ptr
              << setw(10) << *p_ptr << endl;
      return 0;
}
```

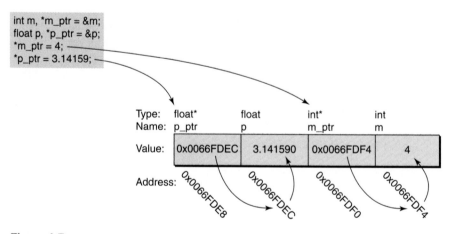

Figure 4-7
Pointers and the Indirection Operator Are Used to Assign Values into the Variables

```
int n, *n_ptr, *pi_wrong_ptr;
double pi, *pi_ptr, *n_wrong_ptr;
n = 5;
pi = 3.14159265;

n_ptr = &n;          //assign int address into int pointer                :-)
pi_ptr = &pi;        //assign double address into double pointer

pi_wrong_ptr = &pi; //assign a double valued address into an int pointer
n_wrong_ptr = &n;    //assign an integer valued address into a double pointer

cout << "\n Write out the values: n = " << n << " pi = " << pi;

cout << "\n Write out the values using *ptr:  n = "
     << *n_ptr << " pi = " << *pi_ptr;

cout << "\n Write out the values using pointers that contain wrong addresses "
          "\n  n = " << *n_wrong_ptr << " pi = " << *pi_wrong_ptr;

cout << "\n All done. \n\n";
return 0;
}
```

The Microsoft Visual C++ compiler reports these two errors and references the
lines where we tried to assign address values into the wrong type of pointer:

Compiling...
Ch4MixedUpPtr.cpp
C:\CBook\TestCases\Ch4MixedUpPtr.cpp(20) : error C2440: '=' : cannot convert from 'double *' to 'int *'
    Types pointed to are unrelated; conversion requires reinterpret_cast, C-style cast or function-style cast
C:\CBook\TestCases\Ch4MixedUpPtr.cpp(21) : error C2440: '=' : cannot convert from 'int *' to 'double *'
    Types pointed to are unrelated; conversion requires reinterpret_cast, C-style cast or function-style cast
Error executing cl.exe.

TestCases.exe - 2 error(s), 0 warning(s)

4.5
Where Are We Going with Pointers?

These initial examples using pointers, addresses, and the indirection operator in a
single main function appear to be more cumbersome than helpful. Why put or get
values into or out of variables through a pointer when you can use the variable
name directly? In fact, C++ programmers never use pointers in a single function as
we have done in these examples. You may ask, "Then what are pointers good for?"
Here are two important pointer topics.

Functions in C++ Return One Piece of Data

When we start working with functions, we will learn two facts. First, it is possible to pass as many input arguments as we want to a function, but the function can return only one piece of data (i.e., one data type element). Second, local data within functions is off limits to other functions; that is, a function's local variables are not seen by other functions. For example, suppose we are writing a program called CooksHelper, and it contains a function called CookTurkey that calculates the time and temperature required for cooking a turkey. (See Figure 4-8 for reference.) The normal, standard return statement does not work for us because we need two pieces of information from CookTurkey. By using pointers, we can have a function return more than one value. CooksHelper has the variables for time and temperature. The variable addresses are sent to CookTurkey, which receives them in pointers. Then CookTurkey can use pointers with the indirection operator to write the necessary information directly into CooksHelper's time and temperature variables.

Efficient Handling of Large Data Structures, Arrays, and Classes

When a programmer works with large data items in a program, such as data records, image files, or complicated scientific data, pointers can be quite useful in saving time and memory. Normally, if a variable is passed to a function, the function makes its own copy of the data. This practice is fine for a few parameters or a

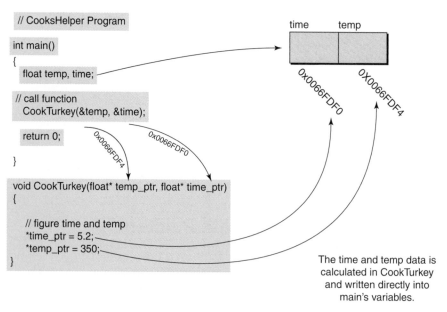

Figure 4-8
The CookTurkey Program with Pointers

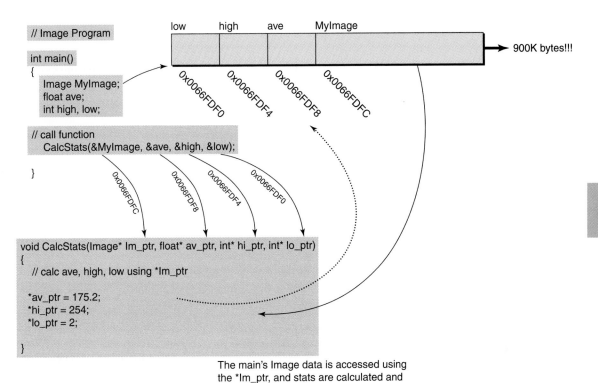

```
// Image Program

int main()
{
    Image MyImage;
    float ave;
    int high, low;

// call function
    CalcStats(&MyImage, &ave, &high, &low);

}
```

```
void CalcStats(Image* Im_ptr, float* av_ptr, int* hi_ptr, int* lo_ptr)
{
    // calc ave, high, low using *Im_ptr

    *av_ptr = 175.2;
    *hi_ptr = 254;
    *lo_ptr = 2;

}
```

The main's Image data is accessed using the *Im_ptr, and stats are calculated and written directly into main's variables.

Figure 4-9
The Image Program with Pointers

small amount of data; however, if the data item is large (i.e., a 640 by 480 pixel color image can easily be 900K bytes), it is best to have only one copy of the data in the program.

Figure 4-9 illustrates a program that contains a large digital image. (C++ allows us to create our own custom data types, so assume that we know how to create the data type Image.) If our program needs to calculate the statistics for the image—such as average pixel value, high and low pixel—we can send the address of the MyImage to the CalcStats function. The CalcStats can then access the MyImage data and return the desired values.

4.6
Summary

All variables in a C++ program are stored in physical bytes of memory located in the RAM of the computer. When you declare and assign a variable in a program, like the example that follows:

```
double MyDouble = 4.63;
int x;
x = 7;
```

there are five items associated with it, shown in Table 4-2.

This chapter introduces the pointer, which is a new type of C++ data type. Important pointer concepts are listed below:

- A pointer is designed to hold a hexadecimal address.
- It is declared using the * operator.
- A variable's address is assigned into the pointer by use of the address operator, &.
- When paired with the indirection operator, the pointer can access the data located at the address that it contains.

There are several important design, memory, and speed issues in which pointers play a very important role. Table 4-3 summarizes and compares numeric variables and pointer variable declaration, assignments, and how the data is accessed.

Do Pointers Early and Often

It's natural to be a bit confused by pointers at this stage of your C++ programming career. You are presently trying to grasp several complex concepts, create the correct program flow, and have your loops stop when they are supposed to stop. Added to this list are pointers. Do not despair! Pointers are basically straightforward and

TABLE 4-2
Items Associated with Each C++ Variable

Item	What Is It?	Example
Data type	Establishes what kind of data the variable will contain	double int
Number of bytes reserved	Quantity of memory used for this type	8 for a double, 4 for an int
Name	How the program normally will reference this variable	MyDouble x
Value	The data held in that variable	4.63 7
Address	The hexadecimal address of the first byte	Unknown, but we can find it using the & operator

TABLE 4-3
Pointer Summary

Item	Numeric	Pointer
Declaration	`float x;` `int m;`	`float *x_ptr;` `int *m_ptr;`

Assign a value	`x = 37.4453;`
	`m = 15;`
		`x_ptr = &x; //pointers are assigned addresses`
		`m_ptr = &m;`

Valid operations	for x—any arithmetic operations except modulus	`*x_ptr = 37.4453; /*assign value where` `                        x_ptr is pointing */`
	for m—all five arithmetic operations	`*m_ptr = 15; /*assign value where m_ptr` `                    is pointing */`

Print values	`cout << x;`	`cout << x_ptr;   // writes address of x`
		`cout << *x_ptr;  // writes 37.4453`

	`cout << m;`	`cout << m_ptr;   // writes address of m`
		`cout << *m_ptr; // writes 15`

Print addresses	`cout <<   &x;` `cout <<   &m;`	`cout <<   &x_ptr;` `cout <<   &m_ptr;`

they are not the difficult nemesis some might have you believe. Besides, you will have plenty of practice along the way.

4.7
Practice

The programs presented in this section are strictly for practice writing code that uses pointers; in reality, however, we never use pointers in a one-function program.

WriteHello and Pointers

In Program 4-7, we ask the user to enter the number of hellos he or she wishes to see and then write them to the screen. All data variables are assigned using pointers and then the variables are used normally.

Knick-Knacking and Pointers

In Program 4-8, a shortened version of the Knick-Knack program (from Chapter 3), we use a pointer to assign the value into the user's input.

```
//Program 4-7  Write Hello and Pointers
#include <iostream.h>
int main()
{
        int number_of_times, go_again;
        int *num_ptr, *go_again_ptr;
        int i, *i_ptr;
                                            //assign the addresses into the pointers
        num_ptr = &number_of_times;
        go_again_ptr = &go_again;
        i_ptr = &i;

        //use the indirection operator and pointer to initialize loop variable
        *go_again_ptr = 1;
        while(go_again == 1 )
        {
                cout << "\n Please enter your desired number of Hellos    ";
                cin >> *num_ptr;
                for(*i_ptr = 0; i < number_of_times; ++(*i_ptr)   )
                {
                        cout << "\n Hello! ";
                }

                cout << "\n\n Want to see more hellos?  1 = YES, 0 = NO ";
                cin >> *go_again_ptr;
        }
        cout << "\n\n Here is a goodbye for you.  \n GOODBYE!  \n ";
        return 0;
}
```

How Big Is Your Pyramid and Pointers

In this last practice program (Program 4-9), we use pointers to access and assign all variables but use the actual variable for writing the values to the screen. The volume of a pyramid is:

$$V\_pyramid = \frac{Ah}{3}$$

where A = area of the base and h = height. We ask our user for the length and width of the base and then the height. Then we can calculate and print the volume.

```
//Program 4-8 Revisit the Knick-Knack program using pointers
#include <iostream.h>
int main()
{
        int number;
        int *num_ptr;
        num_ptr = &number;

        cout << "\n Please enter an integer for knick-knacking     ";
        cin >> *num_ptr;
        cout << "\n\n He played knick-knack ";
        switch(number)    // the number was assigned using the pointer
        {
            case 1:
                    cout << "on my thumb  \n";
                    break;
            case 2:
                    cout << "on my shoe  \n";
                    break;
            default:
                    cout << "\n Whoa! He doesn't play knick-knack there!  \n";
        }
        return 0;
}
```

4

■ REVIEW QUESTIONS AND PROBLEMS

Short Answer

1. Name the five descriptive properties associated with each data variable in C++.

2. What does the address operator do?

3. Where are data variables stored when a program is running?

4. When a pointer variable has the indirection operator in front of it (like *x_ptr), what does this order tell the program?

5. Give three naming conventions for pointers. Describe another possible method for naming pointers.

6. Computer memory is addressed by using what type of notation?

7. In Visual C++, a double variable requires 8 bytes of storage space and an integer requires 4 bytes of storage space. How many bytes of memory are required for a double pointer? For an integer pointer?

```
//Program 4-9   How Big Is Your Pyramid? and Pointers

#include <iostream.h>
int main()
{

        double length, width, height, volume;
        double *l_ptr, *w_ptr, *h_ptr, *v_ptr;
        //assign the addresses into the pointers
        l_ptr = &length;
        w_ptr = &width;
        h_ptr = &height;
        v_ptr = &volume;

        // ask user for pyramid dimensions
        cout << "\n\n Please enter the length and width of your pyramid base   ";
        cin >> *l_ptr >> *w_ptr;
        cout << "\n Great!  How tall is your pyramid?   ";
        cin >> *h_ptr;

        //calculate the volume, accessing all numeric values through their pointers
        *v_ptr = (*l_ptr) * (*w_ptr) * (*h_ptr) / 3.0;

    cout << "\n Your pyramid's base is " << length << " x " << width;
    cout << "\n The height is " << height;
    cout << "\n\n The volume is " << volume << endl;
    return 0;
}
```

8. Write a statement where a pointer and an indirection operator are used to assign a value to a variable. Write a statement where a data value is accessed by using the indirection operator–pointer combination.

9. For C++ programs, why is the stack an important part of the RAM?

10. Name two ways (show statements) in which a value can be accessed in a program.

Reading the Code

For Problems 11 and 12, show the hex addresses and variable values after the statements have been executed. (All pointers are 4 bytes!)

11. The first byte of memory below is xFF2A.

t	s	r	q	x	d	c	b	a

xxFF2A

```
int main()
{
        float a= 32.5, b;
        int c = 5, d = 4.5, x;
        float  *q, *r;
        int *s, *t;
        q = &a;
        r = &b;
        s = &x;
        t = &d;
        *r = c%d;
        *s = *t + c;
```

12.

g_ptr	f_ptr	b_ptr	g	f	e	d	c	b	a

xFF30

```
int main()
{
        float a= 15.1, b, c;
        int d = 4, e = 18, f,g;
        float  *b_ptr;
        int *f_ptr, *g_ptr;
        b_ptr = &b;

        f_ptr = &f;
        g_ptr = &g
        c = e%d + e/d;
        *f_ptr = 2.0*a - 1.0;
        *b_ptr = 7/9*(a*c + d);
```

Debugging Problems

In the source code examples for Problems 13 to 15, identify the compiler errors and state what is needed to eliminate the error(s).

13.
```
#Include <iostream.h>
int main
{
        float x, y;
        float *x, *y;
        cout >> "The value of X is" << x;
```

14.
```
#include <iostream.h>
int main
{
        int *i_ptr, i, m_ptr, m;
        i_ptr = &i;
        m_ptr = &m;
```

15.
```
int main()
{
        double cat, gecko;
        int *cat_ptr, *gecko_ptr;
        cat_ptr = &cat;
        gecko_ptr = &gecko;
        return 0;
```

Programming Problems

16. Write a program that declares a variable and pointer for a long double, float, int, and short int (eight total variables). Write out the addresses of each variable. Use the sizeof operator to state the number of bytes reserved for each type of variable. Then, using pencil and paper, diagram the memory boxes that represent how the program allocated the memory.

17. Write a complete C++ program that declares four integer variables and four integer pointers. Assign the addresses into the pointers and then, using the indirection operator, assign the values 1, 2, 3, and 4 into the four integers. (Use the indirection operator with the pointers to write the integer values.) Your program then should write the addresses and values of all eight variables to the screen in the format shown below:

Variable Type   Variable Value   Variable Address
===

18. Write a program that asks the user to enter the radius and height of a cylinder and calculates the volume. Ask the user if he or she wishes to continue and loop back if the answer is affirmative. All the variables must be assigned and accessed using pointers! Write out the user's input and calculated volume using the variable names. The volume of a cylinder is:

$$\text{Vol\_Cylinder} = \pi r^2 h$$

where π is 3.14159265, r is the radius, and h is the height.

Functions

5

Part I: The Basics

KEY TERMS AND CONCEPTS

arguments
automatic variable
C++ libraries
call by reference
call by value
called function
calling function
call statement
flags
function
function body
function call
function header line
function prototype
global variable
input arguments
local variable
return statement
return type
static variable
variable scope

KEYWORDS AND OPERATORS

return
void

CHAPTER OBJECTIVES

Present the concept of a function—which is a modular block of code—in the C++ language.

Demonstrate the basic format for any C++ function.

Describe how to write functions and how to pass data between them.

Introduce the notion of variable scope—how long a variable is "alive" in a program.

Illustrate how the location of the variable declaration determines the scope of the variable.

Explain when it is necessary to use pointers with functions.

Show the correct use of pointers and functions.

Present many simple program examples to illustrate these basic function concepts.

Building Houses, Building Software

Want to build a house? Call a contractor. The contractor will call a crew. Now the contractor must plan so that the various tasks are completed in the right sequence. The crew members must bring the right tools—some useful for specific tasks and others designed for general use. With good organization and the use of proper tools, the house is built.

Designing and building a house is similar to the overall process of creating a software program. When building software, it is important for the program to be organized, and the program must perform certain tasks in a certain order. Using the right carpentry tools is necessary for building cabinets, and a software program should use customized sections of code to perform certain tasks. If data is to be read from a file, then portions of the code should be set up just to open and read the data. If calculations are to be performed, another part of the program should perform the calculations. Each portion or block of code is known as a function.

5.1
Functions in C++

A *function* is a complete section of C++ code with a definite start point and an end point and its own set of variables. A function should be designed so that it has one primary task to accomplish. Most programs consist of many functions, and each function may pass and receive information from other functions.

function
a discrete module or unit of code that performs specific tasks

Life Before Functions

At this stage in your study of C++ programming, you are familiar with data variables and arithmetic operations, pointers, if and switch statements, and loops. Now suppose you are asked to write a program to assist a student in determining his or her average score for math and science, and both subjects have three scores. Your program must ask the student to enter the scores, and the program will find the

```
//Program 5-1 Calculating Averages for Two Subjects - Brute Force
#include <iostream.h>
int main()
{
        // Declare variables
                float math_sc1, math_sc2, math_sc3, math_ave;
                float sci_sc1, sci_sc2, sci_sc3, sci_ave;

        // Obtain math information and calculate average.
                cout << "\n Please enter your 3 math scores.    ";
                cin >> math_sc1 >> math_sc2 >> math_sc3;
                math_ave = (math_sc1 + math_sc2 + math_sc3)/3.0;
                cout << "\n Your math average is " << math_ave;

        // Obtain science information and calculate average.
                cout << "\n Please enter your 3 science scores.    ";
                cin >> sci_sc1 >> sci_sc2 >> sci_sc3;
                sci_ave = (sci_sc1 + sci_sc2 + sci_sc3)/3.0;
                cout << "\n Your science average is " << sci_ave;
        return 0;
}
```

average value for each subject. The program might look like Program 5-1. Notice that this program repeats essentially the same code. It asks the user for three values, calculates the average, and writes this value to the screen.

Imagine that we need to work with five or six subjects, each having ten to fifteen scores! A more efficient way to write this program is to incorporate a loop for the subjects and generalize the variables. Your new code may look like Program 5-2. This program is more efficient; however, all of the work is still performed in the main function.

Life with Functions

An even more efficient technique for this program uses separate functions for specific tasks. It is possible to separate the tasks so that there is a function to get the scores from the user, another to do the average calculation, and a third to write the average. This technique simplifies the main function greatly, and each task is performed in a separate location in the program. The program below shows a blueprint for a main function that uses customized functions for performing certain tasks. (Many programming details have been left out.)

```
//Program Blueprint Calculating Averages More Efficiently
// This is a blueprint--many details have been left out.
```

```
//Program 5-2 Calculating Averages Using Loops
#include <iostream.h>
int main()
       // Declare variables
       float sc1, sc2, sc3, ave;
       char answer = 'y';            // initialize for while loop
       while(answer == 'y')
       {                             // Obtain 3 scores and calculate average.
              cout << "\n Please enter your 3 scores.    ";
              cin >> sc1 >> sc2 >> sc3;
              ave = (sc1 + sc2 + sc3)/3.0;
              cout << "\n Your average is " << ave;
              cout << "\n Do another calculation?  y = yes   n = no    ";
              cin >> answer;
       }
       return 0;
}


int main()
{
       char answer = 'y';            // initialize for while loop
       while(answer == 'y')
       {
              Get_Three_Scores();
              Find_The_Ave();
              Write_The_Result();
              cout << "\n Do another calculation?  y = yes";
              cin >> answer;
       }
       return 0;
}
```

Now we are getting somewhere! By breaking the different tasks into functions, we organize the program into regions that accomplish specific tasks.

This averaging program can be expanded easily to make use of different functions if the subjects have different grading procedures. The school subjects, as well as the grades, can be maintained in a list. Instead of asking the user to enter each of the grades, we can write the grade information into a data file that the code reads. Our program can be expanded to perform grade calculations for an entire school—thanks to functions!

Functions Are Good

When writing a program, organize the code into logical building blocks and separate the code into functions. A well-written function can be reused in many programs. For example, many software applications can use a function that calculates the average value of a list of numbers. A function that writes a string of text to a file or to the screen can be used in most programs. Use descriptive names for variables, write with an easy-to-read style, and trap for errors you might encounter, and you will be well on your way to writing clearly understood functions.

C programmers concentrated on writing functions. The function is the basic programming unit in a C program. Now that we are heading toward designing and writing object-oriented software (which uses classes and objects), the basic programming unit for C++ is the class. The class descriptions include data and functions, and these functions "work on" the data. (These class functions are also called "methods.") Some might say that all roads lead to Rome; but in the C++ world, all roads lead to classes and objects. Functions are vital elements of classes, and we must have a complete grasp of functions before we jump into classes.

5.2
Functions: Basic Format

The basic format of a function in C++ is:

```
return_type  function_name(input data type and name list)
{
    // Body of function

}
```

return_type

the data type of the variable passed back to the calling function via a return statement

The **return_type** is the data type (such as int, float, or double) of the value returned from the function. Functions in C++ can have only a single return data type. This data is returned to the program in a "return" statement. The function_name is the identifier (name) of the function and is used in the code to access the function. The programmer must follow the rules for naming variables when choosing a name for a function (see Chapter 2). The input data type and name list is the list of the input variable data types and names that the function receives. These inputs are referred to as **arguments** or **input arguments**.

arguments

input values for a function; also known as *input arguments*

Four Simple Functions

All functions in C++ follow the basic format presented above. The rules are simple. The function name must follow standard C++ naming conventions. There may be one return type. If there is no return type, the void data type is used. The input argument list must have data type and names (separated by commas), and you may pass in as many arguments as you like. If your list is empty (no arguments are passed), the parentheses are still required but may be empty ().

The following function, named Add_em_up, is passed three integer values. These input values are then added and the sum is returned. The input argument list shows three integers, and the return type is an integer as well.

```
int Add_em_up(int a, int b, int c)    //input list separated by commas
{
    int sum;                    //local variable for sum
    sum = a + b + c;            //add the 3 input values
    return sum;                 //return the sum
}
```

The Write_em_out function, shown below, receives two input arguments, an integer "small" and a double "big," and the function's job is to write these values to the screen. Since the function simply writes the values and does not return anything, the return type is void and there is no return statement.

```
void Write_em_out(int small, double big)
{
    cout << "\n The big number is " << big
         << "\n and the small number is " << small;
}
```

Get_Age, shown below, does not have any input arguments, but it asks the user for his or her age and returns the value the user entered. The void data type says that there are no input arguments.

```
int Get_Age(void)
{

    int age;
    cout << "\n How old are you?";      //ask the user his or her age
    cin >> age;                         //read in the value
    return age;                         //return the age
}
```

Since the input parameter list for the Get_Age function is empty (no parameters being passed in), it can also be written with empty parentheses:

```
int Get_Age()
{
    int age;
    cout << "\n How old are you?";
    cin >> age;
    return age;
}
```

Functions in C++ are not required to have input arguments or to return anything, as shown below in Write_Hello. However, there must always be a return type for the function. When a function will not return anything, the return type is void. The void data type is not required for an empty input parameter list. This function can be written either way:

```
void Write_Hello(void)
{
        cout << "\n Hello World!";
}

void Write_Hello()
{

        cout << "\n Hello World!";
}
```

calling function

when one function uses (or invokes) a second function, the first function is the calling function

called function

when one function uses (or invokes) a second function, the second function is the called function

function prototype

the C++ statement that contains the function name, input, and return data types

function call statement (same as call statement)

the line of code in a program in which a function is invoked

function header line

the first line of a function

function body

the statements of C++ code inside a function

Calling and Called Functions

The terms *calling function* and *called function* are often used when referring to functions. When a function (e.g., Function1) accesses another function (e.g., Function2), Function1 is the calling function and Function2 is the called function. (Think of using the telephone to call your friend: you are the calling party; your friend is the called party.) It is quite common when a person is writing programs to have a function call a function, and it, in turn, calls another function.

Suppose we are writing a program and our main function calls a Calculate Values function, which in turn calls a WriteAnswers function. When main calls the CalculateValues function, main is the calling function and CalculateValues is the called function. When the CalculateValues function accesses the WriteAnswers function, the CalculateValues function is now the calling function and Write Answers is the called function.

5.3
Requirements for Writing Functions

There are three sets of required statements whenever a function is used in C++. Every function must have a *function prototype* statement, a *function call* statement, and both a *function header line* and a *function body*. The function prototype statement can be thought of as a model or a pattern that tells the compiler the function name, and return and input types. The call statement is the location in the program where the function is used or accessed. The function header line and body is the actual code that is the function.

How Old Are You?

The How Old Are You? program (Program 5-3) illustrates a C++ program with several user-written functions. It writes a greeting to the screen, then asks the user to enter his or her age and writes the age to the screen. This program has four functions. The main function calls the Write_Hello function, which is followed by a call to the Get_Age and Write_Age functions. The function prototypes are located

```
//Program 5-3 Simple Functions and How Old Are You?
#include <iostream.h>
void Write_Hello();        //The three function prototypes.
int Get_Age();
void Write_Age(int);

int main()
{
        int age;
        Write_Hello();          // call--no return or inputs
        age = Get_Age();        // call--the result is assigned into age
        Write_Age(age);         // call--age is passed to the function

        return 0;

}


//Write_Hello writes a greeting message to the screen
void Write_Hello()          //This is the function header line.
{
        cout << "\n Hello World!";
}


//Get_Age asks the user for his or her age, returns age.
int Get_Age()               //No input arguments, but returns an integer.
{
        int age;
        cout << "\n How old are you?   ";
        cin >> age;
        return age;
}
//Write_Age receives the age value, writes it to the screen
void Write_Age(int age)     //Input is an integer, no return value.
{
        cout << "\n You are " << age << " years old!   \n";
}
```

above the main function so that the compiler sees them before it reaches the actual function bodies. Figure 5-1 illustrates the control flow of this program.

Function Prototype

Except for the main function, all functions used in a C++ program must have a function prototype statement. (The main function does not require a prototype because the operating system automatically looks for the main function when the program is executed.) The prototype statement is a declaration statement that provides the compiler with information about the input and return data types. Variable names can be included in the input parameter list. Before a function can be called, the calling function must know about the called function. The prototype may be declared in the calling function before the call, it can appear above the calling function (such as in the How Old Are You? program), or it can appear in an include file. The important point is that the compiler must have seen the function prototype before the function is called.

The form of the function prototype is:

```
return_type  Function_Name(input parameter type list);
```

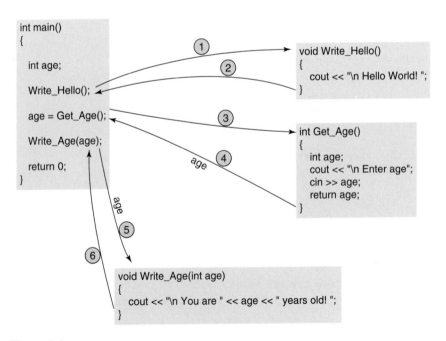

Figure 5-1
Program Control Flow for How Old Are You?

In the How Old Are You? program, the three prototype statements are presented before the main function:

```
#include <iostream.h>

void Write_Hello();        // The three function prototypes.
int Get_Age();             // They should be located so that the compiler "sees" them
void Write_Age(int);       // before it sees the call statements.

int main()
{
```

Function Calls

The **call statement** is the C++ statement (located in the calling function) where the called function is accessed. When a function is called, control is passed to the called function, and the statements inside that function are performed. Control is returned to the calling function when the function tasks are completed. The call statement requires that just the variable names be used.

call statement
the line of code in a program in which a function is invoked

5

The three function calls in the How Old Are You? program are:

```
int main()
{
        int age;
        Write_Hello();       // call to Write_Hello
        age = Get_Age();     // call to Get_Age
        Write_Age(age);      // call to Write_Age

        return 0;
}
```

Input Values When a calling function must pass information to the called function, the actual values or variable names are used in the argument list. In the function Write_Age, we are passing a copy of the variable age to the function:

```
        Write_Age(age);        // a copy of the age value is passed to the function
```

If the called function does not have any input values, the parentheses are left empty, as shown in Write_Hello and Get_Age.

```
        Write_Hello();               // no variable sent to function
        age = Get_Age();             // input list is empty, ()
```

Return Values   Returned values from a function must be assigned to a variable in the calling function. In the Get_Age function, the value returned from the function is assigned to the variable age.

```
age = Get_Age();       // value is assigned into age
```

If the function is not returning a value, no assignment is needed. The Write_Hello and Write_Age do not return a value, so there is no assignment operator in the call.

```
Write_Hello();       // nothing is returned to these functions
Write_Age(age);      // there is no assignment
```

Function Header Lines and Function Bodies

The previous four simple functions and the How Old Are You? program show the function header line and function body. The function header line is the first line of the function. Function header lines have the return type, function name, and input parameter list.

input arguments

variable values (or addresses) that are passed into a function

In the Add_em_up function, the ***input arguments*** or input parameter list has three integers. Writing these three variables (a, b, and c) in the function header line is a declaration for the variables; that is, integers a, b, and c are "owned" by the function Add_em_up.

```
int Add_em_up(int a, int b, int c)   //Function header line has the data declaration.
{
        int sum;
        sum = a + b + c;    // a, b, and c can be used in this function
        return(sum);
}
```

return statement

a line of code where program control leaves a function; an exit point from a function

Return Statement   The ***return statement*** serves three purposes in a C++ function. First, it is required when the function is returning a value to the calling function. If the function is not returning a value, the return statement is not required. Second, many return statements may be included in a function. The return statement causes the program control to exit the function and to return to the calling function. It is possible to "bail out" of a function by using a return statement. (Refer to the examples, Do_It_If_Odd and HowMuchFood, below.) Third, an expression may be evaluated within the parentheses format of the return statement. The return statement in Add_em_up is:

```
return sum;
```

but it could look like this:

```
int Add_em_up(int a, int b, int c)
{
        return(a + b + c);

}
```

The function Write_Hello does not return a value to the calling function, so no return statement is required:

```
void Write_Hello()
{
        cout << "\n Hello World!";

}
```

The return statement also provides the programmer a way to terminate the function and to return to the calling function at any point in the function body. The return statement can be used to return a value or simply to exit the function if nothing is returned. In this vaguely named function, Do_It_If_Odd, the function checks the input value of the number variable to see if it is odd or even and exits the function immediately if the value is even.

```
void Do_It_If_Odd(int number)
{
    if(number%2 == 0) return;        // number is even, we're outta here!

    // Now we know the number is odd so proceed with function.
    // At the end of function--no return is needed.

}
```

In the function HowMuchFood, an integer representing a type of animal and a floating point value for the animal's weight are passed to the function, and the required amount of food per day, in pounds, is returned. The return statements are located within the switch statement.

```
float HowMuchFood(int animal_type, float wt)
{
        switch(animal_type)
        {
            case 1:    //elephant
                    return(wt * 0.2);   //no break needed--exiting the function here
            case 2:    // dog
                    return(wt * 0.25);
            case 3:    //squirrel
                    return(wt * 0.4);

        }

}
```

If a single return statement is located at the end of the HowMuchFood function, break statements are required.

```
float HowMuchFood(int animal_type, float wt)
{
        float total;
        switch(animal_type)
        {
                case 1:    //elephant
                        total = wt * 0.2;
                        break;
                case 2:    // dog
                        total = wt * 0.25;
                        break;
                case 3:    //squirrel
                        total = wt * 0.4;
                        break;
        }
        return total;
}
```

Call by Value

In these function examples, the data are passed to and from the functions, and functions actually have their own copy of the data. When the data is passed to a function, the value of the variable is copied into the input parameter variables of the called function. This type of function call is known as a ***call by value***. When data is passed using a variable name in the call statement, the value of that data is copied into the variables of the called function. In the How Old Are You? program, each function has its own copy of the age variable. This concept is illustrated in Figure 5-2.

call by value

term used when the value of a variable is passed to a function

Another Program Example

Program 5-4, Add Values from 1 to N, has a main function that calls two functions, Get_Number and Add_1_to_N. The user's number is passed to the Add_1_to_N function, which adds the numbers consecutively from 1 to the user's value. For example, if the user enters 5, the function will add $1 + 2 + 3 + 4 + 5$ and return a value of 15. The main function then writes the results to the screen.

In this program, note that the variable names are not the same from function to function. The main function has the variables "x" and "sum." But in the Get_Number function, the variable holding the user's number is "number" and in the Add_1_to_N, it is just "n." The sum value in main is represented as the total value in the Add_1_to_N function.

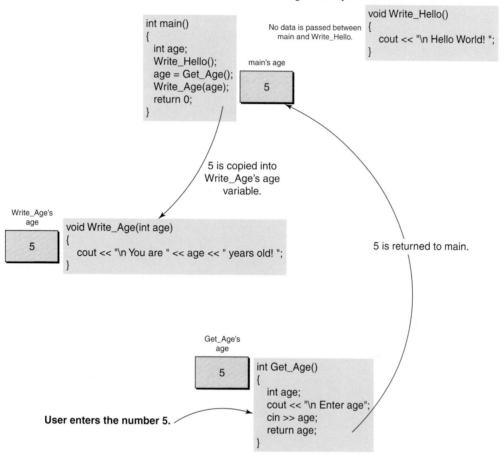

The value of the variable is passed between functions.
There are three different age memory locations.

```
int main()
{
    int age;
    Write_Hello();
    age = Get_Age();
    Write_Age(age);
    return 0;
}
```

No data is passed between main and Write_Hello.

```
void Write_Hello()
{
    cout << "\n Hello World! ";
}
```

main's age

5

5 is copied into Write_Age's age variable.

Write_Age's age

5

```
void Write_Age(int age)
{
    cout << "\n You are " << age << " years old! ";
}
```

5 is returned to main.

Get_Age's age

5

```
int Get_Age()
{
    int age;
    cout << "\n Enter age";
    cin >> age;
    return age;
}
```

User enters the number 5.

Figure 5-2
Program Call by Value for How Old Are You?

When variables are declared in a function header line or within the function itself, the variables are local to (are "owned" by) that function and are not seen by any other function. Figure 5-3 illustrates this concept.

The Add Values from 1 to N program can be rewritten to incorporate another function for writing results to the screen (see Program 5-5). This function, called Write_Values, is called from the Add_1_to_N function. Notice how the Add_1_to_N function return type is now void.

```
//Program 5-4 Add Values from 1 to N
#include <iostream.h>

int Get_Number();          //Prototypes
int Add_1_to_N(int);

int main()
{

        int x,sum;
        x = Get_Number();      //call to get the user's number
        sum = Add_1_to_N(x);   // pass x, adder returns the sum
        cout << "\n The result from adding 1 + 2 + . . . + " << x << " is " << sum << endl;

        return 0;
}

int Get_Number()           //Function header line
{
        int number;
        cout <<"\n Enter a number ";
        cin >> number;
        return number;
}

int Add_1_to_N(int n)
{
        int total = 0,i;
        for(i = 1; i <= n; ++i)    // add numbers 1 to N
        {
                total = total + i;
        }
        return total;
}
```

Review General Format of Functions

Table 5-1 shows several of the example functions from this chapter with the
required prototype and call statements. (The function header line and body of the
function are presented earlier in the chapter.) Remember, the proto*type* requires the
data *type*, and the call requires the variable names. The main problem beginning
programmers have when learning to construct functions is confusing the prototype
and call information. Spend a few minutes reviewing the three types of statements
in Table 5-1.

Each function has its own copy of the data variables.

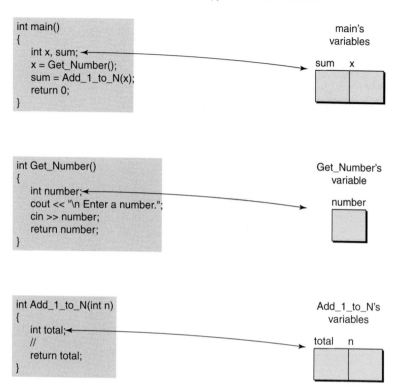

Figure 5-3
Functions and Local Variables

Troubleshooting: Type Mismatch

A common mistake that many C++ programmers make is not matching the data types in their prototypes and function header lines. Another error is that the call statements do not contain the correct data. For example, the return type in the prototype is int, and the return type in the function header line is a float. This example is a type mismatch. The program below contains a type mismatch with the Get_Number and the Add_1_to_N functions.

```
//Revisit Program 5-4x Add Values from 1 to N     COMPILE ERRORS!  Type mismatch
#include <iostream.h>

void Get_Number(int);   //These two prototypes
float Add_1_to_N();     //do not match their function header lines!
```

```cpp
//Program 5-5 Add Values from 1 to N Second Version
#include <iostream.h>

int Get_Number(void);         //Prototypes
void Add_1_to_N(int);
void Write_Values(int, int);

int main()
{

    int x;
    x = Get_Number();   //Get_Number returns user's number
    Add_1_to_N(x);      //Now send user's number to Add function
    return 0;

}

int Get_Number()        //Function header line
{
    int number;
    cout <<"\n Enter a number ";
    cin >> number;
    return number;
}


void Add_1_to_N(int n)
{
    int total = 0,i;
    for(i = 1; i <= n; ++i)    // add numbers 1 to N
    {
        total = total + i;
    }
    Write_Values(n,total);          // call the Write Results function here
}

void Write_Values(int n,int total)
{

    cout << "\n The result from adding 1 + 2 + . . . + " << n << " is " << total;

}
```

TABLE 5-1
Summary of Prototypes, Calls, and Function Header Line Statements

Prototype	Call Statement (in Bold)	Function Header Line

int Add_em_up(int, int, int);	int a, b, c, sum;
	// fill a, b, c with values
	sum = Add_em_up(a, b, c);
	// value for sum returned
		int Add_em_up(int a, int b, int c)
		{

void Write_em_out(int, double);	int small; double big; // fill small and big **Write_em_out(small, big);**	void Write_em_out (int s, double b) {

int Get_Age(void);
or
int Get_Age();
	int age;
	
	age = Get_Age();
	// function returns value for age
		int Get_Age(void)
		{
		
		or
		int Get_Age()
		{

void Write_Hello(void);
or
void Write_Hello();
	Write_Hello();	void Write_Hello(void)
		{
		
		or
		void Write_Hello()
		{

void Do_It_If_Odd(int);	int number; // fill number with value **Do_It_If_Odd(number);**	void Do_It_If_Odd(int n) {

float HowMuchFood(int,float);	float wt, food;
	int a_type;
	// fill wt and a_type with values
	**food = HowMuchFood(a_type,
	wt);**
	// value for food returned
		float HowMuchFood(int t, float w)
		{

5

```
int main()
{
        int x,sum;
        x = Get_Number();
        sum = Add_1_to_N(x);
        cout << "\n The result from adding 1 + 2 + . . . + " << x << " is " <<
sum;
        return 0;
}


int Get_Number()            //Function header line is different than the
prototype!
{

        int number;
        cout <<"\n Enter a number ";
        cin >> number;
        return number;
}


int Add_1_to_N(int n)
{
        int total = 0,i;
        //remainder of function
}
```

The Visual C++ compiler shows these errors:

Compiling...
CH5typemismatch.cpp
C:\CH5typemismatch.cpp(10) : error C2660: 'Get_Number' : function does not take 0 parameters
C:\CH5typemismatch.cpp(11) : error C2660: 'Add_1_to_N' : function does not take 1 parameter
Error executing cl.exe.

TestCases.exe - 2 error(s), 0 warning(s)

The GCC also reports several problems:

login1:johnston:~/gnu:$ g++ G++_Ch5typemismatch.cc
G++_ Ch5typemismatch.cc: In function 'int main()':
G++_ Ch5typemismatch.cc:11: too few arguments to function 'void Get_Number(int)'
G++_ Ch5typemismatch.cc:17: at this point in file
G++_ Ch5typemismatch.cc:17: void value not ignored as it ought to be
G++_ Ch5typemismatch.cc:12: too many arguments to function 'Add_1_to_N()'
G++_ Ch5typemismatch.cc:18: at this point in file
G++_ Ch5typemismatch.cc:18: warning: assignment to 'int' from 'float'

The correct prototype statements for this program are:

```
int Get_Number(void);   //Correct Prototypes—
int Add_1_to_N(int);    //they match their function header lines.
```

> **Helpful Hint** When the compiler reports some form of type mismatch or
> states that a function does not take this type of value or cannot convert from
> one type to another type, the prototype and call and function headers usually
> do not match. Check that the data types in the prototype and function header
> line parameter lists match.

Troubleshooting: Data Type in Call Statement

When the programmer places the data type in the call statement (another common
beginner mistake), the compiler usually reports a syntax error because it assumes
that a data cast is just missing parentheses. For example, if we write the call to
Add_1_to_N with the void and int located in the call statements, like this:

```
int main( )
{
        int x,sum;
        x = Get_Number(void);       //PROBLEM!  Do not put void in empty ().
        sum = Add_1_to_N(int x);    //PROBLEM Do not put int in the call ()
        cout << "\n The result from adding 1 + 2 + . . . + " << x <<
                " is " << sum << endl;

        return 0;
}
```

Visual C++ will report the following errors:

```
Compiling...
Ch5Add_1_to_N.cpp
C:\CBook\TestCases\Ch5Add_1_to_N.cpp(10) : error C2144: syntax error : missing ')' before type 'void'
C:\CBook\TestCases\Ch5Add_1_to_N.cpp(10) : error C2059: syntax error : ')'
C:\CBook\TestCases\Ch5Add_1_to_N.cpp(11) : error C2144: syntax error : missing ')' before type 'int'
C:\CBook\TestCases\Ch5Add_1_to_N.cpp(11) : error C2660: 'Add_1_to_N' : function does not take 0 parameters
C:\CBook\TestCases\Ch5Add_1_to_N.cpp(11) : error C2059: syntax error : ')'
Error executing cl.exe.

Ch5Add_1_to_N.obj - 5 error(s), 0 warning(s)
```

Function Requirements and C++ Libraries

There are eighteen libraries in the C language and nearly fifty in the ISO Standard C++ language. These **C++ *libraries*** provide many commonly used functions. For example, the math library provides a square root function. You may ask yourself, "How do I follow the rules of providing the program with the prototype, call, and function header line and body when using a math or standard library or any other function provided in a C++ library?"

When you need to use a function provided in a C or C++ library, you must include the library's .h file in the file that contains the call to the function. For example, if you are using the square root function, you must write this line at the top of the program file:

```
#include <math.h>
```

This preprocessor directive tells the program to look in the *math.h* file, which contains all the function prototypes for that library.

The C++ compilers include library files (such as *math.lib*) that are the object code version of the actual source code for the library functions. When the compiler sees the include statement for the *math.h* file, it reads the function prototypes in *math.h*. The linker will link the *math.lib* into the executable program file. The function header line and function body are in the library object code.

5.4
Local, Static, and Global Variables

C++ statements within a function are hidden from all other parts of the program and cannot be accessed by any other functions. The only way to get to code or variables in a function is by calling the function and having the program control enter through the function header line. It is impossible to perform a jump or "goto" into the middle of a function.

Now that we have started working with functions, it is time to introduce the concept of variable scope. ***Variable scope*** determines which variables in the program are visible to other portions of the program and which variables are not visible. This variable visibility issue includes the ability for one portion of the code to access a variable in other parts of the code. The scope of the variable is determined by the location where the variable is declared.

Local Variables

The variables declared within the function and in the function header line input list belong to, or are "owned" by, that function. No other function can see, access, or change these variables; they are known as ***local variables*** or ***automatic variables***. These local variables come into existence when the function begins executing and are destroyed once program control exits the function. In the Add Values from 1 to N program example, each function has its own variable that represents the user's number, but each function has a different name for this number. Most programmers will use the same name for a variable throughout the program—this action leads to consistency and easily understood code.

Troubleshooting: Forgetting to Declare Variables

A beginning C++ programmer often forgets that local variables are "private" inside the functions and that a variable declared in main is not seen by any other function. Students will declare a variable in the main function and then use that variable in other functions, believing that one declaration takes care of the program and all other functions can use it. But each variable in each function requires its own declaration.

We revisit the How Old Are You! program (without the Write_Hello function). This code shows the common mistake of forgetting to declare variables locally in functions. The age declared in main is not seen by the other functions. This code has two problems. One is that the function prototype for Write_Age does not match the call in main; the second is that the age in Get_Age is not recognized.

```
//Program 5-x How Old Are You?          WILL NOT COMPILE!!
#include <iostream.h>
int Get_Age();                   // The 2 function prototypes
void Write_Age();
int main()
{
      int age;          // this age is local to main
      age = Get_Age();
      Write_Age(age);
}
int Get_Age()
{
      cout << "\n How old are you?";
      cin >> age;                         //the compiler won't know about this age???
      return (age);
}
void Write_Age()
{
      cout << "\n You are " << age << " years old!";          // or this age???
}
```

The Visual C++ compiler shows these messages:

Compiling...
CH5GetAge.cpp

```
C:\CH5GetAge.cpp(9) : error C2660: 'Write_Age' : function does not take 1 parameters
C:\CH5GetAge.cpp(14) : error C2065: 'age' : undeclared identifier
Error executing cl.exe.

TestCases.exe - 2 error(s), 0 warning(s)
```

The GCC compiler shows the following messages:

```
login1:johnston:~/gnu:$ g++ G++_Ch5GetAge.cc
G++_ Ch5GetAge cc: In function 'int main()':
G++_ Ch5GetAge.cc:13: too many arguments to function 'Write_Age()'
G++_ Ch5GetAge.cc:18: at this point in file
G++_ Ch5GetAge.cc: In function 'int Get_Age()':
G++_ Ch5GetAge.cc:23: 'age' undeclared (first use this function)
G++_ Ch5GetAge.cc:23: (Each undeclared identifier is reported only once
G++_ Ch5GetAge.cc:23: for each function it appears in.)
G++_ Ch5GetAge.cc:24: confused by earlier errors, bailing out
```

The correct way to write this program is shown in Program 5-3, How Old Are You? on page 155.

Static Variables

When a program begins to execute, the local variables inside the main function are created (that is, memory is allocated for them). The storage space for variables within other functions is not allocated until the individual function is called and the program control is passed to it. Once the function statements are completed and we exit, the variables that were declared inside the function are released from memory and the contents of these variables are lost.

static variable

local variable that retains its value until the program is terminated

Functions can retain the variable values by using the static specifier in the variable declaration. Once a variable is declared a *static variable,* the variable contents are retained until the program is terminated. The variable is still visible only to the function and it is not seen by any other parts of the program. The first time the function is entered, the static variable initialization occurs. If there is no initial value assigned in the code, C++ initializes the static variable to zero. The static variable initialization statement is performed only once while the program is running.

The simple program in Program 5-6 illustrates how static variables are used. If a function must "remember" how many times it is called, a static variable can be set up as a counter. The value passed to main from Say_Hello is the static variable count. The Say_Hello function retains the value in count until the program terminates. Here is the output:

```
HELLO!
Number of hellos we've seen: 1
HELLO!
Number of hellos we've seen: 2
```

```
//Program 5-6 Count Hellos using a static variable.
#include <iostream.h>
int Say_Hello();          // prototype
int main()
{
        int how_many, i;
        for(i = 0; i < 10; ++i)
        {
                how_many = Say_Hello();
                cout << "\n Number of hellos we've seen:" << how_many;
        }
        return 0;
}
int Say_Hello()
{
        static int count = 0;          //count is set to zero first time
        cout << "\n HELLO!";
        count++;
        return count;
}
```

HELLO!
Number of hellos we've seen: 3
HELLO!
Number of hellos we've seen: 4
HELLO!
Number of hellos we've seen: 5
HELLO!
Number of hellos we've seen: 6
HELLO!
Number of hellos we've seen: 7
HELLO!
Number of hellos we've seen: 8
HELLO!
Number of hellos we've seen: 9
HELLO!
Number of hellos we've seen: 10

Global Variables

It is possible to declare a variable to be global. A *global variable* is declared outside any function and is visible to all functions in the program; that is, all the functions can use and change a global variable. The Count Hellos program can be rewritten with a global variable for the count (see Program 5-7). When a variable is declared

global variable
variable that is declared outside any function and all functions within the file can access it

```
//Program 5-7 Count Hellos using a global variable.
#include <iostream.h>
void Say_Hello();          // prototype is now void return type
int count = 0;             // global count variable, all can see it
int main()
{

        int i;
        for(i = 0; i < 10; ++i)
        {
                Say_Hello();
                cout << "\n number of hellos we've seen: " << count;
        }
        return 0;
}
void Say_Hello()
{
        cout << "\n HELLO!";
        count++;                            //global variable
}
```

outside a function, all functions in the program can see it. There is no need to pass the count variable now that it is global. The program output is identical to the previous static variable version, but the count variable is not passed between the functions. The variable is stored in a place where both functions may access it.

Global Variables Are Dangerous

When beginning programmers are first introduced to global variables, their initial reaction is that there is no need to pass variables between functions. They can make all the variables global and everybody sees everything. Using global variables can lead to disastrous problems, however, especially when programs are large or several programmers are working on one project. Because global variables are accessible by all functions, every function can change the value.

Global variables should be used sparingly and with considerable thought and subsequent documentation. As a general rule, global variables are used for mathematical constants or universally used values and perhaps file pointers or stream objects. In some instances, global variables are necessary if functions are provided for the programmer, but the input parameter list is fixed. In this case, the variables must be global for the function to be able to access required values. If the program is quite large, with many user-written libraries, it may be best to avoid global declarations altogether.

Troubleshooting: Global Variable y1 and math.h

The TakeASquareRoot program demonstrates how global variables can conflict with C++ libraries. This program uses the global variable "y1." The program needs the *math.h* include file because it uses the square root function.

```
// Program 5-x TakeASquareRoot Program
// Global Variables that conflict with standard C++ libraries.
#include <iostream.h>
#include <math.h>


double y1;


int main()
{


        float x;


        y1 = 25.0;
        x = sqrt(y1);
}
```

The Visual C++ compiler reports these messages:

```
Compiling...
CH5math_conf.cpp
C:\CH5math_conf.cpp(7) : error C2373: 'y1' : redefinition; different type modifiers
    c:\program files\microsoft visual studio\vc98\include\math.h(435) : see declaration of 'y1'
Error executing cl.exe.

TestCases.exe - 1 error(s), 0 warning(s)
```

GCC reports the following errors:

```
login1:johnston:~/gnu:$ g++ G++_Ch5math_conf.cc
G++_Ch5math_conf.cc:14: 'double y1' redeclared as different kind of symbol
/usr/include/bits/mathcalls.h:225: previous declaration of 'double y1(double)'
```

The problem with this small program is that the compiler has already seen a y1 variable in the *math.h* file. The compiler believes we are trying to redefine y1 in our program. It is possible to examine the contents of *math.h*. A few lines are:

```
_CRTIMP double __cdecl _y0(double);
_CRTIMP double __cdecl _y1(double);
_CRTIMP double __cdecl _yn(int, double);
```

TABLE 5-2
Variable Scope Summary

Scope Specifier	Where Declared?	Who Sees It?	Length of Existence
Local, automatic	Inside function in function header line	Only code inside function	It exists only when function is executing and is lost when function is exited.
Static	Inside function	Only code inside function	Once initialized, it exists until program termination.
Global	Outside function	All functions	It exists until program termination.

By placing a global variable in our program, we have a conflict with variables in the math standard library. What is the moral of this story? Always use global variables sparingly and carefully lest you bring on more problems than you can imagine! Table 5-2 summarizes local, static, and global variables.

5.5
Pointers and Functions

Review Call by Value

A call by value occurs when a calling function copies the values of its data into the called function's input variables. Thus, both the calling and called functions have a local copy of the data. If a function's job is relatively straightforward and memory usage and execution speed are not an issue, the call by value approach works well.

Suppose you need a function to calculate the volume of a cylinder, given the radius and height of the cylinder. The calling function can simply pass the called function a copy of the input variables. The called function has its own copy of the variables. In Program 5-8, both the main and CalcCylinderVolume have their own local copies of the radius and height. If the number of variables to be passed to a function is relatively small, call by value is the way to go.

Two Values from a Function?

There are two situations in which call by value is either inefficient or not a workable programming tool. The inefficiency issue involves the need for a function to work on a large piece of data, such as a digital image. For example, if an image is 300K bytes, it is not practical to have local copies of the image data in individual functions. Making copies of large data is too time consuming and requires too much memory. We will examine this situation in more detail in Chapter 7.

```
//Program 5-8 Calculate Cylinder Volume.
// Call by Value
#include <iostream.h>
const double pi = 3.14159265;          //pi is global variable
float CalcCylinderVolume(float,float);   //Prototype

int main()
{
        float radius, height,volume;

        cout << "\n Please enter the radius and height of your cylinder.  ";
        cin >> radius >> height;

        volume = CalcCylinderVolume(radius,height); //call by value
        cout << "\n Your Cylinder Volume = " << volume << endl;
        return 0;
}

float CalcCylinderVolume(float rad, float hgt)  //rad and hgt local variables
{
        float vol;
        vol = pi * rad * rad * hgt;
        return(vol);
}
```

5

The glaring problem facing us right now is that C++ allows the return of only one data item from a function. Often functions need to return more than one item. If we need a function to obtain from the user the dimensions of a cylinder, how will we get both the radius and height back to the calling function? The answer is, by using pointers.

Brief Review of Pointers

Chapter 4 covered pointers in detail, but we can review pointers here briefly. Recall that pointers are variables that hold hexadecimal addresses. We declare pointers using the * operator and data type to which the pointer is supposed to point. Two pointers are declared in these statements:

```
float *a_ptr;
int *b_ptr;
```

We also use the address operator, &, to obtain the address of a data variable and the indirection operator, *, to obtain or assign values where the pointer is pointing.

Programmers can adopt naming conventions to aid them in remembering what type of data the variable is and whether or not it is a pointer. For our examples, we will use the following convention:

```
name_ptr    // _ptr signified the variable is a pointer
```

In the following short program, we shall assign the address of a variable into a pointer and use the indirection operator to access the data value.

```
//Program Review Pointers
#include <iostream.h>
int main()
{
        float a;
        float *a_ptr = &a;          //declare pointers and assign addresses
        *a_ptr = 7.2;          // 7.2 assigned into the address that a_ptr contains
        cout << "\n The value in a is " << *a_ptr;
        return 0;
}
```

The output from this program will show the value of a to be 7.2. It is obtained by using the *a_ptr, which tells the program to get the value in the address contained in a_ptr.

Call by Reference: Variable's Address to a Function

call by reference
term used when the address of a variable is passed to a function

In a *call by reference,* the address of the data variable is passed to a function. The address is copied into a pointer variable that belongs to the called function. The called function accesses the calling function variable via the indirection operator and pointer. (The address of the variable can be thought of as a reference to that variable.) This technique makes the calling function's variable available to the called function, and the called function does not have its own local copy of the variable.

If a called function must return several data items to a calling function, the programmer can use the call by reference technique. The calling function passes the addresses of its variables to the called function, which then writes the data directly into the calling function's variables.

In the Calculate Cylinder Volume program (Program 5-9), we want to use a GetCylinderDimensions function to ask the user to enter the radius and height. To return two pieces of data to main, we shall use a call by reference. Figure 5-4(a) to (d) illustrates the mechanics of the call by reference using pointers. The steps in the process are listed below.

Step 1 (Figure 5-4 [a]): The addresses of the radius and the height are passed to the function and stored in the pointer variables.

```
//Program 5-9 Calculate Cylinder Volume Second Version
// Call by Reference using pointers to functions.

#include <iostream.h>
const double pi = 3.14159265;

void GetCylinderDimensions(float*,float*);   //Prototypes pointers here
float CalcCylinderVolume(float,float);        // Call by value here

int main()
{
        float radius, height,volume;
        GetCylinderDimensions(&radius, &height);       //send addresses
        volume = CalcCylinderVolume(radius,height);    //send values
        cout << "\n Cylinder Volume = " << volume << endl;
}

void GetCylinderDimensions(float *r_ptr, float *h_ptr)  //pointers
{
        float R, H;
        cout << "\n Enter radius and height  ";
        cin >> R >> H;
        *r_ptr = R;         //place value in R where r_ptr is pointing
        *h_ptr = H;         //place value in H where h_ptr is pointing
}

float CalcCylinderVolume(float rad, float hgt)
{
        return (pi * rad * rad * hgt);  //shortcut by doing calcs in return ()
}
```

Step 2 (Figure 5-4 [b]): The values of the radius and the height are obtained and stored in local variables.

Step 3 (Figure 5-4 [c]): The value in R is assigned where r_ptr is pointing. The radius value of 10.0000 is written into main's radius variable.

Step 4 (Figure 5-4 [d]): The value in H is assigned where h_ptr is pointing. The height value of 15.0000 is written into main's height variable.

We pass the addresses of the variables into pointers only for the GetCylinderDimensions function because this function must return two values to main. Call by reference is not needed in CalcCylinderVolume because this function returns only one value. The CalcCylinderVolume needs the radius and height values, which can be passed into the function and used to determine the volume. The volume can then be returned to main.

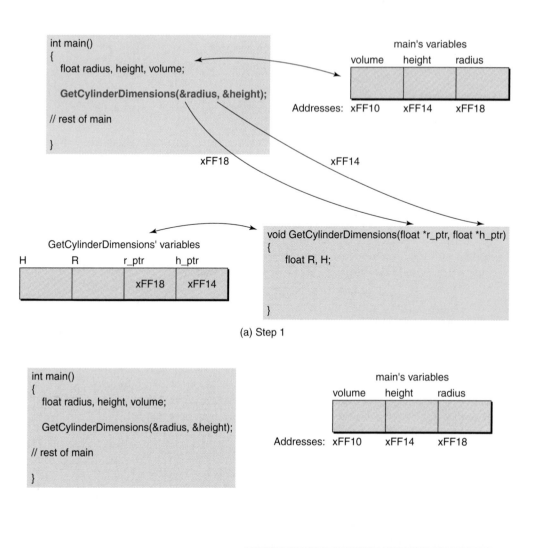

(a) Step 1

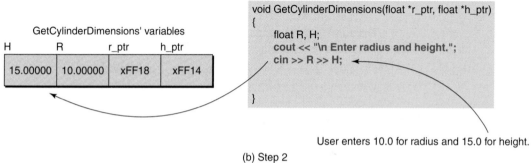

(b) Step 2

Figure 5-4
Data Flow Through Calculate Cylinder Volume Program: Call by Reference

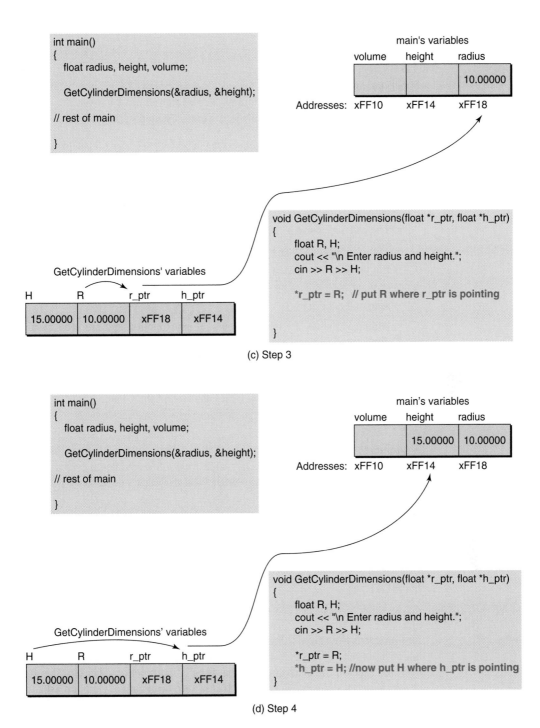

```
int main()
{
    float radius, height, volume;

    GetCylinderDimensions(&radius, &height);

// rest of main

}
```

main's variables

volume	height	radius
		10.00000

Addresses: xFF10   xFF14   xFF18

```
void GetCylinderDimensions(float *r_ptr, float *h_ptr)
{
    float R, H;
    cout << "\n Enter radius and height.";
    cin >> R >> H;

    *r_ptr = R;   // put R where r_ptr is pointing

}
```

GetCylinderDimensions' variables

H	R	r_ptr	h_ptr
15.00000	10.00000	xFF18	xFF14

(c) Step 3

```
int main()
{
    float radius, height, volume;

    GetCylinderDimensions(&radius, &height);

// rest of main

}
```

main's variables

volume	height	radius
	15.00000	10.00000

Addresses: xFF10   xFF14   xFF18

```
void GetCylinderDimensions(float *r_ptr, float *h_ptr)
{
    float R, H;
    cout << "\n Enter radius and height.";
    cin >> R >> H;

    *r_ptr = R;
    *h_ptr = H; //now put H where h_ptr is pointing
}
```

GetCylinderDimensions' variables

H	R	r_ptr	h_ptr
15.00000	10.00000	xFF18	xFF14

(d) Step 4

Figure 5-4 (continued)

Summary

Functions are the backbone of C and C++ programs. To lay the groundwork for learning object-oriented programming, a programmer must have a firm grasp of the basic function. The following key ideas were presented in this chapter:

- Functions require three types of statements: a prototype, call, and function header line and body.
- The function prototype contains the data types for the return value and input parameters.
- The call statement is the location where the function is actually called.
- The call requires only variable names.
- If a value is returned, it should be assigned into a variable.
- Call by reference and pointers are required if the function must return more than one data item.
- Global variables are declared outside any function and are seen by all functions in the file.
- Local variables are declared inside the function or in the function header line and are only accessible within the function.
- Static variables are local variables that retain their value after the function is exited.

A summary of function prototypes, calls, and function header lines and bodies is presented in Table 5-3. The call by value function calculates the area of a circle. The call by reference function calculates the diameter and area of a circle. Both functions are passed the radius of the circle.

5.7
Practice

IsItPrime

The program flow for IsItPrime is illustrated in Figure 5-5. This program determines if a positive integer value is a prime number. It uses a function to get a value from the user. In the GetNum function, it calls the function CheckIt. This function checks to see if the value is positive. If it is zero or negative, GetNum asks the user to re-enter the value. Back in main, we call the IsItPrime function, which deter-

TABLE 5-3

Call by Value and Call by Reference Summary

Example	Call by Value	Call by Reference
Function task	Calculate surface area of a circle given the radius.	Calculate surface area and diameter of a circle given the radius.
Prototype	`float CalcSA(float);`	`void CalcSA_D(float, float*, float*);`

Call	`int main()`
	`{`
	   `float area, r = 5.0;`
	   `area = CalcSA(r);`
	   `return 0;`
	`}`
		`int main()`
		`}`
		   `float area, dia, r = 5.0;`
		   `CalcSA_D(r, &area, &dia);`
		    `return 0;`
		`}`

Function header line and body	`float CalcSA(float rad)`
	`{`
	   `float SA;`
	   `SA = rad*rad*3.141592;`
	   `return SA;`
	`}`
		`void CalcSA_D(float r, float* a_ptr,`
		`float *d_ptr)`
		`{`
		    `*a_ptr = r * r * 3.141592;`
		    `*d_ptr = 2.0 * r;`
		`}`

5

mines if the number is prime[1]. If the number is prime, the IsItPrime function writes the number and prime message. If the number is not prime, it writes the number, a message, and gives one whole number divisor for the number. For example, if the user enters 17, the program reports, "17 is a prime number." If the user enters 24, it reports, "24 is not prime and 2 is one divisor." (Notice how short the main function has become.)

Programming Flags One aspect of creating a program with functions involves determining a value convention for returning indicator variables that relay information concerning the function. These indicator variables are known in computer programming as *flags*. A flag can be any type of variable, but integer, character, and boolean are preferred. There are no hard and fast rules for flags, nor is any magic involved when programming with flags. The programmer simply decides on the type of variables and what each value represents. For example, the return code may indicate that an error occurred in the function. The value of 1 may mean there was an error, whereas the value of 0 means no error. The *bool* data type in C++ allows the programmer to use the *true* and *false* values. The CheckIt function illustrates how to use a bool data type.

flags
variables used in programs to indicate certain events or conditions

---

[1]A whole number is considered prime if it is divisible (using whole number divisors) by only 1 and itself. For example, 7 is a prime number because it can be divided only by 1 and 7 evenly. 24 is not a prime number, because 4 * 6 = 24, 2 * 12 = 24 3 * 8 = 24 (there are many whole number divisors for 24).

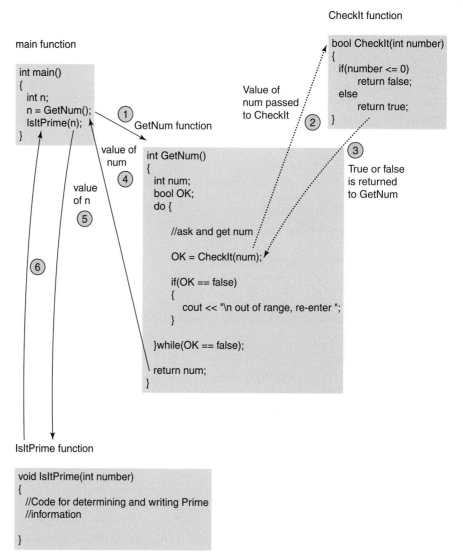

Figure 5-5
IsItPrime Program Flow

```
//Program 5-10 IsItPrime    Phase 1 - Functions called by main.
#include <iostream.h>

int GetNum();           //prototypes
void IsItPrime(int);
bool CheckIt(int);

int main()
{
        cout << "\n I'm in main.";
        int n;
        n = GetNum();
        cout <<"\n Back in main from GetNum and the value of n is " << n;
        IsItPrime(n);
        cout << "\n Back in main, all done!" << endl;

        return 0;
}

int GetNum()
{
        bool OK;
        int num = 1;
        cout << "\n I'm in the GetNum function and will return a 1.";
        OK = CheckIt(num);
        return num;
}

bool CheckIt(int number)
{
        cout << "\n I'm in CheckIt and the number is " << number;
        return true;
}

void IsItPrime(int number)
{
        cout << "\n I'm in the IsItPrime function and the value of number is " <<
        number;
}
```

IsItPrime **Step 1: Program framework.** It is especially important for beginning programmers to get the skeleton of the program in place before implementing the function details. In this first phase seen on page 183, we write shortened versions of the functions. Each function writes a message and the value of the number passed into it. The output from this skeletal program shows that we made round-trips through all the functions.

I'm in main.
I'm in the GetNum function and will return a 1.
I'm in CheckIt and the number is 1.
Back in main from GetNum and the value of n is 1.
I'm in the IsItPrime function and the value of number is 1
Back in main, all done!

Step 2: Complete program. Once the program flow for the main function is working, we can add code to ask the user for a value, send it to the CheckIt function, and add the details of each function. The complete program is shown in Program 5–10 on pages 184–185.

```
//Program 5-10   IsItPrime
#include <iostream.h>

int GetNum();           //prototypes
void IsItPrime(int);
bool CheckIt(int);

int main()
{
      int n;
      n = GetNum();
      IsItPrime(n);
}


int GetNum()
{
      int num;
      bool OK;
      do {
            cout << "\n Please enter a positive integer \n\n==>  ";
            cin >> num;
            OK = CheckIt(num);  // returns 1 if within range, 0 if not
            if(OK == false)
            {
                  cout << "\n Value out of range, please re-enter ";
            }
```

```
        }while(OK == false);

        return(num);
}


bool CheckIt(int number)
{
        if(number <= 0)        return false;
        else    return true;
}


void IsItPrime(int number)
{
        int result,divisor = 0,ctr=2;
        while(ctr < number )  //loop from 2 to n-1 and check remainder from modulus
        {
                result = number%ctr;
                if(result == 0)  // if a number goes into the user's n evenly, not prime
                {
                        divisor = ctr;
                        cout << "\n\n The value " << number << " is NOT prime.";
                        cout << "\n One divisor is " << divisor << endl;
                        return;    // WE'RE all done, get outta here!
                }
                ++ctr;
        }
        cout << "\n\n The value " << number << " is prime.   \n\n";
}
```

Random Numbers

The C language standard library (stdlib) contains the *rand()* function, which is a pseudo–random number generator. The rand() function returns a value between 0 and the maximum range for the system integer. It should be seeded with an integer value that is sent to *srand()* (that is, call srand() with a value and then make calls to rand(), which returns a random number). The random number can be scaled to any range by using the modulus operator. For example, if you want a number between 0 and 9 and if you divide the random number by 10, the possible remainder values will be between 0 and 9. This short program generates and prints 100 random numbers between the values 0 to 9.

Time Conversion

In this program, we ask the user to enter a time in the H:M:S format and then convert it to the total number of seconds. We check the user's values in the GetTime

```
//Program 5-11 Random Numbers

#include <iostream.h>
#include <stdlib.h>        // needed for random number generator
#include <iomanip.h>       // needed for setw()

void Find_100_Random_Num(int);      // pass the seed to the function

int main()
{
        int seed = 123;
        srand(seed);       // seed the random number generator, do this only once
        Find_100_Random_Num(seed);
        return 0;
}

void Find_100_Random_Num(int seed)
{

        int i, rand_num, zero_to_nine;
        for (i = 0; i < 100; ++i)
        {
                rand_num = rand();
                zero_to_nine = rand_num%10;
                cout << "\n " << i+1 << setw(5) << zero_to_nine;
        }
}
```

```
//Program 5-12  Time conversion H:M:S to seconds
#include <iostream.h>
#include <stdlib.h>

void GetTime(int*, int*, int*);          // call by reference
int CalcSeconds(int, int, int);          // call by value

int main( )
{

        int hr, min, sec;
        char another;
        int total_sec;

        cout << "\n\n Welcome to a time-conversion program!     \n\n";
```

```
        do
        {
                GetTime(&hr, &min, &sec);
                total_sec = CalcSeconds(hr, min, sec);

                cout << "\n\n You entered " << hr << ":" << min << ":" << sec;
                cout << "\n It is " << total_sec << " seconds ";

                cout << "\n\n Do another?  y or n ";
                cin >> another;

        } while(another == 'y'|| another == 'Y');

        cout << "\n Thanks for Playing! \n";
        return 0;
}
void GetTime(int *h_ptr, int *m_ptr, int *s_ptr)
{
        int ask_them_again = 1;
        char colon;

        while(ask_them_again == 1)
        {

                cout << "\n Please enter the time in hours minutes seconds ";
                cout << "\n Such as 4:15:34    (Note: Minutes and Seconds < 60)\n\n==>  ";
                cin >> *h_ptr >> colon >> *m_ptr >> colon >> *s_ptr;

                ask_them_again = 0;          //assuming time is OK,
                if(*m_ptr > 59 || *s_ptr > 59)
                {

                        cout << "\n WHOA!!! Invalid Time !!! ";
                        ask_them_again = 1;   //need to ask them again

                }
        }
}


int CalcSeconds(int hr, int min, int sec)
{

        int total_sec;
        total_sec = hr*3600 + min*60 + sec;
        return total_sec;

}
```

5

function to ensure that the numbers for minutes and seconds are between 0 and 59. If the values are out of range, we ask the user to re-enter the values. There are two functions—one is a call by value and the other is call by reference.

Cats and Dogs

This last example illustrates a program written twice—once using pointers to locally declared variables and the second using globally declared variables. This program simply asks the user to enter the number of dogs and cats he or she owns (GetPetInfo) and then reports this information (WritePetInfo). Boolean flags are used to keep track of the user's yes and no answers.

Using Pointers to Local Variables   In this pointer version of Cats and Dogs, the function GetPetInfo must return four pieces of information to the calling function. The addresses of the four variables are sent to GetPetInfo, and the indirection operator is used. In the WritePetInfo function, the values are simply sent to it (not the addresses) because WritePetInfo merely uses the values and returns nothing.

Global Variables   In the global version of Cats and Dogs, the boolean and integer variables are declared globally (above the main function). The functions GetPetInfo and WritePetInfo can access these variables directly. There is no need to pass the variables to the function calls.

```
//Program 5-13 Cats and Dogs with bool operators and pointers
#include <iostream.h>
void GetPetInfo(bool*, int*, bool*, int*);    // dog data, cat data using pointers
void WritePetInfo(bool, int, bool, int);

int main()
{
      bool bDog, bCat;     //flags that are set true or false
      int DogNum, CatNum;

// GetPetInfo places values into these four variables. Pointers are needed.
      GetPetInfo(&bDog, &DogNum, &bCat, &CatNum);
      WritePetInfo(bDog, DogNum, bCat, CatNum);

      if(bDog || bCat)
            cout << "\n Don't you just LOVE owning pets? \n ";
      return 0;
}
```

```cpp
void GetPetInfo(bool *pbDog, int *pDogNum, bool *pbCat, int *pCatNum)
{
    char answer;
// first assume the answers will be no & set flags to false and nums to zero
    *pbDog = false;
    *pbCat = false;
    *pDogNum = 0;
    *pCatNum = 0;

    // Now, ask the questions
    cout << "\n Do you have any dogs?  y = yes, n = no  ";
    cin >> answer;
    if(answer == 'y')
    {
            cout << "\n How many dogs do you have?  ";
            cin >> *pDogNum;
            *pbDog = true;
    }
    cout << "\n Do you have any cats?  y = yes, n = no  ";
    cin >> answer;
    if(answer == 'y')
    {
            cout << "\n How many cats do you have?  ";
            cin >> *pCatNum;
            *pbCat = true;
    }
}


void WritePetInfo(bool bDog, int DogNum, bool bCat, int CatNum)
{

    cout << "\n\n Dog and cat ownership data: ";
    if(bDog == true)
            cout << "\n You own " << DogNum << " dogs. ";
    else
            cout << "\n You don't own any dogs. ";

    if(bCat == true)
            cout << "\n You own " << CatNum << " cats. \n";
    else
            cout << "\n You don't own any cats.\n ";
}
```

```
//Program 5-14 Cats and Dogs with global variables
#include <iostream.h>

void GetPetInfo();
void WritePetInfo();

bool bDog, bCat;      //global variables, all functions see/access them
int DogNum, CatNum;
int main()
{
        GetPetInfo();           //call statements do not pass variables
        WritePetInfo();
        if(bDog || bCat)
                cout << "\n Don't you just LOVE owning pets? \n ";
        return 0;
}

void GetPetInfo()
{
        char answer;
        // first assume the answers will be no & set flags to false and nums to zero
        bDog = false;
        bCat = false;
        DogNum = 0;
        CatNum = 0;
        // Now, ask the questions
        cout << "\n Do you have any dogs?  y = yes, n = no   ";
        cin >> answer;

        if(answer == 'y')
        {
                cout << "\n How many dogs do you have?   ";
                cin >> DogNum;
                bDog = true;
        }

        cout << "\n Do you have any cats?  y = yes, n = no   ";
        cin >> answer;

        if(answer == 'y')
        {
                cout << "\n How many cats do you have?   ";
                cin >> CatNum;
                bCat = true;
        }
}
```

```
void WritePetInfo()
{
        cout << "\n\n Dog and cat ownership data: ";
        if(bDog)
                cout << "\n You own " << DogNum << " dogs. ";
        else
                cout << "\n You don't own any dogs. ";

        if(bCat)
                cout << "\n You own " << CatNum << " cats. \n";
        else
                cout << "\n You don't own any cats.\n ";
}
```

▌ REVIEW QUESTIONS AND PROBLEMS

Short Answer

1. What are the three required statements for every function in C++?

2. Name the three places in a C++ program where variables can be declared.

3. What is the job of the return statement?

4. What is the difference between a prototype statement and a call statement?

5. When should you use pointers in functions?

6. Why is it unnecessary to pass global variables between functions?

7. When you are working with functions, type mismatch compiler errors are usually what type of error?

8. What is the difference between a static local variable and an automatic local variable?

9. Name two reasons why programmers should be careful when using global variables.

10. What is the difference between a calling function and a called function?

Reading the Code

Show the screen output from the code examples in Problems 11 and 12.

11. What output will be generated from the following source code?

C Code	Output
| ```c
#include <iostream.h>
void Red();
int main()
{
  int i = 1;
  while(i < 4)
  {
      Red();
      ++i;
    }
}
void Red()
{
    cout << "\nRed is a great color.";
}
``` | |

12. What output will be generated from the following source code?

C Code	Output
| ```c
#include <iostream.h>
#include <math.h>
int ChangeIt(float );
int main()
{
    int i;
    float x = -3.7755;
    i = ChangeIt(x);
    cout << "The float was" << x;
    cout << "\nIt was changed to" << i;
    return 0;
}
int ChangeIt(float x)
{
    return ( (int) sqrt( x * x));
}
``` | |

Debugging Problems

The source code examples in Problems 13 to 15 are incomplete programs. Identify the compiler errors and state what is needed to eliminate the error(s).

13.

```
#include <iostream.h>
void Func1();
int Func2(float);

int main
{
        Func2();
        n = FUNC1();
}
```

14.

```
include <iostream.h>

Int HowOldAreYou(void);

int main
{
        int age;
        age = HowOldAreYou(void);
}
```

15.

```
#include <iostream.h>

GetTime(float *, int*);
int main
{

        float x = 7;
        int n = 3;
        GetTime(x,n);
}
```

Programming Problems

16. Write a complete C++ program that has a main function, a GetTwoNumbers function, and a FindBigOne function. The main calls the GetTwoNumbers function, which asks the user for two integers. Then the program sends the two ints to FindBigOne, which returns the larger value to main. For example, if the user puts in 19 and 2, FindBigOne will return 19. If the two numbers are the same, it will send back either one. Incorporate a loop in the main function so that the user can keep entering two values as long as he or she desires.

17. Write a program that uses the random number generator functions in the standard library to generate a random sequence of letters from A to Z. The

Get_A_Letter function should return a letter based on the ASCII table; that is, A = 65 and Z = 91. Ask the user to enter a seed value and call srand() with the seed value. Then write out a fifteen-character encoded message based on the seed. *Note*: You will need to place the call to Get_A_Letter inside a for loop and write the message one letter at a time. Continue to loop until the user wishes to stop.

18. Expand the Time Conversion program so that it asks the user if he or she would like to convert H:M:S time to seconds or seconds to H:M:S time. Check that the user has not entered an invalid conversion choice before calling the appropriate functions. You will need to add three functions: CheckInput, GetSeconds, and Sec_to_HMSTime.

5

6

Arrays

KEY TERMS AND CONCEPTS

array
array dimension
array index
array pointers
arrays and functions
atof function
atoi function
atol function
character string
element
multidimensional array
null character
null-terminated string
out of bounds array
single-dimensional array
string class
str functions
zero-indexed

KEYWORDS AND OPERATORS

array index [ ]

CHAPTER OBJECTIVES

Introduce the concept of an array—which is a list of variables with the same name and requires an index value.

Demonstrate how the C++ language automatically creates a pointer to any array that is declared.

Present single (one-dimensional) and multiply dimensioned (two-dimensional, three-dimensional, etc.) array concepts.

Illustrate how arrays are passed and used in functions.

Explore the problems of an array that is out of bounds in a C++ program.

Explain how to read data from a data file, a particularly useful tool when working with arrays.

Present example programs that read data from a file into an array and then pass the array to functions.

Run Faster! Jump Higher!

One part of writing software is designing the data variables to represent accurately the situation the program models. The software may be a computer game, an accounting program, an engineering data analysis package, or drivers for a hardware device. Whatever the application, it is important to spend time during the program design phase thinking about what data variables are needed.

In the previous chapters, we declared variables so that each one provided a location for storing one value. We had variables such as age, number, sum, and count. We asked the user his or her age, counted hellos, and added values. Your work built up your confidence about using different variable types. Now we raise the bar and say, "Jump higher!"

In this chapter and those that follow, we expand our C++ knowledge and learn how to declare a single variable that actually contains a list (array) of data values of the same type or a group of different types of data values (structure). These new data types should be grouped logically; that is, they should relate naturally to each other. For example, you may declare a single array that is actually a list of phone bills for one year. This phone bill array contains twelve values. In the next chapter, we learn how to declare a structure variable that contains different types of variables, such as a mailing list containing names, addresses, zip codes, and age information. It's time to run faster, jump higher, and expand your C++ skills.

6.1
Using Single Data Variables

Let's start with a programming problem that shows how the ability to create a single variable containing a list of values can simplify life. Assume that you need to write a program that averages the phone bills for a year, starting in January and ending with December. You need twelve variables—one for each month in the year—and you need to ask the user to enter these twelve values. Your program calculates and reports the average value. (Eventually it will be nice to have the program read the numbers in from a data file instead of entering the data by hand. We will learn how to read data files later in this chapter.)

First, we must name our twelve variables. How about using abbreviations for the months as variable names to keep track of the twelve months? Then we ask for the numbers and calculate the average cost.

```
//Program 6-Incomplete program for finding the average phone costs for a year.
#include <iostream.h>
int main()
{
    // Declare variables
        float jan, feb, mar, apr, may, jun, jul, aug, sept, oct, nov, dec;
        float ave;

    // Obtain monthly billing information
        cout << "\n Please enter your bill for jan:";
        cin >> jan;
        cout << "\n Please enter your bill for feb:";
        cin >> feb;
        cout << "\n Please enter your bill for mar:";
        cin >> mar;

    // Program needs to ask for values for apr to dec here
    // I am too lazy to type in the code, but you get the idea--right?     ;-)

    // Now average
        ave = (jan + feb + mar + apr + may + ...)/12.0;
    return 0;

}
```

Writing this program is enough to drive someone crazy. It will need twelve input statements, and then the average calculation takes two lines (at least). There must be a better way to do this. We will use an array.

array

list of variables of the same data type referenced with a single name

element

member of an array

array index

the integer value that references a specific element or member of an array

6.2
Array Fundamentals

C++ allows the programmer to declare an *array* (which groups together variables of the same data type), and reference to this group of values can be made with a single name. Each of the array members or *elements* is accessed using an *array index*. An array index is an integer value. The general format for an array declaration is:

```
data_type array_name[ size ];
```

where data_type is the data type (such as float, int, double, etc.), the array_name is the variable name for the array, and size is an integer that represents how many variables are in this array. For the phone bills program, we declare an array of twelve floating point values:

```
float phone_bills[12];
```

The size is often referred to as the ***array dimension***. When a programmer creates a list using one dimension (size) value, as we did with phone_bills, it is referred to as a ***single-dimensional array*** and can be thought of as a single list or as a row of values. These values are stored contiguously in memory.

Figure 6-1 illustrates the phone costs array. It is useful to visualize an array as a group of boxes. Each box represents a separate variable location and each box has its own name. The array index is used to access the individual elements in the array. For example,

```
phone_bills[4] = 34.65;
phone_bills[7] = 83.66;
```

shows how the individual values in the phone bill array are assigned values. More array declaration examples are:

```
int count[1000];        // array of 1000 integers, named count

double rays[200];       // array of 200 double variables, named rays

char name[25];          // array of 25 characters, named name
```

array dimension
the size of the array

single-dimensional array
an array that represents a single list or column of values

6

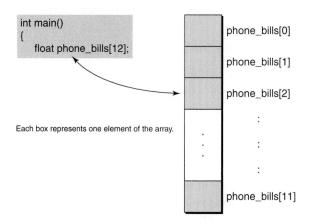

Each box represents one element of the array.

Figure 6-1
Single-Dimensional Array

character string

another name for an array of chars

The last declaration (char name[25];) is an array of characters known as a *character string*. Character strings or character arrays are used for text data such as names, addresses, labels, etc. C++ provides two types of character strings for the programmer. One type is known as a *null-terminated string*. The second type uses the *string class*, which includes object-oriented methods for handling text data. We will cover the null-terminated strings (character string arrays) later in this chapter. The C++ string class is presented in Chapter 10 and Appendix G.

null-terminated string

character string that has a null character at the end of the pertinent data

string class

class in the C++ language for working with text-based information (strings)

zero-indexed

when the first element of an array is referenced using a zero [0]

Arrays in C++ Are Zero Indexed

C++ arrays are referred to as *zero indexed*, which means that the array elements (boxes in Figure 6-1) are numbered starting with zero, *not* one! The name of the first element of any array has zero as the first index, and the last element's name is the size −1 index value. In the phone bill array, the first element (box) is phone_bills[0] and the last element is phone_bills[11].

Some programming languages, such as FORTRAN, allow the programmer to specify the starting array index. C++ does not allow this choice. Some beginning C++ programmers who are used to writing FORTRAN code with a starting index of 1 will try to add an additional array element to the declaration and then ignore the first (index of zero) array element. This technique is not recommended. *All arrays in C++ have the first index value of zero, and the last element is one less than the size.* Do not create your own indexing scheme!

Arrays Are Not Automatically Initialized

Array variables in C++ are not initialized when they are declared, just as singly declared variables in C++ are not initialized. Beginning C++ programmers often assume that numeric arrays are automatically zeroed out (zeros placed in each array element). Be careful not to assume that your arrays are automatically initialized!

One-Dimensional Array Initialization

C++ does not automatically initialize a declared array to any value. However, it is possible to initialize array values (i.e., assign values into the array elements) when the arrays are declared. The general form for initializing the values of a one-dimensional array at the time of declaration is:

```
type array_name [size ] = { list of array values };
```

The list of array values is a list of the initial values for the array elements. Commas must separate the values. The first value in the list is placed in the first element of the array, the second value is placed in the second element, etc.

A floating point array is declared and initialized here:

```
float comp_ratio[4] = { 3.21, 5.32, 0.87, 8.33};
```

This array, named comp_ratio, has four values. Element comp_ratio[0] contains 3.21, comp_ratio[1] contains 5.32, comp_ratio[2] contains 0.87, and comp_ratio[3] contains 8.33.

for Loops and Arrays

When writing software with arrays, the for loop is the programmer's best friend. The for loop provides an efficient method for going through or traversing an array. The index of the loop not only is a counter for the loop, it can also be used as the index value for the array. If you are not comfortable writing for loops, go back to Chapter 3, reread the for loop section, and look at the practice sample programs.

Phone Bills Program   The Phone Bills program can be rewritten with the for loop, and the loop index is used to access each element of our utility costs array. Program 6-1 asks the user to enter the bill amounts for months 1 to 12. Figure 6-2 illustrates how the for loop index variable is used to access the array elements.

```
//Program 6-1 A complete program for finding utility bill average for a year.
#include <iostream.h>
int main()
{
        // Declare variables
                float phone_bills[12];          // sets up an array of 12 elements
                float sum = 0.0, ave;
                int i;                  // loop index will be used to access array elements

        // Obtain monthly billing information
                for(i = 0; i < 12; ++i)
                {
                        cout <<"\n Enter bill for month number: " << i+1 << "=>$";
                        cin >> phone_bills[i];
                }

        // Now calculate the average value. First obtain the sum.
                for(i = 0; i < 12; ++i)
                {
                        sum = sum + phone_bills[i];
                }
                ave = sum/12.0;
                cout << "\n Your average phone bill for 12 months is   $"  << ave;

                return 0;
}
```

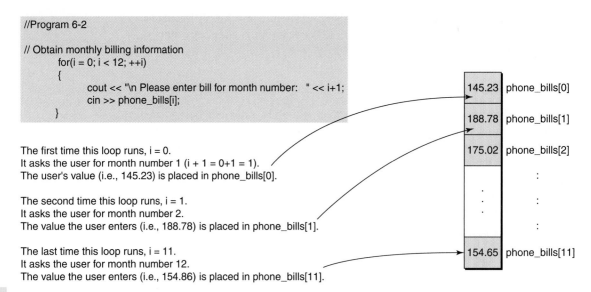

```
//Program 6-2

// Obtain monthly billing information
    for(i = 0; i < 12; ++i)
    {
            cout << "\n Please enter bill for month number:   " << i+1;
            cin >> phone_bills[i];

    }
```

145.23	phone_bills[0]
188.78	phone_bills[1]
175.02	phone_bills[2]

| 154.65 | phone_bills[11] |

The first time this loop runs, i = 0.
It asks the user for month number 1 (i + 1 = 0+1 = 1).
The user's value (i.e., 145.23) is placed in phone_bills[0].

The second time this loop runs, i = 1.
It asks the user for month number 2.
The value the user enters (i.e., 188.78) is placed in phone_bills[1].

The last time this loop runs, i = 11.
It asks the user for month number 12.
The value the user enters (i.e., 154.86) is placed in phone_bills[11].

Figure 6-2
for Loop Index and Array Elements

Figure 6-3 illustrates how this index is then used again when calculating the sum. The for loop index is a convenient tool to use whenever you need to go through an array.

Compression Ratio Example   In Program 6-2, we declare a four-element array (data type = double) and then use four assignment statements to place compression values in each element of the array. Writing the values to the screen, we see that the for loop index is used to access each element. The array is called comp_ratio. The output is shown below:

The compression ratio array contains these four values:
comp_ratio[0] = 3.21
comp_ratio[1] = 5.32
comp_ratio[2] = 0.87
comp_ratio[3] = 8.33

▨ 6.3
A Free Pointer with Every Array

What do you suppose happens if we simply write out the name of the array?

```
cout << comp_ratio;
```

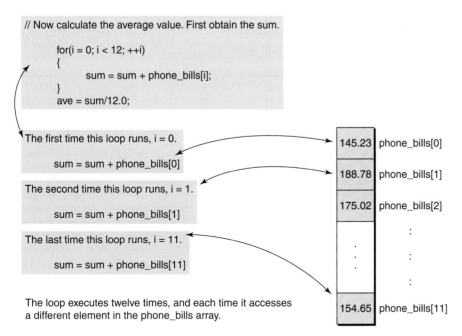

// Now calculate the average value. First obtain the sum.

```
for(i = 0; i < 12; ++i)
{
        sum = sum + phone_bills[i];
}
ave = sum/12.0;
```

The first time this loop runs, i = 0.

    sum = sum + phone_bills[0]

The second time this loop runs, i = 1.

    sum = sum + phone_bills[1]

The last time this loop runs, i = 11.

    sum = sum + phone_bills[11]

The loop executes twelve times, and each time it accesses a different element in the phone_bills array.

145.23	phone_bills[0]
188.78	phone_bills[1]
175.02	phone_bills[2]
154.65	phone_bills[11]

Figure 6-3
Utility Program Sum Calculation

```
//Program 6-2 Compression Ratios
#include <iostream.h>
int main()
{
        // Declare variables
                double comp_ratio[4];        // sets up an array of 4 elements
                comp_ratio[0] = 3.21;
                comp_ratio[1] = 5.32;
                comp_ratio[2] = 0.87;
                comp_ratio[3] = 8.33;

                int i;          // loop index will be used for accessing array elements
                cout << "\n The compression ratio array contains these four values: \n";
                for(i = 0; i < 4; ++i)
                {
                        cout << " comp_ratio[" << i << "] = " << comp_ratio[i] << endl;
                }
                return 0;
}
```

Program 6-3 below declares the comp_ratio array and places a value in each element. We then write the name of the array in the cout statement. Will the C++ compiler stop and give us an error? Will it just write out all the values in the array?

```
//Program 6-3 Compression Ratios without an index
#include <iostream.h>
int main()
{
        // Declare variables
        double comp_ratio[4];           // sets up an array of 4 elements
        comp_ratio[0] = 3.21;
        comp_ratio[1] = 5.32;
        comp_ratio[2] = 0.87;
        comp_ratio[3] = 8.33;


        cout << "\n The compression ratio array without an index: \n";
        cout << " comp_ratio = " << comp_ratio << endl;

        return 0;
}
```

Program 6-3 compiles without error! The output is:

The compression ratio array without an index:
0X0066FDD8

What is going on here? This output looks like a hex address because it *is* a hex address. Actually it is the value of a pointer. Were you thinking, perhaps, that the program would write out all the values in the array? If you did, you have a lot of company. For numeric type arrays, this assumption is wrong. (*Special note:* A character string can be written out just by using the variable's name, as we will soon see. String arrays are handled differently than numeric arrays when doing input and output.)

Array Pointers

array pointer

pointer with the same name as the array that points to the first element of the array

With the declaration of *any* array in C++, the language automatically generates an *array pointer*, which is a pointer of the same data type and the same name, and the pointer will be assigned the address of the zero-element of the array. For example, when you declare the following:

```
float phone_bills[12];
```

your program automatically gets this (see Figure 6-4):

```
float *phone_bills = &phone_bills[0];
```

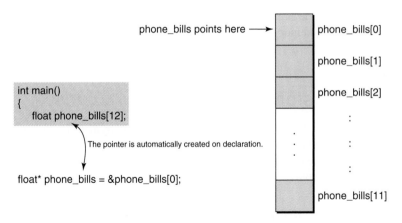

Figure 6-4
An Array Pointer Is Created Whenever an Array Is Declared

This pointer is available and can be used whenever a pointer to the array is needed. If we examine a portion of the compression ratio program one more time, we see that we initially declare our array with this statement:

```
// Declare variables
     double comp_ratio[4];        /* sets up an array of 4 elements
                and a pointer named comp_ratio = &comp_ratio[0]   */
```

and then we assign values into the array elements:

```
          comp_ratio[0] = 3.21;
          comp_ratio[1] = 5.32;
          comp_ratio[2] = 0.87;
          comp_ratio[3] = 8.33;
```

We never actually assign the address of the first element into any pointer—but C++ assigns it automatically. When we write out comp_ratio, the program is writing the value in the array pointer:

```
cout << "\n The compression ratio array without an index: \n";
cout << " comp_ratio = " << comp_ratio << endl;  //writes the pointer value
```

The output is shown below:

The compression ratio array without an index:
0X0066FDD8

The output shows the hexadecimal address contained in the pointer comp_ratio, which is the actual memory address of the element comp_ratio[0].

6.4
One-Dimensional Arrays and Functions

When C was a new language, computer memory was extremely limited and very expensive. The designers of C intentionally created pointers so that a C program would have only one copy of the data, and functions could access this data without having all data variables global to the entire program.

Arrays and Their Pointers

When an array is declared in C++, the language automatically provides a pointer of the same type and name, and it points to the first element of the array. The form is:

```
data_type array_name[ size];      // array declaration
//this occurs too ==>  data_type *array_name = &array_name[0];
```

The usefulness of this pointer will become evident when you learn how arrays and functions work together.

Passing One-Dimensional Arrays to Functions

The name of the array is used in the call statement when an array is passed to a function. Using the name of the array without any array operator brackets [ ] actually passes the address of the array to the function. When the called function uses the array, it is using the calling function's array data. Therefore, sending an array to a function appears to be sending a copy of the array to the function (call by value), but in actuality it is sending an address.

The manner in which C++ handles arrays is memory-efficient. The program has only one copy of an array; the functions do not create their own local copies. This feature of the language is valuable because arrays may be quite large, and creating individual copies of them in functions would be time consuming and a waste of system memory.

A function that uses arrays must indicate the array data type in the prototype and function header line. Using the set of array operator brackets [ ] is how the program identifies the data type as an array. Table 6-1 illustrates two programs: one passing a single float variable to a function and one passing a floating point array. Notice how the square brackets [ ] are used. (Refer to the multidimensional arrays section for two-dimensional or larger arrays and functions.)

The source code in the right column of Table 6-1 contains an array of 100 values. The call statement to Function2 contains the name of the array. This call is

TABLE 6-1

Comparing Single Variables and One-Dimensional Arrays in Functions

Single Float Value Function	Function with a One-Dimensional Array
| ```
// Prototype
void Function1 (float);

int main()
{
   float x;
   Function1(x);   // function call
   return 0;
}

// function body
void Function1(float x)
{
   // function has its own copy of x
   // body of function
}
``` | ```
// Prototype
void Function2 ( float [ ] );

int main()
{
   float q[100];
   Function2( q );    // function call
   return 0;
}

// function body
void Function2(float q[ ] )   //See Note 1
{
   // function actually uses main's q array
   // body of function
}
``` |

Note 1: The address is passed to the function, and main's array data is accessed from the function. Also, for one-dimensional arrays, the size of the array is not needed in the prototype and function header line.

6

actually passing the address, which contains the address of q[0]. In Function2, the declaration of float q[] is declaring a local variable for the Function2, and the function uses normal array syntax to access the elements of the array. However, q in Function2 is really a pointer to main's q array. Function2 is using the calling function's (i.e., main) data directly. This process is illustrated in Figure 6-5.

Array Averaging Program

A common requirement when working with numeric arrays is calculating the average value of the array: a perfect situation for a function. The Average Value of 1D Array program (Program 6-4) uses a function called Ave1D, which returns the average value of a floating point array. We need to pass the array and the number of values in the array to the function, which returns the average value. See Figure 6-6. The output follows:

`The average value of the array is 1049.5`

In this example, the Ave1D function appears to have its own copy of a floating point array, which is incorrect. The function has a pointer only to the calling function's array. If the function changes the array values, it is the calling function's values that have been changed.

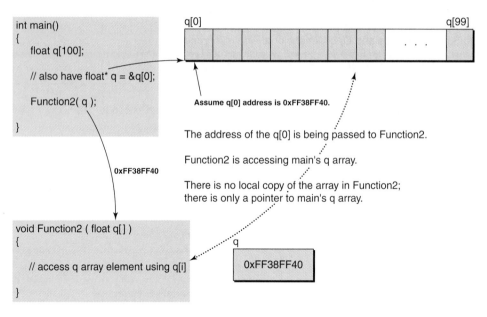

Figure 6-5
Passing Arrays to Functions

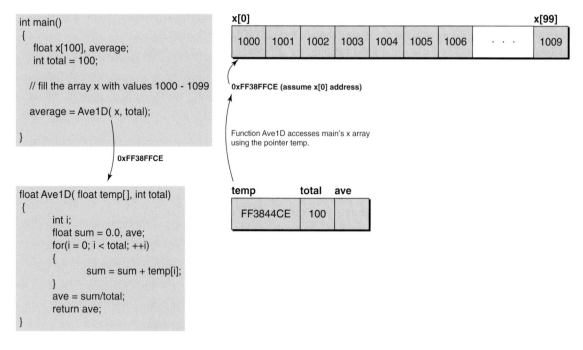

Figure 6-6
Array Averaging Program

Troubleshooting: You Can't "return" an Array from a Function

Beginning C++ programmers often ask, How can I set up a function so that it returns an array to the calling function? The students write perfectly logical source code and attempt to compile it. The compiler blows the whistle and alerts the programmer that he or she is doing something wrong! The two versions of the Gimme5Numbers programs illustrate this situation.

Gimme5Numbers   In the first attempt at writing the Gimme5Numbers program, we try to write the code so that the function returns an array using a return statement. The compiler's messages are listed below the source code, which follows.

```
//Program 6-x Gimme5Numbers First Attempt
//Trying to return an array.  THIS CODE WILL NOT COMPILE!
#include <iostream.h>

int [] Gimme5Numbers( );  //prototype returns an integer array

int main()
{
        int five_nums[5];
        five_nums = Gimme5Numbers();
        return 0;
}


int [] Gimme5Numbers( )
{
        int i, temp[5];
        for(i = 0; i < 5; ++i)
        {
                cout << "\n Enter Number " << i+1;
                cin >> temp[i];
        }
        return( temp );
}
```

The Visual C++ compiler messages appear below:

Compiling...
Gimme5.cpp
Gimme5.cpp(85) : warning C4091: ": ignored on left of 'int' when no variable is declared
Gimme5.cpp(85) : error C2143: syntax error : missing ';' before '['
Gimme5.cpp(85) : error C2143: syntax error : missing ';' before '['
Gimme5.cpp(90) : error C2065: 'Gimme5Numbers' : undeclared identifier
Gimme5.cpp(90) : error C2440: '=' : cannot convert from 'int' to 'int [5]'

```
//Program 6-4  Average Value of 1D Array
#include <iostream.h>

float Ave1D( float [], int);  //prototype passing array to this
int main()
{
        float x[100], average,num = 1000.0;
        int i, total = 100;

//we'll fill x with values 1000 - 1100
        for (i = 0; i < 100; ++ i)
        {
                x[i] = num;
                num++;                // num starts at 1000, incr each time
        }

        average = Ave1D( x, total);
        cout << "\n The average value of the array is " << average << endl;

        return 0;
}

float Ave1D( float temp[], int total)
{
        int i;
        float sum = 0.0, ave;
        for(i = 0; i < total; ++i)
        {
                sum = sum + temp[i];
        }
        ave = sum/total;
        return ave;
}
```

What does GCC have to say about this code?

```
login1:johnston:~/gnu:$ g++ G++_Gimme5.cc
G++_Gimme5.cc:12: parse error before '['
G++_Gimme5.cc: In function 'int main()':
G++_Gimme5.cc:17: warning: implicit declaration of function 'int Gimme5Numbers(...)'
G++_Gimme5.cc:17: incompatible types in assignment of 'int' to 'int[5]'
G++_Gimme5.cc: At top level:
G++_Gimme5.cc:21: parse error before '['
G++_Gimme5.cc:24: parse error before ';'
G++_Gimme5.cc:26: syntax error before '>'
```

Neither compiler says, "You can't return an array." For a function to fill and return an array, the array must be declared initially in the calling function. The array address is then passed to the function. The second version of the code (Program 6-5) will work with no problems, as you can see in Figure 6-7. The output is shown on apge 212:

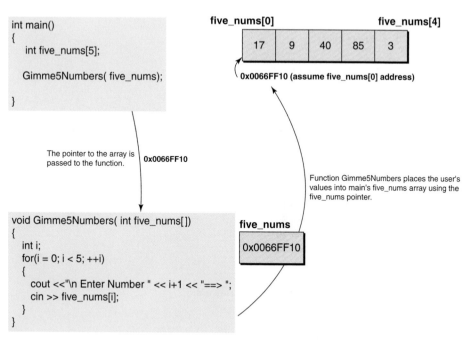

Figure 6-7
Gimme5Numbers Program

```
//Program 6-5 Gimme5Numbers Second Attempt
// Declare the array in the calling function and fill it in the called function.
#include <iostream.h>

void Gimme5Numbers(int [] );   //prototype passes an array to the function

int main()
{
      int five_nums[5], i;

      cout << "\n Welcome to Gimme5Numbers Program \n\n";
      Gimme5Numbers( five_nums );
      cout << "\n The 5 values in the five_nums array are: \n";
      for(i = 0; i < 5; ++i)
      {
            cout << "Element # " << i << " = " << five_nums[i] << endl;
      }
      return 0;
}

void Gimme5Numbers( int five_nums[] )
{
      int i;
      for(i = 0; i < 5; ++i)
      {
            cout << "\n Enter Number " << i+1 << "==> ";
            cin >> five_nums[i];
      }
}
```

Welcome to Gimme5Numbers Program

Enter Number 1 ==> 17
Enter Number 2 ==> 9
Enter Number 3 ==> 40
Enter Number 4 ==> 85
Enter Number 5 ==> 3

The 5 values in the five_nums array are:
Element #0 = 17
Element #1 = 9
Element #2 = 40
Element #3 = 85
Element #4 = 3

In the Gimme5Numbers function, notice that the declaration of the five_nums array does not contain the size value. In the function, we write the code to access the array values as if five_nums was indeed a real array. The five_nums is the name of the pointer that is pointing to main's five_nums array, and the function writes the five numbers directly into main's array. No return statement is required in the function because nothing is returned to the calling function via a return statement.

6.5
Character Strings

Most programs of any size have some sort of character data. This data can range from simple name and address information, to text input from the user, to complicated encryption schemes. If you are writing a program for automobiles, you may have text data in the form of make, model, color, vehicle identification number, and license plate number. Typically, character data are maintained as one-dimensional arrays, and these arrays are known as character strings.

C++ has two ways of handling character strings. The first method described in this chapter is the classic C language character string. It is a one-dimensional character array and is null-terminated; that is, the character array contains the characters and has a zero value, known as the **null character** ('\0'), at the end of the character data. This null character indicates the end of the text data. (The second C++ character string technique is new in C++ and involves using a string class. See Chapter 10 and Appendix G.)

The basic format for declaring a null-terminated character string is

null character
"zero" character, '\0'

6

```
char variable_name[ size ];
```

where the variable_name is the name of the string, and size is an integer value that represents the number of characters in the string. Remember, the string must contain a null character, so always use a size value large enough to include this extra character.

Character String Initialization

Initializing character strings follows the same format as initializing numeric valued arrays. It is possible to initialize this string by using the comma-separated list. Here we illustrate how we initialize the string and put a null character at the end:

```
// Filling line with I love C++! uses 12 of the 15 elements.
// Don't forget, the null character must be placed at the end of the text.
char line[15] = {  'I',  ' ',  'l',  'o',  'v',  'e',  ' ',  'C',  '+',  '+',  '!',  '\0'};
```

Once the program performs this declaration and initialization statement, the line[0] contains the letter I, line[1] contains a space, and so on. If all elements are not initialized, C++ fills the remaining elements with zeros, which effectively null-terminates the string for you.

C++ allows you to initialize a string by using a string constant, and the computer adds the null character for you. See Figure 6-8.

```
char line[15] = "I love C++!";
```

The Null Character

The C++ programmer must ensure that the character string has been null-terminated, which means that the character string has a null character ('\0') at the end of the data. The null character is a zero ('\0'), and C++ uses the null character to indicate where the end of the data is located.

Many of the string functions provided in the string library and the output functions in iostream require a null character to work correctly. The following two sample programs show how important the null character is when writing character strings to the screen. In the first example, the strings are initialized in two ways: one uses the comma-separated list and the second uses a string constant. The program adds null characters to the elements not used in the arrays. Figure 6-9 shows the character strings str and line after they have been initialized. When cout writes a

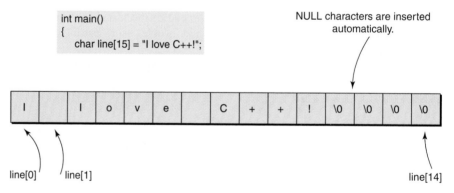

Figure 6-8
Character String Array

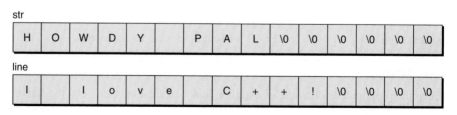

Figure 6-9
str and line Character Strings After Initialization

string to the screen, the null character indicates where the end of the string is located.

```cpp
// Program 6-String and Line
// Our friend, the null character, is put into the strings by C++.
#include <iostream.h>
int main()
{
    // Declare character strings
    char str[15] = { 'H', 'O', 'W', 'D', 'Y', ' ', 'P', 'A', 'L'};
    char line[15] = "I love C++!";

    cout << str << endl;
    cout << line;
    return 0;
}
```

The output appears as follows:

HOWDY PAL
I love C++!

Now we just declare our string and use assignment statements to place elements in the string new_str. We do not put in the null character. When we write this string to the screen, the cout function does not see a null character and it does not know where the end of the string is located. See Figure 6-10 for an illustration.

```cpp
//Program 6-Our friend, the null character, forgotten!
#include <iostream.h>
int main()
{
    // Declare character strings
    char new_str[15];
    new_str[0] = 'H';
    new_str[1] = 'O';
    new_str[2] = 'W';
    new_str[3] = 'D';
    new_str[4] = 'Y';
    cout << new_str << endl;
    return 0;
}
```

The output is:

HOWDYïïïïïïïïï8pe

new_str

| H | O | W | D | Y | ? | ? | ? | ? | ? | ? | ? | ? | ? | ? |

? = not sure what is in the memory. We can regard these entries as trash.
The cout function will print all fifteen characters on the screen.

Figure 6-10
Character String Without Terminating Null Character

As you can see, the computer has trouble determining where the end of the string is located because we did not put a null character in the string. To have our new_str print correctly to the screen, we need to add a terminating null character into the string:

```
new_str[0] = 'H';
new_str[1] = 'O';
new_str[2] = 'W';
new_str[3] = 'D';
new_str[4] = 'Y';
new_str[5] = '\0';   // we add the NULL character to [5]
```

This string is shown in Figure 6-11. Now when cout prints this string, it sees the null character and will print just the following:

HOWDY

Do not despair! The null character will not be your downfall, for there are many "null-helpers" in C++. The majority of string functions and input functions

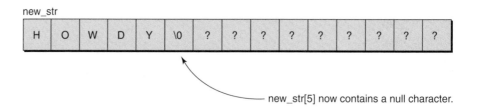

new_str[5] now contains a null character.

The cout function will print the first five characters and stop when it sees the null character.

Figure 6-11
Character String with Terminating Null Character

place a null character in the string automatically for you. You must be aware of the null and be mindful of its importance, but take comfort that helpers are present.

Character String Input

There are several iostream library functions used primarily for receiving character string data. These functions provide methods for reading data into strings. The programmer places the name of the character string in the function call, and the function fills the string variable with character data. When reading the description of these functions, programmers can be confused by the new terminology.

Visualize data that is being read into a program as a stream of characters. These characters will be placed into data variables. The functions that read character data need to know where to put the characters (name of the character string) and when to stop reading the characters for each of the variables. Also, we need to handle the leftover characters in the stream. Before we examine the various functions, review Table 6-2 to be sure that you understand the new terminology. Table 6-3 describes the most commonly used functions. Examples are provided in Table 6-4.

The standard cin function can also be used to read character data, but it should be used with caution. The cin function reads character data until it sees a whitespace character, at which point it stops reading and places a null character in the string.

The get function leaves a newline or the delimiter in the input stream, whereas the getline function removes the newline or delimiter character from the input stream. For this reason, using the getline function is preferable when reading character data from the keyboard or file.

Who Do You Love?   Program 6-6, along with Figure 6-12, illustrates two forms of reading text from the keyboard. The getline and cin functions are employed to

▌ TABLE 6-2
New Terminology for Reading Character Data

Term	Definition
extract	To pull a character out of the stream and put it into a variable.
max	The maximum number of characters to read into a variable.
delimiter	A special character used by the programmer to tell the program when to stop reading characters. If you select an x as the delimiter, the delimiter function will read characters until it sees an x. The function then stops reading the characters for that specific variable.
null-terminated	Having a null character, \0, at the end of the character string.
newline	\n or the Enter key

TABLE 6-3
Character String Functions in iostream Library

Function	Purpose
get(*ch*)	Extracts one character from the stream and places it into the variable named *ch*.
get(*string*, max)	Extracts characters from the stream and places them into variable *string* until either max − 1 characters have been read or a newline is found or an end of file.
	The string is null-terminated by get().
	If the newline is found, it is not extracted and remains in the input stream until the next read operation.
get(*string*, max, delimiter)	Extracts characters from the stream and places them into the variable *string* until either max − 1 characters have been read, the delimiter character has been found, or the end of file is reached.
	The string will be null-terminated by get().
	The delimiter character is left in the stream until the next read.
getline(string, max)	Extracts characters from the stream and places them into the variable string until either max − 1 characters have been read, a newline is found, or the end of file has been reached.
	The string will be null-terminated by getline().
	If a newline is encountered, it is extracted from the stream but not put into the string.
getline(string, max, delimiter)	Extracts characters from the stream and places them into the string until max − 1 characters have been read, the delimiter character has been found, or the end of file has been reached.
	The string will be null-terminated by getline().
	If the delimiter character has been found, it is extracted from the stream and not put in the string.

read text data into character strings. The program asks the user to enter a phrase two times, and each phrase is read by a different method. The program asks the user to enter I love C++! twice. It then writes the following strings to the screen:

Text 1 = I love C++!
Text 2 = I

What happened? The cin.getline(text1,14) reads the eleven characters in our input phrase and once it sees the newline, it null-terminates the text1 string. The cin statement reads until it sees a space and then null-terminates the string. Thus, only

Examples of Character String Functions

Function	Example
get(*ch*)	```char one;``` ```cin.get(one);```

get(*string*, max)	```char name[30];```
	 ```cin.get(name,30);```
	 ```/*reads up to 29 characters and adds terminating null \0 The \n```
	 ```remains in the input stream. */```

get(*string*, max, delimiter)	```char name[30];```
	 ```cin.get(name,30, 'x');```
	 ```/*reads up to 29 characters or until it sees an x in the stream and```
	 ```adds terminating null \0```
	 ```The \n or delimiter remains in the input stream. */```

getline(string, max)	```char name[30];```
	 ```cin.getline(name,30);```
	 ```/*reads up to 29 characters and adds terminating null \0 The \n```
	 ```is removed from the input stream. */```

getline(string, max, delimiter)	```char name[30];```
	 ```cin.getline(name,30, 'x');```
	 ```/*reads up to 29 characters or until it sees an x in the stream and```
	 ```then adds terminating null \0```
	 ```The \n or delimiter is removed from the input stream. */```

the "I" is placed into text2. Again, refer to Figure 6-12. Where is the rest of the second phrase (the "love C++!")? It remains in the input queue until we either read from the keyboard again or terminate the program. Our next example illustrates this situation.

A Handy Tool: cin.ignore   In Program 6-7, we ask the user to enter three phrases. We use the delimiter "C" in the getline statement for text1, a cin statement for text2, and a standard cin.getline for text3. With the delimiter, C++ stops reading when it sees the "C." The remaining characters are left in the input stream. The cin, too, leaves characters in the stream after it sees the first blank. We make use of the cin.ignore function to throw away characters in the stream so that these extra stream characters aren't read accidentally. Figure 6-13 illustrates what would happen without the ignore statements. Program 6-7 shows the correct code.

```
//Program 6-6 Who Do You Love?
//Using cin.getline and cin to read character strings.
#include <iostream.h>
int main()
{
    char text1[15], text2[15] ;
    cout << "\n Using getline(text1,14)  Enter ==> I love C++!    ";
    cin.getline(text1,14);

    cout << "\n Using cin >> text2   Enter ==> I love C++!    ";
    cin >> text2;

    cout << "\n Text1 = " << text1 ;
    cout << "\n Text2 = " << text2 << endl;
    return 0;
}
```

6

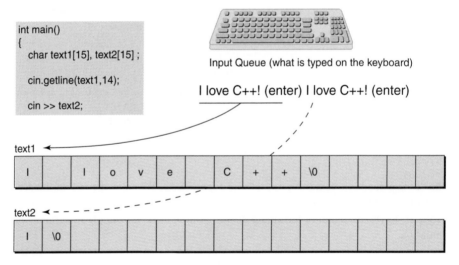

Figure 6-12
Reading Text Data into Character Strings

```
//Program 6-7 Who Do You Love? Part Two
//We will use three different ways to read a phrase.
//We use a cin.ignore to flush the enter key from the input queue.

#include <iostream.h>
int main()
{
      char text1[15], text2[15], text3[15];
      cout <<" \n Who Do You Love? Part Two \n\n";

      cout <<" \n Using getline(text1,14,'C') Enter ==> I love C++!   ";
      cin.getline(text1, 14, 'C');
      cin.ignore(20,'\n')
      cout << "  \223
n                     Output Text1 ==> " << text1;

      cout << "\n\n Using cin >> text2              Enter ==> I love C++!   ";
      cin >> text2;
      cin.ignore(20,'\n');
      cout << "\n                     Output Text2 ==> " << text2;

      cout << "\n\n Using getline(text3,14)      Enter==> I love C++!   ";
      cin.getline(text3, 14);
      cout << "\n                     Output Text3 ==> " << text3;

      cout << "\n\n\n      Don't you love C++?" << endl;
      return 0;
```

The output is shown below:

Who Do You Love? Part Two

Using getline(text1, 14, 'C') Enter ==> I love C++! I love C++!
                   Output Text1 ==> I love

Using cin >> text2   Enter ==> I love C++! I love C++!
                   Output Text2 ==> I

Using getline(text3, 14)   Enter==> I love C++! I love C++!
                   Output Text3 ==> I love C++!

   Don't you love C++?

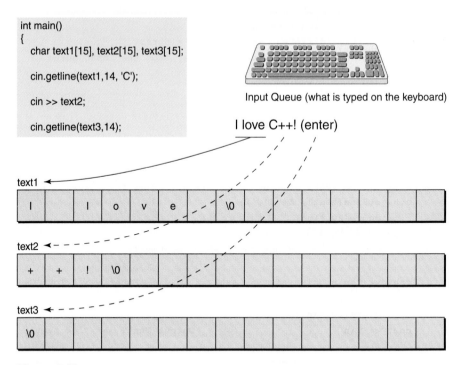

```
int main()
{
    char text1[15], text2[15], text3[15];

    cin.getline(text1,14, 'C');

    cin >> text2;

    cin.getline(text3,14);
```

Input Queue (what is typed on the keyboard)

I love C++! (enter)

text1

| I | | l | o | v | e | | \0 | | | | | | | |

text2

| + | + | ! | \0 | | | | | | | | | | | |

text3

| \0 | | | | | | | | | | | | | | |

Figure 6-13
More Reading Text Data into Character Strings

Your Name Please   If your program needs to read just character data, the get-line function is preferred. In the Your Name Please program, we ask the user for information that is placed into character strings.

```cpp
//Program 6-Short Sample-Your Name Please
//Using cin.getline to read character strings.
#include <iostream.h>
int main()
{
    char name[25], movie[35], color[15];
    cout << "\n Hi User! \n\n Please enter your name:   ";
    cin.getline(name,25);
    cout << "\n Now what is your favorite movie? ";
    cin.getline(movie, 35 );
    cout << "\n Favorite color? ";
    cin.getline(color, 15 );
    cout << "\n Your Name = " << name <<
            "\n Favorite Movie = " << movie <<
```

```
        "\n Favorite Color = " << color;
    return 0;
}
```

If Claire Jaramillo entered her name, *Young Frankenstein*, and blue, the output would be:

Your Name = Claire Jaramillo
Favorite Movie = Young Frankenstein
Favorite Color = blue

Troubleshooting: How Old Are You, Claire?   The next program asks the user to enter both character and numeric data, including his or her name and several more pieces of personal data. We use the cin.getline for character data and the cin statement to read the numeric data. A problem occurs when this program executes (it compiles correctly). Can you find the cause of the problem?

```
//Program 6-8Broken PROBLEM PROGRAM  DOES NOT WORK CORRECTLY
//Using cin.getline and cin to read user information.
#include <iostream.h>
int main()
{
        char name[20], football_team[25];
        int age, num_kids;

// ask user for name, age, football team, and number of kids
        cout<< "\n  Enter your name: ";
        cin.getline(name,20);
        cout << "\n  Enter your age: ";
        cin >> age;
        cout << "\n  What is your favorite football team?     ";
        cin.getline(football_team,25);
        cout << "\n  How many kids do you have?     ";
        cin >> num_kids;

// write info out to screen
        cout << endl << name << ",  your team is " << football_team <<
        "\nYou are " << age << " years old and have " << num_kids << "kids." << endl;

        return 0;

}
```

The code appears straightforward. When the program runs, Claire, the user, can enter her name and age. However, the program does not wait for her to enter

Dallas Cowboys (her favorite team). It does stop for her to enter two kids. The output from the program is:

Claire, your team is
You are 25 years old and have 2 kids.

Have you figured out the error yet? Go back and read how cin and cin.getline handle the Enter key.

Reading Both Numeric and Character Data

Two Approaches   If you need to read integers and character string data (a common occurrence) many techniques are available. First, if you want to use the cin statement, the Enter key that remains in the stream must be removed in some manner. One approach is to use the cin.ignore function to flush the extraneous characters in the stream.

```
// ask user for name, age, football     team, and number of kids
      cout<< "\n  Enter your name:     ";
      cin.getline(name,20);
      cout << "\n  Enter your age:     ";
      cin >> age;
      cin.ignore(10,'\n');
```

Another (less elegant) approach uses a get function to read a single character out of the stream. Here we read the Enter key into the character variable named junk.

```
// One way to get rid of the Enter key in the stream
      char name[20], football_team[25];
      int age, num_kids;
      char junk;
```

```
// ask user for name, age, football team, and number of kids
      cout<< "\n  Enter your name:   ";
      cin.getline(name,20);
      cout << "\n  Enter your age:   ";
      cin >> age;
      cin.get(junk);   //this pulls out the enter key
      cout << "\n  What is your favorite football team?   ";
      cin.getline(football_team,25);
      cout << "\n  How many kids do you have?   ";
      cin >> num_kids;
      cin.get(junk);
```

> **Caution!** Many programs behave badly if the user enters nonnumeric data when cin is expecting a number. It can either lock the program or cause the text to become stuck in an infinite scrolling pattern. Unless the programmer has absolute control over what data is being entered, it is best not to use a cin statement.

Preferred Approach   The safe approach for reading numeric and character data is to use a getline for reading numeric values. This method is accomplished by reading the numeric value into a character string. The *atoi* function converts ASCII characters to integers. The *atol* function converts ASCII characters to a long int. Both the atoi and atol functions are provided in the standard library. The *atof* function converts a string to a double or floating point value. (The atof function is provided in the math library.) Using these functions is preferred because, if the user enters some nonnumeric information, the atoi, atol, and atof functions (in Visual C++) return a zero value. See Program 6-9.

Special note: The atoi function, along with atof and atol, will convert the character data into numeric data—as long as the string contains valid information. If the string contains invalid data, the return value is undefined by the ISO standard; however, many implementations, including Microsoft's Visual C++, will return a zero, which may cause a problem if the program must distinguish between a real zero and an error zero. There are other string-to-number functions (strtod, strtol, etc.) that offer more control over the conversion. These functions return null pointers if the data are invalid, and they are more complicated to use. These functions are also in C's standard library.

atoi function
in the standard library; converts a character string into an integer

atol function
in the standard library; converts a character string into a long integer

atof function
in the math library; converts a character string into a float or double

6

Character String Functions Provided in C++

The C++ standard libraries include two libraries that provide the programmer with several useful functions (such as the atoi function shown above) for working with character strings. Tables 6-5 and 6-6 illustrate the prototype and call statements for these functions. Remember, you need to include only the appropriate library (string.h or stdlib.h). The prototypes are provided as a reference. (You should get used to reading function prototypes to understand fully how the functions work.)

The prototypes for the character string functions show character pointers as input (char*). Remember that C++ provides a pointer to the first element of the array for every array that is declared. When we use the array name, we are simply using the pointer to the array.

The *strcmp* function can determine alphabetical order relationships by using the numeric codes assigned by the ASCII convention; that is, the letter A is assigned decimal value 65, B is 66, C is 67, etc. If we are comparing Apples to Bananas, strcmp will return a negative value because A (97) is less than B (98). Refer to Appendix D, "ASCII Character Codes." The practice programs at the end of this chapter illustrate the use of a few of these functions.

strcmp function
in the string library; compares two character strings for sameness

```
//Program 6-9 How Old Are You? A Better Way
//Using cin.getline to read integer and character strings.
#include <iostream.h>
#include <stdlib.h>          //used for atoi function

int main()
{
      char name[20], football_team[25];
      int age, num_kids;
      char temp[10];

// ask user for name, age, football team, and number of kids
      cout<< "\n  Enter your name:  ";
      cin.getline(name,20);
      cout << "\n  Enter your age:  ";
      cin.getline(temp,10);
      age = atoi(temp);
      cout << "\n  What is your favorite football team?  ";
      cin.getline(football_team,25);
      cout << "\n  How many kids do you have?  ";
      cin.getline(temp,10);
      num_kids = atoi(temp);
// write info out to screen
      cout << endl << name << ",  your team is " << football_team <<
      "\nYou are " << age << " years old and have " << num_kids << "kids." << endl;
      return 0;
}
```

6.6
Multidimensional Arrays

multidimensional array

an array that represents a table (rows and columns) or a layered table

It is possible to declare a ***multidimensional array*** (an array that represents a table with rows and columns) in C++. The declaration for a two-dimensional array is:

```
type array_name [number of rows][number of columns];
```

The only difference between a one-dimensional array and a two-dimensional array is that the two-dimensional array has a second size specification within a second set of brackets. A three-dimensional array is declared with rows, columns, and height (or layers) as:

```
type array_name [number of rows][number of columns][number of layers];
```

TABLE 6-5
Functions in string.h

Function Prototype[a] and Function Name	Purpose and Example[b]

`void strcat(char*, char*);`
 	
`strcat(s1,s2);`
	Concatenates (hooks together) s2 on the end of s1.
	
	`char s1[30] = "I love C++";`
	`char s2[10] = "green tea";`
	
	`strcat(s1,s2);`
	
	`cout << s1;  // writes I love C++green tea`

`void strcpy(char*, char*);`
 	
`strcpy(s1,s2);`
	Copies s2 into s1.
	
	`char s1[30], s2[30] = "I love C++";`
	
	`strcpy(s1, s2);`
	
	`cout << s1;  // writes I love C++`

`int strcmp(char*, char*);`
 	
`int n;`
`n = strcmp(s1, s2);`
or
 	
`if(strcmp(s1,"yes")==0)`
	Compares s1 to s2, returns 0 if same, <0 if s1 < s2 and > 0 if s1 > s2.
	Note: Often used in if or while statements or used to alphabetize words.
	`char s1[15] = "Apples";`
	`char s2[15] = "Bananas";`
	
	`if(strcmp(s1,"Apples") ==0) // checks to see if s1 is Apples`
	
	`if(strcmp(s1, s2) < 0) // if true, s1 is before s2 in the alphabet`

`char * strstr(char*, char*);`
 	
`char *char_ptr;`
 	
`char_ptr = strstr(s1,s2);`
	Returns a pointer to the first occurrence of s2 in s1, or NULL if s2 is not found.
	`char s1[50] = "The rain in Spain is mainly on the plain.";`
	`char s2[10] = "elephant"`
	`char s3[10] = "rain";`
	`char *char_ptr;`
	
	`char_ptr = strstr(s1,s2);  //char_ptr is NULL since elephant is not in s1`
	`char_ptr = strstr(s1,s3); //char_ptr points to "r"`

`int strlen(char *);`
 	
`int length;`
`length = strlen(s1);`
	Returns an integer value length of string not including terminating null.
	`int length;`
	`char s1[25] = "I love C++!";`
	`length = strlen(s1);   // length is 11`

[a]Prototypes are given for reference only. The user needs to include only: `#include <string.h>`
[b]Assumes all strings are null-terminated.

TABLE 6-6
String to Numeric Functions

Prototype[a] and Function Name	Purpose[b] and Example

`double atof(char *);`
`#include <math.h>`
 	
`double x;`
 	
`x = atof(s1);`
	Returns a double value, converts s1 to a double value.
	
	`char s1[30];`
	`double x;`
	`cout <<"\nEnter a double. ";`
	`cin.getline(s1,30);` `// user enters 3.14159`
	`x = atof(s1);` `// x now has 3.14159`

`long atol(char *);`
`#include <stdlib.h>`
 	
`long y;`
 	
`y = atol(s1)`
	Returns a long value, converts s1 to a long integer.
	
	`char s1[30];`
	`long y;`
	`cout <<"\n Enter a long integer. ";`
	`cin.getline(s1,30);` `// user enters 50000`
	`y = atol(s1);` `// y now has 50000`

`int atoi(char *);`
`#include <stdlib.h>`
 	
`int z;`
 	
`z = atoi(s1)`
	Returns an integer value, converts s1 to an integer.
	
	`char s1[30];`
	`int z;`
	`cout <<"\n Enter an integer. ";`
	`cin.getline(s1,30);` `// user enters 3`
	`z = atoi(s1);`

[a]Prototypes are given for reference only. The user needs to include only the appropriate library file.
[b]If the string is not a valid numeric value, then the atof, atol, and atoi functions return a zero value.

Figure 6-14 illustrates one-, two-, and three-dimensional array declarations and the manner in which the elements of the array can be visualized.

Two-Dimensional Array Initialization

Two-dimensional arrays can be initialized so that the rows of the array are filled first. Figure 6-15 shows a two-dimensional array that is three rows by four columns. To initialize this array, the following statement is required:

```
int grid[3][4] = { 1, 2, 3, 4, 5, 6, 7, 8, 9, 10, 11, 12 };
```

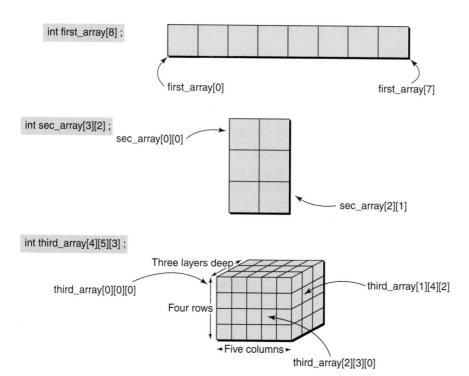

Figure 6-14
One-, Two-, and Three-Dimensional Arrays

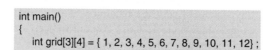

```
int main()
{
    int grid[3][4] = { 1, 2, 3, 4, 5, 6, 7, 8, 9, 10, 11, 12} ;
```

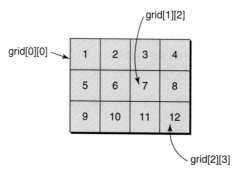

Figure 6-15
Initializing Two-Dimensional Arrays

Another way to write it (to make it easier to visualize) is:

```
int grid[3][4] = { 1, 2, 3, 4,
                   5, 6, 7, 8,
                   9, 10, 11, 12 };
```

Nested for Loops and Two-Dimensional Arrays

Two-dimensional arrays require two indices, and the indices typically need to vary. Nested for loops offer an easy way to set up and keep track of these indices. You may name the integer index variables appropriately so that the code is easy to read.

If we set up a two-dimensional array called grid that is 100 rows by 50 columns, nested for loops will be used to access each array variable and to place zero in each element. In the code below, this set of nested for loops will traverse the array, moving across each row.

```
float grid [100][50];            //2D array of 100 rows by 50 columns
int row, col;
for(row = 0 ; row < 100; ++row)            //outer loop
{
      for(col = 0; col < 50; ++col)            //inner loop
      {
            grid[row][col] = 0.0;
      }
}
```

If we take a closer look at the assignment statement in the inner part of the for loops, we see that this statement will be executed a total of 5000 times. Each time the program reaches this statement, row and column indices are different. Figure 6-16 shows the exact order in which the grid elements are accessed.

Utility Costs Program with Two-Dimensional Array

By expanding the phone bills program, we can add the additional costs for electricity and water for each of the twelve months with a two-dimensional array. This array is shown in Figure 6-17. The array declaration is:

```
float util_costs[12][3];            // set up 12 rows by 3 columns
```

This array now requires two indices to access each element of the array. The rows represent each month, and column 0 holds the phone costs, column 1 holds the electricity costs, and column 2 holds the water costs. (If you wish to build this array so that we keep the variable names "phone," "electric," and "water," you must use a data structure, which is covered in Chapter 7.) Nested for loops are used to traverse

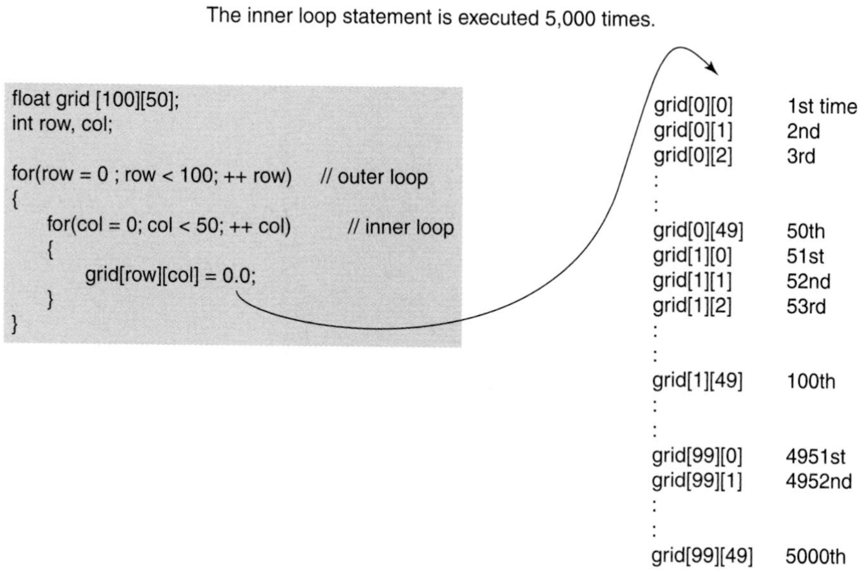

The inner loop statement is executed 5,000 times.

```
float grid [100][50];
int row, col;

for(row = 0 ; row < 100; ++ row)     // outer loop
{
    for(col = 0; col < 50; ++ col)       // inner loop
    {
        grid[row][col] = 0.0;
    }
}
```

grid[0][0]	1st time
grid[0][1]	2nd
grid[0][2]	3rd
:	:
:	:
grid[0][49]	50th
grid[1][0]	51st
grid[1][1]	52nd
grid[1][2]	53rd
:	:
:	:
grid[1][49]	100th
:	:
:	:
grid[99][0]	4951st
grid[99][1]	4952nd
:	:
:	:
grid[99][49]	5000th

Figure 6-16
Accessing Elements 100 × 50 Two-Dimensional Array

6

the two-dimensional array. In the program below, we declare this two-dimensional array and the array is filled with values. (See the comments in the code for descriptions of various techniques for the data input.) Then we calculate the individual total cost for each of the three utilities and a total for all three utilities combined.

```
//Program 6-Utility Costs with Miraculous Input.
#include <iostream.h>
int main()
{
    // Declare variables
    float util_costs[12][3];
    int row, col;                   //loop indices
    float phone = 0.0, water = 0.0, elec = 0.0;
    float sum = 0.0, total_cost;

    /* A miracle occurs here and all 36 values for the year are placed in the
    array elements. This can be accomplished in three ways:
    1. asking the user to enter 36 values or
    2. we can initialize all 36 values with assign statements in the program or
    3. we can read the data from a data file.

    Now we use a nested for loop to traverse the array column by column   */
```

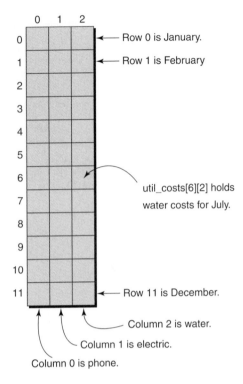

```
int main()
{
    float util_costs[12][3];
```

0   1   2

0   ← Row 0 is January.
1   ← Row 1 is February
2
3
4
5
6   util_costs[6][2] holds
7   water costs for July.
8
9
10
11 ← Row 11 is December.

Twelve rows, one for each month

Column 2 is water.
Column 1 is electric.
Column 0 is phone.

Figure 6-17
Utility Costs Program with a Two-Dimensional Array

```
for(col = 0; col < 3; ++col)  // 1st loop for columns == elec, phone, water
{
        for (row = 0; row < 12; ++row)  // second loop for the 12 months
        {
                sum = sum + util_costs[row][col];     //sum down the column
                        //remember, col stays the same as row goes from 0 to 11
        }

        //assign the sum into the correct total variable
        if(col == 0) phone = sum;
        else if(col == 1) elec = sum;
        else water = sum;

        //zero the sum for the next time column
        sum = 0.0;
}
// Add the three utilities for a total value.
total_cost = elec + phone + water;
```

```
        //write out cost information
        cout << "\n The Total Utility Cost per year:" << total_cost;
        cout << "\n Electric = " << elec << " Phone = " << phone
              << " Water = " << water;
        return 0;
}
```

A nested for loop is the preferred method for accessing a two-dimensional array element. It takes practice to set the loop values and position the indices correctly. We will do another two-dimensional array example in the practice section of this chapter.

6.7
Multidimensional Arrays and Functions

Two-, three-, and higher dimensional arrays require that the programmer specify all but the beginning array size in the prototype and function header line. For example, if a three-dimensional array is passed to a function, the necessary statements are:

```
void MyFunc( float [][3][7] );  // function prototype includes sizes

float m[2][3][7];    // declaration of array

MyFunc( m );   // call uses the array name

void MyFunc ( float m [][3][7] )  // function header line has sizes
```

Revisit Utility Costs Program

The Utility Costs program has been rewritten to use a CalculateTotals function. Because this function must return totals for each utility as well as a total cost, pointers to the individual totals are used.

```
//Program 6-Utility Costs with Calculate Total Function.
#include <iostream.h>
float CalculateTotals(float [][3], float *, float *, float *);
int main()
{
        float util_costs[12][3];                    // Declare variables
        float phone, water, elec;
        float total_cost;
/* A miracle occurs here and all 36 values for the year are placed in the
        array elements. */
        total_cost = CalculateTotals(util_costs, &elec, &phone, &water);
        //write out cost information
```

6

```
            cout << "\n The Total Utility Cost per year:" << total_cost;
            cout << "\n Electric = " << elec << " Phone = " << phone
                    << " Water = " << water;
            return 0;
    }
    float CalculateTotals(float utils[][3], float *e_ptr, float *p_ptr, float *w_ptr)
    {
            float total, sum = 0.0;
            int col, row;
            for(col = 0; col < 3; ++col) // 1st loop for columns == phone, elec, water
            {
                    for (row = 0; row < 12; ++row) // second loop for the 12 months
                    {
                            sum = sum + utils[row][col];        //sum down the column
                                    //remember, col stays the same as row goes from 0 to 11
                    }
                    //assign the sum into the correct total variable
                    if(col == 0) *p_ptr = sum;
                    else if(col == 1) *e_ptr = sum;
                    else *w_ptr = sum;
                    sum = 0.0;                           //zero the sum for the next time column
            }
            // Add the three utilities for a total value.
            total = *e_ptr + *p_ptr + *w_ptr;
            return total;
    }
```

Snow White: Two-Dimensional Array of Names Program

Snow White's software can use an array to keep track of the dwarfs' names. Using a two-dimensional array of character strings in C++ is a convenient way to maintain a list of text-type variables such as names or labels. One technique for initializing a list of names involves declaration and initialization in one statement. Program 6-10 will set up an array for Snow White that will initialize the dwarfs' names and then call a function to print the names to the screen. The program output appears as follows:

Dwarf #1 is Doc
Dwarf #2 is Sleepy
Dwarf #3 is Dopey
Dwarf #4 is Grumpy
Dwarf #5 is Sneezy
Dwarf #6 is Bashful
Dwarf #7 is Happy

```
//Program 6-10 Snow White and Character String Array.
#include <iostream.h>
void WriteNames( char [][15]);    //prototype

int main()
{
    // Declare and initialize the array
    char dwarfs[7][15] = { "Doc", "Sleepy", "Dopey", "Grumpy", "Sneezy",
        "Bashful", "Happy" };

    WriteNames(dwarfs);
    return 0;
}


void WriteNames(char dwarfs[][15])
{
    int i;
    for (i = 0; i < 7; ++i)
    {

        cout << "Dwarf # " << i+1 << " is " << dwarfs[i] << endl;
    }
}
```

6.8
Array Out of Bounds

What happens if you write code like that shown here?

```
float x[100];          //declare an array of 100 elements
```

Then suppose that you proceed to access values beyond the one hundredth element. (Remember x[99] is the last legally declared value in the array.)

```
for(i = 0; i < 500; ++i)
{
    x[i] = 0.0;    // zero out the array values from x[0] to x[499]
}
```

The question is, What does the compiler and program do when this type of C++ code is encountered? The compiler compiles this code. The compiler is reading the code for syntax errors. The declaration:

```
float x[100];                    //declare an array of 100 elements
```

looks correct. The compiler knows what a float is; the variable name is legal; and an array requires square brackets and an integer size, a semicolon at the end, and then a comment. The compiler reports that all is well.

What about the for loop?

```
for(i = 0; i < 500; ++i)
{
        x[i] = 0.0;       // zero values from x[0] to x[499]     |:-0
}
```

The compiler reports that the for loop is acceptable. It is written correctly. If you are wondering about the fact that the loop will run 500 times, this concern is not a compiler issue. The compiler checks to ensure that the syntax of the code is written correctly.

What happens when this program is executed? The computer runs the for loop 500 times, and the program assigns zeros into all of the 500 array elements. Even though the array has only 100 legally declared elements (x[0] to x[99]), the program keeps assigning zeros into the memory locations (see Figure 6-18). The

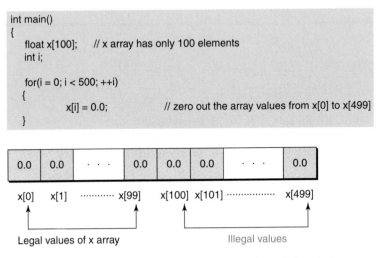

Figure 6-18
Array Out of Bounds!

C++ program simply uses the array index as an offset to access the correct number of bytes from the starting location of the array. We cannot tell what part of the computer memory has been written over by the program or what damage has been done!

Array Out of Bounds == Big Trouble

C++ does not do any type of array boundary checking when a program uses arrays. The program does not warn you or stop the program if a statement causes the program to access an array element that is not legally declared. This *out of bounds array* feature of the C++ language can wreak havoc on your program when the program is executed.

out of bounds array
attempting to access array elements that are not legally declared

In the simple case, accessing an out of bounds array element simply crashes your program or locks your computer, causing you to reboot your system. After the system has been restarted, you should be able to determine quickly where the problem occurs. (*Hint:* Use the debugger, step into your program, and look for an array operation with a for loop that is indexed incorrectly.)

In a not-so-simple (and therefore dreaded) case, the program can perform the portion of the code where the actual illegal, out-of-bounds array access occurs. This action leaves the bad array intact with the appearance that all is well. However, some innocent bystanders (data variables) are victims of this illegal operation. Usually the illegal array activity alters other variable value(s) because these variables are being written over accidentally. Such action will cause the software to run incorrectly. Often the programmer-investigator is led down the wrong path (examining the wrong variables).

The best deterrent is for the programmer to be aware of this potential array out of bounds situation. Keep a close eye on the array indices and be sure that they can take on only the value of the legally declared array bounds. When reading data files into numeric arrays, you must double-check the files to be sure that the array size matches the number of values in the file. Last, do not forget that the character string input functions will place a null character at the end of the string. Be sure to make your strings large enough for your data and the null character.

6.9
Filling Arrays from Data Files

Typically, arrays contain a large number of values. To illustrate and practice using numeric arrays, it is impractical to write programs asking the user to enter the data from the keyboard. (Can you imagine the user having to type in 100 numbers each time he or she ran your program?) In real programs, data are usually read from a data file (or files). C++ provides powerful file input and output tools, and there are several ways to read and to write files. For working with arrays now, we will learn one technique for reading text (both character and numeric) from a data file. We will also write data to an output file.

Using data files in C++ does not require magic, as some programmers may claim. The program needs to be told where the data file is located and it needs to open the file. Once open, the data can be read from the file. We must close the file when we are finished reading the data. (This step is usually performed at the end of the program.)

One last feature when working with data files is that the programmer must know exactly how the data is written in the data file. The read statements must correspond to the way the data is formatted in the file. Appendix F, "File Input/ Output," contains the instructions and example programs for reading textual data from an input file and writing data to an output file. All we need to do is set up input and output streams.

6.10
Summary

Arrays organize and represent data in a C++ program. Key array concepts are presented here:

- An array represents a group of variables that can be thought of as a list of values. This list (or group) is referred to with one name, and each individual value is referenced using an integer index value.

- The array can be set up as a single list or column (one-dimensional), a table (two-dimensional), a stacked table (three-dimensional), and so forth.

- When an array is declared, a pointer of the same name is created automatically, and this pointer contains the address of the zero element of the array.

- An array is passed to a function by using the name of the array (which is actually a pointer containing the address of the first element of the array), and the function accesses the calling function's array. There is only one copy of the array. The function does not have its own copy.

- A function cannot create its own local array and then return it to the calling program.

  Tables 6-7 and 6-8 compare and summarize array properties.

6.11
Practice

Favorite Word

The first practice program in this chapter involves character strings (see Program 6-11). The program asks the user to enter his or her favorite word and then a phrase. Next it calls the function FindFavorite, which determines if the word is contained in the phrase. FindFavorite returns a Boolean value to main, which writes the results

C++ Statements	Individual Data Variables	Arrays

Declaration	`int n,m; // two ints`
	`float x; // one float`
	`char answer;  // one char`
		`int num[10];   //array with 10 values`
		
		`float z[100]; //array with 100 values`
		
		`char name[50];   //string with 50 chars`

Assignment	`n = 7;`
	`m = 3;`
	`x = 3.562434;`
	`answer = 'y';`
		`// assign numeric values using index`
		`num[0] = 7;`
		`num[1] = 9;`
		
		`// can use for loop for ease`
		`for(i = 0; i < 1000; ++i)`
		`{`
		`    z[i] = value;`
		`}`
		
		`// strings initialized on declaration`
		`char name[40] = "Robert Hancock";`
		
		`//or assigned with string.h's strcpy`
		`strcpy(name, "Robert Hancock");`
		
		`//CANNOT DO THIS name = "Robert Hancock";`

Printing	`cout << n << m << x;`
	`cout << answer;`
		`// must use index for each numeric value`
		`cout << num[0] << num[1]; //etc.`
		`// use for loop for all values`
		`for(i = 0; i < 1000; ++i)`
		`{`
		`    cout << z[i] << endl;`
		`}`
		`// just use string if null-terminated`
		`cout << name;`

6

to the screen. The function *strstr* is used to tell us if the word is in the phrase. We pass the phrase and word to strstr, and it returns a null character if the word is not in the phrase. If the word is in the phrase, the pointer points to the first occurrence. Because we do not need to know where the word is located (if it is in the string), we need only to check the pointer to see if it contains a null value. Last, we ask the

strstr function
in the string library; determines if one string is contained in another string

TABLE 6-8
Arrays and Functions

C++ Statements	Two Numeric Arrays	Character String
Prototype	`void Func1 (float[], int [][6]);`	`void Func2(char []);`
Call	`int main()`	`int main()`
	`{`	`{`
	`    float red[25],blue[10][6];`	`    char MyString[50];`
	`    Func1(red, blue);`	`    Func2(MyString);`
	`    return 0;`	`    return 0;`
	`}`	`}`
Function header line and function body	`void Func1(float w[], float y[][6])`	`void Func2(char S[])`
	`{`	`{`
	`    int i,j,k,m;`	`    // body of function`
	`    // body of function`	`    // work with S[i]'s`
	`// work with w[k]'s and y[i][j]'s`	
	`}`	`}`

6

user to enter yes or no and then use the strcmp function to compare what the user enters with the word *yes*. If the user has entered a yes, strcmp returns a zero value.

```
//Program 6-11 Favorite Word   Read in a word and a phrase and determine if
//   the word is in the phrase. Also report length of word and phrase.

#include <iostream.h>
#include <string.h>
bool FindFavorite(char [], char []);

int main( )
{
      char phrase[80], word[15], answer[5];
      bool find_it;
      do
      {
            cout << "\n Please enter your FAVORITE word ===>   ";
            cin.getline(word,15);
            cout << "\n\n Please type in a sentence or a phrase.  \n\n==>   ";
            cin.getline(phrase,80);
            find_it = FindFavorite(phrase,word);
            if(find_it == true)
                  cout << "\n I see it! I see ==> " << word << " <== :-) \n";
            else
                  cout << "\n I don't see ==> " << word << " <==   :-(\n";
```

```
              cout << "\n\n Do it again?  Enter yes or no ==> ";
              cin.getline(answer,5);
       }while(strcmp(answer,"yes")== 0); //strcmp returns 0 is strings match

       cout << "\n\n Aren't strings wonderful?\n\n";
       return 0;
}
bool FindFavorite(char phrase[], char word[])
{
       bool result;
       char* IsItThere;      //declare a character pointer for strstr
       IsItThere = strstr(phrase,word);
       if(IsItThere == NULL)
              result = false;
       else
              result = true;
       return (result);
}
```

6

How's the Weather?

The second practice program involves reading a data file that contains weather information. The file contains character strings with the date (month and year) and location, as well as the high and low temperature readings for that month. The program first reads the data from the file and then calls the FindAve function (which determines the average of a floating point array). We need to call this function twice, once for high and once for low. Then we call the HighLow function that finds the highest high temperature and the lowest low temperature and requires a call by reference (and pointers) because the function must report two values to the calling function. All the information will then be written to an output data file. Refer to Appendix F for information on reading and writing data files.

Finding Array Maximum (or Minimum)   To determine the maximum value in the array, we traverse through the array and compare each value to a maximum variable. If we find an array value higher than the maximum, we place that value in the max variable. The problem is, "What value do we put in max to get started?"

There are two techniques available to us for setting the initial value of max. The first *and not recommended* approach, known as the classic BFMI (brute force, massive ignorance), involves trying to determine a really low value that we know is smaller than the expected highest value in the array. Maybe we can set our weather data to −50,000,000 degrees!

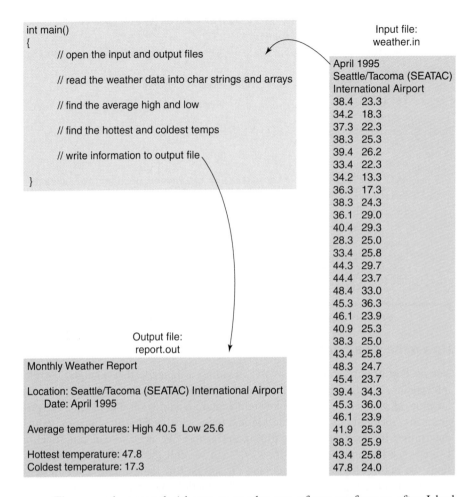

```
int main()
{
        // open the input and output files

        // read the weather data into char strings and arrays

        // find the average high and low

        // find the hottest and coldest temps

        // write information to output file

}
```

Input file:
weather.in

```
April 1995
Seattle/Tacoma (SEATAC)
International Airport
38.4  23.3
34.2  18.3
37.3  22.3
38.3  25.3
39.4  26.2
33.4  22.3
34.2  13.3
36.3  17.3
38.3  24.3
36.1  29.0
40.4  29.3
28.3  25.0
33.4  25.8
44.3  29.7
44.4  23.7
48.4  33.0
45.3  36.3
46.1  23.9
40.9  25.3
38.3  25.0
43.4  25.8
48.3  24.7
45.4  23.7
39.4  34.3
45.3  36.0
46.1  23.9
41.9  25.3
38.3  25.9
43.4  25.8
47.8  24.0
```

Output file:
report.out

```
Monthly Weather Report

Location: Seattle/Tacoma (SEATAC) International Airport
     Date: April 1995

Average temperatures: High 40.5  Low 25.6

Hottest temperature: 47.8
Coldest temperature: 17.3
```

Figure 6-19
Weather Program
Data Files

The second approach (shown to me by one of my professors after I had attempted the BFMI approach) is simply to set the max value to the first element in the array. We read in our array values and set the max to the first value. This technique guarantees that the program always uses a number within range and that the maximum will be determined. This approach is shown in the source code of Program 6-12.[1] Figure 6-19 illustrates the input and output data files. The file *report.out* contains this output:

Monthly Weather Report
Location: Seattle/Tacoma (SEATAC) International Airport
     Date: April, 1995
Average Temperatures: High 40.5 Low 25.6
Hottest Temperature: 47.8
Coldest Temperature: 17.3

---

[1]Thanks to Dr. Delores Etter, my engineering professor, and author of the Foreward of this text.

```
//Program 6-12 Weather, Arrays, Data File I/O

#include <iostream.h>
#include <fstream.h>              //required for file I/O
#include <stdlib.h>              // required for exit()

#define FILE_IN "weather.in"  //be sure to place the data file in the project file
#define FILE_OUT "report.out"

float FindAve(float[], int);
void HighLow(float[], float[], float*, float*, int);

int main()
{
    float high[31],low[31], high_ave, low_ave, hottest, coldest;
    char date[25],location[50];
    int total_days, i=0;

    //first must set up streams for input and output
    ifstream input;                    //set up input stream object
    ofstream output;                   //set up output stream object
    //open for input and don't create if it is not there
    input.open(FILE_IN, ios::in|ios::nocreate);

    //Check to be sure file is opened.  One way, use the fail function.
    if(!input )
    {
        cout << "\n Can't find input file " << FILE_IN;
        cout << "\n Exiting program, bye bye \n ";
        exit(1);
    }
    output.open(FILE_OUT, ios::out); // since we found input file, now open output

    cout << "\nOK found the file, keep going ...";

    //Read the first 2 lines into character strings
    input.getline(date,24);
    input.getline(location,49);
    while(!input.eof() ) //read until we reach the end of file
    {
        input >> high[i] >> low[i];
        ++i;
    }
```

```
            total_days = i;   // value is i, total # of days read in
            cout << "\n All Done Reading!  "<<endl;
            high_ave = FindAve(high, total_days);
            low_ave = FindAve(low, total_days);
            HighLow(high, low, &hottest, &coldest, total_days);

//now write date to output file
            output << "Monthly Weather Report\n\nLocation: " << location <<
                      "\n    Date: " << date;
            output << "\n\nAverage Temperatures:  High " << high_ave <<
                   " Low  " << low_ave;
            output << "\n\nHottest Temperature:  " << hottest <<
                      "\nColdest Temperature:  " << coldest;
            input.close();
            output.close();
            return 0;
}
float FindAve(float x[], int total)
{
            float sum = 0.0;
            int i;
            for(i = 0; i < total; ++i)
            {
                    sum = sum + x[i];
            }
            return(sum/total);
}
void HighLow(float high[], float low[], float *h_ptr, float *l_ptr, int total)
{
            float hottest = high[0], coldest = low[0];
            int i;
            // traverse both arrays, looking for max high and min low
            for(i=0; i < total; ++i)
            {
                    if(high[i] > hottest) *h_ptr = high[i];
                    if(low[i] < coldest) *l_ptr = low[i];
            }
}
```

REVIEW QUESTIONS AND PROBLEMS

Short Answer

1. What type of value must be used as an array index?

2. What is meant by the term *zero-indexed*?

3. What type of array is a character string?

4. Name three situations in which data are maintained ideally as an array.

5. Why is it impossible to return an array from a function using a return statement?

6. What does the size value represent in an array declaration statement?

7. Why is the null character important in character strings?

8. Can you null-terminate a numeric array?

9. When passing an array to a function, what is actually passed to the function?

10. What technique can a programmer use when he or she is trying to find the minimum or maximum value in an array?

Debugging Problems: Compiler Errors

Identify the compiler errors in Problems 11 to 14 and state what is wrong with the code.

11.
```
int list{25},i;
float a, b, c;
for(i = 0, i<25; ++i)
{
    listi = 0.0;
}
```

13.
```
#include <iostream.h>
char [] FillArray();
int main()
{
    int values[75];
    values = FillArray();
    return 0;
}
```

12.
```
#include <iostream.h>
int main()
{
    float numbers[100];
    int j;
    cout << numbers;
}
```

14.
```
char name[50], address[50]
int j,i;
name = "Janis";
address = "1234 Balder Ave";
```

Debugging Problems: Run-Time Errors

Each of the programs in Problems 15 to 18 compiles but does not do what the specification states. What is the incorrect action and why does it occur?

15. Specification: Fill a 100-element floating point array with the values 0.01, 0.02, . . ., 0.99, 1.0.

```
#include <iostream.h>
int main()
{
        float x[100];
        int i;
        for(i = 1; i <= 100;++i)
        {
                x[i] = i/100;
        }
        return 0;
}
```

16. Specification: Ask the user for a character string and then reverse the characters. If the user entered Hello World, the new string would read dlroW olleH.

```
#include <iostream.h>
#include <string.h>
int main()
{
        char string[50],newstring[50];
        int i;
        cout << "\nEnter a string.";
        cin >> string;
        for(i = 0; i< 50; ++i)
        {
                newstring[i] = string[50-i];
        }
        return 0;
}
```

17. Specification: Fill a character array with the uppercase alphabet (place A in [0], B in [1], etc.).

```
#include <iostream.h>
int main()
{
        char alphabet[26];
        int i;
        for(i = 0; i< 26; ++i)
        {
                alphabet[i] = i;
        }
        return 0;
}
```

18. Specification: Assume that two arrays, x and y, are both fifty-element arrays and that they contain double values. This function is supposed to switch the lowest x value with the lowest y value; that is, the lowest value in x is switched with the lowest value in y.

```
void Switcher(double x[], double y[])
{
        double low_x = 0, low_y = 0;
        int i, i_x, i_y;
        for(i = 0; i < 50; ++ i)
        {
                if(x[i] < low_x)
                        low_x = x[i];   //find low x
                        i_x = i;        //remember x index
                if(y[i] < low_y)
                        low_y = y[i];   //find low y
                        i_y = i;        //remember y index
        }
        y[i_y] = low_x;
        x[i_x] = low_y;
}
```

Programming Problems

Write complete C++ programs for Problems 19 to 22. Problems 23 and 24 are continuations of Problem 22.

19. Write a complete C++ program that asks the user to enter a character string. Send the string to a function called ReverseIt. This function will fill a second string so that the original string is reversed (as described in Problem 16). Limit the size of the strings to fifty characters. The last character in the original string (before the null) should be the first character of the second string. Incorporate a loop so that the user can continue to enter strings until he or she chooses to stop.

20. Create a data file with twenty-five values (one value per line) that represent the length of an oak leaf. Have the values range from 1.0 inch to 6.0 inches in the x.xxx format. Write a program that opens and reads these twenty-five values into an array. Then find the average (you may use the FindAve function from Program 6-4). Also, write a function called BigThree that searches the leaf array and returns the three largest values. Below is a classic BubbleSort function that you may find useful. (You can change the data type as needed.)

```
//BubbleSort Function for an array of integers
//sorts an array of integers from low to high

void BubbleSort(int numbers[], int total)
{
     int i, j, temp;
     for(i = 0; i < (total - 1) ; ++i)
     {
          for(j = 1; j < total; ++j)
          {
               if(numbers[j-1] > numbers[j] )
               {
                    temp = numbers[j];
                    numbers[j] = numbers[j-1];
                    numbers[j-1] = temp;
               }
          }
     }
}
```

21. Create a data file with a first line that specifies MALE or FEMALE and a second line that tells how many data values are given (it will be a value between 10 and 20). Following this number are ten to twenty rows of data. Each row has two values, height (inches) and weight (pounds). For example, the file has data for eighteen females:

```
FEMALE
18
63  115
72  165
:
:
60  133
```

Your program should read this data file and place the values into a two-dimensional array. Next, call a function called TallestAndLightest that returns the tallest and lightest values, respectively. Print all the data to the screen.

22. Write a program that declares two twenty-element, one-dimensional integer arrays. Your program should fill these arrays with random numbers by calling a function called Fill_It. You will call Fill_It twice, once for each array, and ask the user to enter two different seed values. Fill_It needs to have a seed value, and low and high range values, and all three integers should be passed to it along with the array. Fill_It will use the seed for srand and then fill the arrays with values between the low and high range. Call Fill_It so that it fills one array with values between 1000 and 2000 and call it again so the range is 0 to 1000. Once both arrays are filled, print them to a data file showing the seed value and the twenty elements. (Refer to the problems in Chapter 5 for a discussion of the random number generator.)

23. Write a function called FindLowValue that will return the lowest value in a one-dimensional array. Call this function twice, once for each array in Problem 22, and write the result to the data file.

24. Write an integer version of the function Switcher described in Problem 18. Switcher switches the lowest value in the first array with the lowest value of the second array. Print both arrays to the data file after calls to Switcher.

7

User-Defined Data Types, struct, and enum

KEY TERMS AND CONCEPTS

array of structures
data structure
data type
enumerated data type
error code or flag
input/output with enums
multiple-file programs
storage specifier
structures within structures
structure tag
tag name
user-defined data types

KEYWORDS AND OPERATORS

enum
struct
dot operator.
right-arrow operator->

CHAPTER OBJECTIVES

Introduce the concept that it is possible for a programmer to build a customized data type (data structure).

Provide the necessary tools so that a programmer may make a data structure and declare and access the data structure elements.

Illustrate how a data structure may be declared as an array.

Demonstrate how structures are passed between functions.

Indicate how pointers to structures are used in functions.

Explore the enumerated data type, which is a numbered list for category values.

Show how enumerated data types are passed between functions.

Create a multifile program using header and source files.

Building a Fort

Did you ever build a fort when you were a kid? Perhaps you used your mother's card table with a blanket draped across it. Your father's borrowed flashlight provided lighting, and you furnished the fort with pillows and all your important possessions. Two chairs and another blanket provided an additional room. It was the most popular spot in the house. The dog, the cat, and your pesky little brother all wanted to play in your fort. Maybe you created a sailing ship with a large cardboard box that once contained a refrigerator. Or you might have built a tree castle from scraps of lumber. Using your imagination and whatever materials at hand, you created wonderful places!

What do forts, sailing ships, and tree castles have in common with programming? You constructed and furnished these childhood retreats with whatever materials you found at hand. In C++, you can also create unique data types (and eventually classes and objects). With the help of a few new keywords and the basic data types already provided in the language, you can build whatever data type you need to accommodate the requirements of your program. Instead of using chairs and blankets, you use ints and floats!

7.1
Customized Data Types

Grouping Data Together

In all our programs, we have used only the standard C++ data types (int, float, double, and char), and all our variables have been declared as either individuals or as arrays.

```
float x, y, z;            // create 3 floats and an int
int count;
```

```
float q[500];            // create a float and character array
char name[80];
```

These six variables (x, y, z, count, q, and name) each represent one type of data. The x, y, z, and count variables may all contain one value, whereas the q and name arrays each hold a group of fifty and eighty values, respectively.

Often, though, programs have data that should be grouped together into logical units or records, and the data is not of the same type. For example, a community college may have a program for maintaining student information. This program undoubtedly has variables for student name, address, identification number, department, and major. If you are writing a student information program, it is necessary to group the student data into a single unit so that one student is contained in one "unit" instead of having many separate variables for each student's record.

We can select the appropriate types of data for the variables in our college program. Character strings are perfect for the student name, address, and identification number. What should we use for the department and major? The college probably has many separate departments, such as Technologies, Arts and Sciences, and Developmental Studies, as well as majors within the departments. Should we use character strings, letters, or numbers to represent the departments and majors (that is, could 1 = Technologies, 2 = Arts and Sciences, etc.)? If we use character strings, we need to incorporate string-handling functions for assignments and comparisons. If we use numbers or letters, we need to keep a list available to remind us what department is represented by each code or letter.

Is it possible to group different types of data together into a single, logical unit? And is there an easy way to set up data categories? Yes, in C++, we can do both.

structs and enums

C++ provides the programmer with the tools to create new, customized data types. A *data structure* in C++ allows various data variables to be grouped together into logical units. We can create a data structure that ties together the student information. (We can call it a Student data type.)

In addition, the programmer can create an *enumerated data type* that represents a numbered list of categories. The items in the enumerated list then can be used in a simple, direct manner to perform assignments and comparisons. (We can develop a College_Dept data type for the list of college departments.)

user-defined data types

structures, classes, and enumerations are all user-defined data types

These two techniques allow a C++ programmer to set up ***user-defined data types*** that precisely fit the programming task. Simply by using the data types at hand (and a few additional keywords and operators), we can build whatever type of data we need. We begin with data structures, and you will soon see that they are fairly simple. A word to the wise—because data structures are the starting-point for classes, getting a good grasp of data structures makes learning classes that much easier.

7.2
Data Structures

Review the Concept of a Data Type

One major concept that C++ programmers must understand is that of a *data type*. A *data type* can be thought of as a ***storage specifier*** for a program variable. What do we mean by a storage specifier? Recall the equipment room story in Chapter 2. You, the new equipment room manager, had to organize storage locations for all the various racquets, clubs, bats, and balls. We used container-doodads that attached to the shelves—one doodad for each piece of equipment. We had various sizes of these storage doodads.

data type
a type of "container" that holds program data

storage specifier
dictates the type of data that will be contained in memory for the program

In C++ programming, we must allocate storage containers for our program data. If our program uses a counting variable, we declare the counter like this:

```
int Counter;
```

and the program then sets aside the necessary memory (4 bytes in Visual C++ systems) to store an integer value. Properties and rules are associated with an integer variable. An integer is a whole number, and we can perform arithmetic operations with it. In C++, several standard data types are provided to us: integers, floats, doubles, and characters. We may modify them by using terms such as short, long, and unsigned, and we can create arrays.

Let's briefly review how data types are used with functions. In C++, we must declare the data type of the input and output variables for the function. For example, if we are returning an integer from a function, the function prototype contains the return data type:

```
int WhatsMyCounter();
```

If we are passing integers to a function, the prototype contains the integer data type in the input list:

```
void TwoInts4You(int, int);
```

The concept of a data type in C++ can be expanded so that programmers create their own data type that fits the specifications of the program. In the equipment room, you may design a special container for golf equipment. This golf-doodad would have space for several woods and irons, golf tees, and balls. If we have 100 sets of golfing equipment, we need 100 of these golf-doodad containers. In a program we perform a similar task. For example, if we write software to track the inventory of a grocery store, we can create a data type called StoreItem. The Store-Item data type may have several character strings for product information: integers and floats that represent volume, size, and price information. Once we have set up a blueprint for a new data type, it is possible to declare variables of that type as well as to pass these data types to and from functions. For example, we can declare two StoreItem variables (MyItem and YourItem) in the same manner as we declare our integer Counter.

```
int Counter;                   //declare an integer Counter
StoreItem MyItem, YourItem;    //declare two StoreItems
```

How do we make our own data types in C++? The next section answers this question.

Creating and Declaring Structures

struct
keyword required to create a data structure

data structure
a grouping of data variables that represent a logical unit

In C++, the keyword *struct* is used to create a **data structure**. A data structure is a group of individual data variables that are grouped together and referenced with a single name. This collection of variables should be related in some way within the program—such as the grocery store items or community college student information. The general form for a structure declaration is:

```
struct structure_type_name
{
        data_type variable_name;
        data_type variable_name;
        .
        .
} structure_variable_name list;
```

The following is an example using grocery store items:

```
struct StoreItem
{
        char product_name[50];
        char UPC[20];
        float unit_price;
} MyItem, YourItem;
```

tag name
data type for variable declarations; is used in the same manner as standard data types in function prototypes and function header lines

The structure_type_name is also known as the **tag name**. The tag name is considered a data type in C++ and can be treated as you would any data type; that is, it is used to declare variables of that type and used in function prototypes and header lines. The data_type variable_name is just standard variable declarations we have been using. The data within a structure can also include structure, enumerated, or class data types. The optional structure_variable_name list contains the actual structure variables.

These statements form a complete data structure declaration, but they are not used in a practical sense. The structure tag style shown in the next section illustrates the preferred method for working with structures.

Structure Tags

There are several ways of creating and employing data structures in C++, but the most practical method is to use a ***structure tag***. A structure tag provides all the utility that you need. It provides the program with a blueprint for the structure, the user-defined date type name of the structure (such as Student), and individual data types and variables for the data included in the structure. Once the tag is created, the program knows of the structure, and the structure may be used throughout the program (assuming that the file containing the structure tag has been included in the appropriate files).

structure tag
blueprint for a structure variable

To make a data structure for our grocery store, we place the structure tag globally (outside any function) and then declare the StoreItem variables locally in the main function.

```
#include <iostream.h>

struct StoreItem          //this is a structure tag
{
      char product_name[50];
      char UPC[20];
      float unit_price;
};


int main()
{
    StoreItem MyItem, YourItem;
```

For the community college student information, we use a structure tag named Student. This structure declaration is located outside any function. Note that there are no structure variable names at the end of the closing brace for either the StoreItem or Student structure tags—just a single semicolon. This single semicolon indicates to the program that this is a blueprint and that no actual memory locations are reserved.

```
#include <iostream.h>

struct Student        // This is a structure declaration.
{
      char name[40];
      char address[80];
```

```
        char ID_Num[15];
        int dept_code;        //Use a code for dept. and major.
        int major;
};


int main()
{
        Student a,b,c;    /*declaration of three variables a, b, c
                               which are of the type Student */
```

Another example shows a data structure for a date that is declared by the use of a structure tag outside the main function. In the main function, two variables of the Date data type are declared.

```
#include <iostream.h>
struct Date                  // structure tag declaration
{
        int month, day, year;
};
int main()
{
        Date hire, birth;    //Declaration of two date variables
```

Data Structures Without Tags

The structure tag technique is the preferred program style, but you may declare individual data structures as either local or global variables. This technique does not provide the program with a tag name or a blueprint of the data structure. For local structure variables, the struct declaration needs to be performed in every function that uses this data structure.

```
#include <iostream.h>
int main()
{
        struct                 // this struct is local to main only
        {

                char name[40];
                char address[80];
                char ID_Num[15];
                int dept_code;
                int major;
        }a, b, c;
  // The main function now has three data
  //structure variables, a, b, and c
```

The following example has the hire and birth data structure variables declared globally. All functions have access to these variables, but there is no Date structure tag.

```
#include <iostream.h>
struct                       // this struct is global to the program
{
      int month, day, year;
}hire, birth;
int main()
{
      // The main function can access hire and birth variables.

}

void F1()
{

      // F1 has access to hire and birth variables.
}
```

7.3
Accessing Structure Elements

Boxes

Can you draw a box? One of the most helpful tools beginning programming students can use when trying to learn data structures is drawing box diagrams. These diagrams represent the data structure. The boxes should be labeled with both the structure type name and the data types of the variables within the structure. Figure 7-1 illustrates the Student data structure. We use box diagrams throughout this text when discussing structures and classes. Now, we return to the topic of structures.

Accessing Structure Elements

Once a structure tag and structure variable(s) are declared, the structure elements are accessed by using the **dot operator**. The form for accessing structure elements is:

dot operator
used with data structure (or class) variables to access structure members (or public class members)

```
structure_variable_name.variable_name
```

The hire Date variables can be accessed by using the following form:

```
hire.month    //each Date variable has three boxes, month, day, and year
hire.day
hire.year
```

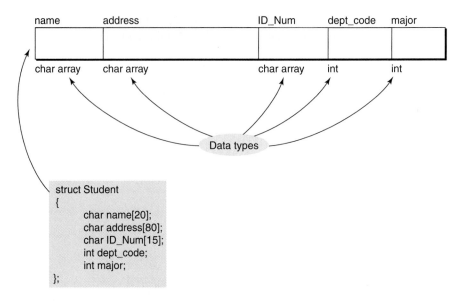

Figure 7-1
Box Diagram of Student Data Structure

Program 7-1 illustrates the use of the dot operator in accessing structure members. To assign values to the structure variables, you simply apply the assignment operator to the name of the "box" where the value is to be placed. Use the box diagram to assist you in remembering the name for the boxes. We declare a single Student variable named MyStudent. Figure 7-2 shows a box diagram for this structure variable with the names of the boxes, and these boxes represent the complete name of the variable.

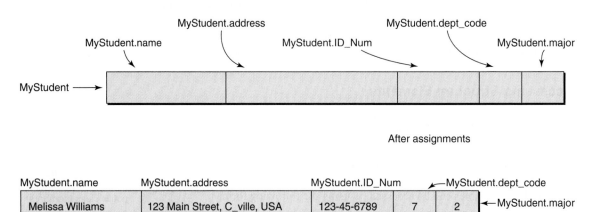

Figure 7-2
Box Diagram of Student Variable Named MyStudent

Chapter 7 ▌ User-Defined Data Types, struct, and enum

```
//Program 7-1 Assigning and printing data structure information.
#include <iostream.h>
#include <string.h>

struct Student     // Using a structure tag for program
{
        char name[40];
        char address[80];
        char ID_Num[15];
        int dept_code;
        int major;
};

int main()
{
        Student MyStudent;    //create a single variable named MyStudent
        strcpy(MyStudent.name, "Melissa Williams");
        strcpy(MyStudent.address, "123 Main Street, C-Ville, USA");
        strcpy(MyStudent.ID_Num, "123-45-6789");
        MyStudent.dept_code = 7;
        MyStudent.major = 2;

        cout << "\n Our student is " << MyStudent.name << "\n Address is " <<
        MyStudent.address << "\n ID number " << MyStudent.ID_Num <<
        "\n Dept Code  " << MyStudent.dept_code << "\n Major Code = " <<
        MyStudent.major << endl;

        return 0;
}
```

The output is shown below.

Our student is Melissa Williams
Address is 123 Main Street, C-Ville, USA
ID number = 123-45-6789
Dept Code = 7
Major Code = 2

A second example (in Program 7-2) shows a portion of a program used for determining race results in running events such as 5K, 10K, and marathon races. A data structure called Person contains the runner's information. The output is shown on page 260.

On your marks, get set....
Runner's name: Jack Rabbit
Sex: m
Age: 17
Age Category: 2
Race Code: 1

GO!

```cpp
//Program 7-2 Race Program with Person data structures.
#include <iostream.h>
#include <string.h>

struct Person
{
     char name[40];
     char sex;              // m = male, f = female
     int age;
     int category;     // racers grouped by age, such as 1 = 0-9, 2 = 10-19, etc.
     int race;         // races have int codes 1 = 5K, 2 = 10K, 3 = marathon
};

int main()
{
     Person runner;
     cout << "\n On your marks, get set....\n\n";
     // We fill the runner and time information in assignment statements.
     strcpy(runner.name, "Jack Rabbit");
     runner.sex = 'm';
     runner.age = 17;
     runner.category = 2;
     runner.race = 1;

     // write out runner's info
     cout << "\n Runner's name: " << runner.name;
     cout << "\n Sex: " << runner.sex << "\n Age: " << runner.age;
     cout << "\n Age Category: " << runner.category;
     cout << "\n Race Code: " << runner.race << endl;

     cout << "\n\n GO! \n\n";

     return 0;
}
```

7.4
Structure Arrays

It is possible to declare an *array of structures* with the standard array declaration. The structure tag is created for a single structure, and then the array declaration is used when the variables are declared. Accessing the elements of the structure array is exactly the same as accessing single data type arrays, and all rules for arrays are applicable to structure arrays.

array of structures
using the [ ] operator(s), declares an array of struct variables

Structure Array Examples

The data in our student grade and race results programs are apt to have arrays of students or runners rather than simply a single instance of the variable. The code below (see also Figure 7-3) shows how to set up the Student data structure and then declare an array of these structures. Program 7-3 uses the cin.getline function to assign values into the structure variables.

```
int main ()
{
  Student MyStudents[100];
```

The name of this box is MyStudents[0].name.

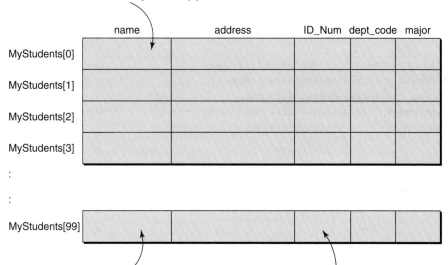

The name of this box is MyStudents[99].name.

The name of this box is MyStudents[99].ID_Num.

Figure 7-3
Box Diagram of Array of Student Variables

```
//Program 7-3 Array of Student data structures.
#include <iostream.h>
#include <string.h>
struct Student     // The tag is created as a single structure.
{
        char name[40];
        char address[80];
        char ID_Num[15];
        int dept_code;
        int major;
};
int main()
{
        Student MyStudents[100];   //create an array of 100 Student structs
// We'll ask the user to enter the information into the first array element
        cout << "\n Enter the student's name:    ";
        cin.getline(MyStudents[0].name,40);
        cout << "\n Enter the student's address:    ";
        cin.getline(MyStudents[0].address, 80);
        cout << "\n Enter the student's ID number:    ";
        cin.getline(MyStudents[0].ID_Num, 15);
        cout << "\n Enter the student's department and major code:    ";
        cin >> MyStudents[0].dept_code >> MyStudents[0].major;
        cin.ignore(10,'\n');

// write out the info
        cout << "\n Student's name: " << MyStudents[0].name;
        cout << "\n Address: " << MyStudents[0].address;
        cout << "\n ID Num: " << MyStudents[0].ID_Num;
        cout << "\n Dept Code: " << MyStudents[0].dept_code;
        cout << "\n Major Code: " << MyStudents[0].major << endl;

        return 0;
}
```

If the programmer needs to access the individual characters in the character strings, the array index is needed, just as it is used to access any character in a string array. Figure 7-4 illustrates the use of array indexes.

The race results program (Program 7-Race Program) is set up in a manner similar to Program 7-3. The structure tag is declared above the main function, and the actual array declaration is in the main function. Figure 7-5 shows the associated box diagram for this array.

```
//Program 7-Race Program with arrays of Person data structure.
#include <iostream.h>
#include <string.h>
struct Person
{
        char name[40];
        char sex;               // m = male, f = female
        int age;
        int category; // races broken into age groups, such as 21-25,
26-30, etc.
        int race;           // races have int codes 1 = 5K, 2 = 10K, 3 =
marathon
};
int main()
{
        Person runner[50];
// We will fill Jack's information into the last array element.
        strcpy(runner.name[49],"Jack Rabbit");
        runner[49].sex = 'm';
        runner[49].age = 17;
        runner[49].category = 2;
        runner[49].race = 1;

// remainder of program

}
```

The M is in MyStudents[0].name[0].   The 2 is in MyStudents[0].ID_Num[1].

	name	address	ID_Num	dept_code	major
MyStudents[0]	Melissa Williams	123 Main Street, C_Ville, USA	123-45-6789	7	2
MyStudents[1]					
MyStudents[2]					
MyStudents[3]					
⋮					
⋮					
MyStudents[99]					

Figure 7-4
Array Indices Are Used to Access Individual Array Elements

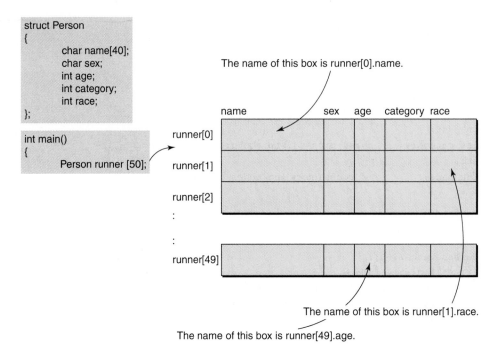

```
struct Person
{
        char name[40];
        char sex;
        int age;
        int category;
        int race;
};

int main()
{
        Person runner [50];
```

The name of this box is runner[0].name.

name   sex   age   category race

runner[0]

runner[1]

runner[2]

:

:

runner[49]

The name of this box is runner[1].race.

The name of this box is runner[49].age.

Figure 7-5
Person Data Structure Array

7.5
Structures Within Structures

Race Program with a Time Structure

When a programmer is organizing the data in a program, it sometimes makes sense to have a data structure within another data structure. In our race program, the runner's time information should be included as part of the Person information. This time information (hours, minutes, and seconds) can be grouped into a data structure, too. To group this information, a Time data structure tag is declared before the Person data structure tag. Then the Time data type is used to declare Time data variables within the Person structure. Figure 7-6 depicts how time is incorporated in the Person data structure.

```
struct Time                    // set up the Time struct
{
        int hr, min, sec;
};
```

```
struct Person
{
        char name[40];
        char sex;
        int age;
        int category;
        int race;
        Time howfast;           //now the Time is part of the Person structure
};


int main()
{
        Person runner;      /* A single Person is declared and it includes the Time
                            information. */
```

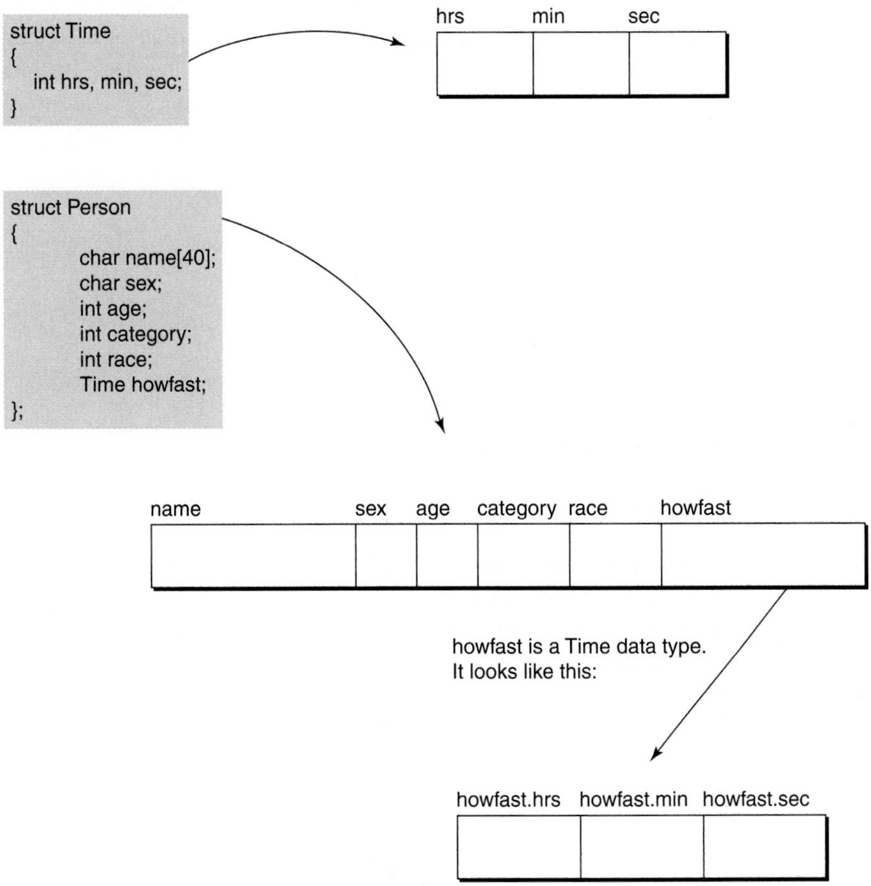

Figure 7-6
Person Data Structure Contains a Time Structure

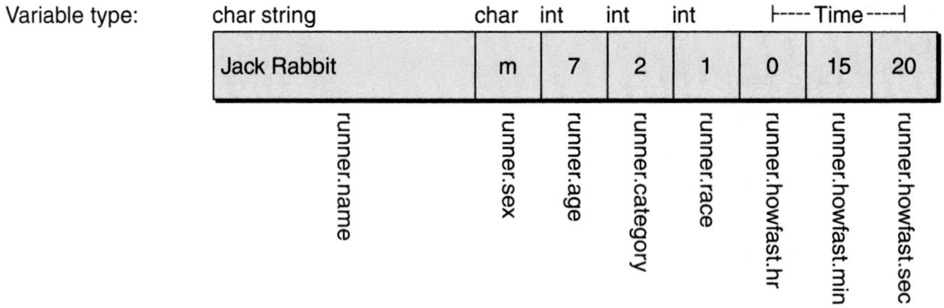

Variable type:	char string		char	int	int	int	├──── Time ────┤		
	Jack Rabbit		m	7	2	1	0	15	20

runner.name
runner.sex
runner.age
runner.category
runner.race
runner.howfast.hr
runner.howfast.min
runner.howfast.sec

Figure 7-7
Assigned Values into Runner

The runner data includes name, sex, age, category, race type, and now a Time data type variable called howfast. The howfast is a Time data type that has hours, minutes, and seconds variables. The time data is assigned into the memory by cascading the structure names and dot operators. Figure 7-7 shows how Jack Rabbit's information is stored in the Person data structure, which also includes the Time structure.

```
// Fill Runner's information.
        strcpy(runner.name,"Jack Rabbit");
        runner.sex = 'm';
        runner.age = 17;
        runner.category = 2;
        runner.race = 1;
        runner.howfast.hr = 0;
        runner.howfast.min = 15;
        runner.howfast.sec = 20;
```

A Structure with Two Structures

In this case, we set up two data structures contained in a third structure. First, we set up a Date data structure and then a Phone struct, including area code, exchange, and number. Last, we build a structure for Employee information, including the Date and Phone structures.

```
struct Date
{
        int month,day,year;
};
struct Phone
{
        int area_code, exch, number;
};
```

```
struct Employee
{
        char name[40];
        Date hire, birth;
        Phone home_ph;
};
```

The Employee data structure has four variables: name, birth, hire, and home_ph (home phone number). The name is a character string, the birth and hire are Date data structures, and the home_ph is a Phone data structure. Figure 7-8 illustrates these structures.

The code below declares one variable of the type Employee and assigns information into it. *Note:* You do not need to declare Date and Phone variables because they are already in the Employee structure. See also Figure 7-9.

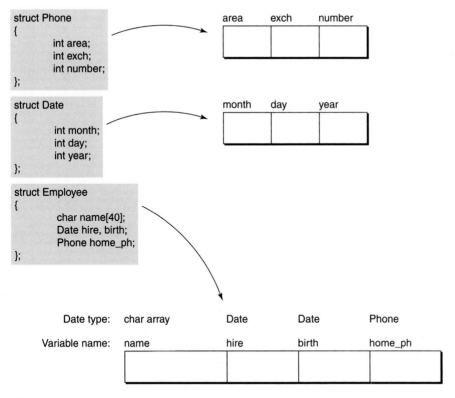

Figure 7-8
Employee Structure Tag Has Two Data Structures, Date and Phone

```
struct Employee
{
        char name[40];
        Date hire, birth;
        Phone home_ph;
};

int main()
{
        Employee worker;
```

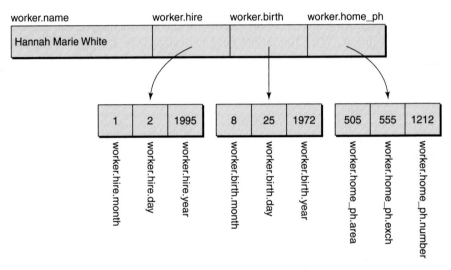

Figure 7-9
Employee Variable Worker Data Assignments

```
int main()
{
      Employee worker;
      strcpy(worker.name, "Hannah Marie White");
      worker.hire.month = 1;
      worker.hire.day = 2;
      worker.hire.year = 1995;
      worker.birth.month = 8;
      worker.birth.day = 25;
      worker.birth.year = 1972;
      worker.home_ph.area_code = 505;
      worker.home_ph.exch = 555;
      worker.home_ph.number = 1212;

//rest of program
```

7.6
Copying Structures

In C++, it is possible to copy the value of one variable to another as long as the data types are the same. When you are using single valued data types, you may do the following:

```
float X, Y = 3.4;
X = Y;               //assignment of Y's value into X
```

This assignment statement is valid, and the program copies the value of 3.4 into the X variable. We can do the same for structures, too, as long as the structure types are the same. In the following example, we use the Date structure from above to illustrate:

```
Date hire, today;
today.month = 8;
today.day = 23;
today.year = 2001;
hire = today;
```

Each member of the today variable is copied into the corresponding members of the hire variable.

If a data structure is contained in another structure, it is still possible to copy similar structures. To explain further, again we use the Date and Employee structures. Recall that the Employee structure has hire and birth Date variables and the home_ph Phone variable.

```
struct Date
{
        int month,day,year;
};

struct Phone
{
        int area_code, exch, number;
};

struct Employee
{
        char name[40];
        Date birth, hire;
        Phone home_ph;
};
```

7

Below we declare local variables of type Date and Phone and assign values to the variables. The Date and Phone values are then copied into the worker variable.

```
int main()
{
        Employee worker;
        Date today;            // Date and Phone structure variables are declared.
        Phone temp;
        today.month = 8;       // Date and Phone variables are assigned values.
        today.day = 23;
        today.year = 2001;
        temp.area_code = 505;
        temp.exch = 555;
        temp.number = 1212;
        worker.hire = today;        // Structure variables are assigned directly to
        worker.home_ph = temp;      // worker structure values of same types.

// rest of program
```

7.7
Structures and Functions

A data structure is treated exactly like any data type when it comes to passing it to and from a function. We can return a floating point value from a function. We can also return a structure from a function. Life is made easier if the structures have been set up with global structure tags. The structure data type is used in the prototype, the variable name is used in the call, and the type and name are used in the function header line.

Tables 7-1 and 7-2 show simple comparisons of two functions with floating point and structure variables. Notice how the data type float and DataStruct are used in the same manner.

Starting Time Program

Program 7-4 returns a structure from a function. The program sets up a structure tag called Time. We have a function called GetStartTime, which asks the user to input a time. The GetStartTime function has a local copy of the Time structure, fills this structure, and then passes the structure back to the calling function. The output is shown below:

Enter start time in hours, minutes, and seconds, such as 9 45 0   5 30 30

The starting time is 5:30:30

Time's Up!

TABLE 7-1
Comparing the Return of a Float and a Data Structure from a Function[a]

C++ Statements	Float and Integer Point Values	User-Defined Data Structure

Prototype	`float Function1 ();`	`struct DataStruct`
		`{`
		`    // structure members`
		`};`
		`DataStruct Function2 ( );`

Call	`int main()`
	`{`
	`    float x;`
	`    x = Function1();`
	`}`
		`int main()`
		`{`
		`    DataStruct MyStruct;`
		`    MyStruct = Function2 ( );`
		`}`

Function header line and function body	`float Function1()`
	`{`
	`    float temp;`
	`    // body of function`
	`    return temp;`
	`}`
		`DataStruct Function2 ( )`
		`{`
		`    DataStruct temp;`
		`    // body of function`
		`    return temp;`
		`}`

[a]Both functions have a local, temporary variable declared.

7

TABLE 7-2
Comparing How to Pass a Float and a Data Structure to a Function[a]

C++ Statements	Float and Integer Point Values	User-Defined Data Structure

Prototype	`void Function3 (float);`	`struct DataStruct`
		`{`
		`    // structure member`
		`};`
		`void Function4 ( DataStruct );`

Call	`int main()`
	`{`
	`    float x;`
	`    Function3(x);`
	`}`
		`int main()`
		`{`
		`    DataStruct MyStruct;`
		`    Function4(MyStruct);`
		`}`

Function header line and function body	`void Function3(float x)`
	`{`
	`    // body of function`
	`}`
		`void Function4(DataStruct MyStruct)`
		`{`
		`    // body of function`
		`}`

[a]Both functions have a local variable declared.

```
//Program 7-4 Time structure returned from a function.
#include <iostream.h>

struct Time
{
        int hr, min, sec;
};


Time GetStartTime(void);   //prototype (must be after structure Tag)

int main()
{
        Time start;

        start = GetStartTime(); //function call, expecting a Time struct in return

        cout << "\n The starting time is " << start.hr << ":" << start.min <<
        ":" << start.sec << endl;

        cout << "\n Time's Up! \n ";
        return 0;
}

Time GetStartTime(void)
{
        Time input;                    //this local variable for the function
        cout << "\n Enter start time in hours, minutes, and seconds, such as 9 45 0 ";
        cin >> input.hr >> input.min >> input.sec;
        return input;                  //now return the input Time structure
}
```

Averaging Two Points Program

Next, we present an example with Cartesian points. Recall that you can graph points on the *x-y* axis with ordered pairs. A point on a graph is represented by (*x, y*) such as (3, 4) or (−8, 4). If you are writing a graphing program, you may need to determine the average point between two points (such as in a smoothing routine). Program 7-5 establishes a structure tag called Point with an Average-TwoPoints function. This function receives two Point variables and returns the

```
//Program 7-5 Average Two Points using a function.
#include <iostream.h>

struct Point
{
        double x, y;
};

Point AverageTwoPoints(Point, Point);   //prototype, receives 2 Points, returns 1

int main()
{
        Point First, Second, Average;
        cout << "\n Please enter the X and Y value for the first point.    ";
        cin >> First.x >> First.y;
        cout << "\n Now enter the X and Y value for the second point.    ";
        cin >> Second.x >> Second.y;
        Average = AverageTwoPoints(First,Second);
        cout << "\n The average point is (" << Average.x << "," << Average.y << ")";

        cout << "\n Don't you wish you were still in high school? \n";
        return 0;
}

Point AverageTwoPoints(Point First, Point Second)
{
        Point temp;             //local copy of a Point
        temp.x = (First.x + Second.x)/2.0;
        temp.y = (First.y + Second.y)/2.0;
        return temp;
}
```

average point. The following output would be the result if the user's points were
(7, 10) and (4, 15):

Please enter the X and Y value for the first point. 7 10

Now enter the X and Y value for the second point. 4 15

The average point is (5.5,12.5)

Don't you wish you were still in high school?

7.8
Call by Reference: Structure Address to a Function

Pointers and Functions: Quick Review

Initially, we discovered how pointers are used in functions when the function needs to return more than one piece of data. We pass the variable address to the function. This address is stored in a pointer variable. Then, via the indirection operator, a value is placed in the address contained in the pointer. (This technique is known as a call by reference because the pointer is referring to the calling function's variable.) The following two short programs illustrate how a function obtains a value for a calling function's variable.

```
//Program 7-Review Call by Value and GiveMeOneFloat
#include <iostream.h>
float GiveMeOneFloat();

int main()
{
     float MyFavoriteNumber;
     MyFavoriteNumber = GiveMeOneFloat();
     cout << "\n My Favorite Number is " << MyFavoriteNumber;
     return 0;
}


float GiveMeOneFloat()
{
     float number;                //local variable to accept input from user
     cout << "\n Enter a favorite number ";
     cin >> number;
     return number;
}


//Program 7-Review Call by Reference and GiveMeOneFloat
#include <iostream.h>
void GiveMeOneFloat(float *);

int main()
{
     float MyFavoriteNumber;
     GiveMeOneFloat(&MyFavoriteNumber);                // pass the address
     cout << "\n My Favorite Number is  " << MyFavoriteNumber;
     return 0;
}
```

```
void GiveMeOneFloat(float *pNumber)
{
        cout << "\n Enter a favorite number  ";
        cin >> *pNumber;
}
```

A structure variable is treated in the same manner as a single variable when the programmer passes the structure address into a pointer in a function. We simply pass the address of the structure variable into the function and use the indirection operator with the pointer to access the structure variables. However, we need to use a new form of the indirection operator: the *right-arrow operator*, –>.

> **Special Consideration**   In some programming applications, data structures can be very large. For example, the information in one 640 by 480 pixel bitmap image file (BMP) can be more than 300K bytes if the image is black and white (900K if the image is in color). Bitmap files are read into programs, and the 300K bytes of information are stored in a set of data structure variables. If we need to pass the bitmap to a function, it is possible to use a call by value; that is, we pass the structure to a function and allow the function to create its own copy of the structure. (The function uses another 300K bytes of memory for this task.) By passing the address of the bitmap data to the function, the programmer eliminates the need to create a second copy of the data—thus saving memory and increasing program execution speed.

7

Filling and Returning Student Data Structure

Call by Value—Two Local Copies of a Structure   Program 7-6 is a parallel design to the first GiveMeOneFloat program on page 274. The main function calls a function called GetStudentInfo, which fills and returns the Student structure. Both the main and GetStudentInfo functions have their own copy of the data structure. The function GetStudentInfo has its own local copy of the Student data structure (temp). The dot operator is used to access temp's variables and then temp is returned.

Call by Reference—One Copy of a Structure   In Program 7-7, the address of MyStudent is sent to the function, and the right-arrow operator and pointer access the structure variables. The program needs only one copy of the data structure.

```
//Program 7-6   Example having local copies of Student and returning it
#include <iostream.h>
#include <string.h>
struct Student     // Using a structure Tag
{
        char name[40];
        char SSN[12];
        int dept;
        float gpa;
};
Student GetStudentInfo(void);   //Prototype, function returns a Student type

int main()
{
        Student MyStudent;                 // main has a copy of data structure
        MyStudent = GetStudentInfo();      //function returns information into A
        return 0;
}

Student GetStudentInfo(void)
{
        Student temp;                  // local copy of Student in function
        strcpy(temp.name,"J. E. White");
        strcpy(temp.SSN,"555-11-5555");
        temp.dept = 1;
        temp.gpa = 3.8;
        return temp;
}
```

Right-Arrow Operator Versus Dot Operator

Recall from the second GiveMeOneFloat program on pages 274–75 that a function uses the indirection operator, *, to place the data where the pointer is pointing. In the following line:

```
cin >> *pNumber;
```

the value entered by the user is placed at the address in the pointer variable pNumber. This expression:

```
cin >> pNumber;  //this is invalid!!
```

```
//Program 7-7 Using a structure pointer to function
#include <iostream.h>
struct Student
{
        char name[40];
        char SSN[12];
        int dept;
        float gpa;
};

void GetStudentInfo(Student*);   //Prototype, input is address to Student struct

int main()
{
        Student MyStudent;
        GetStudentInfo(&MyStudent);     //send the address of MyStudent
}
void GetStudentInfo(Student *temp_ptr) //temp_ptr is pointer with address of A
{
        strcpy(temp_ptr->name,"J. E. White");
        strcpy(temp_ptr->SSN,"555-11-5555");
        temp_ptr->dept = 1;
        temp_ptr->gpa = 3.8;
}
```

7

makes no sense because the user is entering a floating point number, and the pNumber is a float pointer! (A pointer holds a hex address, not a number.) We must have the indirection operator with a pointer variable to direct the program to the address in the pointer.

When using structures, we follow the same procedure. The indirection operator and the pointer access the calling function's structure. However, it is more complicated with the structure because a structure also needs the dot operator. Bear in mind that when we have a local copy of the structure in the function, we use the dot operator.

```
Student GetStudentInfo(void)
{
        Student temp;  //local copy of the structure
        temp.dept = 1; //use the dot operator to access struct elements
        temp.gpa = 3.8;
```

If we pass the address of the structure to a pointer in the function, we expect it to require the indirection operator and the dot operator. A portion of the GetStudentInfo function might look like the following:

```
//Warning:  this code will NOT compile!!
void GetStudentInfo(Student *temp_ptr)
{
        *temp_ptr.dept = 1;   //use the * w/ ptr and . to access struct   :-(
        *temp_ptr.gpa = 3.8;  // WRONG! Can't do this!
}
```

Compiler Error!!! temp_ptr is not a valid structure

What is wrong? The code looks straightforward, but after reviewing the operator precedence table, we see that the dot operator has higher precedence than the indirection operator; that is, the program performs the dot operation first. The dot operator is always used with a structure variable. The compiler thinks you are saying the following:

```
*(temp_ptr.dept) = 1;   //this is what the program thinks
```

Remember, too, that temp_ptr is a pointer to a structure, not a structure itself. To use the indirection operator, *, you need to use the following format:

```
(*temp_ptr).dept = 1;
```

The parentheses have primary precedence. The precedence order directs the program to perform the indirection operator and pointer *first* and then to access the structure element.

Programmer's Shortcut

Because C programmers are always looking for shortcuts, they invented the right-arrow operator, −>, to eliminate the need for typing the parentheses when using pointers and structures. The ***right-arrow operator*** is used with a pointer to a structure (or class) to access the structure (or class) members. The following two statements are equivalent.

right-arrow operator
indirection operator used with a pointer to access structure (or class) members

```
(*temp_ptr).dept = 1;
temp_ptr->dept = 1;
```

A second look at the GetStudentInfo function shows how the pointer and right-arrow operator are used to access the members of the Student data structure:

```
void GetStudentInfo(Student *temp_ptr)  //temp_ptr has the address of
MyStudent
{
      strcpy(temp_ptr->name,"J. E. White");
      strcpy(temp_ptr->SSN,"555-11-5555");
      temp_ptr->dept = 1;
      temp_ptr->gpa = 3.8;
}
```

Figure 7-10 is an illustration of structure addresses to functions.

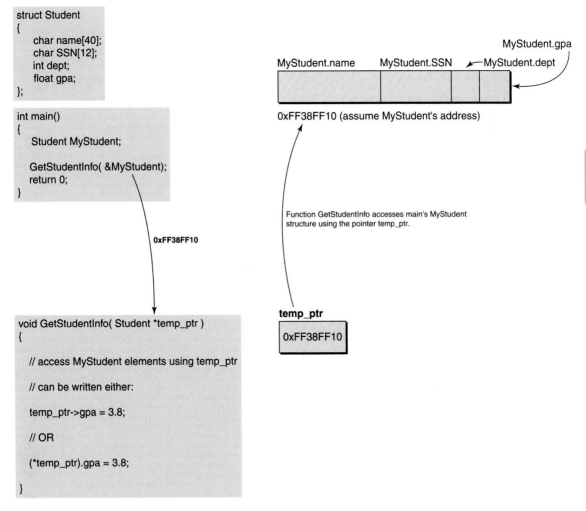

Figure 7-10
Structure Addresses to Functions

Bird-Watching Program

A call by reference is needed if the function must return more than one data item to the calling function. (Remember, a single data structure is considered one data item even though it may contain hundreds of variables.) In Program 7-8, two different

```cpp
//Program 7-8 Example with two structure pointers in a function
#include <iostream.h>
#include <string.h>

struct Bird
{
        char species[25];
        int count;
        char location[25];
};
struct B_Watcher
{
        char name[50];
        int qualification_code;
};

void WatchTheBirdie(Bird *, B_Watcher *);   //prototypes
void WhatDidYouSee(Bird *, B_Watcher *);

int main()
{
        Bird birdie;
        B_Watcher person;
        cout << "\n Watch the Birdie Program  \n";
        WatchTheBirdie(&birdie, &person);   //call sends addresses of structs
        WhatDidYouSee(&birdie, &person);
        return 0;
}


void WatchTheBirdie(Bird *B_ptr, B_Watcher *BW_ptr)
{
        strcpy( B_ptr->species,"sparrow hawk");
        B_ptr->count = 3;
        strcpy( B_ptr->location,"Sandia Mountains");
        strcpy(BW_ptr->name,"Ryan Andrew");
        BW_ptr->qualification_code = 5;
}
```

```
void WhatDidYouSee(Bird *B_ptr, B_Watcher *BW_ptr)
{
        cout << "\n        Watcher: " <<BW_ptr->name;
        cout << "\n Qualification: " << BW_ptr->qualification_code;
        cout << "\n        Species: " << B_ptr->species;
        cout << "\n          Count: " << B_ptr->count << endl;
}
```

data structures are filled by the WatchTheBirdie function. One structure contains information for a species of bird, count, and location. The second structure contains data regarding the individual bird watcher. We also write the information to the screen in the function, WhatDidYouSee. Both functions access these structure members with the right-arrow operator. Figure 7-11 illustrates the process. The output is as follows:

Watch the Birdie Program

Watcher: Ryan Andrew
Qualification: 5
    Species: sparrow hawk
      Count: 3

7.9
Structure Arrays and Functions

Here are some questions for you. If you have an array of structures and you pass it to a function, do you treat it as an array or as a structure? Do you have a pointer to the array of structures? If you pass the array of structures to a function, is a local copy made in the function?

The Bottom Line

When any array is declared in C++, be it an array of floats, a character string, or an array of structures, a pointer to the first element is created. When any array is passed to a function, this address is actually passed and no local copy is created. A structure array is treated exactly like an array of integer values.

How do we access the structure array elements in a function? We access structure array elements in the same manner as we access any array element—by using the array operator, [ ], with an integer index value. To access the individual structure elements, we use the dot operator. *Only* if you pass the address of a single structure do you use the right-arrow operator. To help clear up any confusion, Table 7-3 compares passing the address of a single structure to a function and passing an array of structures to a function.

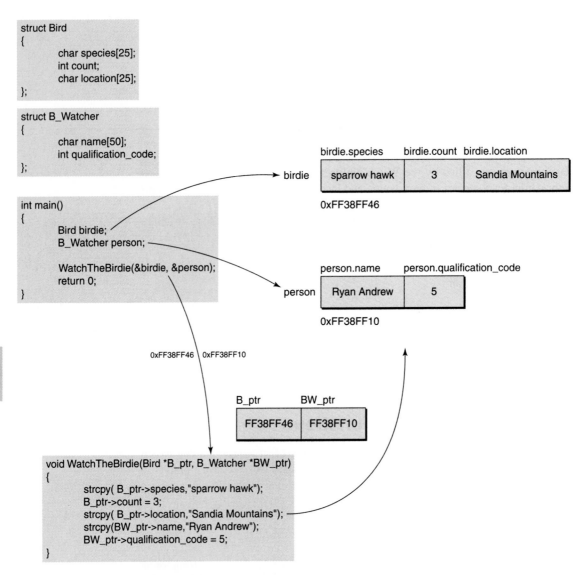

```
struct Bird
{
        char species[25];
        int count;
        char location[25];
};
```

```
struct B_Watcher
{
        char name[50];
        int qualification_code;
};
```

```
int main()
{
        Bird birdie;
        B_Watcher person;

        WatchTheBirdie(&birdie, &person);
        return 0;
}
```

birdie.species   birdie.count   birdie.location

| birdie | sparrow hawk | 3 | Sandia Mountains |

0xFF38FF46

person.name   person.qualification_code

| person | Ryan Andrew | 5 |

0xFF38FF10

0xFF38FF46   0xFF38FF10

B_ptr   BW_ptr

| FF38FF46 | FF38FF10 |

```
void WatchTheBirdie(Bird *B_ptr, B_Watcher *BW_ptr)
{
        strcpy( B_ptr->species,"sparrow hawk");
        B_ptr->count = 3;
        strcpy( B_ptr->location,"Sandia Mountains");
        strcpy(BW_ptr->name,"Ryan Andrew");
        BW_ptr->qualification_code = 5;
}
```

Figure 7-11
WatchTheBirdie Program Illustration

Array of Student structs Program

Let's rewrite the student information and create an array of Student data structures. We add a function called GetInfo, which fills the first two elements of the array. Remember, the function is actually receiving an address to the array. (See Program 7-9.) This function writes its values directly into main's variables. Figure 7-12 illustrates this program.

Functions and Pointer to Single Structure and Structure Array[a]

C++ Statements	Call by Reference (Single Structure)	Structure Array
struct declarations and prototype	```struct StructType { char name[15]; int count; }; void Func1 (StructType *);```	```struct StructType { char name[15]; int count; }; void Func2 (StructType []);```
Call	```int main () { StructType MyStruct; Func1(&MyStruct); }```	```int main () { StructType MyStruct[100]; Func2(MyStruct); }```
Function header line and function body	```void Func1(StructType *w_ptr) { strcpy(w_ptr->name,"Maddie"); w_ptr->count = 11; }```	```void Func2(StructType w[]) { strcpy(w[0].name,"Maddie"); w[0].count = 11; strcpy(w[1].name,"Wally"); w[1].count = 12; }```

[a]Function 1 is passed the address of main's MyStruct structure, and the function uses the indirection operator to access the structure members. Function 2 is passed an address of the MyStruct array (array name holds an address). Both functions access main's variables.

7.10
Enumerated Data Types

It is quite common for a C++ programmer to need to keep track of various conditions or items in a program. Here is an example: let's assume that a program lists several geometric shapes, such as cones, cubes, pyramids, and spheres. Each shape also has a color. What is the best way to keep track of the shapes and colors?

One approach might be simply to assign a number to each item, for example:

Shape	Number
Cone	1
Cube	2
Pyramid	3
Sphere	4

```
//Program 7-9 Structure Array of Student data to a function.
#include <iostream.h>
#include <string.h>
struct Student     // The tag is created as a single structure.
{
        char name[40];
        char ID_Num[15];
        int dept;
        float gpa;
};
void GetInfo(Student [] );  //prototype, sending array of Student data type

int main()
{
        Student MyStudents[100];    //create an array of 100 Student structs
        GetInfo(MyStudents);        // MyStudents is a pointer to MyStudents[] array

        return 0;
}

void GetInfo( Student x[])
{
// We'll fill the first two array elements
        strcpy(x[0].name,"Melissa");
        strcpy(x[0].ID_Num, "123-45-6789");
        x[0].dept = 2;
        x[0].gpa = 3.6;
        strcpy(x[1].name,"Sue");
        strcpy(x[1].ID_Num, "987-65-4321");
        x[1].dept = 1;
        x[1].gpa = 3.7;
}
```

A numbered list can also be used for the colors:

Color	Number
Red	1
Orange	2
Yellow	3
Green	4
Blue	5
Indigo	6
Violet	7

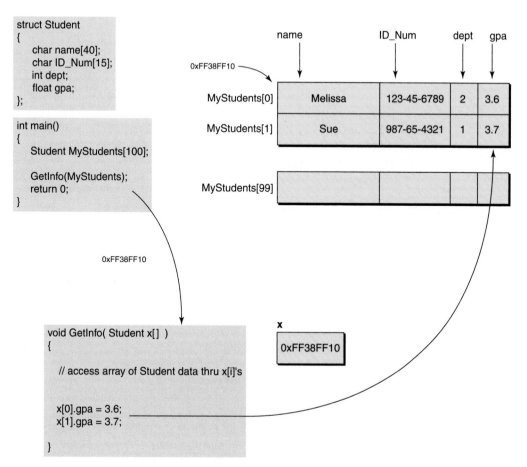

Figure 7-12
Structure Array to a Function

The programmer can then set up a data structure for the Shape that includes two integer values, such as:

```
struct Shape
{
        int ShapeType;      // to be assigned value 1 - 4
        int ShapeColor;     // to be assigned value 1 - 7
};
```

We see that the programmer must document somewhere the numeric values for each shape and color. The following short program shows how a Shape variable is declared and then shows the MyShape values set to blue pyramid:

```
int main()
{
    Shape MyShape;
    MyShape.ShapeType = 3;     // 3 = pyramid's number
    MyShape.ShapeColor = 5;    // 5 = blue color
};
```

Perhaps you are thinking that you need to keep a little note taped to your computer so you can remember the shape and color numbers, which is one way to keep track of these values. But there is a better way.

enums Create Numbered Lists

The C++ language provides the programmer with a tool that creates a numbered list of items (such as shapes and colors). This tool keeps track of the numbers for you; you just use the words (such as "blue pyramid"). The keyword for enumeration is *enum*, and this keyword creates an *enumerated data type* whose variables contain a set of integer-based constants. These constants contain the programmer's specified values. The programmer can create a category-type list, and the list has the actual values that may be assigned into the enum variables.

The basic form for enumeration is:

```
enum enum_data_type_name { constant list };
```

where the enum is the keyword and the enum_data_type_name is the name for the enumeration data type. The constant list lists the values that may be contained by variables of this type. The program maintains integer values for the variables, and the first value in the list is assigned zero. (The enumeration can be thought of as a built-in cross-reference list or list of categories.)

Our shape and color lists are enumerated in the following manner:

```
enum GeometricShape {cone, cube, pyramid, sphere};
enum Color { red, orange, yellow, green, blue, indigo, violet};
```

Once we set up the enumerations, the enumerated data type is used to declare variables. Our Shape structure can be rewritten like this:

```
struct Shape
{
    GeometricShape ShapeType;    // to be assigned cone - sphere
    Color ShapeColor;            // to be assigned red - violet
};
```

The blue pyramid program can then be written as:

enum
keyword used for
creating an
enumerated data type

enumerated data type
user-defined data type
whose variables
contain integer-based
constants

7

```
int main()
{
        Shape MyShape;
        MyShape.ShapeType = pyramid;      //use the enum list values
        MyShape.ShapeColor = blue;
};
```

Can you think of any programming situation where the enum would be helpful? How about using an enumeration variable in a bird-watching program? We can create a BirdType data type with this statement:

```
enum BirdType {robin, rooster, canary, sparrow, roadrunner, finch,
            eagle };
```

This program declares three bird variables of the BirdType data type, and the programmer simply refers to the values in the list in the program. Behind the scenes, the computer keeps an integer-based list, which is demonstrated in Figure 7-13.

```
enum BirdType {robin, rooster, canary, sparrow, roadrunner, finch, eagle };
int main()
{
        BirdType Tweetie, Foghorn, BeepBeep;      // three different BirdType variables

        Tweetie = canary;      // We can now assign one of the enum list values to each
        Foghorn = rooster;       // BirdType variable.
        BeepBeep = roadrunner;
```

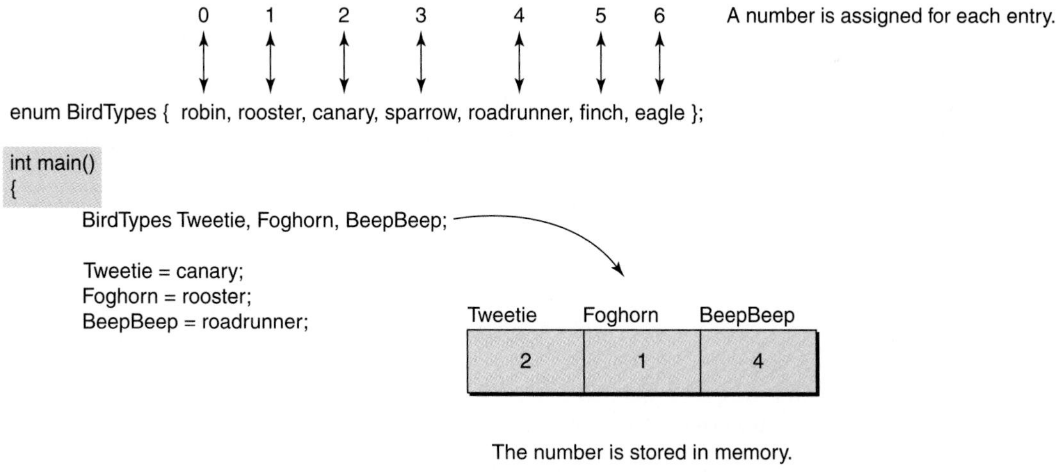

If you write out the values in enumerated variables, you see the integer values.

Figure 7-13
An enum Data Type Is an Integer-Based List

A programmer working on a card game (such as blackjack) might have two enumeration data types, one for the card suit and one for the ranking of the card (i.e., the number). By using the integer-based list, we can set up both the suit and rank of the card in the correct order for comparisons. For example, the suits can be set up in the following order (clubs, diamonds, hearts, and spades). For the card rank, we can assign the first integer in the list to be two instead of the default value of zero. Since the enum values are merely integers, setting up the enums in this fashion lays the groundwork for easily comparing two cards or adding the card values to determine total points. Figure 7-14 illustrates the Suit and Rank enums.

```
enum Rank { two=2, three, four, five, six, seven, eight, nine, ten,
                  jack, queen, king, ace };
enum Suit {club, diamond, heart, spade};
```

enums: Assign and Compare

Enumerated data types in C++ provide an easy way to establish a data type whose variable can contain a programmer-specified value. Enumerated variables are not character strings. Think of them as integers. The enum variables provide an easy and convenient way to read a program variable value—one that makes sense for the programming task. There are two frequently used operations with enums—assignment and comparison.

The Colors data type variables are shown below with assignment statements as well as an if and switch statement:

```
enum Color {red, orange, yellow, green, blue, indigo, violet};

int main()
{
      Color MyColor, YourColor;
      MyColor = red;                         // assign
      YourColor = blue;
```

		3	4	5	6	7	8	9	10	11	12	13	14

enum Rank { two=2, three, four, five, six, seven, eight, nine, ten, jack, queen, king, ace };

enum Suit {club, diamond, heart, spade};

	0	1		2	3

Figure 7-14
Suit and Rank enum Data Types

Chapter 7 ▌ User-Defined Data Types, struct, and enum

```
        3    4   5   6  7    8   9   10  11   12    13   14
enum Rank { two=2, three, four, five, six, seven, eight, nine, ten, jack, queen, king, ace };

enum Suit {club, diamond, heart, spade};

        0    1      2    3
```

Figure 7-14
Suit and Rank enum Data Types

Note: It is possible to assign an integer value directly into an enumerated variable. The integer value must be cast into the enumerated variable. For example, by using a for loop, each element in a Color array can be assigned a different color. Don't forget that the array elements are indexed 0 through 6, and the enumerated color values are also 0 through 6 (0 = red, 1 = orange, etc.).

```
enum Color {red, orange, yellow, green, blue, indigo, violet};

int main()
{
        Color Rainbow[7];
        int i;
        for(i = 0; i < 7; ++i)
        {
                Rainbow[i] = (Color) i;    //cast the integer value into the Color array
        }
```

Community College Departments Example   Creating enumerated data types can be quite useful when the programmer is faced with keeping track of category-type data. Let's refer again to the community college student information program and assume that the college has three departments: Technologies, Arts and Sciences, and Developmental Studies.

Our student information program uses an enumerated data type called Department. The following statement sets up the Department data type:

```
enum Department {Technologies, Arts_and_Sci, Dev_Studies};
```

This enum statement creates the data type Department, and any Department variable can have the value Technologies, Arts_and_Sci, or Dev_Studies.

```
//Program 7-10 Enumerated data in Student data structures.
#include <iostream.h>
#include <string.h>

enum Department {Technologies, Arts_and_Sci, Dev_Studies};
struct Student   // The tag now contains an enum data type.
{
      char name[40];
      char address[80];
      char ID_Num[15];
      Department dept_enrolled;        //this is an enumerated data type variable
};


int main()
{
      Student MyStudent;    //create a single variable
// We'll fill Melissa's information into MyStudent.
      strcpy(MyStudent.name,"Melissa Williams");
      strcpy(MyStudent.address, "123 Main Street, C-Ville, USA");
      strcpy(MyStudent.ID_Num, "123-45-6789");
      MyStudent.dept_enrolled = Technologies;     /* Now assign an enumerated value
                                      directly into the variable. */


      // remainder of program
}
```

Let's see how this works in an example. (See Program 7-10.) We modify our Student data structure to include a dept_enrolled variable instead of an integer department code. When we need to do comparisons, the code will look like this:

```
if(MyStudent.dept_enrolled == Technologies)
{
      cout << MyStudent.name << "is enrolled in the Technologies Dept.";
}
else if( MyStudent.dept_enrolled == Arts_and_Sci)
{
      cout << MyStudent.name << "is enrolled in the Arts and Sciences Dept.";
}
else if(MyStudent.dept_enrolled == Dev_Studies)
{
      cout << MyStudent.name << "is enrolled in the Developmental Studies Dept.";
}
```

A switch statement provides another way to implement comparison code:

```
switch(MyStudent.dept_enrolled)
{
case Technologies:
        cout << MyStudent.name << "is enrolled in the Technologies Dept.";
        break;
case Arts_and_Sci:
        cout << MyStudent.name << "is enrolled in the Arts and Sciences Dept.";
        break;
case Dev_Studies:
        cout << MyStudent.name << "is enrolled in the Developmental Studies Dept.";
}
```

The enumerated constant list is made up of constant values that are basically an integer-based list. The constant values are designed to aid in writing the program, in making comparisons and writing assignment statements, and in acting as case labels in a switch statement. If we write out the enumerated variable, we see only the integer value; that is, if we perform these lines of code:

```
int main()
{
        Student MyStudent;
        MyStudent.dept_enrolled = Technologies;
        cout << "\n The department is " << MyStudent.dept_enrolled;

        //remainder of program
}
```

The output is:

The department is 0

Troubleshooting: enums Are Not Character Strings   The enumeration constant values are not character strings. Programmers often mix up enumerated data and character string data, and attempt to do string copies for enum assignments and string comparisons for variable evaluations. Table 7-4 compares enumerated data and character string data with a shortened Color list.

Enumerated variables are not designed for use in input and output. If you write out an enumerated data value, you find the associated integer constant. (See the next example.) Extra programming effort is required for input and output with enum values, as we shall show later.

TABLE 7-4
Comparing enums and Character Strings

C++ Statements	Enumeration	Character String

Set up data type	`// statement outside main`
	`enum Color {red, blue, green};`
		`/* No setup is necessary because arrays`
		`are part of C++, but we do need the`
		`string.h library for string functions.`
		`*/`
		`#include string.h`

Declaration	`int main()`
	`{`
	`    Color MyColor;`
		`int main()`
		`{`
		`    char YourColor[10];`

Assignment	`/* MyColor can be one of the`
	`three colors in the list. */`
	
	`MyColor = red;`
	
	`/* ALSO can use the integer`
	`value to assign. */`
	
	`MyColor = 0; // red = 0 in list`
		`/* ANY color can be copied into`
		`YourColor using the strcpy function. */`
		
		`strcpy(YourColor, "red");`

Comparison	`/* Compare as you would any`
	`integer variable. */`
	
	`if(MyColor == green)`
	`{`
		`/* Use strcmp function for comparison.`
		`Zero return indicated identical strings.`
		`*/`
		
		`if( strcmp(YourColor, "green") == 0)`
		`{`

Write out value	`/* Must check for each`
	`possibility and "brute force"`
	`writing out the color value. */`
	
	`switch(MyColor)`
	`{`
	`    case red:`
	`      cout << "red"; break;`
	`    case green:`
	`      cout << "green"; break;`
	`    case blue:`
	`      cout << "blue"; break;`
		`/* Write out the string`
		`using cout, as per normal.*/`
		
		`cout << YourColor;`

7

Troubleshooting enums: Choose enum Values Carefully

The enumeration constant values must not have the same identifiers as your program functions, structure tags, class names, or variables. The enumerated constants should be unique to the program. The program below illustrates this problem. The enumerated data contains the value "Corn," but there is also a data structure with the tag name "Corn."

```
//Program 7-x  Problems with enums

#include <iostream.h>
enum BirdFood { SunflowerSeeds, Peanuts, Millet, Corn };

struct Corn
{
        int color;   //1 = white, 2 = yellow, 3 = blue
        float weight;
};

int main()
{
        BirdFood BrandX;
        Corn Jayfood;

        return 0;
}
```

The Visual C++ compiler reports the following error:

```
Compiling...
Ch7EnumProblem_new.cpp
C:\CBook\TestCases\Ch7EnumProblem_new.cpp(18) : error C2146: syntax error : missing ';' before identifier
'Jayfood'
C:\CBook\TestCases\Ch7EnumProblem_new.cpp(18) : error C2065: 'Jayfood' : undeclared identifier
Error executing cl.exe.

Ch7EnumProblem_new.obj - 2 error(s), 0 warning(s)
```

The compiler does not recognize the structure "Corn" because it has already seen the enumerated value "Corn."

Money Makes the World Go 'Round

Imagine that you are writing a money counting program that works with coins, such as pennies, nickels, dimes, quarters, half-dollars, and dollars. You need to keep track of the different types of coins. You immediately recognize this coin problem to be exactly the type of situation for the enum data type, so you set up an enumeration statement. The statement for your money counting program is:

```
enum Coin {pennies, nickels, dimes, quarters, half_dollars, dollars };
```

Once this statement has been set up, you may declare Coin variables in your program.

```
int main()
{
        Coin MyMoney, YourMoney, OurMoney;
```

With an enumerated data type variable, C++ allows you to assign a value in the enumeration list to the variable to make comparisons. The Coin variables MyMoney, YourMoney, and OurMoney can hold the values pennies, nickels, dimes, quarters, half_dollars, and dollars. For example, these are valid statements:

```
YourMoney = nickels;
OurMoney = dollars;
if(MyMoney == dimes)
```

Behind the scenes, C++ is keeping track of the enumerated data, using integers for each value. When the enum Coin is declared, C++ assigns an integer, starting with zero, to the symbols in the enumeration list. The Coin pennies is assigned 0, nickels is assigned 1, dimes is assigned 2, and so on. If you want to print out enumerated values, you see only integers. Refer to Program 7-11. The output appears below:

My Money is 2 and your money is 3

```
//Program 7-11 Money
#include <iostream.h>
enum Coin {pennies, nickels, dimes, quarters, half_dollars, dollars };

int main()
{
        Coin MyMoney, YourMoney;
        MyMoney = dimes;
        YourMoney = quarters;
        cout << "\n My Money is " << MyMoney <<
                " and your money is " << YourMoney;
        return 0;
}
```

You know that enumerated variables store integer values. If you wish to write out the words "dime" and "quarter," you need either an if else or switch statement in the above program. (Enumeration values are not strings and using string functions does not work!)

```
// To write out variable value, an if statement is used.
      if(MyMoney == pennies) cout << " pennies ";
      else if (MyMoney == nickels) cout << " nickels ";
      else if (MyMoney == dimes) cout << " dimes ";
      else if (MyMoney == quarters) cout << " quarters ";
      else if (MyMoney == half_dollars) cout << " half_dollars ";
      else if (MyMoney == dollars) cout << " dollars ";
```

Input and Output for enum Data

A new programmer can become frustrated with enumerated data types because the enums require extra effort for assigning and writing. The usefulness comes for the programmer when he or she is developing and reading/understanding code. An enumerated data type allows the programmer to create code that can be easily read and to simplify the programming tasks.

Now, though, let's concentrate on ways to input and output the values found in the enumerated data lists. As we saw in writing the coin types, we can do a series of checks based on the possible enum values and then write out the word as a string. A more elegant approach for performing enumerated list input and output tasks is to utilize a two-dimensional character array and fill it with the enumerated values. The character string array and enumerated list are both integer-based and, therefore, can cross-reference each other if set up correctly. This technique is especially useful if the enumerated list is long.

Let's use our BirdType list again:

```
enum BirdType {robin, rooster, canary, sparrow, roadrunner, finch, eagle };
```

This new approach involves creating and filling a two-dimensional character string array. Be sure the string array is filled in the same order as the enum list. Figure 7-15 shows how the array and enum list interact.

The two-dimensional character string array is filled in the same order as the enumerated list, and this array can be used for both input and output. We can rewrite our Birds program so that we ask the user to pick the type of bird and then write that bird type to the screen. A for loop aids us in printing out the list of bird types. We read in an integer and then cast it into the BirdType variable. This technique makes the input easy (just enter a number), and writing out the type does not require a long switch statement. Refer to Program 7-12.

```
//Program 7-12 Bird Choices
//Character Strings and enum lists Input and Output
#include <iostream.h>
enum BirdType {robin, rooster, canary, sparrow, roadrunner, finch, eagle };

int main()
{
        char birdlist[7][12] = {"robin", "rooster", "canary", "sparrow", "roadrunner",
                                "finch", "eagle"};
        int i, choice;
        BirdType MyBird;      // One BirdType variable

        cout << "\n Please enter the type of bird \n ";
        for(i = 0; i < 7; ++i)
        {
            cout << i+1 << " " << birdlist[i] << endl;   //writes 1-7 with bird types
        }
        cout << "\n =====> ";
        cin >> choice;
        MyBird = (BirdType)(choice-1);    // must cast integer into BirdType variable

        cout << "\n You entered a(n) " << birdlist[MyBird] << endl;
        return 0;
}
```

The output appears as follows:

Please enter the type of bird
1   robin
2   rooster
3   canary
4   sparrow
5   roadrunner
6   finch
7   eagle
=====> 7

You entered a(n) eagle

This technique combines the strengths of enumerated data types and character strings.

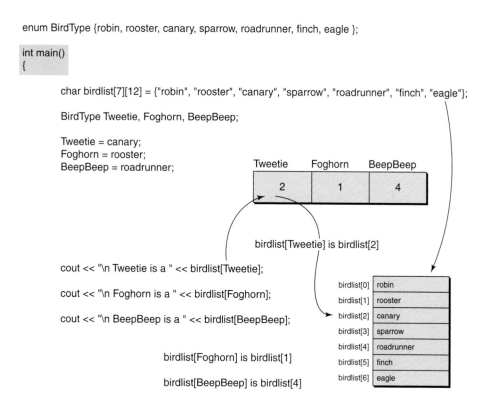

Figure 7-15
Character String Array and enum List Interaction

7.11
Enumerated Data Types and Functions

Enumerated data types are passed to and returned from functions in exactly the same manner as all other data types. They can be passed directly (call by value) or passed by address (call by reference), and they follow the same rules as any other data type in C++. See Table 7-5.

Optics Part Example and Error Codes

In the Optics Parts sample program, we establish an enumerated data type for optical components called Part. This Part data type includes an error code. The function, WhichPart, asks the user to choose a part type. This part is passed to main and then, if it is a valid selection, the part type is passed to the function DoOptics. Program 7-13 illustrates how the enumerated data type is handled in program functions.

```
//Program 7-13 Optics Parts, functions, enums, error codes
#include <iostream.h>
#include <iomanip.h>
enum Part {lens , mirror, prism, error };  // set up the enum data
int WhichPart(Part * );        //prototypes for functions
void DoOptics(Part );

int main()
{
        cout << "\n\nOptics Parts\n";
        int error_code;        // 0 = OK,  -1 = input error
        Part MyPart;
        error_code = WhichPart( &MyPart );

        if(error_code == 0)
                DoOptics(MyPart);  //only call if no input error
        else
                cout << "\n I don't know what that part is!!! \n\n";

        cout << "\n All done with parts! \n";
        return 0;

}

int WhichPart(Part *P_ptr )
{
        int i,choice, error_code = 0;  //assume no error to start

        char Partname[4][10] = {"lens", "mirror", "prism", "error"};

        cout << "\nPlease enter the number of your optics part:\n";
        for(i = 0; i < 3; ++i)
        {
                cout <<setw(2) << i+1 << setw(10) <<Partname[i] << endl;
        }
        cout << "\n =====> ";
        cin >> choice;

        if(choice >= 1 && choice <=3)
        {
                *P_ptr = (Part)(choice-1);                    //valid part
        }
        else
        {
```

```
            *P_ptr = error;
            error_code = -1;      //Whoa!  Had an input error; set the error flag.
        }
        return error_code;
}


void DoOptics(Part new_optic)
{
        switch(new_optic)
        {
            case lens:
                cout << "\n I'm doing lens stuff." << endl;
                break;
            case mirror:
                cout << "\n I'm doing mirror stuff." << endl;
                break;
            case prism:
                cout << "\n I'm doing prism stuff." << endl;
        }
}
```

The WhichPart function is designed to return an ***error code*** or ***error flag***, which is an integer value. No magic is involved with the use of error codes or flags; all functions can be designed to use them. The programmer decides what values to choose for which error code(s), and he or she coordinates the codes between the calling and called functions. It is important to document the error codes in the source code! Typically, a 0 error value reports no errors. A 1 or −1 reports that something is wrong and the function cannot perform as intended or it does not receive expected values. Often several error codes are used, each with a separate meaning. The calling function then checks the error code to determine if a problem occurred. Because the WhichPart function is returning both a Part and an error code, a call by reference (with pointers in WhichPart) is required. The output with a valid part entered is shown below:

error code or flag
set of values specified by the programmer that represents errors discovered in the program

7

Optics Parts

Please enter the number of your optics part
1   lens
2   mirror
3   prism

=====> 3
I'm doing prism stuff.
All done with parts!

Table 7-5 compares enumerated data types and functions.

TABLE 7-5
Enumerated Variable Call by Value and Call by Reference (Pointer)[a]

C++ Statements	Call by Value—Pass from a Function	Call by Reference—Use a Pointer
enum declaration and prototype	`enum Dogs {husky,heeler,mixed };` `Dogs Func3 ( );`	`enum Dogs {husky,heeler,mixed };` `void Func4( Dogs *);`

Call	`int main()`
	`{`
	
	`    Dogs MyDog;`
	`    MyDog = Func3();`
	
	`}`
		`int main()`
		`{`
		
		`    Dogs MyDog;`
		`    Func4(&MyDog);`
		
		`}`

Function header line and function body	`Dogs Func3()`
	`{`
	`    Dogs Puppy;`
	`    // work with enum data directly`
	`    Puppy = husky;`
	`    return Puppy;`
	
	`}`
		`void Func4(Dogs *fido_ptr)`
		`{`
		`    // work with indirection operator`
		`    *fido_ptr = husky;`
		
		`}`

[a]Function 3 has its own local copy of the Dogs variable, and it passes a copy of the Dogs data to main. Function 4 receives the address of main's Dogs variable, and the function uses the indirection operator to access main's MyDog variable.

7.12
Multifile Programs

It is now time to begin organizing our programs into ***multifile programs***, which have separate files as opposed to having the entire source code contained in one *.cpp file. When the program has data structures and associated functions—and classes declarations and definitions—multiple file organization is the only way to construct a program. In real-world applications, it is common to see programs consisting of tens of files if not hundreds of files.

Appendix H, "Multifile Programs," presents the C++ statements necessary to separate your program into many files, as well as two examples from this chapter. It also contains a brief discussion of preprocessor directives.

Although many examples in this text are illustrated in the whole-program-in-one-file format, this style is strictly for simplicity's sake. The reader is encouraged to build all the practice programs in a multifile organizational scheme.

multifile programs
programs consisting of many source and header files created by the programmer

7.13
Practice

What Time Is It?

This program is boring on the outside but exciting on the inside! We ask the user to input a time value based on the twenty-four-hour clock, such as 3:44:32, and we write out whether or not the time is valid. (That's the boring part.) The twenty-four-hour clock is based on twenty-four hours. (Surprised?) Thus, 0:0:1 is one second after midnight and 24:0:0 is midnight. We use a data structure for the time data. Program 7-14 uses the function GetTime, which asks the user to input a time and

```
//Program 7-14 What Time Is It?
#include <iostream.h>

struct Time
{
        int hr,min,sec;
};

Time GetTime();                      //prototypes
bool ValidTime(Time);
void WriteTime(Time);

int main()
{
```

```
        Time MyTime;
        bool GoodTime;

        MyTime = GetTime();
        GoodTime = ValidTime(MyTime);

        WriteTime(MyTime);              // write out the time
        if(GoodTime)
            cout << " is a VALID time. \n";
        else
                cout << " is an INVALID time. \n\n";

        cout << "\n No more time for this program. \n";
        return 0;
}


Time GetTime()
{
        char colon;          //use colon for the input :
        Time local;          // local copy of time structure

        cout << "\n Please enter a time in the format:  HR:MIN:SEC "
        "\n Such as 5:14:43   or 8:33:14  \n\n";
        cin >> local.hr >> colon >> local.min >> colon >> local.sec;

        return local;
}
bool ValidTime(Time T)
{
        // for the twenty-four-hour clock, valid hours are 0 - 23, valid sec/min are 0-59
        // only valid time if hr is 24 is 24:0:0
        // 0:0:0 is invalid

        // first check for the two "edge" times:
        if(T.hr == 0 && T.min == 0 && T.sec == 0) return false;
        if(T.hr == 24 && T.min == 0 && T.sec == 0) return true;

        // now check for all out of bounds cases
        if(T.hr > 24 || T.hr < 0) return false;
        if(T.min < 0 || T.min > 59 || T.sec < 0 || T.sec > 59) return false;

        // if we get to here, we know we have a valid time
        return true;
}
```

```
void WriteTime(Time MyTime)
{
// Write out the time.
        cout << "\n Your Time: "<<MyTime.hr << ":" <<MyTime.min << ":"  << MyTime.sec ;
}
```

returns the structure. A check time function returns a flag indicating whether the time is valid, and a WriteTime function writes the time to the screen. The program execution looks like this (the user enters 24:0:0):

Please enter a time in the format: HR:MIN:SEC
Such as 5:14:43   or 8:33:14
24:0:0

Your time: 24:0:0 is a VALID time.

No more time for this program.

Show Me the Cards

In Program 7-15, we set up a data structure named Card that represents a playing card. Its data is a Suit and a Rank. The main function has an array of fifty-two cards. We simply fill the array values with a suit and a rank value and then print them out to the screen.

```
//Program 7-15 Playing Cards
#include <iostream.h>
#include <iomanip.h>

enum Suit { club, diamond, heart, spade};
enum Rank { two = 2, three, four, five, six, seven, eight, nine, ten, jack, queen,
king, ace};

struct Card
{
        Suit color;
        Rank number;
};

int main()
{
        Card cards[52];   // we have 52 cards, each card will have a suit and rank
        cout << "\n Show Me the Cards!!  \n\n";
```

```
//now use the integer enumeration values to initialize the array element
int i, j, card_ctr = 0;            // array index for cards
for (i = 0; i < 4; ++i)            // this loop is for the four suits
{
        for(j = 2; j < 15; ++j)         // this loop is for the card ranks
        {
                cards[ card_ctr].color = (Suit)i; //cast integer values to assign
                cards[ card_ctr].number = (Rank) j;
                ++ card_ctr;
        }
}

//now let's write out the cards and use the ASCII symbol for card suits
int temp_rank;    // save some typing
card_ctr = 0;  // reset card index to zero
for(i = 0;   i < 4; ++i)
{
        for(j=2 ; j < 15; ++j)
        {                                      // first the number
                temp_rank = cards[card_ctr].number;
                if( temp_rank < 11) cout << cards[card_ctr].number;
                else if(temp_rank == jack) cout << "J";
                else if(temp_rank == queen) cout << "Q";
                else if(temp_rank == king) cout<< "K";
                else cout << "A";

                switch(cards[card_ctr].color)        //now the suit
                {
                        case spade: cout << char(6) << " "; break;    //spades
                        case heart: cout << char(3) << " "; break;    //hearts
                        case diamond: cout << char(4) << " "; break; //diamonds
                        case club: cout << char(5) << " "; break;    //clubs
                }
        ++ card_ctr;
        }
cout << endl;
}
return 0;
}
```

The output from this program uses the ASCII symbols for the four card suits:

2♣ 3♣ 4♣ 5♣ 6♣ 7♣ 8♣ 9♣ 10♣ J♣ Q♣ K♣ A♣
2♦ 3♦ 4♦ 5♦ 6♦ 7♦ 8♦ 9♦ 10♦ J♦ Q♦ K♦ A♦
2♥ 3♥ 4♥ 5♥ 6♥ 7♥ 8♥ 9♥ 10♥ J♥ Q♥ K♥ A♥
2♠ 3♠ 4♠ 5♠ 6♠ 7♠ 8♠ 9♠ 10♠ J♠ Q♠ K♠ A♠

Fun Dog Shows

In this last practice program (Program 7-16), we use two data structures and an enumerated data type in one data structure to model an entrant in a dog show. The data type Contestant contains the owner and dog information. We ask the user to enter the contestant information and the program writes it to the screen. Two functions aid us in this task. The AskUser4Info is passed the address of the structure, and the WriteInfo function is passed a copy of the structure. Furthermore, a two-dimensional character string array handles the input and output of the enumerated data.

```
//Program 7-16 Dog Shows
#include <iostream.h>
#include <stdlib.h>     //for atoi function
enum Breed { husky, heeler, shepherd, pointer, chow, terrier, other};
struct Name
{
        char first[25];
        char last[25];
};
struct Dog
{
        char fido_name[40];
        Breed type;
        int age;
};
struct Contestant
{

        Name owner;
        Dog fido;
};
            // for both functions we'll pass the char strings for enums
void AskUser4Info(Contestant *, char [][15]);  //we use a pointer here
void WriteInfo(Contestant, char[][15] );    // no pointers--send struct to function

int main()
{
```

```
        Contestant Joe;    // Joe is our contestant
        char breedlist[7][15] = {"husky", "heeler", "shepherd", "pointer",
               "chow", "terrier", "other"};
        AskUser4Info(&Joe, breedlist);    // call to get information
        WriteInfo(Joe,breedlist);         // write it out
        cout << "\n All Done with Dogs! \n";
        return 0;
}


void AskUser4Info(Contestant *ptr, char breedlist[][15])
{
        char buf[20];
        cout << "\n Please enter the owner's first name ";
        cin.getline(ptr->owner.first, 25);
        cout << "\n Please enter the owner's last name ";
        cin.getline(ptr->owner.last, 25);
        cout << "\n Please enter the Dog's name ";
        cin.getline(ptr->fido.fido_name,40);
        cout << "\n How old is the dog? ";
        cin.getline(buf,20);
        ptr->fido.age = atoi(buf);

        int i,choice;
        cout << "\n Please select the number of the Dog's breed type: \n\n";
        for(i = 0; i<7; ++i)
        {
               cout << i+1 << " " << breedlist[i] << endl;
        }
        cin.getline(buf,20);
        choice = atoi(buf);
        ptr->fido.type = (Breed)(choice-1);
}
void WriteInfo(Contestant Joe, char breedlist[][15] )
{

        cout << "\n\n This is what you entered:" <<
              "\n     Owner : " << Joe.owner.first << " " << Joe.owner.last <<
              "\n Dog's Name: " << Joe.fido.fido_name <<
              "\n        Age: " << Joe.fido.age <<
              "\n      Breed: " << breedlist[Joe.fido.type] << endl;

}
```

The program execution and output appears as follows:

Please enter the owner's first name   Mike
Please enter the owner's last name   Grobe
Please enter the Dog's name   Kiowa the Wonder Dog
How old is the dog?   7
Please select the number of the dog's breed type
1 husky
2 heeler
3 shepherd
4 pointer
5 chow
6 terrier
7 other
1
This is what you entered:
**   Owner : Mike Grobe**
Dog's Name: Kiowa the Wonder Dog
**   Age: 7**
**   Breed: husky**

All Done with Dogs!

▌ REVIEW QUESTIONS AND PROBLEMS

Short Answer

1. What is the job of the dot operator?

2. Where in the program is a structure tag (description of structure) located?

3. When a structure is passed by a call by value to a function, is a local copy of the structure created in the function? When a structure array is passed to a function, is a local copy of the structure created?

4. Why is the right-arrow operator preferred over the indirection operator, *, when a programmer is working with a pointer that contains an address to a structure?

5. Describe the two items that are located on either side of the dot operator.

6. How can a numbered list be created in a C++ program?

7. If your program has a large data structure, why is it a good idea always to pass the address of the data structure to a function?

8. What is the major drawback to creating a data structure inside a function as opposed to creating it by using a structure tag?

9. Name three differences between a data structure and an array.

10. "Mary" is a variable of type struct A. The struct A has a struct B variable (named b). The B structure has an integer variable named Dot. How many dots does it take to access Mary's Dot? Show the structure declarations and a statement assigning the number 7 into Mary's Dot.

Debugging Problems: Compiler Errors

Identify the compiler errors in Problems 11 to 15 and state what is wrong with the code.

11.
```
#include <iostream.h>
enum Flowers {daisy, rose, tulip, sunflower}
int main();
{
    Flowers bud;
    strcpy(bud, "rose");
    if(bud == "rose") cout << "\n the flower is a rose";
    return 0;
}
```

12.
```
#include <iostream.h>
struct Birds
{
    char name[40];
    float size;
}
int main()
{
    Birds birdies[100];
    birdies[0].name = "robin";
    birdies.size = 5.4;
```

13.
```
struct Ball
{
    Color c;
    float diameter;
};
enum Color { red, green, blue};

int main()
{
    Ball tennis;
    Ball.Color = green;
    tennis.diameter = 2.5;
```

14.

```
#include <iostream.h>
Enum Light {full, partial, shade};
Struct HousePlant
{
    char name[50];
    Light amount;
}
HousePlant GimmeAPlant();
int main()
{
    HousePlant happy
    GimmeAPlant(happy);
```

15.

```
struct Ball
{
    float size;
    Color c;
};

void WhatBall?(Ball *);
int main()
{
    Ball tennis;
    WhatBall?(&tennis);
    return 0;
}
void WhatBall?(Ball *ptr)
{
    *ptr.size = 2.5;
    *ptr.c = red;
}
```

Debugging Problems: Run-Time Errors

Each of the programs in Problems 16 to 18 compiles but does not do what the specification states. What is the incorrect action and why does it occur?

16. Specification: The function ConvertToSeconds should convert the time in the Time structure to total seconds and return it to the calling function. *Note:* Find the error in the function.

```
struct Time
{
    int hr, min, sec;
};
int ConvertToSeconds(Time);       // prototype

int ConvertToSeconds(Time T)      //function body
{
        int total;
        total = T.hr*60.0 + T.min*60.0 + T.sec;
        return total;
}
```

17. Specification: The program should set the color array so that violet is in the first array element and red is in the last array element. The program should then write out the names of the seven colors of the rainbow to the screen.

```
enum Color {red, orange, yellow, green, blue, indigo, violet};
int main()
{
        Color colors[7];
        int i;
        for(i = 0; i < 7; ++i)
        {
                colors[i] = (Color)i;
                cout << "\n That color is" << colors[i];
        }
        return 0;
}
```

18. Specification: The function GimmeAPlant should fill the HousePlant variable with the name "Ivy," and the lighting should be "shade."

```
#include <iostream.h>
#include <string.h>
enum Light {full, partial, shade}
struct HousePlant
{
    char name[50];
    Light amount;
};
void GimmeAPlant(HousePlant *);      // prototype

void GimmeAPlant(HousePlant *plant_ptr)
{
    strcmp(plant_ptr->name, "Ivy");
    plant_ptr->amount = (Light) 3;
}
```

Programming Problems

Write complete C++ programs for Problems 19 to 22.

19. Write a program that sets up a Date structure (integer for month, day, and year) and a Person structure (name and birthday—using the Date struct). The program should have a function (FillPerson) that asks the user to enter all the name and birthday information. The prototype for this function is:

```
Person FillPerson( );
```

You should also have a function called WritePerson that writes out all the person information using the name of the month (as opposed to the integer value) for the birthday month. The prototype for this function is:

```
void WritePerson(Person);
```

Your program should have two Person variables. It should fill these two variables and then call a function called WhoIsOlder, which is sent both Person variables. The function determines who is older and writes the age status to the screen. (*Note:* WhoIsOlder should call WritePerson twice.)

20. Write a C++ program that sets up an enumerated data type for days of the week (Monday, Tuesday, etc.), and then set up a DAYDATE structure. This structure has an enumerated Day variable and a Date struct (see Problem 19). Write a function called WhenDidItHappen. This function receives an address to a DAYDATE structure. This function asks the user to enter a day and date. (Use a two-dimensional character string to assist with the days.) Write the user's day and date in the main function.

21. Write a structure tag and short main program that sets up a struct for a baseball pitcher that contains his name, earned run average (ERA), innings pitched, and strikeout percentage. In the program, declare one pitcher variable and pass its address to a function called Smokin'. This function fills the pitcher variable with the following information:

Name: Smokin' Joe Green	ERA: 1.2
Innings pitched: 55	Strikeout percentage: 0.25

Once the data is in the structure, write the pitcher information to the screen.

22. Create a data file that contains data on football players. The file contains each player's name, height (in feet and inches), and weight in the following format:

```
Deion Husky
6    8.5   325
Cupcake Johnston
5    11    295
Tippy Toe Harte
6    5.5   315
:
:
```

The file may contain information for as many as twenty players. Set up a Foot-ballPlayer structure that holds this information. Your program should declare an array of FootballPlayers and read the data from the file. Next, you should send the array to a function call PlayerAverages. This function determines the average height and weight of your players. (*Hint:* Set up an "Average" football player data variable, fill it, and return that to your calling function.) Write your player information with a function called WritePlayer that receives a single FootballPlayer. Your program should report all the players and the average player information, too.

7

Functions

Part II: C++ Function Enhancements

8

KEY TERMS AND CONCEPTS

call by reference with reference parameters
default parameter list functions
overloaded functions
reference parameters

KEYWORD

inline

CHAPTER OBJECTIVES

Review the general formats for the "classic" C-style function.

Introduce the concept of a reference parameter.

Compare the differences between using pointers and using reference parameters in functions.

Demonstrate how it is possible to overload functions by writing many functions with the same name.

Point out how it is possible to provide default input values for functions.

Show how to prototype an inline function.

Present comparison program examples for examining overloaded functions and default parameter list functions.

Leaving the Structured World Behind

The C language is designed for the top-down structured programming world. Aside from the iostream library we've been using for input and output, the majority of the material in this text (i.e., Chapters 1 to 7) is standard C. By providing tools for building object-oriented software, the C++ language adds new features to the C language.

In Chapter 9, we shall begin to study the C++ language syntax and programming principles required for an object-oriented language. We will discuss program design and implementation with classes and objects. Before you design your first class, you must learn details concerning functions.

This chapter presents four new C++ enhancements to the C language function:

1. A new method of passing the address of a variable to a function (a second *pass by reference* technique); this second technique is more direct and does not require the pointer and indirection operators.

2. *Overloaded functions*, which permit several functions to have the same name.

3. *Default parameter input list functions*, which are special cases of an overloaded function that provide the programmer a way to specify default values for function inputs.

4. *Inline functions*, which produce faster (but larger) executable code.

Before we explore these new features, let's briefly review the C function form and usage.

8.1
Function Review

Basic Requirements

There are three required statements for using a function in C and C++:

1. Prototype.
2. Call.
3. Function header line and function body.

The forms of these three statements are shown below:

```
return_type  Function_name(input data type list);          // Prototype
return_value = Function_name(variable names list);         // Call
return_type  Function_name(input data type and name list)  //F.H.L.
{
    // Body of function
}
```

Call by Value

The call by value parameter passing technique is the most direct approach and the simplest technique in C and C++. In a call by value, a copy of the data is passed from function to function. As shown in the Say Hello program (Program 8-1), the main function calls three functions, Hello, GetNumber, and WriteNumber. Hello simply writes out "hello world" and GetNumber asks the user for a float and returns the value. The main function then calls WriteNumber, which writes this value to the screen. The main, GetNumber, and WriteNumber functions all have their own variable for the number. When this program executes and the user enters 3.2, the screen output is:

A simple program to say "hello world"

Please enter a floating point number   3.2

The number you entered was 3.2
All Done.

In a call by value, copies of the data are passed between functions. As shown in Program 8-1, the main function is passed a copy of the number from GetNumber. The main function then passes a copy of the number to WriteNumber. In all cases, the functions have their own copies of the variable.

Calling and Called Functions

If a function (such as the main) calls another function (such as GetNumber), the main is known as the calling function and GetNumber is known as the called func-

```
//Program 8-1 Review standard C function, Call by Value.
#include <iostream.h>

float GetNumber();           //Prototypes
void WriteNumber(float);
void Hello(void);

int main( )
{
        float num;
        Hello();             //Call statements
        num = GetNumber();
        WriteNumber(num);
        cout << "\n All Done. \n";
        return 0;}

float GetNumber()            //Function header line
{
        float num;
        cout <<"\n Please enter a floating point number   ";
        cin >> num;
        return num;
}
void WriteNumber(float num)
{
        cout << "\n The number you entered was      " << num;
}
void Hello(void)
{
        cout << "\n A simple program to say \"hello world\"\n";
}
```

tion. If GetNumber then calls another function, GetNumber is also a calling function.

Call by Reference: Variable Address to a Function

In a call by reference, the address of a variable is passed to a function and copied into a pointer variable. The function can then access the calling function's variable by using an indirection operator with the pointer. The called function actually accesses and writes data values directly into the calling function's variables.

C and C++ provide the ability for only one data item to be returned from a function via the return statement. A call by reference is needed if the calling function must return more than one item. Remember, a data structure may have many variables included as part of the structure, but the structure is viewed as a single data item.

call by reference with pointers

term used when the address of a variable is passed into a pointer variable in the function

The GiveMe3Floats program (Program 8-2) uses a *call by reference with pointers* to have a called function return three values to the calling function. The calling function passes the addresses of three variables to pointers in a function. This function obtains the three values and then uses the indirection operator and pointers to write the values directly into main's data variables, a, b, and c. The output is shown below:

The GiveMe3Floats using pointers program.
The three floating point values are 6.7 and 8.1 and 33.7

If the data is contained in data structures, addresses to these structures can be passed to functions, and the right-arrow operator is used to access the structure members. The GiveMe2Structs program (Program 8-3) illustrates this situation. The output is shown below:

The GiveMe2Struct program using pointers program.

The first structure contains 7 and 1
The second structure contains 3 and 5
All Done

8

```
//Program 8-2 Review Call by Reference--Pointers
#include <iostream.h>
void GiveMe3Floats(float*,float*,float*);  //Prototype includes pointers, variables

int main( )
{
      float a,b,c;
      cout << "\n The GiveMe3Floats using pointers program.\n";
      GiveMe3Floats(&a, &b, &c);
      cout << "\n The three floating point values are " << a << " and " << b <<
           " and " << c << endl;
      return 0;
}
void GiveMe3Floats(float *a_ptr, float *b_ptr, float *c_ptr)
{
      *a_ptr = (float)6.7;        //indirection operator with pointer
      *b_ptr = (float)8.1;        //cast double values into floats
      *c_ptr = (float)33.7;       //to avoid compiler warnings
}
```

```
//Program 8-3 Review Call by Reference--Pointers with structures
#include <iostream.h>
struct Struct1
{
        int a,b;
};
struct Struct2
{
        int d,e;
};
void GiveMe2Structs(Struct1 *, Struct2 *);  //Prototype includes pointers, variables
int main( )
{
        cout << "\n The GiveMe2Structs using pointers program.\n";
        Struct1 First;
        Struct2 Second;
        GiveMe2Structs(&First, &Second);
        cout << "\n The first structure contains " << First.a << " and " << First.b;
        cout << "\n The second structure contains " << Second.d << " and " << Second.e;
        cout << "\n All Done \n";
        return 0;
}
void GiveMe2Structs(Struct1 *ptr1, Struct2 *ptr2)
{
        ptr1->a = 7;            //indirection operator with pointer
        ptr1->b = 1;
        ptr2->d = 3;
        ptr2->e = 5;
}
```

Global Variables and Functions

Global variables are declared outside any function and are accessible by all functions located within the file containing the global declaration. (The global variables are accessible by the entire program if the declaration is repeated in other files with the keyword *extern* leading the declarative statement. See Appendix H, "Multifile Programs.") When global variables are used, there is no need to pass them between functions. The GiveMe3Floats program (Program 8-4) uses global variables.

Four Methods for Getting Data to and from Functions

There are four basic methods for having the data in the calling function available to the called function. We are familiar with three of these techniques: 1) a copy of the

```
//Program 8-4 Global Variables
#include <iostream.h>

void GiveMe3Floats(void);        //Prototype has void data types, nothing is passed
float a,b,c;                     //variables are global, both main and function see them
int main( )
{
        cout << "\n The GiveMe3Floats using globals program.\n";
        GiveMe3Floats();
        cout << "\n The three floating point values are   " << a << " and " << b <<
                " and " << c << endl;
        return 0;
}

void GiveMe3Floats()
{
        a = (float)6.7;         //values placed in a,b,c
        b = (float)8.1;      //cast double values into floats
        c = (float)33.7;
}
```

variable's value can be passed in a call by value, 2) the address of the variable can be passed in a call by reference using pointers, and 3) the variables can be globally declared. Table 8-1 briefly describes each method. Notice that the last method—call by reference using reference parameters—is a new technique!

8.2
Call by Reference Using Reference Parameters

C++ provides programmers with a new call by reference technique for passing a variable's address to a function that uses reference parameters. A reference parameter is an address; that is, it is implied though not plainly expressed as an address. In the *call by reference with reference parameter* passing technique, the function prototype and function header line contains *reference parameters*—that is, the & is used instead of the *. The & operator in the prototype and function header line is saying "Reference" (as opposed to "Pointer"). In the call statement, just the variable name is used; you do not need to use the & operator.

In this new type of call by reference, the addresses are passed to the called function, and this function accesses the calling function's data. However, the reference parameters make it possible for the call statement to have the call by value notation. In other words, a call by reference with reference parameters really is

Method	Description	Notes
Call by value	Copy of variable value(s) is (are) passed to the function. Functions have their own copies of the data.	Local value used in function is not returned. See Say Hello program (Program 8-1). This technique can be memory consuming and is not recommended for large structures.
Call by reference using pointers	Address of variable passed to function, received by pointer. The indirection operator is used with the pointer to access the calling function's data.	Called function actually accesses local variable of calling function. Only one copy of data in program. See GiveMe3Floats and GiveMe2Structs programs (Programs 8-2 and 8-3).
Global variables	All functions see/use/change global variable values. No input or return data needed. (Void in prototypes.)	Global variables are not recommended for most programming situations. See GiveMe3Floats—global version (Program 8-4).
Call by reference using reference parameters (new!)	Another technique for passing the variable's address to a function. The variable name is used in the call statement, but actually the address of the variable is passed to the function.	Looks like a call by value but works like a call by reference. Reference syntax is used, not pointer or indirection operator. (See Program 8-5.)

sending an address to a function, but the program does not need to use the indirection operator or right-arrow operator to access data.

Reference parameters employ the reference operator, &, in the function declaration. Basically, the reference parameter is saying to the program, "This is really an address. Treat it like one. I'm not going to bother with the address or indirection operators because you and I both know it is an address."

Call by Reference with Reference Parameters

GiveMe3Floats and Structs Again!   The GiveMe3Floats program is rewritten in Program 8-5 using reference parameters instead of pointer variables. Notice how the & replaces the *, and the variables are accessed in the function as if it were a call by value. Figure 8-1 illustrates the underlying process involved.

Data structure reference variables behave in a similar manner. The GiveMe-2Structs program with reference parameters (Program 8-6) illustrates how reference variables simplify accessing data members via the dot operator instead of the right-arrow operator.

```
//Program 8-5 GiveMe3Floats in a Call by Reference with Reference Parameters
#include <iostream.h>
void GiveMe3Floats(float&,float&,float&);   //Prototype has reference types
int main( )
{
        float a,b,c;
        cout << "\n The GiveMe3Floats using reference parameters program.\n";
        GiveMe3Floats(a,b,c);   /* the call just uses the names of the variables,
                        but the addresses are being passed to the function. */
        cout << "\n The three floating point values are  " << a << " and " << b <<
                " and " << c << endl;
        return 0;
}
void GiveMe3Floats(float &a_ref, float &b_ref, float &c_ref)
{

        a_ref = (float)6.7;        //values actually being assigned into main's a,b,c
        b_ref = (float)8.1;        //cast double values into floats
        c_ref = (float)33.7;
}
```

Now that we've seen a few examples, compare the syntax of the call by value, call by reference with pointers, and call by reference with reference parameters. Tables 8-2 and 8-3 compare these techniques. In Table 8-2, the functions F1, F2, and F3 all return the value 5.0 to the main function. In the call by value, the value is returned via a return statement. In the two call by reference examples, the main's variable is accessed by the F2 and F3 functions because both functions have a reference to the main's variable. In Table 8-3, functions F4 and F5 place values in the two members of the struct.

Reference Parameter Limitations   Incorporating reference parameters in calls to functions makes a programmer's life easy—no address operators in the call statement, no indirection operators (either * or ->) in the called function. However, there are several limitations with references. You may not reference another reference. (It is possible to have a pointer to a pointer.) A reference variable must be initialized when declared if it is not part of a function parameter list, or if it is not a return value or class member. It is not possible to create a pointer to a reference or to create an array of references. Every tool has its optimum purpose, and reference parameters work well for functions.

One Downside to Reference Parameters   There is only one slight problem with reference parameters. When you examine a function's calling statement, it is impossible to tell if the function is using a call by value or a call by reference. The

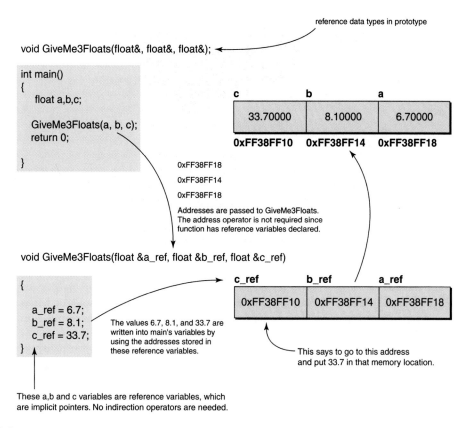

reference data types in prototype

```
void GiveMe3Floats(float&, float&, float&);
```

```
int main()
{
    float a,b,c;

    GiveMe3Floats(a, b, c);
    return 0;

}
```

c	b	a
33.70000	8.10000	6.70000

0xFF38FF10 0xFF38FF14 0xFF38FF18

0xFF38FF18
0xFF38FF14
0xFF38FF18

Addresses are passed to GiveMe3Floats.
The address operator is not required since
function has reference variables declared.

```
void GiveMe3Floats(float &a_ref, float &b_ref, float &c_ref)
```

```
{
    a_ref = 6.7;
    b_ref = 8.1;
    c_ref = 33.7;
}
```

c_ref	b_ref	a_ref
0xFF38FF10	0xFF38FF14	0xFF38FF18

The values 6.7, 8.1, and 33.7 are
written into main's variables by
using the addresses stored in
these reference variables.

This says to go to this address
and put 33.7 in that memory location.

These a,b and c variables are reference variables, which
are implicit pointers. No indirection operators are needed.

Figure 8-1
Call by Reference

8

reference parameters are indicated in the function prototype and function header line—which may be located in other program files. This situation may or may not cause trouble for the programmer. It is always a good idea to understand fully the interface to functions.

Cats and Dogs: Using Reference Parameters   The Cats and Dogs programs, using both pointers and global variables, were presented in Chapter 5 (Programs 5-13 and 5-14). Now we rewrite the program with reference parameters. Recall that the Cats and Dogs program asks the user if he or she has dogs. If the answer is yes, the program then asks, How many dogs? (or, How many cats?). The function GetPetInfo must return four pieces of information to the calling function. In Program 8-7, reference parameters are used, and the addresses of the four variables are implicitly sent to the GetPetInfo (that is, the call statements have the variable names but in reality the variable addresses are being passed). These reference variables are then used and the information returned to the main function without

```
//Program 8-6 GiveMe2Structs in a Call by Reference
#include <iostream.h>

struct Struct1
{
        int a,b;
};
struct Struct2
{
        int d,e;
};
void GiveMe2Structs(Struct1 &, Struct2 &);  //Prototype includes reference data types
int main( )
{
        cout << "\n The GiveMe2Structs using pointers program.\n";
        Struct1 First;
        Struct2 Second;
        GiveMe2Structs( First, Second);  /* the call uses just the variable names
                                            but the addresses are sent to the function */

        cout << "\n The first structure contains " << First.a << " and " << First.b;
        cout << "\n The second structure contains " << Second.d << " and " << Second.e;
        cout << "\n All Done \n";
        return 0;
}

void GiveMe2Structs(Struct1 &rStr1, Struct2 &rStr2)
{
        rStr1.a = 7;            //members accessed via dot operator
        rStr1.b = 1;
        rStr2.d = 3;
        rStr2.e = 5;
}
```

the use of the indirection operator. In the WritePetInfo function, the values are simply sent to it (not their addresses) because WritePetInfo merely uses the values and returns nothing.

Troubleshooting: Using Reference Parameters   By far the most common mistake made by a programmer when first working with reference parameters and variables is that he or she adds the address operator(s) in the call statement. It is as if the programmer understands that a call by reference works like a call by address and he or she accidentally uses the address operator.

TABLE 8-2

Comparing Call by Value, Call by Reference with Pointers, and Call by Reference with Reference Parameters with a Single Variable

Statement	Call by Value	Call by Reference with Pointers	Call by Reference with Reference Parameters
Prototype	`float F1( );`	`void F2(float *);`	`void F3( float &);`

Call	`int main()`
	`{`
	`    float x;`
	`    x = F1( );`
		`int main()`
		`{`
		`    float x;`
		`    F2( &x );`
			`int main()`
			`{`
			`    float x;`
			`    F3( x );`

Function header line	`float F1( )`
	`{`
	`    float x;`
	`    x = 5.0;`
	`    return x;`
	`}`
		`void F2(float *x_ptr)`
		`{`
		`    *x_ptr = 5.0;`
		`}`
			`void F3(float &x_ref )`
			`{`
			`    x_ref = 5.0;`
			`}`

Notes	The main and F1 both have a local copy of x. F1 does not access main's variable. F1 simply passes a copy of x's value to main.	F2's x_ptr contains the address of main's x. With the indirection operator, 5.0 is written into main's x.	F3's x_ref also contains the address of main's x. The x_ref is an implicit pointer.

TABLE 8-3

Comparing Call by Value, Call by Reference with Pointers, and Call by Reference with Reference Parameters with Data structs

Statement	Call by Value	Call by Reference with Pointers	Call by Reference with Reference Parameters

Prototype	`struct SSS`
	`{`
	`    int a, b;`
	`};`
	`SSS F1( );`
		`struct SSS`
		`{`
		`    int a, b;`
		`};`
		`void F1(SSS * );`
			`struct SSS`
			`{`
			`    int a, b;`
			`};`
			`void F1(SSS & );`

Call	`int main()`
	`{`
	`    SSS MyStruct;`
	`    MyStruct = F1( );`
		`int main()`
		`{`
		`    SSS MyStruct;`
		`    F1(& MyStruct );`
			`int main()`
			`{`
			`    SSS MyStruct;`
			`    F1(MyStruct );`

Function header line	`SSS F1( )`
	`{`
	`    SSS F1Struct;`
	`    F1Struct.a = 5;`
	`    F1Struct.b = 6;`
	`    return F1Struct;`
	`}`
		`void F2(SSS *s_ptr)`
		`{`
		`    s_ptr->a = 5;`
		`    s_ptr->b = 6;`
		`}`
			`void F3(float &s_ref )`
			`{`
			`    s_ref.a = 5;`
			`    s_ref.b = 6;`
			`}`

```
//Program 8-7 Cats and Dogs Call by Reference--using reference parameters
#include <iostream.h>
void GetPetInfo(bool&, int&, bool&, int&);    // dog data, cat data using reference
void WritePetInfo(bool, int, bool, int);

int main()
{
        bool bDog, bCat;     //flags that are set true or false
        int DogNum, CatNum;

// The two call statements look identical, but GetPetInfo sends the addresses of the
// variables to the function, and WritePetInfo sends copies of the variables.
        GetPetInfo(bDog, DogNum, bCat, CatNum);
        WritePetInfo(bDog, DogNum, bCat, CatNum);

        if(bDog || bCat)
                cout << "\n Don't you just LOVE owning pets? \n ";
        return 0;
}


void GetPetInfo(bool &rbDog, int &rDogNum, bool &rbCat, int &rCatNum)
{
        char answer;
// first assume the answers will be no & set flags to false and nums to zero
        rbDog = false;
        rbCat = false;
        rDogNum = 0;
        rCatNum = 0;

        // Now, ask the questions
        cout << "\n Do you have any dogs?  y = yes, n = no     ";
        cin >> answer;
        if(answer == 'y')
        {

                cout << "\n How many dogs do you have?  ";
                cin >> rDogNum;
                rbDog = true;

        }
        cout << "\n Do you have any cats?  y = yes, n = no     ";
        cin >> answer;
        if(answer == 'y')
        {
                cout << "\n How many cats do you have?  ";
```

```
                cin >> rCatNum;
                rbCat = true;
        }
}

void WritePetInfo(bool bDog, int DogNum, bool bCat, int CatNum)
{
        cout << "\n\n Dog and cat ownership data: ";
        if(bDog == true)
                cout << "\n You own " << DogNum << " dogs. ";
        else
                cout << "\n You don't own any dogs. ";

        if(bCat == true)
                cout << "\n You own " << CatNum << " cats. \n";
        else
                cout << "\n You don't own any cats.\n ";
}
```

Before we see what is wrong, let's see what is right. In the program How-BigIsYourBox (Program 8-8), we ask the user to enter the three dimensions of a box and then calculate the volume. We declare the GetBoxSize function with reference parameters. Note that we have a call by value for the CalcBoxVol function because its job is to calculate and return only one value.

```
//Program 8-8 How Big Is Your Box?  with Reference Variables  (Correct method!)
#include <iostream.h>
void GetBoxSize(float&, float&, float&);  // using reference parameters
float CalcBoxVol(float,float,float);       // call by value

int main()
{
        float width,length,height,vol;
        GetBoxSize(width,length,height);                       // call statements
        vol=CalcBoxVol(width,length,height);
        cout << "\n Your box dimensions are: " << width << " by " <<
                length << " by " <<  height;
        cout << "\n The volume is " << vol << endl;
        return 0;
}

void GetBoxSize(float &w_ref, float &l_ref, float &h_ref)
{
        cout << "\n Enter the width, length, and height of your box. \n ";
        cin >> w_ref >> l_ref >> h_ref;
}
```

```
float CalcBoxVol(float w, float l, float h)
{

        return (w*l*h);
}
```

The following example of the HowBigIsYourBox program illustrates a common mistake made by programmers. Placing the address operator in the call generates a compiler error. The output from the compilers follows the program.

```
//Program 8-8x How Big Is Your Box?  with Reference Variables     (Incorrect Method!)
//ERROR!  ERROR!! DO not use the & in the call with reference variables.
#include <iostream.h>

void GetBoxSize(float&, float&, float&);   //prototypes
float CalcBoxVol(float,float,float);

int main()
{

        float width,length,height,vol;
        GetBoxSize(&width,&length,&height);    // <= ;-(  Here is the problem
        vol=CalcBoxVol(width,length,height);
        cout << "\n Your box dimensions are: " << width << " by " <<
            length << " by " <<  height;
        cout << "\n The volume is " << vol << endl;
        return 0;
}

void GetBoxSize(float&w_ref, float&l_ref, float&h_ref)
{
        cout << "\n Enter the width, length, and height of your box. \n ";
        cin >> w_ref >> l_ref >> h_ref;
}

float CalcBoxVol(float w, float l, float h)
{
        return (w*l*h);
}
```

The Visual C++ compiler reports the following messages:

```
Compiling...
Ch8BigBox.cpp
C:\Ch8BigBox.cpp(15) : error C2664: 'CalcBoxVol' : cannot convert parameter 1 from 'float *' to 'float'
    There is no context in which this conversion is possible
Error executing cl.exe.

TestCases.exe - 1 error(s), 0 warning(s)
```

The GCC compiler reports the following messages:

```
login1:johnston:~/gnu:$ g++ G++_ Ch8BigBox.cc
G++_ Ch8BigBox.cc: In function 'int main()':
G++_ Ch8BigBox.cc:20: converting to 'float' from 'float *'
G++_ Ch8BigBox.cc:14: in passing argument 1 of 'GetBoxSize(float &, float &, float &)'
```

The compilers are attempting to convert the address of a float to a reference variable. Whenever you see a "cannot convert parameter" compiler error, you always have a mismatch in the data types in your function call, prototype, and function header line.

Reference Variable Arrays

If you stop to think about how arrays are passed to functions, you see that the array is the original reference parameter! The C language automatically constructs a pointer for us, and the name of the array (which contains the address of the first element) is required in the call statement. We do not use the address operator in the call, nor do we need the indirection operator in the function. Arrays to functions use implied pointers. Therefore, it should be no surprise to discover that C++ reference books do not include discussions of arrays using reference parameters.

In fact, let's use our knowledge of reference variables and see what the compiler tells us. We can modify the HowBigIsYourBox program so that the box dimensions are in a floating point array instead of three separate float variables. We'll use the GetBoxSize function.

```
//Program 8-x Let's Try Reference Data Type with an Array.
#include <iostream.h>

void GetBoxSize(float&[]);  //prototype using an array of reference values
int main()
{
    // Declare and initialize the array
    float boxsize[3];

    GetBoxSize(boxsize);
```

```
            cout << "\n Your box dimensions are: " << boxsize[0] << " by " <<
                boxsize[1] << " by " << boxsize[2];
            return 0;
    }
    void GetBoxSize(float& bs[])
    {
            bs[0] = bs[1] = bs[2] = 3.0;
    }
```

The Visual C++ compiler shows the following messages:

Compiling...
Ch8RefV_Array.cpp
C:\Ch8RefV_Array.cpp(5) : error C2234: '<Unknown>' : arrays of references are illegal
C:\Ch8RefV_Array.cpp(12) : error C2664: 'GetBoxSize' : cannot convert parameter 1 from 'float [3]' to 'float *[]'
      Types pointed to are unrelated; conversion requires reinterpret_cast, C-style cast or function-style cast
C:\Ch8RefV_Array.cpp(19) : error C2234: '<Unknown>' : arrays of references are illegal
C:\Ch8RefV_Array.cpp(21) : error C2440: '=' : cannot convert from 'const double' to 'float *'
      There is no context in which this conversion is possible
Error executing cl.exe.

TestCases.exe - 4 error(s), 0 warning(s)

The GCC compiler reports the following:

login1:johnston:~/gnu:$ g++ G++_ Ch8RefV_Array.cc
G++_ Ch8RefV_Array:10: declaration of '' as array of references
G++_ Ch8RefV_Array:10: confused by earlier errors, bailing out

The first set of errors reports that arrays of references are illegal. Remember, when-ever an array is declared in a C++ program, it comes equipped with its own implied pointer.

8.3
Overloaded Functions

In the Old C Days

If you write a C program that must obtain the positive value of a number (the absolute value), C's standard libraries (stdlib and math) provide three different functions for this task. The three functions for the absolute value, abs(), fabs(), and labs(), and the input and return parameter types are integer, float or double, and long, respectively. The function prototypes for these functions are:

```
int abs(int);
double fabs(double);
long labs(long);
```

If you have an integer and you need the absolute value, you must call abs(). If your value is a float or a double, you call fabs(). A long integer requires you to call the labs(). These three functions perform essentially the same action. The programmer must keep track of the type of variable to be able to call the correct absolute value function:

```
//Program 8-Using the three different standard library absolute value functions
#include <iostream.h>
#include <stdlib.h>        // contains abs() and labs()
#include <math.h>          // contains fabs()

int main()
{
        double x = -7.345, y;
        int a = -3, b;
        long l = -44000, n;

        y = fabs(x);        //three different functions are needed
        b = abs(a);
        n = labs(l);
        cout << "\n The positive values are " << y << " and " << b << " and " << n;

        return 0;
}
```

What do you think happens if you accidentally call the abs() function with a floating point value?

```
int main()
{
        double x = -7.345, y;
        y = abs(x);
        cout << "\n The positive value of x is " << y ;

        return 0;
}
```

If you believe that x is 7.00000000, you are correct! The abs() function will return an integer value. Therefore, even if you pass it −7.345, it returns the integer 7.

What would it be like to have one absolute value function? The next section answers this question.

Overloaded Functions

C++ allows the programmer *overloaded functions*, meaning that it is possible to have several functions with the same name but with different parameter declarations. In the C language, each function must have a unique name, but C++ allows several functions to have the same name. Overloaded functions in C++ have the same name but different input parameter data types. To have only the return types differ is not adequate. The C++ compiler keeps track of the different same-name functions. When an overloaded function is called, the program examines the input and return data types in the call statement and accesses the correct function.

Absolute Value Overloaded Functions   In the AbsoluteValue program (Program 8-9), we create three functions, all named AbsoluteValue. Once the functions are in place, the programmer calls the AbsoluteValue function whenever he or she needs to obtain the absolute value of a variable, whether the data type is an int, long, float, or double. C++ keeps track of which function must be called. Behind the scenes, we use the standard library routines because there is no need to reinvent them. Note that there are actually three functions called AbsoluteValue, and their function prototypes have different data types. The output is shown below:

The positive values are 7.345 and 3 and 44000
I'm positive about that!   ;-)

At first glance it appears that setting up overloaded functions creates more work for the programmer instead of less. For each overloaded function, there must be a separately declared and written function. Programmers are soon convinced of the payoff once the overloaded functions are set up and using call statements is made easier.

Say Goodnight   Overloaded functions must have different parameter declarations. In other words, the program must be able to differentiate which call corresponds to which function; therefore, the function prototypes must be unique. Overloaded functions may have the same number of parameters but different types (as in the AbsoluteValue program), or they may have a different number of parameters. In the Say Goodnight program (Program 8-10), there are three overloaded functions, all named SayGoodnight(). If the function has no input parameters, we write "Goodnight!" If the function has a character string, we assume the string is a name (such as Bill) and we write "Goodnight, Bill!" If the function has two character strings, we're saying goodnight to two individuals. The output is shown below:

Goodnight!
Goodnight, Miss Kitty !
Goodnight, Jack Russell and Miss Kitty !

All done saying Goodnight!

```
//Program 8-9 Using overloaded functions for absolute value
#include <iostream.h>
#include <stdlib.h>        //for the abs and labs functions
#include <math.h>          //for the fabs function
int AbsoluteValue(int);    //three different prototypes, same function name
double AbsoluteValue(double);
long AbsoluteValue(long);
int main()
{
      double x = -7.345, y;
      int a = -3, b;
      long l = -44000, n;
      y = AbsoluteValue(x);    //the call is to AbsoluteValue for all 3
      b = AbsoluteValue(a);
      n = AbsoluteValue(l);
      cout << "\n The positive values are " << y << " and " << b << " and " << n;
      cout << "\n I'm positive about that!    ;-)  \n";
      return 0;
}

int AbsoluteValue(int x)       //Here are the three different functions
{
      return(abs(x));
}
double AbsoluteValue(double a)
{
      return(fabs(a));
}
long AbsoluteValue(long l)
{
      return(labs(l));
}
```

8.4
Variable-Length Parameter List Functions

The C++ language provides the programmer a shorthand way to overload functions with the use of the *default input parameter list functions*. This useful C++ feature allows the program to declare a function that has a variable number of input parameters, and the programmer also supplies the default values for the inputs. If the function is called and the values are not passed to it, the function simply uses the

default input parameter list function
default values supplied in the function prototype; used if no values are passed to the function

```
//Program 8-10  Using overloaded functions to say goodnight.
#include <iostream.h>

void SayGoodnight();     //three different prototypes, same function name
void SayGoodnight(char [] );
void SayGoodnight(char [], char[]);


int main()
{
        char dog[25] = "Jack Russell", cat[25] = "Miss Kitty ";

        SayGoodnight();
        SayGoodnight(cat);
        SayGoodnight(dog,cat);
        cout << "\n\n All done saying Goodnight!  \n";
        return 0;
}
void SayGoodnight()
{
        cout << "\n Goodnight!";
}
void SayGoodnight(char one[] )
{
        cout << "\n Goodnight, " << one << "!";
}
void SayGoodnight(char one[], char two[] )
{
        cout << "\n Goodnight, " << one << " and " << two << "!";
}
```

default values supplied in the declaration. The prototype for this type of function may or may not contain the variable name, but the default value must be supplied. Two forms for this type of overloaded function are:

```
return_type  Function_name(type = value  list);
return_type  Function_name(type  variable_name = value  list);
```

where the type = value list and type variable_name = value list is a comma-separated list of data types and default values.

   The compiler requires only the type in prototypes and not the name of the variable. However, it will also accept the name of the variable. Prototypes, which include the names of the variables, are much more meaningful and actually act as a "table of contents" for the program.

DrawLines Program

In the DrawLines program, shown as Program 8-11 below, a default parameter list is declared for a function that prints lines of characters to the screen. The default character is a percent sign (%), the default number of characters is twenty-five, and the default number of lines is one. The function prototype may be in either form:

```
void DrawLines(char = '%', int = 25, int = 1 );    //type = parameter values
```

The following prototype includes the variable names and tells the reader the exact order and variable names for the inputs:

```
void DrawLines(char symbol = '%', int num_symb = 25, int num_lines = 1 );
```

The entire program appears in Program 8-11. The output is shown below:

The DrawLines Program

Default line 25 % on 1 line
%%%%%%%%%%%%%%%%%%%%%%%%%

Change to 30 @ to a line
@@@@@@@@@@@@@@@@@@@@@@@@@@@@@@

Now draw 15 # on 3 lines
###############
###############
###############

Last line has 6 % on 1 line
%%%%%%

No more lines for you.

Parameter Order

Default parameter list functions require the programmer to pass inputs in the declaration order. Starting with the rightmost value, parameters may be omitted from the call. In the DrawLines program above, we called the function in the following four ways.

```
void DrawLines(char symbol = '%', int num_symb = 25, int num_lines = 1 );  //prototype

DrawLines();                //void (empty) list use %, 25, 1

DrawLines('@', 30);         // symbol and number of symbols use @, 30, and 1
```

```
//Program 8-11 DrawLines using variable-length parameter list function.
#include <iostream.h>

void DrawLines(char = '%', int = 25, int = 1 );

/*prototype contains the default parameters for character, number of chars in a line,
and number of lines. *//

int main()
{
        cout << "\n The DrawLines Program \n\n";
        cout << "Default Line 25 % on 1 line";
        DrawLines();
        cout << "\n Change to 30 @ to a line";
        DrawLines('@', 30);
        cout << "\n Now draw 15 # on 3 lines";
        DrawLines('#',15,3);
        cout << "\n Last line has 6 % on 1 line";
        DrawLines('%',6);

        cout << "\n\n No more lines for you. \n";
        return 0;
}
void DrawLines(char symbol, int num_symb, int num_lines)
{
        int i, j;
        cout << "\n";
        for(i=0; i < num_lines; ++i)
        {
                for(j=0; j< num_symb; ++j)
                {
                        cout << symbol;
                }
                cout << "\n";
        }
}
```

```
DrawLines('#',15,3);          // all three input values  use #, 15, 3

DrawLines('%',6);             // need to vary the second value, must have the first
```

The function must be called with input values starting on the left, and input values may not be skipped. If we want to leave the input symbol as the default symbol and change the number of symbols, we need to call the DrawLines function like this:

```
DrawLines('%', 6);            // symbol must be passed with number of symbols
```

The function cannot be called in this manner:

```
DrawLines(, 1);               // Not a valid call :-(
```

If we wish to call the function using the default parameters for the symbol and the number of symbols but change the number of lines, the call must look like this:

```
DrawLines('%', 25, 4);        // symbol must be passed in with number of symbols
```

not like this:

```
DrawLines(, ,4);              //    :-(   invalid call
```

Programming Suggestion When working with default parameter list functions, you should place the value(s) you expect to change in the left side of the list and the values you expect to remain constant in the right side. Since the values in the call may be omitted, beginning from the right, you can design your function to shorten your call list.

Perhaps you have an ogre for a C++ programming instructor, and this ogre requires you to put a header function on all your programs so that your name, assignment number, and due date are written to the screen at the start of your program. To make matters worse, this instructor wishes you to use the same parameter list function for all programs beginning with the fourth assignment. Your header function prototype might look like this:

```
void Header(int ProgNum = 4, int DueDay = 1, int DueMonth = 3, int DueYear = 2001);
```

The corresponding header function is:

```
void Header(int ProgNum, int DueDay, int DueMonth, int DueYear)
{
        cout << "\n Donna Jo Programmer \n Assignment No." << ProgNum;
        cout << "\n Due Date" << DueMonth << "/" << DueDay << "/" << DueYear;
}
```

When this function is called like this:

```
Header();
```

The output is:

Donna Jo Programmer
Assignment No. 4
Due Date 3/1/2001

If Donna Jo's fifth assignment is due on March 15, 2001, the header is called like this:

```
Header(5,15);
```

Now the output is:

Donna Jo Programmer
Assignment No. 5
Due Date 3/15/2001

WriteNumbers Based on a beginning, increment, and ending value, our WriteNumbers program (Program 8-12) writes a sequence of numbers to the screen. For example, if the beginning value is 5, the ending value is 28, and the increment is 5, the program writes 5, 10, 15, 20, and 25. In our parameter list, we expect the starting value usually to be 1 and the increment value to be 3. We set the default list so that the order of parameters is ending value, skip value, and starting value. The output is as follows:

Writing Values Start = 1 End = 10 Incr = 3
1, 4, 7, 10,
Writing Values Start = 1 End = 20 Incr = 3
1, 4, 7, 10, 13, 16, 19,
Writing Values Start = 1 End = 20 Incr = 5
1, 6, 11, 16,
Writing Values Start = 0 End = 15 Incr = 3
0, 3, 6, 9, 12, 15,

Troubleshooting: Overloaded Functions

Beginning programmers often confuse overloaded functions that are written separately with default input parameter list functions. A default parameter list function is merely a special type of overloaded function. The AbsoluteValue, SayGoodnight, DrawLine, and WriteNumbers programs all use a form of an overloaded function. All four functions have several forms of their call statements with different results.

```
//Program 8-12 WriteNumbers Default Parameter List Function
#include <iostream.h>
void WriteNumbers(int = 10, int = 3, int = 1); //end, increment, start

int main()
{
        WriteNumbers();      // use default values, 1 - 10, incr by 3

        WriteNumbers(20);    // now end at 20, write 1 - 20, incr by 3

        WriteNumbers(20, 5); // now go 1 - 20 and incr by 5

        WriteNumbers (15, 3, 0); // now write 0 - 15, incr 3
        return 0;
}

void WriteNumbers(int end, int incr, int start)
{
        int i;
        cout << "\n Writing Values Start = " << start << " End = " << end <<
             " Incr = " << incr << endl;
        for(i = start; i <= end; i = i+incr)
        {
                cout << i << ", ";
        }
}
```

8

The AbsoluteValue and SayGoodnight functions do not have default input values in their parameter lists, and for each version of the call statement, there is a unique corresponding function. The DrawLine and WriteNumbers programs have default input values in the prototype, and each has only one function body.

The C++ programmer should recognize the value in overloaded functions, whether the functions employ a default parameter list or not. In some instances, using a default parameter list function is practical, and in other cases it is not. In the AbsoluteValue program, using a default parameter list is not practical, whereas in the DrawLine program, a default parameter list is the most logical way to write that function.

WriteYourName   To illustrate the difference between using a default list or not, two versions of the WriteYourName program are presented below. The first program has a single function with a default parameter list. The second program has three separate overloaded functions for each call format. The main function and program output are identical in both examples. The output is shown here:

BarbaraBarbaraBarbaraBarbaraBarbara

WayneWayneWayne

MarkMarkMarkMarkMark

Default Parameter List Version of WriteYourName (Program 8-13)

```
//Program 8-13 WriteYourName      Default Parameter List
#include <iostream.h>
void WriteYourName(char * = "Barbara", int = 5 );  //name, # of times


int main()
{

        WriteYourName();                // write Barbara 5 times
        WriteYourName("Wayne", 3);      // write Wayne 3 times
        WriteYourName("Mark");          // write Mark 5 times
        return 0;
}


void WriteYourName(char *name, int count)
{

        int i;
        cout << endl;
        for(i=0; i < count; ++i)
        {
               cout << name;
        }
        cout << endl;
}
```

Individual Functions and Overloaded Version of WriteYourName (Program 8-14)

```
//Program 8-14 WriteYourName      Overloaded Functions
#include <iostream.h>

void WriteYourName();
void WriteYourName(char*, int);
void WriteYourName(char*);
```

```
int main()
{
        WriteYourName();                 // write Barbara five times
        WriteYourName("Wayne", 3);       // write Wayne three times
        WriteYourName("Mark");           // write Mark five times
        return 0;
}


void WriteYourName()
{
        int i;
        cout << endl;
        for(i=0; i < 5; ++i)
        {
                cout << "Barbara";
        }
        cout << endl;
}
void WriteYourName(char *name, int count)
{
        int i;
        cout << endl;
        for(i=0; i < count; ++i)
        {
                cout << name;
        }
        cout << endl;
}


void WriteYourName(char *name)
{
        int i;
        cout << endl;
        for(i=0; i < 5; ++i)
        {
                cout << name;
        }
        cout << endl;
}
```

Can You Mix and Match Overloaded Functions?

Is it possible to have several overloaded function prototypes where some use default parameter lists and others do not use the lists? This is a logical question. Remember, to overload a function, the parameter list data types must be unique and not

```
//Program 8-15 WriteYourName
//Mix and Match Overloaded Function with and without a Default Parameter List
#include <iostream.h>
int WriteYourName(char * = "Barbara", int = 5 ); //name, # of times
void WriteYourName(double);          // this just writes out a number
int main()
{
      int OK;
      double x = 3.4;
      OK = WriteYourName();
      OK = WriteYourName("Wayne", 3);
      OK = WriteYourName("Mark");
      WriteYourName(x);
      return 0;
}
int WriteYourName(char *name, int count)
{
      int i;
      cout << endl;
      for(i=0; i < count; ++i)
      {
            cout << name;
      }
      cout << endl;
      return 1;
}
void WriteYourName(double x)
{
      cout << "\n Barbara, you passed me " << x;
}
```

ambiguous. Let's add a second overloaded function to the default list version of the WriteYourName Program shown above. The output from Program 8-15 is shown below:

BarbaraBarbaraBarbaraBarbaraBarbara
WayneWayneWayne
MarkMarkMarkMarkMark
Barbara, you passed me 3.4

The operation is a success! As long as the input parameter lists are unique, it is possible to have overloaded functions such that one (or more) has a default parameter list.

8.5
Inline Functions

Another C++ enhancement allows a function to be declared an *inline function.* Program control does not jump into inline functions because the compiler places the code from the function at the point where the call is located. The program simply executes the function's code at the location where the function is called. The program does not need to locate the function, step into it, execute it, and return to the call statement. All the same function rules apply to inline functions, and the compiler checks for correct use of the argument (input) list and return value. The good news is that inline functions make the code efficient because the calling and return steps are eliminated and the code executes faster. The bad news is that inline functions create larger code size because function code is replicated at each call location. Therefore, it is important to inline only small functions.

inline functions
functions that contain the inline keyword in the prototype and the inline function body is embedded in the code at the function call location

To declare an inline function, we use the keyword inline in the prototype:

```
inline return_type Function_name(input parameter list);
```

The HowBigIsYourBox program is modified (see Program 8-16) so that the calculation portion of the program is inlined.

```
//Program 8-16 How Big is your Box? Inline function
#include <iostream.h>

inline float CalcBoxVol(float,float,float);

int main()
{
        float width=3.0,length=4.0,height=7.0,vol;
        vol=CalcBoxVol(width,length,height);
        cout << "\n The volume is " << vol << endl;
        return 0;
}
inline float CalcBoxVol(float width, float length, float height)
{
        return (width * length * height);
}
```

The compiler actually sets up the code as shown on the next page:

```
int main()
{

    float width=3.0,length=4.0,height=7.0,vol;
    vol=width * length * height; // Instead of calling CalcBoxVol, the compiler
    //  puts the body of CalcBoxVol where the call // is located.
    cout << "\n The volume is " << vol << endl;
    return 0;

}
```

8.6
Summary

The C++ enhancements to the C function presented in this chapter provide basic building blocks for object-oriented program construction. The overloaded functions are critical for creating classes and are often used for class constructors. Inline functions are used in classes to provide efficient programming techniques, and default parameter list functions bring additional flexibility for the programmer. Table 8-4 summarizes these new function features.

TABLE 8-4
New C++ Function Features

New C++ Function	Characteristic	Notes
Overloaded functions— separate functions for each call	More than one function has the same name. Each function must have a different number of parameters or different data types in parameter list.	Each function has prototype and separate function, but program makes calls using the one name. Parameter lists must be unique.
Overloaded functions—default parameter list function	Prototype has default function input values in the form type = value. The function can be called with no parameters, and default values are used.	Default parameter list functions make it possible to specify all input parameters so that no parameters are required in the call statement.
Inline function	Prototype and function header line statements begin with keyword inline except in class declarations. Code is actually embedded at call location.	Inline functions speed up execution time but can create a larger program file.

REVIEW QUESTIONS AND PROBLEMS

Short Answer

1. What is meant by the term *implied pointer*?

2. What is the role of the indirection operator when you are using reference parameters with a function?

3. Why must the input arguments be unique when you are overloading a function?

4. What C++ statement contains the default parameter values for a default parameter list function?

5. When a structure is passed by a call by reference using reference parameters, is a local copy of the structure created in the function? How are the structure elements accessed?

6. What steps are saved during program execution when an inline function is used?

7. If you use a call by reference function, can it contain a return statement? That is, can a call by reference function return a value (via a return statement), too?

8. Describe how the * and & are related in the two types of call by reference functions.

9. Describe the differences among passing an array to a function using call by value, using call by reference using pointers, and using call by reference using reference parameters.

10. Is it possible to pass an enumerated variable to a function using reference parameters? If you believe the answer is yes, write a simple function illustrating this situation.

Debugging Problems: Compiler Errors

Identify the compiler errors in Problems 11 to 15 and state what is wrong with the code.

11.
```
#include <iostream.h>
int GetIt(int);
float GetIt(int);
double GetIt(int);
int main();
{
```

```cpp
    int n = GetIt();
    float x = GetIt();
    double y = GetIt();
    return 0;
}
```

12.
```cpp
#include <iostream.h>
void Swap(float&, float&);

int main()
{
    float a = 2, b = 6;
    Swap(&a, &b);
    return 0;
}
void Swap(float &x float &y)
{
    float temp = x;
    x = y;
    y = temp;
    return;
}
```

13.
```cpp
enum Color { red, blue, green}
struct Ball
{
    Color c;
    float diameter;
};
int Bounce(Ball *);
int main()
{
    Ball 4tennis;
    int flag;
    flag = Bounce(4tennis);
    return 0
}
void Bounce(Ball &tennis)
{
    tennis.c = red;
    tennis.diameter = 2.5;
}
```

14.
```
#include <iostream.h>
struct Bridge;
{
   double span, height, width;
}
void SwayFactor(Bridge);
Bridge SwayFactor()
int main()
{
   int lanes = 3;
   bridge Brooklyn, Skyway;
   SwayFactor(&Skyway);
   Brooklyn = SwayFactor(lanes);
   return 0;
}
void SayFactor(Bridge &)
{
    // function
}
Bridge SwayFactor()
{
   Bridge temp;
   // function
   return &temp;
}
```

15.
```
include <iostream.h>
void PayCheck(float OT_hrs = 0.0, float rate = 8.50, float hrs = 40);
int main()
{
    PayCheck( , 10.50);
    PayCheck(10.5);
    return 0;
}
float PayCheck(float, float, float)
{
    float pay = hrs * rate + 1.10 * rate * OT_hrs;
    return pay;
}
```

Debugging Problems: Run-Time Errors

Each of the programs in Problems 16 to 18 compiles but does not do what the specification states. What is the incorrect action and why does it occur?

16. Specification: The function CalcPaint is sent the dimensions of a room—length, width, and ceiling height—and the number of square feet a gallon of paint covers. (For example, Brand X paint can cover 250 square feet. If a room has 1,000 square feet, it would need four gallons of paint.) The function CalcPaint should return the required number of gallons of paint for the dimensions of the room.

```
struct Room
{
    float length, width, height;
};
float CalcPaint(Room&, int coverage);
int main()
{
    float paint;
    Room bedroom;
    bedroom.length = 12.0;
    bedroom.width = 10.5;
    paint = CalcPaint(bedroom,225);
    return 0;
}
float CalcPaint(Room &R, int coverage)
{
    int paint;
    paint = R.length * R.width + R.height / coverage;
    return paint;
}
```

17. Specification: The program uses a default parameter input list for writing out an n by n square of characters. The default character is * and there are three lines. A 3 by 3 square is:

```
***
***
***
```

```
#include <iostream.h>
void WriteBlock(char = '*', int = 3);
int main()
{
    cout << "\n The first block :" << endl;
    WriteBlock();
```

```
            cout << "\n The second block :" << endl;
            WriteBlock('$', 12);
            return 0;
}
void WriteBlock(char symbol, int number)
{
    int i,j;
    for(i = 0; i < number; ++i)
    {
        for(j = 0; j < number; ++i)
        {
            cout << symbol;
        }
    }
}
```

18. The function SetColor assigns three colors to a Shape variable by using randomly generated numbers. The stdlib's srand() and rand() functions are used. Any three colors may be assigned into the Shape color array, but the colors must be different.

```
#include <stdlib.h>
enum Color {red, orange, yellow, green, blue, indigo, violet};
struct Shape
{

    Color color[3];
    // assume other shape variables
};
void SetColor(Shape &);
int main()
{
        Shape MyShape;
        srand(123);            //seed the number generator
        SetColor(MyShape);
        return 0;
}


void SetColor(Shape &MyShape)
{
        MyShape.color[1] = (Color)(rand()%6);
        MyShape.color[2] = (Color)(rand()%6);
        MyShape.color[3] = (Color)(rand()%6);
}
```

Programming Problems

Write complete C++ programs for Problems 19 to 21.

19. Write a program that sets up an overloaded function set called GetRandom-Num. These functions return a random number that is generated with stdlib.h's srand() and rand(). You will need to use the modulus function to do a little math to obtain the desired results. There are three different prototypes for the GetRandomNum function:

1. Pass in a positive integer m and it returns an integer value between 0 and $m - 1$.

```
int GetRandomNum(int m);
```

2. Pass in two integers (assume i and j are zero or positive and $i < j$) and receive a random integer between but not including i and j.

```
int GetRandomNum(int i, int j);
```

3. Void call returns a random number between 0.000 and 1.000. Assume that three digits of precision are necessary.

```
double GetRandomNum();
```

Your program should make three calls to GetRandomNum: once obtaining a number between 0 and 27, once obtaining a number between 3 and 73, and last obtaining a number between 0.0 and 1.0. Write all three numbers to the screen. (Can you combine the first and second GetRandomNum calls into one default parameter list function?)

20. Write a program that has a function called WriteHellos and uses a default input parameter list in the prototype. The default parameters include an integer for the number of hellos on the line and an integer for the number of lines. The default function result shows five hellos on three lines. This call:

```
WriteHellos();
```

results in output like this:

hello hello hello hello hello
hello hello hello hello hello
hello hello hello hello hello

If either input value is zero, write "No Hellos for You." Your main function should call this program four times—once using the default values, once so that you see twelve hellos on three lines, once so that you see five hellos on eleven lines, and once showing the "No Hellos for You" message.

21. Create a data structure called Phone that contains integer variables for area code, exchange, and phone number. Create an enumerated data type called Rating, and the values are NoWay, SoSo, Nice, and PopTheQuestion. Next, create a structure called BeMyDate that contains a character string for the BeMyDate's name, a Phone variable, and a Rating variable. (The outline for this program is shown below.) Write two functions called SetUpDate. This overloaded function has two forms; one has a reference parameter to a BeMyDate structure. This function asks the user to enter the BeMyDate data. The second form of the SetUpDate has no inputs in the call and simply returns a BeMyDate structure. This version of the SetUpDate function loads the BeMyDate structure variable with your ideal person's information. Last, write a function called WriteItOut that receives a reference parameter to a BeMyDate structure and writes out the structure information. Your main function has two BeMyDate variables, and main calls both versions of the SetUpDate function; then the main function calls WriteItOut twice. Feel free to create a character string to make the enumerated data-handling easier. (This program may also be written using pointers instead of reference parameters if you'd like more practice with pointers.)

```
//Chapter 8, Problem 21-Outline

#include <iostream.h>
struct Phone
{
    //you fill this in
};

enum Rating {  /* you fill this in */  };

struct BeMyDate
{
    //you fill this in
};

//overloaded function prototypes
void SetUpDate(BeMyDate &);
BeMyDate SetUpDate();

//date write function
void WriteItOut (BeMyDate &);
```

8

```
int main()
{
    BeMyDate ideal, non_ideal;

    ideal = SetUpDate();  //this function fills a BeMyDate w/ your perfect date

    SetUpDate( non_ideal); //this function asks user for date information

    cout << "\n My Ideal Date Information: ";
    WriteItOut(ideal);

    cout << "\n My Non-Ideal Date Information: ";
    WriteItOut(non_ideal);

    cout << "\n Isn't Dating fun? ";
    return 0;
}
```

9

Classes and Objects

KEY TERMS AND CONCEPTS

access specifiers
array of objects
class
class constructor
class declaration
class definition
class destructor function
class members
instance of a class
method
object
obtaining computer system time
operator function
overloaded constructors
overloaded operators
private
public
qsort

KEYWORDS AND OPERATORS

class
operator
private
public
scoping operator ::

CHAPTER OBJECTIVES

Introduce the principles and definitions used in object-oriented programming.

Illustrate how classes incorporate data and functions.

Explain the relationship between the class declaration and objects.

Demonstrate how a class declaration is written.

Show how the world may access class members.

Present several simple program examples that illustrate the mechanics of working with objects.

Describe the purpose of class constructor and destructor functions, and illustrate how these functions are used in a program.

Illustrate how pointers to objects work.

Wax On, Wax Off

In the movie *Karate Kid*[1] Daniel and Mr. Miyagi strike a deal. Mr. M will teach Daniel karate and Daniel must do everything Mr. M asks him to do, without question. Daniel's first task is to wax the cars. Wax on, wax off. Big circles; wax on, wax off. Sanding the floors is Daniel's next task. Again, big circles. Mr. M then tells him to paint the fence. Brush goes up, brush goes down. The last task is to paint the house; side to side, side to side. Daniel is respectful and does as he is told. However, after many days he becomes frustrated and wants to know when he is going to start learning karate. As it turns out, Daniel's car waxing, floor sanding, fence painting, and house painting have trained him to perform the correct movements for karate.

You may be feeling like Daniel felt when he painted the house. Pointers, integers, operators, functions, and structures—when are we going to get to the good stuff? You are so close. You now have all the tools you need to begin writing object-oriented programs. Your patience will be rewarded very soon.

9.1
Object-Oriented Principles and Definitions

A Brief Introduction

Let's describe a modeling problem. Have you ever parked your car in a metered parking space? You must be sure you have change in your pocket because the parking meter always needs to be fed. Imagine yourself finding a parking spot, parallel parking, and knowing it's time to pay the meter. What do you do? The meter has a little sign on it telling you how much time you can buy. You put a coin in the meter, twist the knob, and the clock starts ticking.

Now, you are asked to write a program to model the parking meter. In a structured C program, the design and program flow follows a sequential chain of events:

---

[1] *Karate Kid*, a 1984 film produced by Jerry Weintraub and directed by John G. Avildsen, Columbia Pictures.

read in the data, perform calculations on or manipulate the data, write the answers. The functions are called in the order necessary to "do things" to the data. A structured parking meter program undoubtedly has functions for obtaining the money, calculating the amount of time purchased based on the money fed to the meter, ticking off the purchased time, and indicating that the meter is out of time.

Object-oriented (OO) methods are a natural way to think about a problem or to model a situation. The OO program design is centered about actual things (objects) and how these things act and interact with each other. When a programmer is presented with a problem to solve, he or she must first ask many questions. What objects do we need? What do the objects do? When do they do their tasks? Who tells each object to perform its task(s)? Object-oriented program design is not a programming style, nor are programs written in C++ necessarily object-oriented.

To start an object-oriented design, you must examine the program components required by the project and examine how these components need to interact with each other. For our parking meter problem, there are three main components:

1. A meter, to coordinate all of the meter and user interactions.
2. A bank, to handle the money.
3. A timer, to count off the purchased time.

We can model the parking meter as a group of three "things": a "Meter," a "Bank," and a "Timer." Our user is a Parker and, yes, the Parker is a "thing," too. Let's define the tasks that the four "things" do. In fact, let's get four volunteers to stand up and play the "Parking Meter Game." Mike will be our automobile driver. Mike has the job of a Parker and has parked his car by the meter. John is our Meter. Mike, our Parker, interacts with John, our Meter. Jerry is our Banker and Ruth is our Timer. John also interacts with Jerry and Ruth. (Mike, our Parker, doesn't see Jerry or Ruth. He sees just John, our Meter.) You can think of the Meter as the master coordinator for meter functions. Before we continue, suppose we summarize our four players as shown in Table 9-1.

It is important to keep in mind that each of our players has specific jobs to perform. The Banker must keep track of the money, and he or she knows the total amount that has been received from the Parker. The Banker does not deal with the Parker directly, nor does he or she calculate how much time the Timer must count. The Timer's job is to count down the allotted time. It is not the Meter's job to keep track of the money but simply to ask the Banker how much money it has received. The Meter must determine how much time the Parker has purchased, and the Meter then asks the Timer to count down the time.

The parking rate at the C++ Parking Meter is three seconds for five cents. (In Chapter 10, you will write the program. The Timer will use the system time to count the time.) In our Parking Meter Game, the players could have the following conversation:

TABLE 9-1

The Parking Meter Game Players

Player	Description	Role
Mike	Parker	Park the car beside the meter. (Parking is not modeled here.) Put money in the meter and twist the knob.[a]
John	Meter	Take the money from the Parker. Give the money to the Banker. Ask the Banker how much money he has from the Parker. Figure out how much time the Parker has purchased based on each coin. Keep a running total for seconds. Tell the Timer how much time to tick off the clock.
Jerry	Banker	Take the coins from the Meter. Keep track of the total money received from the Meter. When asked, state the total amount of money the Banker has.
Ruth	Timer	Count off the time requested by the Meter. Report to the Meter when the time has been completed.

[a]We'll assume that the meter's coin slot allows only valid coins to be inserted into the meter.

John:	I'm ready for a coin. (The Meter is clear and ready for its next Parker.)
Mike:	Here is a coin for you, John. (The Parker twists the knob after giving the Meter a quarter.)
John:	Here is a coin for you, Jerry. (Meter gives the Banker the quarter.)
Jerry:	Thank you. (Banker starts a running total of the money: total = $0.25.)
John:	Want to insert another coin?
Mike:	Here is a coin for you, John. (The Parker twists the knob after giving the Meter a dime.)
John:	Here is another coin for you, Jerry.
Jerry:	Thank you. (Banker adds $0.10 to the total: total = $0.35.)
John:	Want to insert another coin?
Mike:	No. I'm ready to start the clock.
John:	Hey, Jerry, how much money do we have? (Meter asks the Banker for the total amount of money.)
Jerry:	I have thirty-five cents.
John:	Let's see, thirty-five cents buys twenty-one seconds.
John:	Ruth, start the timer and set it for twenty-one seconds.
Ruth:	Got it, twenty-one seconds. I'm now ticking off twenty-one seconds.
Twenty-one seconds later:	
Ruth:	Ding! Time's up, John.
John:	Jerry, time to clear out bank and wait for our next Parker. I'm setting Total Seconds to zero. I'm ready for a coin.

When you begin to identify the components for your program and then assign tasks to each component, you are essentially defining a ***class***. (We described this

class
a "job description" for a program object

process as writing a job description in Chapter 1.) In object-oriented programming, a class is the basic component that represents a set or a group with similar characteristics (or attributes) and behaviors. For example, we can set up a Bank class for this problem. A Bank class defines the jobs that our banker performs. A banker can validate coins, keep a running total of the money, and tell how much money it has. Jerry, our fellow student who plays the role of a banker, is an ***instance of a class***, which is an ***object***. Jerry is a Bank object, Mike is a Parker object, Ruth is a Timer object, and John is a Meter object.

instance of a class

another term for an object

object

a program component with data and functions

This simple example illustrates how an object-oriented program works. What are the important points for a beginning C++ programmer to note?

1. The program, which models a Parking Meter, is designed with individual classes. Initially we specified our classes (Parker, Meter, Bank, Timer), and the actual implementation uses individual objects (Mike, John, Jerry, and Ruth).

2. Each of the parking meter tasks is assigned to be the job of a class; that is, the Bank handles the money, the Timer handles the time, etc.

3. The tasks are defined in the class.

4. The objects perform the actual program tasks.

5. Each object has a name and is a unique entity.

6. An object may use other objects (or a group of objects) to accomplish certain tasks. John (the Meter) has Jerry (a Bank) and Ruth (a Timer) assist him in his duties as a Meter.

7. The objects interact with each other and tell each other what to do.

8. The Timer object can be used in any program that requires the counting of a given amount of time, such as that found in an oven or microwave.

9. The Bank object can be used in any program that requires coins to be totaled, such as that found in a vending machine.

10. We can set up another Parking Meter by asking four more people to play the roles of Parker, Meter, Bank, and Timer. The roles of the Parker, Meter, Bank, and Timer are fixed, but these four new people are new instances of these classes.

Principles of an Object-Oriented Language

For a computer language to be object-oriented, it must support several programming principles or tenets. There are a total of seven principles, five of which are mandatory for the language to be truly object-oriented. This text will refer continually to these principles as the object-oriented material is presented. They are listed in Table 9-2.

▌ TABLE 9-2

Principles Required of an Object-Oriented Language

Principle	Description	Notes
Modularity	Creates logically separate units (objects) that are well defined and interact through the use of functions. Ideally, objects should have minimum dependence on each other.	Extends the idea of a function or subroutine so that data are included.
Encapsulation	The ability to package or wrap things together into a well-defined unit or class.	The encapsulation concept allows the internal architecture and data to be hidden from other classes.
Abstraction	The ability to hide the complexity of the design and processes that carry out the operations on an object.	The abstraction concept deals with hiding how the functions work on the data. A class function is like a black box that performs its job without letting the world "see" how it does it.
Polymorphism	One interface, many methods (or implementations).	C++ implements polymorphism with inherited classes. (See Chapter 11.)
Inheritance	The ability to create new (derived) classes from existing (base) classes. Inheritance represents an "is a" class relationship.	Classes form a hierarchical relationship.
Persistence[a]	In distributed or database applications, the object states are retained (persist) after the program has been terminated.	C++ can mimic persistence using files or databases to store object states.
Concurrency[a]	In client/server applications, the objects are distributed across different hardware platforms.	A banking system mainframe computer and ATM machines are distributed across different platforms. The objects need to interact with each other through the use of well-defined interfaces (functions).

[a]Optional object-oriented language requirement.

Objects Are Real-World Things

Let's look at a real-world item before we jump into class and object syntax. Go outside and borrow your dog's tennis ball for a few moments. This tennis ball is a real-world object, although it might be slimy and dirty. You can roll it in your hands, feel the fuzzy outer layer, bounce it, squeeze it, or toss it for your pup. It has certain characteristics and has certain behaviors.

What are the characteristics of the tennis ball? The ball has many dimensions, including diameter, radius, circumference, volume, surface area, and weight. Because it is hollow, we know there is a certain thickness to the rubber shell. The ball has a color and perhaps a brand label printed on it.

What are the behaviors of the tennis ball? It can roll, spin, and bounce. It can also be still and not move. Depending on the age and use, it may not bounce as well as it once did. See Figure 9-1 for a depiction of the ball's characteristics and behaviors.

If we want to write a computer program to model how the tennis ball reacts in a tennis game, we need to know many characteristics of the tennis ball as well as how the ball behaves. We need to be able to calculate how the tennis ball bounces and how it reacts when it is struck with a racquet.

This tennis game-modeling program brings up other object questions—such as what about the tennis player and the tennis racquet? These are real-world objects, too. We can describe the tennis player in terms of characteristics (physical dimensions, strength, and speed with which he or she can swing a racquet) and behaviors (reaction time and type of shots, such as lob, drop, pass, and down-the-line).

The racquet itself has many characteristics, too. Talk to any tennis pro and you will get a description of string material and tension, racquet head material, hitting surface area, length, and grip material, not to mention a physics lesson involving the amount of power the racquet imparts on the ball. See Figure 9-2 for an illustration of the tennis game objects.

Object Definition

In object-oriented programming, the software requirements are analyzed and designed in terms of classes and objects instead of data or process flow. The program is built with a collection of objects that work together to perform the program tasks. If we were to model a tennis game in software, we would describe the ball object, player objects, and racquet objects.

Characteristics	Behaviors
Diameter	No movement
Outer radius	Roll
Thickness of rubber shell	Bounce
Inner radius	Spin
Circumference	Can be compressed
Weight	
Surface area	
"Bounce factor"	
Color	
Brand name	
Age (usage amount)	
Altitude rating	

Figure 9-1
Tennis Ball Characteristics and Behaviors

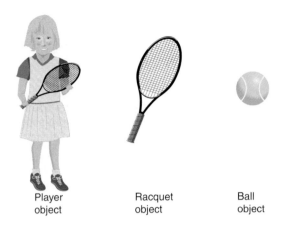

| Player | Racquet | Ball |
| object | object | object |

Figure 9-2
Tennis Game Objects

The definition of an object has been formalized in object-oriented design terminology as "an entity that has a state, behavior, and an identity."[2] Descriptions of these object definitions are shown in Table 9-3. The tennis game objects are used as an example.

When first learning object-oriented programming, the programmer must view the world in terms of real-world objects—what characteristics the objects possess and how they behave. Before we continue, read Table 9-4 to learn several new terms.

9.2
Classes and Objects

Object-Oriented Analysis: Characteristics, Behaviors, and Functions

Object-oriented programming involves examining the objects and determining the characteristics and behaviors. First, we need to identify an object. How about using the dog's tennis ball? Second, we must perform an object-oriented analysis task and identify the characteristics and behaviors of our object. Table 9-5 lists both.

There are many redundant characteristics in our list. Once you know one of the radius values and the thickness, the diameter, circumference, both radii, volume, and surface area can be calculated. It is common for the programmer to find redundant characteristics and behaviors when first analyzing an object. Sometimes your

---

[2]The object definition is taken from the text *Unified Objects Object-Oriented Programming Using* C++ by Babak Sadr, IEEE Computer Society, 1998.

TABLE 9-3
Object Definition State, Behavior, and Identity

Term	Description	Tennis Game Example
State	The value of the member data variable.	A tennis player object can exist in one of many states. At any time the player can be serving or receiving a serve, hitting the ball, or standing and doing nothing else.
Behavior	The functions or operations that are needed to perform the object's tasks or to change the state of the object.	The ball object has many behaviors. In our game we need functions to model how the ball object bounces and spins.
Identity	A system may contain several of the same types of object, but each object is unique and has its own identity.	In the tennis game program, we need one ball object, two (or four) player objects, and two (or four) racquet objects. Each object is unique and has its own name. The two player objects are based on the same class (blueprint), but each is unique.

TABLE 9-4
Object-Oriented Terminology

Term	Description	Notes
Class	The data variables and functions that describe the job of a program component.	The format of a class is similar to that of a data structure. The keyword "class" is used instead of the keyword "struct." A class sets up a blueprint for an object, whereas a struct sets up a blueprint for a data structure.
Object	An instance of a class. It is not "real" until the program is executed.	As in a data structure, the class name is used to declare actual objects.
Method	An Ada[a] language term for a function. It is often used in C++ to describe a function that belongs to a class.	In C++, functions can be referred to as methods or operations.
Member or class member	Either a data variable or function that belongs to a class.	In the tennis example above, the bounce and spin functions are referred to as member functions.
Object-oriented analysis (OOA)	When determining program requirements, the programmer must identify the necessary objects along with their characteristics and functions.	This task is usually accomplished with pencil and paper. Redundant characteristics are often discovered.
Object-oriented design (OOD)	Once the objects for a program are identified, the required functions and characteristics are refined and the interfaces to the objects are identified.	Object-oriented principles should be considered when designing the class.

[a]The Ada programming language was developed in the 1970's and named after Lady Ada Lovelace, daughter of poet Lord Byron.

TABLE 9-5
Tennis Ball Characteristics and Behaviors

Characteristics	Behaviors
Diameter of entire ball	Still; no movement
Outer radius (based on one-half the diameter)	Roll
Thickness of rubber and fuzz	Bounce
Inner radius	Spin
Volume based on inner radius	Can be compressed
Circumference	
Weight	
Surface area	
"Bounce factor"	
Color	
Brand name	
Age (usage amount—such as new, old, chewed-on)	
Altitude rating (such as high altitude or sea level)	

object has nebulous features that are difficult to quantify ("bounce factor") or behaviors that may be ignored. The lists are often refined in the design stage.

Object-Oriented Design

During the object-oriented design stage of your program, you narrow the necessary object characteristics and functions or ***methods***. To simplify our tennis ball object, we calculate only how high the ball bounces when we drop it from a given height. We will assume here that if we know the "age" of the ball, distance of the drop, initial spin rate, and the surface hardness, we have enough information to determine how high the ball bounces. Also, we determine the new spin rate after the bounce.[3] See Figure 9-3.

    To determine the bounce, we use a CalculateBounce function for our object. We need a function to calculate the new spin rate and a function to characterize the age of the ball (based on the number of hours played). See Figure 9-4. With this program criteria, we can shorten our list of required data items and functions. This shortened list is shown in Table 9-6.

    Upon examining the characteristics, you may ask, Why aren't the bounce distance or surface hardness included in the list? This list contains physical aspects of the object itself. The tennis ball object has a radius, weight, age, and some rate of

method
another term for a class member function

9

---

[3]The Swiss mathematician, Daniel Bernoulli, describes the relationship of pressure and velocity in reference to horizontal fluid (air) movement. This mathematical description (along with other laws of physics) can be used to calculate the tennis ball's spin and bounce.

We will assume that if we know the age, original drop distance, initial spin rate, and playing surface hardness, we can calculate how high the ball bounces and its new spin rate.

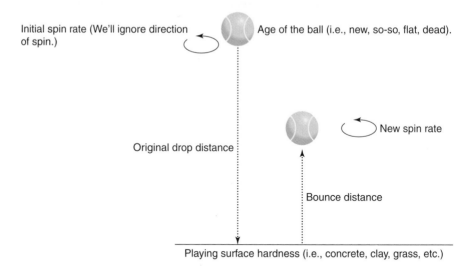

Figure 9-3
Tennis Ball Bounce Calculation Factors

Modeling how a ball object bounces is complex. The initial drop and spin will determine the bounce height and new spin. These values are then used for the next bounce calculation.

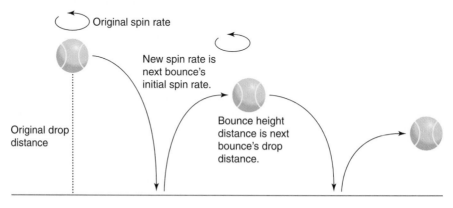

Figure 9-4
Bouncing Tennis Ball

Shortened List of Tennis Ball Characteristics and Functions

Characteristics (Object Variables)	Functions
Radius Weight Age Spin rate	Calculate Bounce Height (Returns a height distance based on ball age, initial drop height, spin rate, and surface hardness.)
	Calculate New Spin Rate (Determines the new spin rate based on prebounce spin rate, weight, radius, and surface hardness.)
	Calculate Age (Establishes an age characterization from the enumerated list based on hours of play.)

spin. The bounce distance calculation is based on the ball properties and surface hardness, yet the distance and the surface property are not part of a ball object.

Structured TennisBall

Once you mastered structs in Chapter 7, you could have written a program modeling the bouncing tennis ball. You know how to set up this information with an enumerated data type and a data structure. To characterize the age of the ball and surface hardness, you can use enumerated data types as follows:

```
enum TBall_Age {like_new, so_so, flat, dead};
struct TennisBall
{
    double radius, weight, spin_rate;
    TBall_Age age;
};
enum Surface {concrete, clay, grass};
```

For the actual functions, you could have used a pointer to the structure. You could pass in the drop height and surface hardness. The prototypes for these functions are shown here:

```
double CalcBounceHeight(TennisBall *pBall, double InitHeight, Surface type);
void CalcNewSpinRate(TennisBall *, Surface type);
void CalcAge(TennisBall *, int HoursPlayed);
```

In the actual program, you could initialize the data and then call the functions. We do not write the actual functions here but show only how main might call them.

```
// Review C data structures and functions for a bouncing tennis ball.
#include <iostream.h>
#include <string.h>

enum TBall_Age {like_new, so_so, flat, dead};
struct TennisBall
{
      double radius, weight, spin_rate;
      TBall_Age age;
};


enum Surface {concrete, clay, grass};

double CalcBounceHeight(TennisBall *pBall, double InitHeight, Surface type);
void CalcNewSpinRate(TennisBall *, double InitSpin);
void CalcAge(TennisBall *, int HoursPlayed);

int main( )
{
      TennisBall ball;                        // create an instance of the data struct
      int hours_played = 5;
      CalcAge(&ball, hours_played);                // now characterize the ball age
      ball.spin_rate = 0.0;    // initial spin rate is zero, initial struct value
      ball.radius = 1.5;       // initialize radius
      ball.weight = 0.25;      // initialize weight (pounds)
      double new_height;
// drop the ball from 6 feet onto concrete
      new_height = CalcBounceHeight(&ball, 6.0, concrete );
// now calculate the new spin rate in preparation for next bounce
      CalcNewSpinRate(&ball, concrete);
      return 0;
}
```

class declaration

the source code that
contains the keyword
class and members,
including the private,
protected, and public
sections, with data and
function prototypes

Class Declaration

To create an object in our program, we must first tie together the necessary data variables and functions into a class. The class format is similar to setting up a data structure. This format is known as a *class declaration* and uses the keyword class. The data (characteristics) and functions (behaviors) are grouped together. Two new keywords, *private* and *public*, are used in the declaration. The general format for a class declaration is shown here:

```
class Class_Name
{
private:     //List the private class members
        int a;     // class variables are declared in the usual manner

public:      //List the public class members
        void Function1(); // function prototypes are used
};
```

All the data and functions listed within the class declaration belong to that class and are known as *class members*. The class members can see and access each other. What does this last statement mean? All the functions in the class have access to the class data variables. These class variables do not need to be passed to the class functions. (Think of class data as global variables for the class functions.) The keywords *private* and *public* are *access specifiers*, which dictate the accessibility of the members to the "world." Any area of the program outside the class cannot access private class members; that is, the "world" cannot use the private class members (such as assigning a value to one or writing one to the screen). We will see many examples of private class members soon. Table 9-7 summarizes class members' private and public access in a formal manner.

The class name is used to declare an instance of an object. (This procedure is exactly like using a data structure Tag name to declare a data structure variable.) The object name and dot operator together access the public members of the class. Table 9-8 compares classes and structures.

TennisBall Class

The tennis ball data and function specifications from above can now be incorporated into a TennisBall class. We enumerate the TBall_Age data type outside the class declaration.

TABLE 9-7
Private and Public Access

Keyword	Definition
private	An access specifier used in classes. The private members can be seen, used, assigned, and/or changed only by other members of the class.
public	An access specifier used in classes. The public members may be seen, used, assigned, and/or changed by all parts of the program providing that these other program parts can find the class object.

TABLE 9-8
Structures and Classes

Item	Structures	Classes

Declaration	`struct TheStruct`
	`{`
	    `int a, b;`
	`};`
		`class NewClass`
		`{`
		    `private:`
		        `int a;`
		    `public:`
		        `void Functionl();`
		`};`

Use	`int main ()`
	`{`
	    `TheStruct MyStruct;`
	
	    `MyStruct.a = 3;`
	    `MyStruct.b = 4;`
	`}`
		`int main ()`
		`{`
		    `NewClass MyObject; // instance of an object`
		
		    `MyObject.Functionl();  // see Note`
		`}`

Note: Only the public members of NewClass can be accessed by the "world." The compiler does not allow us to write this statement: `cout << MyObject.a;` because the a variable is private.

```
enum TBall_Age {like_new, so_so, flat, dead};
class TennisBall
{
private:
        double radius, weight, spin_rate;
        TBall_Age age;
public:
        double CalcBounceHeight(double InitHeight, Surface type);
        void CalcNewSpinRate(Surface type);
        void CalcAge(int HoursPlayed);
};
```

In the TennisBall class declaration, the data and functions are declared within the class { } framework. The data and functions are all members of the class TennisBall. The functions can see and access the data; therefore, there is no need to pass any ball data. See Figure 9-5 for an illustration.

The main function can declare an object of the type TennisBall, and only the public members of the class may be accessed. The data is encapsulated (hidden) within the class. See Figure 9-6.

We begin our program by declaring a class TennisBall and then creating a TennisBall object in the main function. We soon see that, because we have hidden our data in the class, we cannot initialize the spin rate, radius, or weight.

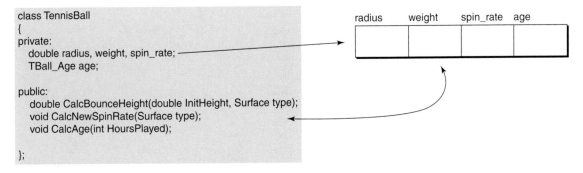

The data inside the class can be seen and accessed by the class functions.
There is no need to pass any class data between class functions.

```
class TennisBall
{
private:
    double radius, weight, spin_rate;
    TBall_Age age;

public:
    double CalcBounceHeight(double InitHeight, Surface type);
    void CalcNewSpinRate(Surface type);
    void CalcAge(int HoursPlayed);

};
```

radius	weight	spin_rate	age

Figure 9-5
Tennis Ball Class

```
//Program Outline for TennisBall Class
enum TBall_Age {like_new, so_so, flat, dead};
enum Surface {concrete, clay, grass};
class TennisBall
{
private:
        double radius, weight, spin_rate;
        TBall_Age age;
public:
        double CalcBounceHeight(double InitHeight, Surface type);
        void CalcNewSpinRate(Surface type);
        void CalcAge(int HoursPlayed);
};


int main()
{
        TennisBall MyBall;          // this creates an object of the class TennisBall

// We use the object and dot operator to access the public Calculate Age function.
// Assume the ball has been used for 5 hours. Pass 5 to TennisBall's HoursPlayed.
        MyBall.CalcAge(5);

/* In the struct program we could just assign the rate, radius, and weight directly,
but in this program, if we try to do this:
        MyBall.radius = 1.5;
we get a compiler error.   HELP!!!   */
```

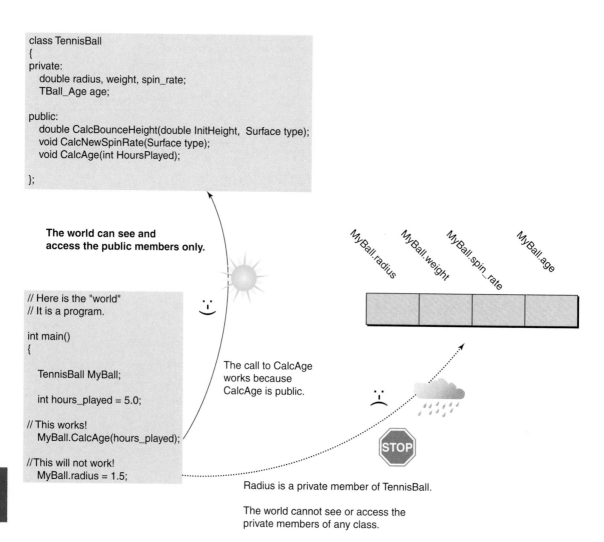

```
class TennisBall
{
private:
    double radius, weight, spin_rate;
    TBall_Age age;

public:
    double CalcBounceHeight(double InitHeight,  Surface type);
    void CalcNewSpinRate(Surface type);
    void CalcAge(int HoursPlayed);

};
```

The world can see and access the public members only.

MyBall.radius MyBall.weight MyBall.spin_rate MyBall.age

```
// Here is the "world"
// It is a program.

int main()
{

    TennisBall MyBall;

    int hours_played = 5.0;

// This works!
    MyBall.CalcAge(hours_played);

//This will not work!
    MyBall.radius = 1.5;
```

The call to CalcAge works because CalcAge is public.

STOP

Radius is a private member of TennisBall.

The world cannot see or access the private members of any class.

Figure 9-6
Tennis Ball Class and the World

How to Get Values into the Data Members

At this stage of our TennisBall program, we are stuck. We wish to follow the object-oriented principles and hide our data from the world (by making it private), but how do we get values into the private members?

The direct approach is to have a public member function whose job is simply to assign the input value into the data member. This scheme can also be used to obtain the value of a private data member. It is common to see "Set" and "Get" functions for these tasks. (Set and Get are not C++ keywords nor are they reserved functions. They are simply an easy convention to use in naming the member functions that assign values to data variables and retrieve them as well.) Simple one-line functions do the trick for us. For example, "Set" and "Get" functions can look like the following:

```
void Set_Radius(double r)
{
        radius = r;
}

double Get_Radius()
{
        return radius;
}
```

These two functions can be written in one line:

```
void Set_Radius(double r){ radius = r; }

double Get_Radius() { return radius;}
```

Although this isn't the best style, it is a convenient form when working with class declarations. One-line functions are often incorporated directly into the class declaration. Table 9-9 illustrates the Set functions for the radius, spin rate, and weight in both the conventional and one-line formats.

▌ **TABLE 9-9**
Conventional and One-Line Function Formats

Conventional	One-Line

`void Set_Radius(double r)`
`{`
`    radius = r;`
`}`
	`void Set_Radius(double r) {radius = r;}`

`void Set_Weight(double wt)`
`{`
`    weight = wt;`
`}`
	`void Set_Weight(double wt) {weight = wt; }`

`void Set_SpinRate(double sr)`
`{`
`    spin_rate = sr;`
`}`
	`void Set_SpinRate(double sr) {spin_rate = sr;}`

We can use the one-line format as an efficient method of writing complete functions located in a class declaration. Here is the TennisBall declaration with six member functions. The Calculate functions merely have the prototype, but the Set functions contain the complete function.

```
enum TBall_Age {like_new, so_so, flat, dead};
enum Surface {concrete, clay, grass};
class TennisBall
{
private:
        double radius, weight, spin_rate;
        TBall_Age age;
public:
        double CalcBounceHeight(double InitHeight, Surface type);
        void CalcNewSpinRate(Surface type);
        void CalcAge(int HoursPlayed);

        void Set_Radius(double r) {radius = r;}
        void Set_Weight(double wt) {weight = wt; }
        void Set_SpinRate(double sr) {spin_rate = sr;}
};
```

The TennisBall class now has the required functions to initialize the data variables and to calculate bounce and spin information. We have not written the Calculate functions here.

```
//Program 9-TennisBall Class and main function INCOMPLETE PROGRAM
#include <iostream.h>
#include <string.h>

enum TBall_Age {like_new, so_so, flat, dead};
enum Surface {concrete, clay, grass};
class TennisBall
{
private:
        double radius, weight, spin_rate;
        TBall_Age age;
public:
        double CalcBounceHeight(double InitHeight, Surface type);
        void CalcNewSpinRate(Surface type);
        void CalcAge(int HoursPlayed);
        void Set_Radius(double r) {radius = r;}
        void Set_Weight(double wt) {weight = wt; }
        void Set_SpinRate(double sr) {spin_rate = sr;}
};
```

```
int main()
{
        TennisBall MyBall;           // this creates an object of the class TennisBall
        int hours_played = 5;        // initialize the hours for determining ball age

        MyBall.CalcAge(hours_played);        //characterize the age value

        MyBall.Set_SpinRate(0.0);            //Set functions to initialize private data
        MyBall.Set_Radius(1.5);
        MyBall.Set_Weight(0.25);
        double new_height;
        // drop the ball from 6 feet onto concrete
        new_height = MyBall.CalcBounceHeight(6.0, concrete );

                              //  now determine new spin rate
        MyBall.CalcNewSpinRate(concrete);

        return 0;
}
```

Advanced Programming Note: A better programming design involves having a private CalcNewSpinRate function that is called by the Bounce function. In this design, the bounce and spin calculations are handled in a logical sequence instead of requiring the user to make a separate function call to update the spin rate value.

9.3
Writing Member Functions

Two Different Formats/Locations

There are two techniques for writing the actual source code for member functions. One approach is to write the entire function body within the class declaration. Simply write the function header line and function body within the framework of the class ClassName {   }. (This technique was used in the Set functions for the tennis ball program above.) This straightforward approach is recommended when the member functions are very short (i.e., one or two lines).

In reality, member functions are larger than a few lines. Programmers often refer to the class declaration for a concise description of the class members. When the larger member functions are written inside the class declaration, the declaration is difficult to read. Often programmers do not need to see the actual function bodies. It is good programming practice to write the class declaration in a concise and simple-to-read format located in one file and to place the member functions in a separate file.

```
//Program 9-1    Complete Sphere program in one file and writing the
//functions within the class declaration

#include <iostream.h>
#include <math.h>

const double pi = 3.14159265;

class Sphere
{
private:
        double radius, volume, s_area;
public:
        void Set_Rad(double r) { radius = r; }
        void CalcVolume()
        {
                volume = 4.0/3.0 * pi * pow(radius,3);
                // pow is the power function provided math.h
        }
        void CalcSurfaceArea()
        {
                s_area = 4.0*pi* pow(radius,2);
        }
        void PrintSphere()
        {
                cout << "\n The sphere data is \n radius = " << radius <<
                "\n volume = " << volume << "\n surface area = " << s_area;
        }
};
int main()
{
        cout << "\n Welcome to the Sphere Program!  \n ";
        Sphere MySphere;

        MySphere.Set_Rad(5.0);    // the sphere radius will be 5.0
        MySphere.CalcVolume();
        MySphere.CalcSurfaceArea();
        MySphere.PrintSphere();
        cout << "\n\n All done \n";
        return 0;
}
```

Class Sphere Example

The tennis ball goes back to the dog. Now we create a new class for a generic sphere. The equations for the volume and surface area of a sphere are shown in Table 9-10. The first requirement is to set up class functions for calculating surface area and volume and a function for setting the radius. A print function writes all the object values to the screen.

An Example: Function Source Code Inside Declaration Writing the member functions within the class declaration is straightforward, but functions longer than a few lines can make the code difficult to read. In Program 9-1, we write the class functions within the class declaration. The output from this program is:

Welcome to the Sphere Program!

The sphere data is
radius = 5
volume = 525.265
surface area = 315.159

All done

File Organization The class declaration and the actual class function source code should be separated into two files. The class declaration should be in an include file (ClassName.h), and the source code should be in its own source file (ClassName.cpp). When working with many classes, the programmer should organize each class into its own set of *.h and *.cpp files. If you decide in the future you do not need a class, it will thus be easy to remove the files from the project.

9

An Example: Place Member Functions in a Separate File To write the member functions in a separate file, we need to introduce a new format and operator. The member functions belong to a class, and we need to tell the compiler which

▊ **TABLE 9-10**
Sphere Formulas

Surface Area of a Sphere[a]	Volume of a Sphere[a]
$SA = 4\pi r^2$	$Vol = \dfrac{4}{3}\pi r^3$

[a]r is the radius and π (pi) is the constant 3.14159265.

class "owns" the functions. For this task, we use the *scoping operator, ::,* which tells the compiler who owns the function. The scoping operator is used in the following format:

```
return_type Class_Name::FunctionName(input parameter list)
{
// function body
}
```

The complete Sphere program is illustrated in Figure 9-7.

The Sphere class can be separated into two different files: Sphere.h and Sphere.cpp. The class declaration is in the include file, and the *class definition* (source code) is in the *.cpp file. Notice that we leave the Set function in the class declaration because the functions are short and the Sphere declaration file, Sphere.h, must be included in both the driver and definition files. Both the main function and the class functions need to see the Sphere declaration.

Figure 9-8 illustrates how a Sphere object (MySphere) may access the public functions of the Sphere class. These functions can access the private data members in the class.

Class declaration

```
// Sphere.h

#ifndef _SPHERE_H
#define _SPHERE_H

class Sphere
{
    private:
            // private members here
    public:
            //public members here

};

#endif
```

```
// Driver.cpp

#include "Sphere.h"
#include <iostream.h>

int main()
{

        Sphere MySphere;

        // statements

        cout << "\n\n All done \n";
        return 0;
}
```

Class definition

```
// Sphere.cpp

#include <iostream.h>
#include <math.h>

#include "Sphere.h"

double const pi = 3.14159265;

void Sphere::CalcVolume()
{
        //function lines
}

void Sphere::CalcSurfaceArea()
{
        //function lines
}

void Sphere::PrintSphere()
{
        //function lines
}
```

The project will keep track of the *.cpp and *.h files.

The Sphere.h file must be included in both *.cpp files because both files need to know what a Sphere is.

Figure 9-7
Sphere Program Organized in Separate Files

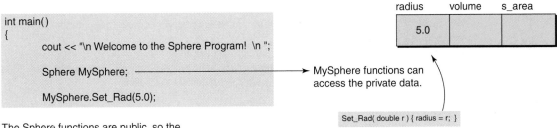

A sphere object named MySphere is created in the main function.

MySphere data is private.

```
int main()
{
        cout << "\n Welcome to the Sphere Program! \n ";

        Sphere MySphere;

        MySphere.Set_Rad(5.0);
```

MySphere functions can access the private data.

The Sphere functions are public, so the MySphere object can call the functions.

The MySphere object can access the Set_Rad function. It passes the value 5.0 into the function.

Set_Rad(double r) { radius = r; }

Figure 9-8
Sphere Program Data Flow

9.4
Class Constructors

How to Initialize Class Data Members

When an object is created in a program, we often need to set the object variables to initial values. How can we assign initial values into the object variables? The C++ compiler does not allow us to assign initial values into data variables in the class declaration. If we try to assign initial values in the Sphere class declaration, we receive many compiler errors.

```
// ILLEGAL ASSIGNMENTS IN CLASS DECLARATION
class Sphere
{
        private:
                double radius = 5.0; // initial assignment for the radius
                double volume, s_area;
        public:
                void Set_Rad(double r) { radius = r; }
                void CalcVolume();
                void CalcSurfaceArea();
                void PrintSphere();
};
```

The Visual C++ compiler believes we are trying to declare virtual functions when we accidentally initialize data variables in a class declaration. (Virtual functions are presented in Chapter 11.) It reports errors in both the *.h file and *.cpp file compilation:

```
Compiling...
Driver.cpp
c:\testcase\sphere.h(11) : error C2258: illegal pure syntax, must be '=0'
c:\testcases\sphere.h(11) : error C2252: 'radius' : pure specifier can only be specified for functions
Sphere.cpp
c:\testcases\sphere.h(11) : error C2258: illegal pure syntax, must be '=0'
c:\testcases\sphere.h(11) : error C2252: 'radius' : pure specifier can only be specified for functions
c:\testcases\sphere.cpp(14) : error C2065: 'radius' : undeclared identifier
Error executing cl.exe.

Sphere.exe - 5 error(s), 0 warning(s)Error executing cl.exe.
```

GCC reports that C++ forbids in-class initializations of the members:

```
login1:johnston:~/gnu:$ g++ G++_Ch9sphere.cc
G++_Ch9 sphere.cc:12: warning: ANSI C++ forbids initialization of member 'radius'
G++_Ch9 sphere.cc:12: warning: making 'radius' static
G++_Ch9 sphere.cc:12: ANSI C++ forbids in-class initialization of non-const static member 'radius'
```

We cannot initialize a class member within the class declaration statement.

Class Constructor Functions

class constructor function

class member called automatically when an object is created

Programmers should always initialize the data variables to avoid unpredictable program behaviors. The designers of C++ recognized the need to initialize the object states (to assign initial values into object variables) when the objects come into existence. When an object is created, the system automatically calls the *class constructor function*. The constructor is a member function whose job is to initialize the object variables upon object creation.

The constructor function must have the same name as the class. C++ permits the constructor function to be overloaded because many possible ways exist for the programmer to initialize the object data. The prototype in the class declaration for the class constructor function is:

```
class ClassName
{
    public:
    ClassName (input list);      // constructor function prototype
};
```

Notice that there is no return type in the prototype. Constructors do not return any value to the calling function. Our Sphere class can have a constructor that looks like the following:

```
class Sphere
{
private:
        double radius, volume, s_area;
public:
        Sphere();               // constructor prototype
                //other public functions
};


Sphere::Sphere()
{
        radius = 5.0;           // initialize the radius to 5.0 in the constructor
        volume = 0.0;
        s_area = 0.0;
}
```

Constructors and the Seven-Day/Twenty-Four-Hour Clock

To illustrate how class constuctor functions work, we use the twenty-four-hour clock. Three integers represent the hour, minute, and second (HR:MIN:SEC). The time value 0:0:1 is a second after midnight and 24:0:0 is midnight. Our new class is named DayTime and an enumerated value is designated for the day of the week (Sunday, Monday, etc.).

In our program we may have objects initialized with default values, such as Sunday 0:0:1. Or we may wish to have an object initialized with a day and time other than the default, such as Tuesday 12:0:0. Our class DayTime contains two constructor functions. One constructor simply sets the time values to Sunday 0:0:1. The second constructor sets the day and time to the constructor input values—such as Tuesday 12:0:0. Also, we have a ShowDayTime function that writes the data to the screen. The last member function, ResetDayTime, resets the object variables according to the values in the input list.

The DayTime class declaration is shown below:

```
//Program 9-2 Class DayTime with two Constructor Functions
enum Day {Sun, Mon, Tue, Wed, Thur, Fri, Sat, Sun};
class DayTime
{
private:
        int hr, min, sec;
        Day whichday;
public:
        DayTime();              //first constr, sets object vars to Sun 0:0:1
        DayTime(Day WD, int h, int m, int s); // second constr
                                        // initializes the object vars to WD h:m:s
```

```
      void ShowDayTime();  //write the DayTime values
// Resets the DayTime variables
      void ResetDayTime(Day WD, int h, int m, int s );
};
```

 Important Note: The second constructor function and the ResetDayTime member function both have the same input parameter list and source code, but they are fundamentally different. The constructor creates a new object whose initial values are set to the input list values. The ResetDayTime function is used on an existing object.
The implementation of the first constructor function is shown below:

```
DayTime::DayTime()
{
      hr = min = 0;
      sec = 1;
      whichday = Sun;
}
```

The implementation of the second constructor function is shown below:

```
DayTime::DayTime(Day WD, int h, int m, int s)
{
      hr = h;
      min = m;
      sec = s;
      whichday = WD;
}
```

The following main function has two DayTime objects (named initial and later), which were created by using different constructor functions:

```
//Program 9-2 Class DayTime with two Constructor Functions
int main()
{
      DayTime Initial;    /* calls the first constructor
                          default values used to set Initial object to Sun 0:0:1 */

      DayTime Later(Tues, 12, 0, 0); /* calls the second constructor
                          "Later" object is initialized to Tues 12:0:0   */
```

The DayTime declaration and definition are in the DayTime.h and DayTime.cpp files, respectively, and a Driver.cpp sample program is illustrated in Figure 9-9.

Class declaration

```
// DayTime.h
// Program 9-3

#ifndef_DAYTIME_H
#define_DAYTIME_H

enum Day {Sun, Mon, Tues, Wed, Thur, Fri, Sat};

class DayTime
{
        //private data

    public:

        // two constructor functions
        DayTime();
        DayTime(Day WD, int h, int m, int s);

        //other public data and functions
};

#endif
```

Class definition

```
// DayTime.cpp
// Program 9-3

//include statements

DayTime::DayTime()              // 1st constructor
{
        hr = min = 0;
        sec = 1;
        whichday = Sun;
}

// 2nd constructor
DayTime::DayTime(Day WD, int h, int m, int s)
{
        hr = h;
        min = m;
        sec = s;
        whichday = WD;
}

// other DayTime functions
```

Driver program

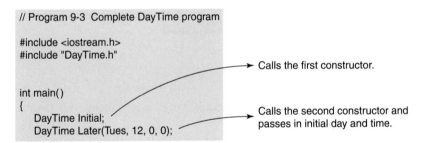

```
// Program 9-3  Complete DayTime program

#include <iostream.h>
#include "DayTime.h"


int main()
{
        DayTime Initial;
        DayTime Later(Tues, 12, 0, 0);
```

→ Calls the first constructor.

→ Calls the second constructor and passes in initial day and time.

Figure 9-9
DayTime Program with Two Constructor Functions

Figure 9-10 illustrates how the constructors build objects with initial values and how the Reset function can change the object values.

Constructor Notes

Class constructors are used to initialize member data variables and usually do not have input or output tasks. Beginning C++ programmers can add an output state-

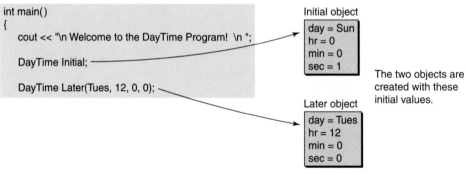

Driver program

Two new objects

```
int main()
{
    cout << "\n Welcome to the DayTime Program! \n ";

    DayTime Initial;

    DayTime Later(Tues, 12, 0, 0);
```

Initial object

| day = Sun |
| hr = 0 |
| min = 0 |
| sec = 1 |

The two objects are created with these initial values.

Later object

| day = Tues |
| hr = 12 |
| min = 0 |
| sec = 0 |

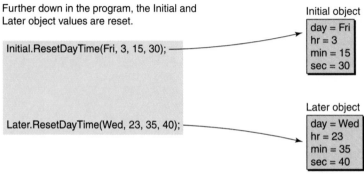

Further down in the program, the Initial and Later object values are reset.

Initial.ResetDayTime(Fri, 3, 15, 30);

Later.ResetDayTime(Wed, 23, 35, 40);

Initial object

| day = Fri |
| hr = 3 |
| min = 15 |
| sec = 30 |

Later object

| day = Wed |
| hr = 23 |
| min = 35 |
| sec = 40 |

Figure 9-10
DayTime Program Function Calls

ment in the constructor ("I'm in the constructor") to convince themselves that the construct function is called.

A class constructor's job is only to create objects. It should *not* be called whenever the programmer wishes to re-initialize the object variables. The Set and Reset member functions can be used to alter the values in existing objects.

Constructor functions do not have a return data type (unlike all other functions in C++). If an error occurs when the constructor is executed, there is no direct way to issue an error code to the calling function. The means to trap for an error during the constructor execution is to make use of exception handling. (Exception handling is presented in Chapter 12.)

Two Dates Program

The Two Dates program shown below illustrates a class declaration that contains two constructor functions, as well as ShowDate and SetDate functions. In the short main function, we declare two Date objects, each using a different constructor function. We then change each object using the SetDate function.

Note: One naming convention for classes asks the programmer to place a capital "C" at the start of the class name. We shall do this in this example and periodically in other text examples. See what you think.

First, let's set up the CDate class declaration and functions. Refer to Program 9-3. For the main function, notice in the code below how we declare two Date objects, and each Date object uses the ShowDate, SetDate, and WriteDate function. When we write out which Date object we're working with, we need to print this message from the main function—*not* from within a class function. This issue is sometimes confusing. The class functions are generic functions for the class, and any object-specific information is handled elsewhere.

```
int main()
{
        cout << "\n The Two Dates Program.   \n";

        CDate MyDate;        //calls the default constructor, sets date to 1/1/2001
        CDate YourDate(5,5,1955);    //calls constructor that sets date to 5/5/1955

        cout << "\n\n The original dates are: ";
        cout << "\n The MyDate date is    ";
        MyDate.ShowDate();
        cout << "\n The YourDate date is ";
        YourDate.ShowDate();

        cout << "\n Now we'll change the dates.";
        MyDate.SetDate(1,2,1956);
        YourDate.SetDate(3,14,1994);

        cout << "\n\n The new dates are: ";
        cout << "\n The MyDate date is    ";
        MyDate.ShowDate();
        cout << "\n The YourDate date is ";
        YourDate.ShowDate();
        cout << "\n No more dates for you. "    << endl;

        return 0;
}
```

```
//Program 9-3    Two CDate Objects and Constructor functions
#include <iostream.h>

class CDate
{
private:
        int mon, day, year;
public:
        CDate();
        CDate(int m, int d, int y);
        void ShowDate();
        void SetDate(int m, int d, int y);
};

CDate::CDate()
{
        cout << "\n I'm in the default constructor.";
        mon = 1;
        day = 1;
        year = 2001;
}

CDate::CDate(int m, int d, int y)
{
        cout << "\n I'm in the constructor where we pass m/d/y to me.";
        mon = m;
        day = d;
        year = y;
}

void CDate::ShowDate()
{
        cout <<  mon << "/" << day << "/" << year << endl;
}
void CDate::SetDate(int m, int d, int y)
{
        mon = m;
        day = d;
        year = y;
}
```

The output is shown below:

The Two Dates Program.

I'm in the default constructor.
I'm in the constructor where we pass m/d/y to me.

The original dates are:
The MyDate date is   1/1/2001
The YourDate date is 5/5/1955

Now we'll change the dates.

The new dates are:
The MyDate date is   1/2/1956
The YourDate date is 3/14/1994
No more dates for you.

9.5
Class Destructors

An object is "born" when it is created (and the constructor function initializes variables) during program execution. Just as the object is "born," it also "dies" when the program terminates or if it is no longer required while the program is running. At program termination or when the object goes out of scope, the object may be destroyed. Some programming situations call for the object to perform certain tasks when it is destroyed. These tasks may include closing a data file if the object had opened one or freeing memory that the object had allocated with the new operator. C++ provides a *class destructor function* that is called automatically (if it exists) when the object is destroyed. Global object destructors are called when the program terminates. If a function creates a local copy of an object, this local copy is destroyed when the function is exited.

class destructor function

class member called automatically when an object goes out of scope

9

The form of the destructor function is similar to that of a constructor function. The class name is used with a ~ in front of the name, and there is no return value. There is only one destructor function in a class. The programmer may issue a call to the destructor if necessary; however, typically the program automatically issues the call.

The prototype of the destructor is shown below:

```
class ClassName
{
    public:
    ~ClassName ();   //destructor function prototype
};
```

In our DayTime program, there is no real need for a destructor function, but we can add one to illustrate how it is used.

```cpp
// Class Constructor and Destructor Functions with DayTime class

enum Day {Sun, Mon, Tue, Wed, Thur, Fri, Sat, Sun};
class DayTime
{
    private:
        int hr, min, sec;
        Day whichday;
    public:
        DayTime();                              // two constructors
        DayTime(Day WD, int h, int m, int s);

        ~DayTime();    // destructor function

        void ShowDayTime();
        void ResetDayTime(Day WD, int h, int m, int s );
};
```

The implementation of this destructor is as follows:

```cpp
DayTime::~DayTime()
{
    cout << "\n Parting is such sweet sorrow. Goodbye! \n";
}
```

The short program below and its corresponding output, which follows the program, illustrate the constructor and destructor functions:

```cpp
int main()
{
    DayTime OneObject;

    cout << "\n A short program. ";

    cout << "\n All done now! \n";
    return 0;
}
```

The output is shown here:

Hi there! I'm in the constructor!
A short program.
All done now!

Parting is such sweet sorrow. Goodbye!

9.6
A Simple Example

Common Stumbling Blocks

In the first seven chapters, we lived in a structured world. We built a function that served the entire program. We were careful to pass data into and out of our functions. We did not use globally declared data variables. Now we are stepping into the object-oriented world and the rules are changing. Data within classes can be thought of as global data for the member functions, and each object has its own set of functions, serving only itself.

The most difficult concept for beginning C++ programmers is the idea that each object comes equipped with its own set of member functions which may be called in two different ways. Public class functions may be called by using the object name and dot operator from a location outside a member function (such as the main function). Class functions may also be called directly from within other member functions. Each object's functions "work on" that object's data. Class data is accessible (consider it global) to all member functions. Class data does not need to be passed into and out of class functions.

Often C++ novices are not sure how or if the correct function is called or how he or she knows which object is doing what. Remember, a class is a blueprint for objects. Setting up a class declaration is like drawing a blueprint for a house. You can build many houses from that blueprint, and each house has all the features in that blueprint. When you declare objects, each object has all the features in that class.

9

```
//Program 9-4 Two Gadgets
//File:  Ch9Gadgets.h
#ifndef _GADGETS_H
#define _GADGETS_H

class Gadget
{
private:
        int x,y,z,sum;
        bool good;                 //set to true if data is valid
        void Validate();           //check to see if x,y,z are positive
        void SumData(){ sum = x + y + z; }

public:
        Gadget();                  //constructor
        ~Gadget();                 //destructor
        bool GetData();            //asks for x,y,z and returns true if data is good
        void WriteData();          //writes data to the screen
};
#endif
```

The Gadgets Program

Here is another "boring on the outside, exciting on the inside" program. A Gadget class is declared. (A Gadget is like a widget or a thing-a-ma-jig.) The private class members are four integers, x, y, z, and a sum variable, and a boolean flag that is set to true if the three ints are positive. Two functions are also private, Validate and SumData. Public members include a constructor, destructor, GetData, and Write Data. The class declaration, located in the Ch9Gadgets.h, is shown in Program 9-4.

The member functions are located in a separate file, Ch9Gadgets.cpp, except for the SumData function. The SumData function is a one-liner that is included in the class declaration. The constructor initializes the values to 0 and false, and the destructor merely says goodbye. The exciting portion of the program is seen in the GetData function. GetData asks the user for the three integers and then calls the Validate function. Notice that there is no dot operator with Validate. One member function may call another member function directly. Validate checks to see if the data is positive, and sets the good flag. Back in GetData, if the good flag is true, the SumData function is called. Since the x, y, z, sum, and good data are class members, all the class functions may see and access them! There is no need to pass any data between these functions.

```
//Program 9-4
//File: Ch9Gadgets.cpp
#include <iostream.h>
#include "Ch9Gadgets.h"

Gadget::Gadget()
{
      cout << "\n I'm in the Gadget constructor, setting all values to 0 ";
      x = y = z = sum = 0;
      good = false;
}


Gadget::~Gadget()
{
      cout << "\n I'm in the Gadget destructor. "
              "\n Nothing to do but say Goodbye. Goodbye! \n";
}

bool Gadget::GetData()
{
      good = false;                     //set to false initially

      cout << "\n Please enter your Gadget's x, y, and z integers => ";
      cin >> x >> y >> z;
      Validate();                       //call to Validate, to check values
      if(good == true)
      {
            SumData();                  //if data is good, then sum values
      }
      return good;
}


void Gadget::Validate()
{
      //data is valid as long as all three integers are positive
      if(x > 0 && y > 0 && z > 0)
            good = true;
      else
            good = false;
}


void Gadget::WriteData()
{
      cout << "\n Gadget Data:   x = " << x << " y = " << y << " z = " << z;
      cout << "  The sum is " << sum << endl;
}
```

9

In our main function, we create two different Gadget objects (red and blue). The GetData returns the boolean value (the good variable) so that the main function knows whether the object data is valid. Only valid data is written to the screen.

Notice that there is no need to write two sets of GetData, WriteData, Validate, and SumValues functions, even though we have two different Gadget objects. Remember that the code we have written in the Ch9Gadget.cpp file is a blueprint for every Gadget object. If you wish to see the Red Gadget message written for the red gadget's data, you must write that message from the main function. The code in the void Gadget::WriteData function is executed whenever any gadget object calls it.

```cpp
//Program 9-4 Gadgets
//File: GadgetsDriver.cpp
#include <iostream.h>
#include "Ch9Gadgets.h"

int main()
{
        cout << "\n\n The Gadgets Program!  \n\n";

        Gadget red,blue;                  //declare two Gadget objects
        bool goodred, goodblue;
// write out Red message, then call red's GetData();
        cout << "\n Red Gadget:  ";
        goodred = red.GetData();

        cout << "\n Blue Gadget:  ";              // same idea for the Blue Gadget
        goodblue = blue.GetData();

        if(goodred == true && goodblue == true)
        {
                cout << "\n Both sets of gadget data are good! ";
                cout << "\n Red Gadget: "; //call to red's WriteData();
                red.WriteData();

                cout << "\n Blue Gadget:  ";
                blue.WriteData();                        //call to blue's WriteData();
        }
        else if(goodred && !goodblue)
        {
                cout << "\n The red data is good, but the blue data is bad. ";
                cout << "\n Red Gadget: ";
                red.WriteData();
        }
```

```
        else if(!goodred && goodblue)
        {
                cout << "\n The red data is bad, but the blue data is good. ";
                cout << "\n Blue Gadget: ";
                blue.WriteData();
        }
        else
        {
                cout << "\n BAD GADGET DATA    :-(     ";
        }
        cout << "\n\n What to do with all these gadgets????    \n\n";
        return 0;
}
```

The program output below shows that the two different constructor functions are called. The user has entered valid data for the red object and invalid data for the blue object. Only the red's WriteData function is called. The destructors are called when the program terminates.

The Gadgets Program!

I'm in the Gadget constructor, setting all values to 0
I'm in the Gadget constructor, setting all values to 0
Red Gadget:
Please enter your Gadget's x, y and z integers => 7 8 9

Blue Gadget:
Please enter your Gadget's x, y and z integers => 0 1 2

The red data is good, but the blue data is bad.
Red Gadget:
Gadget Data: x = 7 y = 8 z = 9   The sum is 24

What to do with all these gadgets????

I'm in the Gadget destructor.
Nothing to do but say Goodbye. Goodbye!

I'm in the Gadget destructor.
Nothing to do but say Goodbye. Goodbye!

Troubleshooting: Common Errors with Classes

Beginning object-oriented programmers make a few common mistakes as they start to write classes and objects. These errors are more annoying than life-threatening because the compiler or linker often catches them, but they result in compiler or linker reports that may be misleading to the new programmer.

Scoping Operator ::   The programmer should separate his or her code into different files by placing the class declaration in the *.h file and the class definition in the *.cpp file. The programmer often forgets the class name and scoping operator in the function header line. The Phone class below illustrates this mistake. The following class declaration looks correct:

```
//Program 9-x Forgotten Scoping Operator
//File: Ch9_PhoneX.h
#include <iostream.h>
class Phone
{
private:
        int area, exc, number;
public:
        Phone(){area = exc = number = 0; }
        void SetPhoneNumber(int, int, int);
        void WritePhoneNumber();
};
```

The problem is here with the class definition; the class functions do not have the class name and scoping operator:

```
//File: Ch9_PhoneX.cpp
#include "Ch9_PhoneX.h"
void SetPhoneNumber(int a, int e, int n)
{
        area = a;
        exc = e;
        number = n;
}

void WritePhoneNumber ()
{
        cout << endl << area << "-" < exc << "-" < number;
}
```

The main driver is written correctly:

```
//File:  Ch9_PhoneXDriver.cpp
#include "Ch9_PhoneX.h"
```

```
int main()
{
        Phone Jason, Ryan;

        Jason.SetPhoneNumber(555,111,2222);
        Ryan.SetPhoneNumber(555,222,3333);

        cout << "\n Jason's number is ";
        Jason.WritePhoneNumber();

        cout << "\n Ryan's number is ";
        Ryan.WritePhoneNumber();

        cout << "\n Don't you love to call your friends?" << endl;
        return 0;
}
```

The Visual C++ compiler reports that the class variables in the PhoneX.cpp file are undeclared, meaning that the compiler believes these variables are local to these functions and are not members of the Phone class:

Compiling...
Ch9_PhoneX.cpp
c:\cbook\testcases\ch9_phonex.cpp(8) : error C2065: 'area' : undeclared identifier
c:\cbook\testcases\ch9_phonex.cpp(9) : error C2065: 'exc' : undeclared identifier
c:\cbook\testcases\ch9_phonex.cpp(10) : error C2065: 'number' : undeclared identifier
Ch9_PhoneXDriver.cpp
Error executing cl.exe.

TestCases.exe - 3 error(s), 0 warning(s)

The contents of the three files were placed in the Ch9_PhoneXDriver.cpp file and compiled by GCC. It also believes that area, exc, and number are undeclared:

login1:johnston:~/Phone:$ g++ Ch9_PhoneXDriver.cc
Ch9_PhoneXDriver.cc: In function 'void SetPhoneNumber(int, int, int)':
Ch9_PhoneXDriver.cc:35: 'area' undeclared (first use this function)
Ch9_PhoneXDriver.cc:35: (Each undeclared identifier is reported only once
Ch9_PhoneXDriver.cc:35: for each function it appears in.)
Ch9_PhoneXDriver.cc:36: 'exc' undeclared (first use this function)
Ch9_PhoneXDriver.cc:37: 'number' undeclared (first use this function)
Ch9_PhoneXDriver.cc: In function 'void WritePhoneNumber()':
Ch9_PhoneXDriver.cc:42: confused by earlier errors, bailing out

The correct way to write the functions in the PhoneX.cpp file is shown as:

```
//File: Ch9_PhoneX.cpp
#include "Ch9_PhoneX.h"


void Phone::SetPhoneNumber(int a, int e, int n)
{
        area = a;
        exc = e;
        number = n;
}
void Phone::WritePhoneNumber()
{
        cout << area << "-" << exc << "-" << number << endl;
}
```

With these functions written correctly, the program compiles with no errors or warnings. The output is seen below:

Jason's number is 555-111-2222
Ryan's number is 555-222-3333
Don't you love to call your friends?

Type Mismatches Reported as Overloaded Function Problems   The data type and variables in the function prototype and function header line must match, or the programmer is guaranteed problems. In our previous chapters, these types of errors were reported as type mismatches. (See Troubleshooting: Type Mismatch in Chapter 5.) When programming classes, the programmer will find a "new" type of error for this "old" problem.

Using the Phone class again, we illustrate this error by writing the Set-PhoneNumber prototype with only two integer inputs, while the function header line has three. The compiler is not happy with the code because it is expecting a second form of the SetPhoneNumber function, and it reports that it cannot find an overloaded function. The Phone declaration is shown below:

```
//Program 9-x Forgotten Scoping Operator
//File: Ch9_PhoneX.h
#include <iostream.h>

class Phone
{
private:
        int area, exc, number;
public:
        Phone(){area = exc = number = 0; }
        void SetPhoneNumber(int, int);    //Error! We need three ints.
        void WritePhoneNumber();
};
```

The function header line for SetPhoneNumber contains three integers:

```cpp
//File: Ch9_PhoneX.cpp
#include "Ch9_PhoneX.h"

void Phone::SetPhoneNumber(int a, int e, int n)
{
        area = a;
        exc = e;
        number = n;
}

void Phone::WritePhoneNumber()
{
        cout << area << "-" << exc << "-" << number << endl;
}
```

The Visual C++ compiler reports the following:

Compiling...
Ch9_PhoneX.cpp
c:\cbook\testcases\ch9_phonex.cpp(7) : error C2511: 'SetPhoneNumber' : overloaded member function 'void (int,int,int)' not found in 'Phone'
        c:\cbook\testcases\ch9_phonex.h(7) : see declaration of 'Phone'
Ch9_PhoneXDriver.cpp
C:\CBook\TestCases\Ch9_PhoneXDriver.cpp(10) : error C2660 : 'SetPhoneNumber' : function does not take 3 parameters
C:\CBook\TestCases\Ch9_PhoneXDriver.cpp(11) : error C2660 : 'SetPhoneNumber' : function does not take 3 parameters
Error executing cl.exe.

TestCases.exe - 3 error(s), 0 warning(s)

The GCC compiler finds a similar problem:

login1:johnston:~/Phone:$ g++ Ch9_PhoneXDriver.cc
Ch9_PhoneXDriver.cc: In function 'int main()':
Ch9_PhoneXDriver.cc:20: no matching function for call to 'Phone::SetPhoneNumber (int, int, int)'
Ch9_PhoneXDriver.cc:11: candidates are: Phone::SetPhoneNumber(int, int)
Ch9_PhoneXDriver.cc:21: no matching function for call to 'Phone::SetPhoneNumber (int, int, int)'
Ch9_PhoneXDriver.cc:11: candidates are: Phone::SetPhoneNumber(int, int)
Ch9_PhoneXDriver.cc: At top level:
Ch9_PhoneXDriver.cc:34: prototype for 'void Phone::SetPhoneNumber(int, int, int)' does not match any in class 'Phone'
Ch9_PhoneXDriver.cc:11: candidate is: void Phone::SetPhoneNumber(int, int)

Forgotten Functions   Another common mistake that programmers make is forgetting to provide the function body for class functions. Building the program in steps is the correct approach, but forgetting to enter the function header line and body yields an unhappy linker. The Phone class is shown below with the constructor prototype, but there is no function in the corresponding *.cpp file:

```
//Program 9-x  Forgotten Scoping Operator
//File: Ch9_PhoneX.h

#include <iostream.h>

class Phone
{
private:
        int area, exc, number;
public:
        Phone();     //Error!  No associated function to be found!
        void SetPhoneNumber(int, int, int);
        void WritePhonenumber();
};
```

The Visual C++ compiler finds nothing wrong, but the linker cannot find the Phone constructor function:

```
Compiling...
Ch9_PhoneX.cpp
Ch9_PhoneXDriver.cpp
Linking...
Ch9_PhoneXDriver.obj : error LNK2001: unresolved external symbol "public: _thiscall Phone::Phone (void)"
(??0Phone@@QAE@XZ)
Debug/TestCases.exe : fatal error LNK1120: 1 unresolved externals
Error executing link.exe.

TestCases.exe - 2 error(s), 0 warning(s)
```

The GCC compiler reports the following:

```
login1:johnston:~/Phone:$ g++ Ch9_PhoneXDriver.cc
/tmp/cc4yFF19.o: In function 'main':
/tmp/cc4yFF19.o(.text+0xb): undefined reference to 'Phone::Phone(void)'
/tmp/cc4yFF19.o(.text+0x17): undefined reference to 'Phone::Phone(void)'
collect2: ld returned 1 exit status
```

Building your program in stages is exactly the correct way to develop software. You should always write your complete class declaration and place empty functions in the declaration so that the linker is happy. (Empty functions can be written with an empty set of braces, as in Phone(){}.)

9

9.7
Array of Objects

A C++ programmer may declare an array of objects in the same manner as he or she would declare an array of integers or structures. The individual objects in the array are accessed with the use of an integer index value.

The first step in declaring an array of objects is to declare the class. This declaration defines the blueprint for a single object, such as:

```
class Doodad
{
     private:
            int doodad_number;
     public:
            Doodad();   //constructor
            void Set_A_Doodad(int n) { doodad_number = n ; }
            void WriteDoodad();
};
```

The array is specified in a function, such as:

```
int main()
{

        Doodad MyDoodads[100];     // sets up an array of 100 Doodad objects
```

An individual object is then accessed with an integer array index:

```
MyDoodads[0].Set_A_Doodad(6857);   // sets doodad[0] doodad number to 6857
MyDoodads[1].Set_A_Doodad(6164);   // sets doodad[1] doodad number to 6164
```

Array of PhoneList Objects

The PhoneList class represents a single entry for a telephone book listing, including two character strings for the name and address and three integer values for the area code, exchange, and phone number. The PhoneList is used to create an array of objects in a program.

What functions do we need for our phone data? The data is private, so we must be able to fill all the object variables. (A "set" function does the trick.) A print function allows us to write the listings to the screen. We shall read the phone information from the data file, phonebook.dat. See Program 9-5. This program is illustrated in Figure 9-11.

```
//Program 9-5    Array of Objects
//This program uses a class PhoneList that represents a telephone book entry.
//Then it reads five entries from a data file, filling the array of objects.
#include <iostream.h>        // for cout
#include <string.h>          // for strcpy
#include <iomanip.h>         // for setw()
#include <fstream.h>         // for file i/o
#include <stdlib.h>          // for exit(); and atoi();
#define FILE_IN "phonebook.dat"

class PhoneList
{
private:
        char name[25], address[30];
        int areacode, exchange, number;
public:
        PhoneList();
        void SetName(char n[]) { strcpy(name, n); }
        void SetAddress(char addr[]) { strcpy(address, addr); }
        void SetPhone(int a, int ex, int num );
        void ShowListing();
};

PhoneList::PhoneList()    // constructor null's strings and zero's integers
{
        name[0] = '\0';
        address[0] = '\0';
        areacode = exchange = number = 0;
}

void PhoneList::SetPhone( int a, int ex, int num)
{
        areacode = a;
        exchange = ex;
        number = num;
}

void PhoneList::ShowListing()
{
        cout << endl << setw(25) << name << setw(30) << address << "   ";
        cout << areacode << " - " << exchange << "-" << number;
}
```

```cpp
int main()
{
        PhoneList mylist[5];    // we have five entries in our phone book

//first must set up streams for input
        ifstream input;                     //setup input stream object
//open for input and don't create if it is not there
        input.open(FILE_IN, ios::in|ios::nocreate);
//Check to ensure the file was opened.
        if(!input )
        {
                cout << "\n Can't find input file " << FILE_IN;
                cout << "\n Exiting program, bye bye \n ";
                exit(1);
        }

        int i, a, ex, num;
        char buf[35];

        for (i = 0; i < 5; ++i)  // this loop reads each entry in phone book file
        {
                input.getline(buf,25);
                mylist[i].SetName(buf);
                input.getline(buf,30);
                mylist[i].SetAddress(buf);
                input.getline(buf,4);     // need to read in each part of the number
                a = atoi(buf);            // ASCII to integer conversion function used
                input.getline(buf,5);
                ex = atoi(buf);
                input.getline(buf,7);
                num = atoi(buf);
                mylist[i].SetPhone(a,ex,num);
        }

        cout.setf(ios::left);     //left justify the output
        cout << "\n Your Address Book contains these listings: \n\n";
        for(i=0; i< 5 ; ++i)
        {
                mylist[i].ShowListing();
        }
        input.close();
        cout << "\n\n And a gracious Goodbye!  \n";
        return 0;
}
```

9

Class declaration
Each PhoneList object looks like this:

phonebook.dat

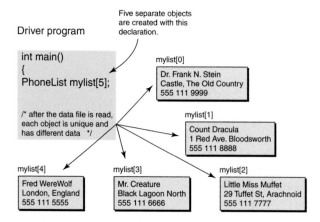

```
class PhoneList
{
    private:
        char name[25], address[30];
        int areacode, exchange, number;
    public:
        PhoneList();
        void SetName(char n[]) { strcpy(name, n); }
        void SetAddress(char addr[]) { strcpy(address, addr); }
        void SetPhone(int a, int ex, int num );
        void ShowListing();

};
```

Dr. Frank N. Stein
Castle, The Old Country
555 111 9999
Count Dracula
1 Red Ave. Bloodsworth
555 111 8888
Little Miss Muffet
29 Tuffet St, Arachnoid
555 111 7777
Mr. Creature
Black Lagoon North
555 111 6666
Fred WereWolf
London, England
555 111 5555

Driver program

Five separate objects
are created with this
declaration.

```
int main()
{
PhoneList mylist[5];

/* after the data file is read,
each object is unique and
has different data   */
```

mylist[0]

Dr. Frank N. Stein
Castle, The Old Country
555 111 9999

mylist[1]

Count Dracula
1 Red Ave. Bloodsworth
555 111 8888

mylist[4]

Fred WereWolf
London, England
555 111 5555

mylist[3]

Mr. Creature
Black Lagoon North
555 111 6666

mylist[2]

Little Miss Muffet
29 Tuffet St, Arachnoid
555 111 7777

Figure 9-11
PhoneList Array of Objects

Array of Objects and Show Me the Cards

Chapter 7 illustrated an array of structures in the Show Me the Cards example. We used a data structure that represented a single card and then declared an array of these structures. In the Chapter 7 program, we were able to use a nested for loop to assign directly the Suit and the Rank for each card.

The Card class incorporates all the necessary functions for an individual card. Because we hide our data, SetSuit and SetRank member functions are required. The class declaration and member functions are shown below:

```
//Program 9-6 Show Me the Cards
#include <iostream.h>
enum Suit { club, diamond, heart, spade};
enum Rank { two = 2, three, four, five, six, seven, eight, nine, ten, jack, queen,
king, ace};
```

```
class Card
{
        private:
                Suit color;
                Rank number;
        public:
                Card();
                void SetSuit(Suit s ){ color = s; }
                void SetRank(Rank r ){ number = r; }
                void ShowCard();
};

Card::Card()            // constructor, initially set it to the 2 of clubs
{
        cout << " Hi, I'm in the constructor.\n";
        color = club;
        number = two;
}

void Card::ShowCard()
{
        if(number < 11) cout << number;
        else if(number == jack) cout << "J";
        else if(number == queen) cout << "Q";
        else if(number == king) cout<< "K";
        else cout << "A";

        switch(color)
        {
                case spade:      cout << char(6) << " "; break;
                case heart:      cout << char(3)<< " "; break;
                case diamond:    cout << char(4)<< " "; break;
                case club:       cout << char(5)<< " "; break;
        }
}
```

In the main function, we declare an array of fifty-two card objects. With the use of a nested for loop, each card is then accessed, and the suit and rank are set. All the cards are then printed to the screen.

```
int main()
{
        Card card[52];    // we have 52 cards; each card has a suit and rank
        //now use the integer enumeration values to initialize the array element
        int i, j, card_ctr = 0;   // array index for cards
        for (i = 0; i < 4; ++i)  // this loop is for the 4 suits
        {
                for(j = 2; j < 15; ++j)        // loop for card rank 2 - Ace
                {
                        card[ card_ctr].SetSuit((Suit) i);
                        card[ card_ctr].SetRank((Rank) j);
                        ++ card_ctr;
                }
        }
//now write out the cards by using the ASCII symbol for card suits
        card_ctr = 0;
        for(i = 0;     i < 52; ++i)
        {
                card[i].ShowCard();
                card_ctr++;
                if( card_ctr == 13 )
                {
                        cout << endl;    // newline if new suit
                        card_ctr = 0;
                }
        }
        return 0;
}
```

9

The program output includes fifty-two "Hi, I'm in the constructor" statements because we create fifty-two card objects.

Hi, I'm in the constructor.
Hi, I'm in the constructor.
:
: **[Fifty-two of these Hi statements.]**
:
Hi, I'm in the constructor.
2♣ 3♣ 4♣ 5♣ 6♣ 7♣ 8♣ 9♣ 10♣ J♣ Q♣ K♣ A♣
2♦ 3♦ 4♦ 5♦ 6♦ 7♦ 8♦ 9♦ 10♦ J♦ Q♦ K♦ A♦
2♥ 3♥ 4♥ 5♥ 6♥ 7♥ 8♥ 9♥ 10♥ J♥ Q♥ K♥ A♥
2♠ 3♠ 4♠ 5♠ 6♠ 7♠ 8♠ 9♠ 10♠ J♠ Q♠ K♠ A♠

9.8
Overloaded Operators and Objects

The C++ language provides many symbol operators. The C++ operators are designed for specific tasks and data types. There are relational ($<$, $>$, $<=$, $>=$, $==$, $!=$), logical (&&, ||, !) and arithmetic ($+$, $-$, $*$, $/$, %) operators. Programmers find the increment and decrement ($++$, $--$) operators convenient to use when working with integers. The modulus (%) operates only on integers.

Is it possible to use operators with objects? Can we increment an object? Is it possible to know if one object is greater than another? Can we add two objects together?

The good news is that there is a technique in C++ to overload operators. Just as we overloaded functions in the previous chapter, we can also overload operators. Recall that when we overloaded a function, we had more than one implementation but only one interface; that is, we had several functions with the same name, such as DrawLine, SayGoodnight, and WriteYourName.

We already have some *overloaded operators* in C++. An asterisk, *, tells the program to perform multiplication when the asterisk is used with two numbers. When the asterisk is paired with a pointer, the asterisk is the indirection operator and accesses the memory to which the pointer is pointing.

It is possible to overload operators in C++. C++ operators (which are just symbols) perform different tasks, depending on how they are used. To overload an operator, we must write a specific operator function that is a class member. This *operator function* defines a valid C++ operator that performs the tasks when it is working with an object of that class. You may use only valid C++ operators. *Note:* You cannot use characters that are not already operators in C++.

The prototype format for an overloaded operator function contains the keyword *operator* and is followed by the desired operator symbol:

```
return_type operator symbol (input parameter list);
```

If we were to overload the increment operator in our Doodad class, the prototype in the class declaration would be the following:

```
class Doodad
{
        private:
                int doodad_number;
        public:
                Doodad();   //constructor
                void operator ++ ();            // keyword operator is used
        // other Doodad functions go here
};
```

overloaded operator
a valid C++ symbol (operator) that has been assigned a specialized task when the operator is used with objects

operator function
a class member function that is required to specify the task(s) for overloading an operator

operator
C++ keyword for designating class member operator functions

9

```
// Program 9-7  Overloaded operators with the class Counter
#include <iostream.h>

class Counter
{
private:
        int count;
public:
        Counter() {  count = 0;  }              // constructor inits count to zero
        void operator ++ () { ++count;  }    // defines the ++ to add one to count
        void operator -- ()   { --count;  }    // defines the -- to sub one from count
        void Reset() { count = 0;  }              // resets the counter to zero
        int GetCount () { return count; }      // returns the value in count
};
```

Unary Overloaded Operators

The class Counter illustrates how to overload the increment (++) and decrement
(--) operator. A unary operator is an operator requiring only one operand. We establish this class Counter so that a single integer represents the count. The class functions
include a constructor that zeros the count, a reset function, and increment and decrement operator functions. The Counter class is declared as shown in Program 9-7.

   The ++ and -- operators now have new definitions when used with a Counter
object. These operators still work in the same manner as before with integers. In the
following sample program, we have Counter objects and individual integers.

```
int main()
{
        Counter MyCount, YourCount;        // both objects are initialized to zero
        int number = 0;

        ++MyCount;
        ++YourCount;
        ++number;
        cout << "\n MyCount = " << MyCount.GetCount();
        cout << "\n YourCount = " << YourCount.GetCount();
        cout << "\n Number = " << number;

        ++MyCount;
        --YourCount;
        --number;
```

```
        cout << "\n MyCount = " << MyCount.GetCount();
        cout << "\n YourCount = " << YourCount.GetCount();
        cout << "\n Number = " << number;

        cout << "\n\n Enough counting for me! \n";
        return 0;
}
```

The output is shown below:

MyCount = 1
YourCount = 1
Number = 1
MyCount = 2
YourCount = 0
Number = 0

Enough counting for me!

Prefix Versus Postfix with Increment/Decrement Operators

The Counter example begs the issue: "What if we enter the code by typing a postfix operator instead of a prefix operator?" In other words, what if we type the code like this:

```
MyCount++;
YourCount++;
```

instead of this?

```
++MyCount;
++YourCount;
```

By placing the ++ to the right of the object, the C++ compiler considers it a postfix operator. (When typed with the ++ to the left of the object, the ++ is considered a prefix operator.) The Visual C++ compiler issues the following warning when the code uses a postfix unary operator:

Compiling...
Ch9Counter.cpp
C:\TestCases\Ch9Counter.cpp(30) : warning C4620: no postfix form of 'operator ++'
found for type 'Counter', using prefix form
        C:\TestCases\Ch9Counter.cpp(6) : see declaration of 'Counter'
Linking...

TestCases.exe - 0 error(s), 1 warning(s)

The Visual C++ compiler uses the prefix form of the operator function here.

Binary Overloaded Operators

A binary operator requires two operands. Let's review an example with integers. To add two integer values, the addition operator (+) must have two integers, one on either side of it. The assignment operator is required so that the addition result is stored into a new value, for example:

```
int a = 7, b = 8, c;
c = a + b;
```

The ability to define binary operators for objects makes possible the addition of two objects, such as:

```
Doodad MyDoodad, YourDoodad, OurDoodad;      // we don't know
OurDoodad = MyDoodad + YourDoodad;           // what a doodad is    ;-)
```

The mechanics for performing binary operations with objects (i.e., requiring two operands) are a bit more involved than those for unary operators, but the end result yields the same convenient tool for working with objects. There is no magic here—the programmer specifies exactly what steps the program performs for each overloaded operator.

Add Two Time Objects   The twenty-four-hour clock illustrates how to overload the addition (+) operator for an object. The twenty-four-hour clock uses the HR:MIN:SEC notation; 0:0:1 is one second after midnight, and 24:0:0 is midnight. We declare an addition operator so that we add two times together. For example, 3:4:5 added with 10:11:12 yields 13:15:17. If we add 15:30:55 and 3:45:15, we obtain 19:16:10. Remember—when creating the operator functions, the programmer must do all the work to obtain the correct results.

First we specify the overloaded operator prototype in the class declaration (see Figure 9-12):

```
class Time
{
private:
        int hr, min, sec;
public:
        Time();      //initializes the time object to 0:0:1
        Time(int h, int m, int s);    //initializes object to h:m:s
        void Reset(int h, int m, int s); // resets time to h:m:s
        void ShowTime();
        Time operator + (Time N);         //overload the + operator
};
```

Time Object Operator + Prototype ⟶ Time Operator + (Time N);

This function returns a Time object.

The input to this function is a Time object.

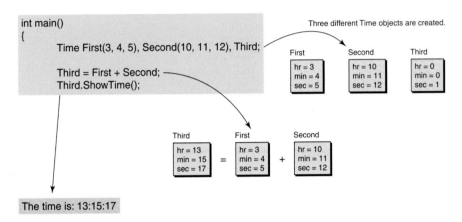

```
int main()
{
        Time First(3, 4, 5), Second(10, 11, 12), Third;

        Third = First + Second;
        Third.ShowTime();
```

Three different Time objects are created.

First	Second	Third
hr = 3	hr = 10	hr = 0
min = 4	min = 11	min = 0
sec = 5	sec = 12	sec = 1

Third		First		Second
hr = 13		hr = 3		hr = 10
min = 15	=	min = 4	+	min = 11
sec = 17		sec = 5		sec = 12

The time is: 13:15:17

Figure 9-12
Add Two Time Objects

The main function in Program 9-8 shows the instantiation of three objects (First, Second, and Third), as well as the addition statement. The output is shown below:

The time is: 13:15:17
The time is: 19:16:10
All done adding Time objects!

When two objects are added, the result is another Time object. The return type from the addition operation function is another Time object. The call to the adding function is:

```
Third = First + Second;
```

Now comes the tricky part. The Time class has an addition function. Whenever a Time object is created, the object has its own addition function. This program has three Time objects: First, Second, and Third. When we add the First and Second object, which object's addition function is actually called?

With binary operators, the object on the left-hand side of the operator owns the function that is called when the program encounters the operator. First's + oper-

```
//Program 9-8 Adding Time objects
int main()
{
        Time First(3,4,5), Second(10, 11, 12), Third;
        Third = First + Second;    // juicy part of the whole program  ;-)
        Third.ShowTime();
        First.Reset(15,30,55);
        Second.Reset(3,45,15);
        Third = First + Second;
        Third.ShowTime();
        cout << "\n All done adding Time objects!  \n\n";
        return 0;
}
```

ator function is called when we add our two Time objects. Figure 9-13 illustrates this process.

The actual operator function must perform the addition and handle the situation when the seconds or minutes are more than 59. Here is the source code for the addition function:

```
Time Time:: operator +(Time N)
{
        Time result;
        int divisor;

        result.sec = sec + N.sec;              // add the seconds
/*if more than 60, divide to get minutes, remainder is new seconds
        add additional minutes to new minute  */
        divisor = result.sec/60;
        result.sec= result.sec%60;
        result.min = min + N.min + divisor;
// same thing if minutes are over 60
        divisor = result.min/60;
        result.min = result.min%60;
        result.hr = hr + N.hr + divisor;
        return (result );
}
```

Is This Card Bigger Than That Card?   It is often necessary to compare objects and thus determine whether one object is "bigger" than another or to determine if two objects are the "same." We can overload any of the relational or logical

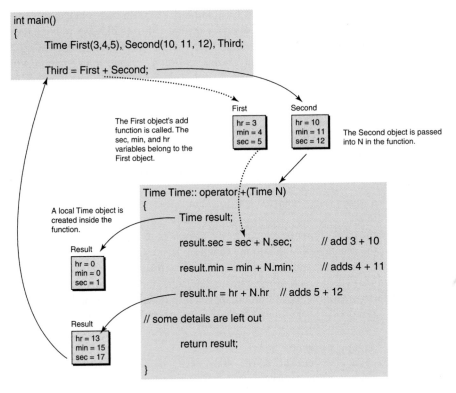

```
int main()
{
        Time First(3,4,5), Second(10, 11, 12), Third;

        Third = First + Second;
```

First
```
hr = 3
min = 4
sec = 5
```

Second
```
hr = 10
min = 11
sec = 12
```

The First object's add function is called. The sec, min, and hr variables belong to the First object.

The Second object is passed into N in the function.

A local Time object is created inside the function.

Result
```
hr = 0
min = 0
sec = 1
```

```
Time Time:: operator +(Time N)
{
        Time result;

        result.sec = sec + N.sec;       // add 3 + 10

        result.min = min + N.min;       // adds 4 + 11

        result.hr = hr + N.hr   // adds 5 + 12

// some details are left out

        return result;

}
```

Result
```
hr = 13
min = 15
sec = 17
```

Figure 9-13
The First Operand Object's Operator Function Is Called

operators and perform object comparisons in the operator function. Typically, the return value from the comparison function is either a 1 (true) or a 0 (false). We may use Boolean return types, too.

Recall our "normal" greater than operator works as follows:

```
int a, b;
//assign values to a and b
if(a > b)
        cout << " \n a is greater than b";
else
        cout << "\n a is not greater than b";
```

The Card class from the Show Me the Cards example can have a comparison function with the greater than ($>$) symbol. We can compare the rank (number) and suit to determine if one card has a greater value than another. In many card games, one suit is designated "trump"—it takes precedence over the other suits.

Our next move is to set up the Card class declaration and include an overloaded > operator. We model our > operator so that it works like any relational or logical operator. Our function returns an integer value 1 (true) and 0 (false). We use this operator in the same manner that we use a normal "greater than" operator. In our card example, our operator returns a 1 or a 0, and then we use the operator in the same manner as above:

```
Card first_card, second_card;
// set rank and suit for both cards
if(first_card > second_card)
        cout << "\n The first card is greater than the second card.\n";
else
        cout << "\n The first card is not greater than the second card.\n";'
```

The comparison function requires two operands, as in the Time class, so we need to pass the second operand into the function. In our program, a card is considered "greater" if its rank is higher; that is, an ace is greater than a king—no matter what the suits are. If the rank of the cards is the same, then the suits are to be considered. We use the following suit order: spades (high), hearts, diamonds, and clubs (low).

```
enum Suit { club, diamond, heart, spade};
enum Rank { two = 2, three, four, five, six, seven, eight, nine,
ten, jack, queen, king, ace};
class Card
{
        private:
                Suit color;
                Rank number;
        public:
                Card();
                void SetSuit(Suit s ){ color = s; }
                void SetRank(Rank r ){ number = r; }
                void ShowCard();
                int operator > (Card X);    // for card comparison
};
```

Notice how the enumeration lists are set up so that the actual card numbers are lower in the enum list than the face cards and ace (that is, the three has an enum value of 3 and four has an enum value of 4, etc.). The suits are in order of actual playing rank. (The club suit is the lowest ranking suit and has an enum value of 0.)

The comparison function assumes that the ranking of the suits is spades, hearts, diamonds, and clubs. The function is illustrated in Figure 9-14 and the

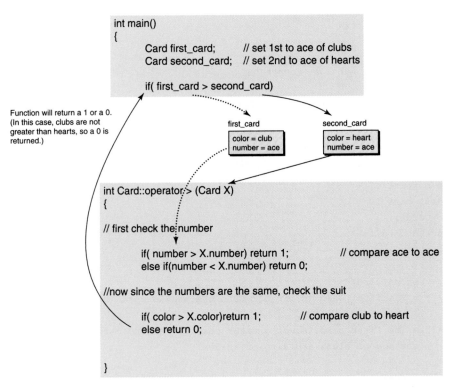

Figure 9-14

The first_card Object's Operator Function Is Called

source code is shown below.

```
int Card::operator > (Card X)
{
                                        // first check the number
    if( number > X.number) return 1;
    else if(number < X.number)return 0;

//now since the numbers are the same, check the suit
    if( color > X.color)return 1;
    else return 0;
}
```

The main function that illustrates this operator is shown in Program 9-9.

```
//Program 9-9  Comparison of objects
int main()
{
       Card first_card, second_card;    // we have two cards

       first_card.SetRank(ace);    // the second card has a higher value than the first
       first_card.SetSuit(club);
       second_card.SetRank(ace);
       second_card.SetSuit(heart);

// Show the cards and compare
       cout << "\n First card is ";
       first_card.ShowCard();
       cout << "\n Second card is ";
       second_card.ShowCard();

       if(first_card > second_card)
              cout << "\n The first card is greater than the second card.\n";
       else
              cout << "\n The first card is not greater than the second card.\n";
// now set the cards to the ace of clubs and king of spades

       first_card.SetRank(ace);
       first_card.SetSuit(club);
       second_card.SetRank(king);
       second_card.SetSuit(spade);

       // Show the cards and compare
       cout << "\n First card is ";
       first_card.ShowCard();
       cout << "\n Second card is ";
       second_card.ShowCard();

       if(first_card > second_card)
              cout << "\n The first card is greater than the second card.\n";
       else
              cout << "\n The first card is not greater than the second card.\n";
       cout << "\n\n Aren't overloaded operators great? \n";
       return 0;
}
```

The output is shown here:

First card is A♣

Second card is A♥
The first card is not bigger than the second card.

First card is A♣

Second card is K♠
The first card is greater than the second card.

Aren't overloaded operators great?

9.9
Pointers and Classes

C++ allows an object's address to be passed to a function in the same fashion as we passed data structure addresses. The object's address may be passed to a pointer, or an implicit address is passed into a reference variable. With either the right-arrow operator (pointers) or the dot operator (reference), the public members of the class are accessible. Tables 9-11 and 9-12 compare data structures and classes using

▌ TABLE 9-11
Pass by Reference with Pointers, Objects to Functions

Item	Data Structure	Class

Declaration	```struct TheStruct```
	 ```{```
	    ```int a, b;```
	 ```};```
		```class TheClass```
		 ```{```
		 ```private:```
		    ```int a,b;```
		 ```public:```
		    ```void SetValues(int aa, int bb)```
		    ```{ a = aa; b = bb; }```
		 ```};```

Function prototype	```void Func1(TheStruct*);```	```void Func2(TheClass*);```

Call	```int main ()```
	 ```{```
	    ```TheStruct str_var;```
	    ```Func1(&str_var);```
	 ```}```
		```int main ()```
		 ```{```
		    ```TheClass obj;```
		    ```Func2(&obj);```
		 ```}```

Function	```void Func1(TheStruct *ptr)```
	 ```{```
	    ```ptr->a = 5;```
	    ```ptr->b = 6;```
	 ```}```
		```void Func2(TheClass *ptr)```
		 ```{```
		    ```ptr->SetValues(5,6);```
		 ```}```

9

Item	Data Structure	Class
Declaration	```struct TheStruct\n{\n int a, b;\n};```	```class TheClass\n{\nprivate:\n int a,b;\npublic:\n void SetValues(int aa, init bb)\n {\n a = aa;\n b = bb;\n }\n};```
Function prototype Call	```void Func1(TheStruct &);\nint main ()\n{\n TheStruct str_var;\n Func1(str_var);\n}```	```void Func2(TheClass &);\nint main ()\n{\n TheClass obj;\n Func2(obj);\n}```
Function	```void Func1(TheStruct &ref)\n{\n ref.a = 5;\n ref.b = 6;\n}```	```void Func2(TheClass &ref)\n{\n ref.SetValues(5,6);\n}```

pointers and reference variables. The only new point here is that the public member functions of the class can now be called by using the pointer or reference variable. Notice how data structures and classes are treated in an identical manner.

Program Examples

It is possible to pass the object's address to a single, stand-alone function or pass the address into another object's member function. (That sounds confusing!) In either case, the mechanics of pointers and public members work in exactly the same manner as we've seen with conventional C functions.

Hair Ball Example   This example contains a Kitty class and a separate (non-Kitty class) function, FillCatInfo, that fills the Kitty object information. This FillCatInfo function asks the user to enter the information. Do not expend energy wondering why this function is not a member of the Kitty class (where it should be), but do spend time examining the mechanics of passing an address of an object to a function.

First, declare the Kitty class. We need three Put functions to place information into the private data variables and a print function. See Program 9-10. This program is illustrated in Figure 9-15.

The GetCatInfo function receives the address of the object.

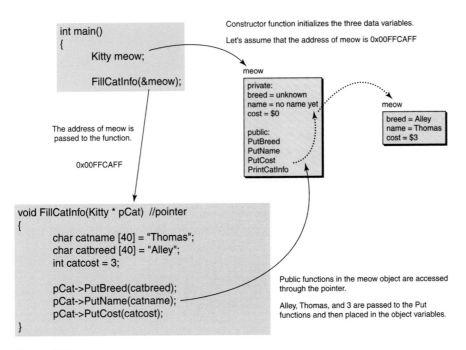

Figure 9-15
Hair Ball Program

```
//Program 9-10 Kitty, Kitty
//Pass the address of a Kitty object to a function.
#include <iostream.h>
#include <string.h>
class Kitty
{
private:
        char breed[40], name[40];
        int cost;

public:
        Kitty();
        void PutBreed(char b[]){strcpy(breed,b);}
        void PutName(char n[]) {strcpy(name,n); }
        void PutCost(int c) {cost = c; }
        void PrintCatInfo();
};
```

```
Kitty::Kitty()        //constructor
{
        strcpy(breed,"unknown");
        strcpy(name, "not named yet");
        cost = 0;
}

void Kitty::PrintCatInfo()
{
        cout << "\n Breed " << breed << "\n  Name " << name;
        cout << "\n  Cost $ " << cost;
}
```

The FillCatInfo function's prototype and function are located outside the class declaration. Notice that the input argument for the function is a pointer to a Kitty.

```
void FillCatInfo(Kitty *);    // prototype
int main()
{
        Kitty meow;

        cout << "\n Hair Ball Program \n\n Before the function call:\n";
        meow.PrintCatInfo();

        FillCatInfo(&meow);    // address of Kitty object is passed into the function

        cout << "\n\n After the function call:\n";
        meow.PrintCatInfo();
        cout << "\n\n No more kitties for you.  \n";

        return 0;
}

void FillCatInfo(Kitty * pCat)  //pointer
{
        char catname[40] = "Thomas", catbreed[40] = "Alley";
        int catcost = 3;

        pCat->PutBreed(catbreed);  // public Kitty functions accessed with pointer
        pCat->PutName(catname);
        pCat->PutCost(catcost);
}
```

The output is shown below:

Hair Ball Program

Before the function call:

Breed   unknown
Name   not named yet
Cost $ 0

After the function call:

Breed   Alley
Name   Thomas
Cost $ 3

No more kitties for you.

This program can be written with a reference parameter instead of a pointer. The differences are seen below in the FillCatInfo function prototype, call, and actual function. There are no changes to the class Kitty.

```
// prototype
void FillCatInfo(Kitty &);

// call statement in the main program
FillCatInfo(meow);

//function using a reference variable instead of a pointer
void FillCatInfo(Kitty &rCat)
{
        char catname[40] = "Thomas", catbreed[40] = "Alley";
        int catcost = 3;

        rCat.PutBreed(catbreed);    // public Kitty functions
        rCat.PutName(catname);      // accessed with dot operator
        rCat.PutCost(catcost);
}
```

SetTimeObject Function   A stripped-down version of the Time class (from earlier in this chapter) illustrates how to use pointers and objects in a program. See Program 9-11. The first step is to make a Time object and then to send its address to a function called SetTimeObject. The SetTimeObject function accesses the computer system time using functions found in the C++ standard time library (time.h) and places the system time into the object values. Figure 9-16 illustrates this concept. The initial portion of the program file contains the two include files and Time class declaration. The necessary Time member functions follow the declaration.

```
//Program 9-11 Pointers to objects--set a time object to the system time.
#include <iostream.h>
#include <time.h>                      //This is the C++ library's time.h file.

class Time
{
private:
        int hr, min, sec;
public:
        Time();      //sets the time object to 0:0:1
        void Reset(int h, int m, int s); // resets time to h:m:s
        void ShowTime();
};

Time::Time()
{
        hr = min = 0;
        sec = 1;
}

void Time::Reset(int h, int m, int s)
{
        hr = h;
        min = m;
        sec = s;
}

void Time::ShowTime()
{
        cout << "\n The time object: " << hr << ":" << min << ":" << sec;
}
void SetTimeObject(Time *pWatch);//Function prototype, receives ptr to Time object

int main()
{
        Time MyWatch;                   // MyWatch is an object of class Time
        cout << "\n What time is it?  \n\n";
        SetTimeObject(&MyWatch);        // pass the object's address to function
        MyWatch.ShowTime();             // use Mywatch's function to show time
        cout << "\n\n OK  Thanks!  \n\n";
        return 0;
}
```

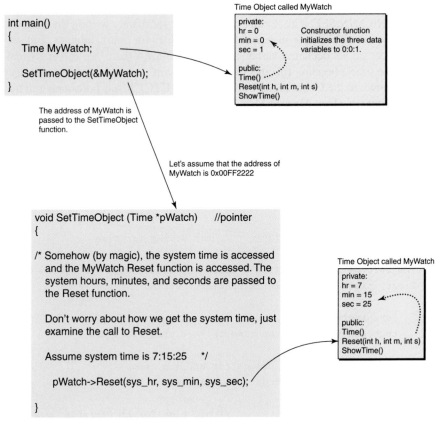

We create a Time object and then send its address to a function that sets the time to the computer's system time.

Time Object called MyWatch

```
private:
hr = 0          Constructor function
min = 0         initializes the three data
sec = 1         variables to 0:0:1.

public:
Time() ·····
Reset(int h, int m, int s)
ShowTime()
```

```
int main()
{
    Time MyWatch;

    SetTimeObject(&MyWatch);
}
```

The address of MyWatch is passed to the SetTimeObject function.

Let's assume that the address of MyWatch is 0x00FF2222

```
void SetTimeObject (Time *pWatch)      //pointer
{

/* Somehow (by magic), the system time is accessed
and the MyWatch Reset function is accessed. The
system hours, minutes, and seconds are passed to
the Reset function.

Don't worry about how we get the system time, just
examine the call to Reset.

Assume system time is 7:15:25    */

    pWatch->Reset(sys_hr, sys_min, sys_sec);

}
```

Time Object called MyWatch

```
private:
hr = 7
min = 15
sec = 25

public:
Time()
Reset(int h, int m, int s)
ShowTime()
```

Figure 9-16
Time Object and Computer System Time

9

The system time is reported in the SetTimeObject function; following this action, it is written again by the Time object. The output from this program is shown below:

What time is it?

The system time is 13:22:43
The Time object: 13:22:43

OK Thanks!

The SetTimeObject function uses data types and functions that are defined in the C++ standard library time.h file. We first access the system time with a character string and_strtime function. This function fills a string with the system time in the form HR:MIN:SEC. This format is convenient for merely writing the time, but we need to access the time in terms of integer values for hours, minutes, and seconds. To do so, we declare a variable of the type time_t (here, we call it System-Time). The time() function fills this data variable with the number of seconds since 1/1/70, known as the Coordinated Universal Time (UTC). It was previously referred to as Greenwich Mean Time (GMT). We convert this time value to a struct tm by calling the localtime function found in the time library. Once we have filled the OStime structure, we can access the hours, minutes, and seconds.

```
//Demonstrates two ways to access the computer system time.
void SetTimeObject(Time *pWatch)
{

        char time_right_now[20];    //char string for time

// The_strtime function fills a character string with the system time.
// First, place system time in character string

        _strtime(time_right_now);
        cout << "\n The system time is " << time_right_now;

// We need to get integer values for hr, min, sec.
// Need to use a time_t struct that is defined in time.h

        time_t SystemTime;          // UTC time format variable

// Passing the address of SystemTime to time function.
// The time function fills the SystemTime with UTC seconds

        time (&SystemTime);

// Need to convert UTC to something we can use.
// The localtime function does that.
// Declare struct tm ptr to hold individual time info

        struct tm *OStime;
```

```
// Pass the address of SystemTime to localtime to convert to tm struc
// and it fills OStime with all we need.

    OStime = localtime(&SystemTime);

/* Now we can access the hr, min, sec of system time, and
send them to the object's Reset function. (whew)
The tm struct has tm_hour, tm_min and tm_sec variables. */

    pWatch->Reset(OStime->tm_hour, OStime->tm_min, OStime->tm_sec);
}
```

9.10
Summary

In object-oriented programming, the design of the software is based on real-world objects instead of data flow. It is possible to incorporate the data and functions together in a class declaration and, that accomplished, the programmer may create and use these class objects. The classic C structure syntax is extended so that the programmer uses the dot operator to access the public members of the class.

There are several software development principles in object-oriented programming. One principle is encapsulation, which means that the class data is "hidden" (placed in the private section of the class declaration). This step ensures that only class member functions can use the data and that the object data are not accessed by parts of the program that have no business tinkering with them.

New functions are associated with classes. Class constructors are executed automatically when an object is declared. The purpose of the constructor is to initialize the object data (or states) to known values. Destructor functions are executed when the object is destroyed or the program is terminated. Overloaded operator functions allow any C++ operators to be defined tasks with objects.

Comparing Structures and Classes

What is the difference between the two declarations shown in Table 9-13? There is a critical difference between the two declarations. The data in the structure is treated as public. The data in the class is (by default) private. Supporting the encapsulation rules for object-oriented programming, the designers of C++ specify that the C++ language makes the data private if the access specifier for data is not given by the programmer.

Table 9-14 illustrates the similarities between the structure and class syntax. Note how the structure data variables are accessible in the main function, whereas the class data are private and must be accessed through the public member functions. The class has a one-line constructor function that sets the private data to zero.

TABLE 9-13

Comparing a Simple Structure and Class

Structure	Class
| ```
struct A
{
    int b;
};
``` | ```
class A
{
    int b;
};
``` |

TABLE 9-14

Structure and Class Function Comparison

Item	Structure	Class
| Declarations and prototypes | ```
struct TheStruct
{
    int a,b;
};
void WriteEm(TheStruct);
``` | ```
class TheClass
{
private:
    int a, b;
public:
    TheClass(){a = 0, b = 0;}
    void SetEm(int, int);
    void WriteEm();
);
``` |
| Call | ```
int main()
{
    TheStruct MyStruct;
    MyStruct.a = 5;
    MyStruct.b = 6;
    WriteEm(MyStruct);
}
``` | ```
int main()
{
    TheClass MyObject;
    MyObject.SetEm(5,6);
    MyObject.WriteEM();
}
``` |
| Function | ```
void WriteEm(TheStruct ms)
{
    cout << ms.a " and "
        << ms.b;
}
``` | ```
void TheClass::SetEm(int x, inty)
{
    a = x;
    b = y;
}
void MyClass::WriteEm()
{
    cout << a " and " b;
}
``` |

9.11
Practice

Big, Bigger, Biggest Football Players

Our practice example in this chapter has something for everyone! Program 9-12 has a FootballPlayer class that contains data and functions for a football player. The player information is read into an array from a data file called players.dat. The program should first report the player information as read from the file, sort the players (from smallest to largest), and report the sorted information.

An overloaded greater than operator, $>$, in the FootballPlayer class enables us to write a function to compare two players. A modified Bubble Sort function is used to sort FootballPlayers. One player is greater than another player if he (or she) is taller; if they are the same height, the heavier player is deemed greater. The program writes out the sorted players and reports the players in order from smallest to largest.

Note: We use the notoriously inefficient but easy-to-understand Bubble Sort routine in this example. The reader is encouraged to investigate the Quick Sort function provided in the standard library (stdlib). The **qsort** function is versatile and efficient.

qsort
a general sorting routine located in the C++ standard library (stdlib.h)

In Program 9-12, we declare the FootballPlayer (FPlayer) class in the fplayer.h file. The associated class functions are shown on page 424 in FPlayer.cpp:

9

```
//Program 9-12 Football Players
//File:  FPlayer.h
#ifndef _FPLAYER_H
#define _FPLAYER_H

#include <string.h>
#include <iostream.h>

class FPlayer
{
private:
        int weight, feet, inches, totalinches;
        char name[25];
public:
        FPlayer(){ cout << "\n I'm in the constructor. ";};
        void SetName(char* n) { strcpy(name,n);}
        void SetWeight(int w) { weight = w;}
        void SetHeight(int ft, int in);
        void WriteInfo();
        bool operator > (FPlayer p);
};
#endif
```

```
//File:  FPlayer.cpp
#include "FPlayer.h"
#include <iostream.h>
#include <iomanip.h>

bool FPlayer::operator > (FPlayer p)
{
            // if two players are the same height, the heavier player is "bigger"
        if(feet > p.feet) return true;

        if(feet == p.feet)
        {
            if(inches > p.inches) return true;
            else if(inches == p.inches)
            {
                    if(weight > p.weight) return true;
                    else return false;
            }
            else return false;
        }
        else
            return false;
}

void FPlayer::SetHeight(int ft, int in)
{
        feet = ft;
        inches = in;
}

void FPlayer::WriteInfo()
{
        cout << endl << setw(25) <<    name << setw(8) << feet << "' " << setw(3) <<
            inches << "\" " << setw(8) << weight << " pounds";
}
```

The player information file contains an integer in the first line that represents the number of players, followed by each player's name, height (feet and inches), and weight. This format is seen in player.dat:

5
Deion Husky
6 8 275
Robert Steamroller
6 5 320
TippyToe Harte
6 8 332
Cupcake Johnston
6 5 265
Dave KnockemDown
5 11 275

The main function and the file reading and sorting functions are in the Fplayer-Driver.cpp file. Notice that these two supporting functions are *not* class members for FPlayer! The FPlayer class contains code pertinent to one player. Reading the file and sorting the array do not belong in the Football Player class.

```cpp
//Program 9-12 Big, Bigger, Biggest Football Players
#include <iostream.h>
#include <fstream.h>
#include <stdlib.h>
#include "FPlayer.h"

int ReadFootballPlayers(char *input, FPlayer team[], int* total);
void SortEm(FPlayer [], int total);

int main()
{
        FPlayer team[5];   // a team of football player objects
        int total;

        cout << "\n\n  Sorting Football Player Objects  \n" <<
               "\n Hit an enter to continue: ";

        char enter;
        cin.get(enter);
        char *input = "Players.dat";

        int error = ReadFootballPlayers(input, team, &total);
        if(error)
        {
                cout << "\n\n couldn't find file " << input;
                exit(1);
        }
}
```

```
        cout << "\n\n The original Players.dat file is: ";
        for (int i= 0; i < total; ++ i)
        {
                team[i].WriteInfo();
        }

        SortEm(team, total);

        cout << "\n\n The sorted Players array is: ";
        for ( i= 0; i < total; ++ i)
        {
                team[i].WriteInfo();
        }

        cout << "\n\n These are big fellows! \n\n";

        cin.get(enter);
        return 0;
}


void SortEm(FPlayer team[], int total)
{
// a classic bubble sort, using FPlayers object, sorts from low to high

        int i, j;
        FPlayer temp;
        for(i = 0; i < (total - 1) ; ++i)
        {
                for(j = 1; j < total; ++j)
                {
                        if(team[j-1] > team[j] )
                        {
                                temp = team[j];
                                team[j] = team[j-1];
                                team[j-1] = temp;
                        }
                }
        }
}


int ReadFootballPlayers(char *filename, FPlayer team[], int *total)
{
        //opens and reads the input filename, and fills the team data
        int wt, ft, in;
        ifstream input;
```

```
input.open(filename, ios::in|ios::nocreate);
if(!input)return 1;

char buf[50], junk;
input.getline(buf,50);
*total = atoi(buf);

for(int i = 0; i < *total; ++ i)
{

        input.getline(buf,50);
        team[i].SetName(buf);
        input >> ft >> in >> wt;
        input.get(junk);
        team[i].SetWeight(wt);
        team[i].SetHeight(ft,in);
}
input.close();
return 0;

}
```

In the program output, we see (initially) the constructor message five times because our array has five players. We hold the screen by waiting for an Enter key and then list the unsorted and sorted information. It is important to note that another constructor message is seen in the output. This message is written to the screen when a local, temporary FPlayer object (temp) is created in the SortEm function. The output is shown below:

I'm in the constructor.
I'm in the constructor.
I'm in the constructor.
I'm in the constructor.
I'm in the constructor.

Sorting Football Player Objects

Hit an Enter to continue:

The original Players.dat data file is:

Deion Husky	6'	8"	275 pounds
Robert Steamroller	6'	5"	320 pounds
TippyToe Harte	6'	8"	332 pounds
Cupcake Johnston	6'	5"	265 pounds
Dave KnockemDown	5'	11"	275 pounds

I'm in the constructor.

The sorted players array is:

Dave KnockemDown	5'	11"	275 pounds
Cupcake Johnston	6'	5"	265 pounds
Robert Steamroller	6'	5"	320 pounds
Deion Husky	6'	8"	275 pounds
TippyToe Harte	6'	8"	332 pounds

These are big fellows!

■ REVIEW QUESTIONS AND PROBLEMS

Short Answer

1. What is the purpose of the Set and Get functions in classes?

2. Who may access the private data members in a class?

3. What is the difference between a class declaration and class definition?

4. What are the steps a programmer must take when creating an array of objects?

5. When is the constructor function executed? What is its primary purpose?

6. Describe the "ideal" file organization scheme to use with classes.

7. If the Parking Meter needs to print for the Parker a receipt that shows the amount of money received, describe how you might integrate a Printer object in the program. What are the tasks for the Printer and who tells the Printer what to do?

8. A class may have only one destructor function. What is the main purpose of the destructor? When is this function called and who may call it?

9. Declaring a class with all the data and functions public violates which principle(s) of object-oriented programming?

10. Describe the difference in the call statement if a public class member function is called from within another class function versus via an object.

Debugging Problems: Compiler Errors

Identify the compiler errors in Problems 11 to 15 and state what is wrong with the code.

11.
```
#include <iostream.h>
class Ball
{
   private:
      Color shade;
```

```
        Ball(){ shade = green;}
        WhatColor{}{cout << shade;}
}
enum Color {red, blue, green};
int main();
{
    Ball MyBall;
    MyBall.WhatColor();
}
```

12.
```
#include <iostream.h>
Class Birds
{
private:
    char name[40];
    float size;
public:
    Birds();
    void SingASong();
}
void SingASong()
{

    cout << "cheep cheep";
}
int main()
{
    Birds Sparrows[100];
    Sparrows.SingASong[0];
}
```

13.
```
#include <iostream.h>
class Printer
{
private:
    int pages = 0;
    int mode = 2;
public:
    Printer();
};

int main()
{
    Printer 4HP2;
```

14.

```
#include <iostream.h>
enum Light {full, partial, shade};
class Photo
{
private:
    char subject[50];
    Light amount;
public:
    Photo();
    Void SetLight(Light x){amount = x;}
}
int main()
{
    Photo OneOfMe;
    strcpy(OneOfMe.subject, "Joshua DotCommer");
    OneOfMe.SetLight(bright);
```

15.

```
#include <Iostream.h>
class Dolphin
{
private:
    float size;
    char name[45];
public:
    Dolphin(){ strcpy(Dolphin.name, "Tosser");    }
    void SetSize(float s) { size = s;}
    bool operator > ();
};
void Dolphin::operator > ()
{
    if(X.size > size) return false;
    else return true;
}
int main()
{
    Dolphin Big, Little;
    Big.SetSize(20);
    Small.SetSize(15);
    if(Big > Little) cout << "bigger";
    else cout << "smaller".
}
```

Debugging Problems: Run-Time Errors

Each of the programs in Problems 16 to 18 compiles but does not do what the specification states. What is the incorrect action and why does it occur?

16. Specification: The following program should set the dimensions of a Cube object to 3 and calculate the volume and surface area.

```
#include <iostream.h>
#include <math.h>
class Cube
{
private:
   float side;
public:
   Cube() { side = 0.0; }
   void SetSide(float s) {side = s; }
   float Volume(){ return pow(side,2); }
   float SurArea() { return 8.0 * side*side; }
};
int main()
{
    Cube MyCube;
    float CubeVol, CubeSA;
    MyCube.SetSide(5);
    CubeVol = MyCube.Volume();
    CubeSA = MyCube.SurArea();
    return 0;
}
```

17. Specification: When the object is created, the program below should set the time to HR:MIN:SEC. The ++ operator should increment the minute value. When the fifty-ninth minute is incremented, the HR is incremented and the MIN is reset to 0. *Note:* Only the class functions are presented here.

```
class Time
{
private:
   int hr, min, sec;
public:
   Time(int h, int m, int s) { hr = h; min = m; sec = m; }
   void operator ++ ();
};
void Time::operator ++ ()
{
   min++;
```

```
      if(min == 59)
      {
         hr++;
         min = 0;
      }
}
```

18. Specification: The Convert class performs conversions from miles to inches. We need to convert 2.5 miles to inches. (Recall that there are 5,280 feet in a mile, 12 inches in a foot.)

```
#include <iostream.h>
class Convert
{
private:
   double miles, inches;
public:
   Convert(){ miles = 0.0; inches = 0.0; }
   Convert(double m){miles = m; }
   double Miles2Inches();
};
double Convert::Miles2Inches()
{
   inches = miles * 5208.0 * 12.0;
   return inches;
}
int main()
{
   Convert MyMiles(2.5), MyOtherMiles;
   double MyInches;
   MyInches = MyOtherMiles.Miles2Inches();
   cout << "\n Total inches are " << MyInches;
   return 0;
}
```

Programming Problems

Write complete C++ programs for Problems 19 and 20.

19. Write a program that sets up a Date class with private ints for month and day—no year. (You may thank me later because this deletion simplifies the date validation process!) Other class data members are needed; I'll let you figure out what they are.

• One contructor function sets the date to January 1.

- Also needed is a GetDate class function that asks the user to input a date in an integer format. Another requisite is a WriteDate function that writes the date using the month name, such as January 1 instead of 1/1.

- Include a Validate function that returns a false (bool) value if the date is invalid and it writes an "invalid date" message to the screen. This function also resets this invalid date to January 1. (Thirty days hath September, April, June, and November. All the rest have thirty-one—except February, which has twenty-eight days.) You may assume this program is not dealing with a leap year.

- The Date class should also have a private HowManyDays function that calculates the number of days the date object is in a 365-day year. For example, January 31 is the thirty-first day and February 1 is the thirty-second day. This function is not called from the main but is called by the class functions.

- A last necessity of your program is an overloaded operator, $<$, that compares which day is "sooner" in the year. For example, January 31 is less than February 1 because January 31 occurs earlier in the year; however, November 3 is not less than March 8 because March 8 occurs sooner.

- Write a driver program that sets up two Date objects. The user will input two dates. If both dates are valid, the main should compare the dates and report which date occurs sooner in the year. Include a loop so that the user can input several sets of dates.

20. Write a C++ program that sets up a class Sailboat containing private data for a boat's manufacturer and name, length, beam (width), and draught (water depth required to float the boat). The class has set functions for all data as well as a Write Info that reports all the Sailboat object data to the screen. It also has a $>$ operator that compares Sailboat objects. One boat is greater than another if it is longer. If the boats are the same length, then the larger beamed boat is bigger.

    Create a data file of boat data called boats.dat so that the first line is the total number of boats in the file; the next line is the manufacturer; followed by the name; and then the boat length, beam, and draught on the fourth line. For example, this file has three boats:

```
3
McGregor 25
The Sparkly Lady
25   8   3.5
Victoria
WayLay
18   6   3
Hobie
Lazy Days
18   8   1.0
```

9

Your main program should set up an array of five boat objects. Place five boat objects in your boats.dat file. Open your data file and fill your Sailboat array with the boat data from the file. Report the boat information in the order of the data file (unsorted) and then sort the array by using a bubble sort function. Write the boat objects to the screen in the order from smallest to largest boat.

9

10

Class Relationships

KEY TERMS AND CONCEPTS

class relationships
complex class
has a
is a
numeric classes
object model
polling loop
setting random number generator
with system time
string class and objects
uses a
using namespace std
valarray class

CHAPTER OBJECTIVES

Introduce the three basic class relationships: has a, uses a, and is a.

Describe how we have been using C++ classes in earlier chapters.

Present the C++ using namespace standard reference and explain its importance.

Reference the C++ string class, which contains a new C++ tool for handling string/text data.

Explore several demonstration programs that illustrate the has a and uses a class relationship.

Show how it is possible to access the computer system time and use it to seed a random number generator.

Demonstrate how the system time can be used to create a stopwatch class that performs timing operations.

Explain how classes may have classes as data members or that classes simply may use other classes to provide a service.

It's Time to Have Fun!

Clowns have fun, sea lions have fun, and now you know enough object-oriented programming fundamentals to have fun, too. Can you believe it? To get off to a good fun start, the programmer needs to identify the necessary objects for his or her program and to understand the relationship between the objects. Sounds daunting but in reality it is quite simple.

10.1
Object Model and Class Relationships

An *object model* is a software design technique that uses a collection of objects to represent the items in a program. Designing a program with the object model involves examining what objects are required and the relationships between them. These relationships and interactions specify how the objects use each other's services.

> Imagine an automobile as an object. The automobile itself *has* many different components: the engine, transmission, wheels, braking system, frame, and body. When a person examines the relationships among the components, he or she knows that the automobile must have the engine, transmission, braking system, etc. Without these items, the car cannot function as required. However, the automobile *uses* a radio. (Many of us consider the car radio a necessity, but the radio is not an integral component in the automobile.) Now imagine a sports car with wishbone suspension, rack and pinion steering, tachometer, RAM air intake, and convertible top. The sports car is a special kind of an automobile, yet the sports car *is* an automobile. In object-oriented design terms, does a person use an automobile or does a person have an automobile?

> Many advanced computer science courses and textbooks describe system design with the object model notation and custom-diagram formats. For us, it is important to recognize the object relationships and to see that these relationships make sense in our programs. There are three basic class relationships: *uses a*, *has a*, and *is a*. A brief summary of these relationships is shown in Table 10-1.

object model
a software design technique that uses a collection of objects to represent the items in a program

uses a
a class relationship in which an object makes use of another object to accomplish a task

has a
a class relationship in which one object (first) contains another object (second) and the second object is an integral part of the first object

437

Term	Description	Example
uses a	An object can use another object to accomplish a task.	An automobile uses a radio. A computer object uses a printer object to print a document. The computer uses a printer. A computer uses a monitor to display messages to the user. A person uses an automobile.
has a (composition)	One object (first) contains another object (second) and the second object is an integral part of the first object. (If the second object were removed from the first object, the first object could not perform as expected.)	A computer has a motherboard. An automobile has an engine. A tennis player has a tennis racquet.
is a (inheritance)[a]	A new (derived) class is created from an existing (base) class by inheriting properties from the base class. The new class is a special case of the base class.	A computer disk may be a general object that stores information. There are several types of disks—including floppy, hard disks, zip disks, and CDs. A floppy disk is a computer disk. A hard disk is a computer disk. A sports car is a car. A boss is a company employee.

[a]Inheritance is presented in Chapter 11.

is a

a class relationship established when a new (derived) class is created from an existing (base) class when the new class inherits properties from the base class

class relationships

the interactions and connections or associations that classes may have with each other

As we design programs with object-oriented techniques, we examine the *class relationships*. It is convenient to describe (in plain English) the objects and their relationships. The computer *uses a* printer. The boss *is an* employee. The automobile *has an* engine. Often great discussions can ensue: for example, does the computer have a monitor or does a computer use a monitor? At this stage of the C++ game, we do not need to split hairs about the monitor. It is important to recognize that there are two objects—the computer and the monitor!

10.2
Using C++ Language Classes

The C++ language provides several ready-made classes for our use. There are classes for input and output and for handling character strings, and numeric classes providing tools for working with complex numbers and arrays. When we employ one of these ready-made objects in one of our programs or program objects, we are using the C++ object.

iostream

The concept of using classes and objects to perform tasks for us may sound like a new topic, but we have been using the iostream class since Chapter 2. The iostream class is a complicated series of classes that support input and output routines for programs. We have written data to the screen with the cout << statement. Reading data from the keyboard has been accomplished with the cin >> or cin.getline. The cout object is predefined in the ostream (output stream) class, and the cin object is predefined in the istream (input stream) class. The insertion operator (<<) is an ostream overloaded operator, and the extraction operator (>>) is an ifstream overloaded operator. The ostream and istream classes are inherited from (are special cases of) the iostream. The functions we have been using—precision, getline, and setioflags—are all public member functions. (This discussion is a simplified view of the ios class.) By including the iostream header at the top of our programs, we essentially declare these objects for our program's use.

C++ String Class

The designers of C++ added to the language a *string class* that provides tools for making string handling very simple. This new class gives the programmer the ability to declare a *string object*. The class has various overloaded operators and member functions that make working with strings a snap!

    Appendix G presents an overview of the string class and several example programs; however, the appendix is not complete. This class is very large and has many functions. The C++ programmer is encouraged to become familiar with a complete C++ reference text or the on-line help that accompanies his or her C++ compiler.

string class
a C++ library class that provides string objects

string object
objects that contain character data, such as text, and have operators and functions for easy string manipulation

numeric classes
C++ classes for working with specialized numeric data, including the complex and valarray classes

C++ Numeric Classes

The C++ language also provides several types of *numeric classes*, including numeric arrays and complex numbers. The *valarray class* provides software tools for one-dimensional arrays. Functions for determining the maximum and minimum values in the array and overloaded operators that perform arithmetic, logical, and bitwise operations relieve the programmer of writing these commonly used functions. The *complex class* offers the programmer the ability to declare complex numbers and to work with these values as well as with the real and imaginary portions. (Anyone who has ever programmed complex numbers equations will appreciate this versatility.) For further information regarding the valarray and complex classes, refer to a C++ reference text.

valarray class
a class provided in the C++ standard libraries for working with arrays

complex class
a class provided in the C++ language for working with complex numbers

10

using namespace std

The standard C language program format has been discussed in the previous chapters of the text. In a C program, we place the #include statements at the top of each file, as shown below:

```
// C style include file format
#include <iostream.h>
#include <stdlib.h>
#include <string.h>

int main()
{
```

The C++ standard defines a new header format. These header lines do not require the .h extension in the library names. It does require a new line, one that we have not seen before—a namespace declaration.

```
//C++ Standard header formats
#include <iostream>
#include <string>
using namespace std;
int main()
{
```

using namespace std
directing the compiler to employ the standard (std) namespace, which includes the standard C++ libraries

The ***using namespace std*** statement informs the compiler that you wish to employ the standard (std) namespace, which includes the standard C++ libraries. To be able to use the string class or the numeric classes provided in the C++ standard library, the headers must be declared in the new format. As you examine the sample programs in Appendix G, "C++ String Class," and other programs in later chapters of this text, you will see this new header format.

The idea of a namespace is new. A namespace declaration aids in the program organization. The standard (std) namespace contains the C++ standard library. Large programs may have function name conflicts. For example, if your program defines a function called strlen(), the compiler might confuse your function and the same-named function in the string library. Furthermore, if you use a third-party library that contains a function with the same name as one of your functions, compiler confusion results.

Simple namespace Example

It is possible for the C++ programmer to create his or her own namespace and then to employ the scoping operator (::) to aid the compiler in finding the correct function. The simple program in Program 10-1 illustrates how a custom namespace may contain functions that have the same name as functions in the C++ libraries. In this

```
//Program 10-1 Program to illustrate different namespaces
#include <iostream>
#include <math.h>
using namespace std;

namespace MyOwn
{
        int rand();
        int sqrt();
};

int MyOwn::rand()
{
        return 42;   // my number is always 42
}

int MyOwn::sqrt()
{
        return 52;    //sqrt always returns a 52
}

int main()
{
        srand(123);

        int StdNumber = rand();
        cout << "\n The number from the standard rand is " << StdNumber;

        int MyNumber = MyOwn::rand();                    //scoping operator
        cout << "\n The number from my own rand is " << MyNumber;

        double RealSqrt = sqrt(25.0);
        cout << "\n The real square root is " << RealSqrt;

        int MySqrt = MyOwn::sqrt();
        cout << "\n My square root is " << MySqrt;
        cout << "\n All done. ";

        return 0;
}
```

program, we create our own namespace region, called MyOwn. It contains two functions, rand and sqrt. The scoping operator enables us to call both the standard and custom rand and sqrt functions. The output is shown below:

The number from the standard rand is 440
The number from my own rand is 42
The real square root is 5
My square root is 52

Setting up and using your own namespace is an advanced C++ topic. What you need to know now regarding namespaces is just this: if you wish to use a C++ class, such as string class, you need to write your include statements in the new header formats.

10.3
Having and *Using* User-Defined Classes

Now it is time to have fun! The four examples in this section illustrate classes that have classes and classes that use classes. When a programmer designs his or her classes correctly, the programming becomes concise and easy to implement. However, we are about to venture into the thick forest of object-oriented details and to spend time examining individual trees. Try not to lose sight of the forest!

In Chapter 9, we examined the interactions between the classes in a Parking Meter. A few of the important points are repeated here:

1. The tasks are defined in the class, which is accomplished in the class declaration.

2. The objects perform the actual program tasks. We ***instantiate*** objects and use the objects.

3. Each object has a name and is a unique entity.

4. The objects interact with each other and tell each other what to do.

5. An object may have an object as part of its own description or an object may use another object to perform a task.

instantiate
a C++ term referring to the declaration of an object—that is, making an instance of a class, which is an object

The typical design found when one object *has* another object is that the second object is declared as a data member of the first class. The second object's member functions are called when needed to work with the data.

There are two possible ways for a class to *use* another user-defined class. A class may simply access another class's function for the services it may provide, or a class may use another class by declaring a local object within its member function. Inside the member function, the local object provides its services. The servicing object is not an integral part of the first object—it simply performs a task and that's that.

This material is very esoteric (and may be over all our heads), so let's work through a few examples. What is important to focus on in these examples is the manner in which the objects relate to each other. Notice where the objects are declared and how they are used.

Example 1

Part 1: The Shopper and the Checkout Clerk   Imagine that you are ready to go shopping. You remember your list of items to buy, place some money in your wallet, and off you go. Once you have parked the car away from the loose carts in the lot, you stroll into the store, grab a cart of your own, and head toward your listed items. When you have finished selecting your stuff, you find the shortest checkout line. What happens next? You wheel the cart into the checkout area, and the clerk removes the items one at a time and scans them through the register. The clerk tells you the total cost of your purchases. You reach into your wallet and (assuming you have enough money) give the clerk the balance due, get the bags, and leave the store.

Now we need to think about a program design that models this shopping scenario. What are all the real-world objects? There is a shopper. There is a checkout clerk. The shopper has a wallet. There is also a shopping cart. And there are items that the shopper wants to buy. Figure 10-1 illustrates this scenario.

How are all these objects related? The shopper has a wallet. The shopper interacts with (uses a) checkout clerk. These relationships are fairly obvious. However, the relationship between the shopper and the shopping cart is not so clear. (Remember, in a *has a* relationship, the object is an integral part of the containing object, whereas in the *uses a* relationship, the second object provides a service to the first object.) The shopper uses a cart (true enough). We can argue that the shopper must carry his or her items and the cart does this task for the shopper; therefore,

This is Ed, our shopper. Ed has a wallet and a cart full of stuff.

This is Gladys, our checkout clerk. Gladys will check out the items in Ed's cart and tell Ed the total cost.

Figure 10-1
The Shopper and the Checkout Clerk

the cart is an integral part of the shopper. For this example, we decree that the shopper has a cart. Figure 10-2 illustrates these relationships. (Part 2: The Shopper and the Checkout Clerk sets up the program so that the Shopper uses a Cart.)

Before we get into the classes, below is an Item data structure that contains the information related to each of the purchases. This data structure has only two variables, but the Item could be much more complicated if necessary.

```
struct Item
{
      string name;
      float price;
};
```

The Cart class can now be started. Assuming a Cart object is capable of holding up to fifty Items, we establish an Item array (Item stuff[50]). The software cart also needs to keep track of how many items it contains and to have the ability to add an item into the stuff array. Also, because the data is private, we need to access the array of items. The counter variable (here it is called HowMany) is the index into the Item array. We start the HowMany variable at 0 and place the first item in stuff[0] (stuff[HowMany]). The HowMany counter is then incremented and is now ready for the next item. (For completeness, we should check that we do not allow the HowMany counter to be above forty-nine. Recall that we have an array of fifty items and that arrays in C++ are zero-indexed. The first element is stuff[0], and the last element is stuff[49]. If the items in the cart exceeded fifty, we would have an array out of bounds, run-time error. This error would most likely show itself by overwriting another variable.) The RetrieveNextItem function employs the WhichItem variable to keep track of the next item that is retrieved. WhichItem is initialized to zero in the constructor, and hence the zero item is retrieved first.

```
class Cart
{
private:
      Item stuff[50];
      int HowMany;
      int WhichItem;

public:
      Cart() { HowMany = 0;  WhichItem = 0;}
      void AddItemToCart(Item newthing);
      Item RetrieveNextItem();
      int HowManyInCart(){return HowMany; }
};
```

```
struct Item
{
        string name;
        float price;
};
```

```
class Cart
{
private:
        Item stuff[50];
        int HowMany;
        int WhichItem;

public:
        Cart() { HowMany = 0; WhichItem = 0;}
        void AddItemToCart(Item newthing);
        Item RetrieveNextItem();
        int HowManyInCart(){return HowMany;}
};
```

```
class Shopper
{
private:
        float wallet;
public:
        Shopper() { wallet = 100.00; }

        Cart SqueakyWheels;
        float GetMoneyFromWallet(float);
};
```

```
class Clerk
{
private:
        float total;

public:
        Clerk() { total = 0.0; }
        float FigureTotal(Cart*);
};
```

Here is an item, a can of coffee.

The cart can hold items.

Our shopper has a wallet and a cart full of items.
Our shopper can remove money from his wallet.

Our checkout clerk will total the purchases in the cart.
The checkout clerk will look in the cart.

Figure 10-2
Item, Cart, Shopper, and Clerk Relationships

```
void Cart::AddItemToCart(Item newthing)
{
        stuff[HowMany] = newthing;
        ++ HowMany;
}
Item Cart::RetrieveNextItem()
{

        Item next;
        next = stuff[WhichItem];
        ++WhichItem;
        return next;
}
```

For the Shopper class, we have a floating point data type for the wallet variable (no need to be fancy here). For this example, the Shopper has a Cart; therefore,
the Cart is a data member of the Shopper class. The Shopper's Cart is also public
because the "world" (in this case, our Clerk) needs to interact with the Cart. (If the
Cart were private, the world would have to go through the Shopper object to interact with his cart.)

```
class Shopper
{
private:
        float wallet;  // nobody's business--keep the wallet private

public:
        Shopper() { wallet = 100.00; }   // set the wallet to $100
        Cart SqueakyWheels;         // our shopper has a Cart
        float GetMoneyFromWallet(float);
};


float Shopper::GetMoneyFromWallet(float cost)
{
        if(cost > wallet)
        {
                cout << "\n Not enough money!  Put something back! \n";
                return 0;
        }
        else
        {
                wallet = wallet - cost;
                return cost;
        }
}
```

The Clerk class is fairly simple. The Clerk has a variable (total) that represents the sum of the prices of the items in the cart. The FigureTotal function receives a pointer to a Cart object and then accesses the total items in the cart. The function then executes a for loop, retrieving each item from the cart and adding the price to the total.

```cpp
class Clerk
{
private:
        float total;
public:
        Clerk() { total = 0.0; }
        float FigureTotal(Cart*);
};
float Clerk::FigureTotal(Cart *pCart)
{
        int i, CheckOutTotal;
        Item TheItem;
        CheckOutTotal = pCart->HowManyInCart();
        for (i = 0; i < CheckOutTotal; ++i)
        {
                TheItem = pCart->RetrieveNextItem();
                total = TheItem.price + total;
        }
        return total;
}
```

Now that we have the framework built, the main function shows how the objects interact. We instantiate a Shopper object (Ed) and a Clerk object (Gladys), and then we set up local variables, including a local Item called LemmeSeeIt. We fill the LemmeSeeIt with item data and then add the item to Ed's cart.

Once Ed is ready to check out, he passes the address of his cart to Gladys's FigureTotal function. Gladys returns Ed's total. Ed then gets his money from his wallet for Gladys. (Notice that the wallet is private—Ed does not want the world looking in his wallet.)

```cpp
//Program 10-2 The Shopper Has a Cart
int main()
{
        Shopper Ed;
        Clerk Gladys;
        float HowMuchEdOwes, PayOut;
        Item LemmeSeeIt;
        // Ed's first item is potato chips
        LemmeSeeIt.price = 2.99;
        LemmeSeeIt.name = "potato chips";
```

```
        Ed.SqueakyWheels.AddItemToCart(LemmeSeeIt);    //put the chips in Ed's cart

        // Ed's second item is coffee
        LemmeSeeIt.name = "coffee";
        LemmeSeeIt.price = 8.99;
        Ed.SqueakyWheels.AddItemToCart(LemmeSeeIt);

// Ed is now ready to check out. Gladys looks into Ed's cart and figures the total.
        HowMuchEdOwes = Gladys.FigureTotal(&Ed.SqueakyWheels);
        cout << "\n Ed owes Gladys " << HowMuchEdOwes;
        PayOut = Ed.GetMoneyFromWallet(HowMuchEdOwes);
        cout << "\n Ed can pay Gladys " << PayOut;
        cout << "\n\n Shopping is hard work! \n";
        return 0;
}
```

The output is shown below:

Ed owes Gladys 11.98
Ed can pay Gladys 11.98

Shopping is hard work!

In this example, Gladys (our Clerk object) provides a service to Ed (our Shopper object). Our Shopper has a Cart and uses a Clerk.

Part 2: The Shopper and the Checkout Clerk   The second version of the Shopper and the Checkout Clerk differs only because the program is designed with the Shopper using a Cart instead of having a Cart. Reviewing the has a relationship, we see that the Cart is simply declared as a data member of the Shopper class.

```
                    // Previous Example
class Shopper    // The Shopper has a Cart
{
private:
        float wallet;
public:
        Shopper() { wallet = 100.00; }
        Cart SqueakyWheels;    // our shopper has a Cart
        float GetMoneyFromWallet(float);
};
```

Now we design the program so that the Shopper uses a Cart. The Cart class remains the same:

```
class Cart
{
private:
        Item stuff[50];
        int HowMany;
        int WhichItem;
public:
        Cart() { HowMany = 0; WhichItem = 0;}
        void AddItemToCart(Item newthing);
        Item RetrieveNextItem();
        int HowManyInCart(){return HowMany; }
};
```

The Shopper class does not have a Cart object declared as a member variable, but the Shopper needs a new function that allows the Shopper object to place an item in the Cart. (In the previous example, the Shopper merely used the Cart's AddItemToCart function.) The new Shopper class is shown here:

```
class Shopper
{
private:
        float wallet;

public:
        Shopper() { wallet = 100.00; }
        float GetMoneyFromWallet(float);
        void PutItemInCart(Item, Cart*);          //new function
};

void Shopper::PutItemInCart(Item newthing, Cart *pCart)
{
        pCart->AddItemToCart(newthing);
}
```

The main function is also changed slightly. The Cart object, SqueakyWheels, is declared within the main function and our Shopper object, Ed, uses Squeaky-Wheels to hold his potato chips and coffee. The Clerk class is not changed. The Clerk needs the address of a Cart and it doesn't care if the Shopper uses a Cart or the Shopper has a Cart.

```
//Program 10-3 The Shopper Uses a Cart
int main()
{
        Shopper Ed;
        Clerk Gladys;
```

10

```
        Cart SqueakyWheels;    // our shopper uses a cart called SqueakyWheels

        float HowMuchEdOwes, PayOut;
        Item LemmeSeeIt;

        // Ed's first item is potato chips
        LemmeSeeIt.price = 2.99;
        LemmeSeeIt.name = "potato chips";

/* In order to put the chips in the cart, we need to call Ed's function and give
        it the item and cart address. We wouldn't want Ed to put his chips in
        someone else's cart!    */

        Ed.PutItemInCart(LemmeSeeIt, &SqueakyWheels);

        // Ed's second item is coffee
        LemmeSeeIt.name = "coffee";
        LemmeSeeIt.price = 8.99;

        Ed.PutItemInCart(LemmeSeeIt, &SqueakyWheels);

// Ed is now ready to check out.  Gladys looks in Ed's cart and figures the total.

        HowMuchEdOwes = Gladys.FigureTotal(&SqueakyWheels);
        cout << "\n Ed owes Gladys " << HowMuchEdOwes;

        PayOut = Ed.GetMoneyFromWallet(HowMuchEdOwes);
        cout << "\n Ed can pay Gladys " << PayOut;

        cout << "\n\n Shopping is hard work! \n";
        return 0;
}
```

10

People may argue about which Shopper and Cart relationship design is "better." One programmer might say that the has a relationship is cleaner code. When the Shopper uses a Cart, the Shopper class requires a wrapper function (PutItemInCart), which then calls the Cart function (PutItemInCart). This wrapper function is extraneous code and is not required when a Shopper has a Cart.

A good check for a programmer to perform when he or she designs and builds programs is to examine the code for the extra wrapper functions. If you have wrapped many member functions of a class in another class's functions, you might want to rethink the class relationships you have designed.

Example 2: DicePlayer Has Dice

Object-oriented software provides a wonderful and powerful tool set for modeling real-world processes. It is important always to view the program components as objects and base your class design on individual objects, even if the program has many of the same objects. This example models Johnston's Dice Game. Each player has five white dice. The player rolls his or her five dice and adds the points on the face of each die. A running total is maintained and the first player reaching 100 (or more) points wins the game. If a player hits exactly 50 points, he or she wins $1 million! Figure 10-3 illustrates the game objects.

We can define a Die class (which represents a single cube). A single Die has an integer value that represents the value of the Die when a player rolls it and an

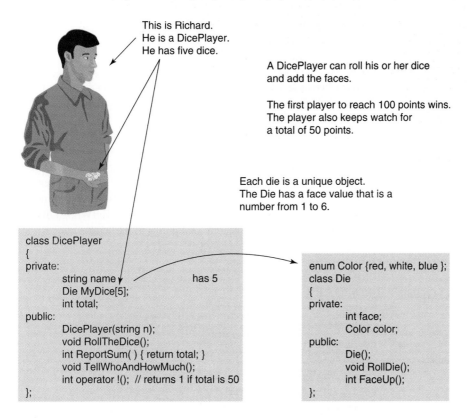

Each player has five dice. The first player rolling 100 points wins.
If a player rolls exactly 50 points, that player wins $1,000,000.

This is Richard.
He is a DicePlayer.
He has five dice.

A DicePlayer can roll his or her dice
and add the faces.

The first player to reach 100 points wins.
The player also keeps watch for
a total of 50 points.

Each die is a unique object.
The Die has a face value that is a
number from 1 to 6.

```
class DicePlayer
{
private:
        string name            has 5
        Die MyDice[5];
        int total;
public:
        DicePlayer(string n);
        void RollTheDice();
        int ReportSum( ) { return total; }
        void TellWhoAndHowMuch();
        int operator !();  // returns 1 if total is 50
};
```

```
enum Color {red, white, blue };
class Die
{
private:
        int face;
        Color color;
public:
        Die();
        void RollDie();
        int FaceUp();
};
```

Figure 10-3
Johnston's Dice Game Objects

enumerated color—red, white, or blue. (The colors play an important role in Johnston's Enhanced Dice Game, which is based on inheritance. Johnston's Enhanced Dice Game is described in the next chapter.) The default constructor sets the value to 1 and the color to white. The RollDie function calls the random number generator to obtain a number between and including 1 and 6. This value is placed into the Die object's face member variable. (For our purposes, we have the main function seed the generator with the system time.) A FaceUp function returns the face value of the Die object to the calling function.

```
enum Color {red, white, blue };
class Die
{
private:
        int face;
        Color color;
public:
        Die() { face = 1; color = white; }
        void RollDie(){ face = rand()%6+1; }
        int FaceUp() { return face;}
};
```

The DicePlayer class represents a person who plays Johnston's Dice Game. A C++ string stores the player's name, and this name is passed to the DicePlayer constructor function. The player rolls his or her five dice (MyDice) and then adds the total on the faces. The player keeps track of the total points. The DicePlayer class must have a RollTheDice function that rolls the dice and a ReportSum function that returns the sum total to the calling function. (Notice that the ReportSum function does not add the dice values but merely reports the total. The total is obtained when the dice are rolled.) The class also has overloaded the ! operator. This function returns a 1 if the sum is 50, or a 0 if the sum is not 50. Last, the class has a TellWhoAndHowMuch function that writes the player's name and total points to the screen.

```
class DicePlayer
{
private:
        string name;
        Die MyDice[5];   // the DicePlayer has five Die objects
        int total;
public:
        DicePlayer(string n);   //set the player's name
        void RollTheDice();   // rolls dice, adds faces to total
        int ReportSum( ) { return total; }
        void TellWhoAndHowMuch();
        int operator !();   // return a 1 if the total is 100
};
```

```
DicePlayer::DicePlayer(string n)
{
        name = n;
        total = 0;
}
void DicePlayer::RollTheDice()
{

        int i;
        for (i = 0; i<5; ++i)
        {
                MyDice[i].RollDie();    // roll each die and add
                total = total + MyDice[i].FaceUp(); //face to total
        }
}


void DicePlayer::TellWhoAndHowMuch()
{
        cout << endl << name << " has " << total << " points.";
}
int DicePlayer::operator ! ()
{
        if (total==50)return 1;
        else return 0;
}
```

The main function instantiates two DicePlayer objects called First and Second. We assign the player name into each object. (Richard is our First object and Steve is our Second object.) We then obtain the system time to use to seed the random number generator. This ensures each game has a unique seed value. The system time is placed in the time_t structure. (This system time is the time in seconds since January 1, 1970, 00:00:00 GMT, and is a large integer value.)

A while loop is started and each player rolls his or her dice. The scores are shown, and each player checks his or her point total. If his or her point total is fifty, the player wins $1 million! If both players reach 100 (or more) on the same roll, the game is a tie and no one wins. (*Note:* There is no interaction with the user—the program simply runs until there is a winner or a tie.)

```
//Program 10-4 Johnston's Dice Game
int main()
{
        cout << "\n Welcome to Johnston's Dice Game \n\n";
        DicePlayer First("Richard"), Second("Steve");    // We have two DicePlayers
```

Section 10.3 ▌ *Having* and *Using* User-Defined Classes

453

```
time_t ltime;
time( &ltime );    // fills ltime with the UTC time, a large integer value
int seed = (int)ltime;    // cast the ltime into an integer
srand(seed);    // seed the random number generator with the system time

bool go = true;
int score1, score2;
while(go)
{
        First.RollTheDice();
        Second.RollTheDice();
        score1 = First.ReportSum();
        score2 = Second.ReportSum();
        First.TellWhoAndHowMuch();
        Second.TellWhoAndHowMuch();
        if(!First || !Second)
        {
                cout << "\n SOMEONE HAS EXACTLY 50 POINTS! ";
                if(!First) First.ReportSum();
                else Second.ReportSum();
                cout << " AND WINS $1,000,000!!  \n";
                go = false;
        }
        else if(score1 >= 100 && score2 >= 100)
        {

                cout << "\n BOTH PLAYERS ARE OVER 100, IT'S A TIE";
                go = false;
        }
        else if(score1 >= 100 || score2 >= 100)
        {
                cout << "\n SOMEONE HAS REACHED 100 POINTS! \n\n  ";
                if(score1 >= 100) First.TellWhoAndHowMuch();
                else Second.TellWhoAndHowMuch();
                cout << " He/She is the winner! \n";
                go = false;
        }
}
cout << "\n Game Over " << endl;
return 0;
}
```

One round of this game has the following output:

Welcome to Johnston's Dice Game
Richard has 20 points.
Steve has 12 points
Richard has 40 points.
Steve has 31 points
Richard has 61 points.
Steve has 50 points
SOMEONE HAS EXACTLY 50 POINTS!
Steve has 50 points. AND WINS $1,000,000!!

Game Over

In Johnston's Dice Game, we have a Die class and a DicePlayer class. The DicePlayer has five Die objects; that is, the DicePlayer class contains an array of Die objects. The DicePlayer function RollTheDice calls each of the five Die objects' RollDie functions. It is common for object-oriented programs to have an object use another object's function(s) to perform the lion's share of the work.

Example 3: A Track_Coach Has a StopWatch; the StopWatch Uses a MasterClock

Do you remember running races in elementary school? If you were lucky, your physical education teacher encouraged you by calling out times. He or she used a stopwatch for keeping track of times during the races. Let's refer to this teacher as our Track Coach.

Suppose we model the track coach and have him or her time us performing 100,000,000 floating point multiplication operations! Our Track_Coach has a Stop-Watch object and is fairly small. It has only two public members, the StopWatch object and a function to yell out the time.

```
class Track_Coach
{
public:
        StopWatch Watch;        // the watch is public to allow access
        void YellOutTime();     // reports the elapsed time
};


void Track_Coach::YellOutTime()
{
        cout << "\n YOUR ELAPSED TIME IS ";
        Watch.ReportTime();     // use the watch's report time function
}
```

10

The StopWatch class uses the computer system time for its clock. The Stop-Watch needs three Time objects to perform its job. When the watch is started, the system time is obtained for the start time. When the watch is stopped, the system time is obtained once again, and the difference of the times is calculated and reported. (This difference is elapsed time.) Before we get into the details of obtaining the system time, let's review the Time class, which we saw in the previous chapter. For this example, the Time class contains an overloaded subtraction operator that is used to calculate the elapsed time. The class declaration is presented here:

```
class Time
{
private:
        int hr, min, sec;
public:
        Time();     //sets the time object to 0:0:1
        void Reset(int h, int m, int s);    // resets time to h:m:s
        void ShowTime();
        Time operator -(Time N);   // need to be able to subtract times
};
```

The StopWatch class member functions use a MasterClock object to set the times. The StopWatch class is the beefy part of this example. This class has three Time objects, which are integral pieces of the StopWatch's object. The Start and Stop functions use a MasterClock object to set the times. Notice that the Master-Clock is not part of the member data, but a local MasterClock object (called clock) is declared as a local variable inside the Start and Stop functions.

```
class StopWatch
{
private:
        Time Begin, Finish, Elapsed;
public:
        StopWatch() {};
        void Start();  // obtains the Beginning time
        void Stop();    // obtains the Finish time and calc Elapsed time
        void ReportTime();
};

void StopWatch::Start()
{
        MasterClock clock;              // we create a temp MasterClock
        clock.SetTimeObject(&Begin);    // and use it to set the time
        cout << "\n The starting time is:  ";
        Begin.ShowTime();
}
```

```
void StopWatch::Stop()
{
        MasterClock clock;
        clock.SetTimeObject(&Finish);
        cout << "\n The stopping time is:  ";
        Finish.ShowTime();
        Elapsed = Finish - Begin;       // calculate elapsed time
}


void StopWatch::ReportTime()
{
        Elapsed.ShowTime();
}
```

The MasterClock class contains the necessary data and functions to access the system clock and assign the system time into a Time object. (The SetTime function was presented in the previous chapter but was not included as a class member function.). The address of a Time object can be passed to the MasterClock member function, and the object's time values are then set.

```
class MasterClock
{
private:
        time_t SystemTime;           // time_t format
public:
        MasterClock(){ };            // empty constructor
        void SetTimeObject(Time *N);
};

void MasterClock::SetTimeObject(Time *N)
{
        time(&SystemTime);   // fill the time_t struct with system time

        struct tm *OStime;
        OStime = localtime(&SystemTime);   //convert system time to tm
        N->Reset(OStime->tm_hour, OStime->tm_min,OStime->tm_sec);
}
```

Figure 10-4 shows the various classes and objects. The MasterClock class utilizes functions available in the time library for obtaining the computer's system time.

The main function is quite simple. A Track_Coach object (called John) is made. John starts his watch at the start of our calculations and stops it after we have finished. John then yells out our time. The StopWatch is a public member of the Track_Coach class, so we can access the watch functions (Start, Stop) directly.

10

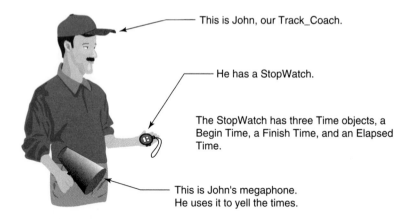

The StopWatch has three Time objects.
The StopWatch uses a MasterClock.

This is John, our Track_Coach.

He has a StopWatch.

The StopWatch has three Time objects, a Begin Time, a Finish Time, and an Elapsed Time.

This is John's megaphone.
He uses it to yell the times.

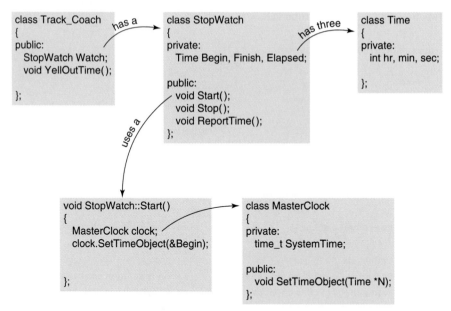

```
class Track_Coach
{
public:
    StopWatch Watch;
    void YellOutTime();

};
```

has a

```
class StopWatch
{
private:
    Time Begin, Finish, Elapsed;

public:
    void Start();
    void Stop();
    void ReportTime();
};
```

has three

```
class Time
{
private:
    int hr, min, sec;

};
```

uses a

```
void StopWatch::Start()
{
    MasterClock clock;
    clock.SetTimeObject(&Begin);

};
```

```
class MasterClock
{
private:
    time_t SystemTime;

public:
    void SetTimeObject(Time *N);
};
```

The MasterClock provides the service of setting the Time object to the computer's system time.

Figure 10-4
Track_Coach, StopWatch, Time, and MasterClock Classes

```
//Program 10-5 Track Coach
int main()
{
        Track_Coach John;      // John is our track coach. He has a stopwatch.

// John is going to time us doing 100,000,000 floating point multiplications
        int i;
        double result;

        John.Watch.Start();   // John starts his watch.
        for(i=0; i < 100000000 ; ++i)
        {
                result = 5.234 * 4.23546;   // multiply 2 numbers together, 100,000,000 times
        }
        John.Watch.Stop();
        John.YellOutTime();
        return 0;
}
```

This program was executed on a Pentium II-350, and the output is shown below:

The starting time is: 13:0:10
The stopping time is: 13:0:12
YOUR ELAPSED TIME IS: 0:0:2

The main function is essentially the tip of the object-oriented iceberg. The Track_Coach object calls its member function (YellOutTime) or the member functions of its own member data (Watch.Start() and Watch.Stop()). The StopWatch objects contain Time objects and use MasterClock objects locally in their functions. The objects in this program are short and elegant.

Example 4: Cola Vending Machine

Thirsty for knowledge? Soon object-oriented programming will be as simple for you as twisting a cap off a bottle.

Fact Finding Field Trip   Dig out some quarters, dimes, and nickels from your pocket or backpack. Stroll down to the cafeteria and gaze at the soft-drink vending machine. You are on a very important fact-finding programming mission. Stand back for a few minutes and observe the machine patrons. A person plunks in his or her coins, and the machine reports the total amount entered with each coin. The person then selects a button for the drink of choice. If the person has entered enough money and the item is in stock, the can or bottle drops into the bin and change is dispensed. If the person has not entered enough money, nothing happens (or perhaps a message is presented). If the item is out of stock (if a light isn't reporting this fact), an out-of-stock message appears.

User Interaction   Using an object-oriented design, we can model the vending machine. Initially, we examine the way our user interacts with this program.

Welcome to the Acme Vending Machine Program!
Please enter your coin value in pennies Quarter = 25, Dime = 10, etc.

Our user enters the coins, one at a time. This programmatic action is accomplished in a while loop. Assuming the user entered four quarters, the program then shows:

You entered $1.00
Enter the number of your item   (cost)
0   Coke   ($1.00)
1   Pepsi   ($1.00)
2   BrandX Cola   ($0.80)
3   Blue Sky Cola   ($1.25)
4   Jolt   ($2.50)

5   Return Money and Exit

Now the user makes his or her selection. There are several cases to consider. If the user selects a Pepsi, the program shows:

You selected a Pepsi ENJOY!
Chug-a-lug! Goodbye.

If the user enters $1.00 and selects BrandX Cola, the program reports the following:

You selected a BrandX Cola ENJOY!
Your change back is: 0.20
Chug-a-lug! Goodbye.

The third case involves selecting an item that costs more money than the user enters. Assume that the user enters $1.00 and selects a Blue Sky Cola:

Not enough cash!

Another selection? y = yes

In this case the user did not enter enough money. The program reports this fact and then asks the user if he or she would like to enter another selection. If the answer is yes, the program places control in the money-entering loop. If the user does not want another selection (and enters an n for no), the program returns his or her money.

Another case to consider is if the user selects an item that is out of stock. In the following example, the Jolt Cola is out of stock. The program issues this message:

OUT OF STOCK!

Another selection? y = yes

The last case to examine is if the user decides he or she does not want a drink and simply wants the money returned.

Your change back is: 1.00
Chug-a-lug! Goodbye.

Figure 10-5 illustrates the possible program flow. This program control is performed in our main function.

Program Design   What are the necessary objects for our vending machine program? Let's start with the obvious—a vending machine object. A vending machine has two basic components: (1) a money counter that handles the money and (2) a rack of dispensers where the cans and bottles are placed. (Our machine has five dispensers.) What are the necessary tasks that our machine must perform? It must accept the money, show the user the choices, dispense the item, and return money. The declaration for our vending machine shows that our machine has a MoneyCtr object (we call it bank) and an array of five Dispenser objects (D[i]).

Do not lose any sleep over visualizing a MoneyCtr and Dispenser! Examine the following declaration and understand that it represents a vending machine. (Remember, design one object at a time and have faith that the details will work out.)

```
class VendingMachine
{
private:
        MoneyCtr bank;
        Dispenser D[5];
public:
        VendingMachine();
        void ShowChoices();
        void InsertMoney(){ bank.GetMoney();} // Call the bank's function.
        bool DispenseItem(int selection);
        void ReturnAllMoneyAndExit();
};
```

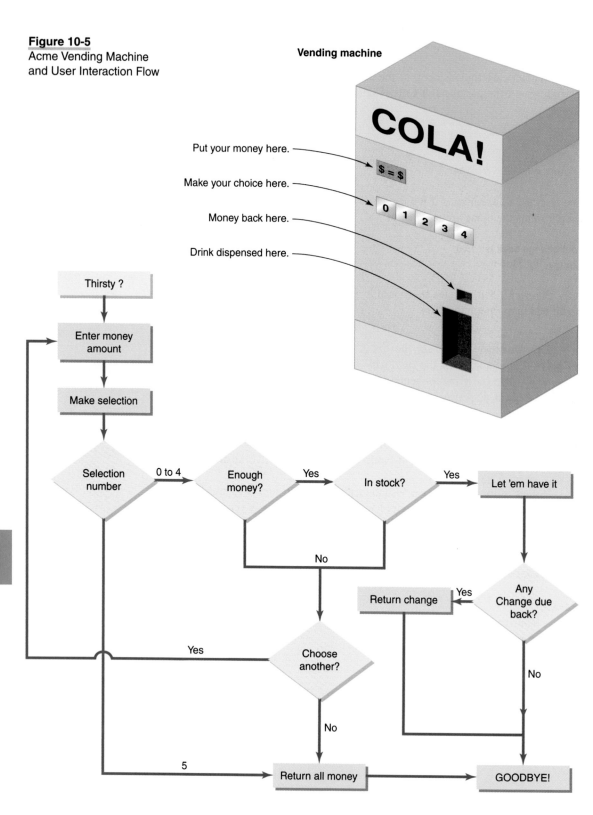

Figure 10-5
Acme Vending Machine
and User Interaction Flow

The beauty of an object-oriented program lies in the ability of an object to contain another object and to let that second object do the work. The workhorses of the vending machine class are the MoneyCtr and Dispenser objects. The Vending-Machine functions are quite short.

The MoneyCtr object must handle all the financial transactions for our VendingMachine. This class must get the money, tell the VendingMachine how much money it has, return a specified amount to the user, and clear the input amount. The declaration for this class is shown here:

```
class MoneyCtr
{
private:
        float input_amount;

public:
        MoneyCtr(){ input_amount = 0;}
        void GetMoney();                // ask user for coins
        float HowMuchDoWeHave() { return input_amount;}
        void Clear(){ input_amount = 0;}
        void ReturnMoney(float );  // returns the amount of money
};
```

Our VendingMachine has five Dispenser objects. Let's concentrate on one Dispenser for now. What must each Dispenser do? The Dispenser must know what it contains (a string can hold the name of the beverage), plus the cost and total number of items the Dispenser holds. We need to be able to initialize the Dispenser (this task is performed by the SetStock function), report what the item is and how much it costs, check whether there are items to dispense, and dispense the item requested. The declaration for the Dispenser is shown below:

```
class Dispenser
{
private:
        string Beverage;
        float cost;
        int total;
public:
        Dispenser(){cost = 0; total = 0;}
        void SetStock(string n, float c, int t) ;
        float HowMuchDoICost( ){ return cost;}
        void WhatAmI(){ cout << setw(15) << Beverage ; }
        void LetEmHaveIt();
        int CheckStock() { return total; }
};
```

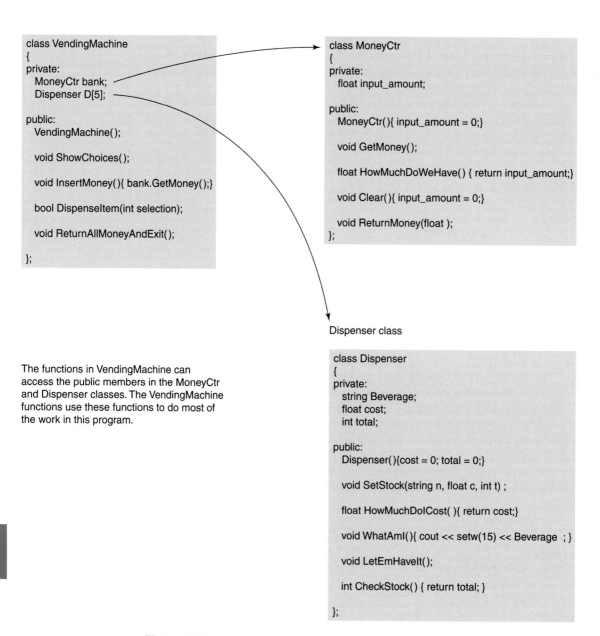

```
class VendingMachine
{
private:
    MoneyCtr bank;
    Dispenser D[5];

public:
    VendingMachine();

    void ShowChoices();

    void InsertMoney(){ bank.GetMoney();}

    bool DispenseItem(int selection);

    void ReturnAllMoneyAndExit();

};
```

```
class MoneyCtr
{
private:
    float input_amount;

public:
    MoneyCtr(){ input_amount = 0;}

    void GetMoney();

    float HowMuchDoWeHave() { return input_amount;}

    void Clear(){ input_amount = 0;}

    void ReturnMoney(float );
};
```

Dispenser class

```
class Dispenser
{
private:
    string Beverage;
    float cost;
    int total;

public:
    Dispenser(){cost = 0; total = 0;}

    void SetStock(string n, float c, int t) ;

    float HowMuchDoICost( ){ return cost;}

    void WhatAmI(){ cout << setw(15) << Beverage  ; }

    void LetEmHaveIt();

    int CheckStock() { return total; }

};
```

The functions in VendingMachine can
access the public members in the MoneyCtr
and Dispenser classes. The VendingMachine
functions use these functions to do most of
the work in this program.

Figure 10-6
VendingMachine Class Relationships

10

Program Implementation   Our main function has a VendingMachine object (we call our object cola) and this object can see and access the class's public functions. The VendingMachine class has both the bank and the dispenser array objects and can access the public functions of these classes. The bank and dispenser objects do most of the work in this program. Figure 10-6 illustrates this relationship.

The main function drives the program. Most of this function contains loop-handling code, but notice how the VendingMachine functions are simple to call.

```
//Program 10-6 Vending Machine
int main()
{
        VendingMachine cola;
        char answer[5], selectbuf[5];
        int selection;
        bool gimme_cash = true, Got_it, go_again;
        cout << "\n Welcome to the Acme Vending Machine Program \n\n";
        do
        {
                while(gimme_cash)
                {
                        cola.InsertMoney();
                        cout << "\n Again?  yes or no   ";
                        cin.getline(answer,5);
                        if(strcmp(answer,"no")==0)gimme_cash = false;
                }
                cola.ShowChoices();
                cin.getline(selectbuf,5);
                selection = atoi(selectbuf);
                if(selection == 5)
                {
                        cola.ReturnAllMoneyAndExit();
                        go_again = false;
                }
                else
                {
                        Got_it = cola.DispenseItem(selection);
                        if(Got_it==true) go_again = false;
                        else
                        {
                                cout << "\n Another selection?  yes or no";
                                cin.getline(answer,5);
                                if(strcmp(answer,"yes")==0)
                                {
                                        gimme_cash = true;
```

```
                                        go_again = true;
                        }
                        else
                        {
                                cola.ReturnAllMoneyAndExit();
                                go_again = false;
                        }
                }
        }
    }while(go_again == true);
    cout << "\n Chug-a-lug! Goodbye. \n\n";
    return 0;
}
```

The initial task of the VendingMachine cola object is the execution of the constructor functions of the VendingMachine's two objects. The constructors are executed, and the MoneyCtr constructor sets the input amount variable to zero.

```
MoneyCtr(){ input_amount = 0;}
```

The Dispenser constructor is executed five times, once for each element in the dispenser array. The VendingMachine constructor function sets the items in each dispenser.

```
VendingMachine::VendingMachine()
{
    D[0].SetStock("Coke", 1.00, 25);
    D[1].SetStock("Pepsi", 1.00, 25);
    D[2].SetStock("BrandX Cola", 0.80, 25);
    D[3].SetStock("Blue Sky Cola", 1.25, 22);
    D[4].SetStock("Jolt", 2.50, 0);
}
```

The SetStock function is a Dispenser function:

```
void Dispenser::SetStock(string n, float c, int t)
{
    Beverage = n;
    cost = c;
    total = t;
}
```

The first task for our user is to enter his or her money. The program calls the VendingMachine's InsertMoney function,

```
cola.InsertMoney();
```

which in turn calls the bank's GetMoney function.

```
void InsertMoney(){ bank.GetMoney();}
```

The bank's GetMoney function asks the user for the money. Then the face value of
the money is added to the input_amount variable. This input_amount variable's
value is the total money amount from the user.

```
void MoneyCtr::GetMoney()
{
   float coin;
   cout << "\n Please enter coin value in pennies"
           "Quarter = 25, Dime = 10, etc. ";
   cin >> coin;
   input_amount += coin/100.0;
   cout << "\n Total Money $" << input_amount;
}
```

Now the program must show the user the choice of items. Displaying the
choices is performed in the main with the call to the VendingMachine's Show-
Choices.

```
cola.ShowChoices();          // show the choices
```

In turn, the ShowChoices function calls the Dispenser's WhatAmI and HowMuch-
DoICost functions.

```
void VendingMachine::ShowChoices()
{
     int i;
     cout.precision(2);
     cout.setf(ios::fixed);
     cout << "\n You entered $" << bank.HowMuchDoWeHave();
     cout << "\n Enter the number of your item  (cost) ";
     for(i = 0; i < 5; ++i)
     {
          cout << endl << i << " ";
          D[i].WhatAmI();
          cout << "  ($" <<   D[i].HowMuchDoICost() << ")";
     }
     cout << "\n\n5    Return Money and Exit  ";
}
```

When the user selects an item, the VendingMachine's DispenseItem is called with the selection number. A boolean flag is returned, and this flag indicates whether or not an item has been delivered to the user.

```
Got_it = cola.DispenseItem(selection);          // dispense the item
```

The DispenseItem function checks initially to see if it has enough drinks to dispense. If the InStock value is greater than zero, the DispenseItem function must be sure the user has entered enough money. The function then calls the bank's How-MuchDoWeHave function and the Dispenser's HowMuchDoICost function to determine if the user may receive a drink. (The user's money total must be greater than or equal to the cost of the item.) If the amount of the money is enough, the selection number is used as an array index for the appropriate Dispenser array item. The following DispenseItem function illustrates the beauty and power of object-oriented programming:

```
bool VendingMachine::DispenseItem(int selection)
{
    int InStock;
    InStock = D[selection].CheckStock();
    if(InStock > 0)                             // enough drinks to dispense?
    {
        if(bank.HowMuchDoWeHave() >= D[selection].HowMuchDoICost() ) //enough $$ ?
        {
            D[selection].LetEmHaveIt();
            float change = bank.HowMuchDoWeHave() - D[selection].HowMuchDoICost();
            if (change > 0) bank.ReturnMoney(change);
            return true;
        }
        else
        {
            cout << "\n Not enough cash! \n";
            return false;
        }
    }
    else
    {
        cout << "\n OUT OF STOCK";
        return false;
    }
}
```

Notice how the VendingMachine's DispenseItem function uses the bank and dispenser functions to perform its tasks. The if statement compares the bank's total with the selected cola's cost: one object using other objects to perform its task, which is object-oriented programming at its best!

10.4
Summary

Object-oriented programming bases software design on individual objects and the objects' relationships to each other. It is important that each object, in a sense, takes care of itself. In this chapter, we have looked at several examples illustrating various ways of object interaction. Table 10-2 presents a summary.

TABLE 10-2
Chapter Examples and Class Relationships

Example	Description
Shopper, Cart, and Clerk (Part 1)	The Shopper has a wallet and has a Cart. The Shopper uses a Clerk.
Shopper, Cart, and Clerk (Part 2)	The Shopper has a wallet and uses a Cart. The Shopper uses a Clerk.
	The Shopper must have an extra wrapper function to call the Cart function.
DicePlayer and Die	The Die class represents a single die object. The DicePlayer object has an array of five Die objects.
	The DicePlayer functions employ the Die object's functions.
Track_Coach, StopWatch, Time, and MasterClock	The Track_Coach class has a StopWatch object. The StopWatch has three Time objects.
	The StopWatch functions use a local copy of a MasterClock object to set the Time objects.
VendingMachine, MoneyCtr, and Dispenser	The VendingMachine class has a MoneyCtr object and an array of five Dispenser objects.
	The VendingMachine functions all employ the MoneyCtr and Dispenser member functions to perform their jobs.

10

There is no absolute formula that programmers may follow to ensure the best program design. Often a programmer starts down one path and discovers that a better way can be found down a different one. Your goal for software is simplicity and, if possible, elegance.

▌ PROBLEMS

1. A Parking Meter model was described at the beginning of Chapter 9. In this problem, you will build the Parking Meter program. We'll get you started by providing the main function and three of the four classes for the Parking Meter scenario. (This version does not incorporate a Parker object; the user can be considered the Parker.) A typical interaction with this program is shown below:

Welcome to C++ Parking !!!
Lucky you, you found a meter.

Parking Rates: 5 cents = 3 seconds

The meter is ready. Want to insert a coin? y = yes n = no y

Please insert your coin into the slot < q, d, n >   q

Your $0.25 has purchased 15 seconds.
Insert another? y = yes   n = no   y

Please insert your coin into the slot < q, d, n >   d

Your $0.35 has purchased 21 seconds.
Insert another?   y = yes   n = no   n

Hit the Enter key to start your countdown.

ticktick
ticktick   (ticks for 21 seconds)

Ding!   Time's Up!

Want to park some more?   y = yes,   n = no   n

Parking sure is expensive!

The main function is shown as:

```
int main()
{
        ParkingMeter WillGrabIt;        // name our parking meter after a fictitious mayor
        bool IAmParking = false;
        char answer,more_coins = 'y';
        cout << "\n Welcome to C++ Parking !!! " <<
                        "\n Lucky you, you found a meter.\n\n" <<
                        "\n Parking Rates:  5 cents = 3 seconds \n\n";
        do
        {
                cout << "\nThe Meter is ready.    Want to insert a coin? y = yes, n = no";
                cin >> more_coins;

                while(more_coins == 'y')    //keep looping until parker says no more coins
                {
                        IAmParking = true;          //indicates we have a parking situation
                        WillGrabIt.TwistKnob();
                        cout << "\n Insert another???  y = yes, n = no      ";
                        cin >> more_coins;
                }
                if(IAmParking)              //we know we are parking
                {
                        WillGrabIt.TimeToPark();
                        IAmParking = false;
                }
                cout << "\n Want to park some more?? y = yes, n = no ";
                cin >> answer;
        }while (answer == 'y');
        cout << "\n\n Parking sure is expensive! \n";
        return 0;
}
```

As you can see the Meter has two functions, TwistKnob and TimeToPark. Do you think about how you (a potential Parker) interact with a meter? You simply insert your coin and twist the knob, and the meter tells you how much time you have purchased. You continue to feed coins into the meter and then it ticks off the time.

The ParkingMeter class has Bank and Clock objects. Notice that the TwistKnob function calls the Bank's GetACoin function. The TwistKnob function must call the FigureHowManySeconds function to calculate and report the total money and time to the Parker. The Bank's job is to ask for and obtain the Parker's money. The TimeToPark function merely calls the Clock's CountDownSeconds function.

```
class ParkingMeter
{
private:
        Bank banker;
        Clock ticker;
        int HowManySeconds;

        void FigureHowManySeconds();
        void ResetMeter() { HowManySeconds = 0; }

public:
        ParkingMeter()  { HowManySeconds = 0; }
        void TwistKnob();    //calls the Bank's GetACoin() and FigureHowManySeconds()
        void TimeToPark();   //is called when the user is done inserting coins
};
class Bank
{
private:
        float totalmoney;         // total amount of money user enters
        char coin;                //actual coin that was entered
public:
        Bank() { totalmoney = 0.0; }    // constructor zero's total money
        bool GetACoin();        // asks user for d, n, q
        float TotalMoney() { return totalmoney; }
        void ResetToZero() {totalmoney = 0.0;}
};
class Clock
{
private:
        int seconds;
public:
        Clock(){ seconds = 100; }
        bool CountDownSeconds(int s);
};
```

The Clock's CountDownSeconds accesses the system time and actually counts off the purchased number of seconds. Build a "polling loop" that will poll the system time until it reaches a specific time; that is, get the system UTC time and add the Parker's seconds to it. This total is the ending time. Then start a while loop and obtain the system time (again) and check if that new system time is greater than the ending time. Continue to allow the loop to execute until the system time is greater than the ending time. (Refer to the way the Track Coach's StopWatch and Johnston's Dice Game access the computer's system time.) A skeleton of the CountDownSeconds function is shown as:

```
bool Clock::CountDownSeconds(int seconds)
{
        time_t ltime;
        int system_time, end_time;
        //obtain system time in ltime and cast it into the system_time
        end_time = system_time + seconds;
        while ( end_time >= system_time)     //polling loop
        {
                // obtain system time again
                system_time = yada, yada    ;-)
        }
        return true;         // all done!
}
```

2. Expand the Shopping example so that the Shopper reads the items from a data
   file called StuffToBuy.dat. This file contains the item name, price, and quantity.
   For example, our Shopper might have a list that looks like the one here:

whole wheat bread	1.99	2
vanilla ice cream	4.59	1
honey	2.69	1
apples	0.25	6
decaf coffee	5.99	1

   When the items are placed in the Cart and checked out, each item (whether the
   Shopper purchased one or many) is treated as a single item. Add the ability for
   the Clerk to report the item name and price as the items are scanned during the
   checkout procedure. Also, have the Clerk add a 5 percent sales tax to the total
   purchase amount and report the number of items scanned. The Shopper should
   write out the amount of money in his or her wallet before and after the shopping experience.

3. Here are new rules for Johnston's (modified) Dice Game. There are three players, each with five white dice. All three players roll their dice. The players who
   roll the highest and lowest totals are not allowed to keep their points for that
   roll; only the middle roller has that right. If two (or three) players roll the same
   total, that roll does not count for any player. The first player reaching fifty
   points wins the game. Use the system time to seed the random number generator for each game.

10

11

Inheritance and Virtual Functions

KEY TERMS AND CONCEPTS

base class
base class access specifiers
child class
commercial off-the-shelf (COTS) software
compile-time polymorphism
constructor rules for inheritance
derived class
destructor rules for inheritance
inheritance
is a relationship
multiple inheritance
parent class
passing parameters to base constructors
private specifier
protected specifier
public specifier
pure virtual function
run-time polymorphism
virtual functions

CHAPTER OBJECTIVES

Explain the concept of inheritance in C++ programs.

Present the basic format required for deriving new classes from base classes.

Explain how the different access specifiers dictate properties of members in the derived classes.

Discuss briefly multiple inheritance schemes.

Explain what constructor and destructor functions are called in C++ inheritance.

Introduce the concept of polymorphism and virtual functions.

Demonstrate how virtual functions are used in base and derived classes.

Parents and Children

The Oxford Dictionary of Current English defines *inherit* as "(1) receive property, rank, title, etc., by legal succession. (2) derive (a characteristic) from one's ancestors."[1] *Webster's Ninth New Collegiate Dictionary* defines *inheritance* as "1 a: the act of inheriting property; b: the reception of genetic qualities by transmission from parent to offspring; c: the acquisition of a possession, condition or trait from past generations."[2]

What do these definitions have to do with C++? Imagine having the ability to create a class (a parent class), then being able to derive a new class (a child class) from the parent. This child class has the properties and characteristics of the parent, and the programmer can add additional components unique to the child class. It is time to wade out into deeper programming waters and see if all our object-oriented and C++ programming skills will keep us afloat.

11.1
Why Is Inheritance So Important?

Counter Class Example

Imagine you are a member of a software development team and this team has spent countless hours designing, implementing, and testing a Counter class. This Counter class has an integer count variable. The constructor zeros the count value. An overloaded operator, "++," increments the count value, and a GetCount function returns the count value. Last, there is a PrintCount and a SetCount function. The class Counter declaration, located in the file Counter.h, is shown below:

---

[1] *The Oxford Dictionary of Current English*, Oxford Press, 1992.
[2] *Webster's Ninth New Collegiate Dictionary*, 1984.

```
// File: Counter.h
class Counter
{
private:
        int count;
public:
        Counter(){count = 0;}
        void operator ++(){ ++count; }    // add one to the count
        int GetCount() { return count; }
        void SetCount( int c ) { count = c; }
        void PrintCount () { cout << "\n The count is" << count; }
};
```

Your programming team has operational code on the system. Many portions of your programs use the Counter class and objects. One sample program with a Counter object is shown in Program 11-1. The sample program output is shown below:

Sample program with class Counter
The count is 0
Increment HowMany twice:
The count is 2
Now set the count back to zero.
The count is 0
All finished counting!

```
//Program 11-1 with class Counter
#include <iostream.h>
#include "Counter.h"
int main()
{
      Counter HowMany;                    // constructor sets HowMany count = 0
      cout << "\n Sample program with class Counter  \n";
      HowMany.PrintCount();
      cout << "\n Increment HowMany twice: ";
      ++HowMany;
      ++HowMany;
      HowMany.PrintCount();
      cout << "\n Now set the count back to zero. ";
      HowMany.SetCount(0);                 // set count value back to zero
      HowMany.PrintCount();
      cout << "\n\n All finished counting! \n";
      return 0;
}
```

Your software is thoroughly tested, it is stable, and it works well and makes your users happy. You have archived the Counter class into a library.

Scenario 1: The Wrench in the Gears One day you and your team discover that you must add an additional function to your Counter class. You need to decrement the count. What happens if you add another overloaded operator for the "− −" in the class declaration?

Many problems are associated with adding this one simple new feature. The least are the three new lines of code. In the real world, classes can be very complex. Indeed, hours of time are spent designing, implementing, testing, and releasing operational software. Whether the software is a commercial product, the front end to a database, or a piece of flight control software, baseline code versions are put in place and programmers do not just tinker with this operational, baselined code. The risk is quite high that something might break in the process of adding new features. Many government software systems (as well as industry systems) are required to go through an operational test and evaluation (OT&E) phase accompanied by a detail test plan.

Scenario 2: Can I Use Your Counter Class? A second situation arises when the software folks across the hall, who have seen your Counter class, wish to use it as a basis for their new DoodadCounter class. The project leader asks you for the Counter software. Your Counter class has everything your neighbors want, and they wish to add a few items in the class specific to their Doodads.

Now you and your team have spent much time working on the Counter functions, some of which are quite complicated. (The actual Counter is not complicated, but for the sake of the example, play along with me.) You are flattered that the people across the hall want your software, but you fear they might mess it up. What to do?

Inheritance Is the Answer

In both scenario 1 and scenario 2, the modifications to the Counter class can be added easily without touching the Counter class (or perhaps by changing only one line in the class declaration). C++ provides the ability to create a new derived (child) class from an existing base (parent) class. The derived class can inherit all the functionality in the base class. In scenario 1, the new decrement feature can be placed in a NewCounter class, which has all the parts and pieces of the Counter class. This NewCounter class will need only the decrement function, and the software in the Counter class is not touched. The Doodad programmers can create a new DoodadCounter class based on your Counter class. You can give them the library (object) code; they do not need your actual function source code.

11

11.2
Inheritance Basics

The class relationship that models *inheritance* is the *is a relationship*. The *base class*, typically, is a general-purpose class and the *derived class* is a special case of the base class. The phrase *is a* describes how the classes are related. The New-Counter is a Counter. The DoodadCounter is a Counter, too. The relationship is not true in the reverse. The Counter is not a NewCounter, and the Counter is not a Doo-dadCounter.

When a new class is "inherited" from a base class, the new class automatically receives members of the base class. There is no need to write these members in the new class declaration. The format for class inheritance is shown below:

```
class Base_class_name
{
        // members of the base class
};
class Derived_class_name : access_specifier Base_class_name
{
        // members of the derived class
        // inherit certain members of the base
        // as determined by the access_specifier
};
```

Once the derived class is declared, derived class objects may be instantiated and used in the normal fashion.

Counter and NewCounter Example

Our Counter class allows the programmer to increment, set and get the count value, and print the value to the screen. The decrement function will be a member of the derived class, NewCounter. Recall the Counter class, which is shown below:

```
class Counter
{
private:
        int count;
public:
        Counter(){count = 0;}
        void operator ++(){ ++count; }  // add one to the count
        int GetCount() { return count; }
        void SetCount( int c ) { count = c; }
        void PrintCount () { cout << "\n The count is" << count; }
};
```

The format for declaring a derived class for NewCounter is shown here:

```
class NewCounter : public Counter
{
public:
        void operator --();   // subtract one from count
};
```

The first line in the declaration, class NewCounter : public Counter, states that the class NewCounter is derived from the class Counter. The term *public* is a *base class access specifier*. (We will examine its purpose in Section 11.3.) The public and protected members of Counter are inherited by NewCounter, but the base constructor functions are not. The only declared member of the NewCounter class is the new overloaded operator function that decrements the count value. In reality, the NewCounter class has all the public members of the Counter class. Figure 11-1 illustrates this situation.

We cannot forget one detail in all this inheritance business: the fact that the variable count in the Counter class is private. No one but the Counter functions may access or change this variable. Even though the NewCounter class inherits the public member functions of Counter (and these functions may access count), NewCounter does not have access to the private members of the class.

The following short program assumes incorrectly that the count value is available to the NewCounter class and that the decrement function is similar to the increment function in Counter:

```
//Program 11-1x with class NewCounter derived from Counter
//DOES NOT COMPILE!!!   :-(
#include <iostream.h>
#include "Counter.h"       // has the class Counter declaration
class NewCounter:public Counter
{
public:
      void operator --() { --count;}   // decrement count here
};

int main()
{
      // main statements
      return 0;
}
```

The NewCounter class is derived from the Counter class.
The NewCounter class has all the public members of the Counter class
except for the base class constructor.

This is the declaration for the Counter class.

```
class Counter
{
private:
        int count;
public:
        Counter(){count = 0;}
        void operator ++(){ ++count; }
        int GetCount() { return count; }
        void SetCount( int c ) { count = c; }
        void PrintCount() { cout << "\n The count is " << count; }
};
```

This is the declaration for the NewCounter class.
It is derived from the Counter class.

```
class NewCounter:public Counter
{
public:
        void operator --(); // prototype
};
```

The NewCounter class has the public members of Count.
You may visualize the NewCounter class looking like this:

```
public:
        void operator --() ;  // prototype

        void operator ++(){ ++count; }
        int GetCount() { return count; }
        void SetCount( int c ) { count = c; }
        void PrintCount() { cout << "\n The count is " << count; }
```

Figure 11-1
Counter and NewCounter Classes

```
//Program 11-2 with class NewCounter derived from Counter    :-)
//Counter class has private count variable.
//NewCounter uses Counter's GetCount and SetCount functions.
#include <iostream.h>
#include "Counter.h"
class NewCounter:public Counter
{
public:
      void operator --()
};
void NewCounter::operator --()
{
      int c = GetCount();
      --c;
      SetCount(c);
}

int main()
{
      NewCounter nctr;   // new counter object

      cout << "\n Sample program with class NewCounter \n";
      cout << "\n What is in the nctr?";
      nctr.PrintCount();

      cout << "\n Increment the new counter object twice: ";
      ++nctr;
      ++nctr;
      nctr.PrintCount();

      cout << "\n Now decrement the new counter: ";
      --nctr;
      nctr.PrintCount();

      cout << "\n\n All finished counting! \n";
      return 0;
};
}
```

The Visual C++ compiler shows us this error:

```
Compiling...
Ch11NewCounter.cpp
C:\TestCases\Ch11NewCounter.cpp(25) : error C2248: 'count' : cannot access private member declared in class 'Counter'
        C:\TestCases\Ch11NewCounter.cpp(11) : see declaration of 'count'
Error executing cl.exe.

TestCases.exe - 1 error(s), 0 warning(s)
```

GCC tells us that count is private:

```
login1:johnston:~/gnu:$ g++ G++_Ch11NewCounter.cc
G++_Ch11NewCounter.cc: In method 'void NewCounter::operator --()':
G++_Ch11NewCounter.cc:29: member 'count' is private
```

For the NewCounter function to decrement the count variable, the Counter's Set and Get functions must be used. The complete program, which implements correctly the NewCounter's decrement function, is shown in Program 11-2. The output is shown below:

Sample program with class NewCounter

What is in the nctr?
The count is 0
Increment the new counter object twice:
The count is 2
Now decrement the new counter:
The count is 1

All finished counting!

Protected Members

The ability of a new class to inherit functionality from a base class is a powerful feature in C++ programming. However, if the data of the base class is all privately declared (as in the Counter class above), the derived class will have extra work for obvious tasks. We do not want to make the data public because that action defeats the data-hiding principle of object-oriented programming. There is a third specifier in C++ designed just for inheritance.

The protected access specifier provides the programmer greater flexibility when he or she is working with inherited classes. When a class member is specified as *protected*, that member then is inherited in the derived classes, but the member is not accessible outside the base, or derived class. The Counter class can declare the count variable as protected, the NewCounter class inherits it, but the world cannot access it. Figure 11-2 illustrate this situation. Table 11-1 compares these two ways to write the Counter class.

The Counter class has a protected count variable, and the count variable is inherited by the NewCounter class.

This is the declaration for the Counter class.

```
class Counter
{
protected:
        int count;
public:
        Counter(){count = 0;}
        void operator ++(){ ++count; }
        int GetCount() { return count; }
        void SetCount( int c ) { count = c; }
        void PrintCount() { cout << "\n The count is " << count; }
};
```

This is the declaration for the NewCounter class.
It is derived from the Counter class.

```
class NewCounter:public Counter
{
public:
        void operator --(); // prototype
};
```

Since the Counter's count variable is protected,
the NewCounter class receives the count variable.

```
protected:
        int count;

public:
        void operator --() ; // prototype

        void operator ++(){ ++count; }
        int GetCount() { return count; }
        void SetCount( int c ) { count = c; }
        void PrintCount() { cout << "\n The count is " << count; }
```

Figure 11-2
Counter and NewCounter Using Protected Count Variable

11

TABLE 11-1
Two Ways to Write the Counter Class

	Private and Public Members	Protected and Public Members

Class declaration	```class Counter```
	```{```
	```private:```
	``` int count;```
	```public:```
	``` // Counter Functions```
	```};```
		```class Counter```
		```{```
		```protected:```
		``` int count;```
		```public:```
		``` // Counter Functions```
		```};```

What does a derived class get?	The public Counter Functions, but not the constructor.	The protected int count and the public Counter Functions, but not the constructor.
How does a derived class access the count variable?	The derived class uses the public Get and Set functions, just like the rest of the world.	The derived class has the protected int count and can access it directly.
What can the world see?	All the public members	All the public members

Now we can rework the Counter and NewCounter classes so that the New-Counter inherits the count variable, and then the NewCounter decrement function can access count directly. Figure 11-3 illustrates the program organization incorporating the same main function from above.

Employees, Bosses, and CEOs

Another Example Let's examine a second example before delving into the object and inheritance details. We begin by building a class for employee information (name, social security number, department, and salary). From there, we derive a new class for boss information. The boss is an employee. Lastly, we derive a CEO class. The CEO is a boss; the boss is an employee. The employee is the boss's base class and the boss is the CEO's base class.

Starting with basic employee information for the class CEmployee, we specify the data that is normally private to be protected. This specification allows the derived class to receive the following information:

```
class CEmployee
{
protected:
      char name[50], SSN[15];
      int dept;
      float yearly_salary;
```

```
// File:  Counter.h
#ifndef_COUNTER_H
#define_COUNTER_H
#include <iostream.h>

class Counter
{
protected:
        int count;
public:
        Counter(){count = 0;}
        void operator ++(){ ++count; }
        int GetCount() { return count; }
        void SetCount( int c ) { count = c; }
        void PrintCount() { cout << "\n The count is " << count; }
};
#endif
```

This is the declaration for the Counter class, with the protected specifier for the data.

This is the declaration for the NewCounter class. It is derived from the Counter class.

```
// File:  NewCounter.h
#ifndef_NEWCTR_H
#define_NEWCTR_H

#include "Counter.h"

class NewCounter:public Counter
{
public:
        void operator --() { --count;}
};
#endif
```

```
//Program with class NewCounter derived from Counter and protected count variable.

#include <iostream.h>
#include " NewCounter.h"

int main()
{

        NewCounter nctr;      // new counter object

        // rest of program
        return 0;
}
```

Figure 11-3
Program Organization Using the Counter and NewCounter Classes, and the Protected Specifier for the Count Variable

```
public:
        CEmployee();
        GetEmpInfo();
        WriteEmpInfo();
};
```

The CEmployee class has only three member functions. The constructor function will initialize values to NULL and zero. The Get and Write functions ask for information from the user and write it to the screen, respectively. The class declaration is placed in a separate include file, and the corresponding source code is

```
//Program 11-3 Employee
int main()
{
        cout << "\n\n Work, Work, Work. \n";
        CEmployee worker;
        worker.GetEmpInfo();
        worker.WriteEmpInfo();

        cout << "\n\n No more work to do.\n\n";
        return 0;
}
```

placed in a *.cpp file. A sample main function (shown in Program 11-3) is located in a third file. The file relationships are shown in Figure 11-4. The program input and output are shown here:

Work, Work, Work.

Enter the employee's name Joe Smith
Enter the employee's SSN   111-11-1111
Enter the dept code and salary 34 25000

Employee: Joe Smith
        SSN: 111-11-1111
        Dept: 34
      Salary: $25000

No more work to do.

The boss is an employee. Therefore, we derive a new child class from the CEmployee class that contains the boss information (his or her yearly financial bonus). Our CBoss class needs all the employee information. The data in CEmployee is protected, so the CBoss class inherits this data.

```
class CBoss: public CEmployee
{
protected:
        float bonus;
public:
        WhatsMyBonus();
        WriteBonus();
};
```

```
//File: Ch11CEmployee.h

#ifndef _CEMPLOYEE_H
#define _CEMPLOYEE_H


class CEmployee
{
protected:
        char name[50],SSN[15];
        float salary;
        int dept;
public:
        CEmployee();
        void GetEmpInfo();
        void WriteEmpInfo();
};

#endif
```

```
//File: Ch11CEmployee.cpp

#include "Ch11CEmployee.h"
#include <iostream.h>
#include <string.h>

CEmployee::CEmployee()
{
        // statements
}

void CEmployee::GetEmpInfo()
{
        // statements
}

void CEmployee::WriteEmpInfo()
{
        //statements

}
```

```
//Program with class CEmployee
//File: Ch11CEmployeeMain.cpp

#include <iostream.h>
#include "Ch11CEmployee.h"

int main()
{

        cout << "\n\n Work, Work, Work. \n";

        CEmployee worker;

        worker.GetEmpInfo();
        worker.WriteEmpInfo();

        cout << "\n\n No more work to do.\n\n";
        return 0;


}
```

Figure 11-4
Program Organization for the CEmployee class and Sample Program

11

```
//File: Ch11CBoss.h

#ifndef _CBOSS_H
#define _CBOSS_H

#include "Ch11CEmployee.h"


class CBoss: public CEmployee
{
protected:
        float bonus;
public:
        void WhatsMyBonus();
        void WriteBonus();
};

#endif
```

```
//File: Ch11CBoss.cpp

#include <iostream.h>
#include "Ch11CBoss.h"

void CBoss::WhatsMyBonus()
{
        cout << "\n\n What is my bonus this year? $$$$$$  ";
        cin >> bonus;
}

void CBoss::WriteBonus()
{
        cout << "\n   Bonus:  $" << bonus;
}
```

The CBoss class is derived from the CEmployee class.
The CEmployee.h file must be included in the CBoss header file.

```
//Program with class CEmployee and CBoss
//File: Ch11CBossMain.cpp


#include <iostream.h>
#include "Ch11CBoss.h"


int main()
{
        CBoss manager;

        // statements

        return 0;
}
```

Figure 11-5
Program Organization for the CBoss Class and Sample Program

In our program, we create a boss object that has inherited all the employee information, plus it contains the yearly bonus data (specific only to boss objects). The program file organization is illustrated in Figure 11-5. A sample main function for the CBoss class and its output is shown in Program 11-4:

```
//Program 11-4  Boss
int main()
{
        cout << "\n\n Work, Work, Work. \n";
        CBoss manager;
        manager.GetEmpInfo();   // inherited from the CEmployee class
        manager.WhatsMyBonus();
        manager.WriteEmpInfo();
        manager.WriteBonus();
        cout << "\n\n No more work to do.\n\n";
        return 0;
}
```

The program input and output are shown below:

Work, Work, Work.

Enter the employee's name   Mary Jones
Enter the employee's SSN   222-22-2222
Enter the dept code and salary   34 40000
What is my bonus this year? $$$$$$ 25000

Employee: Mary Jones
      SSN: 222-22-2222
      Dept: 34
    Salary: $40000
   Bonus: $25000
No more work to do.

Taking inheritance one step further, we now create a CEO class for the company's chief executive officer. Our CCEO class is a child class of the CBoss class (which is derived from the CEmployee class). Our CEO needs to have all the data in the employee and boss classes as well as the CEO specific stock option data.

```
class CCEO: public CBoss
{
protected:
        int stock_options;
public:
        void HowManySharesDoIGet();
        void WriteShares();
};
```

11

The CCEO class is derived from the CBoss class, which is derived from the CEmployee class. The CCEO has all the data and functions from these two classes because the employee and boss data and functions are declared as either protected or public. The CCEO file organization and sample program are shown in Figure 11-6. The sample program input is shown in Program 11-5.

```
//File: Ch11CCEO.h

#ifndef _CCEO_H
#define _CCEO_H

#include "Ch11CBoss.h"


class CCEO: public CBoss
{
protected:
        int stock_options;
public:
        void HowManySharesDoIGet( );
        void WriteShares( );
};

#endif
```

```
//File: Ch11CCEO.cpp

#include <iostream.h>
#include "Ch11CCEO.h"

void CCEO::HowManySharesDoIGet( )
{
        cout << "\n How many shares do I get?  ";
        cin >> stock_options;

}

void CCEO::WriteShares( )
{
        cout << "\n  Shares: " << stock_options;
}
```

The CCEO class is derived from the CBoss class.
The CBoss.h file must be included in the CCEO header file.

```
//Program with class CEmployee and CBoss and CCEO
//File:  Ch11CCEOMain.cpp


#include <iostream.h>
#include "Ch11CCEO.h"


int main( )
{
        CCEO BigCheese;

        // statements

        return 0;
}
```

Figure 11-6
Program Organization for the CCEO Class and Sample Program

Chapter 11 ▌ Inheritance and Virtual Functions

```
//Program 11-5 CEO
#include <iostream.h>
#include "Ch11CCEO.h"
int main()
{
        cout << "\n\n Work, Work, Work. \n";
        CCEO BigCheese;
        BigCheese.GetEmpInfo();                // inherited from CEmployee
        BigCheese.WhatsMyBonus();         // inherited from CBoss
        BigCheese.HowManySharesDoIGet();

        BigCheese.WriteEmpInfo();
        BigCheese.WriteBonus();
        BigCheese.WriteShares();
        cout << "\n\n No more work to do.\n\n";
        return 0;
}
```

The output is shown below:

Work, Work, Work.

Enter the employee's name Delores White
Enter the employee's SSN   333-33-3333
Enter the dept code and salary   34 75000
What is my bonus this year? $$$$$$ 25000
How many shares do I get? 500

Employee: Delores White
      SSN: 333-33-3333
     Dept: 34
   Salary: $75000
   Bonus: $25000
  Shares: 500

No more work to do.

Figure 11-7 illustrates how the employee, boss, and CEO classes interact. The BigCheese object in the main program (above) has all the data and functions of the three classes.

Derived Functions Calling Base Functions   Another design approach for the employee, boss, and CEO programs streamlines the process of obtaining and writing information. It is more logical to have a GetEmpInfo and WriteEmpInfo function for all three classes that takes care of asking for and reporting all the

File: *Ch11CEmployee.h*

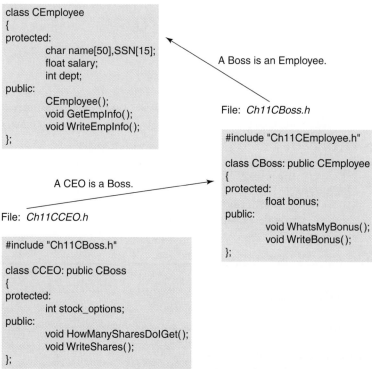

```
class CEmployee
{
protected:
        char name[50],SSN[15];
        float salary;
        int dept;
public:
        CEmployee();
        void GetEmpInfo();
        void WriteEmpInfo();
};
```

A Boss is an Employee.

File: *Ch11CBoss.h*

```
#include "Ch11CEmployee.h"

class CBoss: public CEmployee
{
protected:
        float bonus;
public:
        void WhatsMyBonus();
        void WriteBonus();
};
```

A CEO is a Boss.

File: *Ch11CCEO.h*

```
#include "Ch11CBoss.h"

class CCEO: public CBoss
{
protected:
        int stock_options;
public:
        void HowManySharesDoIGet();
        void WriteShares();
};
```

Figure 11-7
Summary of CEmployee, CBoss, and CCEO Classes

employee information. This consolidation eliminates the need for the separate Bonus and Shares functions. What do we mean? Let's look at each of the class declarations:

```
class CEmployee
{
protected:
        char name[50], SSN[15];
        int dept;
        float yearly_salary;
public:
        CEmployee();
        GetEmpInfo();          //asks for name, SSN, dept, and salary
        WriteEmpInfo();        //write info to screen
};
```

For the CBoss class, we also include GetEmpInfo and WriteEmpInfo functions. These functions are called using a CBoss object.

```
class CBoss: public CEmployee
{
protected:
        float bonus;
public:
//This GetEmpInfo calls the CEmployee GetEmpInfo function,
//then asks for bonus info
        GetEmpInfo();
//This WriteEmpInfo calls the CEmployee WriteEmpInfo function,
//then writes the bonus.
        WriteEmpInfo();
};
```

The code for the boss's Get and Write functions shows how the base class functions are called:

```
void CBoss::GetEmpInfo()
{
        CEmployee::GetEmpInfo();
        cout << "\nWhat is my bonus this year? $$$$$$     ";
        cin >> bonus;
}

void CBoss::WriteEmpInfo()
{
        CEmployee::WriteEmpInfo();
        cout << "      Bonus: $" << bonus;
}
```

The main function for the CBoss object is cleaner and shorter.

```
//Program 11-6 Boss Part 2
int main()
{
        cout << "\n\n Work, Work, Work. \n";
        CBoss manager;
        manager.GetEmpInfo();  // asks for all info including bonus
        manager.WriteBonus();  // writes all info including bonus
        cout << "\n\n No more work to do.\n\n";
        return 0;
}
```

The program output (shown below) is similar to the previous example:

Work, Work, Work.

Enter the employee's name   Mary Jones
Enter the employee's SSN   222-22-2222
Enter the dept code and salary   34 40000
What is my bonus this year? $$$$$$ 25000

Employee: Mary Jones
**   SSN: 222-22-2222**
**   Dept: 34**
**   Salary: $40000**
**   Bonus: $25000**

No more work to do.

Following this same technique, the CCEO class is built with Get and Write functions that call the parent class functions.

```
class CCEO: public CBoss
{
protected:
        int stock_options;
public:
        //This GetEmpInfo calls the CBoss GetEmpInfo
        //which in turn calls the CEmployee GetEmpInfo.
        //Finally, this asks for the stock information.
        GetEmpInfo();
        WriteEmpInfo();     //same logic as GetEmpInfo function
};
```

The CCEO functions are shown here:

```
void CCEO::GetEmpInfo()
{
        CBoss::GetEmpInfo();
        cout << "\nHow many shares do I get?     ";
        cin >> stock_options;
}


void CCEO::WriteEmpInfo()
{
        CBoss::WriteEmpInfo();
        cout << "     Shares: " << stock_options;
}
```

11.3
Access Specifier Specifics

There are three access specifiers for classes: private, protected, and public. We are familiar with the role these three play when they are used inside a class declaration, such as:

```
class C
{
private:
      // members accessible only to class members
protected:
      // members that are inherited in children classes
public:
      // members that are accessible to the world
};
```

Another place we use these specifiers is in the first line of a class declaration. When used in the first line of a declaration, they are known as **base class access specifiers**. The format is shown below:

```
class A : public B
{
      :
      :
};
```

base class access specifier

an access specifier used in the first line of a declaration dictates how the base members are treated in the derived classes

The "public B" is the base class access specifier. It is possible to create derived classes by using all three of the specifiers: public, protected, and private. This base specifier dictates how the base members are treated in the derived classes. Table 11-2 summarizes the base class specifiers if class A (below) is used as a base class.

```
class A
{
private:
      // private members
protected:
      // protected members
public:
      // public members
};
```

11

TABLE 11-2

Base Class Specifiers in Derived Class Declarations[a]

public	protected	private
```class B: public A { };```	```class C: protected A { };```	```class D: private A { };```
All public members of class A become public members of class B. All protected members of class A become protected members of class B.	All public and protected members of class A become protected members of class C.	All public and protected members of class A become private members of class D.

[a]Private members of base class A are not inherited by class B, C, or D. Private class members (data and functions) are never passed to derived classes.

11.4
Multiple Inheritance

multiple inheritance

two or more classes used as base classes for a new class

Beginning C++ programmers often ask if it is possible to have *multiple inheritance*, that is, to derive a new class from two or more base classes. The answer is yes, it is possible to have multiple parents for a child class. The syntax for this type of inheritance is shown here:

```
class A
{
        // base class
        :
        :
};

class B
{
        // base class
        :
        :
};
```

```
class C : public A, public B
{
        // derived class from two base classes
        // class C has both public and protected members from A and B
        :
        :
};
```

The derived class must have the parent classes in a comma-separated list, and base access specifiers are needed. To design a class with multiple base classes, you should be sure that the new class does indeed have an *is a* relationship with both base classes. For example, if you are writing a program for Pets (e.g., cats, dogs, hamsters, etc.) you may derive a class Cats by using both a HousePet class and a Mammal class because a cat is a HousePet and a cat is a Mammal. Beginning C++ programmers may believe that using a multiple-base inherited derived class is a time-saving solution for their program. In truth, multiple derived classes pose rather complicated design and implementation issues, and should be attempted with extreme caution.

11.5
Inheritance, Constructors, and Destructors

Perhaps by now you have noticed that we have not mentioned constructors (and destructors) and inheritance. There are several rules in C++ concerning base and derived class constructor relationships, when constructors are called and when they are not, and parameter passing between base and derived constructors. It is important for the new programmer to get the hang of inheritance and base and derived classes before learning these rules. The counter and employee examples are good places to start.

Review of Constructors and Destructors

A constructor function is a class member function that has the same name as its class, and this function is executed when the object is created. The main job of a constructor is to initialize object data to known values and thus avoid unexpected behavior from the object. It is possible to overload class constructors. Overloading class constructors offers the programmer many ways to create new objects.

A destructor function is a class member that also has the same name as its class, and this function is executed when the object is destroyed. The destructor function's job is to perform any clean-up activity (such as closing files or freeing memory) before the object goes out of existence. The destructor function cannot be overloaded.

Base and Derived Classes and Constructor Functions

Constructor functions may be placed in both base and derived class declarations. A specific order of execution occurs when a derived object comes into existence.

When a derived object is created, the base class constructor function (if it exists) is executed first, followed by the derived class's constructor. The simple program below illustrates this process:

```
#include <iostream.h>
class Base
{
public:
        Base() { cout << "\n Executing Base class constructor "; }
};

class Derived: public Base
{
public:
        Derived() { cout << "\n Executing Derived class constructor ";
}
};
int main()
{
        Derived TheKid;

        cout << "\n All done. \n\n";
        return 0;
}
```

The output is shown below:

Executing Base class constructor
Executing Derived class constructor
All done.

The base constructor function was executed first, followed by the derived constructor function. Because the derived class depends on the base class, the base class constructors must be executed before the derived constructor. As long as there are no input parameters to either the derived or base class constructor functions, the program will execute the base constructor and then the derived constructor.

Base and Derived Classes and Destructor Functions

Class destructor functions may also be placed in both base and derived class declarations. The order of execution for the destructors is opposite that of constructor function execution when the derived object is destroyed; that is, the derived object destructor is called before the base class destructor function. Expanding the previous simple program illustrates the order of constructor and destructor execution:

```cpp
#include <iostream.h>
class Base
{
public:
        Base() { cout << "\n Executing Base class constructor "; }
        ~Base() { cout << "\n Executing Base class destructor "; }
};

class Derived: public Base
{
public:
        Derived() { cout << "\n Executing Derived class constructor "; }
        ~Derived() { cout << "\n Executing Derived class destructor "; }
};

int main()
{
        Derived TheKid;

        cout << "\n All done. \n\n";
        return 0;
}
```

The output is shown below:

Executing Base class constructor
Executing Derived class constructor
All done.

Executing Derived class destructor
Executing Base class destructor

The derived class destructor function is executed first, followed by the base class destructor function. (The destructor functions are executed in the reverse order of the constructor functions.) Remember that the object destructor functions are called when the program terminates (and the objects go out of existence) or when local copies of objects are destroyed. We see the "All done." statement before the destructor function messages because the destructors are called once program termination is initiated.

Parameter Passing and Base and Derived Constructor Functions

It is wonderful to build a base class and then to have a derived class inherit the data and functions of the base class. Programmers often find they create only derived class objects in programs, yet the programmers still need to initialize the base class variables when the derived object comes into existence. Remember, a child class inherits the protected and public members of the class, and these base class members are contained in the derived class.

When working with inherited classes and constructors, a programmer can take two possible routes for data initialization. First, the programmer can write the derived class constructor to perform the initializations for all the variables (base and derived). But if the base class already has appropriate constructor functions, why reinvent the wheel? Also, with complicated classes, it is unwise to risk handling base class initialization in the derived class constructor. The second and preferred route is for the programmer simply to allow the derived class constructor function to call the base constructor function and to pass the initial values to it. This programming technique is more efficient and typically involves less risk.

An example is needed to illustrate this principle. Let's get out the old nine-iron and take a walk on the golf course.

A Golfer Is a Person   A base class, CPerson, is shown below with two protected data members (name and age), a WritePerson function, and two constructor functions. One constructor function is a do-nothing constructor: no initialization statements are executed when this function is called. The second constructor function requires two input parameters that are used to initialize the CPerson data members. When this constructor executes, it calls WritePerson, which writes the name and age to the screen along with entrance and exit messages. The very short program in Program 11-7 shows the use of creating a CPerson object with the overloaded constructor.

```
//Program 11-7 CPerson
#include <iostream>
#include <string>

using namespace std;

class CPerson
{
protected:
        string name;
        int age;
public:
        CPerson(string n, int a);
        CPerson(){ cout << "\nI'm in the do-nothing CPerson constructor \n"; };
        void WritePerson(){ cout << name << " is " << age << " years old. \n"; }
        ~CPerson() { cout << "\nDestructing CPerson object \n"; }
};
```

```
CPerson::CPerson(string n, int a)
{
        cout << "\nIn the CPerson constructor \n";
        name = n;
        age = a;
        WritePerson();
        cout << "Leaving the CPerson constructor  \n";


}


int main()
{
        CPerson somebody("Vincent", 29);

        cout << "\nNo more people around here. \n\n";
        return 0;
}
```

The program output is shown below:

In the CPerson constructor
Vincent is 29 years old.
Leaving the CPerson constructor
No more people around here.
Destructing CPerson object

The First Route—Make the Children Do All the Work!   The CPerson is now used as a base class for a new class, CGolfer. The golfer class has the person's golf handicap score. We'll assume the handicap is an integer value.

In Program 11-8, the CGolfer constructor function initializes all the object data. This code is perfectly legal and will execute without problem. Note that C++ requires a base class constructor if the derived class constructor has input parameters. The empty CPerson constructor is required for this method. The output is shown below:

In the do-nothing CPerson constructor
In the CGolfer constructor
Vincent is 29 years old.
Handicap: 15
Head over to the 19th hole!
Destructing Golfer object
Destructing CPerson object

```
//Program 11-8 CGolfer
//Make the Children Do All the Work!
#include <iostream>
#include <string>
#include "CPerson.h"
using namespace std;

class CGolfer:public CPerson
{
private:
        int handicap;
public:
        CGolfer(string n, int a, int h);
        void WriteGolfer();
        ~CGolfer() { cout << "\nDestructing Golfer object \n"; }
};

CGolfer::CGolfer(string n, int a, int h) //Route 1 this inits all
{
        name = n;
        age = a;
        cout << "\nIn the CGolfer constructor \n";
        handicap = h;
}

void CGolfer::WriteGolfer()
{
        CPerson::WritePerson();
        cout << "\n Handicap: " << handicap;
}

int main()
{
        CGolfer AlmostPro("Vincent", 29, 15);
        AlmostPro.WriteGolfer();
        cout << "\n\n Head over to the 19th hole! \n\n";
        return 0;
}
```

 The Second Route As we asked earlier, why not use perfectly good code? The CPerson class has a constructor function that initializes the name and age variables. We should use this constructor! This second approach to getting the initial values into name and age uses the base class constructor function. The only way our program can access the base class constructor is through the derived constructor. When

CGolfer constructor function passes the name and age
to the CPerson constructor function.

```
int main( )
{

        CGolfer  AlmostPro("Vincent", 29, 15);
```

"Vincent", 29, and 15 are passed to the CGolfer constructor.

CGolfer Constructor Function

```
CGolfer::CGolfer(string n, int a, int h) : CPerson(n, a)
{
        cout << "\nIn the CGolfer constructor \n";
        handicap = h;

}
```

The CGolfer function in turn passes the name (in "n") and age (in "a") to the CPerson constructor.

Notice the new syntax for the derived constructor function.

```
CPerson::CPerson(string n, int a)
{
        cout << "\nIn the CPerson constructor \n";
        name = n;
        age = a;
        cout <<  name << " is " << age << " years old.  \n";
        cout << "Leaving the CPerson constructor  \n";

}
```

Figure 11-8
The Derived Class Constructor Passes Initial Values to the Base Class Constructor

the object is created, the parameters are passed to the derived class constructor, which in turn passes the arguments to the base class constructor. Figure 11-8 illustrates this concept.

The CGolfer constructor function prototype contains only the inputs to the function, but the derived constructor function header line has new notation. This notation is required for calling the base class constructor and passing the base constructor parameters to the base constructor. This new code is shown in the constructor definition.

```
class CGolfer:public CPerson
{
private:
        int handicap;
public:
        CGolfer(string n, int a, int h);    // prototype
        void WriteGolfer();
        ~CGolfer() { cout << "\nDestructing Golfer object "; }
};
CGolfer::CGolfer(string n, int a, int h) : CPerson(n, a)
{
        cout << "\nIn the CGolfer constructor \n";
        handicap = h;
}
```

The CGolfer constructor calls the CPerson constructor, passing the name and age to the routine. This method of writing software is more efficient than repeating initialization statements found in the base class constructor. The main function using the CPerson constructor is shown below:

```
//Program 11-8
int main()
{
        CGolfer AlmostPro("Vincent", 29, 15);
        AlmostPro.WriteGolfer();
        cout << "\n\n Head over to the 19th hole! \n\n";
        return 0;
}
```

The output is shown below:

In the CPerson constructor
Vincent is 29 years old.
Leaving the CPerson constructor

In the CGolfer constructor
Vincent is 29 years old.

Handicap: 15

Head over to the 19th hole!
Destructing CGolfer object
Destructing CPerson object

Rules for Derived Class—Base Class Constructors   The way to a base class constructor is through the derived class constructor if we need to pass parameters to the base class constructor. The programmer should keep several points in mind while using a derived class constructor:

1. The base class constructor function will be called automatically if there is no derived class constructor—as long as the derived object does not require input parameters.

2. If you need the services only of the base class constructor and there are no inputs to the derived class upon creation, a derived class constructor is not required.

3. If your derived object needs to pass parameters to the base class constructor (and there are no specific inputs for the derived class), a derived class constructor must be present. This derived constructor merely acts as a conduit for the parameters.

We'll let the CXYPoint and CCustomDataPoint classes illustrate this constructor and parameter pass-through technique. Many graphics software interfaces use the Cartesian coordinate system to describe points that are plotted on the x and y axes. Each point on the x-y coordinate system is represented as a pair of points, such as (3, 4) and (6, 2). The CXYPoint class declaration has two double valued variables representing a point on the xy-axis system. Two constructors are provided in this class.

```
class CXYPoint
{
protected:
        double x, y;
public:
        CXYPoint();
        CXYPoint(double x1, double y1);
        void ShowThePoint() {cout << "\n (" << x << "," << y << ")"; }
};

CXYPoint::CXYPoint()
{
        cout << "\n In CXYPoint constructor x=y=0";
        x = 0.0; y = 0.0;
}
CXYPoint::CXYPoint(double x1, double y1)
{
        cout << "\n In the CYXPoint constructor x=x1, y=y1";
        x = x1; y = y1;
}
```

11

Suppose a famous statistician (who moonlights as a software engineer) discovers that she needs specialized data point objects in her stats software. She is familiar with the famous CXYPoint class and recognizes that the famous point functions are the best in the business. She decides to use the CXYPoint as a base class for her CCustomDataPoint class.

First, she decides to let the base class constructor initialize her custom points. She writes the custom point class and uses the short main in Program 11-9 to test her software. Her output shows that the points are (0, 0), as expected.

Welcome to the Infamous Point Program Part 1

In CXYPoint constructor x=y=0
In the CYXPoint constructor x=y=0
Point 1 is
(0,0)
Point 2 is
(0,0)

This works famously!!!

```
//Program 11-9 Famous Points Part 1
class CCustomDataPoint: public CXYPoint
{
public:
//      no constructor function here
};

int main()
{
        cout << "\n Welcome to the Infamous Point Program Part 1 \n\n";

        CCustomDataPoint point1;    //derived object, base class constructor called
        CCustomDataPoint point2;

        cout << "\n Point 1 is ";
        point1.ShowThePoint();
        cout << "\n Point 2 is ";
        point2.ShowThePoint();

        cout << "\n\n This works famously!!!    \n\n";
        return 0;
}
```

```
//Program 11-10      Famous Points Part 2
class CCustomDataPoint: public CXYPoint
{
public:
        CCustomDataPoint(double x1, double y1): CXYPoint(x1, y1) {}
        CCustomDataPoint(){}
};


int main()
{

        cout << "\n Welcome to the Infamous Point Program Part 2 \n\n";

        CCustomDataPoint point1;
        CCustomDataPoint point2(10,12);

        cout << "\n Point 1 is ";
        point1.ShowThePoint();
        cout << "\n Point 2 is ";
        point2.ShowThePoint();

        cout << "\n\n This works famously!!!  \n\n";
        return 0;
}
```

Now she decides to pass in the values for her points when the point objects are created. She must modify her custom point class to include two constructor functions. Refer to Program 11-10. The output is shown below:

Welcome to the Infamous Point Program Part 2

In CXYPoint constructor x=y=0
In the CYXPoint constructor x=x1, y=y1
Point 1 is
(0,0)
Point 2 is
(10,12)

This works famously!!!

Troubleshooting: Inheritance

Beginning C++ students have two main problems with inheritance and with parent and children classes. These problems do not involve syntax or link errors but center on understanding the concept of inherited classes. When asked to describe the members of a derived class, novice programmers will respond correctly, reciting the derived class members, but will forget that the derived classes have inherited the protected and public members of the base class.

The second problem is that of trying to design base and derived classes. It is difficult for the new programmer to visualize how the base class members will be inherited by the derived classes. This stumbling block is illustrated in the following example.

Pet Store Inventory   Suppose that you are asked to design classes that represent the items found in a pet supply store. What are the characteristics of all items in the pet store? All items have a manufacturer's brand, a universal price code, and wholesale and retail costs. The base class for our pet store items is shown below:

```
class PetStoreItem
{
protected:
   float retail_cost, wholesale_cost;
   char UPC[15], brand [30];
public:
   PetStoreItem();
   Display()
};
```

As we refine our program design, we need to think about the data and pertinent functions for the children classes. Every item in the store *is a* PetStoreItem object. What is the best way to categorize the items in the store and separate them into children classes? Let's keep it simple and design classes for only two types of items: food and training equipment (such as leashes and collars). What data are specific only to the pet food but not to training equipment? Pet food may be canned or dry, it is identified by its ingredients (such as chicken, lamb and rice, etc.), and it is sold by weight. Training equipment, on the other hand, may be made of nylon or leather, its size is important, and it is made in various styles. Class declarations for Food and TrainingItems are shown below. Notice that both these classes are derived from PetStoreItem.

```
class PetFood : public PetStoreItem
{
private:
   char flavor[30];
   bool bDry;               //true = dry food, false = canned
   float weight;
public:
   void DescribeFood();  //writes pet food information
   //other food functions
};
```

```
class TrainingItem : public PetStoreItem
{
private:
    float length:    // in inches
    int equipment_type;        // 1 = collar, 2 = leash, 3 = harness
    bool bNylon;    //true = nylon, false = leather
public:
    void DescribeTrainingItem();
    //other training item functions
};
```

We have left out details and perhaps missed opportunities where enumerated data types would make our programming life easier. However, it is important to notice how the two classes appear to contain only food or training equipment information when, in fact, these two classes have also inherited the PetStoreItem members! A collar for your cat has a length, it is made of a certain material, and it is made in a certain style, but it also has a brand name, associated costs, and a universal price code (UPC).

Remember the following facts when working with inheritance:

1. The children inherit the protected and public members of the parent class.
2. You can examine the base class to learn what members will be inherited in the derived classes.
3. The derived classes should be designed so that they are special cases of the base class.
4. If you find yourself duplicating a data member in derived classes, that data member most likely belongs in the base class.

11.6
Inheritance Program Examples

Class relationships can range from simple and straightforward to a complicated chain of objects that are objects having objects and using more objects. There are three main goals in any well-written program:

1. To perform as required.
2. To be error-free.
3. To be written so that another programmer can read and understand the program details.

For object-oriented programs, we can add a fourth goal: the object relationships must make sense in real-world terms.

The Animals Program

The Animals program is a simple (and maybe a bit silly) example that has a base class Animal and several derived classes for various types of animals. The base class contains information for all Animals including the type (i.e., mammal, bird, etc.), species (i.e., dog, scrub jay, etc.), name, and birthday. The Animal class declaration has a Date object and two enumerated variables. Notice that the Animal constructor function requires four input parameters.

```
class Date
{
private:
        int mon,day,yr;
public:
        Date(){mon = 1; day = 1; yr = 2000; };
        void SetDate(int m, int d, int y);
        void ShowDate();
};


enum Category { mammal, fish, bird, reptile, amphibian, insect };
enum Species { dog, cat, scrubjay, sparrow, frog, toad };

class Animal
{
protected:
        string name;
        Species whatIam;
        Date birth;
        Category type;
public:
        Animal(Category t, Species s, string n, Date b);
        void Write();
};
```

The Write function incorporates character string arrays for writing the enumerated values for the type and species of animal. The birthday is written via the Date's ShowDate function.

```
void Animal::Write()
{
        char AnimalType[6][15] = {"mammal", "fish", "bird", "reptile",
                                  "amphibian", "insect"};
        char SpeciesTypes[6][15] = { "dog", "cat", "scrubjay", "sparrow",
                                  "frog", "toad" };
```

```
        cout << "\nThis animal is a(n) " << AnimalType[type] <<
            " (" << SpeciesTypes[whatIam] << ")";
        cout << "\nName: " << name << " born on ";
        birth.ShowDate();
}
```

There are three derived classes, Mammal, Amphibian, and Bird. The three children classes all contain a variable specific to that type of animal as well as a SayHello and FavoriteFood function. Notice how each constructor function has five input parameters, four of which are passes to the base class constructor. The three child classes are:

```
class Mammal : public Animal
{
private:
        double height;
public:
        Mammal(Category t, Species s, string n, Date b, double h);
        void SayHello();
        void FavoriteFood();
};


class Bird: public Animal
{
private:
        double wingspan;
public:
        Bird(Category t, Species s, string n, Date b, double w);
        void SayHello();
        void FavoriteFood();
};


class Amphibian: public Animal
{
private:
        double length;
public:
        Amphibian(Category t, Species s, string n, Date b, double l);
        void SayHello();
        void FavoriteFood();
};
```

The Mammal, Bird, and Amphibian classes appear very small, but they all have the protected and public members of the Animal class. To avoid redundancy, let's examine just the Mammal functions because the Bird and Amphibian functions have similar features. The Mammal constructor function passes all but the height value to the Animal constructor.

```
Mammal::Mammal(Category t, Species s, string n, Date b, double h)
      :Animal(t, s, n, b)
{
      height = h;
}


void Mammal::SayHello()
{
      if(whatIam == dog)
             cout << "\n Bark Bark hello!";
      else if( whatIam == cat)
             cout << "\n Meeeeooowwww hello! ";

      cout << " and I'm " << height << " feet tall. ";
}


void Mammal::FavoriteFood()
{
      if(whatIam == dog)
             cout << "\n I love to eat cookies! \n";
      else if( whatIam == cat)
             cout << "\n I love to eat birds! \n" ;
}
```

The main function simply declares three animals: a dog, a scrub jay, and a frog. The Write function is a base class function and it reports the base class parameters. The SayHello and FavoriteFood are child-specific functions. A temporary Date variable is created so that the different birthdays may be passed into the constructor functions. Refer to Program 11-11. The program output is shown below:

The Animals Program

This animal is a(n) mammal (dog)
Name: Noel born on 12/25/1995
Bark Bark hello! and I'm 2.5 feet tall.
I love to eat cookies!

This animal is a(n) amphibian (frog)
Name: Spooky born on 6/10/1999
Ribbit hello SPLASH! and I'm 0.4 feet long.
I love to eat flies!

```
//Program 11-11 The Animals Program
int main()
{
        cout << "\n The Animals Program " << endl;

        Date temp;
        temp.SetDate(12,25,1995);
        Mammal Fido(mammal, dog, "Noel", temp, 2.5);
        Fido.Write();
        Fido.SayHello();
        Fido.FavoriteFood();

        temp.SetDate(6,10,1999);
        Amphibian GreenGuy(amphibian, frog, "Spooky", temp, 0.4);
        GreenGuy.Write();
        GreenGuy.SayHello();
        GreenGuy.FavoriteFood();

        temp.SetDate(4,25,1998);
        Bird Noisy(bird, scrubjay, "Mrs Blue", temp, 1.8);
        Noisy.Write();
        Noisy.SayHello();
        Noisy.FavoriteFood();

        cout << "\n What a busy place! \n\n";
        return 0;
}
```

This animal is a(n) bird (scrubjay)
Name: Mrs Blue born on 4/25/1998
SqqqquuuuAAAAKKK hello! and my wingspan is 1.8 feet
I love to eat peanuts!

What a busy place!

Shuffle and Deal the Cards

This program example models the process of shuffling and dealing playing cards. There are two players in this game—one is the Dealer. The Dealer has fifty-two cards. The Dealer object shuffles the cards by placing them in a random order. Once the Dealer has shuffled the cards, he or she draws the top card and passes it to the Player, who picks up the card and places it in his or her hand. The Dealer takes the next card and gives it to him- or herself. Then the Player receives the third card; the dealer, the fourth; and so on. For this example, we have both players receiving four cards. Once both players have four cards, each shows the other his or her cards.

Imagine you and your friend sitting down with a deck of cards. You have the cards and are the Dealer. Once you have shuffled the cards, you deal four cards (alternately) to the Player and yourself and then both of you show your hands. This program simulates the shuffle, the deal, and showing the cards. This card game may not be ready for Las Vegas, but it does lay the groundwork for many card games.

Program User Interface   The user interface for this program is shown below. The Shuffle and Deal Program asks the user for a random number seed value and then presents the user with five choices in a simple menu. Card-handling routines in addition to the deal option are presented.

Welcome to the Shuffle and Deal Program!

Please enter an integer for the random number generator seed.

Pick your option:

1 Show Original Deck	**3 New Shuffle**	
2 Show Shuffled Cards	**4 Deal 4 Cards and Show Hands**	**5 Exit**

The random number generator is seeded only once in the main driver function. The menu items show the user's five options. A switch statement handles the user's input.

Object-Oriented Program Design

The first question asked by a programmer when designing an object-oriented program is: "What objects are needed?" Design your program based on single objects—do not worry about how many of each type are needed. The Shuffle and Deal Program needs the Card class, which we developed in the previous chapter. A single card has a suit (such as diamonds) and rank (such as 2). Each card must be able to set the suit and rank and to display itself. (The program's Dealer object will have fifty-two of these Card objects.) The cards do not deal themselves; the dealer deals the cards. There is no deal function with the cards.

We must have an object that represents your friend, the Player. What does the Player have and what does the Player do? The Player has a four-card hand. The Player must have the ability to add a card to the hand and keep count of the number of cards in the hand, and the Player must show his or her hand. Figure 11-9 illustrates this situation.

The last object in our program design is the Dealer. The Dealer must perform several tasks. The Dealer has an array of fifty-two cards. He or she must shuffle the cards and deal them to him- or herself and the player. For our program, we give the

Card object

Each card has a rank and a suit,
such as the two of diamonds.

We need to be able to
set the suit and rank and
to show the card.

Player object

Each player has a hand of four cards.

We need to know how many cards are in the hand.

We need to be able to give the
player a card. When the player is
given a card, the card is placed
in the hand array.

Last, we need to be able to
show the hand.

11

Figure 11-9
Card and Player Objects

Dealer the ability to show the fifty-two cards (both shuffled and in the original order). You should be saying, "Hey, isn't the Dealer a Player?" The Dealer *is a* Player. We will create a CPlayer class and then derive a CDealer class. The data and functions that the player has will be inherited by the CDealer, and additional deal and show cards functions will be added to the CDealer class. See Figure 11-10.

CDealer object

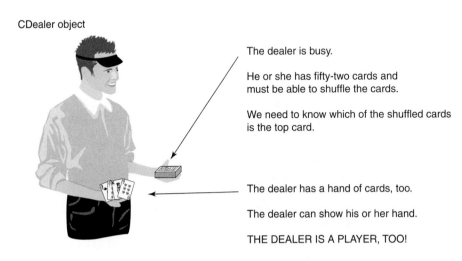

The dealer is busy.

He or she has fifty-two cards and must be able to shuffle the cards.

We need to know which of the shuffled cards is the top card.

The dealer has a hand of cards, too.

The dealer can show his or her hand.

THE DEALER IS A PLAYER, TOO!

The dealer must deal cards to her- or himself and to the player.

Figure 11-10
CDealer Object

The Driver Source Code   Before we get to the details of the class functions, let's look at the main function, which acts as our driver. After a greeting is presented and the user enters a seed value for the random number generator, the program creates two objects, a CDealer named Bob and a CPlayer named Lucy.

```
//Program 11-12 Shuffle and Deal
int main()
{
        CDealer Bob;    // we have Bob, our CDealer Object; he has 52 Cards
        CPlayer Lucy;   // we have Lucy, our CPlayer Object
```

Bob, our Dealer, shuffles the cards before we start. A while loop allows the user to continue selecting an option until exiting. The user's menu choice is handled with the following switch statement.

```
        Bob.Shuffle();  // Our Dealer shuffles the deck before we start

        int choice, enough;
        bool goodbye = false;
        while (goodbye == false)
        {
                choice = ShowMenu();   // Shows user options
                switch(choice)
                {
                    case 1:    // show cards
                          Bob.ShowOrigCards();
                          break;
                    case 2:    // show shuffled cards
                          Bob.ShowShuffledCards();
                          break;
                    case 3:
                          Bob.Shuffle();
                          Bob.ShowShuffledCards();
                          break;
                    case 4:    // deal four cards to the dealer and player
                          enough = Bob.WhereIsTheTop();
                          if(enough < 43)
                          {
                                  Bob.Deal4Cards(&Lucy);
                                  cout << "\n Player--Lucy's Hand: ";
                                  Lucy.ShowHand();  // Player shows her hand
                                  cout << "\n Dealer--Bob's Hand: ";
                                  Bob.ShowHand();   //Dealer shows his hand
                          }
```

```
            else
                    cout << "\n\n Not enough cards to deal, sorry.  \n";
            break;
    case 5:
            goodbye = true;
            break;
    default:
            cout << "\n I don't do that option!   \n ";
  }
}
```

Class Declarations

The Card declaration is straightforward and includes enumerated data types for the rank and suit as well as Set and Show card functions. The CPlayer class declaration has an array of Cards that is the Hand of cards. When the Dealer deals a card to the Player, the card is placed into the hand. A counter variable is used to keep track of the number of cards in the hand (cards_in_hand). Notice that the data is protected—not private—in the CPlayer class. The Player must be able to show the hand. The ShowHand function will use the ShowCard function in the Card class. See Figure 11-11. The CDealer class is inherited from the CPlayer. The CDealer has an array of fifty-two Cards, and additional functions in the CDealer class are used for shuffling, showing, and dealing the cards. See Figure 11-12.

CPlayer Functions   The CPlayer functions are short. The constructor sets the cards_in_hand counter to zero. The GetCard function has a single Card as the input. This new card is placed in the Hand array, and the cards_in_hand counter is incremented. The ShowHand function performs a loop and shows each of the cards in the hand. The Card function, ShowCard, is called for each card. Once the Player shows the hand, the cards_in_hand counter is reset to zero in anticipation of the next hand.

```
//File:  CPlayer.cpp

#include <iostream.h>
#include "Card.h"
#include "CPlayer.h"

CPlayer::CPlayer()
{
      cout << "\n In the CPlayer constructor. ";
      cards_in_hand = 0;;
}
```

Card class declaration

```
//File: Card.h

#ifndef_CARD_H
#define_CARD_H

enum Suit { club, diamond, heart, spade};
enum Rank { two = 2, three, four, five, six, seven, eight, nine, ten, jack, queen, king, ace};

class Card
{
private:
        Suit color;
        Rank number;
public:
        Card();
        void SetSuit(Suit s ){ color = s; }
        void SetRank(Rank r ){ number = r; }
        void ShowCard();
};

#endif
```

Each card has a rank and a suit, such as the two of diamonds.

We need to be able to set the suit and rank and to show the card.

CPlayer class declaration

```
//File: CPlayer.h

#ifndef_CPLAYER_H
#define_CPLAYER_H

#include "Card.h"

class CPlayer
{
protected:
        Card Hand[4];   // the players have a hand of cards
        int cards_in_hand;
public:
        CPlayer();
        void GetCard( Card X );
        void ShowHand();
};
#endif
```

Each player has an array of card objects (hand of cards).

We need to know how many cards are in the hand.

We need to be able to give the player a card. When the player is given a card, the card is placed in the hand array.

We need to be able to show the hand.

Figure 11-11
Card and CPlayer Class Declarations

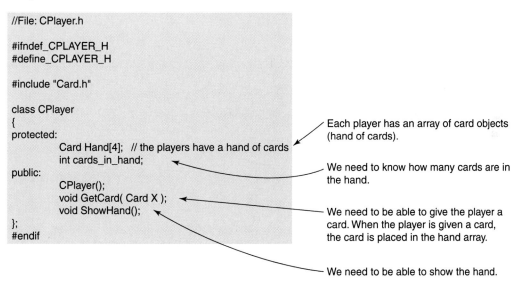

CDealer class declaration

```
//File: CDealer.h

#ifndef_CDEALER_H
#define_CDEALER_H

#include "Card.h"
#include "CPlayer.h"

class CDealer: public CPlayer
{
private:
        Card card[52];
        int index[52];
        int top_card;  // index that points to the top card in the deck

public:

        CDealer() ;

        void Shuffle();
        void ShowOrigCards();
        void ShowShuffledCards();
        void Deal4Cards(CPlayer* X);
        int WhereIsTheTop() { return top_card;}

};

#endif
```

The dealer is a player, too. The CDealer is derived from the CPlayer class. It inherits the hand of cards, cards_in_hand variable, and ShowHand and GetCard functions.

The dealer has fifty-two cards and an index array that contains the shuffle order for the fifty-two cards.

We need to know which of the shuffled cards is the top card.

The dealer constructor must set up the fifty-two cards.

The dealer shuffles the cards, shows both shuffled and unshuffled cards.

The dealer deals a card to a player. We need to know which player gets the card (use the address operator). The dealer can deal a card directly into his or her hand.

Figure 11-12
CDealer Class Declaration

```
void CPlayer::GetCard(Card newcard)
{
        Hand[cards_in_hand] = newcard;
        ++cards_in_hand;
}
void CPlayer::ShowHand()
{
        int i;
        for(i=0; i < cards_in_hand; ++i) Hand[i].ShowCard();
        cards_in_hand = 0; //reset count for next hand
}
```

CDealer's Constructor Function   The Dealer's constructor function sets the suit and rank of the fifty-two Cards in the order of ace of spades to deuce of clubs. A card_ctr variable is the array index, and the Card's SetSuit and SetRank functions are called for each of the fifty-two card objects. There are four suits for the cards (spades, hearts, diamonds, and clubs) and thirteen cards for each suit (2, 3, 4, . . . , king, ace). A nested for loop runs through the four suits, setting each of the thirteen card ranks. (The enumerated data for Suit and Rank allows us to use just the integer value to set the card values.) The first Card[0] is assigned a suit value of 3 (spades) and a rank value of 14 (ace). The last card, Card[51], is assigned the suit value 0 (clubs) and rank value of 2. Therefore, our array is filled from ace of spades to two of clubs. When the user views the original cards, he or she sees the order just described.

```
CDealer::CDealer()
{
//The CDealer constructor will set up the 52 cards
//and set top of deck to zero
        cout << "\n In the Dealer constructor.    ";

        top_card = 0;
        int i, j, card_ctr = 0;  // array index

        for (i = 3; i >= 0; --i)  // four suits
        {
                for(j = 14; j >=2; --j) // ace to two
                {
                        card[card_ctr].SetSuit((Suit) i);
                        card[card_ctr].SetRank((Rank) j);
                        ++ card_ctr;
                }
        }

        for (i=0; i<52; ++i) index[i]=i;  // fill index array 0 to 51
}
```

There is also an index array in the CDealer class. This array actually holds the index values for the shuffled cards.

Shuffling the Cards The random number generator is used to shuffle the cards. The shuffling scheme we use is simple. We generate a random number between and including 0 and 51 (for example, 17). This value represents the card in the original array that is the first card in the shuffled deck. The second random number is the index of the original card that is our second shuffled card.

Instead of mixing up the cards in the card array, we mix up integer values in an indexed array. The index array represents the order of the shuffled cards and is referenced when accessing the shuffled cards. This technique of using an index array is hard to visualize at first. Let's take it a step at a time. Initially, we fill the fifty-two cards with a suit and a rank, and we fill the index array with integer values from 0 up to and including 51. Figure 11-13 shows the initial array values.

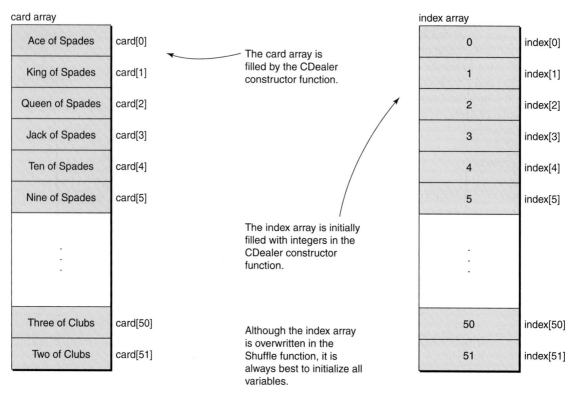

card array

Ace of Spades	card[0]
King of Spades	card[1]
Queen of Spades	card[2]
Jack of Spades	card[3]
Ten of Spades	card[4]
Nine of Spades	card[5]
. . .	
Three of Clubs	card[50]
Two of Clubs	card[51]

The card array is filled by the CDealer constructor function.

The index array is initially filled with integers in the CDealer constructor function.

Although the index array is overwritten in the Shuffle function, it is always best to initialize all variables.

index array

0	index[0]
1	index[1]
2	index[2]
3	index[3]
4	index[4]
5	index[5]
. . .	
50	index[50]
51	index[51]

Figure 11-13
Initial Card and Index Array Values

The shuffle function obtains fifty-two different random numbers between and including 0 and 51 and places them in the index array. The value in the index[0] element represents the first card in the shuffled deck. The value in index[1] represents the second card in the shuffled deck. If 5 is in index[0], the sixth card in the card array (remember that zero begins the indexed arrays) is the top card in the shuffled deck. When the program accesses the shuffled card, the index array is used. Figure 11-14 shows this relationship.

This technique of mixing or sorting an array of items with an index array is commonly used in applications. It is quicker and easier to sort or mix integer array values than it is to sort or mix large structures or classes. Several techniques are used for obtaining values for the index array. The trick, of course, is in not using the same number twice. In this example, we use a local Boolean array named "check" that is size 52 and is initially filled with the false values. The check array element is set to true if a value has been placed in the index array. (For instance, if our random number is 17, we place 17 in index[0] and set check[17] to true.) Each time we get a random number between 0 and 51, we check the check array. If the check value is

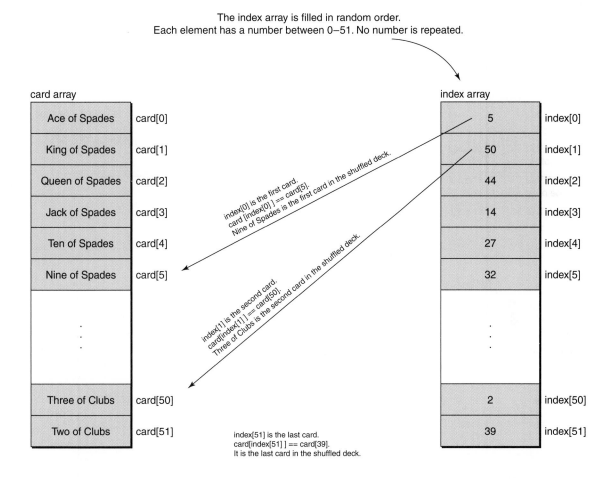

The index array is filled in random order.
Each element has a number between 0–51. No number is repeated.

card array

Ace of Spades	card[0]
King of Spades	card[1]
Queen of Spades	card[2]
Jack of Spades	card[3]
Ten of Spades	card[4]
Nine of Spades	card[5]

index array

5	index[0]
50	index[1]
44	index[2]
14	index[3]
27	index[4]
32	index[5]

index[0] is the first card.
card [index[0]] == card[5].
Nine of Spades is the first card in the shuffled deck.

index[1] is the second card.
card[index[1]] == card[50].
Three of Clubs is the second card in the shuffled deck.

| Three of Clubs | card[50] |
| Two of Clubs | card[51] |

| 2 | index[50] |
| 39 | index[51] |

index[51] is the last card.
card[index[51]] == card[39].
It is the last card in the shuffled deck.

The index array is used when the program is accessing the shuffled cards.

card[index[i]].ShowCard( ); // where i is the card we want to show

Figure 11-14
Index Array and Shuffled Cards Relationship

false, we place the number in the index array, set the check value to true, and generate another random number. The check array ensures that each value in the index array is unique and between and including 0 and 51. See Figure 11-15. Here is the source code for the Dealer's Shuffle function:

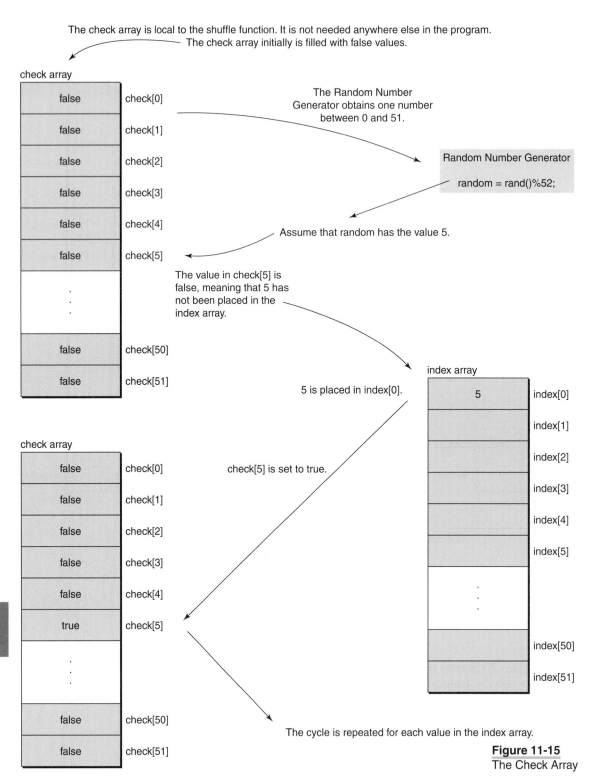

The check array is local to the shuffle function. It is not needed anywhere else in the program.

The check array initially is filled with false values.

check array

false	check[0]
false	check[1]
false	check[2]
false	check[3]
false	check[4]
false	check[5]
. . .	
false	check[50]
false	check[51]

The Random Number Generator obtains one number between 0 and 51.

Random Number Generator

random = rand()%52;

Assume that random has the value 5.

The value in check[5] is false, meaning that 5 has not been placed in the index array.

index array

5	index[0]
	index[1]
	index[2]
	index[3]
	index[4]
	index[5]
. . .	
	index[50]
	index[51]

5 is placed in index[0].

check array

false	check[0]
false	check[1]
false	check[2]
false	check[3]
false	check[4]
true	check[5]
. . .	
false	check[50]
false	check[51]

check[5] is set to true.

The cycle is repeated for each value in the index array.

Figure 11-15
The Check Array

```
void Dealer::Shuffle()
{
        int i, random, top_card = 0;
        bool check[52];

//zero all values in the check array--
//this keeps track of numbers we've used
        for(i=0; i<52; ++i) check[i] = false;

        int got_a_good_one = 0;
        for(i=0; i < 52 ; ++i)
        {

                // loop until we get a number not yet used
                while( got_a_good_one == 0)
                {
                        random = rand()%52;    // returns from 0 to 51
                        if(check[random] == false)
                        {
                                index[i] = random;
                                check[random] = true;  // set check to true
                                got_a_good_one = 1;    // stop the loop
                        }
                }
                got_a_good_one = 0;  // ready for next one

        }

}
```

Dealing the Cards   The deal task, which includes interaction between the Dealer and the Player, is the most complicated function (syntactically speaking) in this program, yet it is implemented exactly as you would normally deal a card in an actual game. You will be the Dealer to help illustrate what we mean. First, shuffle the cards. Then take the first card from the top of the deck and pass it to the Player. The Player then picks up that card and puts it in his or her hand. Take the next card and add it to your hand. Next, take the top card from the deck (the third card in the shuffled deck) and pass it to the Player. The Player places the card in his or her hand (it is the second card in the hand). This routine continues until each of you has four cards.

The Deal4Cards function is structured in the same way. First we must check to see if there are enough cards to deal. The WhereIsTheTop function returns the value in top_card. Recall that the top_card variable points to the index array element representing the shuffled deck. If there are less than eight cards in the shuffled deck, we cannot deal another hand. The deal function is invoked (if there are enough cards to deal), using Bob, our Dealer object.

11

```
case 4:      // deal four cards to the dealer and player
        enough = Bob.WhereIsTheTop();
        if(enough < 43)
        {
               Bob.Deal4Cards(&Lucy);
               cout << "\n Player--Lucy's Hand: ";
               Lucy.ShowHand();   // Player shows her hand
               cout << "\n Dealer--Bob's Hand: ";
               Bob.ShowHand();   //Dealer shows his hand
        }
        else
               cout << "\n\n Not enough cards to deal, sorry.  \n";

        break;
```

Notice that we pass the Player's address to the function. The Deal4Cards must be given the address of the Player to be able to deal cards to that Player. Then, using the right-arrow operator, the function calls the Player's GetCard function—placing the card into the Player's hand. Figure 11-16 describes this process.

11.7
Polymorphism and Virtual Functions

Polymorphism—One Interface, Many Forms

polymorphism

one interface, many implementations

Polymorphism is a concept supported by object-oriented languages. A literal definition of *polymorphism* is "one interface, many forms or methods." What does this definition mean? A computer's CD drive provides an easy way to illustrate polymorphism. To operate a computer's CD drive, you press a button on the front of the player and the door glides open. You place a compact disk on the rack and push a button to close the door. The drive starts, whether it is playing music or accessing computer data. No matter who makes CD drives for computers, the drives all operate in the same manner; that is, there is "one interface" (one way to interact with it) and there are "many methods" (different vendor CD drives).

Another example of a single interface, multiple forms, is a key and lock. There are many different types of lock and key systems, such as the lock on your front door, the lock on your car door, or a padlock. The interface for whatever type of key and lock is the same: you insert the key in the lock and turn the key to unlock the door or padlock. Although locks have different mechanisms and keys look different, the key and lock interface is the same.

How do these concepts relate to C++ programming? In C++ programs, it is possible to create several implementations that have the same name, thus reducing program complexity. For example, borrowing from our lock and key idea, it is possible to build several CLockandKey classes (i.e., padlock key, door key, car key,

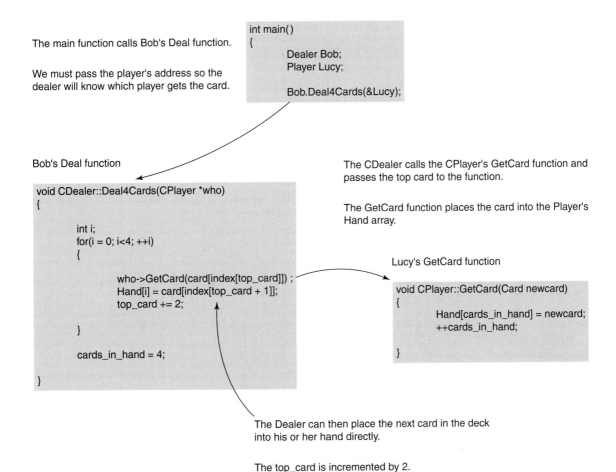

The main function calls Bob's Deal function.

We must pass the player's address so the dealer will know which player gets the card.

```
int main()
{
        Dealer Bob;
        Player Lucy;

        Bob.Deal4Cards(&Lucy);
```

Bob's Deal function

The CDealer calls the CPlayer's GetCard function and passes the top card to the function.

The GetCard function places the card into the Player's Hand array.

```
void CDealer::Deal4Cards(CPlayer *who)
{

        int i;
        for(i = 0; i<4; ++i)
        {

                who->GetCard(card[index[top_card]]) ;
                Hand[i] = card[index[top_card + 1]];
                top_card += 2;

        }

        cards_in_hand = 4;

}
```

Lucy's GetCard function

```
void CPlayer::GetCard(Card newcard)
{
        Hand[cards_in_hand] = newcard;
        ++cards_in_hand;

}
```

The Dealer can then place the next card in the deck into his or her hand directly.

The top_card is incremented by 2.

Figure 11-16
Mechanics of Dealing a Card in the Shuffle and Deal Program

etc.). Each class contains a Lock and an Unlock function specific for that type of lock. If our program then has many different types of CLockandKey objects, we simply call the Lock and Unlock functions as needed for each of the different types of objects. Behind the scenes, the correct function is accessed for each object.

You may ask yourself, "Aren't overloaded functions providing us with multiple implementation with a single function name?" Yes! Overloaded functions and operators are referred to as **compile-time polymorphism**. When the program is compiled, the compiler and the linker work together so that the location (address) of each function is known for each call. (The computer term for this process is "early binding.") At program execution time, there is no question about which one of the overloaded functions is to be called. Chapter 8 had three forms of the Say-

compile-time polymorphism
the condition in which the program knows exactly which function will be called at each call statement

Goodnight function. When we compile and link a program that has SayGood-night();, SayGoodnight("Dick");, and SayGoodnight("Dick", "Jane");, the program knows exactly which SayGoodnight function is to be called in each call statement once the program is linked.

A second form of polymorphism, known as *run-time polymorphism*, uses inheritance and virtual functions. (The computer term for this is "late binding.") The program sometimes does not know exactly which function is to be called until the program is executing. Why do we care about this? Imagine a base class, such as Shape, that is used to derive many new classes, such as Sphere, Pyramid, Cone, and Box. Assume that each of the Shape children classes have a same-name function, such as DrawMyself. If the program user can select one of the Shapes, then the program will be calling one of the DrawMyself functions, but we aren't sure which shape is drawn until the program executes. This programming method is accomplished by "virtual" functions. These special functions provide a way to access a derived class function via a pointer during run-time. This ability provides a very powerful and flexible programming tool.

run-time polymorphism

the condition in which the program does not know which function will be called until execution

What Is a Virtual Function?

virtual function

function in a base class; the child class redefines this function for its specific use

A *virtual function* is a class member function located in a base class. When this base class is used to derive a new class, this new child class redefines the virtual function to fit its specific needs. Virtual functions are accessed by objects in the usual fashion; however, the power in virtual functions is achieved when a program uses a pointer to access the functions.

Virtual Shapes: Part 1 Let's use an example to show how virtual functions operate. We make a base class called Shape that has a virtual function WhatAmI. Note that the keyword *virtual* is used in the class member prototype. We derive two classes from Shape: Sphere and Pyramid. Both children classes have WhatAmI functions (no virtual keyword) and the functions have been rewritten specifically for each shape.

```
class Shape
{
public:
        //Note: virtual keyword here and not in children
        virtual void WhatAmI() { cout << "\n I am the basic shape. \n "; }
};
class Pyramid:public Shape
{
public:
        void WhatAmI() { cout << "\n I am a pyramid. \n"; }
};
```

```
class Sphere : public Shape
{
public:
        void WhatAmI() { cout << "\n I am a sphere. \n"; }
};
```

Here comes the hard part. If a programmer declares a pointer to the base class and assigns the address of a derived class into that pointer (legal in C++), then the derived class virtual function is accessed via that pointer. In the short main program in Program 11-13, we declare a Shape, Sphere and Pyramid objects, as well as a pointer to the base class. The addresses of the various objects are assigned into this pointer, and the WhatAmI function is called. Notice that the call to WhatAmI is identical for all three objects. The output below shows what the different WhatAmI functions are called:

```
//Program 11-13 Virtual Functions and Shapes
int main()
{
        cout << "\n The Virtual Shapes Program " << endl;

        Shape *ptr_to_base, MyShape;
        Sphere MySphere;
        Pyramid MyPyramid;

        ptr_to_base = &MyShape;     // base pointer points to Base class
        ptr_to_base->WhatAmI();

        ptr_to_base = &MySphere;   // pointer now points to the Sphere
        ptr_to_base->WhatAmI();

        ptr_to_base = &MyPyramid;   // pointer now points to the Pyramid
        ptr_to_base->WhatAmI();

        cout << "\n Ohhh This is hard! \n\n";
        return 0;
}
```

The Virtual Shapes Program

I am the basic shape.
I am a sphere.
I am a pyramid.

Ohhh This is hard!

Virtual Shapes: Part 2   By expanding the Virtual Shapes: Part 1 example, we can derive two more shapes, a Cone and a Box, and include the WhatAmI function for both. If we place the addresses of our four derived objects into an array of Shape pointers, we can use the base pointer and a for loop to access all WhatAmI functions. See the main function in Program 11-14 for an illustration. The output is shown below:

The Virtual Shapes Program — Part 2

I am a cone.

I am a sphere.

I am a pyramid.

I am a box.

Ohhh This is getting easier!

```
//Program 11-14 Virtual Functions and Shapes Part 2
int main()
{
        cout << "\n The Virtual Shapes Program -- Part 2" << endl;

        Shape *ptr_to_base[4];       //WOW! An array of pointers!
        Sphere MySphere;
        Pyramid MyPyramid;
        Cone MyCone;
        Box MyBox;

        ptr_to_base[0] = &MyCone;            //each element gets a different Shape
        ptr_to_base[1] = &MySphere;
        ptr_to_base[2] = &MyPyramid;
        ptr_to_base[3] = &MyBox;

        for(int i = 0; i < 4; ++i)           //access all four WhatAmI functions
        {
                ptr_to_base[i]->WhatAmI();
        }

        cout << "\n Ohhh This is getting easier! \n\n";
        return 0;
}
```

Purely Virtual Functions

A virtual function does not require that an actual function body exist in the base class. The derived class functions often contain all the required code to perform whatever action is desired, and no code is needed in the base class. If a base class virtual function does not have an associated function body, it is said to be a *pure virtual function*. This type of function is designated in the base class declaration as shown here:

pure virtual function
no actual function implementation in the base class

```
class Base
{
public:
        // the = 0; means virtual
        virtual return_type FunctionName() = 0;
};
```

If we wish to have a pure virtual function in our Shape class, the declaration is:

```
class Shape
{
public:
        virtual void WhatAmI() = 0;    // virtual function
};
```

How Are Virtual Functions Useful?

Game Programming   Many different programming scenarios using virtual functions make a programmer's life much easier. Let's pretend you are writing the software for an adventure game based in New Mexico in the 1700s. In this game, there are different characters that may be drawn into the playing window, depending on the conditions in the current scene. These characters include our hero, her band of traveling companions, a dog, a pack of burros, a herd of sheep, and a handsome man—our hero's love interest. At any given time, you expect to have anywhere from one to thirty characters on the screen.

There are several design approaches for this game. One approach involves setting up a base class for all the characters in the game. We place several virtual functions in this base class, including AmIOnScreen (keeps track of whether the character is currently drawn on the screen), WhereAmI (reports screen location), and Draw (contains drawing information for the character). The base class and two children classes are shown here:

11

```
class GameCharacter
{
private:
        Screen Location;        // Screen is struct for coordinates
                                // other general data
public:
        virtual Screen WhereAmI();
        virtual bool AmIOnScreen();
        virtual void Draw();
};


class Hero : public GameCharacter
{
        // Hero data
public:
        Screen WhereAmI();
        bool AmIOnScreen();
        void Draw();
};


class Sheep: public GameCharacter
{
        // Sheep data
public:
        Screen WhereAmI();
        bool AmIOnScreen();
        void Draw();
};
```

The main part of the game declares not only a hero object but all the supporting characters listed above as well. A graphics game such as this one probably will be built in the Windows environment (if the target platform is a personal computer), and the graphics may be either OpenGL or DirectX. For our example, we simply pretend there is a main function:

```
int main()
{
        Hero Rosita;            //All game character objects declared here.
        Sheep BaaBaa[5];
        Dog Perro;
        //etc.
        :
        :
```

In the screen-handling portion of the game, we need to create an array of Game-Character pointers and assign the addresses of all the character objects.

```
GameCharacters *ptr_GameChar[100];
int NumberCharacters;
ptr_GameChar[0] = &Rosita;       //first pointer holds the hero's address
ptr_GameChar[1] = &Perro;        //next pointer holds the dog's address
for(i = 0; i < NumSheep; ++i)    //fill the next NumSheep with sheep's addresses
{
        ptr_GameChar[i+2] = &BaaBaa[i];
}
```

Once the GameCharacter pointer array contains the addresses of all the character objects, the drawing portion of the game can be handled in a simple for loop.

```
Screen place;         //local variable to hold screen coords
for (i = 0; i < NumberCharacters; ++i)
{
        //if true this char is on the screen
        if(ptr_GameChar[i]->AmIOnScreen())
        {
                //each object knows where it is
                place = ptr_GameChar[i]->WhereAmI();

                // use the screen coords and check for placement
                // conflict and then draw
                ptr_GameChar[i]->Draw();    //calls correct drawing routine
        }
}
```

Each game character object knows its location, whether it is on the screen at the current time, and how to draw itself. The programmer does not need to use large switch statements to determine which routine must be called; virtual functions handle that detail. There is always a small amount of overhead associated with setting up pointer arrays and filling them with addresses, but the payoff is great!

One Last Example: Two Vehicles   Let's do one last program and illustrate inheritance, array of pointers to base classes, and virtual functions one more time. The Two Vehicles program contains a base class for vehicle information. From this class, we derive two different vehicle classes: recreational (RV) and commercial (Semi). The base class has character strings for owner and license information. The member functions include virtual functions for obtaining and writing the information. To keep our example simple, we have an empty base class constructor. The Vehicle base class is:

```
class Vehicle
{
protected:
        char owner[50], license[20];
public:
        Vehicle(){};
        virtual void GetInfo();
        virtual void WriteInfo();
};
```

The RV and Semi children classes also have empty constructors. The RV class contains an integer category. The Semi class contains a double-valued weight-capacity variable.

```
class RV:public Vehicle
{
private:
        int category;          //RV size 1, 2, or 3
public:
        RV(){}  // empty constructor
        void GetInfo();
        void WriteInfo();
};

class Semi:public Vehicle
{
private:
        double weight_cap;                      //weight capacity
public:
        Semi(){}
        void GetInfo();
        void WriteInfo();
};
```

The Vehicle class function GetInfo asks the user to enter the owner and license information. The WriteInfo function uses a character string array to write the type to the screen.

```
void Vehicle::GetInfo()             //This is the Base class.
{
        cout << " \nEnter owner's name:  ";
        cin.getline(owner,50);
        cout << "\nEnter license plate, such as NM 123 ABC :  ";
        cin.getline(license,50);
}
```

```
void Vehicle::WriteInfo()
{
        cout << "\n\n          Owner: " << owner <<
        "\n      License: " << license;
}
```

Both the RV and Semi GetInfo and WriteInfo functions call the base class member functions for obtaining and writing the vehicle information. The RV functions are shown here:

```
void RV::GetInfo()
{
        char enter;
        cout << "\n Please enter information for the recreational vehicle.";
        Vehicle::GetInfo();        //call the base class GetInfo first
        cout << "\nEnter RV category  1, 2, or 3 ";
        cin >> category;
        cin.get(enter);            // pull off Enter key left by cin
}
```

```
void RV::WriteInfo()
{
        Vehicle::WriteInfo();
        cout << "\n This RV is a category " << category;
}
```

The main function in Program 11-15 shows the power that virtual functions provide for the C++ programmer. The RV object is assigned into the base[0] element. When this element's virtual functions are called, the RV functions are executed. The Semi object is assigned into base[1]. Again, note that the Semi functions are executed when the virtual functions are called. The use of for loops provides a simple way to call the appropriate functions. The program output is shown below:

The Two Vehicles Program
Please enter information for the recreational vehicle.
Enter owner's name: Jennifer Marie
Enter license plate such as NM 123 ABC : GA 999 XYZ
Enter RV category 1, 2, or 3 3

Please enter information for the commercial vehicle.
Enter owner's name: Hannah Marie

Enter license plate such as NM 123 ABC : NM 987 ABC

Enter the weight capacity 45000

```
//Program 11-15 Two Vehicles and Virtual Functions
int main()
{
        cout << "\n The Two Vehicles Program \n " << endl;
        int i;

        Vehicle *base[2];    //two pointers to the base class
        RV HaveFun;          // HaveFun and GoToWork are derived class objects
        Semi GoToWork;

        base[0] = &HaveFun; //assign RV and Semi addresses into base class pointers
        base[1] = &GoToWork;

        //obtain the information using the virtual functions
        for(i = 0; i < 2; ++i)
        {
                base[i]->GetInfo();
        }

        //now write the information
        for(i = 0; i < 2; ++i)
        {
                base[i]->WriteInfo();
        }
        cout << "\n\n Let's go camping!  \n\n";
        return 0;
}
```

Owner: Jennifer Marie
License: GA 999 XYZ
This RV is a category 3

Owner: Hannah Marie
License: NM 987 ABC
This commercial vehicle has a weight capacity of 45000

Let's go camping!

▓ 11.8
Summary

Inheritance is an important principle in object-oriented software and involves the ability to take an existing class and derive new classes from it. This ability to create new classes from existing ones opens the door to writing software that is modular and expandable. It allows the programmer to customize and/or modify code through the use of derived classes, with minimal modifications to the base classes.

Also, many commercial software businesses build ***commercial off-the-shelf (COTS) software*** libraries that may be incorporated into software projects. COTS software often provides complete tools with specialized software functionality. Software developers often use a COTS product whenever possible because it is usually much cheaper to buy a package than to write code from scratch. For example, if you are writing a program that requires two-dimensional x-y plots, several COTS graphing products are relatively easy to hook into the code. (Figuring out the hooks is much easier than writing your own two-dimensional graphics package.) Many of the tools available today are object-oriented and provide the developer with classes that can be used either directly or as base classes for custom work. Other COTS software products include translator software that reads and writes certain types of data files (such as image files or computer-aided design files). If your software needs to support industry standard file formats, chances are excellent that translator packages are available. It is not uncommon for translator software developers to add custom features on request—for a fee, of course.

commercial off-the-shelf (COTS) software products that may be purchased by software developers to use in the developer's own software

One last note before we leave the subject of inheritance, remember to KISS your software—that is, Keep It Simple, Sweetie. Classes and inheritance are powerful software tools that may easily be misused and made overly complex. It is possible to write C++ code that contains derived classes many layers deep. (You may have great-great-great-grandchildren classes!) After the first two or three layers, a programmer may forget what data and functions an object contains. Design your software in a straightforward manner, document your source code, and limit your class derivations, and you will be a much happier software developer. (And the person who has to maintain your code in the future will be happy, too!)

▮ REVIEW QUESTIONS AND PROBLEMS

Short Answer

1. Is it possible for children classes to access the private data in their base class?

2. What must happen to allow private members of a class to be inherited by a derived class?

3. If a child class is to contain the public and protected members of its base class as protected members, which access specifier must be used?

4. When is an empty base class constructor function necessary?

5. What is meant by a purely virtual function?

6. Describe the order of function execution for base and derived constructor functions and for destructor functions.

7. Locks and keys and CD players are examples of polymorphism: "one interface, many methods." Can you think of another example?

8. Name three goals for well-written software.

9. Describe how a pure virtual function (the prototype) is written.

10. Search the Internet for two COTS packages that provide C++ classes.

Programming Problems

Write complete C++ programs for Problems 11 to 13.

11. Write a program that sets up a base class Sailor containing protected data for name, rank, and serial number. There should be two constructor functions: one is empty and the other has the three data values as inputs. (Look at the CPerson class for assistance.) The other member functions should include a GetInfo function (asks the user for Sailor information) as well as a WriteInfo (writes all the Sailor data to the screen).

Next derive a new class from Sailor. The Sailor_At_Sea class has the name of the ship to which the Sailor has been assigned, as well as the name of the ship's home port. The Sailor_At_Sea class also has two constructor functions: one that does nothing and the other that receives *all* the possible Sailor data. This constructor passes the Sailor data to the base class constructor. There are also WriteInfo and GetInfo functions that call the associated Sailor functions before handling the derived class specific data.

The main function has several steps. Initially it should declare one Sailor and one Sailor_At_Sea object. Simply make up all the data and pass it into the objects when they are created. Call the WriteInfo functions and verify that the objects were created with the data you passed into them. Next, change the information in both objects by calling the GetInfo functions, and then call the WriteInfo function to verify that the object data has been changed.

12. Use the Shuffle and Deal Program as a starting point for building your own blackjack card game that allows you (the user) to play blackjack against the computer. The Dealer is the computer and you are the Player. Here are the rules for a simplified version of the game:

- Both the Player and Dealer are dealt two cards to start.
- The game should tell the Player how many points he or she has based on the following scheme: aces count eleven points, face cards count 10, other cards are counted at face value.
- The Player is asked if he or she would like to be "hit" (i.e., dealt another card).
- The Player continues to be asked to receive cards until he or she "busts" (goes over twenty-one points) or "holds."
- If the Player busts, the game is over.
- If the player holds, the Dealer draws until it has eighteen points or higher (or it may bust). The game then reports who won the hand.
- No money is bet.

- The Player is asked if he or she would like to play another hand.
- A new game cannot begin if there are less than nine cards remaining in the deck.
- The main function will control the game using a series of while loops and a switch statement.
- Whenever the Dealer or the Player is dealt a card, both the Dealer and Player hands are written to the screen, along with the total points in each hand.

You can put the necessary logic in the main function for decision making and messages written to the screen (such as "You bust"). All card-handling and point-counting functions *must* be member functions.

13. Write a C++ program that sets up a base class BankAcct containing the protected data of a basic bank savings account (name, account number, and savings account balance). Your constructors should be set up so that the initial data is passed into them. The BankAcct class has three virtual functions: Deposit (add money to the savings account balance), Withdraw (subtract money from the saving account balance), and ShowAll (report all information).

Derive an ATM_BankAcct class from the BankAcct class that contains an ATM account number and personal identification number (PIN). The ATM_BankAcct class member functions (Withdraw and Deposit) have built-in fees associated with all the basic banking functions. The Withdraw function subtracts $2.50 from the balance as a bank fee. The Deposit function charges $1.00 if the deposit amount is less than $1,000. The fee is based on the balance prior to the transaction. The ATM_BankAcct class constructor is passed all the account information (name, account number, savings balance, ATM account number, and PIN).

Derive a third class, Gold_BankAcct, from the ATM_BankAcct. The Gold objects have all the ATM data, but the ATM fees are not charged if the current savings account balance is $20,000 or more. Gold accounts earn interest on the account if the balance is $5,000 or more. The interest rate is a Gold member variable, and it is passed into the Gold constructor with the other data. The interest is added into the base balance before any deposit is made.

In the main function, create one of all three types of bank account objects. Fill in the names and account numbers values for each object when it is created. Initialize the balances as follows:

BankAcct	$500
ATM_BankAcct	$1,500
ATM_GoldAcct	$25,000

Make an array of BankAcct pointers and assign each of the three object addresses into this array. Set up a loop that asks the user what type of banking transaction he or she wants. For whatever type of transaction, run a for loop and call the appropriate function. After each transaction, call the ShowAll functions, which report all data associated with each object. For example, if the user wishes to deposit $100, then $100 is deposited into each account. (Try to conserve screen space so that all the data may be written on the screen for each transaction.) Be sure to place error messages if the user attempts to perform an illegal transaction (i.e., not enough money in the account to make the requested withdrawal). Your program should ask the user if he or she wishes to perform another transaction. Quit the program when the user is finished.

14. Review Johnston's Dice Game presented in Chapter 10. Using inheritance, derive a new class called SuperDicePlayer from the DicePlayer class. A SuperDicePlayer is a DicePlayer. In addition to the DicePlayer's five white dice, a SuperDicePlayer has two red dice. When a SuperDicePlayer plays Johnston's Dice Game, the two red dice are rolled along with the five white dice, and the face values of all seven dice are added to the total. The risk associated with being a SuperDicePlayer is that, if the two red dice show the same value (for example, both show 5), the player automatically loses and his or her opponent wins.

Write a new SuperDicePlayer class (which is a child of the DicePlayer) and include an overloaded operator * (asterisk) that checks to see if the two red dice are the same. This operator returns a true if the values of the red dice are the same, a false if the values of the red dice are different. Set up a main function that has a DicePlayer versus a SuperDicePlayer. Use the system time to seed the random number generator for each game. Modify the DicePlayer and SuperDiceplayer classes and the main function presented in Chapter 10 so that you can watch each throw of the dice and see the face value of each die. Have the program wait for an Enter key before each round of dice tossing.

12

Advanced Topics in C++

KEY TERMS AND CONCEPTS

bytecode
dynamic memory allocation
exception handling
free
heap
Java™
Java Virtual Machine
just in time compilers
Microsoft Foundation Class
pointers to pointers
stack
templates
Windows Application Program
Interface (Win32 API)
Windows Messages

KEYWORDS AND OPERATORS

catch
delete
new
throw
try

CHAPTER OBJECTIVES

Present a brief description and program examples of many important advanced C++ topics.

Introduce the concept of dynamic memory allocation and the use of the new and delete operators.

Demonstrate how pointers to pointers are used in C++ programs.

Explain the exception-handling basics along with the use of the try, throw, and catch keywords.

Illustrate how the Microsoft Foundation Class Library (MFC) is an object-oriented tool set for Microsoft Windows application development.

Explore the Java™ Programming Language.

Introduce briefly the concept of a template and standard template library.

The Tip of the Iceberg!

We have worked hard in the last eleven chapters covering the basics of C++, but by no means have we presented all the language features. You can imagine yourself standing on an iceberg, having just walked around its entire peak. But an iceberg is like a mountain and there's a lot more to it than what you can see above the water! Your hard work learning the language will pay off, whether you are continuing your C++ studies or moving on to a different object-oriented language.

This final chapter presents several topics that a C++ programmer is sure to encounter if he or she continues in this field. We could write an entire book covering this material. In fact, there are many books that cover these topics in great detail. Trying to present all of C++ in one book is like trying to taste every dish at one of those country kitchen buffet restaurants! In this chapter we will sample the following programming topics:

1. *Dynamic memory allocation* is a method that allows the programmer to obtain and release memory as the program executes (via the keywords *new* and *delete*). For example, suppose you had to read a list of numbers from a data file and place these values into an array. You do not know how many numbers you have until your program is running. Dynamic memory allocation makes it possible for your program to obtain the necessary memory "on the fly" for your values. If you need memory for ten values or 10,000, you simply allocate what you need as you go.

2. A *star wars* section presents many ways in which pointers and indirection operators can be used in a program. Software design may dictate that you pass a pointer to a pointer or have a pointer to an array of pointers.

3. *Exception handling* is a graceful way to manage errors instead of having your program crash. In other words, the program can be set up to throw an exception when an error happens. An exception-handling routine is then called to let your program recover from the error. Exception handling has been incorporated into the C++ language and uses the keywords *try, catch*, and *throw*.

4. *Microsoft Foundation Class (MFC)* is one implementation of an object-oriented environment for the development of application programs for Microsoft Windows. All MFC items are derived from several base classes. If you need a dialog box in your application, you customize an MFC dialog box. Your dialog box comes complete with the necessary code. Some programmers love MFC and some don't. All we will do is provide an overview of this object-oriented area and allow you to make your own judgments.

5. The *Java*™ programming language is object-oriented by design. Its principal goal is to provide a tool for building highly portable applications. A better word to describe Java is that it is cross-platform—it is possible to compile your code once and then run it anywhere. We'll take a brief look at the language.

12.1
Dynamic Memory Allocation

Overview

dynamic memory allocation

the program obtaining memory for program variables "on the fly" (as the program executes)

Dynamic memory allocation means that memory for variables in your program is obtained "on the fly" (as your program executes). Two operators in C++ are used to perform dynamic memory allocation: new and delete. The new operator allocates memory and returns an address to that memory. The address is then stored in a pointer variable. The delete operator frees the memory allocated by the new operator.

Before we jump into the new and delete details, we should clarify the concept of memory allocation. Up to now, we have declared all our variables in declaration statements, such as

```
float numbers[100];         //all of these are valid declarations
Fplayer team[5];
Counter MyCounter, YourCounter;
int a,b,c;
```

All the array variables need the size value in the declaration statement. We have never tried to use a variable in an array declaration like the following:

```
int size;
cout << "\n Enter the size for the array.  ";
cin >> size;
float numbers[size];                //invalid declaration statement!!!!
```

This type of declaration is illegal. To have a variable size array, we must allocate memory with the new operator as the program executes. Once we have finished using the array, we de-allocate (or free) the memory by using the delete operator. In the C language, the functions that perform memory allocation are malloc and free, and they are located in C's stdlib library.

New and Delete Operators

The formats for the new and delete operators are

```
type *pointer_var;
pointer_var = new type;
delete pointer_var;
```

where the type is the data type for the allocated memory, and pointer_var is a pointer to the reserved memory. If we need to reserve memory for an integer value, we follow that format. To access the memory, we use the pointer and the indirection operator.

```
int *int_pointer;        //set up a pointer to an integer

int_pointer = new int;   //pointer receives the address to reserved memory

*int_pointer = 5;        //assign 5 where the pointer is pointing

delete pointer;          //to free the memory, we use delete
```

To allocate memory for an array, we use the array operator [] in the new and delete statements. Once we have the memory, we can access the array elements in the usual manner. (Remember, the array name is always a pointer to the [0] element.) Let's assume we wish to allocate memory for 1,000 doubles:

```
int i;
double *d_pointer;           //set up a pointer to a double

d_pointer = new double[1000];    //pointer receives the address
for(i = 0; i < 1000; ++i)   //assign 0.0 into each element
{
     d_pointer[i] = 0.0;
}

//release the memory when finished using the array
delete [] d_pointer;
```

How Big an Array Would You Like?   The simple array program in Program 12-1 asks the user to enter a size value for an array of random numbers. We'll use the modulus operator to scale the numbers generated by the rand function to something the user desires. The new operator lets us allocate the exact size for the array.

```
//Program 12-1   How big an array would you like?
//File Ch12HowBigOfAnArray.cpp

#include <iostream>
using namespace std;

int main()
{
        int i, size, limit;

        cout << "\n What size array would you like?   ";
        cin >> size;
        cout << "\n\n Now, your random numbers should go from 0 to what integer? ";
        cin >> limit;

        int *pArrayOfRands;
        pArrayOfRands = new int[size];

        srand(123);                       //seed the random number generator
        for (i= 0; i < size; ++i)
        {
                pArrayOfRands[i] = rand()%limit;
                cout << "\n i = " << i << " Rand# = " << pArrayOfRands[i];
        }

        cout << "\n Wow. That was a lot of numbers. " << endl;
        delete [] pArrayOfRands;
        return 0;
}
```

The program output for five random numbers ranging from 0 to 25,000 is shown below:

What size array would you like? 5

Now, your random numbers should go from 0 to what integer? 25000

i = 0 Rand# = 440
i = 1 Rand# = 19053
i = 2 Rand# = 23075
i = 3 Rand# = 13104
i = 4 Rand# = 7363
Wow. That was a lot of numbers.

New with Classes and Structures   The new and delete allocation schemes are also used for classes and structures. The programmer needs to remember that the handle to our object or structures is through the pointer that is returned by the new operator. Therefore, we access the object or structure members using the right-arrow operator—just as we did when we passed an address of an object to a function. The class constructor function is called when the object is created, and the destructor function is called when the object goes out of scope.

Let's look at a few examples from our past programs. To allocate memory for a football player object and to access public functions, we do the following:

```
FPlayer *FP_ptr;          //here's our pointer to a Football player

FP_ptr = new Fplayer;     //allocate memory for one player

FP_ptr->SetName("Deion Husky");  //can access the public functions
FP_ptr->SetWeight(285);
FP_ptr->SetHeight(6,8);
FP_ptr->WriteInfo();

delete FP_ptr;            //free the memory when finished with our player
```

Initialization of Objects   Since the class constructor function is called when the new operator allocates memory, it is possible to initialize objects by providing the parameters in the new statement. In Chapter 9, the TwoDates program had a Date class with an overloaded constructor, as well as basic support functions. The class declaration is:

```
class CDate
{
private:
        int mon, day, year;
public:
        CDate();                   //set date to 1/1/2001
        CDate(int m, int d, int y);     //user's input
        void ShowDate();
        void SetDate(int m, int d, int y);
};
```

In the Chapter 9 version of the program, the main function declared two date objects. One object was created using the default constructor and the other used the overloaded constructor. The program then showed the dates, changed the dates, and showed them once again. We can rewrite this program so that the new operator allocates memory for our date objects. Refer to Program 12-2.

```
//Program 12-2  Rewrite of Two Date Objects (from Chapter 9)
//Reworked using new and delete operator.
int main()
{
        cout << "\n The NEW Two Dates Program.  \n";

        CDate *pMyDate, *pYourDate;     //sets up two pointers to Cdate

        pMyDate = new CDate;                   //calls the default constructor
        pYourDate = new CDate (5,5, 1955);     //calls the overloaded constructor

        cout << "\n\n The original dates are: ";
        cout << "\n The MyDate date is  ";
        pMyDate->ShowDate();                    //access member function through pointer

        cout << "\n The YourDate date is ";
        pYourDate->ShowDate();

        cout << "\n Now we'll change the dates.";
        pMyDate->SetDate(1,2,1956);
        pYourDate->SetDate(3,14,1994);

        cout << "\n\n The new dates are: ";
        cout << "\n The MyDate date is  ";
        pMyDate->ShowDate();

        cout << "\n The YourDate date is ";
        pYourDate->ShowDate();

        cout << "\n No more dates for you. " << endl;
        delete pMyDate;
        delete pYourDate;

        return 0;
}
```

heap

the portion of the
computer memory
where global and static
program variables are
stored along with the
memory reserved
during dynamic
memory allocation

What if New Fails?

The new operator reserves its memory in a location other than the local function variables. The local variables are held in the *stack*, whereas the allocated variables are stored on the **heap**. (The stack is changing constantly while your program runs. Local function variables are "stacked in" this memory when the function comes into scope, and they are "tossed off" the stack when the function is out of scope.)

The heap memory is quite large, but it is limited and may not be available when you request memory via the new operator.

If the new operator requests memory that is not available, the new operator fails. Aside from letting the program crash, the programmer can handle this error in one of two ways. The ISO Standard C++ dictates that when a new fails, a *bad_alloc* exception is generated and the program should handle this exception. If the exception is not handled, the program terminates. (We cover exactly how to do exception handling later in this chapter.)

A second way to trap for this error is to have the new operator return a NULL instead of throwing an exception. The pointer is assigned a NULL, which the programmer may check directly. (The malloc function in C returns a NULL if there isn't enough memory.) To use this form of error checking, the programmer may use the nothrow form of the new operator, which is:

```
pointer_var = new(nothrow) type;      //nothrow general form
```

The C++ new library must be included in your program. A specific example is shown below:

```
//Program 12-3 new with nothrow option
#include <iostream>
#include <new>                 //for the nothrow new operator
using namespace std;
int main()
{
        int *int_pointer;

        int_pointer = new(nothrow) int[100];          //memory for 100 ints
        if(int_pointer == NULL)                  //check the value in the pointer
        {
                cout << "\n NO MEMORY, BAIL OUT!";
                exit(1);
        }
        return 0;
}
```

The program should always trap for this potential run-time error!

12.2
Star Wars

How do you allocate memory for a two-dimensional array of numbers? How do you declare a pointer to a pointer? Do you use one * or two? If you pass an address to a function, which in turn passes that address to another function, do you use the & or not? Let's tackle one question at a time.

Allocating Memory for a Two- or Three-Dimensional Array

We know the following declarations reserve the same amount of memory:

```
int a,b,c,d,e,f,g,h;            //8 individual ints
int numbers[8];                  //a 1D array of 8 ints
int numbers2D[2][4];       //a 2D array, 2 rows x 4 cols
int numbers3D[2][2][2];    //a 3D array, 2 rows x 2 cols x 2 layers
```

And we know that if we declare a two- or three-dimensional array in this manner, we can access any element using the proper number of indices, such as:

```
numbers2D[0][0] = 5;
numbers3D[0][0][0] = 5;
```

When the C++ programmer uses the new operator in his or her code, the new operator allocates a continuous block of bytes that is adequate to hold either one data type's worth of data or [size]-number of data types. The format for the new operator is either one of the following:

```
int *ptr1, *ptr2;    //2 pointers to ints

ptr1 = new int;          //memory for one int
ptr2 = new int[8];       //memory for 8 ints
```

However, the new operator does not provide a way for the programmer to allocate easily a two- (or more) dimensional array. (It can be finessed in software—but it can't be allocated directly.) If we have a programming situation where the user wants to specify the size of a two-dimensional integer array that represents a sampling grid, how would we include this situation in our program? Figure 12-1 illustrates the problem.

The way to solve this problem is to determine the total number of array elements needed (this number is the number of rows multiplied by the number of columns) and allocate this total number. The new operator returns the address to the start of this reserved memory. The programmer must keep track of the rows and columns, a task that can be done in two ways. Before we show how to keep track of rows and columns, let's be sure that we understand what we are doing. Refer to Figure 12-2.

The grid could be any size:

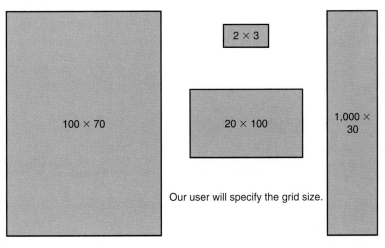

Figure 12-1
User Defined Sizes for Two-Dimensional Array

Assume that the user specifies a 20 × 100 size for the grid.

20 × 100

We allocate 20 × 100 = 2,000 integers.

2,000 integers

Solution:
We let the first 100 elements represent row 0.
The next 100 elements represent row 1.
The last 100 elements represent row 99.

0–99	100–199	. . .	1900–1999
(row 0)	(row 1)		(row 99)

Figure 12-2
Allocate Total Number of Array Elements Required

12

Two-Dimensional Array Allocation: Scheme 1 One way to work this problem in software is to keep two variables that represent the desired row and column, but use a third variable to access the array. (Remember, the memory on the heap is like a one-dimensional array.) We have our desired two-dimensional indices, but we calculate the one-dimensional index we need for the allocated array. The row size will act as a multiplicative offset value. Refer to Figure 12-3 and Program 12-4. The output for a 2-row $\times$ 4-column array is shown below:

Enter the row and column size for your 2D array 2 4

i (row) = 0 j (col) = 0 Array Value = 0
i (row) = 0 j (col) = 1 Array Value = 1
i (row) = 0 j (col) = 2 Array Value = 2
i (row) = 0 j (col) = 3 Array Value = 3
i (row) = 1 j (col) = 0 Array Value = 4
i (row) = 1 j (col) = 1 Array Value = 5
i (row) = 1 j (col) = 2 Array Value = 6
i (row) = 1 j (col) = 3 Array Value = 7
The End.

Two-Dimensional Array Allocation: Scheme 2 Our second approach for allocating a two-dimensional array is a bit more elegant because we develop an array that acts like a normal two-dimensional array and we use two indices instead of a single index. We allocate the memory for the data array that is the total size (as in Scheme 1). The catch in this new approach is that we also allocate memory for

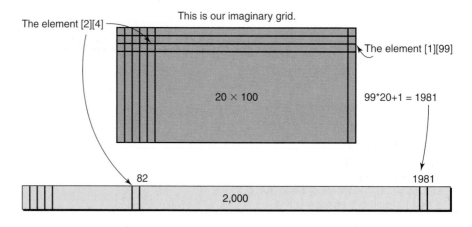

Our imaginary element in [2][4] is actually the 4 * 20 + 2 = 82 element.

Formula: desired column * row size + desired row

Figure 12-3
Scheme 1: Use a Formula to Determine Element Location

```
//Program 12-4  Two-Dimensional Array Using Offset Multiplier
//File Ch12TwoDArrayScheme1.cpp

#include <iostream>
using namespace std;

int main()
{
      int rowsize,colsize, totalsize;
      int index, i,j;

      cout << "\n Enter the row and column size for your 2D array";
      cin >> rowsize >> colsize;

      totalsize = rowsize * colsize;
      int *pArray;
      pArray = new int[totalsize];

      //fill the array with integers from 0 to totalsize
      // fill across the rows, moving down the columns

      int arrayvalue = 0;
      for (i = 0; i < rowsize; ++i)       //outer loop--traverse down the "rows"
      {
              for (j = 0; j < colsize; ++j)    //inner loop--move across each "column"
              {
                    // calculate array index
                    index = rowsize * j + i;
                    pArray[index] = arrayvalue;
                    cout << "\n i (row) = " << i << " j (col) = " << j <<
                            " Array Value = " << pArray[index];
                    ++ arrayvalue;
              }
      }

      cout << "\n The End." << endl;
      delete [] pArray;
      return 0;
}
```

an array of pointers that will contain the address of the start of each row. We fill this second array with the row addresses, and we can access the data array through this address array. Figure 12-4 illustrates the idea.

Program 12-4 showed some new code. There are two *'s in one line!

```
int *pArray; //pointer to an integer
int **pPointerArray; //pointer to an integer pointer

pArray = new int[totalsize]; //memory for totalsize integers
pPointerArray = new int* [rowsize]; //memory for row # of int pointers
```

Remember, to declare a pointer variable, we use the following code:

```
int *pArray;                   //pointer to an integer
```

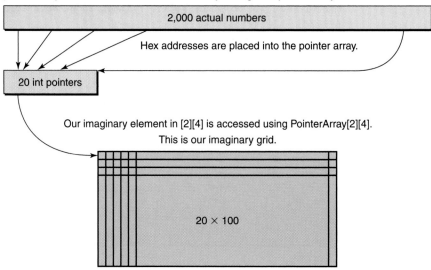

Our desired grid is 20 × 100.
The actual data array has 2,000 integer elements in it.

2,000 integers

20 int pointers
We allocate memory for twenty integer pointers.

We'll assign the address of each data element that corresponds to the first column into the pointer array. We can then access the data array through the pointer array.

2,000 actual numbers

Hex addresses are placed into the pointer array.

20 int pointers

Our imaginary element in [2][4] is accessed using PointerArray[2][4].
This is our imaginary grid.

20 × 100

Figure 12-4
Scheme 2: Use an Array of Pointers to Access the [Row][Column] Data Values

Now, if we need a pointer to a pointer, we use this code:

```
int **pPointerArray;        //pointer to an integer pointer
```

The memory allocation scheme follows the same idea. To allocate memory for an array of integers, we use the following:

```
pArray = new int[totalsize];    //memory for totalsize integers
```

For an array of pointers to integers, we use the following:

```
pPointerArray = new int* [rowsize];     //memory for rowsize # of int pointers
```

The entire program and output is shown in Program 12-5.

```
//Program 12-5  Two-Dimensional Array Using an Array of Pointers
//File Ch12TwoDArrayScheme2.cpp

#include <iostream>
using namespace std;

int main()
{
        int rowsize,colsize, totalsize;
        int i,j;

        cout << "\n Enter the row and column size for your 2D array  ";
        cin >> rowsize >> colsize;

        totalsize = rowsize * colsize;

        int *pArray;                    //pointer to an integer
        int **pPointerArray;            //pointer to an integer pointer

        pArray = new int[totalsize];            //memory for totalsize integers
        pPointerArray = new int* [rowsize];     //memory for rowsize # of int pointers

        //fill the pointer array with the pArray[i][0] addresses
        int index = 0;
```

```
for (i = 0; i < rowsize; ++i)     //outer loop--traverse down the "rows"
{
        pPointerArray[i] = &pArray[index]; //place the address into the pointer
        index = index + colsize;
}

//now fill the pArray by using the pPointerArray to access elements.
int arrayvalue = 0;
for (i = 0; i < rowsize; ++i)      //outer loop--traverse down the "rows"
{
        for (j = 0; j < colsize; ++j)     //inner loop--move across each "column"
        {
                pPointerArray[i][j] = arrayvalue;
                cout << "\n i (row) = " << i << " j (col) = " << j <<
                    " Array Value = " << pPointerArray[i][j];
                ++ arrayvalue;
        }
}
cout << "\n The End. " << endl;
delete [] pArray;
delete [] pPointerArray;
return 0;
}
```

Passing an Address to a Function and Beyond

Occasionally programmers encounter a situation where a function passes an address to a function, which in turn passes that address to a third function. We have a program that will ask the user to enter two pieces of data. We'll pass the variable addresses to one function that, in turn, passes the addresses to separate Get functions. The code is shown in Program 12-6. Figure 12-5 illustrates this program.

```
//Program 12-6  Addresses to Functions to Functions
//File Ch12PointertoFuncToFunc.cpp

#include <iostream>
using namespace std;

void GetXandY(double *x_ptr, double *y_ptr);
void GetX(double *x_ptr);
void GetY(double *y_ptr);
```

```
int main()
{
        double x,y;

        GetXandY(&x, &y);    // pass the address of x and y
        cout << "\n X = " << x << " and Y = " << y << endl;
        cout << "\n Missouri is the Show Me! state. " << endl;
        return 0;
}

void GetXandY(double *x_ptr, double *y_ptr)
{
        GetX(x_ptr);          //x_ptr & y_ptr contains the addresses
        GetY(y_ptr);          //just pass the value in x_ptr and y_ptr
}

void GetX(double *x_ptr)
{
        cout << "\n Please enter the value for X ";
        cin >> *x_ptr;
}

void GetY(double *y_ptr)
{
        cout << "\n Please enter the value for Y ";
        cin >> *y_ptr;
}
```

12.3
Exception Handling

Exception handling is a way to deal with run-time errors gracefully. When an error occurs, an exception is "thrown" and "caught" by an exception handler. The C++ language has exception-handling classes, and there are several ways to implement exception handling. The keywords are *try, throw*, and *catch*. We test for an error inside a "try" block. If we find the error, we "throw" an exception, which is handled in the "catch" block The general format for the try, throw, and catch is shown here:

exception handling
a fancy name for handling errors encountered when the program executes

12

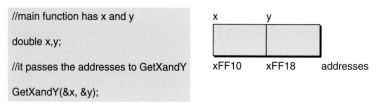

```
//main function has x and y

double x,y;

//it passes the addresses to GetXandY

GetXandY(&x, &y);
```

x   y

xFF10   xFF18   addresses

This is a call by reference—the addresses of x and y are being passed.

```
void GetXandY(double* x_ptr double* y_ptr)
{
        GetX(x_ptr);
        GetY(y_ptr);
}
```

x_ptr   y_ptr

FF10   FF18

These two calls are call by value. The value of the variable is being passed to the functions.
(The variable is a pointer and its value is an address.)

```
void GetX(double *x_ptr)
{
        cout << "\n Enter a value for X ";
        cin >> *x_ptr;
}
```

x_ptr

FF10

```
void GetY(double *y_ptr)
{
        cout << "\n Enter a value for Y ";
        cin >> *y_ptr;
}
```

y_ptr

FF18

The GetX and GetY functions use the indirection operator with the pointer and access main's memory directly.

Figure 12-5
Pointers to Functions and Beyond

```
try
{
    //test for your error, throw exception if found
    throw argument
}
catch(type argument)
{
    //catch statements
}
```

KISS Examples

We follow the KISS approach (Keep It Simple, Sweetie) and show a few short examples. In Program 12-7, we ask the user to enter a positive number, and we test to see if it is positive. If the number is zero or negative, we throw an exception. If we run our program and enter a positive number, the number's value is tested in the try block. Because the value is positive, the catch statements are skipped, as you

```
//Program 12-7  Exception Handling
//File Ch12ExcHandPosNumber.cpp
#include <iostream>
using namespace std;

int main()
{
        cout << "\n A Simple Exception-Handling Program\n";
        int number;
        cout << "\n Please enter a positive number  ";
        cin >> number;

        try                     //we test for our error in the try block
        {
                if(number <= 0)
                        throw number;       //WHOA! not positive, throw an exception!
                else
                        cout << "\n You entered a " << number;
        }

        catch (int i) //catch the exception, we pass the number to the catch statement
        {
                cout << "\n You entered " << i << " that is not positive! \n";
        }

        cout << "\n\n That wasn't so bad, was it? " << endl;
        return 0;
}
```

can see in the following output:

A Simple Exception-Handling Program
Please enter a positive number 5
You entered a 5
That wasn't so bad, was it?

The following output shows that the catch statement is executed when we enter a negative number:

A Simple Exception-Handling Program
Please enter a positive number −5
You entered −5 that is not positive!
That wasn't so bad, was it?

It is possible to have several catch statements in a program. C++ requires that the catch statement input data type be unique and that the program execution jump to the correct catch statement. (The unique data types are similar to overloaded functions because the parameter list must be different—but we are *not* calling the catch statements, merely jumping to them.) Refer to Program 12-8.

We'll run this program three times to show how the catch statements are either executed or skipped. First, we enter "red" and see the following output:

An Exception-Handling Program with Several Catches
Please enter one of these colors: red, blue, or green red
Oh Happy Day! You entered my favorite color!
Throwing and Catching is Fun!

Next, we enter "blue":

An Exception-Handling Program with Several Catches
Please enter one of these colors: red, blue, or green blue
You entered blue or green.
Throwing and Catching is Fun!

Last, we enter "yellow":

An Exception-Handling Program with Several Catches
Please enter one of these colors: red, blue, or green yellow
You entered yellow and that wasn't a choice!
Throwing and Catching is Fun!

Exception Handling with New Operator

Earlier we mentioned that exception handling is one technique to use when the new operator fails to allocate the requested memory. Visual C++ will automatically set the pointer to NULL if the new operation fails (the nothrow option is not needed). The attempted allocation should be performed in the try block. This situation is illustrated in Program 12-9. If we enter 100000000 (that is eight zeros: 100,000,000), we cannot allocate the memory.

Enter the size for your 1D array   100000000
Not enough memory, sorry.
Check out that catch!

If we enter the value 10000000 (that is seven zeros: 10,000,000), our new operator is successful.

Enter the size for your 1D array   10000000
If we made it to this line, no exception was thrown.
Check out that catch!

```
//Program 12-8  Exception Handling can have several catches
//File Ch12ExcHandManyCatch.cpp
//we'll throw one exception if the color is blue or green (i.e., not red)
//we'll throw a different exception if the color is not red, blue, or green

#include <iostream>
#include <string>
using namespace std;

int main()
{
        cout << "\n An Exception-Handling Program with Several Catches\n";

        char input_color[10];
        string color;

        cout << "\n Please enter one of these colors: red, blue, or green   ";
        cin.getline(input_color,10);
        color.assign(input_color);        // assign the user's color to the string

        try
        {
                if(color == "red")
                        cout << "\n Oh Happy Day! You entered my favorite color!  \n ";
                else if(color == "blue" || color == "green")
                        throw 100;    //throw an exception--we can just use an integer
                else
                        throw color;  // throw an exception--we pass the string
        }
        catch (int i)//catch the exception, we pass the number to the catch statement
        {
                cout << "\n You entered blue or green. \n";
        }

        catch (string s)
        {
                cout << "\n You entered " << s << " and that wasn't a choice! \n";
        }

        cout << "\n\n Throwing and Catching is Fun!"  << endl;
        return 0;
}
```

```
//Program 12-9 Exception Handling and new
#include <iostream>
using namespace std;
int main()
{
        int *int_pointer, size;

        cout << "\n Enter the size for your 1D array    ";
        cin >> size;
        try
        {
                int_pointer = new int[size];            //memory for a lot of ints
                if(int_pointer == NULL) throw 100;

                cout << "\n If we made it to this line, no exception was thrown. \n";
        }
        catch(int i)
        {
                cout << "\n Not enough memory, sorry.";
        }

        cout << "\n Check out that catch!" << endl;
        return 0;
}
```

12.4
Microsoft Foundation Class Library (MFC)

Brief Overview

**Microsoft Foundation
Class Library (MFC)**
an object-oriented
development
environment for
creating Microsoft
Windows applications

The *Microsoft Foundation Class Library (MFC)* provides C++ developers a set of prebuilt C++ components for building applications in Microsoft Windows®. The MFC components contain code for the common Windows-based features found in any Windows application. These components include toolbars and status bars, form and edit views, print and print preview, multiple-document interface, splitter and scroller windows, dialog boxes, database access, context-sensitive help, and more.

The Microsoft Windows operating system issues all sorts of **Windows Messages** that let the user know, for example, when the mouse moves, when a mouse button is clicked, or when a key has been struck. The **Windows Application Program Interface (Win 32 API)** has specific program requirements. It is possible to use the low-level API software to write a Windows program. MFC has packaged, ready-to-go classes that provide Windows components as well as functions that handle the underlying window messages. A programmer can use MFC to develop a Windows application without being an expert in Windows API.

To illustrate what we mean, we will use the example demonstrating that a Windows message is issued when the left mouse button is pressed. The message is WM_LBUTTONDOWN. In Windows API, if we need to know when the left mouse button is pressed, we would have a large switch statement checking for this case. Using MFC, we just add the function OnLButtonDown, which is called automatically when the button is pressed. (This view of the world is very simple.)

MFC is written in C++ and is structured around several base classes. The MFC Hierarchy Chart can be viewed by accessing Visual C++ –> Help –> Contents –> Visual C++ Documentation –> Microsoft Foundation Class Library and Templates –> Microsoft Foundation Class Library –> Hierarchy Chart. This chart shows that many classes are derived from CObject.

Build a Beeping Windows Program in a Few Mouse Clicks

To get an idea of the power of MFC, we'll create one Windows program that will be up and running after a few clicks of the mouse. Follow these steps:

1. To start a new project, select –> MFC AppWizard (exe). Name it WindowsEx. Press OK.
2. Select Single Document and leave Document/View Architecture checked in the step 1 window. Hit Next.
3. Leave "none" checked for database support in the step 2 window. Hit Next.
4. In steps 3 through 6, leave the default settings checked, but notice how the program allows you to customize your application.

Once you have finished the setup, pop open the FileView tab and notice that there are several *.ccp and *.h files. The ClassView tab shows several classes, including CAboutDialog, CMainFrame, CWindowsExApp, CWindowsExDoc, and CWindowsExView. Press the build key, and it will compile and link with no errors or warnings. Press the execute key and you'll see your windows application program.

Let's request that the computer beep at us if we press the left mouse button. We need to tell our Windows program to "listen for" the WM_LBUTTONDOWN message. Visual C++ has the Class Wizard, which makes this job easy. Follow these steps:

12

1. Under View -> ClassWizard -> make sure the Class Name is CWindowsExView. Scroll through the Messages and find WM_LBUTTONDOWN. Click it.

2. Press Add Function. Visual C++ automatically adds the OnLButtonDown function into the CWindowsExView.cpp file. This function will be called whenever the left mouse button is pressed.

3. Press Edit Code. You will see the following function.

```
/////////////////////////////////////////////////////////////////////////
// CWindowsExView message handlers

void CWindowsExView::OnLButtonDown(UINT nFlags, CPoint point)
{
    // TODO: Add your message handler code here and/or call default

    CView::OnLButtonDown(nFlags, point);
}
```

4. We'll use the MessageBeep function with the MB_OK argument. (Use the Visual C++ Help to see the full documentation for MessageBeep.) The MB_OK is the default system beep. Add the single line into the function above.

```
/////////////////////////////////////////////////////////////////////////
// CWindowsExView message handlers

void CWindowsExView::OnLButtonDown(UINT nFlags, CPoint point)
{
    // TODO: Add your message handler code here and/or call default
    MessageBeep(MB_OK);

    CView::OnLButtonDown(nFlags, point);
}
```

5. Compile and run your program. When you press the left mouse button, you will hear the system beep.

Spend some time looking through the files of your Windows program. A lot of it looks foreign, but you should see class declarations showing that your WindowsEx classes are derived from MFC base classes. For example, your WindowsExDoc class is derived from MFC's CDocument class.

12

```
// WindowsExDoc.h : interface of the CWindowsExDoc class
//
//////////////////////////////////////////////////////////////////////
#if !defined(AFX_WINDOWSEXDOC_H__53BBD90A_75E4_11D4_803D_00A0CC5774AA__INCLUDED_)
#define AFX_WINDOWSEXDOC_H__53BBD90A_75E4_11D4_803D_00A0CC5774AA__INCLUDED_

#if _MSC_VER > 1000
#pragma once
#endif // _MSC_VER > 1000

class CWindowsExDoc : public Cdocument
{
protected: // create from serialization only
       CWindowsExDoc();
       DECLARE_DYNCREATE(CWindowsExDoc)
```

And your WindowsExView class is derived from the CView class.

```
// WindowsExView.h : interface of the CWindowsExView class
//
//////////////////////////////////////////////////////////////////////
#if !defined(AFX_WINDOWSEXVIEW_H__53BBD90C_75E4_11D4_803D_00A0CC5774AA__INCLUDED_)
#define AFX_WINDOWSEXVIEW_H__53BBD90C_75E4_11D4_803D_00A0CC5774AA__INCLUDED_

#if _MSC_VER > 1000
#pragma once
#endif // _MSC_VER > 1000

class CWindowsExView : public CView
{
protected: // create from serialization only
      CWindowsExView();
      DECLARE_DYNCREATE(CWindowsExView)
```

If you are interested in learning how to program Windows applications using MFC, excellent MFC books are available.

12.5
The Java™ Programming Language

Java™ is an object-oriented programming language that was designed to run on many different kinds of computers, consumer electronics, and other devices. With Java technology, you use the same application on any kind of machine—a PC, a Macintosh computer, a network computer, or even new technologies like Internet

Java™

an object-oriented programing language originally developed by Sun Microsystems

screen phones. Developed by Sun Microsystems beginning in 1991, the Java™ technology was designed for transferring media across networks. In 1995 the Sun engineers made the first version of the Java source code available to developers, who downloaded it from the Internet. Java is a popular programming language, and currently there are thousands of Java developers.

The Java language produces portable software. The Java source code is compiled on one machine, and it can then run the code on any machine. (This portability differs from C++ because C++ must be compiled on each type of machine.) Java achieves this portability by producing **bytecode**—which includes instructions for the **Java Virtual Machine (JVM)**. The JVM resides on the computer platform that will run the Java program and acts as an interface between the bytecode and machine processor. (The JVM is machine dependent!) A machine that has a Java Virtual Machine will be able to run a Java program. Java is referred to as an interpreted language because running a Java program involves having the JVM read the Java bytecode and issue processor instructions. Java running in this manner does not run as fast as resident compiled code; however, **just in time compilers** that build bytecode into code specific for the resident processor are in development.

One last general statement concerning Java—the Java programmer may write two types of programs: applications and applets. Application programs are stand-alone, and applets are embedded in HTML code and require a Web browser.

bytecode

produced by the Java compiler and interpreted by the Java Virtual Machine

Java Virtual Machine (JVM)

program that interprets Java bytecode and issues machine instructions

just in time compilers

Java compilers that build bytecode into code specific to the resident processor

Java™ Is C++ Without Pointers

When C++ programmers take a Java programming course, they have two immediate reactions: "Java looks just like C++" and "No pointers!" Java was built with the C++ language as a starting base. If you consider how Java runs—bytecode that is interpreted by the Java Virtual Machine, which issues processor commands—pointers as we know them are an impossibility in Java. C++ allows us to access the memory and addresses directly. Table 12-1 compares the language syntax for C++ and Java.

Hello World in Java™

The Sun Microsystems' Web site (www.java.sun.com) has a wealth of information on the Java programming language. At this Web site, you may download and install the Java compiler. Our first program in this text was the C++ version of Hello World, so it is only fitting that our last program is Hello World in Java.[1]

The steps for creating a Java program are similar for a C++ program. We need to enter our Java source code in a text editor and save the file.

---

[1]The Java Hello World application program was provided by Steve Parratto, Instructor, Albuquerque TVI.

TABLE 12-1
Language Syntax Comparison for C++ and Java

Characteristics Common to C++ and Java	Characteristics Specific to Java
for, while, and do while loops	Each application must contain at least one class.
if and switch statements	Everything in Java is an object.
Relational operators (same)	No pointers, but does include reference variables
Arithmetic operators (same)	No structures, unions, or enumerated data types
Overloaded functions	Strings are not null-terminated.
Both support inheritance and polymorphism.	Java provides graphics, network, and multimedia as part of its standard library.
	Java's inheritance allows inheritance from one superclass.

```
//JavaProgram 12-1  Displays "Hello World!" to the standard output.

//Filename:  SamplePrgm.java
//This is a Sample Java Program

public class SamplePrgm {
    public static void main( String args[] )
    {
      System.out.println("Hello World from Java!");
      System.out.println("Goodbye for now!");
      System.out.println("Hope to see you soon!");
    }
}
```

Once the source code file is compiled, a new file called SamplePrgm.class is created. This file is the bytecode and is the file that is run.

12.6
Summary: Templates, Standard Template Library, and Friends

Note that three other C++ topics will not be covered here, but we'll mention them so you can say that you have heard of them. Advanced C++ texts and reference books include discussions of templates and the Standard Template Library.

C++ *templates* give the programmer a way to create generic functions and classes. The keyword *template* is used to set up the framework for a function or a

templates
formats used to create generic functions and classes

12

class. In a function or class template description, the data type is actually passed in as an argument. It is possible to build a function or a class that performs the same action and is general enough not to be bound specifically to a data type. For example, a general one-dimensional array sort function is a good candidate for serving as a template function. You may think of a generic function as a cousin to an overloaded function; however, the generic function performs the same action for all functions.

The Standard Template Library (STL) is a set of routines (part of the C++ language) that provide many useful data manipulation tools. There are three fundamental components of the STL—containers, algorithms, and iterators. Containers are objects that hold other objects and have functions applied to the container. The algorithms operate on the data within the container. The iterators are objects that allow you to cycle through the container's contents. It would be easy to spend an entire semester exploring C++'s STL.

Friend functions are nonmember functions that have been granted access to private members of a class. The keyword *friend* is used with the function prototype inside the class declaration. Friend functions are useful in certain programming situations because they grant the friends access to otherwise private data. Friend classes are also possible, but they are seldom used. A friend class has access to the private members of another class.

cout<< "\n Goodbye!";

Time to send you out into the world as a C++ programmer! Remember to follow Johnston's Nine Rules for Programmers from Chapter 1. And don't get mad, save early, save often, and keep your sense of humor. We want to wish you great luck in your programming endeavors!

Getting Started with Visual C++

C++ Development Environment Tools

The C++ programmer must learn and become efficient with the tools of his or her development environment, just as the home construction worker must know how to use his or her tools. Software development environments, including Microsoft's Visual C++, provide an integrated set of tools for writing, editing, debugging, and running programs. Table A-1 summarizes the development environment features.

TABLE A-1
Software Development Environment Tools

Tool	Use
Editor	The programmer writes the source code using the editor environment and saves the source file to disk. Editing tools specifically for writing C++ code are often available.
Compiler	The source code is read by a compiler, which checks to see that the source code is grammatically correct and does not violate any rules of syntax. If there are no errors, the compiler produces object or machine code. The compiler results are listed to the screen. Compiler errors in the source code are explained in a different window and a line number is given for reference. The Help section can be accessed for additional description of the error.
Linker	The linker hooks the object code and library code together and builds an executable file. This executable file runs the program.
Debugger	Once the program is running (that is, there are no compile or link errors), the debugger allows the programmer to single-step through the program, providing the ability to watch variables and to follow the flow of the program. Breakpoints can be set in the program so that the program runs and stops at these points.
Help	The package provides help reference for the C++ language as well as the error messages generated by the code.

Installing Visual C++

The Microsoft Visual C++ Version 6.0 Introductory CD that accompanies this book is used to install the Visual C++ software on your personal computer. System requirements for this software are listed below:

- Personal computer with a 486DX/66 (Pentium 90 or higher microprocessor recommended)
- Microsoft Windows 95 or later, Windows NT 4.0, with service pack 3 or later (service pack 3 included)
- Minimum memory: 24 MB for Windows 95 or later, 24 MB for Windows NT 4.0 (32 MB recommended for all)
- Hard-disk space required:

    Typical installation: 225 MB
    Maximum installation: 305 MB
    Microsoft Internet Explorer 4.01 Service Pack 1 (included)

- Additional hard disk space required for Microsoft Internet Explorer: 43 MB typical, 59 MB maximum
- CD-ROM drive
- VGA or higher-resolution monitor (Super VGA recommended)
- Microsoft Mouse or compatible pointing device

It is recommended that you do the "typical" installation for both the Visual C++ and Microsoft Developer's Network (MSDN) software. The MSDN includes extensive help and reference sections.

Program Construction Steps

The programmer takes several steps to build a program. In some older C and C++ development environments, it is possible to build a program by using a single source file. The C++ source files should have the .cpp extension. Figure A-1 shows these steps.

Visual C++ Projects and Workspaces   The majority of C++ programs consists of many source files, not just one. A programmer can organize his or her software into separate files according to what the program must do. For example, a program for the Automatic Teller Machine software can be organized into banking files, hardware control files, customer files, and so on.

Most development environments expect programs to be constructed with many source files. These environments, including Microsoft Visual C++, require the programmer to create a project and to add the program files to the project. The project folder contains the source files (or knows where they are located). The workspace keeps track of the entire set of program files. The compile, link, and run

A

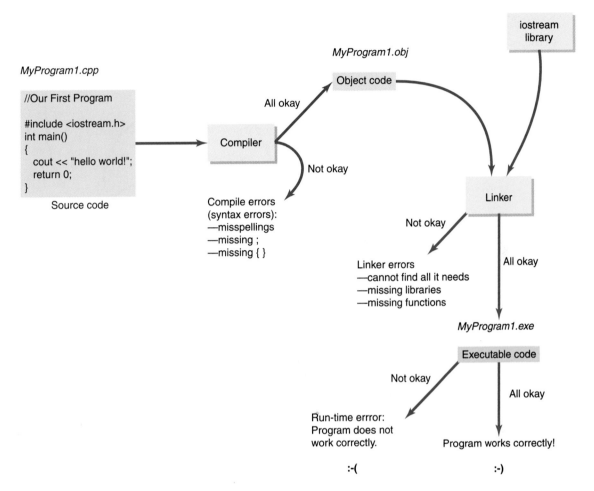

Note: Visual C++ requires an active workspace and project folder.
This example is for illustration purposes only!

Figure A-1
Software Build Steps: The Simple (One File) Case

steps are also performed via this project environment. These project steps are illustrated in Figure A-2.

The Visual C++ documentation, which is located in the Help pull-down menu, includes a complete reference section for working with projects. Under Help –> Contents –> Visual C++ User's Guide –> Working With Projects, several topics offer much detail. There is an Overview section as well as How Do I … topics section.

A

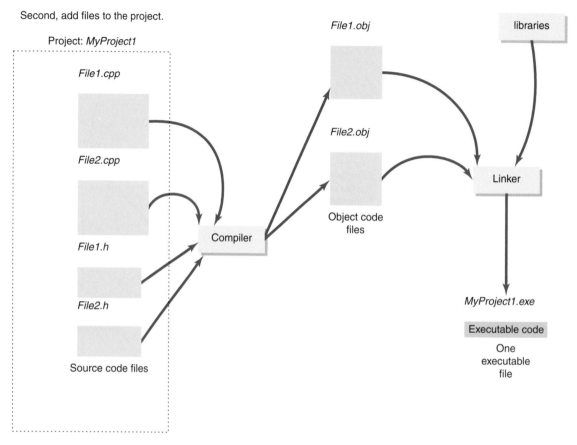

Must be performed when using Visual C++

First, create the project
MyProject1.

Second, add files to the project.

Project: *MyProject1*

File1.cpp

File2.cpp

File1.h

File2.h

Source code files

Compiler

File1.obj

File2.obj

Object code
files

libraries

Linker

MyProject1.exe

Executable code

One
executable
file

Figure A-2
Software Build Steps for Multifile Projects

We show a simple example below and try to answer all your "getting started" questions. Once you work through several of the practice programs and programs in the chapters, you can return to the Visual C++ Help and review all this information on projects.

An Example: Hello World from Scratch   Microsoft Visual C++ requires that the program be contained in a project. A project must be set up before a program can be compiled and run. The project folder contains the source code files (including the *.cpp and *.h files) as well as several project specific files, such as *.ncb, *.opt, *.dsw, and others.

Warnings:

1. Do *not* set up your program project on a floppy disk. Visual C++ will not work well (if at all) if you set up the project on the floppy disk. Always create your project on a hard disk or zip disk!

2. If you are working at home and at school, you will need to transport only your source files (*.cpp and *.h) between home and school. You should plan to create separate projects at your home and school accounts and then copy the source files from your zip or floppy disk into your project folder.

In this example, we set up a new project in Microsoft Visual C++. The program writes "hello world" to the output screen. The project has the following characteristics:

- Designated Working Directory: C:
- Project name: JohnstonEx1
- Program file: hello.cpp

Start the Visual C++ Program   Visual C++ may be accessed via the Start menu. You may also add it to a toolbar or create a shortcut to the program and place the shortcut on your desktop. Make use of the Start menu: Start –> Programs –> Microsoft Visual C++ 6.0 –> Microsoft Visual C++ 6.0. See Figure A-3.

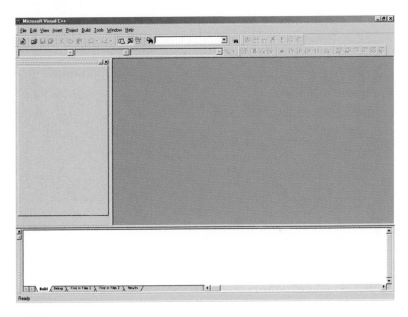

Figure A-3
Visual C++ Environment

A

Step 1: Create the project.   You need to do this step *only once* for each program! Once you have it set, you can work on your program as often as necessary.

Start Visual C++.

Under FILE –> New –> Select Project –> Win32 Console Application

Location: C: [Don't enter anything here.]

Project Name: [Enter this:] JohnstonEx1

When you finish this list, Visual C creates a new directory (see Figure A-4) and the location will read:

C:\JohnstonEx1

Hit OK. Then select "An Empty Project." Hit Finish. Visual C will show you the "New Project Information Window." Hit OK. You are now ready to start entering source code.

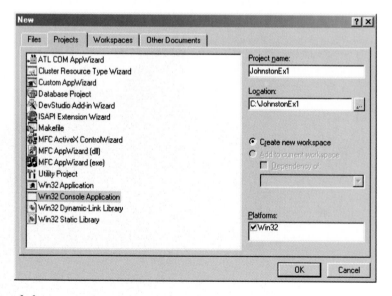

Figure A-4
Create a New Project[a]

[a]As you type in the project name, a new folder name is entered automatically in the Location field.

Step 2: Create a new source file.   To create a file for source code, complete this list (see Figure A-5):

> Under File –> New –> Select C++ Source File, enter the file name: hello (Visual C automatically adds the .cpp extension). Hit OK.

A window will come up with the file name in the window bar at the top (see Figure A-6):

> hello.cpp

Now enter the following source code:

```
//This is my first program. It will write out hello world! to the screen.

#include <iostream.h>
int main(void)
{
        cout << "\n hello world!    \n" ;
        return 0;
}
```

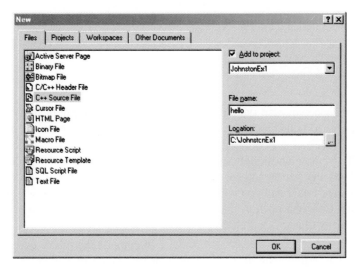

Figure A-5
File –> New[a]

[a]Select C++ Source File, and enter the File name.

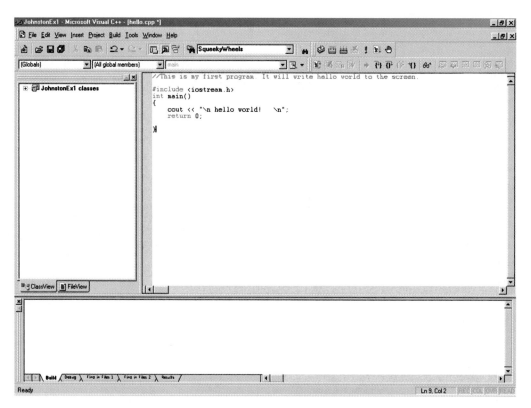

Figure A-6
Enter the Program into the Edit Window[a]

[a]You should see the Source, Header, and Resource folders in the FileView section on the left.

Notice that once you start typing in the window, the file name at the top of the window changes to hello.cpp*. The * indicate that this file has new contents since it was last saved.

The window on the left shows a "FileView" and a "ClassView" tab. If you look at FileView, you should see three folders: Source, Header, and Resource. Click on the Source folder and you will see your *hello.cpp* file. You can click on the file, and Visual C++ will open to that file. This procedure is useful when your project contains many files.

Step 3: Compile your source code. To compile the source code, you may hit either the "Build" button on the toolbar or Build –> Compile hello.cpp. (Place the cursor over each toolbar button, and Visual C++ displays its title.) Any compile errors are shown in the lower window. You may double click the line in the error window, and it will put the cursor on the line in the source code where it believes the problem exists. If there are no errors, it will show the following message:

JohnstonEx1.obj 0 error(s) 0 warning(s)

If you select the FileView tab in the window on the left, you should see the Header, Source, and Resource folders. These folders are shown in Figure A-7.

Step 4: Run your program. To build and execute the program, you may hit the Execute button (red exclamation point) or Build –> Execute JohnstonEx1.exe. The first time you run the program, you may be told that JohnstonEx1.exe does not exist and asked, Do you want to build it? Answer yes.

If you are running the Visual C++ that accompanies this text, an informational window is presented telling you that your executable file cannot be run on other machines. Press OK. Then the console window will be displayed by Visual C with your program results (see Figure A-8). When your program is finished, it will display the following message.

Press any key to continue

When you hit the Enter key, this window disappears.

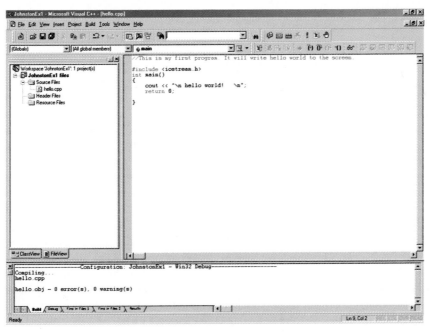

Figure A-7
The Program Compiled with No Errors and No Warning

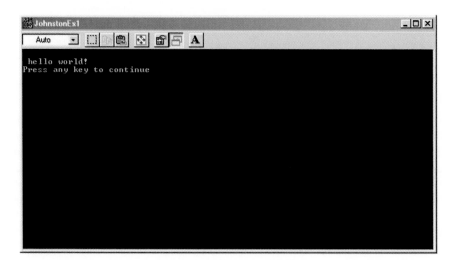

Figure A-8
The Console Window Shows the Output of Your Program

Step 5: All finished for the day. To exit Visual C++, you should save your workspace. This action causes Visual C++ to "remember" everything about your project. The next time you work on the project, it will be exactly as you left it.

To save your workspace, enter File –> Save Workspace.

To close your workspace, enter File –> Close Workspace.

To exit Visual C++, enter File –> Exit.

Step 6: Check to see what files Visual C has set up for you. Because we are just beginning with Visual C++, now is a perfect time to examine the files that Visual C++ has set up in the project folder. Using My Computer or Explorer, examine the files in your JohnstonEx1 project. You will see a Debug folder, as well as hello.cpp, JohnstonEx1.dsp, JohnstonEx1.dsw, JohnstonEx1.ncb, and JohnstonEx1.plg. The Debug folder contains several files, including the JohnstonEx1.exe and JohnstonEx1.obj.

Visual C creates a project and the default build mode is Debug. When compiling a program in the debug configuration, Visual C provides the necessary "hooks" for the debugger. This provision makes the program executable file a fairly large one. Once your program is working well, you may select the configuration option of Release, which compiles and builds your program without the debugging hooks. At this point, the project folder should contain a Release folder that contains an obj and an exe file. The size of the executable file is smaller here.

Step 7: Save early, save often. You need to copy only the *.cpp and *.h files (and any program data files) to your floppy or zip disk for work at home or for safekeeping. The project folder can always be rebuilt if necessary.

A

Exit Warning: It is a *bad idea* to close Visual C++ by pressing the X button in the top right corner of the window. Save your workspace and then close it. By saving and closing your workspace, you ensure that Visual C++ is shut down properly, your files and workspace are saved, and everything can be located when Visual C++ is restarted.

Step 8: Start working on your program again.

This part of Appendix A is crucial. When you start working on your project, you must open your workspace, *not* your cpp file! Remember, always go through your workspace when working on a program!

Bring up Visual C.

File –> Open Workspace –> Go through the directory structure to locate your project file with the .dsw extension. For example, we'll need to find: C:\JohnstonEx1\JohnstonEx1.dsw.

Select JohnstonEx1.dsw (see Figure A-9). This step brings you right into your project and you are ready to go.

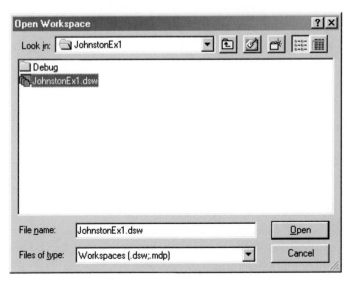

Figure A-9
Starting Your Project: Open Workspace, Select the .dsw File

Frequently Asked Questions

1. I typed my hello.cpp file at home. How can I set up my project at school and use this file in it?

For any programming project you will need to create the project once (see step 1 on page 574).

Once the project is created, minimize Visual C++.

Use My Computer or Explorer to copy and paste your source file(s) into the project directory.

Once your files are located inside your project folder, maximize Visual C++.

Project –> Add to Project –> Files: select the file to add.

Another Important Note: Be sure that the source file is located *inside* the project file!

---

2. I took my hello.cpp file home and improved it. How can I use it in the project on the school computer?

You can simply copy over your old hello.cpp file (use My Computer or Explorer). Because the project knows to look for hello.cpp, you won't need to add the file again to the project.

3. How can I use a new hello file (call it new_hello.cpp) instead of the one already there?

Use My Computer or Explorer and copy the *new_hello.cpp* into your project folder.

Open Visual C++.

Open your desired workspace.

You may delete your *hello.cpp* file from the file list. (To do this, use the File-View window on the left).

Add the *new_hello.cpp* file to the project (Project –> Add to Project –> Files).

A Warning

Opening the source code file (with a double click while in My Computer or Explorer) automatically opens Visual C++. But be warned! You do not have an active workspace. See Figure A-10. Notice that the window on the left is gray instead of white. The gray indicates that you have not opened a workspace. If you compile this file, you will see the warning in Figure A-11. If you answer yes to this message, Visual C++ creates a second workspace file—an unfortunate predicament!

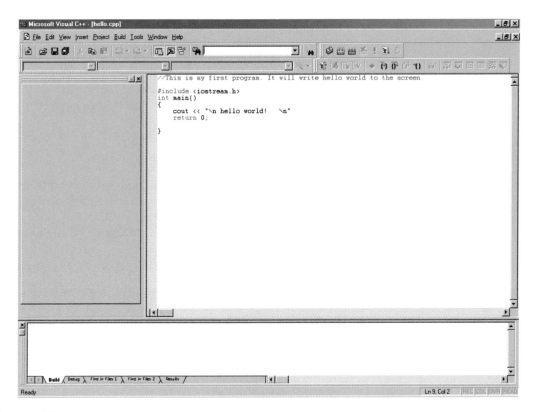

Figure A-10
Results of Opening hello.cpp by Double Clicking the File from My Computer or Explorer[a]

[a]The grayed out window on the left indicates there is no active workspace.

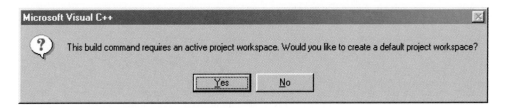

Figure A-11
Default Workspace Warning[a]

[a]The default workspace warning indicates that you have not opened your workspace but have opened your .cpp file. This action leads to an incorrectly built project.

A

When you have multiple source files in a project, the project workspace file (*.dsw) must be opened so that Visual C++ sees all the files. If you open one *.cpp file and build a new workspace, this workspace knows of this one *.cpp file only. You should always open Visual C++, open your workspace, and then open your .cpp file.

Figure A-12 shows an incorrectly built workspace. The window on the left does not contain the Header, Source, and Resource folders. When a project is built correctly, these folders are present.

Help

Visual C++ provides an extensive Help system that may be accessed in several ways. The first and most obvious way is through the pull-down menu on the Visual C++ main window. Three of the Help menu options are Contents, Index, and Search. When you bring up help, you will see the MSDN Library Visual Studio 6.0, which is shown in Figure A-13.

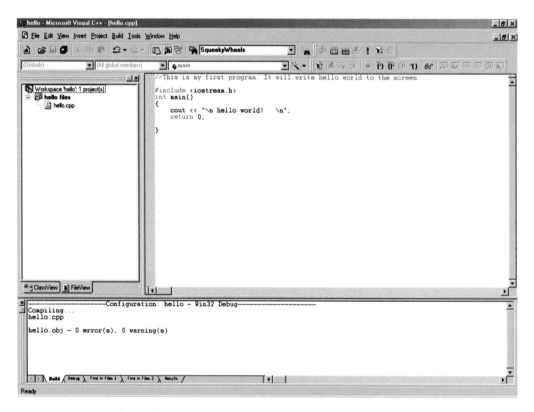

Figure A-12
Incorrectly Built Workspace[a]

[a]You should see the Source, Header, and Resource file folders in the FileView on the left when the workspace is built correctly.

The Contents tab provides a table of contents for all the reference material available to you. Under the Visual C++ Documentation is a Reference tab. Here you will find the C/C++ Language and C++ Libraries documentation. This documentation provides a wealth of information, including sample programs, for all features of the C++ language.

The Index tab provides a quick and easy way to find a topic if you know what you are looking for. For example, in the Index keyword field, you can enter "ASCII" and the index shows all the reference listings for ASCII. The Index is an incredibly useful developer's tool.

The Search tab allows you to enter a phrase that will search all the reference material for you and provide a list for you to examine. For example, you can enter "formatted output" or "memory leak," and the Search engine produces a multitude of articles for you.

Finally, whenever you have either a compile or link error, a number is always associated with the error. If you highlight the error number and press F1, the documentation on the error is presented for you.

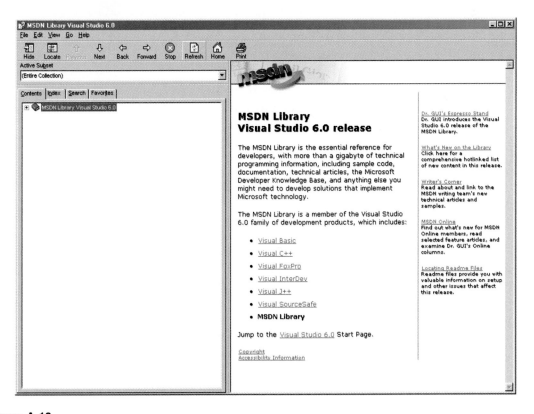

Figure A-13
The Microsoft Developer's Network Library Visual Studio 6.0 Contains all the Help
Features in Visual C++

A

You should spend some time looking through the different Help options. The Visual C++ Help is a powerful feature of this software. Learn how to use it!

Practice

1. Create a project called QUOTES and a .cpp file called FourScore. Here is the program for you to enter in your FourScore.cpp file:

```
//Gettysburg Address.

#include <iostream.h>

int main(void)
{
        cout << "\n Four score and seven years ago our fathers "
                << "\n brought forth on this continent, a new nation,"
                << "\n conceived in liberty and dedicated to the proposition"
                << "\n that all men are created equal. \n\n";

        cout << "\n\n Author:  A. Lincoln  \n";
        return 0;
}
```

2. Create a project called BUGS and a .cpp file called APoem. Enter the following poem in the APoem.cpp file:

```
//BUGS Program.

#include <iostream.h>

int main(void)
{
        cout << "\n\n Spiders, Roaches, Ants and Ticks"
                << "\n Centipedes and Flies"
                << "\n Have many legs to walk upon."
                << "\n Just so they walk outside.";

                cout << "\n\n Author:  B. Johnston  \n";
        return 0;
}
```

3. Go back to the QUOTES project and add a title line that will be shown in the output window. The title should be something about the Gettysburg Address.
4. Return to the BUGS project and add your own verse.

C++ Keyword Dictionary

A total of sixty-three keywords are part of the current ISO/ANSI C++ Standard. The ISO C standard has thirty-two keywords, and the C++ Standard added thirty-one. The language reserves these keywords, and they cannot be used as program identifiers; that is, keywords cannot be used in a program as function or variable names. The sixty-three C and C++ keywords are listed below:

asm	auto	bool	break	case	catch
char	class	const	const_cast	continue	default
delete	do	double	dynamic_cast	else	enum
explicit	export	extern	false	float	for
friend	goto	if	inline	int	long
mutable	namespace	new	operator	private	protected
public	register	reinterpret_cast	return	short	signed
sizeof	static	static_cast	struct	switch	template
this	throw	true	try	typedef	typeid
typename	union	unsigned	using	virtual	void
volatile	wchar_t	while			

The thirty-one keywords specific to C++:

asm	bool	catch	class	const_cast	delete
dynamic_cast	explicit	export	false	friend	inline
mutable	namespace	new	operator	private	protected
public	reinterpret_cast	static_cast	template	this	throw
true	try	typeid	typename	using	virtual
wchar_t					

Each of the sixty-three keywords is presented in Table B-1 with a brief definition, and most keyword entries contain sample usage. Where applicable, chapter references are also listed. A few topics are presented only in the keyword dictionary, and the reference is shown as "C++ Ref," which indicates that the reader should consult a complete C++ reference for discussion and examples. (See the bibliography in this textbook.) A brief definition of terms frequently used in the dictionary is presented below:

access modifier	controls how a variable may be used or changed in a program
access specifiers	controls how data or functions are available (or not) to the program
casting operator	transforms one type of variable into another
control statement	directs flow of the program execution steps
data type declaration	statement that creates data variable(s) and associated memory for storage of variable values
jump statement	causes execution of the program to move to another part of the program
label statement	a valid identifier followed by a colon
modifier	alters or provides additional capability for a keyword
operator	a word or a symbol that is reserved in C++ and that performs a specific task
storage specifier	dictates the manner in which the compiler stores the variables

▌ TABLE B-1
Keyword, Use, Example, and Reference

Keyword	Use and Example	Refer to Chapter
asm	To embed assembly language directly into C++ programs. ```asm{` ` instruction sequence` `}```	C++ Ref[a]
auto	Data type declaration for local variables. *Note*: Locally declared variables are assumed to be automatic by default and auto declaration is not needed. Therefore, auto is one of the least used keywords. `auto int x;`	2
bool	Data type declaration for true or false valued variables. ```bool OK, Flag; // declare boolean variables OK and Flag` `OK = true; // assign true to OK` `Flag = false; // assign false to Flag```	2

[a]The reader should consult a complete C++ reference for discussion and examples. See the bibliography in this textbook.

(continued)

B

Keyword	Use and Example	Refer to Chapter
break	A jump statement commonly used in switch statements. *See* switch.	3
case	A label statement used in a switch statement. *See* switch	3
catch	Used in exception handling. Statement used to handle the error. *See* try.	12 C++ Ref

char	A data type declaration for variables that hold characters. Can be single variable or array, which is a character string.
	
	`char answer;      // single variable`
	
	`char name[50];    // character string`
		2, 6

class	A declaration used for creating classes. It defines a new type combining data and functions.
	
	<pre>class X
	{
	    private:
	        int a,b;
	    protected:
	        DoSomething();
	    public:
	        X();
	        DoSomethingElse();
	};</pre>
		9, 10, 11

const	An access modifier that controls how variables may be changed. A program cannot change the value of a const variable after it has been initialized. The const modifier may be used in variable declarations or in function header lines to keep the function from changing a value.
	
	`const double pi = 3.14159265;  // variable cannot be changed`
	
	`Function1(const char[]);       // function cannot change this`
	`                               // char string.`
		2

B

(continued)

Keyword	Use and Example	Refer to Chapter
const_cast	A casting operator that overrides const and volatile declared variables. As shown here, the const_cast allows the const pointer that contains the address of pi to be assigned into a non-const variable, n.	C++ Ref

```
void ChangePi(const double *);
int main()
{
        double pi = 3.14159;
        cout <<"pi = " << pi;       //writes 3.14159
        ChangePi(&pi);
        cout <<"\npi = " << pi;   //write 27
        return 0;
}

void ChangePi(const double *newpi)
{
        double *n;
        n = const_cast<double *>(newpi);
        *n = 27;
}
```

Keyword	Use and Example	Refer to Chapter
continue	A jump statement used in loops. A continue statement forces the next iteration of the loop and will skip any code remaining in the loop. As shown here, the for loop is used to count the letters in the string. If a space is found, a continue is used to skip the remaining statements and iterate the loop.	C++ Ref

```
char string[40] = "A bird in the hand is worth two in the bush.";
int count_letters;
for(i = 0; i < 40; ++i)
{
    if(string[i] ==' ') continue;

    ++count_letters;
}
```

Keyword	Use and Example	Refer to Chapter
default	A label statement used in a switch statement. If none of the cases in the switch statements are true, the statement(s) in the default block are performed. *See* switch	3
delete	An operator that frees memory allocated by the new operator. It cannot be used with any other type of pointer. *See* new	12 C++ Ref (continued)

B

Appendix B ∎ C++ Keyword Dictionary

Keyword	Use and Example	Refer to Chapter
do	A loop/iteration control statement used in conjunction with a while statement. A do while loop will execute the loop statements once before checking the condition. The loop statements are repeated as long as the condition is true.	3

```
int number = 0;

do {

   cout << "\n The number is "<< x;
   ++ number;
}
while(number < 100);
```

| double | A data type declaration for variables that hold numeric values with decimal precision. The ISO C++ Standard states that a double must maintain at least ten digits of decimal precision. | 2 |

```
double x, y;
```

| dynamic_cast | A casting operator that performs run-time verification of a polymorphic casting operation. A dynamic_cast is used with base and derived class pointers. One example that is legal: it is possible to cast a derived class pointer into a base class pointer. | C++ Ref |

```
BaseClass *pB, Bobject;
DerivedClass *pD, Dobject;
pB = &Dobject;  //base class pointer points to derived object

// legal to cast base into derived pointer
pD = dynamic_cast < DerivedClass * > pB;
```

Many variations of this cast are legal, but here is an illegal cast:

```
BaseClass *pB, Bobject;
DerivedClass *pD, Dobject;
pB = &Bobject;  //base class pointer points to base object

pD = dynamic_cast < DerivedClass * > pB;  // can't do this
```

You cannot cast a base object into a derived object.

Consult a C++ reference for further explanation.

(continued)

B

Keyword	Use and Example	Refer to Chapter
`else`	A conditional control statement used with an if statement. There are two formats using the else keyword. It may be used in conjunction with an if or used separately. There can be only one else condition block for an if. If none of the conditional statement in the if statements are true, the statement(s) in the else block are performed. *See* if.	3
`enum`	A data type declaration statement that creates an integer-based (numeric) list of constants. The constant values are assigned integers beginning with 0 (zero) unless otherwise specified.	7

```
enum DogBreed { Husky, Heeler, Collie, Boxer, Mixed };

enum Cards { two = 2, three, four, five, six, seven, eight };

int main()
{
    DogBreed MyDog;
    MyDog = Husky;
    Cards MyCard;
    MyCard = two;
    if( MyCard == three) cout << "\n The card is a three";
```

Keyword	Use and Example	Refer to Chapter
`explicit`	The explicit keyword is used only with converting constructors. It allows the programmer to create nonconverting constructors. Constructors with one input argument are known as converting constructors. For example, if a class constructor can be called like this:	C++ Ref

```
class NewClass
{
private:
    int x;
public:
    NewClass(int y) { x = y; }
);

int main()
{
    NewClass NC(5);    // could also  NewClass NC = 5;
```

It is possible not to allow this automatic conversion by writing:

```
explicit NewClass(int y) { x = y; }
```

in the class definition.

(continued)

B

export
The export keyword is used in a template declaration so that other files are allowed to use the declared template. When an export template is declared in another file, the second file may use the original template without duplicating the template definition.

C++ Ref

```
// File1.cpp  Template function definition
// Place the y into the x[num] element of the array
template <class A> void PutIntoTheArray(A *x, A y, int num)
{
    x[num] = y;
}

// File2.cpp  exported to another file
export template <class A> void PutIntoTheArray(A *x, A y, int num);
```

extern
A storage class specifier for variables to be shared by routines in multifile or multilibrary programs. A variable is originally declared globally in one file and can be globally extern'd in another file. For example:

App. H

```
//File1.cpp
double x;      // declared globally

//File2.cpp
extern double x;        // File2.cpp can now use the x variable.
```

false
The keyword false is a Boolean constant with a zero value.

See bool.

2

float
A data type declaration for numeric values with decimal precision. The C++ language requires five digits of decimal precision with a float variable.

2

for
A loop/iteration control statement. The for statement contains three parts: initialization, conditional check, and increment.

3

```
cout << "\n Counting 0 to 9 ";
int i;
for(i = 0; i < 10; ++i)
{
    cout << "\n The number is " <<i;
}
```

(continued)

B

friend

A friend function is declared in a class declaration. A friend function has access to all private and protected members of that class but is not a member of the class.

C++ Ref

```
class A
{
private:
   int x, y;
public:
   friend void WriteValues();    //declared as friend
}

void WriteValues()   // since it's a friend, it can access x and y
{
   cout << "\n The values are " << x << " and " << y;
}
```

goto

A jump statement that requires an associated label statement. The goto and its label must be in the same function. The goto can be used to skip statements.

C++ Ref

```
int count;
// code that establishes value for count

if( count < 10) goto next1;
// code that will be skipped if count is less than 10

next1:
```

if

A conditional/decision control statement.

3

```
if(a > 0)
{
   // statements
}
else if( a == 0)
{
   // statements
}
else
{
   // statements
}
```

B

(continued)

Keyword	Use and Example	Refer to Chapter
inline	The inline keyword is placed in function declarations. This placement causes the compiler to place the function at the point in the software where the function is called.	8

```
inline void SwitchEm(float *x, float *y);   //prototype

int main()
{
    float sum, a = 4.0, b = 5.0;
    SwitchEm(&a,&b);              // call to the function
}

inline void SwitchEm(float *pX, float *pY)
{
    float temp = *pX;
    *pX = *pY;
    *pY = temp;
}
```

Keyword	Use and Example	Refer to Chapter
int	A data type declaration for whole numbers. The range of values for an integer variable depends on the machine architecture.	2

```
int number;   // minimal range -32767 to 32768
              // range on Visual C++ ~-2 billion to 2 billion
```

Keyword	Use and Example	Refer to Chapter
long	A data type declaration for integers and doubles. In some machine architectures, the long declaration provides twice the memory space (and increases the range) for the variable values.	2

```
long int number;   // minimal range ~-2 billion to 2 billion
long double x;      // minimal range 10 digits of precision
```

Keyword	Use and Example	Refer to Chapter
mutable	The mutable keyword, when used in a class declaration, allows a member of an object to modify a variable modified by const.	C++ Ref

B

(continued)

| namespace | The namespace defines the scope or region of a program. It is possible to have separate namespace regions to avoid confusion—especially if functions have the same name. Here is a namespace region called MyOwn that contains a rand function. (See the example in Chapter 10.) | 10 C++ Ref |

```
namespace MyOwn
{
      int rand();
};

int MyOwn::rand()
{
      return 42; // my number is always 42
}
```

| new | The new operator allocates memory at run-time. The new operator returns a pointer to the allocated memory. The delete operator is used to free the memory and should be used only with valid pointers. If adequate memory is not available, this operation fails and in Visual C++ returns a NULL pointer. Other C++ compilers may issue a bad_alloc exception. (The reader should refer to Chapter 12 and a C++ reference for complete discussion.) | 12 C++ Ref |

```
class Xclass
{
  // description
};

int main()
{
    int *ptr;       // pointer to an integer
    Xclass *xptr    //pointer to an Xclass
    ptr = new int; // allocate memory for an integer
    xptr = new Xclass;  //allocate memory for Xclass object

    delete ptr;       // free the memory
    delete xptr;
}
```

B

(continued)

Keyword	Use and Example	Refer to Chapter
operator	Creates a new definition of a function for a given operator. It is possible to create class member operator functions and non-class member operator functions—or overloaded friend functions. The operator keyword is used in the function prototype. This example shows how to build a class member overloaded operator function.	9 C++ Ref

```
class Xclass
{
   public:
   void operator ++ ();     // create a ++ operator for the Xclass.
};
void Xclass::operator ++( )
{
    //function code here
}
```

(The reader should consult a C++ reference for a description of a non-class operator function.)

Keyword	Use and Example	Refer to Chapter
private	An access specifier used in classes. The private members are accessible only by other members of the class. *See* class	9
protected	An access specifier used in classes and inheritance. The protected members are accessible by members of the class and are inherited in derived classes. *See* class.	9
public	An access specifier used in classes. The public members are accessible by all parts of the program. *See* class.	9
register	A storage specifier for variables that allows the program faster access to variables. Register memory is located so that the program requires fewer steps to access the stored values.	C++ Ref
reinterpret _cast	A casting operator that changes one data type into a completely different data type.	C++ Ref

```
char *s = "this is a string";
int pinteger;

pinteger = reinterpret_cast <int> (s);
```

(continued)

B

Keyword	Use and Example	Refer to Chapter
return	A return is a jump statement used to return program execution from a calling function to the called function.	2, 5
short	A data type modifier for integers. A short int is half the number of bytes as the normal int. In Visual C++ an int is 4 bytes. A short int is 2 bytes and has a range from −32768 to +32767.	2
signed	A data type modifier for integers and chars. A signed variable includes negative values.	2
sizeof	An operator that computes the actual size, in bytes, of any variable or data type. Can be used with either data type or data variable, such as:	2

```
double x;

cout << sizeof(double);  //writes 8 since doubles are 8 bytes long
cout << sizeof(x);       // same result as above
```

| static | A storage class modifier for local variables so that variable values are maintained until program termination. | 5 |
| static_cast | A casting operator can be used for standard casting or nonpolymorphic cast of a base class into a derived class. The static_cast is essentially the C language casting operator. | 2 C++ Ref |

```
int n = 5;;
double x;

x = static_cast <double> (n);
```

| struct | A declaration used to create data structures, such as: | 7 |

```
struct Ball
{
   float radius, surface area:
};
```

B

(continued)

Keyword	Use and Example	Refer to Chapter
switch	A conditional/decision control statement.	3

```
switch(variable)
{
   case 1:
      // code executed if variable's value is 1
      break;
   case 2:
      // code executed if variable's value is 2
      break;
   default:
      //code executed if no case values are found
}
```

Keyword	Use and Example	Refer to Chapter
template	A declaration statement used to create a generic class or function.	C++ Ref
this	When a member function is called in objects and classes, there is an implicit pointer. The implicit pointer is the "this" pointer. It points to the invoking object. For example:	C++ Ref

```
class MyClass
{
   public:
   void Function1();
};

int main()
{
   MyClass MyObject;
   MyObject.Function1();
```

When the Function1 function is called, the "this" pointer points to the MyObject object.

Keyword	Use and Example	Refer to Chapter
throw	Found in exception handling, a throw statement must be executed when an error is found. *See* try	12 C++ Ref
true	The keyword true is a Boolean constant with a nonzero value. *See* bool	2

B

(continued)

Keyword	Use and Example	Refer to Chapter
try	Keyword found in exception handling. The try is a block of statements used to monitor code when looking for errors. When an error is encountered, we throw an exception, which is "caught" by the catch statement. In this example, we ask the user to enter a positive number. We check the number in the try block and if it is not positive, we throw an exception.	12 C++ Ref

```
int number;
cout << "\n Enter a positive number. ";
cin >> number;

try    //try block
{
    if(number <=0) throw number;
}
catch( int i )  // caught an exception
{
    cout << "\n ERROR, your number is not positive.";
}
```

Keyword	Use and Example	Refer to Chapter
typedef	The typedef defines new data type names. For example, it is possible to typedef int's as WHOLE_NUMBERS, as follows:	C++ Ref

```
typedef int WHOLE_NUMBERS;
```

You can then declare variables of type WHOLE_NUMBERS like this:

```
int main()
{
    WHOLE_NUMBERS x, y, z;
```

The typedef is a required statement in C code (not C++) to define a structure tag as a data type. (This statement is not required in a C++ compiler!)

```
struct MyStruct
{
// struct members
};
```

```
typedef MyStruct MYSTRUCT;
```

Then use MYSTRUCT to declare structure variables.

Keyword	Use and Example	Refer to Chapter
typeid	Provides the type of an object during program execution. Must include TYPEINFO.H header.	C++ Ref

(continued)

B

Keyword	Use and Example	Refer to Chapter
typename	The typename keyword has two purposes. First, it can be substituted for the keyword class in the template declaration. Second, it tells the compiler a name is a type name instead of an object name.	C++ Ref
union	A declaration for memory location that is shared by two or more different variables or variable types at different times.	C++ Ref
unsigned	A data type modifier for integers and chars. An unsigned variable does not contain negative values. Can be used with char and int.	2
using	A directive statement used with namespace objects. The using statement tells which namespace (or region of the program) that the compiler must read. `using namespace std;` *See* namespace	10 C++ Ref
virtual	The virtual keyword is used in function declarations in base classes for functions that will be redefined in inherited classes.	11

```
class Base
{
  public:
  virtual void WhatAmI();
};
class Derived : public Base
{
  public:
  void WhatAmI(); // actual function implementation found here
};
```

Keyword	Use and Example	Refer to Chapter
void	A data type that represents "nothing," such as in a function prototype. Here the function FUNC does not return anything; therefore, it has a void return type. `void FUNC();`	2
volatile	An access modifier for variables whose value may be changed by ways not specified by the program.	C++ Ref
wchar_t	A data type declaration for variables that hold wide characters. Wide characters are needed in character sets of languages that have more than 255 characters.	C++ Ref

(continued)

B

Keyword	Use and Example	Refer to Chapter
while	A loop/iteration control statement. The while loop continues to execute as long as the condition remains true.	3

```
int count;

while (count < 10)
{
  cout << "\n Counting " << count;
  ++ count;
}
```

B

Operators in C++

The operator precedence (or priority) of operations is listed in Table C-1 in descending order. The highest priority is at the top of the list and the lowest priority is at the bottom. The associativity refers to the position of the operator in the C++ statement, not in this table. For example, in the following statement, the division will be performed before the multiplication because the associativity for these two operators is left to right.

```
x = a / b * c;    // division is performed first, then multiplication
```

TABLE C-1
Operators in C++

Type	Symbol	Associativity
Resolution	`::`	Left to right
Primary	`() [] .-> casting operators`	Left to right
Unary	`++ -- & * ! ~ sizeof (type)`	Right to left
Arithmetic	`* / %`	Left to right
Arithmetic	`+ -`	Left to right
Shift	`<< >>`	Left to right
Relational	`< <= > >=`	Left to right
Relational	`== !=`	Left to right
Bitwise	`& (AND)`	Left to right
Bitwise	`^ (XOR)`	Left to right
Bitwise	`| (OR)`	Left to right
Logical	`&& (AND)`	Left to right
Logical	`|| (OR)`	Left to right
Conditional	`?:`	Right to left
Assignment	`= += -= *= /= %= etc.`	Right to left
Comma	`,`	Left to right

ASCII Character Codes

Table D-1 shows the ASCII character codes for decimal 0 to 127 (a few symbols have not been included here.). On the source code CD, a project folder in Appendix D provides a short program that writes out the decimal, hex, octal, and symbol for the entire ASCII code for 0 to 255. Also, Visual C++ Help provides a complete description of the 255 ASCII codes, including the control sequences. Refer to the MSDN Visual Studio 6.0 and find the index listing for "ASCII Character Codes."

TABLE D-1
ASCII Character Codes for 0 to 127

Decimal	Hex	Octal	Symbol
0	0	0	NULL
1	1	1	☺
2	2	2	[See C++ reference]
3	3	3	♥
4	4	4	♦
5	5	5	♣
6	6	6	♠
7	7	7	Beep or bell
8	8	10	Backspace
9	9	11	Horizontal tab
10	A	12	\n newline
11	B	13	♂ vertical tab
12	C	14	♀ form feed
13	D	15	↵Enter key or carriage return
14	E	16	[See C++ reference]

Decimal	Hex	Octal	Symbol
15	F	17	[See C++ reference]
16	10	20	[See C++ reference]
17	11	21	[See C++ reference]
18	12	22	[See C++ reference]
19	13	23	[See C++ reference]
20	14	24	[See C++ reference]
21	15	25	[See C++ reference]
22	16	26	[See C++ reference]
23	17	27	[See C++ reference]
24	18	30	[See C++ reference]
25	19	31	[See C++ reference]
26	1A	32	[See C++ reference]
27	1B	33	Escape
28	1C	34	[See C++ reference]
29	1D	35	[See C++ reference]
30	1E	36	[See C++ reference]
31	1F	37	[See C++ reference]
32	20	40	Space
33	21	41	!
34	22	42	"
35	23	43	#
36	24	44	$
37	25	45	%
38	26	46	&
39	27	47	'
40	28	50	(
41	29	51	)
42	2A	52	*
43	2B	53	+
44	2C	54	,
45	2D	55	-
46	2E	56	.

D

Decimal	Hex	Octal	Symbol
47	2F	57	/
48	30	60	0
49	31	61	1
50	32	62	2
51	33	63	3
52	34	64	4
53	35	65	5
54	36	66	6
55	37	67	7
56	38	70	8
57	39	71	9
58	3A	72	:
59	3B	73	;
60	3C	74	<
61	3D	75	=
62	3E	76	>
63	3F	77	?
64	40	100	@
65	41	101	A
66	42	102	B
67	43	103	C
68	44	104	D
69	45	105	E
70	46	106	F
71	47	107	G
72	48	110	H
73	49	111	I
74	4A	112	J
75	4B	113	K
76	4C	114	L
77	4D	115	M
78	4E	116	N

D

Decimal	Hex	Octal	Symbol
79	4F	117	O
80	50	120	P
81	51	121	Q
82	52	122	R
83	53	123	S
84	54	124	T
85	55	125	U
86	56	126	V
87	57	127	W
88	58	130	X
89	59	131	Y
90	5A	132	Z
91	5B	133	[
92	5C	134	\
93	5D	135	]
94	5E	136	^
95	5F	137	_
96	60	140	`
97	61	141	a
98	62	142	b
99	63	143	c
100	64	144	d
101	65	145	e
102	66	146	f
103	67	147	g
104	68	150	h
105	69	151	i
106	6A	152	j
107	6B	153	k
108	6C	154	l
109	6D	155	m
110	6E	156	n

D

Decimal	Hex	Octal	Symbol
111	6F	157	o
112	70	160	p
113	71	161	q
114	72	162	r
115	73	163	s
116	74	164	t
117	75	165	u
118	76	166	v
119	77	167	w
120	78	170	x
121	79	171	y
122	7A	172	z
123	7B	173	{
124	7C	174	I
125	7D	175	}
126	7E	176	~
127	7F	177	Delete

D

Bits, Bytes, Memory, and Hexadecimal Notation

Overview

When C/C++ programs are compiled and executed, physical memory in the computer is reserved and used for the program's variables and other program components. It is important for the C++ programmer to understand a few details about computer memory and how it is addressed with hexadecimal notation. This information is especially helpful when learning about pointers and how they work.

Computer Memory and Disks

Computers store pieces of information in the form of bits, which are commonly referred to as 1s and 0s. Computer systems use several types of physical materials for storing and accessing data. Fundamentally, all these systems maintain the bits of data in one of two states, which are interpreted as 1s and 0s. For example, magnetic media such as floppy and hard disks are similar to old phonograph records, and the tracks are charged into positive or negative states. Random access memory (RAM) in personal computers is made up of computer chips that have digital logic with two distinct voltage states, often referred to as high and low. This two-state representation for data storage is known as binary. Table E-1 summarizes the two-state storage methods for computers.

Bits and Bytes

When data is read from a floppy disk, the positive and negative regions are interpreted as a series of 1s and 0s. This continuous stream of 1s and 0s is grouped into 8-bit sections, or bytes. Eight bits make up 1 byte of data, and 4 bits represent $\frac{1}{2}$ byte, or a nibble.

Byte Formats: ASCII and EBCDIC   There are two standard conventions for interpreting the series of bits: the American Standard Code for Information Interchange (ASCII) and the Extended Binary Coded Decimal Interchange Code (EBCDIC). The personal computer uses the ASCII notation for interpreting bits, whereas mainframes and some minicomputers use the EBCDIC format. (Appendix D, "ASCII Character Codes," presents a complete set of codes.)

Table E-2 shows how the same bit patterns have different meanings on two different systems. The hexadecimal notation for the bit pattern is presented and will be discussed in detail below. The *0x* prefix is used to indicate hex notation.

Hexadecimal Notation   To read the series of 1s and 0s, computer scientists have adopted *hexadecimal (hex) notation* as a way to write and understand bit patterns in bytes. This *hex* notation provides an easy and efficient way to interpret bit patterns and is used when addressing computer memory. The C++ programmer will see hex notation when he or she writes out the address of a variable or the value of a pointer.

Memory Is in Hex   All programmers should have an appreciation of the complex science underlying the computer programming languages. What the programmer needs to know is that computer memory is addressed and reported in hexadecimal notation. When the programmer examines addresses in C++ (in pointer

▌ **TABLE E-1**
Computer Media

Type of Material	Where Is It?	How Does It Work?	Note
Magnetic material	Floppy disk, zip disks, computer hard disks	Disk head sets the polarity on the media	Very important to keep magnets away from disks and computers because they can remagnetize them.
Digital logic	Random access memory (RAM)	Electronic chips have voltage values set high or low	Data in RAM is lost if the power is turned off.

▌ **TABLE E-2**
Byte Format Conventions

Bit Pattern	Hex Notation	In ASCII (on a PC)	In EBCDIC (on a Mainframe)
0101 0000	0x50	P	&
0110 0001	0x61	a	/
0100 1100	0x4C	L	<
0110 1111	0x6F	o	?

variables), the addresses will be shown in hex. Program E-1 writes the addresses of two floating point values. The input and output are shown below:

Please enter 2 floating point values 3.6 8.2

You entered 3.6 and 8.2
The addresses in hex of the numbers are 0x0066FFD4 and 0x0066FDF0

Not bad, huh?

The variable num1 has the value 3.6 and its address is 0x0066FFD4. This address is eight hex digits. The *0x* is the computer's way of indicating that this address is a hex value. These eight digits represent 4 bytes because it takes two hex digits to represent 1 byte of computer memory. Each address shown is 4 bytes. Is this material confusing? Let's examine hexadecimal notation in more detail.

Base 10 Decimal, Base 2 Binary, Base 16 Hexadecimal   We are all familiar with counting in decimal notation (base 10) because that notation is our normal counting method. The symbol *0* represents none and the symbol *1* represents one. We use the symbol *5* to represent the number of fingers on one hand. But when asked how many eggs in a dozen, we do not have one symbol to represent twelve. We need to use two of our symbols, a 1 and a 2, to represent twelve. Ten different symbols are used for writing numeric values. These symbols are 0, 1, 2, 3, 4, 5, 6, 7, 8, and 9. Our counting scheme has an individual symbol for representing zero through nine, but when we need to represent ten objects, we must use a combination of our symbols. We write ten using 10 (we have started reusing our symbols).

```
//Program E-1 Writing out hex addresses for two numbers.
#include <iostream.h>
int main()
{
        float num1, num2;
        cout << "\n Please enter 2 floating point values ";
        cin >> num1 >> num2;
        cout << "\n You entered " << num1 << " and " << num2;
        cout << "\n The addresses in hex of the numbers are " <<
        &num1 << " and " << &num2 << endl;

        cout << "\n Not bad, huh?" << endl;
        return 0;
}
```

E

Because computer data is stored in bits, we have only two symbols, 1 and 0, with which to write all the information for the computer. (Our alphabet uses twenty-six symbols to represent the English language.) All computer data is written in this two-symbol language known as *base 2* or *binary*. Since binary notation is so cumbersome, computer scientists use *base 16*, also known as *hexadecimal*, as a shorthand notation for representing the binary data. Hexadecimal notation uses sixteen separate symbols, 0 to 9 and A, B, C, D, E, and F. Table E-3 shows the different base representations for the numeric values 0 to 20.

By combining the 8-bit byte and hexadecimal notation, computer scientists have a method where one digit (or symbol) can be used to represent 4 bits, and two

▌ TABLE E-3
Numeric Values and Different Bases

Numeric Amount	Base 2	Base 10	Base 16	Notes
Zero	0	0	0	
One	1	1	1	
Two	10	2	2	Base 2: start reusing symbols
Three	11	3	3	
Four	100	4	4	Base 2: we now use three symbols
Five	101	5	5	
Six	110	6	6	
Seven	111	7	7	
Eight	1000	8	8	
Nine	1001	9	9	
Ten	1010	10	A	Base 10: start reusing symbols
Eleven	1011	11	B	
Twelve	1100	12	C	
Thirteen	1101	13	D	
Fourteen	1110	14	E	
Fifteen	1111	15	F	
Sixteen	10000	16	10	Base 16: carry the 1 and start reusing symbols
Seventeen	10001	17	11	
Eighteen	10010	18	12	
Nineteen	10011	19	13	
Twenty	10100	20	14	Base 10: increment 1 to 2 and start the ones column at 0 again.

E

hex digits (symbols) can be used to represent 1 byte of data. Decimal notation (0 to 9) would not be practical to use because it requires two digits to represent ten through fifteen.

Individual bit patterns can be obtained from hexadecimal notation. Two examples are shown in Table E-4. (Refer to Table E-3 for actual hex values shown in detail.)

Counting in Hex   It is not necessary for the C++ programmer to become an expert in hex arithmetic unless he or she is planning to do assembler-level programming or to work on programming hardware devices. It is important for the C++ programmer to be able to recognize hex notation and count in hex so that he or she can fully understand pointers and addresses.

Learning to count in hex (base 16) is similar to learning to count in decimal (base 10). The difficult part is remembering that there are sixteen symbols in hex instead of the ten symbols in decimal. Let's practice counting in both base 10 and base 16. First, we will count from one to twenty-three in both base 10 and base 16:

```
Base 10   1,2,3,4,5,6,7,8,9,10,11,12,13,14,15,16,17,18,19,20,21,22,23
Base 16   1,2,3,4,5,6,7,8,9, A, B, C, D, E, F,10,11,12,13,14,15,16,17
```

Now we'll count from 90 to 106 in base 10 and match these values to the comparable values in hex. Notice that in base 10, we run out of digits at ninety-nine and begin using a third digit.

```
Base 10    90,91,92,93,94,95,96,97,98,99,100,101,102,103,104,105,106
Base 16    5A,5B,5C,5D,5E,5F,60,61,62,63, 64, 65, 66, 67, 68, 69, 6A
```

Now we'll count from 250 to 259 in base 10. In the base 16 counting, we run out of digits at base 10 255 (0xFF) and begin using a third hex digit for base 10 256 (100).

```
Base 10    250,251,252,253,254,255,256,257,258,259
Base 16     FA, FB, FC, FD, FE, FF,100,101,102,103
```

Hex and Bit Patterns

Hex Pattern	Number of Bytes	Details	Bit Pattern
0xFF24	2	0xF = 1111, 0x2 = 0010, 0x4 = 0100.	1111 1111 0010 0100 F F 2 4
0xFA1E	2	0xA = 1010, 0x1 = 0001, 0xE = 1110	1111 1010 0001 1110 F A 1 E

E

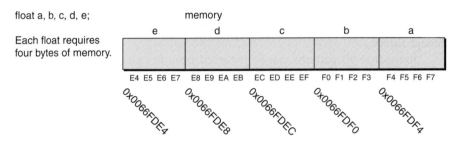

float a, b, c, d, e;

Each float requires
four bytes of memory.

memory

e   d   c   b   a

E4 E5 E6 E7   E8 E9 EA EB   EC ED EE EF   F0 F1 F2 F3   F4 F5 F6 F7

0x0066FDE4   0x0066FDE8   0x0066FDEC   0x0066FDF0   0x0066FDF4

Figure E-1
Five Floating Point Variables in Memory

Data Variables and Hex   In Chapter 4, many sample programs showed memory locations and their corresponding hex addresses. With pointers it is helpful to have a minimal understanding of hexadecimal notation and memory. A C++ program must reserve memory to store the variables and know the location (or address) of each variable. This location or address is in hexadecimal notation.

The programmer need not worry about where in memory the variables are stored because that is the job of the operating system. However, it is convenient to know that each floating point variable requires 4 bytes of memory and each double requires 8 bytes, and when the programmer examines a variable's address (be it directly or in a pointer), it will be in hexadecimal notation.

Practice

In Figure E-1, we have five floating point variables, and the beginning address for the first variable is 0x0066FDE4. What are the other variables' starting addresses? Here is the declaration:

```
float a,b,c,d,e;
```

Note that variables are stacked in memory from last to first. The last declared variable, "e," is the first one in memory and it has the lowest address. Figure E-1 illustrates the computer memory.

The Most Common Mistake When Counting in Hex   The most common mistake made when learning to count in hex is forgetting that there are sixteen symbols in hex. The order of the sixteen symbols (from smallest to largest) is shown here:

0, 1, 2, 3, 4, 5, 6, 7, 8, 9, A, B, C, D, E, F

E

Always refer to base 10 counting as a guide and remember to carry one when you run out of symbols. When counting in hex, remember that the symbols go up to F instead of just 9. Table E-5 illustrates common mistakes made when counting in hex.

TABLE E-5

Right and Wrong Way to Count in Base 10 and Base 16 (Hex)

Technique	Count from Seven to Eighteen[a]
Right way: base 10	7, 8, 9, 10, 11, 12, 13, 14, 15, 16, 17, 18
Right way: base 16	7, 8, 9, A, B, C, D, E, F, 10, 11, 12
Wrong way: base 16	7, 8, 9, ⊗, 10, ⊗, 1A, 1B, 1C, 1D, 1E, 1F, 20, 21
Technique	**Count from Fourteen to Twenty-Seven**
Right way: base 10	14, 15, 16, 17, 18, 19, 20, 21, 22, 23, 24, 25, 26, 27
Right way: base 16	E, F, 10, 11, 12, 13, 14, 15, 16, 17, 18, 19, 1A, 1B
Wrong way: base 16	E, F, 10, 11, 12, 13, 14, 15, 16, 17, 18, 19, ⊗, 2A, 2B

[a] ⊗ indicates incorrect counting sequence.

E

C++ provides several methods for reading and writing information from and to a data file. This appendix provides one technique for handling text-based data that is similar to reading data from the keyboard. The data in a text-based file is in ASCII format, and these data files can be created in a simple text-editor program—such as Microsoft's Notepad. Before we present the C++ statements needed for reading and writing data files, we must understand data files in general.

Know the File Format

When reading data from a file, you must know how the data is arranged in the file. This arrangement isn't magic—it is part of the program design. Just as you decide how to organize your program and which functions to use, you also decide how the data files are to be formatted. Your program must have the read statements arranged so that they match the file layout, or your data will not be read correctly. Several general file format schemes are available.

Header Line   The data file contains a header line(s) that relays information to the program concerning the data file. One example of this file type has an integer value in the first line. This value represents the number of lines following or other pertinent data. The program reads the first line into an integer variable and then uses it in a for loop. Figure F-1 shows the general flow of a program and a data file that has a header line and data.

Trailer or Sentinel   Another file format scheme involves placing a special value at the end of the data file and having the program check the values as they are read in from the file. When the program sees this special *trailer value* or *sentinel value*, it stops reading from the data file. Figure F-2 shows the program flow and data file in which the sentinel value is −99. The program continues to read the data file until it finds this value.

When using this technique, the programmer needs to pick a trailer value that is not within the range of the actual data. Also, if the program needs to read in sev-

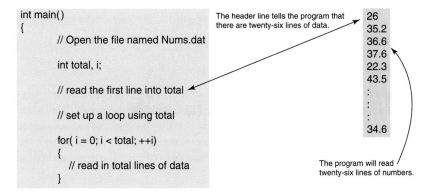

Figure F-1
Header Line Data File Scheme

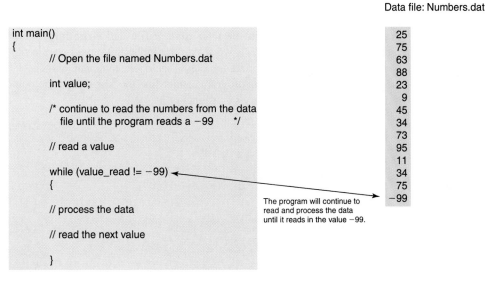

Figure F-2
Trailer Line Data File Scheme

eral pieces of information on a line, such as a record of data, the programmer can designate one of the data items to be the trailer and trap for a special value.

Read Until End of File   A very common technique used when reading data files is to have the program read until it reaches the end of the file. Data files contain an end of file marker (it is a special character), and C++ recognizes that marker when it reads it. The end of file marker is automatically placed at the end of the file when the file is closed; the programmer does not need to enter it into the file. For our purposes, this marker is designated as EOF. This type of file reading works exactly like the trailer or sentinel value approach and is illustrated in Figure F-3.

File I/O Using iostream

In C++, we originally introduced the data stream concept for input from the keyboard and output to the screen. We include the iostream library and use the cin and cout functions. When working with data files, we establish input and output stream objects and use these objects in the same manner as we used cin and cout. Open the stream object and use them exactly as we used our old pals cin and cout, and we're "in there" reading data from files!

Steps for Text-Based File Input/Output

Step 1: Open the file. The program must first locate and open the data file. Files must be opened before data can be read. The required functions are in the fstream library. It is also convenient to use a #define statement near the top of your program so the file names can be found easily when reading source code. Assume that we will read data from the *wthr_sum.in* file and write information to the *report.out* file. In Program F-1, we set up the input and output stream objects and open the files, set the appropriate ios flag in the open statement, and check also that the input file is located. If the program cannot find the file, there is no point in continuing; so the standard library's exit function is used.

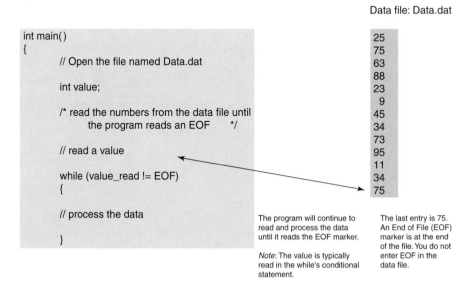

Data file: Data.dat

```
int main( )
{
        // Open the file named Data.dat

        int value;

        /* read the numbers from the data file until
            the program reads an EOF      */

        // read a value

        while (value_read != EOF)
        {

        // process the data

        }
```

```
25
75
63
88
23
9
45
34
73
95
11
34
75
```

The program will continue to read and process the data until it reads the EOF marker.

Note: The value is typically read in the while's conditional statement.

The last entry is 75. An End of File (EOF) marker is at the end of the file. You do not enter EOF in the data file.

Figure F-3
Read End of File Marker Scheme

```
//Program F-1 Weather Statistics
#include <iostream.h>            //required for cout
#include <fstream.h>             //required for file I/O
#include <stdlib.h>              //required for exit

#define FILE_IN "wthr_sum.dat"     // place the data file in the project folder
#define FILE_OUT "report.out"

int main()
{
        //first must set up streams for input and output
        ifstream input;           //set up input stream object
        ofstream output;          //set up output stream object

        //open for input and don't create if it is not there
        input.open(FILE_IN, ios::in|ios::nocreate);

        //Check to be sure file is opened.  Use the ! operator with input object.
        if(!input )
        {
                cout << "\n Can't find input file" << FILE_IN;
                cout << "\n Exiting program, bye bye \n ";
                exit(1);
        }

        //Open the output file for the output
        output.open(FILE_OUT, ios::out);

        //Now the files are open and ready to go.
```

Step 2: Read the data into variables. Once the input and output stream objects have been created and opened successfully, the data can be read from the input file and written to the output file. To continue with this example, suppose the weather data input file was set up as shown in Figure F-4. We want our program to read in this data and report the temperature range, humidity (dry, nice, muggy), and whether or not it rained that day at the reporting station.

We need to declare the following data variables in the program:

```
char date[25], station[50];
int high,low;
float humidity, rain;
```

Data file: *wthr_sum.in*

September 13, 2001	Date
Albuquerque International Airport	Reporting station
83	High temperature
60	Low temperature
0.18	Relative humidity
0.00	Rainfall

Figure F-4
Contents and Format of *wthr_sum.in* File

Now, using the input stream object, we can just read in the data:

```
//Read the first 2 lines into character strings
input.getline(date,25);
input.getline(station,50);

//Read the numeric values
input >> high >> low >> humidity >> rain;
```

Remember that the cin function reads numeric data separated by whitespace values, as does the input stream object. We could also use the following format:

```
//Set up a character string temporary buffer
char buf[15];
//Read each line of numeric values into buffer
//and use atoi and atof functions.
input.getline(buf, 15);
high = atoi(buf);
input.getline(buf, 15);
low = atoi(buf);
input.getline(buf,15);
humidity = atof(buf);
input.getline(buf,15);
rain = atof(buf);
```

Step 3: Write output.   To write data to the output file, we use the output stream in a manner similar to cout:

```
output << "Date:" << date << "\nStation:" << station;
if(rain == 0.0)
        output << "\n    No Rain";
else
        output << "\n    It rained today.";
```

```
        int range = high - low;
        output << "\nThe temperature range was " << range;

        if(humidity < 0.33)
                output << "\nDry";
        else if(humidity < 0.66)
                output << "\nNice";
        else
                output << "\nMuggy";

        //Now close the files.
        input.close();
        output.close();

        return 0;
}
```

The output from this program is in the *report.out* file in Figure F-5.

Complete Example: Student Grades   The file *student_gd.dat* contains student information on each line. The first line contains the number of student "records" in the file. In Program F-2, we read in the data, calculate the average, and print the student's name and grade in the *Grades.out* file. The *student_gd.dat* file is shown in Figure F-6. The student's grades are read into an array and we use the FindAve function. We need to declare array sizes. We write this program so that we read in eight grades for each student.

It is important to remember that the end of line characters must be handled correctly when one is reading data files. If we have character data and numeric data and use a cin-like read for the numbers, the end of line must be pulled out of the input stream. (When reading just numeric data, as in the previous weather example above, the cin-like read statements ignore the whitespace characters.) Program F-2 illustrates the use of getline and character strings as well as the use of an individual get statement. Also, the data file is constructed carefully so that no extra spaces are accidentally placed at the end of the lines. The output data file is shown in Figure F-7.

Data file: *report.out*

Date: September 13, 2001
Station: Albuquerque International Airport
No Rain
The temperature range was 23
Dry

Figure F-5
Contents and Format of *report.out* File

F

```
//Program F-2 Calculate Student Grades
#include <iostream.h>
#include <iomanip.h>              // required for setw
#include <fstream.h>             //required for file I/O
#include <stdlib.h>              // required for exit() and atoi

#define FILE_IN "Student_gd.dat"   //be sure to place the data file in the project file
#define FILE_OUT "Grades.out"

float FindAve(float[], int);      //function prototype

int main()
{
        float grades[8], ave;
        char name[25];
        int total_students, total_grades = 8;
//first must set up streams for input and output
        ifstream input;
        ofstream output;

//open for input and don't create if it is not there
        input.open(FILE_IN, ios::in|ios::nocreate);

//Check to be sure file is opened.
        if(!input )
        {
                cout << "\n Can't find input file " << FILE_IN;
                cout << "\n Exiting program, bye bye \n ";
                exit(1);
        }
        output.open(FILE_OUT, ios::out);

//Write a header out to the output file before we begin reading
        output << "\n The Most Fantastic Grading Program Ever Written  ;-) \n\n"
                << "Student Name          Average Grade\n";

//Read the first line to determine number of students
//Use the getline so that it will pull out the end of line character.
        char buf[15];
        input.getline(buf,15);
        total_students = atoi(buf);
```

```
// Set the numeric output flags for 3 decimal digits of precision
        output.precision(3);
        output.setf(ios::fixed);

// Now read each line of student data and calculate and print ave.
        char junk;
        int i, j;
        for(i = 0; i<total_students; ++i)
        {
                input.get(name,25);    // read in the name
                                //use a for loop to read in the 8 grades
                for(j = 0; j < 8; ++j)
                {
                        input >> grades[j];
                }
                input.get(junk); //pull out end of line char
                ave = FindAve(grades, total_grades);

//now write date to output file
                output << name << setw(10) << ave << endl;
        }
        output << "\n How do you like them apples??? Bye! ";
        cout << "\n All Done! \n";
        input.close();
        output.close();
        return 0;
}


// Find Average function
float FindAve(float x[], int total)
{
        float sum = 0.0;
        int i;
        for(i = 0; i < total; ++i)
        {
                sum = sum + x[i];
        }
        return(sum/total);
}
```

F

Data file: *Student_gd.dat*

6										Number of students in file	
Janet McCarthy	98	74	96	97	95	89	78	98		First student	8 grades
John Glover	99	97	97	69	96	88	95	99		Second student	8 grades
Mister Freecell	84	75	80	78	58	68	75	88		Third student	8 grades
Mike Cary	94	70	100	88	82	93	83	79		Fourth student	8 grades
Jason Thomas	78	88	98	84	89	88	92	93		Fifth student	8 grades
Carol Hoffhill	99	82	92	67	105	84	91	90		Sixth student	8 grades

Figure F-6

Contents and Format of *Student_gd.dat* File

Data file: *Grades.out*

The Most Fantastic Grading Program Ever Written ;-)

Student Name	Average Grade
Janet McCarthy	90.625
John Glover	92.500
Mister Freecell	75.750
Mike Cary	86.125
Jason Thomas	88.750
Carol Hoffhill	88.750

How do you like them apples??? Bye!

Figure F-7

Contents and Format of *Grades.out* File

Read Until End of File   The file *Whole_Lotta_Numbers.dat* contains a list of integer values. We do not know how many numbers are in this file, only that there is one number on each line. The program AddAllThoseNumbers opens the file and reads and adds these values (one at a time). Program F-3 demonstrates how to continue reading a data file until we reach the end of file (EOF) marker. The output is shown below:

> The file is Whole_Lotta_Numbers.dat
> Total Numbers in file 250
> The sum is 125024

How do you like them numbers??? Bye!

Binary File Input and Output: Overview

The secret to success with binary files is understanding pointers and addresses! (Are you surprised?) To *write* a binary file, we essentially open a file as binary and tell the program to write a chunk of data from memory into the file. We tell the

```
//Program F-3 Read Until EOF
#include <iostream.h>
#include <fstream.h>                    //required for file I/O
#include <stdlib.h>                     // required for exit() and atoi

#define FILE_IN "Whole_Lotta_Numbers.dat"
int main()
{
        int total_numbers = 0, number_du_jour, sum;

        //first must set up stream for input
        ifstream ILoveNumbers;                          //set up input stream object

        //open for input and don't create if it is not there
        ILoveNumbers.open(FILE_IN, ios::in|ios::nocreate);

        //Check to be sure file is opened.  One way, use the fail function.
        if(!ILoveNumbers )
        {
                cout << "\n Can't find input file " << FILE_IN;
                cout << "\n Exiting program, bye bye \n ";
                exit(1);
        }

        sum = 0;
        while(!ILoveNumbers.eof() )      //read until we reach the end of file
        {
                ILoveNumbers >> number_du_jour;                 // read the number
                sum = sum + number_du_jour;
                ++total_numbers;
        }

        cout << "\n          The file is " << FILE_IN;
        cout << "\n Total Numbers in file " << total_numbers;
        cout << "\n          The sum is " << sum;

        cout << "\n\n How do you like them numbers??? Bye! " << endl;

        ILoveNumbers.close();
        return 0;
}
```

F

write function the address of the data and how many bytes of memory to write. Then the binary data is packed into the file. When we *read* a binary file, we do just the opposite. We must provide the address of the memory where we wish the file data to be placed. To demonstrate, Program F-4 uses a simple data structure, and we write the data to a file and then read it back into the program.

```
//Program F-4 Write and Read Binary Files

#include <iostream.h>
#include <fstream.h>              //required for file I/O
#include <stdlib.h>              // required for exit() and atoi
#include <string.h>

#define FILE_IN "TestBinaryOutput.dat"   //we'll write and read the same file
#define FILE_OUT "TestBinaryOutput.dat"

struct Person
{
        char name[50];
        int age;
        char sex;    // M or F
};

int main()
{
        Person people;
        strcpy(people.name,"Claire J");
        people.age = 25;
        people.sex = 'F';
        cout << "\n Our person is " << people.name;
        cout << "\n His/Her sex is " << people.sex;
        cout << "\n His/Her age is " << people.age;

        ofstream output;                  //set up output stream object
        output.open(FILE_OUT, ios::out|ios::binary);

        output.write((char *) &people, sizeof(Person) );    //give the address & size

        cout << "\n All done writing our person to the file! \n";
        output.close();
```

F

```
//Now let's open and read the file

        cout << "\n\n Now let's read our file. \n ";
        Person Newperson;
        ifstream input;                         //set up output stream object

        //open for input and don't create if it is not there
        input.open(FILE_IN, ios::out|ios::binary);

        //Check to be sure file is opened.
        if(!input )
        {
                cout << "\n Can't find input file " << FILE_IN;
                cout << "\n Exiting program, bye bye \n ";
                exit(1);
        }

        input.read((char *) &Newperson, sizeof(Person) );

        cout << "\n The new person is " << Newperson.name;
        cout << "\n His/Her sex is " << Newperson.sex;
        cout << "\n His/Her age is " << Newperson.age;

        input.close();
        cout << "\n\n WOW!   Wasn't that amazing? " << endl;
        return 0;
}
```

The screen output shows that we have read the new data into Newperson.

Our person is Claire J
His/Her sex is F
His/Her age is 25
All done writing our person to the file!

Now let's read our file.

The new person is Claire J
His/Her sex is F
His/Her age is 25

WOW! Wasn't that amazing?

F

Arrays, structures, objects, and individual variables may be written into and read from binary files using this same write and read scheme. Program F-5 is an expanded version of Program F-4. In this expanded version, we use an individual write and read statement for each variable. The read and write functions are members of the stream class. The C++ programmer is encouraged to refer to a complete C++ reference for additional details.

```cpp
//Program F-5 More with Binary Files

#include <iostream.h>
#include <fstream.h>                //required for file I/O
#include <stdlib.h>                 // required for exit() and atoi
#include <string.h>

#define FILE_IN "BinaryOutput2.dat"   //we'll write and read the same file
#define FILE_OUT "BinaryOutput2.dat"

 struct Person
{
        char name[50];
        int age;
        char sex;     // M or F
};

int main()
{
        Person people;
        strcpy(people.name,"Claire J");
        people.age = 25;
        people.sex = 'F';

        int numbers[4] = {23, 235, 36, 9433 };
        int counter = 43;
        ofstream output;                    //set up output stream object

        output.open(FILE_OUT, ios::out|ios::binary);
        output.write((char *) &people, sizeof(Person) );      //write the struct
        output.write((char *) &numbers, sizeof(numbers) );    //write the array
        output.write((char *) &counter, sizeof(int) );        //write the integer

        cout << "\n All done writing data to the file! \n";
        output.close();
```

```
//Now let's open and read the file
        cout << "\n\n Now let's read our file. \n ";
        Person Newperson;
        int Newnums[4];
        int Newcounter;

        ifstream input;                       //set up input stream object

        //open for input and don't create if it is not there
        input.open(FILE_IN, ios::out|ios::binary);

        //Check to be sure file is opened.
        if(!input )
        {
                cout << "\n Can't find input file " << FILE_IN;
                cout << "\n Exiting program, bye bye \n ";
                exit(1);
        }

        input.read((char *) &Newperson, sizeof(Person) );     //the data must be read
        input.read((char *) &Newnums, sizeof(Newnums) );      //in the order that it
        input.read((char *) &Newcounter, sizeof(int) );       //was written

        cout << "\n The new person is " << Newperson.name;
        cout << "\n His/Her sex is " << Newperson.sex;
        cout << "\n His/Her age is " << Newperson.age;

        cout << "\n Newnumbers are " << Newnums[0] << "," << Newnums[1]
             << "," << Newnums[2] << "," << Newnums[3];
        cout << "\n Newcounter is " << Newcounter;

        input.close();
        cout << "\n\n WOW!  More amazing file feats! " << endl;
        return 0;
}
```

The output for Program F-5 is shown below:

All done writing data to the file!

Now let's read our file.

The new person is Claire J
His/Her sex is F
His/Her age is 25
Newnumbers are 23,235,36,9433
Newcounter is 43

WOW! More amazing file feats!

F

APPENDIX
G

C++ String Class

The designers of C++ added a string class to provide tools to make string handling very simple. The C++ string class gives the programmer the ability to declare a string object. The class has various overloaded operators and member functions that make working with strings a snap!

String Objects

Creating a String   The string class handles the memory management and frees the programmer from worrying about the details of allocating enough memory. The three constructors for the string class and examples for these constructors are shown in Table G-1.

String Operators   Many overloaded operators are found in the string class, and they perform the commonly used operations. Table G-2 summarizes these string operators.

TABLE G-1
String Class Constructors

Constructor	Job	Example
string();	Creates an empty string.	`string S1;`

string(const char *str);	Creates a string object from a null-terminated character array. It provides a conversion from a class C character array to a string. It is also used to create and initialize a string object.	`// conversion from char array`
		`char MyCString[25] = "I Love C++";`
		`string S2(MyCString);`
		`//S2 now contains I Love C++`
		`// create and initialize`
		`string S3("What a great day.");`

string(const string &str);	Creates a string from another string.	`string S1;`
		`S1 = "I love C++";`
		`string S2(S1);`
		`// S2 now contains "I love C++."`

Operator	Job	Example
=	assignment	S1 = "What a great day."; S2 = "Do you love C++?";

+	concatenate
	
	 Can be used with C-style character strings and C++ strings.
		S3 = S1 + S2; //hooks S2 on end of S1
		 // S3 now has What a great day.Do you love C++?
		 S3 = S1 + MyOldString;
		 // S3 now has What a great day.Howdy Partner

+=	concatenation and assignment	S1+=S2; // hooks Do you love C++? onto What a great day.
		 // S1 now contains What a great day.Do you love C++?

==	same as	if(S1 == S2) // compares the strings, 1 if same, 0 if not

!=	not same as	if(S1 != S2) // compares the strings, 1 if not the same,
		 0 if same

<	less than	if (S1 < S2) // compares the string for alphabetical order based on the ASCII code, where A to Z is lower than a to z and A is less than B. (See Appendix D, "ASCII Character Codes.")
<=	less than or same as	if (S1 <= S2) // see <
>	greater than	if(S1 > S2) // see <
>=	greater than or same as	if(S1 >= S2) // see <
[]	subscripting Allows an array of strings to be created.	string S[10]; // creates an array of 10 strings
<<	output	cout << S1;
>>	input[b]	cin >> S1;

[a]MyOldString is declared by char MyOldString [25]="Howdy Partner";
[b]cin will read to first whitespace character and terminate the reading process.

G

Program G-1 shows the use of several string constructor functions and operators. (Refer also to Figure G-1.)

```
// Program G-1    String Example Program with Overloaded Operators

#include <iostream>   //C++ header style since using C++ string class
#include <string>
using namespace std;

int main()
{
      string S1("What a great day."), S2, S3;
      char MyOldString[20] = "Howdy Partner";

      string S4(MyOldString);   // create a string object S4 and fill with MyOldString
      S2 = "Do you love C++?";                    //assignment
      S3 = S1 + S2;                    // add two strings and assign into S3

//Write the initial string values
      cout << "\n          S1 = " << S1;
      cout << "\n          S2 = " << S2;
      cout << "\n          S3 = " << S3;
      cout << "\n          S4 = " << S4;
      cout << "\n MyOldString = " << MyOldString << endl;

      if(S1 > S2)cout << "\n S1 is greater than S2";
      else cout << "\n S1 is not greater than or the same as S2";

      S1 = "\nAll done with strings.";
      cout << S1 << endl;

      return 0;
}
```

The output for Program G-1 is shown below:

```
        S1 = What a great day.
        S2 = Do you love C++?
        S3 = What a great day.Do you love C++?
        S4 = Howdy Partner
MyOldString = Howdy Partner

 S1 is greater than S2
All done with strings.
```

G

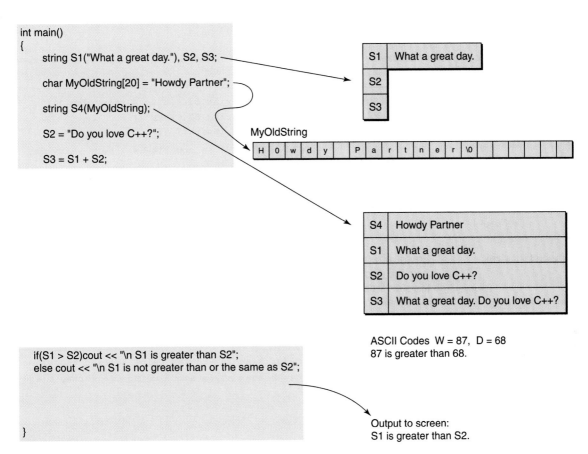

```
int main()
{
    string S1("What a great day."), S2, S3;

    char MyOldString[20] = "Howdy Partner";

    string S4(MyOldString);

    S2 = "Do you love C++?";

    S3 = S1 + S2;
```

S1	What a great day.
S2	
S3	

MyOldString

| H | o | w | d | y | | P | a | r | t | n | e | r | \0 | | | | | |

S4	Howdy Partner
S1	What a great day.
S2	Do you love C++?
S3	What a great day. Do you love C++?

ASCII Codes W = 87, D = 68
87 is greater than 68.

```
    if(S1 > S2)cout << "\n S1 is greater than S2";
    else cout << "\n S1 is not greater than or the same as S2";



}
```

Output to screen:
S1 is greater than S2.

Figure G-1
String Example Program

String Functions: Editing The string class contains many member functions, several of which are overloaded. The programmer should become familiar with a good C++ reference book or check the on-line help for a complete listing of all the string functions. Table G-3 shows three commonly used string functions. Note that all string index values are based on the first character referenced as zero. The examples in Table G-3 are presented in Program G-2, shown on page 632, and illustrated in Figure G-2. The output from Program G-2 is shown here:

       S1 = It is a rainy day.
       S2 = very
       S3 = sunny
       S1 = It is a very rainy day.
       S1 = It is a very sunny day.
       S1 = It is a sunny day.
All done with strings.

G

TABLE G-3
Partial Listing of String Class Editing Functions

Function	Job	Example
insert(start, string);	Place the string into the invoking string object at the start index.	```string S1("It is a rainy day.");``` ```string S2("very");``` ```S1.insert(7,S2);``` ```//S1 is now "It is a very rainy day."```
replace(start, size, string)	Replaces size number of characters of invoking string object at the start index.	```//S1 is "It is a very rainy day."``` ```// S3 is "sunny"``` ```S1.replace(13, 6, S3);``` ```// S1 is "It is a very sunny day."```
erase(start, size);	Erases size number of characters from the invoking string object at the start index.	```S1.erase(8, 5);``` ```// S1 is "It is a sunny day."```

```
// Program G-2   String Class Example Program Using Editing Functions
#include <iostream>    //C++ header style since using C++ string class
#include <string>
using namespace std;
int main()
{
        string S1("It is a rainy day.");
        string S2("very ");
        string S3("sunny ");
//Write the initial string values
        cout << "\n         S1 = " << S1;
        cout << "\n         S2 = " << S2;
        cout << "\n         S3 = " << S3;
// Insert "very" into S1
        S1.insert(8,S2);
        cout << "\n         S1 = " << S1;
// Replace "rainy" with "sunny" in S1
        S1.replace(13, 6, S3);
        cout << "\n         S1 = " << S1;
// Erase "very" from S1
        S1.erase(8, 5);
        cout << "\n         S1 = " << S1;
        S1 = "\nAll done with strings.";
        cout << S1 << endl;
        return 0;
}
```

G

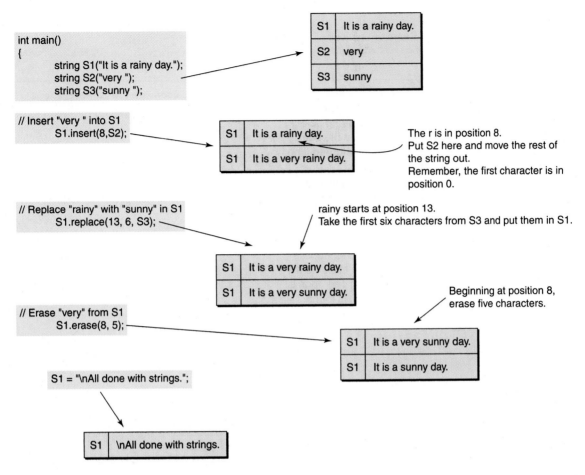

```
int main()
{
        string S1("It is a rainy day.");
        string S2("very ");
        string S3("sunny ");
```

S1	It is a rainy day.
S2	very
S3	sunny

// Insert "very " into S1
        S1.insert(8,S2);

S1	It is a rainy day.
S1	It is a very rainy day.

The r is in position 8.
Put S2 here and move the rest of
the string out.
Remember, the first character is in
position 0.

// Replace "rainy" with "sunny" in S1
        S1.replace(13, 6, S3);

rainy starts at position 13.
Take the first six characters from S3 and put them in S1.

S1	It is a very rainy day.
S1	It is a very sunny day.

Beginning at position 8,
erase five characters.

// Erase "very" from S1
        S1.erase(8, 5);

S1	It is a very sunny day.
S1	It is a sunny day.

S1 = "\nAll done with strings.";

S1	\nAll done with strings.

Figure G-2
String Class Editing Functions

Searching a String   Several search functions are included in the string class. A partial list appears in Table G-4. It is possible to search a string for the first occurrence of an item within that string, both in the forward and the reverse directions. Once again, you must provide the function with the starting position. Program G-3, shown on page 635, illustrates the find and rfind functions. Note that the string class defines the npos as the length of the string. Figure G-3 shows the details for Program G-3.

Function	Job	Example
find(string,start);	Returns the first occurrence index position of the string located within the invoking string object. The search begins at the start index. The npos is returned if no match is found.	```//Refer to code sample in Program E-3.``` ```First_pos = S1.find(S2,0);```
findr(string,start);	Returns the index of the string located within the invoking string object searching in reverse order. The search begins at the start index. (Note that string::npos is defined in the string class as the length of the string.) The npos is returned if no match is found.	```//Refer to code sample in Program E-3.``` ```Last_pos = S1.findr(S2,string::npos);```

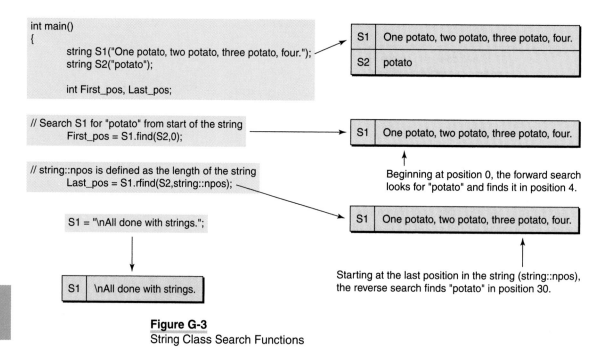

Figure G-3
String Class Search Functions

```
// Program G-3    String Class Program Example Using Search Functions

#include <iostream>    //C++ header style since using C++ string class
#include <string>
using namespace std;

int main()
{
        string S1("One potato, two potato, three potato, four.");
        string S2("potato");
        int First_pos, Last_pos;
//Write the initial string values
        cout << "\n          S1 = " << S1;
        cout << "\n          S2 = " << S2;
// Search S1 for "potato" from start of the string
        First_pos = S1.find(S2,0);
        cout << "\n The first \"potato\" is at " << First_pos;
// string::npos is defined as the length of the string
        Last_pos = S1.rfind(S2,string::npos);
        cout << "\n The last \"potato\" is at " << Last_pos;
        S1 = "\nAll done with strings.";
        cout << S1 << endl;
        return 0;

}
```

The output is shown below:

```
          S1 = One potato, two potato, three potato, four.
          S2 = potato
 The first "potato" is at 4
 The last "potato" is at 30
All done with strings.
```

Miscellaneous String Functions   This appendix presents several commonly used string operators and functions, but we have scratched only the surface of the string class. A complete C++ reference gives details for the approximately eighty forms of the string functions. Table G-5 presents more string functions, which the reader may find helpful.

G

Miscellaneous String Class Functions

Function	Job	Example

assign(char [])	Copy the contents of the character array into the invoking string.	```string S1;```
		 ```char MyArray = "I love C++";```
		 ```S1.assign(MyArray);```
		 ```//S1 now contains I love C++```

assign(string, start, number)	The number of characters from the string will be assigned into the invoking string, beginning at the start index. This function is normally used when a partial string assignment is needed. Use the = to assign an entire string.	```string S1, S2("I want a new car.");```
		 ```S1.assign(S2,7,9);```
		 ```//S1 now contains a new car```

assign(char [] , start, number)	Assigns the number of characters from a character string array into the invoking string, beginning at the start index.	```char MyArray[20] = "Turtles are green.";```
		 ```string S1;```
		 ```S1.assign(MyArray,8,9);```
		 ```// S1 now contains are green```

append(string, start, number)	Appends the number of characters from the string to the invoking string, beginning at the start index.	```string S1("I like to eat");```
		 ```string S2("peanuts and popcorn");```
		 ```S1.append(S2, 11, 8);```
		 ```//S1 now contains```
		 ``` I like to eat popcorn```

append(char [], start, number)	Appends the number of characters from the character string array to the invoking string, beginning at the start index.	```string S1("Birds like to eat");```
		 ```char MyArray[20] = "fruit and nuts";```
		 ```S1.append(MyArray, 0, 5);```
		 ```//S1 now contains```
		 ``` Birds like to eat fruit```

Conversion Between Character String Arrays and Strings   If you have a character string array, you usually need a string. If you have a string, you need a character string array. This predicament can be a millstone around the neck of any programmer! It is time to summarize conversion between the two.

First, it is possible simply to assign the char array into the string by using the assign operator. In Program G-4, we use the c_str( ) function to convert a string to a

G

const char*. The c_str( ) function returns a pointer to a null-terminated string; however, you may not change the contents of this string. (C++ does not guarantee the contents if you change the value; hence it requires the char* to be a const char*.)

```
// Program G-4    Convert Between Strings and Character String Arrays
#include <iostream>    //C++ header style since using C++ string class
#include <string>
using namespace std;

int main()
{
        string S1("I like the sea and C, you see.");
        string S2;
        char MyArray[50] = "Is C++ really a B-?";
        const char MyOtherArray;

        cout << "\n The original string and array";
        cout << S1 << endl;
        cout << MyArray << endl;

        //First we place MyArray contents into S2 using the assign
        S2.assign(MyArray);

        //Next, we'll stuff the contents of S1 into MyOtherArray
        MyOtherArray = S1.c_str();

        cout << "\n The converted array and string";
        cout << MyOtherArray << endl;
        cout << S2 << endl;

        return 0;
}
```

The output from Program G-4 is shown below:

```
The original string and array
I like the sea and C, you see.
Is C++ really a B-?

The converted array and string
I like the sea and C, you see.
Is C++ really a B-?
```

Reading into a String Students usually ask, "How can you read data into a string from the keyboard?" Well, you may use a cin, but it only reads until the first whitespace character and then stop reading. If you need to read text with white-space characters (e.g., blanks), you must use the get or getline functions with character arrays and then assign the contents into a string. Program G-5 shows how to do this task.

```
// Program G-5  Reading into a String
#include <iostream>
#include <string>
using namespace std;

int main()
{
        string S1;
        char MyArray[50];

        cout << "\n Enter your favorite string saying " << endl;
        cin.getline(MyArray,50);

        //Assign the array contents into S1
        S1.assign(MyArray);
        cout << "\n Here is your saying twice! "<< endl;
        cout << MyArray << endl;
        cout << S1 << endl;

        return 0;
}
```

The output is shown below:

Enter your favorite string saying
I love the sea and C, you see.

Here is your saying twice!
I love the sea and C, you see.
I love the sea and C, you see.

G

Multifile Programs

C++ programs should be constructed so that the program components are organized and grouped together into individual files. In general, include files (named with a *.h extension) contain #define statements, necessary #include statements, function prototypes, class declarations, and structure tags. Source files (named with a corresponding *.cpp extension) contain necessary #include statements and the source code for all functions. Ideally, the *.h and *.cpp file set should have the same name (and different extensions) and contain the necessary source code for one structure or one class. Often this setup is not practical, but the file-set program components must be related to each other.

Simple Example: hello world!

To illustrate how to break a program into multiple files, we revisit the classic "hello world!" program. This program has the function SayHello, which writes "hello world!" to the screen. The single-file version of this program appears in Program H-1.

```
//Program H-1 Single-File version of hello world!
// File SayHello.cpp

#include <iostream.h>

void SayHello();            // prototype

int main()
{
       cout << "\n Hi, this is the SayHello program. \n";
       SayHello();          // call to the function
       return 0;
}
```

```
void SayHello()                  // actual function
{

        cout << "\n hello world!  \n";

}
```

In breaking this program into multiple files, we place the function prototype into the *hello.h* file and its associated function into the *hello.cpp* file. The main function then must include the *hello.h* file so that it knows about the SayHello function. The multiple-file version of this program (Program H-2) now contains two *.cpp files and one *.h file.

```
//Program H-2 Multifile version of hello world!
// File: SayHello.cpp

#include <iostream.h>
#include "hello.h"           // include file uses " " not < >

int main()
{
        cout << "\n Hi, this is the SayHello program. \n";
        SayHello();          // call to the function
        return 0;
}

// File: hello.h
void SayHello();

// File: hello.cpp
#include <iostream.h>
void SayHello()
{
        cout << "\n hello world!  \n";
}
```

Preprocessor Directives

Before we jump into the details of the #include statement, let's review the preprocessor directive. A preprocessor directive is a statement that provides instructions to the compiler. Each directive statement begins with a # and must be on its own line (that is, you cannot write: #include <math.h> #include <iostream.h>). There are twelve preprocessor directive statements in C and C++:

#define   *#endif*   *#ifdef*   *#line*
#elif   *#error*   *#ifndef*   *#pragma*
#else   *#if*   *#include*   *#undef*

Each directive serves a purpose. We require (and illustrate the use of) four of these statements (#include, #define, #ifndef, and #endif) when creating multifile programs. The reader should refer to a complete C++ reference for a full description and usage examples for all the preprocessor directive statements.

#include Statements and < > and " "

An *#include* statement tells the compiler to read another source file. In essence, it is saying, "Go read this file so that you know all of its contents." The file that is in the #include line must be contained in either angle braces < > or double quotes " ", such as:

```
#include <iostream.h>
#include "hello.h"
```

A file enclosed in < > tells the compiler to look for the file in the language's standard location for include files. For example, Microsoft Visual C++ places the language's include files in the \Program File\Microsoft Visual Studio\VC98\Include directory. Whenever Visual C++ encounters a <*filename*> , it looks in this directory automatically.

If a file is enclosed in double quotes, the compiler expects the full path for that file. If the file is located in the project folder (in Visual C++), no formal path description is necessary:

```
#include "hello.h"
```

The compiler expects this *hello.h* file to be located in the project folder.

Large programs often have all the include files located in a separate "Include" directory (which is a practical program design). In this case, the include statement must include the path, such as:

```
#include "\Includes\hello.h"
```

It is possible to "nest" include statements. An include file can have an #include statement that contains a file with an #include statement (and so on). The number of layers of nesting that the ISO C language allows is eight, and the ISO C++ language provides for 256. Although 256 levels are possible, programmers are encouraged to nest their #include statements only a few layers deep.

H

What Do I Include Where?

One of the most confusing aspects of organizing a program with multiple files is knowing what needs to be included in what file. Beginning C++ programmers often take the shotgun approach and include everything in every file, which is a bad habit!

For each file in your program, the compiler must have the complete library and include information. For example, if you are writing output to the screen in a function, the file containing that function must have the #include <*iostream.h*> statement, even if you have already included it in another file. Look back at the "hello world" example. The iostream library is included in both the *hello.cpp* and *SayHello.cpp* files because both files contain a cout statement. Notice that the *hello.h* file does not contain the #include <*iostream.h*> statement. The *hello.h* file does not contain any iostream function calls; therefore, iostream is not needed.

As you are learning to put multifile programs together, you should ask yourself: What does this file need to know? If the file is performing a square root function, it needs C++'s math library and must have the #include <*math.h*> statement. If the file is referencing a data structure or class that is defined in *MyNewThing.h*, then you must include the MyNewThing.h file. It is common to have an include file included in several program files.

One last programming issue—you do not need to (nor should you include) *.cpp files within *.cpp files. It is the job of the project to keep track of your source files, and the project reads them automatically when the program is compiled.

#ifndef, #define, and #endif

It is important to understand that the compiler needs to read through a file only once during the compilation process. When the compiler sees an #include statement, it reads that file. If the compiler rereads the same file, it believes you are redefining something it has already read. (Compiler Errors!) This practice results in an unhappy compiler, which results in an unhappy programmer.

If an include file is to be included in several files, conditional directive statements must be used in that include file. Basically, if an include file is to be included more than once, you must tell the compiler, "Compiler, if you haven't read this yet, read it, *but* if you have read it, don't read it again."

Here is where the #ifndef, #define, and #endif directive statements come into play. Assume that we need to include the SayHello function prototype in several files because several files will call the function SayHello. We need to wrap these statements around the prototype, as shown here:

```
// File: hello.h

#ifndef    _HELLO_H
#define    _HELLO_H

void SayHello();

#endif
```

The #ifndef statement (if not defined) is saying to the compiler, "If you haven't seen this item I'm calling _HELLO_H, that is, if it isn't defined yet...." (The compiler knows if it has seen the _HELLO_H.) The #define line is telling the compiler, "Okay, define all the lines you read between this #define and #endif as _HELLO_H." The compiler then knows what _HELLO_H is, and if it encounters another #ifndef_HELLO_H statement, the compiler does not reread it.

Note that the _HELLO_H label (actually it is a macro name) must be the same in both the #ifndef and the #define line. A C++ convention for this label uses all capital letters, and the name should match the file name or give some indication about what it is. This idea is only a convention, not a requirement. If you examine some of the C++ library *.h files, you will see the following:

```
// math.h contains this set of statements
#ifndef _INC_MATH
#define _INC_MATH
```

Creating a Multifile Project in Visual C++

This part is the easiest of the whole discussion. As you construct your *.cpp and *.h files, the files must be added to the Visual C++ project (Project → Add to project → Files). In the FileView for the workspace, you can see your *.h files in the Header folder and your *.cpp files in the Source folder. You may then double click on any of the file names and Visual C++ opens that file for your use. In theory you do not need to add the *.h files to the project (they are included in the source files), but it is good practice because Visual C++ can thus provide quick access to the files. Figures H-1 and H-2 show the Visual C++ project workspace for the FootballPlayer (Chapter 9) and Shopper (Chapter 10) programs. The source and header files are seen in the left-hand window. Be sure that your files are organized and placed in the correct directories.

extern Global Variables in Multiple Files

It is common in the structured programming world (and at times in the object-oriented world) to have variables declared in one file that are accessed by the program routines located in other files. In this situation, the variables must be declared globally and declared with the extern keyword in the second file.

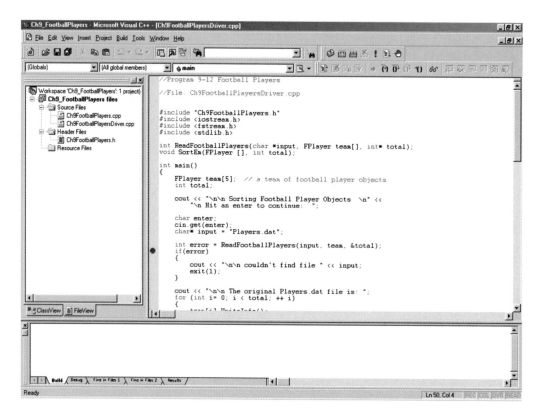

Figure H-1
The Visual C++ Project Workspace for the FootballPlayer Program in Chapter 9

Let's look at an example. Suppose a program contains a data variable, "total," and assume that our program needs to see the total in another routine located in a separate file. The "total" declaration looks like the following:

```
// File1.cpp
// Contains the original global declaration for total

double total;

int main()
{
        // code for calculating total
        total = //some magic formula
}
```

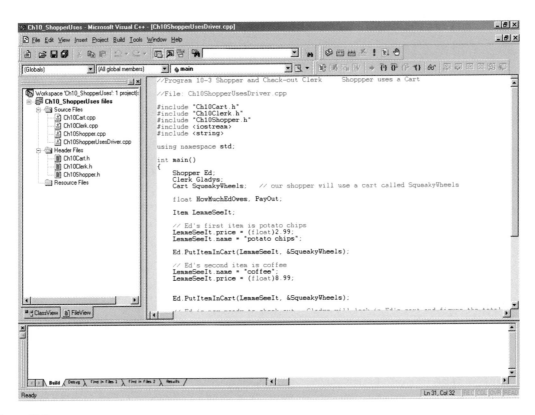

Figure H-2
Visual C++ Project Workspace for the Shopper Program Example in Chapter 10

In the second source file, the *total* variable must be declared again with the extern keyword, like this:

```
// File2.cpp
// Contains the extern declaration for total

extern double total;

void Function1()
{
    // code that uses total
}
```

The extern statement basically tells the compiler, "Somewhere else in this program is a global declaration for a double named total." Remember, there can be only one global declaration of a variable and there may be many extern declarations in many files.

extern Output Stream Example   Suppose you wish to write your program output to a data file. Your program is set to have several source files, and it is logical to have information written from these program locations. One way to make the output stream object available to many program locations is to declare the output stream globally and then extern it in other program files. In the following short program, we declare the output stream object global to the main function and then extern it to the second file. The initial declaration is seen here:

```
//File:  SayHelloMain.cpp
#include <iostream.h>
#include <fstream.h>
ofstream Output;               //globally declared output stream object

void SayHelloToAFile();
int main()
{

        Output.open("TestOutputFile.txt",ios::out);
        Output << "\n This is a test. This is written from main.\n";
        SayHelloToAFile();
        return 0;

}
```

The output stream is written with the extern keyword in the file containing the SayHelloToAFile function:

```
//File:  SayHello.cpp
#include <iostream.h>
#include <fstream.h>

extern ofstream Output;

void SayHelloToAFile()
{
        Output << "\n\n Hello World in an output file.";
}
```

Examples from Chapter 7

Two program examples are presented in Figures H-3 and H-4. Both figures indicate
how these programs can be broken into multifile programs.

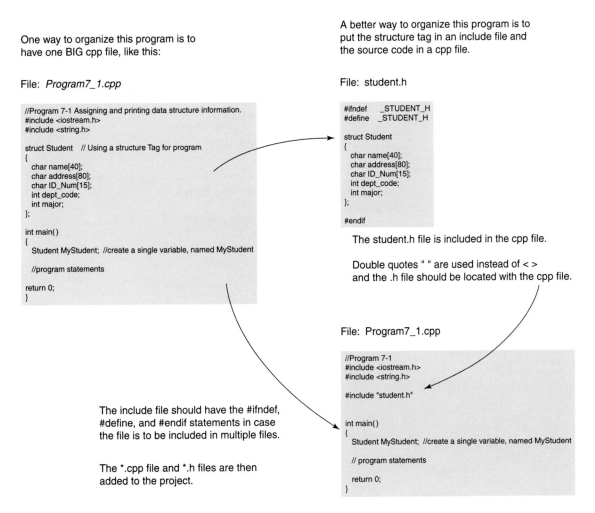

One way to organize this program is to
have one BIG cpp file, like this:

A better way to organize this program is to
put the structure tag in an include file and
the source code in a cpp file.

File: *Program7_1.cpp*

File: student.h

```
//Program 7-1 Assigning and printing data structure information.
#include <iostream.h>
#include <string.h>

struct Student    // Using a structure Tag for program
{
  char name[40];
  char address[80];
  char ID_Num[15];
  int dept_code;
  int major;
};

int main( )
{
  Student MyStudent; //create a single variable, named MyStudent

  //program statements

  return 0;
}
```

```
#ifndef     _STUDENT_H
#define     _STUDENT_H

struct Student
{
  char name[40];
  char address[80];
  char ID_Num[15];
  int dept_code;
  int major;
};

#endif
```

The student.h file is included in the cpp file.

Double quotes " " are used instead of < >
and the .h file should be located with the cpp file.

File: Program7_1.cpp

```
//Program 7-1
#include <iostream.h>
#include <string.h>

#include "student.h"

int main( )
{
  Student MyStudent; //create a single variable, named MyStudent

  // program statements

  return 0;
}
```

The include file should have the #ifndef,
#define, and #endif statements in case
the file is to be included in multiple files.

The *.cpp file and *.h files are then
added to the project.

Figure H-3
Student Data Structure (Program 7-1)

H

Program 7-4 is shown here in one file.

A better way to organize this program is to place the prototypes and structure tags in one include file, the functions in a separate cpp file, and the main in a cpp file. All three files are added to the project.

File: *Program7_4.cpp*

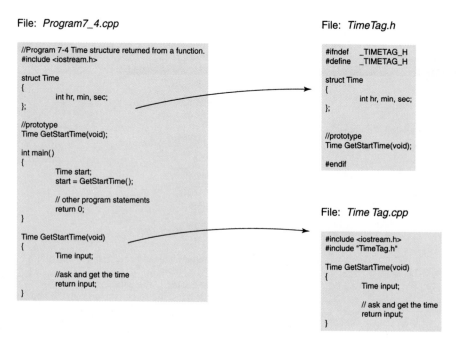

```
//Program 7-4 Time structure returned from a function.
#include <iostream.h>

struct Time
{
        int hr, min, sec;
};

//prototype
Time GetStartTime(void);

int main()
{
        Time start;
        start = GetStartTime();

        // other program statements
        return 0;
}

Time GetStartTime(void)
{
        Time input;

        //ask and get the time
        return input;
}
```

File: *TimeTag.h*

```
#ifndef    _TIMETAG_H
#define    _TIMETAG_H

struct Time
{
        int hr, min, sec;
};


//prototype
Time GetStartTime(void);

#endif
```

File: *Time Tag.cpp*

```
#include <iostream.h>
#include "TimeTag.h"

Time GetStartTime(void)
{
        Time input;

        // ask and get the time
        return input;
}
```

File: *Driver.cpp*

```
//Program 7-4 Time structure returned from a function.
#include <iostream.h>
#include "TimeTag.h"

int main()
{
        Time start;
        start = GetStartTime();

        // other program statements
        return 0;
}
```

Each file must have whatever include files it needs. For example, if there is a call to cout in the file, you must include iostream. Both the Driver.cpp and the TimeTag.cpp need to know what a Time is, so TimeTag.h is included in both files.

Do *not* include cpp files in #include statements! The project will keep track of the cpp files.

Figure H-4
GetStartTime Program as a Multifile Program (Program 7-4)

Keyboard Input, Screen Output

To begin writing programs, you must learn how to enter data from the keyboard and to write output to the screen. The C++ iostream library makes this task easy. Already we have written "hello world!" with the cout function. In real-world situations, this type of input and output is impractical. User interfaces to programs are Windows-based and mouse-driven, or data is read from a file or database. To start, however, this keyboard input and screen output is just what we need!

C++ Streams

A stream in C++ is a device that either uses data (such as input) or produces data (such as output). Streams in C++ are connected to a physical device by the operating system. For example, an output stream can be the screen, a data file, or a printer. C++ stream functions are identical, even though the physical devices are quite different.

cout and cin

The two functions we use initially in the iostream library are cout and cin. As we have seen, cout (pronounced "C out") writes stream output to the screen. The cin (pronounced "C in") function reads stream input into our program from the keyboard. The concept of an input or output stream can simply be thought of as a stream or flow of characters.

The cout function uses the insertion operator, < < , to direct the data from the right side of the operator to the left. In the following statement:

```
cout << "\n hello world!";
```

the characters "\n hello world!" are sent to the cout function, where they are then written to the screen. This insertion operator can string together output and write text information and numeric data to the screen:

```
int X = 5, Y = 7;
cout << "\n X = " << X << " and Y = " << Y;
```

The screen output is shown below:

X = 5 and Y = 7

In the statement above, notice that the variables X and Y are not written within the quotation marks. When the variable name, such as X, is inserted into the stream, it is telling the program to "go get the value of X and place it in the stream." The value in the variable is written to the screen.

To obtain input from the keyboard, the cin function is used with the extraction operator, $>>$.

```
int n, m;
cout << "\n Please enter two integers.";
cin >> n >> m;
```

If the user enters 8 and 9, the 8 is placed in n and the 9 is placed in m.

Program I-1 uses cout and cin to obtain data from the user and to write arithmetic results to the screen. The cout statements above were combined into one statement (on many lines) in Program I-1 by using the $<<$ operator:

```
cout << "\n Your two integers were" << a << " and " << b <<
        "\n The sum is " << sum << " and the difference is " << diff;
```

Escape Sequences

As a general rule, C++ takes the stream output in the cout function and displays what it receives. The cout function handles the string input (such as writing Hello World), using the double quotes to indicate the start of the string and then again to find the end of the string. In this statement:

```
cout << "Hello World";
```

the double quotes (" ") show the start and end of the string to be printed.

When the backslash, \, is combined with certain characters inside the string, the cout function knows to escape from the normal interpretation and to do something special when writing output. For instance, when the output must start on a new line, we use the \n. The \n is known as an escape sequence.

This cout statement does not contain any \n escape sequences:

```
cout << "What a wonderful day! What will we do? Get some ice cream!";
```

```
//Program I-1 Example using cin and cout to obtain input and write output.
#include <iostream.h>                        // needed for cout and cin

int main()
{
        int a,b,sum,diff;
        cout << "\n Please enter two integers";
        cin >> a >> b;
        sum = a + b;
        diff = a - b;
        cout << "\n Your two integers were " << a << " and " << b;
        cout << "\n The sum is " << sum << " and the difference is " << diff;
        return 0;
}
```

The output from this code is shown below:

What a wonderful day! What will we do? Get some ice cream!

The same statement is rewritten with \n newline escape sequences inserted:

```
cout << "What a wonderful day! \nWhat will we do? \nGet some ice cream!";
```

The output from this code is shown here:

What a wonderful day!
What will we do?
Get some ice cream!

Another commonly used escape sequence is the \", which prints a double quote. The following example prints the words "Four score and seven years" to the screen:

```
cout << "\"Four score and seven years\"";
```

Here is the output from this statement:

"Four score and seven years"

Table I-1 lists the escape sequence in C++. It is important to note that these escape sequences are used only in cout and *not* in cin. If we want to see "Oh Boy! Here's a backslash \ !" written to the screen, the cout statement must be:

```
cout << "\"Oh Boy! Here\'s a backslash \\ !\"";
```

TABLE I-1

Escape Sequences in C++

Escape Sequence	Purpose
\a	Beep
\b	Backspace
\f	Formfeed
\n	Newline
\r	Return
\\	Backslash
\'	Single quote
\"	Double quote
\xdd	Hexadecimal notation
\ddd	Octal notation

The output is shown here:

"Oh Boy! Here's a backslash \!"

The endl Manipulator

C++ provides an alternative to the \n escape sequence for inserting a new line into an output stream. This alternative involves using a stream manipulator. When the manipulator *endl* is inserted into the stream, it causes the output to go to a new line. The previous ice cream example can be written by using the endl manipulator.

```
cout << "What a wonderful day!" << endl << "What will we do?" << endl
   "Get some ice cream!";
```

Here we are using \n instead:

```
cout << "What a wonderful day! \nWhat will we do? \nGet some ice cream!";
```

The endl manipulator is convenient when a programmer is writing variables in output streams. It avoids writing \n in the stream. Compare these two examples, first—the endl:

```
cout << endl << "The value in X is " << x << endl
      "The value in Y is " << y << endl;
```

Now, the \n:

```
cout << "\nThe value in X is " << x <<
      "\nThe value in Y is " << y << "\n";
```

You can use both:

```
cout << "\nThe value in X is " << x <<
      "\nThe value in Y is " << y << endl;
```

Basic Formatted Output Using cout

The cout function in the iostream library writes variable values in the simplest form possible with only the necessary space to show the data. Decimal points are not printed with float or double if no decimal precision is in the variable, as seen in Program I-2. The output is shown here:

Sample Output
Cost = 5 Price = 5.5
pi = 3.14159 and count = 75
The symbol is +

ios Formatting Flags

How do we get the decimal point with floating point data, such as with the cost variable? How do we see the price as "5.50" or pi written to four digits of precision? How can we line up the output? Various techniques are used for writing formatted data, and we present one method here.

Several flags can be used in association with the cout function. These flags are known as ios formatting flags and they can be turned on and off. To see a deci-

---

```
//Program I-2 Program showing cout output with no format commands.
#include <iostream.h>

int main ()
{
      double cost = 5.00, price = 5.50, pi = 3.14159265;
      int count = 75;
      char symbol = '+';
      cout << "\n Sample Output \n Cost = " << cost << " Price = " << price <<
            "\n pi = " << pi << " and count = " << count
            << "\n The symbol is " << symbol;
      return 0;
}
```

TABLE I-2
ios Formatting Flags

ios Flag	Purpose
skipws	Leading whitespace characters are discarded.
left	Output is left justified.
right	Output is right justified.
internal	A numeric value is padded to fill a field.
dec	Write output in decimal.
hex	Write numeric output in hexadecimal.
oct	Write numeric output in octal.
showbase	Shows the base of numeric values (such as 0x for hex).
showpoint	Shows a decimal point and trailing zeros for all floating point values.
uppercase	Shows scientific and hex notation in uppercase, such as 3.4E3 or 0XF2.
showpos	Shows leading plus sign.
scientific	Floating point data is displayed in scientific notation, such as 3.4e4.
fixed[a]	Floating point values are displayed in normal notation.
unitbuf	I/O system is flushed after each output operation.

[a]Default shows six decimal places. If neither fixed nor scientific is set, compiler chooses the appropriate method.

mal point in floating point data, the showpoint flag must be turned on. The ios formatting flags can be turned on by the setf function:

```
cout.setf(ios::showpoint);
```

Once a flag is turned on, it stays on until it is turned off by the unsetf function. The following statement turns off the fixed flag:

```
cout.unsetf(ios::showpoint);
```

Table I-2 lists the various ios formatting flags and their functions.

Flags may be set in one setf call. Here, we turn on the hex and showbase flag:

```
cout.setf(ios::hex | ios::showbase);
```

In Program I-3, we modify the output program so that the decimal point can be seen in the double variables. The output is shown below:

Sample Output
Cost = 5.0000 Price = 5.50000
pi = 3.14159 and count = 75
The symbol is +

```
//Program I-3 Example showing cout output using format commands.
#include <iostream.h>

int main ()
{
        double cost = 5.00, price = 5.50, pi = 3.14159265;
        int count = 75;
        char symbol = '+';
        cout.setf(ios::showpoint);
        cout << "\n Sample Output \n Cost = " << cost << " Price = " << price <<
              "\n pi = " << pi << " and count = " << count
              << "\n The symbol is " << symbol;
        return 0;

}
```

Precision

Setting the ios flags solved the decimal point problem, but how do we see just two digits of precision? This precision is accomplished by using the cout.precision function in conjunction with the ios fixed flag. If the precision is set without the fixed flag, we see just the number of digits specified by precision.

```
cout.precision(2);
cout.setf(ios::showpoint);
cout << "\n Sample Output \n Cost = " << cost << " Price = " << price <<
      "\n pi = " << pi << " and count = " << count
      << "\n The symbol is " << symbol;
```

The output is shown here:

Sample Output
Cost = 5.0 Price = 5.5
pi = 3.1 and count = 75
The symbol is +

Now we add the fixed flag to the source code:

```
cout.precision(2);
cout.setf(ios::showpoint | ios::fixed);
cout << "\n Sample Output \n Cost = " << cost << " Price = " << price <<
      "\n pi = " << pi << " and count = " << count
      << "\n The symbol is " << symbol;
```

The output is shown below:

Sample Output
Cost = 5.00 Price = 5.50
pi = 3.14 and count = 75
The symbol is +

To write the cost and price values with two digits and pi with five, the code requires the following statements:

```
cout.precision(2);
cout.setf(ios::showpoint | ios::fixed);
cout << "\n Sample Output \n Cost = " << cost << " Price = " << price;
cout.precision(5);
cout <<"\n pi = " << pi << " and count = " << count
<< "\n The symbol is " << symbol;
```

The output is shown below:

Sample Output
Cost = 5.00 Price = 5.50
pi = 3.14159 and count = 75
The symbol is +

Specify the Width setw( )

A stream manipulator *setw*( ) sets the field width for the variable output that follows. The following line of code uses a setw( ) manipulator to reserve five spaces in which to write the value of the variable x:

```
cout << "\n The value of x is" << setw(5) << x;
```

The setw( ) is a member of the iomanip library; therefore, the iomanip.h must be included in an #include statement. If we want our money output in six spaces and pi to be in ten spaces, we can insert setw( ) before the values are written out. See Program I-4. The output from Program I-4 is shown below:

Sample Output
Cost =   5.00 Price =   5.50
pi =   3.141593 and count = 75
The symbol is +

Whitespace Characters and cin

Whitespace characters are spaces, carriage returns, line feeds (the Enter key), tabs, vertical tabs, and form feeds. The cin function ignores the whitespace characters; it

```
//Program I-4 Example showing formatted output.
#include <iostream.h>
#include <iomanip.h>          // for the setw()
int main ()
{
        double cost = 5.00, price = 5.50, pi = 3.14159265;
        int count = 75;
        char symbol = '+';
        cout.precision(2);
        cout.setf(ios::showpoint | ios::fixed);
        cout << "\n Sample Output \n Cost = " << setw(6) << cost <<
            " Price = " << setw(6)<< price;
        cout.precision(5);
        cout <<"\n pi = " << setw(10) << pi << " and count = "
            << count<< "\n The symbol is " << symbol;
        return 0;
}
```

does not place them into your program variables. The cin function knows what type of data it is supposed to read, such as an integer, as it examines the contents of the stream one character at a time. If cin sees a whitespace character, it tosses it out (ignores it). The cin function works well for entering simple numeric or character data but does not work if the program needs to see an Enter key.

The cin function uses the whitespace data to help it read the input stream. It uses the whitespace characters to know where the data begins and ends. For example, if we want to read in four integer values, we use the following statements:

```
int a, b, c, d;
cout << "\n Please enter 4 integers.";
cin >> a >> b >> c >> d;
```

If you type this:

18 45 9 36 ↵ **(Enter)**

the characters and the Enter key are stored in the input buffer. Once the Enter key is hit, data is extracted from the stream and placed into the variables. The Enter key generates a carriage return line feed (CRLF) character. The blanks and CRLF characters are ignored by cin. The same data could be entered in this manner:

18 45 ↵
9 36 ↵

When the cin function is in use, the last CRLF character in the input buffer is not "flushed" out of the input buffer. Figure I-1 illustrates this process.

Use Caution When Reading Numeric and Character Data   To get started, the simple programs that we write shall read numeric and single character data with cin. The cin does not do any error trapping for incorrect user input. Also, cin goes crazy if the user accidentally enters a character when it is expecting an integer! Other methods are more appropriate for reading in data, and as we gain knowledge and skills with C++, we'll start using those methods.

Beware! If the program must read numeric and character *array* data, do *not* use the cin function with the character array functions cin.get or cin.getline because the remaining CRLF character left over from the cin will cause trouble. We will not go into detail about that topic now. We cover this topic in detail in Chapter 6.

What's Our Goal?   Keep in mind that as we write C++ programs, we wish to be able to handle whatever input the user enters, no matter what. Error trapping for user input can be a major part of some programs. We want our programs to recover gracefully whenever the user enters an incorrect value. Although many of our sample programs do not incorporate error-trapping code (because the error code might obscure the current topic or make the program too long), you should always error trap your user's input.

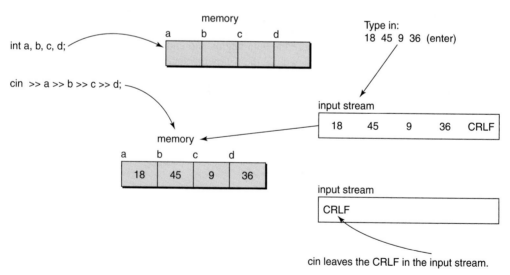

Figure I-1
Reading Variables with cin Function

Reading an Enter Key (or Other Whitespace Data)

If you are trying to read in an Enter key, the cin function is not going to work because it ignores whitespace characters. The function cin.get, found in the iostream library, reads any character. The iostream class provides many functions for program input and output. One such function is the get function. (It has many different formats.) One form of the cin.get function is:

```
cin.get(character_variable);
```

The portion of code below shows how a program can ask the user to hit an enter key to continue running the program. Note: two cin.get statements are needed for most situations.

```
char input;
cout << "\n Pausing the program."
       "\n Please Hit the Enter key to continue.";
cin.get(input);
cin.get(input);
```

The cin.get places the Enter key character into the input variable.

Two Examples

Programs I-5 and I-6 illustrate writing formatted text to the screen. The second example (Program I-6) incorporates stream manipulators. The manipulators set the ios flags, too, but instead of using the cout.setf function, the flags are set directly in the stream. First, let's examine writing output with the cout.set functions in Program I-5. The output from this program is shown below:

Example 1 Output and cout functions

First, write out the values

Pi = 3.14159   Sq Feet in Acre = 43560   Feet in a mile 5280

Now set show point to see the dec.pt in feet in a mile

Pi = 3.14159   Sq Feet in Acre = 43560   Feet in a mile 5280.00

Now set fixed and precision of 3. We'll see .xxx in doubles.

Pi = 3.142   Sq Feet in Acre = 43560   Feet in a mile 5280.000

Now, unset fixed, we'll just see 3 digits

Pi = 3.14   Sq Feet in Acre = 43560   Feet in a mile 5.28e+003

```
//Program I-5  Practice with iosflags
#include <iostream.h>

int main()
{
        double pi = 3.141592653589793;
        double feet_in_a_mile = 5280.0;
        int sq_ft_in_acre = 43560;

        cout << "\n  Example 1   Output and cout functions " << endl;

//First, just write out all three values to see what we get
        cout << "\n\n First, write out the values" <<endl;
        cout<< "\nPi = " << pi <<    "      Sq Feet in Acre = " << sq_ft_in_acre <<
            "      Feet in a mile " << feet_in_a_mile << endl;

//Second, set showpoint to see the feet in a mile decimal point
        cout << "\n\n Now set show point to see the dec.pt in feet in a mile\n";
        cout.setf(ios::showpoint);
        cout<< "\nPi = " << pi <<    "      Sq Feet in Acre = " << sq_ft_in_acre <<
            "      Feet in a mile " << feet_in_a_mile << endl;

//Next, set fixed flag and 3 precision
        cout << "\n\n Now set fixed and precision of 3. We'll see .xxx in doubles.\n ";
        cout.setf(ios::fixed);
        cout.precision(3);
        cout<< "\nPi = " << pi <<    "      Sq Feet in Acre = " << sq_ft_in_acre <<
            "      Feet in a mile " << feet_in_a_mile << endl;

//Now, unset the fixed flag and we'll just see 3 digits
        cout << "\n\n Now, unset fixed, we'll just see 3 digits \n ";
        cout.unsetf(ios::fixed);
        cout<< "\nPi = " << pi <<    "      Sq Feet in Acre = " << sq_ft_in_acre <<
            "      Feet in a mile " << feet_in_a_mile << "\n\n";
        return 0;
}
```

```
//Program I-6  Example 2   Formatted output using manipulators
/* Manipulators can be set directly in the stream.  Once an IOS formatting
flag is set, it remains set until you unset it.
Character strings are covered in Chapter 6 */
```

```
#include <iostream.h>
#include <iomanip.h>                    //include manipulator library

int main()
{
        double pi = 3.141592653589793;
        double feet_in_a_mile = 5280.0;
        int sq_ft_in_acre = 43560;
        char Getty[15] = "4 score and 7";

        cout << "\nExample 2:  Output using manipulators " << endl;

//First, just write out all four values to see what we get
        cout << "\n1. Write out the values" <<endl;
        cout<< "\n  Pi = " << pi <<   " Sq Feet in Acre = " << sq_ft_in_acre <<
                "\n  Feet in a mile = " << feet_in_a_mile << " Gettysburg = " << Getty
<<endl;

//Next, set fixed flags in the output stream. No need for cout.setf!!!
        cout << "\n2. Set fixed, showpoint and precision=4 \n ";
        cout<< setiosflags(ios::fixed | ios::showpoint) << setprecision(4) <<
                "\n  Pi = " << pi << " Sq Feet in Acre = " << sq_ft_in_acre <<
                "\n  Feet in a mile " << feet_in_a_mile << " Gettysburg = " << Getty <<
endl;

//Next, work on justification
        cout.setf(ios::left);
        cout << "\n3. Text to be written always left just, ios::left works on variables
\n " <<
"\n=========|=========|=========|=========|=========|=========|=========|";
        cout << setw(20) << "\nGettysburg = " <<   setw(20)<< Getty
                << setw(20) << "\nSqFt/AcresPi = " << setw(20)<<  sq_ft_in_acre << endl;
        //Next, work on justification
        cout.unsetf(ios::left);
        cout.setf(ios::right);
        cout << "\n4. Unset left, set right \n "
                <<
"\n=========|=========|=========|=========|=========|=========|=========|";

        cout<< setw(20) << "\nGettysburg = " <<   setw(20)<< Getty
                << setw(20) << "\nSqFt/AcresPi = " << setw(20)<<    sq_ft_in_acre <<
endl<<endl;

        return 0;
}
```

In Program I-6, we use manipulators and place the fix and precision commands in stream. The output from Program I-6 is shown below:

Example 2: Output using manipulators

1. Write out the values

Pi = 3.14159 Sq Feet in Acre = 43560
Feet in a mile = 5280 Gettysburg = 4 score and 7

2. Set fixed, showpoint and precision = 4

Pi = 3.1416 Sq Feet in Acre = 43560
Feet in a mile 5280.0000 Gettysburg = 4 score and 7

3. Text to be written always left just, ios::left works on variables

```
=========|=========|=========|=========|=========|=========|=========|
Gettysburg =      4 score and 7
SqFt/AcresPi =    43560
```

4. Unset left, set right

```
=========|=========|=========|=========|=========|=========|=========|
Gettysburg =      4 score and 7
SqFt/AcresPi =              43560
```

Microsoft Visual C++ Debugger

Aside from knowing the language and the problem and the software goals, knowing how to use the debugger is most important. The C++ programmer *must learn* how to use the debugging tools in whatever environment he or she is working.

The debugger allows you to step into your program and stop at any given line of code. You may run your program by stepping through it one line at a time and see the value for any and all variables in your program. In this manner, it is possible to follow exactly how the code executes and to see which lines are skipped. You write your software with certain expectations, and the debugger gives you the means to verify that the code is performing as anticipated—and to locate the point where logic or calculation failures occur.

Debugging Concepts

The Visual C++ debugger tool is powerful and easy to use. We should examine a list of new terms before we jump into an example. A complete listing and description of these tools is in the Visual C++ Help –> Index –> Debugger Window. Table J-1 covers the basic terms.

When your program compiles and runs but is not working correctly, use the debugger to examine how your program runs. You set one breakpoint (or several) in the program and then single-step through lines of your code, watching the variable values and seeing how the program flows. You may either step into functions or step over them. You may enter variables in the Watch window to monitor the program execution.

A Simple Example

We can use the complete version of the Time Conversion program, located in the Practice section of Chapter 3. Figure J-1 shows this project open and the start of the program.

Putting a breakpoint at the beginning of the switch statement will cause the program to stop at this point. By stopping the program at that point, we can see how our program executes after the user has selected an option. To toggle on a break-

Term	Icon/F Key Location	Use
Breakpoint	Hand icon or F9	A breakpoint is placed at a line of code in a program where you want the program to stop so that you may examine variables. Also, you may set a breakpoint where you wish to begin single-stepping through the code.
Go	Sheet of paper with arrow or F5	Start the debugger.
Stop	Paper with red slash across it or Shift F5	Stop the debugger.
Step into	F11	Step into a function.
Step over	F10	Step over a function (function is executed).
Step out	Shift F11	Step out of a function.
Run to cursor	Ctrl F10	Run the program and stop at the line where the cursor is located.
Auto, locals, and "this"	View –> Debug Windows –> Variables	This window has tabs for showing either the local variables that are in the current function or the auto variables, which are the currently changing variables. The "this" window presents whatever object is currently held in the "this" pointer.
Watch	View –> Debug Windows –> Watch	Allows you to enter up to four different sets of watch variables. A watch variable is simply a variable that the programmer enters and then can watch its value continuously.
Debug windows	View –> Debug Windows	Six different debug windows are available to the programmer. Aside from the Variables and Watch windows, there are the Call Stack, Registers, Memory, and Disassembly windows.

point, we put the cursor on the line below the switch (where the switch's brace is located) and press the hand icon. A red dot is placed on the left—which indicates that a breakpoint has been placed at that line. Figure J-2 illustrates the breakpoint.

Now start the debugger by pressing the F5 key or pressing the icon that shows a sheet of paper with an arrow pointing down (Go). Since we have a breakpoint after the cin statement, the console window pops up and waits for our input. We'll

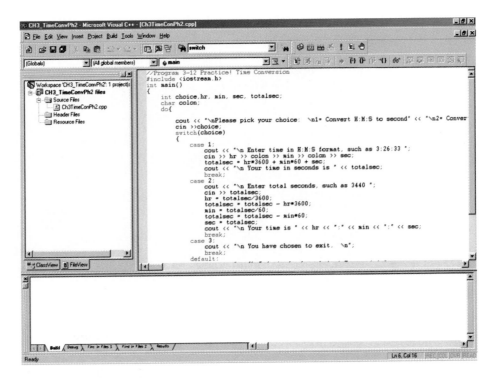

Figure J-1
Time Conversion Program in Visual C++

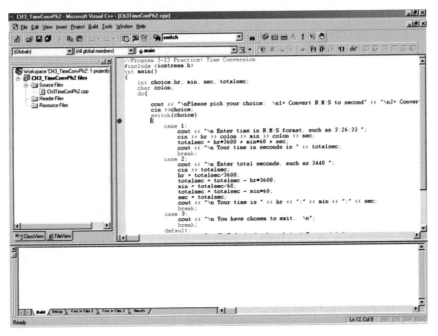

Figure J-2
Breakpoint Set at the Beginning of the Switch Statement

J

Figure J-3
We Must Enter Our Option First

select a number, in this case 1 (convert H:M:S to seconds). Figure J-3 shows the selection of our option.

Once we have entered our choice, the program stops at the breakpoint placed at the switch statement. Figure J-4 shows the debugger environment. The lower left window shows the Variables window. The Auto tab is selected and we see only two variables, choice (which is a 1) and cin. The lower right window is the Watch window. The default windows you see depend on what debug windows you have selected (through the View option) and how you have saved your workspace. Notice that there is a yellow arrow on the red breakpoint dot. This arrow indicates the line of code that is the next line to be executed.

Hitting the F10 (Step) key a few times, we can see that we step into the case 1 statements. If we stop at the cin line (before the user has entered any numbers), we see that the values for hr, min, and sec are −858993460. This number indicates that these variables have not yet been initialized and Visual C++ sets them to a large negative value. (Think of it as "trash" in the variable.) See Figure J-5.

When we continue to step, the program executes and the cin line expects input from the user. The console window does not automatically pop up! Notice that the Context: bar is grayed out in Figure J-6. (The Context bar is located in the middle left portion of the screen, above the Variables window.) When this bar is grayed out, the program is expecting input, and you must double click the MSDOS window icon to bring up your console window.

Proceeding with our program, we enter the time, 6:7:8. We can see that the program places these values correctly into the hours, minutes, and seconds variables. In the Variables window, these variables contain the values 6, 7, and 8, as well as

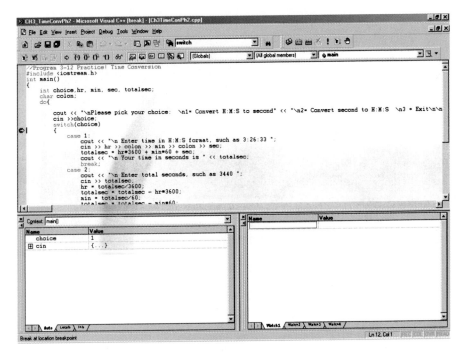

Figure J-4
Debugging Environment

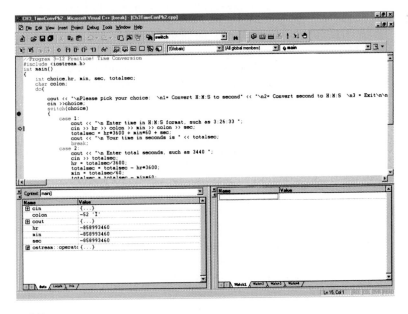

Figure J-5
Step to the cin Line

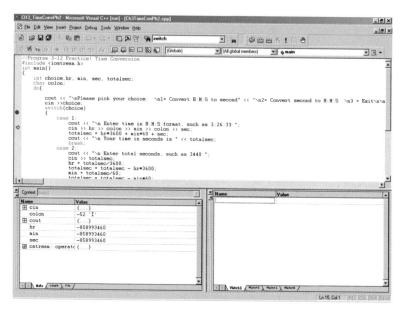

Figure J-6
Grayed out Context Bar Indicates Time to Enter Data

the colon character (ASCII 58). These variables are in red, which indicates that the line of code just executed has changed these values. See Figure J-7.

One more step and we calculate the total seconds. In Figure J-8, notice how the total seconds value is now red and the hours, minutes, and seconds have been changed to black.

If we change the tab to Locals in the Variables window, we can see all the variables for this main function. It is possible for us to enter a variable name in the Watch window (here we put in total seconds) and to watch it throughout the program execution. See Figure J-9.

To exit the debugger, you can press the Debugger –> Stop Debugging menu option or the icon with the sheet of paper with the red slash across it.

Features to Know

The Visual C++ debugger has several convenient features for the developer:

1. If you place the cursor over a variable in the debugger, a little window pops up and tells you the current value of that variable. This same feature will show you what data type the variable is when you are in the edit (nondebugger) mode. You can always use this cursor trick to see what the functions are for all the Visual C++ icons, including all the debugging icons.

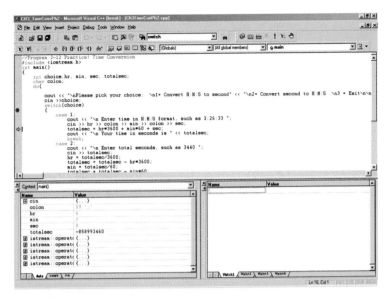

Figure J-7
The Time 6:7:8 Has Been Entered into the Program and Is Shown in Red

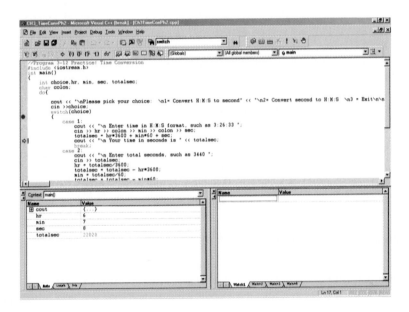

Figure J-8
The Total Seconds (totalsec) Variable Has Been Calculated and Now It Is Shown in Red

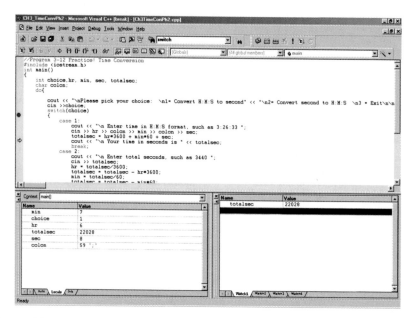

Figure J-9
Viewing the Local Variables and Setting Total Seconds in the Watch1 Window

2. It is possible to set several breakpoints in your code and subsequently use the F5 key to run from breakpoint to breakpoint. Set the breakpoints, then start the debugger (hit F5 or the Go icon). You may just hit the F5 key again to run to the next breakpoint.

3. You may set up Visual C++ so that all debugging icons are located in their own window. Go to Tools –> Customize –> Toolbars –> and check the Debug box. (See Figure J-10.)

4. The other handy debug window is the Call Stack window. It lists the order of the calls for the various functions. If a function calls a function that calls another function, it is easy to lose track of the order of the calls. By examining the Call Stack, you can see what has called which.

Debugging with Pointers, Arrays, Classes, and Structures

Visual C++ shows all the data members for both structures and classes. Let's examine the FootballPlayer program from Chapter 9. Figure J-10 shows that we have our debugging tools separated into the Debug window and that we have a breakpoint following the function where we have read the player data into the team array.

When we run the debugger and stop at the breakpoint, we may examine the array of football players by switching to the Locals tab in the Variables window. Notice how the team variable, which is a pointer (and shows a hex address), has a

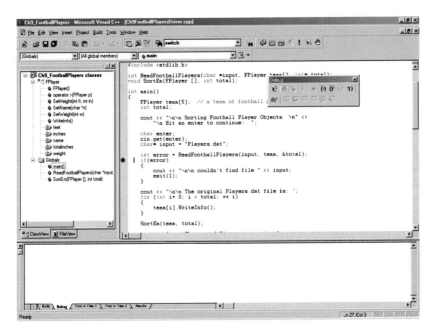

Figure J-10
FootballPlayer Program from Chapter 9

+ beside it. (Remember, the FPlayer team[5] is an array of football player objects. The team is the pointer to the [0] value.) Whenever you see the + beside a variable (be it array, struct, or class) you may then "mouse" (left-click) it and show the various members. In Figure J-11, we have "mouse'd" the team[0] member, which expands to show Deion Husky's information.

When you pass an array into a function and step into that function using the debugger, you will see only the pointer to that array. Figure J-12 shows the results after we stepped into (F11) the SortEm function. The team variable in the Variables window shows only the pointer (which points to team[0]). If you wish to examine a different team member, the team variable (team[array index]) must be entered in the Watch window. Figure J-12 shows the team[2] player information in the Watch window.

J

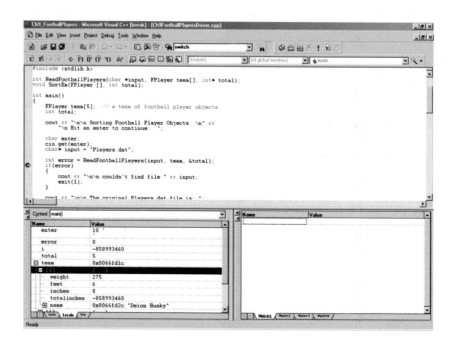

Figure J-11
Examine One Team Member

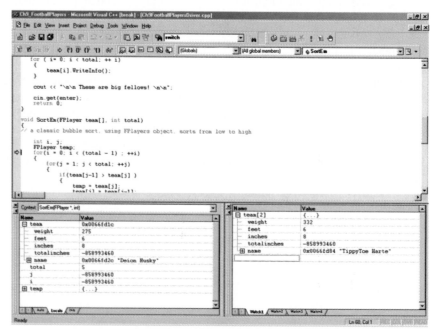

Figure J-12
The Team Array Pointer in the SortEm Function

J

Program Index

The majority of the sample programs in this text are found on the accompanying CD, and this appendix lists the programs found there. The program number (text reference), project title, and a brief description are summarized in the following tables on a chapter-by-chapter basis.

▌ TABLE K-1
Chapter 2: Getting Started

Number	Title	Description
2-1	HelloWorld	Writes hello world! to the screen.
2-2	HowsTheWeather	Writes weather comments to the screen.
2-3	OneLineHello	The source code for Hello World (Program 2-1) rewritten in one line.
2-4	WeatherRewritten	The Weather source (Program 2-2) rewritten so that the source code fits into a few statements.
2-5	StyleToHate	Program illustrates poor coding style.
2-6	StyleToLove	Program 2-5 rewritten with good coding style.
2-7	CalcTemp	Illustrates problems with integer division in temperature conversion. Shows correct and incorrect output.
2-8	CalcSphere	More problems with integer division in sphere calculations. Shows correct and incorrect output.
2-9	UsingDefines	Uses #defines for PI and MyPay.
2-10	AppleBananas	Compares const versus #define.
2-11	DataCasting	Casting not performed and program gives wrong answer.
2-12	EquStatement	Correctly placed equation in program.
2-13	CalcCyl	Practice with I/O and calculates the volume of a cylinder
2-14	ConvertTotalInches	Uses integer division and the modulus operator to calculate total inches from feet and inches.
2-15	CharsToInts	Casting chars to ints to be able to write character data as decimal.

TABLE K-2
Chapter 3: Control Statements and Loops

Number	Title	Description
3-1	KnickKnack_IfElse	Knick Knack program with if else.
3-2	NestedIfs	Nested if statements sample program.
3-3	KnickKnack_Switch	Knick Knack program with switch.
3-4	FamousYear	Program with switch
3-5	HowManyHellos_For	Using a for loop sample program.
3-6	WritingABC_For	Using a for loop and writing the ABCs using integers cast into ASCII characters.
3-7	Poetry_While	Write the poem using a while loop.
3-8	HowManyHellos_While	Write hellos using a while loop.
3-9	Poetry_DoWhile	Write the poem using a do while loop.
3-10	ABCs_DoWhile	Write the ABCs using a do while loop and casting integers to ASCII characters.
3-11	SemiAndWarnings	Does not run correctly due to misplaced semicolons.
3-12	TimeConvPh2	Using a switch statement with a do while loop to convert between H:M:S and Total seconds.
3-13	NumPh2	Sample program with while loop and if else statements.
3-14	SimplePattern	Write a simple pattern using nested for loops.

TABLE K-3
Chapter 4: Pointers, Addresses, and the Indirection Operator

Number	Title	Description
4-1	SizeOper	Using sizeof operator with variables and data types to determine bytes of memory.
4-2	AddressOperator	Shows the address of each variable.
4-3	AddressOperatorsLucky	Shows the address of the variables lucky, PI, and money.
4-4	VarsAddsPtrs	Assign addresses of variables into pointers.
4-5	AddPtrsAndIndirectionOpers	Access data values and perform addition using pointers and the indirection operator.
4-6	MorePtrs	What are pointers pointing to?
4-7	WriteHelloAndPtrs	Assign addresses into pointers and use the indirection operator and pointer to perform the WriteHello program.
4-8	KnickKnack	Knick Knack program rewritten using pointers and the indirection operator and a switch statement.
4-9	PyramidAndPtrs	Uses pointers with indirection operators to access and assign all variables as well as perform calculations. Uses the actual variable for writing the values.

K

Chapter 5: Functions, Part 1: The Basics

Number	Title	Description
5-1	CalcAvgsBruteForce	Calculate Averages for two subjects by brute force technique.
5-2	CalcAvgsLoops	Uses a while loop to calculate course averages—still with brute force.
5-3	GetAge	Demonstrates simple functions to write message, ask for user's age, and then write age to screen.
5-4	Add1toN	Uses functions to ask for number, then adds the numbers and writes results. The main function calls all functions.
5-5	Add1ToN_Second Version	Rewrite of Program 5-4 so that the calculate function calls the write function.
5-6	CountHelloStatic	Demonstrates use of a static variable in a function.
5-7	CountHellosGlobal	Rewrite of Program 5-6 using a global variable.
5-8	CalcVolCyl	Calculates the volume of a cylinder; demonstrates call by value
5-9	CalcVolCylPtrs	Demonstrates call by reference with pointers to receive two values from a function.
5-10	PrimPh1	Demonstrates use of bool variables. Program has many functions, and it determines whether a number is prime or not.
5-11	Random	Demonstrates the use of the srand and rand random number generators.
5-12	TimeConversion	Demonstrates call by value and call by reference to get time and convert H:M:S to seconds. Pointers and indirection operators are used.
5-13	CatsAndDogsPtrs	Uses bool variables and call by reference with pointers to pass several pieces of data between functions. Demonstrates concept of boolean flags.
5-14	CatsAndDogsGlobal	Uses bool variables and global variables. No data is passed between functions. Demonstrates the concept of boolean flags.

K

Number	Title	Description
6-1	PhoneBill	A complete program for finding utility bill average for a year. Uses a one-dimensional array.
6-2	CompRatio	Shows an array of four elements. Each element is assigned a number. A for loop is used to write the numbers to the screen.
6-3	CompRatioPtr	A free pointer with every array. Writes the array name without an index value, and we see the hex address in the array pointer.
6-4	Ave1DArray	Demonstrates passing an array to a function. Uses a function to calculate the average of a one-dimensional array.
6-5	GimmeFiveNum	Declares an array in the calling function and fills it in the called function.
6-6	WhoDoYouLove	Uses cin.getline and cin to read character strings from the keyboard.
6-7	WhoDoYouLovePart2	Uses cin.getline with a delimiter and cin to read character strings. Makes use of the cin.ignore function. Demonstrates how cin stops reading at a blank.
6-8	HowOldAreYouClaire	Broken program—does not work correctly reading text and numeric data.
6-9	HowOldBetterWay	Program 6-8 is rewritten, using cin.getline with atoi functions for reading all integer and character strings
6-10	SnowWhite	Uses a two-dimensional character string array. Demonstrates how to handle a list of textual values and how to pass two-dimensional arrays to functions.
6-11	FavoriteWord	Reads in a word and then a phrase and determines if the word is in the phrase. Passes character arrays to functions and uses a character pointer and the strstr function.
6-12	HowsTheWeather	Reads several columns of data from a file into one-dimensional arrays. Arrays are passed to functions. The program demonstrates a way to determine the max and min of an array. Writes data to an output file.

K

Chapter 7: User-Defined Data Types, struct, and enum[a]

Number	Title	Description
7-1	AssignDataStruct	Assigns and prints data structure information for a Student.
7-2	JacksRace	Assigns and prints data structure information for a Person in a race.
7-3	StudentArray	Demonstrates how to access elements in a structure array.
7-4	GetStartTime	Demonstrates how to return a structure from a function.
7-5	AvePoints	Demonstrates how to pass structures to functions and return a third structure. The function receives two points structs and returns the average point.
7-8	WatchTheBirdies	Demonstrates how to pass addresses of two structures to a function and access structure elements with the right-arrow operator.
7-12	BirdChoices	Contains an enumerated variable and uses a corresponding two-dimensional character string for program input and output. Also shows how to cast an integer into an enumerated data variable.
7-13	OpticParts	Demonstrates call by value and call by reference with pointers using an enumerated data variable. Corresponding two-dimensional character string array is used for input and output.
7-14	WhatTimeIsIt	Demonstrates passing a structure variable between functions. Boolean flags are used.
7-15	PlayingCards	Sets up a playing card struct and fills an array of fifty-two playing cards and prints them to the screen. Enumerated data is used for card suit and card rank.
7-16	DogShows	Demonstrates how structs may contain struct and enum variables. A data structure, Contestant, contains Name and Dog structures. The Dog struct has an enumerated Breed variable. Call by reference and call by value, and passing two-dimensional character string arrays are used in this program.

[a]Programs 7-6, 7-7, 7-9, 7-10, and 7-11 are previous programs with slight modifications and are not included on the source CD.

K

Number	Title	Description
8-1	ReviewHelloWorld	Review call by value.
8-2	ReviewGiveMe3Floats	Review call by reference with pointers.
8-3	GiveMe2Structs	Call by reference with pointers and structures.
8-4	GiveMe3Floats—Global	Uses global variables. No data is passed between functions.
8-5	GiveMe3Floats—Reference	Demonstrates call by reference with reference parameters and single data variables.
8-6	GiveMe2Structs—Reference	Demonstrates call by reference with reference parameters and struct variables.
8-7	CatsAndDogsReference	Rewrite of Dogs and Cats program from Chapter 6 using reference parameters.
8-8	HowBigIsYourBox	Calculates the volume of a box using a call by reference with reference parameters.
8-9	AbsoluteValue—Overloaded	Demonstrates overloaded functions. Program has three AbsoluteValue functions.
8-10	SayGoodnight—Overloaded	Demonstrates overloaded functions that write Goodnight to no one or one or two people.
8-11	DrawLines	Demonstrates a variable-length parameter list function to write lines of characters to the screen.
8-12	WriteNumbers	Demonstrates a default parameter list function for writing a series of numbers to the screen.
8-13	WriteYourName—Default	Demonstrates a default parameter list function for writing names to the screen.
8-14	WriteYourName—Overloaded	Rewrite of Program 8-13 using three overloaded functions.
8-15	WriteYourName—MixAndMatch	Combination of overloaded functions with and without default parameter list inputs.
8-16	HowBigIsYourBox—In-line	Demonstrates an inline function.

Number	Title	Description
9-1	Sphere	Demonstrates a class declaration and uses it in a program. The class functions are written inside class declaration.
9-2	Daytime	Demonstrates how to break a program into .cpp and .h files. Program has overloaded class constructor functions.
9-3	TwoDates	Demonstrates a program with two different CDate objects.
9-4	Gadgets	A simple program example with two objects. Demonstrates a constructor and destructor function.
9-5	ArrayOfObjects	The PhoneList program that reads entries from a data file and fills an array of objects.
9-6	ShowMeTheCards	Has enumerated data as class member data. Creates an array of fifty-two card objects and fills the array with enumerated data.
9-7	Counter	Has overloaded operators (unary operators $++$ and $--$) in a class. Demonstrates how overloaded operators are used with objects.
9-8	AddingTimes	Demonstrates binary overloaded operators with objects. Adds time objects to determine the sum.
9-9	CompareCards	Demonstrates how to overload an operator to perform a relational comparison between two objects.
9-10	KittyKitty	Demonstrates how to pass the address of an object to a function.
9-11	SetTime	Passes the address of an object to a function. The function uses utilities in the Time.h function to access the system time.
9-12	BigBiggerBiggestFootballPlayers	A program that demonstrates reading football player data into an array of FPlayer objects from a data file. The class declaration contains an overloaded greater than operator (>) to compare football players. A standard bubble sort function is used to sort the array of objects.

K

Number	Title	Description
10-1	Namespace	Illustrates using different namespace regions.
10-2	Shopper	Program classes include Shopper, Clerk, and Cart. A data struct for an Item is described as well. Demonstrates how an object can be a data member of another class. The Shopper class has a Cart object. The Shopper places Items in the Cart. The Shopper uses the services of the Clerk. The Clerk removes the Items and determines the total cost of the Shopper's Items.
10-3	ShopperUses	Program 10-2 is rewritten so that the Shopper is using a Cart instead of having a Cart. This change requires additional wrapper functions for the Cart and Shopper.
10-4	DiceGame	Program classes include Die (representing a single six-sided die) and a DicePlayer. The DicePlayer has an array of Die objects. Illustrates a class that has an array of objects as part of its declaration. Uses a random number generator to simulate rolling the dice. The computer system time is used to reseed the random number generator before each game of dice.
10-5	TrackCoach	Program classes include a Track_Coach, StopWatch, Time, and MasterClock. Demonstrates both has a and uses a class relationships. The Track_Coach has a StopWatch object. The Stop_Watch has three Time objects, and the Stop_Watch uses the MasterClock object for setting the Time objects. The system time is accessed by the MasterClock and sets the Stop_Watch Time objects.
10-6	VendingMachine	Program classes include a VendingMachine, Dispenser, and MoneyCtr (bank). The VendingMachine has one MoneyCtr object, and the VendingMachine has an array of Dispenser objects. Simulates how a vending machine operates. The MoneyCtr object and Dispense objects perform the majority of the work.

K

Number	Title	Description
11-1	Counter	A short review program with a counter object.
11-2	NewCounter	Demonstrates inheritance. A NewCounter is a Counter. A NewCounter is derived from Counter.
11-3	CEmployee	A program that contains a CEmployee class.
11-4	CBoss	The CBoss class is derived from the CEmployee class using inheritance. A boss is an employee. Demonstrates also how to organize files when inheritance is being used.
11-5	CCEO	A CCEO class is derived from the CBoss class. The chief executive officer is a boss.
11-6	CBoss2	The CBoss class member functions from Program 11-4 have been rewritten so that they call the (CEmployee) base class functions. The programmer should always use the base class functions wherever possible.
11-7	CPerson	A review program demonstrating a class with two constructor functions and a destructor function. The data members are protected.
11-8	CGolfer	The CPerson class is used as a base class for the CGolfer class. A golfer is a person. The CGolfer class contains constructor and destructor functions. Demonstrates the order of how base and derived class constructors and destructors are called, and how base class constructors are called from derived class constructors.
11-9	CXYPointsPart1	CCustomDataPoint is derived from CXYPoint class. The derived class does not contain a constructor function. As long as the derived objects are created with no input parameters, the derived class constructor is not required and the base class constructor is called automatically.
11-10	CXYPointsPart2	Constructor input parameters are used to initialize the CCustomDataPoint objects. Derived class constructors are required to pass input parameters to the base class constructor.
11-11	Animals	Several animal classes are derived from the Animal class, including Mammal, Amphibian, and Bird. The program demonstrates creating different types of derived class objects and how the base class functions are used.
11-12	Shuffleand DealCards	A fairly large program that contains Card, Player, and Dealer classes. The Dealer is a Player and hence is derived from the Player class. The Dealer has the deck of cards, which is represented by an array of fifty-two Card objects. Demonstrates how the address of the Player object is passed into the Dealer's deal function. The card-shuffling algorithm is discussed also. The use of an index array that keeps track of the order of the shuffled cards is used.

(continued)

Number	Title	Description
11-13	VirtualShapes: Part 1	A Shape class is used as a base class. Sphere and Pyramid classes are derived from the Shape class. The base class contains virtual functions, which are redefined in the Sphere and Pyramid classes. Demonstrates how the addresses of the derived classes are placed in pointers to the base class and the virtual functions are then accessed.
11-14	VirtualShapes: Part 2	Program 11-13 with additional new Shapes.
11-15	TwoVehicles	A base class, Vehicle, is used to derive two new classes, Semi and RV. The main function contains only Semi and RV objects, and the virtual functions are accessed.

TABLE K-11
Chapter 12: Advanced Topics in C++

Number	Title	Description
12-1	HowBigOfAnArray	Demonstrates how to use the new operator to allocate memory for a one-dimensional array.
12-2	TwoDates	Rewrite of Program 9-3 allocating two Dates in memory using the new operator.
12-3	NewNoThrow	Demonstrates the nothrow option that can be used with the new operator so that an exception is not thrown if the operator fails.
12-4	2DArrayScheme1	Demonstrates one technique to allocate memory for a two-dimensional array. Uses an offset value and calculates the array index.
12-5	2DArrayScheme2	Demonstrates a different technique for handling a two-dimensional allocated array using an array of pointers.
12-6	AddrtoFunctoFunc	Demonstrates how to pass an address to a function and then pass it to another function.
12-7	ExcHandPosNumber	Demonstrates basic exception handling and how to write a condition so that it throws an exception and catches and handles the exception.
12-8	ExcHandManyCatches	Demonstrates how a try block can have many catch statements for handling various exceptions.
12-9	ExcHandNewOperator	Demonstrates how to perform exception handling if the new operator fails. This feature is specific to Visual C++ because C++ automatically returns a NULL if memory is not available.
Last One	WindowsEx	A document/view architecture sample Windows program that beeps if the left mouse button is pressed.

K

Appendix	Program Number	Title	Description
D: ASCII Character Codes	D-1	ASCII_Codes	Writes the decimal, hex, octal, and ASCII character symbols for 0–255.
F: File Input/ Output	F-1	WeatherStats	Reads weather data from a text data file and writes summary information to an output file.
	F-2	StudentGrades	Demonstrates header line in a data file. Reads grade data from a file into an array and determines the grade average. Data are written to an output file.
	F-3	AddAllThoseNumbers	Demonstrates reading until the End Of File (EOF) is reached for a text file.
	F-4	BinaryFiles	Demonstrates how to open, write to, and read from a binary file. Writes data to a binary file, then reads the data from the file.
	F-5	MoreBinaryFiles	Writes array, struct, and single variables to a binary file and then reads the data from the file.
G: C++ String Class	G-1	StringOperators	Demonstrates the use of some basic C++ string class operators.
	G-2	StringEdit	Demonstrates C++ string class edit operators.
	G-3	StringSearch	Demonstrates C++ string class search functions.
	G-4	ConvertBetween	Demonstrates how to convert C++ string class objects and character array variables.
	G-5	ReadingIntoString	Demonstrates how the getline must be used to read text data from the keyboard/file and convert to C++ string object.

K

(continued)

Appendix	Program Number	Title	Description
I: Keyboard Input, Screen Output	I-2	OutputNoFormatting	Basic numeric and character output. No formatting.
	I-4	OutputWithFormatting	Basic numeric and character output with formatting, including set precision and set width.
	I-5	OutputWithISOFlags	Numeric and character data are written to the screen using set precision and set width.
	I-6	OutputWithManipulators	Numeric, character, and character array data are written using set precision, width, and justification. IOS manipulators are used instead of the cout.setf function in the stream.

Bibliography

The reader should consult the documentation that accompanies this text on the Visual C++ CD-ROM. The Microsoft Visual C++ Version 6.0, MSDN Library Visual Studio 6.0, C/C++ Language, and C++ Libraries contain descriptions and usage examples.

Bronson, Gary, and Menconi, Stephen, *A First Book of ANSI C: Fundamentals of C Programming,* Minneapolis/St. Paul, MN: West Publishing Company, 1996.

Deital, H. M., and Deital, P. J., *C++ How to Program,* Upper Saddle River, NJ: Prentice Hall, 1998.

Eckel, Bruce, *Thinking in C++,* 2nd Edition, Upper Saddle River, NJ: Prentice Hall, 2000.

Etter, Delores M., *Introduction to C++ for Engineers and Scientists,* Upper Saddle River, NJ: Prentice Hall, 1977.

Kernighan, Brian W., and Ritchie, Dennis M., *The C Programming Language,* Englewood Cliffs, NJ: Prentice Hall, 1978.

LaFore, Robert, *Object-Oriented Programming in C++,* 3rd Edition, Indianapolis, IN: Sams Publishing, 1999.

Sadr, Babak, *Unified Objects Object-Oriented Programming Using C++,* Los Alamitos, CA: IEEE Computer Society, 1998.

Schlidt, Herbert, *C++: The Complete Reference,* 3rd Edition, Berkeley, CA: Osborne McGraw-Hill, 1998.

Staugaard, Andrew C., Jr., *Structured and Object-Oriented Techniques*, Upper Saddle River, NJ: Prentice Hall, 2000.

Glossary

access specifier   Dictates the accessibility of class members to the world. Access specifiers are private, protected, and public.

address operator: &   When used with a variable name, the address operator returns the hex address of the memory location for that variable, for example: &number;

algorithm   A process or set of rules for solving a problem.

ANSI/ISO standard   American National Standards Institute/International Standards Organization. Oversees the committee that standardizes the C++ language.

arguments   Input or return values for a function.

array   A list of variables of the same data type that are referenced with a single name. Each element or member of an array is accessed by using an integer index value. The [] operators are used in the declaration statement. For example, an array of 100 doubles named "numbers" is declared by using: doublenumber[100];

array dimension   The size of the array. Arrays can be single-dimensional (list), two-dimensional, (table), or multi-dimensioned.

array index   The integer value that references a specific element or member of an array.

array pointers   When an array is declared, C++ automatically creates a pointer of the same name that "points to" the first element of the array.

ASCII   American Standard Code for Information Interchange (ASCII). The personal computer uses the ASCII notation for interpreting bits.

associativity   When two (or more) operators that have the same procedure are found in a C++ expression, associativity specifies the order of operations, such as left to right or right to left.

automatic variable   Variables that are declared inside functions. Automatic variables are also known as local variables.

base access specifier The three access specifiers, private, protected, and public, can also be used in the first line of a class declaration. When used here, the specifiers dictate how the base class members are treated in the derived classes.

base class A general-purpose class—also known as the "parent" class. New classes are derived from the base class. These new classes (children classes) are special cases of the base class. This principle is known as inheritance. For example, a vehicle class (which describes data and functions for motor vehicles) can be a base class. A Recreational Vehicle class can be derived from the Vehicle class. An RV is a Vehicle. The RV inherits properties from the Vehicle class.

base 16 Uses sixteen different symbols to represent a quantity of items. The sixteen symbols are 0, 1, 2, 3, 4, 5, 6, 7, 8, 9, A, B, C, D, E, F. Also known as hexadecimal notation.

base 10 Our common counting system, with ten different symbols to represent a quantity of items. The ten symbols are 0, 1, 2, 3, 4, 5, 6, 7, 8, 9. Also known as decimal notation.

base 2 Uses two different symbols to represent a quantity of items. The two (most common) symbols are 0 and 1. Also known as binary notation.

binary operator An operator that requires two operands, such as the addition operator a + b or greater than operator a > b.

bit A unit of data that exists in one of two states, such as 1 or 0, on or off.

body of function The statements of C++ code inside a function.

bool A data type used to declare boolean variables. A boolean variable contains the value true or false.

breakpoint A line of source code that is identified by the programmer while he or she is using the debugger. A breakpoint tells the debugger to stop the program on that line of code to enable the programmer to examine program variables.

byte Consists of 8 bits and is the basic unit of computer memory.

bytecode The Java compiler produces bytecode. The Java Virtual Machine program interprets the bytecode and issues machine instructions.

call by reference A term used when the address of a variable is passed to a function.

call by reference with pointers A term used when the address of a variable is passed into a pointer variable in the function. The address operator is required in the call statement and the indirection operator is required in the function.

call by reference with reference parameters The address of a variable is passed to a reference variable in the function. Just the name of the variable is required in the call statement and no indirection operator is required in the function.

call by value The value of a variable is passed to a function.

called function When one function uses (or invokes) a second function, the second function is the called function.

calling function When one function uses (or invokes) a second function, the first function is the calling function.

call statement The line of code in the program where a function is invoked.

case sensitive Recognizing upper- and lowercase letters to be different. C++ is a case-sensitive language. TOTAL, Total, and total are three different names in C++.

casting An operation in which the value of one type of data is transformed into another type of data.

C++ class The fundamental unit in object-oriented programming; contains the "job description" (member data and functions) for a program object.

char A data type used to declare a variable that contains one character symbol. The value 'y' can be stored in a char variable.

character string A character array, such as char name[50];.

child class A derived class. *See* derived class *and* base class.

class A "job description" for a program object. The class contains member data and functions. See C++ class.

class constructor A function that has the same name as the class and is automatically called when objects are declared. The main job of a constructor function is to initialize object member data. It may be overloaded.

class declaration The source code that contains the class members, including the private, protected, and public sections with data and functions. Typically, the class declaration is contained in a *.h file.

class definition The source code that contains the implementation of member functions. Typically, the class definition is contained in a *.cpp file.

class members Either data or functions that are declared within a class.

class relationships The interactions and connections or associations that classes have with each other. There are three class relationships: uses a, has a, and is a.

comment Lines in source code, ignored by the compiler, in which programmers may write information concerning the file or program.

commercial off-the-shelf (COTS) software The general term for products offered by software developers. COTS is ready to use in the developer's own software; for example, COTS software can be file translators, image processing, or graphics software.

compiler A software program that reads source code and produces object or machine code.

compile-time polymorphism Illustrated in either overloaded functions or overloaded operators. (*See* polymorphism *for complete discussion.*)

complex class   A class provided in the C++ language for working with complex numbers. (Complex numbers are represented as a + bi, where i is the sqrt(− 1).)

conditional statement   A statement in C++ in which a condition is evaluated. The result determines which path the program control takes.

const   A modifier specifying that the variable is to remain a constant value, such as const double pi = 3.14159265;

constructor function   *See* class constructor.

data structure   A grouping of data variables that represents a logical unit, such as the data describing an item in a grocery store, including name, brand, price, UPC code, etc. The keyword struct is required.

data type   A type of "container" holding program data. There are several different data types in C++, including int, float, double, char, and bool.

debugger   The portion of the development environment that allows the programmer to step into a program and run the program line by line. The programmer can set breakpoints and watch how the values of variables change. It is possible to watch the order of statement execution in the debugger.

default input parameter list function   Default input values may be supplied in the function prototype. If the variables (or values) are not provided in the function call, the default input values are used in the function.

delimiter   A character specified in a read statement; the reading is concluded when the delimiter character is found.

derived class   A new class created by inheriting data and functions from a base or parent class. *See* base class.

destructor function   A function that has the same name as the class with a ~ character, such as ~Date or ~Player. The destructor is called automatically when the object goes out of scope. It cannot be overloaded.

double   A data type used to declare variables with up to ten places of decimal precision. The value 3.9342431337 can be stored in a double variable.

dynamic memory allocation   Occurs when the program obtains memory for program variables "on the fly" as the program executes.

EBCDIC   Extended Binary Coded Decimal Interchange Code. Mainframes and some minicomputers use the EBCDIC format for interpreting bits.

elements   Members of an array.

enumerated data type   A user-defined type; a numbered list of categories or items, such as days of the week, types of coins, or dog breeds.

error code   A set of values specified by the programmer that represents errors discovered in the program. For example, error codes could be 1 for invalid user input, 2 for file not found, etc.

error flag   The variable containing the error code.

error trap   Term used by programmers that means "be on the look-out" for a possible error, such as an invalid user input or a divide by zero. Error trapping code checks and avoids invalid code operation.

exception handling   A way to deal with run-time errors gracefully. When an error occurs, an exception is "thrown" and "caught" by an exception handler. An exception is another name for an error.

extract   When characters are pulled out of the stream of data, and placed into variables, these characters are said to be extracted from the stream.

flags   Variables used in programs to remember items or conditions in a program. Flags are usually integers or boolean variables. For example, set a flag = 0 if no errors occurred or flag = 1 if an error occurred.

float   A data type used to declare variables with up to five places of decimal precision. The value 6.24313 can be stored in a floating point variable.

free   The C standard library function that releases (frees) allocated memory from the program and returns it to the system.

function   A discrete module or unit of code that performs specific tasks.

function body   Consists of the statements of C++ code inside a function.

function header line   The first line of any function in C/C++ contains the input types and arguments and return type.

function prototype   The C++ statement that contains the function name, input, and return data types. The prototype informs the compiler that the function exists in the program.

GCC GNU C compiler   A C++ development environment produced by the GNU project.

global variable   A variable declared outside any function. All functions within the file can access global variables.

has a relationship   The "has a" relationship is a class relationship in which one object (first) contains another object (second), and the second object is an integral part of the first object. If the second object were removed from the first object, the first object could not perform as expected. For example, a tennis player has a tennis racquet.

heap   The portion of the computer memory in which global and static program variables are stored, along with the memory reserved during dynamic memory allocation (using the new operator).

hex address   The address of a memory location.

hexadecimal notation   The mathematical notation that describes how computer memory is referenced. Base 16 is hexadecimal notation.

identifier In C++, the name of a variable, label, function, or object that the programmer defines.

indirection operator: * When used with a pointer, it directs the program to go to the address held in the pointer variable. The $->$ is also an indirection operator used with a pointer to a struct or a class.

inheritance The inheritance process in an object-oriented language is demonstrated when a new class is created from an existing class—and this new class contains data and functions from the existing class. *See* base class.

inline functions Inline functions contain the inline keyword in the prototype. When the executable file is produced, the inline function body is embedded in the code at the function call location.

input arguments The variable values (or addresses) passed into a function.

instance of a class (or instantiation of a class) When a class variable is declared, an object is created. This object is known as an instance of a class.

int A data type used to declare variables that are whole numbers. The value of 42 can be contained in an integer variable.

is a relationship The "is a" relationship is found when one class is derived from a second class (inheritance-type class relationship). The second class becomes a first class. For example, an Animal class can be a base class for a Bird class. The Bird object is a(n) Animal.

Java™ An object-oriented programming language originally developed by Sun Microsystems. Java programs can run on many different kinds of computers, consumer electronics, and other devices.

Java Virtual Machine A program that interprets Java bytecode and issues machine instructions.

Just in Time compilers Java compilers that build bytecode into code specific for the resident processor.

keywords In C++, words reserved by the language that have specific syntax and actions. They may not be used as variable or function names. For example, switch, for, if, and float are keywords in C++. (There are a total of sixty-three keywords in C++.)

linker A software program that hooks or links machine code and library code together to form an executable file.

local variable A variable declared either inside a function or in the function header line. Local variables exist only while the program control is in the function. The variables are lost when the function is exited.

logical operator An operator that evaluates AND, OR, or NOT conditions. The resultant value is either a 1 (true) or 0 (false).

loop   A series of C++ statements enabling the program to repeat line(s) of code until a certain condition is met.

loop altering statement   A line of C++ code that changes the value of a variable used in the condition-checking decision for a loop.

loop index   A variable used as a counter in a loop.

lvalue   A C++ entity that may be found on the left side of an assignment operator.

make file   In the UNIX environment, a make file specifies the files and libraries for a program.

malloc   The C standard library function that allocated memory as the program is executing.

memory   The physical location in the computer that provides storage space for program data and variables.

method   A class member function.

Microsoft Foundation Class (MFC)   One implementation of an object-oriented environment for the development of application programs for Microsoft Windows. A programmer can use MFC to develop a Windows application without being an expert in Windows API. MFC has packaged, ready-to-go classes that provide Windows components as well as functions that handle the underlying window messages. See Windows API.

Microsoft Project   Microsoft Visual C++ requires that the program files be contained in a project.

multiple-file programs   Programs consisting of many source and header files that are created by the programmer.

multiple inheritance   A term used to describe how two or more classes are used as base classes for a new class.

nested statements   When one set of statements is located inside another set of statements, these statements are said to be nested.

newline   \n or an Enter key.

null character   A "zero" character; '\0'.

null-terminated string   A character string has a null character that indicates the end of the pertinent data in the character array.

numeric classes   C++ provides several classes for working with specialized numeric data, including the complex and valarray classes.

object   A single instance of a class.

object model   A software design technique that uses a collection of objects to represent the items in a program. Designing a program with the object model involves determining what objects are required and the relationships between them.

object-oriented program   A program based on real-world items (objects) and how these objects interact with each other.

operand   C++ operators work on operands. In the expression a + b, a and b are operands and + is the operator.

operator function   A class member function required to specify the task(s) for overloading an operator.

operators   Symbols that direct certain operations to be performed, such as + for addition, = for assignment, etc.

out of bounds array   When the program accesses array elements not legally declared, the program has gone out of bounds.

overloaded functions   Functions that have the same name but different input parameter lists.

overloaded operator   A valid C++ symbol (operator) that has been assigned a specialized task when the operator is used with objects.

parent class   A base class. *See* base class.

pointer   A variable that "points" to another variable. A pointer is a variable that "holds" another variable's hex address. When an indirection operator is used with a pointer, it directs the system to go where the pointer is pointing.

polling loop   A loop in which the condition is based on continually checking the status of a variable until a certain condition is met. For example, a polling loop can be used to count off a certain number of seconds by getting the system time, adding the "waiting period" to the time, and then continually polling (asking) the system time until the waiting period has been reached.

polymorphism   In an object-oriented language, allows the programmer to develop one interface and many implementations. There are two types of polymorphism in C++: compile time (overloaded operators and functions) and run-time (virtual functions).

portable language   A language in which the source code does not need to be changed when it is moved from one type of computer to another.

precedence of operations   A set of rules that dictates the order in which operations are performed.

preprocessor directives   Lines in the source code that give the compiler instructions, such as #include or #define lines.

private specifier   Used in class declarations as either an access specifier or as a base access specifier. The private access specifier dictates that only the member of the class can see and access the private members. Private members are not visible outside the class, and private members are not inherited in children classes. When private is used as a base access specifier, all public and protected members of the base class become private members of the derived class.

protected specifier   Used in class declarations as either an access specifier or as a base access specifier. When used in a base class, the protected members are inherited in children classes. Protected members can be seen and accessed by all members of the class but are not visible outside the class. When protected is used as a base access specifier, all public and protected members of the base class become protected members of the derived class.

public specifier   Used in class declarations as either an access specifier or as a base access specifier. When used in a base class, the public members are visible outside the class and are inherited in children classes. When public is used as a base access specifier, all public members of the base class become public members of the derived class. Protected members of the base class become protected members of the derived class.

pure virtual function   Does not have an actual function implementation in the base class.

qsort   A general sorting routine located in the C standard library (stdlib.h).

reference parameter   Declared by using the & operator. It is an implicit pointer.

relational operator   An operator that evaluates >, >=, < , <=, ==, != conditions. The resultant value is either a 1 (true) or 0 (false).

return type   The data type of the variable that is passed back to the calling function via a return statement.

rule of thirds   A software development theory stating that software project time should be divided into three parts: designing, writing, and implementing/testing.

run-time polymorphism   Illustrated in virtual functions. (*See* polymorphism *for complete discussion.*)

rvalue   A C++ entity that may be found on the right side of an assignment operator.

sentinel value   A trailer value.

sizeof   In C++, returns the number of bytes reserved for the variable or for data type. For example, the statement:

int bytes = sizeof(float);

returns the value of 4 into the bytes variable.

software development skill set   A list of the necessary skills a person should possess to become a successful programmer.

software development steps   A series of logical steps followed to design and build software.

source code   The file(s) that contain the C/C++ statements that provide program instructions.

stack   The portion of the computer memory where local program variables are stored.

standardized libraries   Libraries found in C++ that provide useful functions for mathematics, file I/O, text operations, etc. The math.h is a standard library.

static variable   A local variable that retains its value until the program is terminated.

storage specifier   A data type.

string class   A class provided in the C++ language for working with text-based information (strings).

structure array   Structures may be declared as arrays in the same manner that standard C++ data type arrays are declared.

structured programming   A software design technique in which the program is based on the flow of the data through the program.

structure tag or **template**   A blueprint for a structure variable. The structure tag is considered a data type in C++ and is used wherever data types are required (in variable declarations and functions).

syntax   The grammatical rules required by the language. For example, after most C++ statements, the programmer must place a semicolon. If the semicolon is omitted, a syntax error is reported.

tag name   A data type for variable declarations; used in the same manner as standard data types in function prototypes and function header lines.

templates   Used to create generic functions and classes. The keyword, *template*, is used to set up the framework for a function or a class. In a function or class template description, the data type is actually passed in as an argument.

ternary operator   An operator requiring three operands. The ? : operators together are considered ternary operators because there are three operands. In the statement

```
int a, b;
a = 50;
b = a > 100 ? 200 : 0 ;
```

the three operands are a $>$ 100, 200, and 0.

top-down   Top-down programming is a software design technique in which the program is based on the flow of the data through the program.

trailer value   Used when reading data files. The trailer value is the last value in the data file and is different from the other data values in the file. The program can be structured to read until it sees the trailer value. For example, a $-$ 1 can be a trailer value for a file of positive integers.

true (1), false (0)   Relational and logical operators return 1 if true and 0 if false.

unary operator   An operator that requires only one operand, such as the increment operator, ++.

user-defined data types   Data structures, classes, and enumerations are all considered to be user-defined data types.

uses a relationship   A relationship in which an object makes use of another object to accomplish a task. For example, a computer uses a printer.

using namespace std   Directs the compiler to employ the standard (std) namespace, which includes the standard C++ libraries. To use the string class or the numeric classes provided in the C++ standard library, the headers must be declared in the new style format.

valarray class   A class provided in the C++ standard libraries for working with arrays.

value   The actual data stored in the variable is called the variable's value.

variable declaration   The C++ program statement that dictates the type and name for a variable.

variables   Memory locations reserved by the program for storing program data. The variable has a name and type, such as int, float, etc.

variable scope   The length of time a variable is in existence as the program runs. Local variables in a function are in scope only when program control is in the function. Global and static variables are in scope until program termination.

Visual C++   A development environment product from Microsoft.

watch variable   A program variable that the programmer wishes to examine while the program is being run in the debugger. (The watch variable is being "watched" or examined.)

whitespace characters   Spaces (blanks), tabs, line feeds, Enter key, control characters, vertical tabs, and form feed characters.

Windows Application Program Interface (Win32 API)   The program interface that enables a programmer to develop Windows-based programs.

Windows messages   Issued by the Windows operating system when certain events have occurred, such as a mouse click, keystroke, etc.

zero-indexed   The first element of an array is referenced by using a zero [0] value. Such arrays are said to be zero-indexed.

Index

A

absolute value overloaded functions, 332
abstraction, 359
access specifiers, 367
    base class, 479, 495–96
    inheritance and, 495–96
    protected access specifier, 481–84
    public access specifier, 479
accumulation operators, 56–57
address operator (&), 127–29
    pointers and, 130–32
addresses
    of data variables, 127–29
    hex addresses, 126–27
    passing to functions, 176–80, 556–57
advanced topics, 543–44
    dynamic memory allocation, 544–49
    exception handling, 557–62
    friends, 568
    Java programming language, 565–67
    Microsoft Foundation Class Library (MFC), 562–65
    Standard Template Library (STL), 568
    * operator, 550–57
    templates, 567–68
algebraic expressions, 52
ALGOL 60 language, 7
algorithm design, 22–24
algorithms, 22

American National Standards Institute (ANSI), 7
angle braces, and #include statements, 643
ANSI (American National Standards Institute), 7
ANSI/ISO standard, 7
applets, 566
arguments, 152, 158
Ariane 5 rocket, 43
arithmetic operators, 48–53
    algebraic expressions, 52
    intermediate results with, 49
    math library (math.h), 52
    modulus operator, 48–49, 66–67
    operator precedence and math expressions, 52–53
    troubleshooting
        fractional calculations, 53
        using fractions, 49–52
array declarations, 198–200
array dimension, 199
array index, 198, 521–23
array of characters. *See* character strings; string class; string objects
array of objects, 397–402
array pointers, 138–39, 202–6
arrays, 197–238. *See also*
    multidimensional arrays;
    one-dimensional arrays
    array declarations, 198–200
    array dimension, 199
    array index, 198, 521–23

array pointers, 138–39, 202–6
compression ratio array, 202
debugging with, 672–74
defined, 198
elements, 198
filling, from data files, 237–38
fundamentals of, 198–202
initialization, 200–201, 228–30
for loops and, 201–2
maximum or minimum value, finding, 240–44
out of bounds array, 235–37
properties of, 239
reference variable arrays, 329–30
returning from functions, 208–13
single data variables and, 197–98
size value for, 545–46
structure arrays, 259–62, 281–83
summary of, 238
valarray class, 439
zero-indexed, 200
ASCII character codes, 602–6
ASCII format, 607–8
asm keyword, 586
assignment, with enum keyword, 288–92
assignment operator, 46–48, 102
    data types and stored values, 47
    in declarations, 47
    lvalue and rvalue, 48
    problems with, 61–62
associativity, 46
atof function, 225
atoi function, 225

atol function, 225
AT&T Bell Labs, 8
auto keyword, 586
automatic variables, 168–69
averaging, 207, 272–73

B

B language, 7
base 2 notation, 609–11
base 10 notation, 609–11
base 16 notation, 609–11
base class, 478
    access specifiers, 479, 495–96
    constructor functions and,
        497–98, 505–7
    destructor functions and, 498–99
base functions, calling derived
        functions, 491–94
BCPL language, 7
beeping Windows program,
        building, 563–65
Bell Laboratories, 7
binary file input and output, 622–26
binary notation, 609–11
binary operators, 74–75
bits, 40–41
bool keyword, 586
box diagrams, 257
braces, 31
    angle braces and #include
        statements, 641
    with if statements, 80–81
    in loops, 91, 104–6
    in Visual C++, 108
break keyword, 587
break statement, 88–90
bugs, 28. *See also* debugger
byte formats, 607–8
bytecode, 566
bytes, 40–41
    sizeof operator, 124–26

C

C language, 6–10
    as compiled language, 8
    history of, 7–8
C++ language, 6–10
    advantages of, 8, 10

compared with Java, 566, 567
    as compiled language, 8
    history of, 7–8
C Programming Language, The
        (Kernighan & Ritchie), 7
call by reference, 176–80, 317–18.
        See also user-defined data
        types
    filling and returning a data
        structure, 275–76
    large data structures and, 275
    reference variable arrays, 329–30
    right-arrow operator, 278–79
        versus dot operator, 276–78
call by reference with pointers, 318
call by reference with reference
        parameters, 320–30
    disadvantage of reference
        parameters, 322–23
    limitations of reference
        parameters, 322
    troubleshooting with reference
        parameters, 324–29
call by value, 160, 174, 275, 316
call statement, 157
    data types in, 167
    function call statement, 154
called functions, 154, 316–17
calling functions, 154, 158–59,
        316–17
case keyword, 587
case sensitivity, 37
casting, 61–63, 67
    const_cast keyword, 588
    data casts, 61–63
    dynamic_cast keyword, 589
    reinterpret_cast keyword, 595
    static_cast keyword, 596
catch exception handling, 557–62
catch keyword, 587
char data type, 39
char keyword, 587
character arrays. *See* character
        strings; string class; string
        objects
character data
    character string functions, 218,
        219

converting, 67
reading
    both numeric and character
        data, 224–25
    terminology for, 217
    whitespace characters and, 658
character string functions, 225–27
    example, 219
    in iostream library, 218
character string input, 217–24
character strings, 200, 213–26. *See
       also* string class; string
       objects
    character string functions, 218,
        219, 225–27
    character string input, 217–24
    compared with enum keyword,
        291–92
    initialization, 213–14
    null character, 213, 214–17
    reading both numeric and
        character data, 224–25
child classes. *See* derived classes
cin function, 217, 225, 649–50,
        656–658
cin.ignore function, 219–21
class constructor functions. *See*
        constructor functions
class data members, 377–78
class declaration, 366–67, 518–26
class definition, 376
class destructor functions, 385–87
class keyword, 587
class members. *See* members
class relationships, 438
    classes having classes, 442–68
    classes using classes, 438–42
        examples, 443–50
        iostream class, 439
        numeric classes, 439
        string class, 439
        using namespace std statement,
        440–42
    has a, 437–38
    is a, 437–38, 478
    object model and, 437–38
    summary of, 469
    uses a, 437–38

classes, 11, 357–58, 362. *See also* class relationships; object-oriented programming; string class; string objects
base class, 478, 479, 495–99, 505–7
complex class, 439
debugging with, 670–72
declaring, 366–67, 518–26
derived class, 478, 497–507
errors with, 391–96
functions and, 152
instance of a class, 358
iostream class, 439
Microsoft Foundation Class Library, 5, 562–65
new operator with, 547
numeric classes, 439
pointers and, 138–39, 413–21
valarray class, 439
code, 28
bytecode, 566
function source code, 374
object code, 28
source code, 5, 8, 28, 576–77
spaghetti code, 12
code portability, 8
comments, 30, 34, 38
commercial off-the-shelf (COTS) software, 537
comparison, with enum keyword, 288–92
compiled languages, 8
compilers, 8, 28
error messages, 106, 164, 167, 169, 173
GCC compiler, 5, 35
Java, 566
just in time compilers, 566
syntax errors, 34–36
Visual C++, 35, 36, 576–77
compile-time polymorphism, 527–28
compiling source code, Visual C++, 576–77
complex class, 439
complex numbers, 439
compression ratio array, 202

computer media, 607, 608
computer system time, accessing, 417, 420
concatenation of character strings, 227
concurrency, 359
conditional statements, 74. *See also* control statements; if statements; loops
common mistakes in, 100–103
relational and logical operators, 74–77
summary of, 109
switch operator and, 88–90, 109
const keyword, 587
const modifier, 59–60
versus #define statement, 60
const_cast keyword, 588
constructor functions
base class and, 497–98, 505–7
class constructor functions, 377–85
derived class and, 497–98
inheritance and, 497–509
initializing class data members, 377–78
parameter passing and, 499–507
string constructors, 629
twenty-four-hour clock and, 379–81
continue keyword, 588
control statements, 73
if statements, 77–88
loops, 90–100
relational and logical operators, 74–77
summary of, 108, 109–10
switch statement, 88–90
troubleshooting, 100–108
conversion
character data, 67
character string arrays and strings, 632–33
time conversion, 110–11, 185–88
COTS (commercial off-the-shelf) software, 537
cout function, 649–50, 653
CPL language, 7

.cpp files, 641
cylinder volume, 65–66

D

data, 38–39
data accessibility methods, for functions, 319–20, 321
data casts, 61–63
data files, filling arrays from, 237–38, 614–27
data initialization, and inheritance, 499–500
data structures, 252, 253–57. *See also* user-defined data types
compared with classes, 421–22
creating and declaring, 254–55
debugging with, 670–72
filling and returning, 275–76
large data structures, 138–39, 275
passing to and from functions, 270–73
structure address to a function, 274–81
structure tags, 255–56
without tags, 256–57
data type modifiers, 41–42
data types, 39–43, 253–54. *See also* user-defined data types
assignment statement and, 47
in call statements, 167
char data type, 39
data type modifiers, 41–42
double data type, 39
enumerated data type, 252, 283–97
float data type, 39, 102–3
input data type and name list, 152
int data type, 39, 102–3
memory bytes for, 124
stored values and, 47
data variables
address of, 127–29
arrays and single data variables, 197–98
hex notation and, 612
memory and, 124–27
rules for naming, 44

debugger, 28, 663–72
  debugging
  concepts, 106–8, 663
  with pointers, arrays, classes, and
    structures, 670–72
  example, 663–68
  features of, 668–70
  terminology, 664
decimal notation, 609–11
declarations
  array declarations, 198–200
  assignments in, 47
  class declarations, 366–67,
    518–26
  function source code inside, 374
  namespace declaration, 440
  pointer declarations, 130
  structure declarations, 254–55
  variables declaration, 43–45,
    169–70
decrement operators, 53–56, 405–6
default keyword, 588
default parameter list function,
  333–34
#define statement, 57–59
  versus const modifier, 60
delete keyword, 588
delete operator, 545–48
  initialization of objects, 547
  size value for arrays, 545–46
derived class, 478
  constructor functions and, 497–98
  destructor functions and, 498–99
  parameter passing and, 499–507
derived class construct, 505–7
derived functions, calling base
  functions, 491–94
destructor functions
  base class, 498–99
  class destructor functions, 385–87
  derived class and, 498–99
  inheritance and, 497–509
development environment tools,
  569
directives, 640–41
  #define directive, 642–43
  #endif directive, 642–43
  #ifndef directive, 642–43
  #include directive, 30, 641

preprocessor directives, 30,
  640–41
do keyword, 589
do while loops, 97–100
dot operator, 257–58
  versus right-arrow operator,
    276–78
double data type, 39
double keyword, 589
double quotes, and #include
  statements, 641
dynamic memory allocation,
  544–49
  heap memory, 548–49
  new and delete operators, 545–48
dynamic_cast keyword, 589

E
EBCDIC format, 607–8
elements, 198
else keyword, 590
encapsulation, 359, 421
end of file marker, 615–16, 622
  unexpected end of file, 106–8
endl manipulator, 652–53
Enter key, reading, 659
enum keyword, 286, 590
  assignment and comparison with,
    288–92
  choosing enum values, 293
  compared with character strings,
    291–92
  input and output for enum data,
    295–97
  struct keyword and, 252
  troubleshooting, 291–92, 293
enumerated data type, 252, 283–97
  creating numbered lists, 286–88
  functions and, 297–300
  input and output for enum data,
    295–97
equations, 52–53, 64–65
error checking, for new operator,
  548–49
error codes, 299
error flags, 299
error handling, 382
error messages from compiler, 106,
  164, 167, 169, 173

error trapping, for user input, 658
errors, 5. *See also* exception
    handling
  with classes, 391–96
  syntax errors, 34–36
escape sequences, 652–54
evaluation tools, 73
example programs index, 673–84
exception handling, 557–62
  examples, 558–60
  with new operator, 560–62
executable files, 28
explicit keyword, 590
export keyword, 591
expressions, 75–77
  algebraic expressions, 52
  math expressions, and operator
    precedence, 52–53
extern global variables, 643–46
extern keyword, 319, 591, 643–46
extern output stream, 646

F
false keyword, 591
file formats, 614–16
  header lines, 614
  read until end of file, 615–16
  trailer value or sentinel value,
    614–15
file input/output, 614–27
  binary file input and output,
    622–26
  example, 619–22
  file formats, 614–16
  with iostream library, 616
  opening files, 616
  read until end of file, 622
  reading data into variables,
    617–18
  steps for, 616–22
  writing output, 618–19
files
  .cpp files, 641
  executable files, 28
  filling arrays from data files,
    236–38
  .h files, 639
  include files, 639
  make file, 29

opening, 616
source files, 639
flags, 181
    error flags, 299
    ios formatting flags, 653–55
float data type, 39
    versus int data type, 102–3
float keyword, 591
for keyword, 591
for loops, 91–95
    altering the loop index, 93–94
    arrays and, 201–2
    examples, 94–95
    nested, and two-dimensional
        arrays, 230
fractional calculations,
        troubleshooting, 53
fractions, troubleshooting with,
        49–52
friend functions, 568
friend keyword, 592
function body, 154, 158–60
function call statement, 154
function calls, 157–58
function header lines, 31, 154,
        158–60
function prototype, 154, 156–57,
        162, 165
function source code, 374
function_name, 152
functions, 10, 149–52, 274–75,
        316–20
    atof, atoi, atol functions, 225
    C++ enhanced features, 344
    call by reference, 176–80,
        317–18, 320–30
    call by value, 160, 174, 275, 316
    called functions, 154, 316–17
    calling functions, 154, 158–59,
        316–17
    character string functions, 218,
        219, 225–26
    cin function, 217, 225, 649–50,
        656–58
    cin.ignore function, 219–21
    class constructor functions,
        378–79
    class destructor functions, 385–87
    classes and, 152

constructor functions, 378–79,
        497–507
cout function, 649–50, 653
data accessibility methods for,
        319–20, 321
default parameter list function,
        333–34
derived functions calling base
        functions, 491–94
destructor functions, 385–87,
        498–99
enumerated data type and,
        297–300
examples, 152–54, 160–62
format of, 152–54, 162–64
friend functions, 568
get function, 217
global variables and, 171–74,
        188, 319
inline functions, 343
large pieces of data and, 174
libraries and, 168
local variables and, 168–69
main function, 31
member functions, 373–77
multidimensional arrays and,
        233–35
object-oriented analysis and,
        361–63
one-dimensional arrays and,
        206–13
one-line function formats, 370–72
operator function, 403
overloaded functions, 330–33,
        338–42, 394–95
pass by reference, 413, 414
passing addresses to, 176–80,
        556–57
passing data structures to and
        from, 270–73
passing one-dimensional arrays
        to, 206–7
pointers and, 138, 174–80, 274–75
prototype *versus* call information,
        162, 165
pure virtual functions, 531
qsort function, 423
reference variable arrays, 329–30
returning a value to the calling

function, 158–59
    returning arrays from, 208–13
    returning data with pointers, 138,
        175–80
    static variables and, 170–71
    strcmp function, 225
    string class editing functions,
        629, 633, 634
    string class functions, 632, 638
    string class search functions, 631,
        636
    string to numeric functions, 228
    in string.h library, 225, 227
    strstr function, 239–40
    structure arrays and, 281–83
    structures and, 270–73
    summary of, 180, 343–44
    terminating, 159
    troubleshooting
        data type in call statement, 167
        forgetting to declare variables,
            169–70
        forgotten functions, 396
        type mismatch, 164–67,
            394–95
    variable scope and, 168, 174
    variable-length parameter list
        functions, 333–42
    virtual functions, 528–36
    writing, 154–68
        call by value, 160
        example, 155–56
        function body, 158–60
        function calls, 157–58
        function header lines, 158–60
        function prototype, 156–57

G
game programming, 531–33
GCC (GNU C Compiler), 5
get function, 217
global variables, 171–74
    cautions for using, 172
    extern global variables, in
        multifile programs, 643–46
    functions and, 171–74, 188, 319
    h1 and math.h library, 173
GNU C Compiler (GCC), 5
goto keyword, 592

H

.h files, 639
h1 global variable, and math.h library, 173
has a (class relationship), 437–38
header lines, 614
    function header lines, 31, 154, 158–60
heap memory, 548–49
hex addresses, 126–27
hexadecimal notation, 126–27, 608–13
    counting in, 611, 612–13
    data variables and, 612

I

identifiers, 44
if else statements, 79–80, 84–85
    illegal else, 106–8
    misplaced else, 106–8
    nested, 86
if keyword, 592
if statements, 77–88
    braces with, 80–81
    if else statements, 79–80, 84–85, 86, 106–8
    if-else if-else statements, 81–83
    inefficient programming techniques for, 83–84
    nested if else statements, 86
    ? operator, 87–88
    summary of, 109
if-else if-else statements, 81–83
illegal else, 106–8
include directory, 641
include files, 639
#include statement, 30, 643
increment operators, 53–56, 405–6
indention style, 108
index of sample programs, 675–86
indexed array, 198, 521–23
indirection operators
    right-arrow operator, 275
    *, 132–35, 550–57
infinite loops, 91
inheritance, 359, 478–94. *See also* polymorphism; virtual functions

access specifiers, 495–96
class declarations, 518–26
constructors and destructors, 497–509
data initialization and, 499–500
defined, 478
derived functions calling base functions, 491–94
examples, 475–77, 478–81, 484–94, 509–26
importance of, 475–77
multiple inheritance, 496–97
object-oriented design, 514–18
protected members, 481–84
summary of, 536–37
troubleshooting, 507–9
initialization
    arrays, 200–201, 228–30
    character strings, 213–14
    class data members, 377–78
    inheritance and, 499–500
    objects, 547
    one-dimensional arrays, 200–201
    string objects, 547
    two-dimensional arrays, 228–30
inline functions, 343
inline keyword, 593
input. *See also* file input/output; keyboard input/screen output
    binary file input, 622–26
    character string input, 217–24
    for enum data, 295–97
    error trapping for user input, 658
input arguments, 152, 158
input data type and name list, 152
instance of a class, 358
int data type, 39
    versus float data type, 102–3
int keyword, 593
integer arithmetic, 50
integers, 42–43
International Standards Organization (ISO), 5, 7–8
I/O. *See* file input/output
ios formatting flags, 653–55
iostream class, 439
iostream library
    character string functions in, 218

file input/output with, 616
is a (class relationship), 437–38, 478
ISO C standard, 7–8
ISO C++ standard, 5, 8
ISO (International Standards Organization), 5, 7–8

J

Java language, 8, 565–67
    applets, 566
    applications programs, 566
    bytecode, 566
    as C++ without pointers, 566
    compared with C++, 566, 567
    example, 566–67
    just in time compilers, 566
    Website for, 566
Java Virtual Machine (JVM), 566
Johnston's Dice Game, 451–55
Johnston's Rules for Programmers, 6
just in time compilers, 566
JVM (Java Virtual Machine), 566

K

Kernighan, Brian W., 7
keyboard input/screen output, 64, 649–62
    basic formatted output, using cout function, 653
    cout and cin functions, 649–50, 653
    endl manipulator, 652–53
    escape sequences, 650–52
    examples, 659–62
    ios formatting flags, 653–55
    precision, 655–56
    streams, 649
    whitespace characters, 656–58, 659
    width specification setw(), 656
keyword dictionary, 585–600
keywords, 36

L

large data structures
    call by reference and, 275

functions and, 174
pointers and, 138–39
late binding, 528
libraries
defined, 168
functions and, 168
iostream library, 218, 616
math library (math.h), 52, 173
Microsoft Foundation Class
Library (MFC), 5, 562–65
Standard Template Library
(STL), 568
standardized libraries, 10
string.h library, 225, 227
link error, 571
linker, 8, 28
local variables, 168–69
logical operators, 74–77
expressions, 75–77
precedence of operators, 75–77
long keyword, 593
loop altering statements, 91
loop index, 91
loop tools, 73
loops, 90–100. *See also* control
statements
braces in, 91, 104–6
do while loops, 97–100
infinite loops, 91
for loops, 91–95, 201–2, 230
repeating, 103–4
semicolons in, 104–6
summary of, 110
while loops, 95–97
lvalue, 48

M

main function, 31
make file, 29
math expressions, and operator
precedence, 52–53
math library (math.h), 52, 173
maximum value, of arrays, 240–44
member functions, writing, 373–77
file organization, 374
function source code inside
declaration, 374
place member functions in a

separate file, 374–77
two different formats/locations,
373
members, 362, 367
class data members, 377–78
getting values into data members,
370–73
member functions, 373–77
protected members, 481–84
memory, 40–41, 126, 607–13. *See
also* dynamic memory
allocation
accessing variables in, 132
allocating, for multidimensional
arrays, 550–56
byte formats, 607–8
data variables and, 124–27
heap memory, 548–49
hexadecimal notation and,
126–27, 608–13
memory bytes for data types,
124
physical memory, 607–12
reserving, 126, 127
sizeof operator, 124–26
storage methods, 607, 608
memory stack, 126, 548
methods, 355–61, 362, 363
Microsoft Foundation Class Library
(MFC), 5, 562–65
Microsoft Visual C++. *See* Visual
C++
minimum value, of arrays, 240–44
misplaced else, 106–8
modifiers
const modifier, 59–60
data type modifiers, 41–42
modularity, 359
modulus operator, 48–49, 66–67
multidimensional arrays, 226–33.
See also two-dimensional
arrays
functions and, 233–35
memory allocation, 550–56
multifile programs, 639–48
creating a multifile project in
Visual C++, 643
examples, 639–40, 647–48

extern global variables in, 643–46
extern output stream, 646
#ifndef, #define, and #endif
directives, 642–43
#include statements and, 641
preprocessor directives, 640–41
program design, 642
user-defined data types and, 301
multiple inheritance, 496–97
mutable keyword, 593

N

namespace declaration, 440
namespace keyword, 594
naming rules, 44
nested for loops, 230
nested if else statements, 86
nested include statements, 641
new keyword, 594
new operator, 545–48
with classes and structures, 547
error checking for, 548–49
exception handling with, 560–62
failure of, 548–49
initialization of objects, 547
size value for arrays, 545–46
Nine Commandments for
Programmers, 6
nonnumeric data, and cin, 225
notation
base 2, 609–11
base 10, 609–11
base 16, 609–11
binary, 609–11
decimal, 609–11
hexadecimal, 126–27, 608–13
null character, 213, 214–17
null-terminated strings, 200
numbered lists, 286–88
numeric classes, 439
numeric data
reading, 224–25, 658
string to numeric functions, 228
whitespace characters and, 658

O

object code, 28
object definition, 360–61, 362

object model, and class
relationships, 437–38
object-oriented analysis (OOA),
361–63
object-oriented design (OOD), 362,
363–65, 514–18
object-oriented languages, 358–59
object-oriented methods, 355–61,
362, 363
object-oriented programming,
10–12
advantages of, 11–12
array of objects, 397–402
class constructors, 377–85
class destructors, 385–87
classes and objects, 361–73
class declaration, 366–67
examples, 365–70
getting values into data
members, 370–73
object-oriented analysis,
361–63
object-oriented design, 362,
363–65
classes and pointers, 413–21
examples, 414–21
pass by reference with
pointers, 413
pass by reference with
reference parameters, 414
comparing structures and classes,
421–22
examples, 11, 365–70, 387–96,
423–28
member functions, writing,
373–77
overloaded operators and objects,
403–13
versus structured programming,
12–15
summary of, 421–22
terminology, 362
versus top-down programming,
12–15
troubleshooting, 387
errors with classes, 391–96
forgotten functions, 396
scoping operator ::, 392–94
objects, 11, 358, 359–60, 362. *See*

also object-oriented
programming; string objects
array of, 397–402
initialization, 547
overloaded operators and, 403–13
one-dimensional arrays, 199, 439
functions and, 206–13
array averaging program, 207
arrays and pointers, 206
passing one-dimensional arrays
to functions, 206–7
returning arrays from
functions, 208–13
troubleshooting, 208–13
initialization, 200–201
one-line function formats, 370–72
OOA (object-oriented analysis),
361–63
OOD (object-oriented design), 362,
363–65, 514–18
opening files, 616
operands, 74
operator function, 403
operator keyword, 403, 595
operators, 8, 10, 45–57, 601
accumulation operators, 56–57
address operator (&), 127–32
arithmetic operators, 48–53
assignment operator, 46–48,
61–62, 102
binary operators, 74–75
decrement operators, 53–56,
405–6
delete operator, 545–48
dot operator, 257–58, 276–78
increment operators, 53–56,
405–6
indirection operators, 132–35,
275
logical operators, 74–77
modulus operator, 48–49, 66–67
new operator, 545–49
overloaded operators, and classes,
403–13
postfix operators, 56, 405–6
precedence of, 45–46, 52–53,
75–77
prefix operators, 56, 405–6
? operator, 87–88

relational operators, 74–77
right-arrow operator, 275–79
same as operator, 102
scoping operator ::, 374–76,
392–94
sizeof operator, 124–26
* operator, 132–35, 550–57
string operators, 628–29
switch operator, 88–90, 109
ternary operators, 87
unary operators, 74–75
unary overloaded operators,
404–5
out of bounds array, 235–37
output, 5. *See also* file input/output;
keyboard input/screen output
binary file input and output,
622–26
for enum data, 295–97
extern output stream, 646
output patterns, 113–16
overloaded functions, 330–33
absolute value overloaded
functions, 332
mixing and matching, 341–42
troubleshooting, 338–41, 394–95
type mismatches reported as,
394–95
overloaded operators, and objects,
403–13
binary overloaded operators,
406–13
examples, 406–13
prefix *versus* postfix operators,
with increment/decrement
operators, 405–6
unary overloaded operators,
404–5

P
parent class. *See* base class
pass by reference
with pointers, 413
with reference parameters, 414
passing
addresses, to functions, 176–80,
556–57
data structures, to and from
functions, 270–73

one-dimensional arrays, to
functions, 206–7
parameter passing and
constructor functions,
499–504
variables, to functions, 176–80
persistence, 359
physical memory, 607–12
pointers, 8, 123, 129–37, 274–75
accessing variables in memory,
132
address operator (&) and, 130–32
array pointers, 138–39, 202–6
call by reference with, 318
classes and, 138–39, 413–21
debugging with, 670–72
functions and, 138, 174–80,
274–75
importance of, 123–24
indirection operator (*) and,
132–35
large data structures and, 138–39
locating variables with, 188
mixing up, 135–37
pass by reference with, 413
pointer declarations, 130
pointer to pointer, 552–54
returning data from functions,
138, 175–80
summary of, 139–41
polymorphism, 359, 526–28. *See
also* virtual functions
compile-time, 527–28
run-time, 528
portable languages, 8
postfix operators, 56, 405–6
precedence of operators, 45–46,
52–53, 75–77
precision, 655–56
prefix operators, 56, 405–6
preprocessor directives, 30, 640–41
prime numbers, 180–85
private access specifier, 367
private keyword, 595
program data, 38–39
program format, 29–38
program index, 673–84
programming fundamentals, 21–28
algorithm design, 22–24

example, 25
rule of thirds, 25–27
software development steps,
27–28
steps to programming success,
24
programming style, 37–38, 106–8
programming techniques, 16, 17
projects, 28–29
protected access specifier, 481–84
protected keyword, 595
public access, 367
public access specifier, 479
public keyword, 595
pure virtual functions, 531

Q

qsort function, 423
? operator, 87–88

R

random numbers, 185, 521–22
read until end of file, 615–16, 622
unexpected end of file, 106–8
reading data. *See also* file
input/output
character data, 217, 224–25, 658
numeric data, 224–25, 658
into variables, 617–18
reading whitespace characters, 658,
659
reference parameters, 320
call by reference with, 320–30
disadvantage of, 322–23
limitations of, 322
pass by reference with, 414
troubleshooting with, 324–29
reference variable arrays, 329–30
register keyword, 595
reinterpret_cast keyword, 595
relational operators, 74–77
expressions, 75–77
precedence of operators, 75–77
repeating loops, 103–4
reserving memory, 126, 127
return keyword, 596
return statement, 158–60
returning
arrays from functions, 208–13

data from functions, with
pointers, 138, 175–80
data structures, 275–76
values to calling functions,
158–59
return_type, 152
Richard, Martin, 7
right-arrow operator, 275, 278–79
versus dot operator, 276–78
Ritchie, Dennis M., 7
rule of thirds, 25–27
run-time errors. *See also* exception
handling
general description, 571
run-time polymorphism, 528
rvalue, 48

S

same as operator, 102
sample programs index, 673–84
scope of variables, 45, 168, 174
scoping operator ::, 374–76,
392–94
screen output, 64. *See also* keyboard
input/screen output
searching strings, 631, 636
semicolons, in loops, 104–6
sentinel value, 614–15
setw() width specification, 656
short keyword, 596
signed keyword, 596
single-dimensional arrays. *See* one-
dimensional arrays
sizeof keyword, 596
sizeof operator, 124–26
software
commercial off-the-shelf (COTS),
537
construction techniques, 16, 17
developer skill set, 3–4
development, 27–28
source code, 5, 8, 28
source files, 639
spaghetti code, 12
stack, 126, 548
Standard Template Library (STL),
568
standardized libraries, 10
star (*) operator, 132–35, 550–57

statements, 31–32. *See also*
    conditional statements;
    control statements; if
    statements
  break statement, 88–90
  call statement, 154, 157, 167
  #define statement, 57–59, 60
  function call statement, 154
  #include statement, 30, 641
  loop altering statements, 91
  return statement, 158–60
  switch statement, 88–90, 109
  using namespace std statement,
    440–42
static keyword, 596
static variables, 170–71
static_cast keyword, 596
STL (Standard Template Library),
  568
storage methods, 607, 608
storage specifier, 253
stored values, 47
strcat function, 227
strcmp function, 225
streams, 651
string class, 200, 628–40
  as a class using a class, 439
string class editing functions, 629,
  633, 634
string class functions, 632, 638
string class search functions, 631,
  636
string constructors, 629
string objects, 439, 628–40. *See also*
  character strings
  combining string objects and
    character strings, 629
  conversion between character
    string arrays and strings,
    632–33
  creating strings, 628
  initialization, 547
  overloaded operators and,
    403–13, 630
  reading into a string, 633
  string class editing functions,
    629, 633, 634
  string class functions, 632, 638

string class search functions, 631,
  636
string constructors, 629
string operators, 628–29
string operators, 628–29
string to numeric functions, 228
string.h library, 225, 227
strings
  creating, 628
  searching, 631, 636
Stroustrup, Bjarne, 8
strstr function, 239–40
struct keyword, 254, 596. *See also*
  data structures
  enum keyword and, 252
structure tags, 255–56
structured programming, 10–11
  versus object-oriented
    programming, 12–15
structures. *See* data structures
style, 37–38, 106–8
Sun Microsystems, 566
switch keyword, 597
switch operator, 88–90, 109
switch statement, 88–90, 109
syntax, 28, 34
syntax errors, 34–36
system time, accessing, 417–420

T

tag name, 254
template keyword, 597
templates, 567–68
terminating functions, 159
terminology
  C++, 28
  debugger, 664
  object-oriented programming,
    362
  reading character data, 217
ternary operators, 87
this keyword, 597
Thompson, Ken, 7
throw exception handling, 557–62
throw keyword, 597
time conversion, 110–11, 185–88
top-down programming, 10–11
  versus object-oriented

    programming, 12–15
trailer value, 614–15
troubleshooting, 17
  arithmetic operators, 49–53
  control statements, 100–108
  enum keyword, 291–92, 293
  fractional calculations, 53
  with fractions, 49–52
  functions, 164–67, 169–70,
    394–95, 396
  inheritance, 507–9
  integers, 42–43
  object-oriented programming,
    387, 391–96
  one-dimensional arrays, 208–13
  overloaded functions, 338–41,
    394–95
  with reference parameters,
    324–29
true keyword, 597
try exception handling, 557–62
try keyword, 598
twenty-four-hour-clock, 379–81,
  406–8
two-dimensional arrays. *See also*
  multidimensional arrays
  example, 230–33
  initialization, 228–30
  memory allocation, 550–56
  nested for loops and, 230
type mismatch, 164–67, 394–395
typedef keyword, 598
typeid keyword, 598
typename keyword, 599

U

unary operators, 74–75
unary overloaded operators, 404–5
unexpected end of file, 106–8
union keyword, 599
UNIX operating system, 7
unsigned keyword, 599
user-defined data types. *See also*
  data structures; data types
  accessing structure elements,
    257–59
  call by reference, 274–81
  call by value, 275

dot operator, 276–78
examples, 280–81
filling and returning a structure, 275–76
large data structures, 275
one copy of a structure, 275
pointers and functions, 274–75
right-arrow operator, 276–79
two local copies of a structure, 275
copying structures, 269–70
data structures, 253–57
box diagrams representing, 257
creating and declaring, 254–55
data types and, 253–54
structure tags, 255–56
without tags, 256–57
defined, 252
enum keyword, 252
enumerated data type, 283–97
functions and, 297–300
examples, 270–73, 301–7
grouping data together, 251–52
multifile programs, 301
struct keyword, 252
structure arrays, 259–62
functions and, 281–83
a structure with two structures, 266–68
structures and functions, 270–73
structures within structures, 262–68
uses a (class relationship), 437–38
using keyword, 599
using namespace std statement, 440–42

V

valarray class, 439
values, 43
variable declaration, 43–45
variable names, 40, 44
variable scope, 45, 168, 174
variable-length parameter list

functions, 333–42
default parameter list function, 333–34
examples, 335, 338, 339–41
mixing and matching overloaded functions, 341–42
parameter order, 335–38
troubleshooting overloaded functions, 338–41
variables, 43. *See also* data variables
accessing, in memory, 132
automatic variables, 168–69
declarations, 43–45, 169–70
extern global variables, 643–46
forgetting to declare, 169–70
global variables, 171–74, 188, 319
local variables, 168–69
locating, with pointers, 188
passing addresses to functions, 176–80
reading data into, 617–18
rules for naming, 44
scope of, 45, 168, 174
static variables, 170–71
virtual functions, 526–36. *See also* polymorphism
defined, 528–30
example, 533–36
game programming with, 531–33
pure virtual functions, 531
uses for, 531–36
virtual shapes, 528–30
virtual keyword, 599
Visual C++, 4–5, 569–84. *See also* debugger
braces in, 108
compiler, 35, 36, 576–77
compiling source code, 576–77
creating projects, 573–74
creating source files, 575–76
development environment tools, 569
examples, 572–73, 584

exit warning, 579
exiting, 578
frequently asked questions, 580
generated files, 578
Help system, 582–84
installing, 570
multifile project in, 645
program construction steps, 570–79
running programs, 577
saving data, 578
starting, 573–79
syntax errors, 35, 36
workspaces, 570–72, 579, 580–82
void keyword, 599
volatile keyword, 599

W

warnings, 5, 579
wchar_t keyword, 599
while keyword, 600
while loops, 95–97
whitespace characters, 32–34, 656–59
cin function and, 656–58
error trapping for user input, 658
reading, 658, 659
reading Enter key, 659
reading numeric and character data, 658
width specification setw(), 656
Windows, building applications in, 562–65
Windows Application Program Interface (Win32 API), 563
Windows Messages, 563
writing data. *See* file input/output
writing functions, 154–68
writing member functions, 373–77
writing output. *See* file input/output

Z

zero-indexed arrays, 200